Traumatic Brain Injury

The past 15 years have seen many developments in the knowledge, research and rehabilitation of individuals following traumatic brain injury (TBI). The second edition of this book provides an updated guide for health professionals working with individuals with such injuries.

Its uniquely clinical focus provides both comprehensive background information, and practical strategies for dealing with common problems with thinking, memory, communication, behaviour and emotional adjustment. The book addresses a wide range of challenges, from those which begin with impairment of consciousness, to those occurring for many years after injury, and presents strategies for maximising participation in all aspects of community life, in both adults and children.

The book will be of use to practising clinicians, students in health disciplines relevant to neurorehabilitation, and also the families of individuals with traumatic brain injury.

Jennie Ponsford is Professor in the School of Psychology and Psychiatry at Monash University, and Director of the Monash-Epworth Rehabilitation Research Centre at Epworth Hospital in Melbourne, Australia. Over the past 30 years she developed rehabilitation programmes and conducted research investigating outcomes following head injury and evaluating rehabilitative therapies. She has written two books and over 120 journal articles on the subject.

Sue Sloan is an accredited Occupational Therapist and Clinical Neuropsychologist. She has worked in private practice for the past 15 years and provided community rehabilitation services to people with severe acquired brain injury. Sue also provides clinical supervision to students at La Trobe University and Monash University, Australia.

Pamela Snow is an Associate Professor in the School of Psychology and Psychiatry at Monash University. She is a psychologist and speech pathologist, and has an extensive clinical and research history in the field of TBI, and a current research focus on language competence in high-risk adolescents.

Traumatic Brain Injury

Rehabilitation for everyday adaptive living

Second edition

Jennie Ponsford, Sue Sloan and Pamela Snow

First published 1995
by Psychology Press

This edition published 2013
by Psychology Press
27 Church Road, Hove, East Sussex BN3 2FA

Simultaneously published in the USA and Canada
by Psychology Press
711 Third Avenue, New York NY 10017

Psychology Press is an imprint of the Taylor & Francis Group, an informa business

British Library Cataloguing in Publication Data
A catalogue record for this book is available from the British Library

Library of Congress Cataloging-in-Publication Data
Ponsford, Jennie.
Traumatic brain injury rehabilitation for everyday adaptive living / Jennie Ponsford, Sue Sloan, and Pam Snow.—2nd ed.
p. cm.
Includes bibliographical references and index.
ISBN 978-1-84872-027-5 (hardback)
1. Brain damage—Patients—Rehabilitation. 2. Vocational rehabilitation. 3. Neuropsychological tests. 4. Psychotherapy. I. Sloan, Sue. II. Snow, Pamela. III. Title.
RC387.5.P66 2012
617.4'8103—dc23

2011051871

ISBN13: 978-1-84872-027-5 (hbk)
ISBN13: 978-0-20308-280-5 (ebk)

Typeset in Times
by RefineCatch Limited, Bungay, Suffolk

Printed and bound in Great Britain by
TJ International Ltd, Padstow, Cornwall

This book is dedicated to those traumatically brain-injured individuals and their families, who have taught us so much.

Contents

Illustrations

Figures

Tables

Boxes

Preface to the first edition

Over the past three decades there has been a growing awareness of the needs of those who experience traumatic brain injury and their families. Initially the emphasis was on defining the nature of sequelae. More recently, there has been much written regarding rehabilitative strategies. A number of different approaches to management have been advocated, based on the development of some excellent model rehabilitation programmes, most notably those of Yehuda Ben-Yishay and colleagues, George Prigatano and colleagues, Peter Eames and Rodger Wood, and McKay Moore Sohlberg and Catherine Mateer. These programmes target different types of problems at different levels. Whilst these approaches have much to offer clinicians, we felt there was a need for more comprehensive guidelines, covering a broader spectrum, in terms of severity, problems and time frames.

With the growth of services for those with traumatic brain injury, increasing numbers of rehabilitation professionals are being employed in traumatic brain injury rehabilitation programmes, often with limited education and experience in this area. There was, therefore, a perceived need for a book which provided comprehensive and practical guidelines for psychologists and therapists in training, and practitioners working in this complex and stressful area.

When we set about doing this, there was a growing realisation that it would not be possible to cover every aspect of traumatic brain injury. Reflecting the expertise of the authors, this book focuses on the psychological consequences of traumatic brain injury, rather than the medical or physical consequences. This should not imply that medical or physical consequences are less important or significant in their impact on certain traumatically brain-injured individuals. However, these have been explored comprehensively elsewhere. Moreover, there is now substantial evidence to show that, in the majority of cases, the psychological consequences of traumatic brain injury have the most significant and pervasive impact on the rehabilitation process and, more importantly, on the lifestyle of the person who is injured.

Whilst it is acknowledged that some of those who sustain mild traumatic brain injury will have ongoing difficulties and require interventions along the lines outlined in this book, those who sustain moderate and severe injuries more commonly have ongoing problems. Hence, greater emphasis has been placed on dealing with the difficulties presented by those who sustain moderate and severe injuries.

Chapter 1 discusses the epidemiology, pathophysiology, sequelae and psychosocial consequences of traumatic brain injury. Using this as a basis, it also outlines the principles of the approach recommended to rehabilitation following traumatic brain injury. We have termed this the REAL approach, signifying Rehabilitation for Everyday Adaptive Living.

Chapter 2 covers assessment and management of individuals with impaired consciousness, incorporating both coma and post-traumatic amnesia. Chapters 3 and 4 provide guidelines for the assessment and management of cognitive problems and the facilitation of participation in life roles. Chapter 5 deals with communication and interpersonal difficulties, and Chapter 6 with behaviour problems. The emphasis in managing all of these problems, both within a rehabilitation setting and in the community, is on effective teamwork, focusing on participation in the real world, involving the injured person and family in therapy, and taking a long-term view.

In Chapter 7, issues involved in returning to the community are explored. These include return to independent living, work, study, avocational interests and driving. Chapter 8 explores the nature of and methods of assisting with emotional and social problems, which tend to arise or have a greater impact after return to the community, including problems with self-awareness and self-esteem, depression, anxiety, anger control, relationship problems and sexual difficulties.

Chapter 9 addresses the impact of traumatic brain injury on the families, caregivers and others close to the person who is injured. It outlines methods of minimising this impact, with emphasis on the need for their involvement in all aspects of the rehabilitation process, and the need for support to continue indefinitely.

The impact of traumatic brain injury on children is, in some respects, different from that in adults. Chapter 10 explores these differences and discusses approaches to assessment and rehabilitation which take account of the special needs of children. Detailed guidelines for return to school are also provided in this chapter.

A significant challenge in writing this book has been to strike a suitable balance between research findings and clinical practice. Every effort has been made to base our recommendations on evidence from research studies. We cannot overemphasise the need to evaluate the effectiveness of interventions. We also acknowledge that there is a significant need for further research into many aspects of traumatic brain injury, particularly the development of better methods of measurement, exploration of long-term sequelae and scientific evaluation of the impact of different methods of intervention in terms of their effectiveness in alleviating disability and handicap in individuals with different types of injury and impairment.

However, given the perceived need for detailed and practical guidelines for those working with traumatically brain-injured individuals, the book is essentially clinically driven. The content is largely based on our experience in working with individuals with traumatic brain injury over many years. As such, not all the recommendations have been scientifically evaluated, although ongoing attempts are being made to do this. Every effort has been made to illustrate guidelines with case material. Whilst the majority of these case descriptions are based on real interventions, we have tried to preserve confidentiality by using pseudonyms and altering certain details.

It is important to acknowledge that the extent to which the guidelines recommended in this book may be implemented will be largely determined by the institutional, social and, above all, financial resources available to traumatically brain-injured individuals, their families, and clinicians. In many cases these are very limited, and significant adaptations will need to be made accordingly. It is, unfortunately, something of a paradox that these resources tend to diminish over time, whilst some of the problems experienced, or the injured person's receptivity to intervention, may actually increase over time. Rehabilitation professionals have an obligation to draw this to the attention of funding bodies, so that models of service delivery may be adjusted. A significant, unresolved issue within the existing framework of services is that of how services should be co-ordinated over the longer term. It is not desirable to maintain the dependency of traumatically brain-injured individuals and their families on hospitals or rehabilitation centres. This is an area which policy-makers need to address.

Traumatic brain injury can have a devastating impact on those who are injured and their relatives. It creates complex and stressful challenges for those involved with any aspect of their rehabilitation or long-term care. We hope that this book will, in some way, alleviate the burden of traumatically brain-injured people, their families, and the rehabilitation professionals assisting them.

Preface to the second edition

In the fifteen years which have elapsed between these editions there has been a burgeoning growth in the literature on traumatic brain injury. There has also been considerable expansion of treatment programmes and community-based services. Despite this, there is still a lack of community awareness of the needs of individuals with these injuries, and meeting their needs poses many challenges for therapists. Research studies have shed some light on the effectiveness of various approaches to management. However, our understanding of the processes of recovery from these injuries remains limited and the quality and amount of research evidence supporting current clinical practice disappointing. In this edition we have updated the evidence base supporting a broad range of intervention strategies for cognitive, behavioural and emotional sequelae of traumatic brain injury. It has been heartening to see that the REAL approach advocated in the first edition of this book, which focuses on maximising the injured person's participation in the context of the community and the family, is as relevant as ever, and has been adopted increasingly by traumatic rehabilitation programmes worldwide. We have included a greater emphasis on participation in this edition, both from the perspectives of assessment and treatment. We have also expanded the discussion of mild traumatic brain injury. The chapter on psychological issues has expanded, reflecting the growth of evidence in this domain and awareness of its significance. There are still many challenges. The first is to scientifically evaluate which elements of our rehabilitative interventions, or approaches to maximising participation, are most efficacious and for whom. The second is to create greater equity and consistency of service provision in order to provide broader access to skilled clinical assistance for individuals with traumatic brain injury worldwide. We have a very long way to go.

Acknowledgments

This book is born of a very special colleagueship, which has spanned 30 years since we were members of the Head Injury Team at Bethesda Hospital, now Epworth Healthcare, in Melbourne. We have spent many hours collaborating on the themes, content and case material, which has brought both depth and breadth of experience and expertise to the book. We also owe a great deal to many fellow members from the Head Injury team at Epworth Healthcare, and clinicians at Osborn Sloan Associates in Melbourne who have participated in the evolution of the approach to traumatic brain injury rehabilitation which is recommended in this book.

Kate Gould and Michele Grant gave invaluable assistance with referencing and proof-reading. We would also like to acknowledge the tolerance of other members of the School of Psychology and Psychiatry at Monash University, who covered for me (Jennie Ponsford) through my absences. Margaret Mealings, Pam Ross, Helen Harrington and Ali Crichton also gave helpful feedback on particular chapters. We gratefully acknowledge the contribution of case studies by the staff of the Epworth Transitional Living Centre, particularly Helen Harrington, and by Pam Ross and Jan Mackey.

Finally, we all acknowledge the love, support and, above all, tolerance of our respective husbands, Lew, Rick and Stuart, our children, Isabelle and Alice, William and Jack, and Alexandra and Katie, and our parents.

"How to get there" by Michael Leunig, from *A Bunch of Poesy.* Reproduced with permission of Michael Leunig and the publishers, Collins Angus & Robertson, Sydney, Australia.

1 Mechanism, recovery and sequelae of traumatic brain injury

A foundation for the REAL approach

Jennie Ponsford

Introduction

Over the past three decades, there has been a significant growth of interest in the study of traumatic brain injury (TBI). The literature now abounds with studies of its epidemiology, pathophysiology, neuropsychology and outcome, and there have been numerous texts written on the subject. In spite of this, rehabilitation professionals remain uncertain in dealing with the challenging and complex problems presented by those who have sustained TBI, and most find it stressful. Moreover, outcome studies suggest that in spite of rehabilitative efforts, many people with severe TBI remain significantly handicapped, often causing great stress to their families. The reasons for this lie largely in the unique epidemiological, pathophysiological and neuropsychological characteristics of this population.

Before examining these characteristics more closely, it is important to be clear as to what is meant by the term "traumatic brain injury". The Brain Injury Association of America describes a TBI as "an alteration in brain function, or other evidence of brain pathology, caused by an external force" (Brain Injury Association of America, 2011). Such an injury may result from a blow to the head from a relatively blunt object or from blunt impact of the head with a stationary object. TBIs may also result from penetration by a sharp instrument or a missile. These are termed open head injuries. However, penetrating injuries result in a somewhat different pattern of neurological deficit. The present text will deal with the consequences of TBI which have resulted from blunt impact, where the brain itself is not penetrated, otherwise known as closed head injuries. These represent approximately 70 per cent of all head injuries.

Epidemiology

Most studies suggest that the majority of moderate to severe TBIs result from motor vehicle accidents. Other causes include falls, bicycle accidents, assault, and sports injuries (Kraus and McArthur, 1999). In recent years the use of explosive devices in armed conflict has added a new mechanism of injury – blast injury, the effects of which are the focus of considerable current research interest, particularly in the USA (Tabar, Warden, and Hurley, 2006). It is difficult to obtain precise data regarding the incidence of TBI, due to variations in definition and methods of data collection. In the US, between 100 and 250 per 100,000 are admitted to hospital each year, and 20–30 per cent die (50 per cent in hospital and 50 per cent out of hospital). Other industrialised nations have similar rates (Bruns and Hauser, 2003). The Australian Institute of Health and Welfare has reported a rate of 107 TBIs per 100,000 population in Australia (Australian Institute of Health and Welfare, 2004; O'Rance and Fortune, 2007). Figures for China are relatively lower, at 56 per 100,000, and for South Africa and some European countries they are closer to 300 per 100,000 (Bruns and Hauser, 2003). Most studies suggest that approximately 20 per cent of TBI patients admitted to hospital have sustained moderate or severe head injuries (Bruns and Hauser, 2003), with the other 80 per cent representing mild injuries. Nevertheless, this represents a sizeable number. Moreover, a significant proportion (15–25 per cent) of those who sustain mild head injuries suffer ongoing cognitive difficulties (Carroll, Cassidy, Peloso et al., 2004b; Ponsford et al., 2000).

The highest overall incidence of TBI is in the age-group from 15 to 24 years, with other peaks in early childhood and in the elderly. In recent years there has been a rise in the proportion of those in older age groups sustaining TBI (O'Rance and Fortune, 2007). Most estimates indicate that between 1.5 and three males sustain TBI for every female, with the highest ratio evident in late adolescence/early adulthood, lower ratios in countries with less violence, and a more even ratio in the elderly (Bruns and Hauser, 2003). Studies focusing on other characteristics of the TBI population have suggested that a greater than average proportion have pre-existing maladaptive problems, such as psychopathology and substance abuse (Parry-Jones, Vaughan, and Cox, 2006; Rimel and Jane, 1984; Robinson and Jorge, 2002). TBI has also been shown to occur more commonly in the lower socio-economic classes, in people who are less educated and who are unemployed (Kraus and McArthur, 1999; Rimel and Jane, 1984).

Improvements in the acute management of TBI, particularly more rapid transfer to hospital and the use of measures to monitor and reduce intracranial pressure, have resulted in a reduction in mortality rates. The death rate from TBI in the US decreased from 25 per 100,000 to 19 per 100,000 between 1979 and 1992, although the death rate from firearm-related TBI has risen significantly in the USA (Bruns and Hauser, 2003). The declining death rate, together with the relative youth of those who sustain TBI, has led to a growth in the number of survivors of TBI in the community. They will be confronting their disabilities for decades in a society which still has a limited understanding of and facilities to cater for the needs of people with TBI.

Pathophysiology

Blunt trauma to the head associated with acceleration or deceleration forces results in a combination of translation and rotation, which may cause laceration of the scalp, skull fracture and/or shifting of the intracranial contents, with resultant focal and diffuse changes.

Skull fractures result from deformation of the skull at the time of impact. The majority of skull fractures are linear fractures, in which the area of impact is bent inwards and the surrounding skull is bent outwards. Fractures of the base of skull are common in the most severe head injuries. They carry a risk of intracranial infection via the sinuses or the middle ear and of cranial nerve injury. In a depressed skull fracture the bone has been pushed inwards beyond the level of the skull, and in a comminuted fracture the bone has broken into fragments. Both of these fractures may result in laceration of the cerebral cortex or haemorrhage and a possible focus for post-traumatic epilepsy and/or infection. They require surgery to lift and stabilise the bone segment (Roth and Farls, 2000). Fractures over the middle meningeal groove or the sagittal sinus may lead to the formation of an extradural haematoma.

The mechanisms whereby damage occurs within the brain tissue as a result of TBI are extremely complex, involving multiple, interactive pathological processes. These result in both focal changes, including contusion and haematoma formation, and diffuse changes, including diffuse axonal injury (DAI) and diffuse microvascular damage, as well as widespread neural excitation and metabolic changes (Povlishock and Katz, 2005). A distinction is drawn between primary and secondary brain injury resulting from blunt trauma, the former resulting directly from the trauma and the latter as a result of systemic complications, which are potentially treatable.

Primary brain injury mechanisms – Focal

Cerebral contusion

Contusions are haemorrhagic lesions resulting when acceleration/deceleration forces cause differential movements between the brain and the skull or at grey–white matter interfaces. They may occur at the site of impact, referred to as a "coup" injury, if local deformation has been sufficiently severe (Gaetz, 2004). Contre-coup contusions may be found on the opposite side to that of the impact, but are usually found on the crests of the gyri of the cerebral hemispheres, especially in those areas most likely to have contact with bony skull protuberances: the orbital plate of the frontal bone, the sphenoidal ridge, the petrous portion of the temporal bone and the sharp edges of the falces (Le and Gean, 2009). As a result, the basal and polar portions of the frontal and temporal lobes are most susceptible to contusions. However, contusions may also be found on the medial surfaces of the cerebral hemispheres and along the upper surface of the corpus callosum (Graham, 1999). They contribute to local neuronal destruction and ischaemia, or reduced blood supply, depriving neurons of oxygen and glucose.

Mechanisms of cell death occurring in contusional and pericontusional areas are termed *necrosis* and *apoptosis*. Necrosis occurs more quickly, as a result of membrane failure and ionic disruption, which degrade the neuronal cytoskeleton and cytoplasm and cause swelling and dilation of the mitochondria. Apoptosis occurs slowly over a longer period, without disruption of the cell membrane. It may be caused by neural excitation, radical-mediated injury or a disruption of calcium homeostasis (Povlishock and Katz, 2005; Raghupathi, 2004).

Intracranial haematoma

Vascular injury may be seen as multiple tiny "petechial" haemorrhages throughout the cerebral hemispheres. Tearing of larger blood vessels at the time of impact results in bleeding inside the skull and the formation of a clot, which can eventually cause compression of the brain and ischaemia. This may lead to the development of coma after a delay or to a deterioration in conscious state, necessitating prompt surgical intervention to stop the bleeding and evacuate the haematoma. Intracranial haematomas are classified according to their anatomical location. An *extradural haematoma* results from bleeding between the skull and outer covering of the brain, known as the dura mater. This is most commonly a complication of a temporal skull fracture, where meningeal vessels have been torn. A *subdural haematoma* is a collection of blood between the dura mater and the arachnoid mater. The elderly are at increased risk of chronic subdural haematoma because of their increased risk of falls and the greater intracranial space caused by cerebral atrophy. A *subdural hygroma* is a collection of cerebrospinal fluid in the subdural space through a tear in the arachnoid mater. It develops days or weeks after injury, and may form after the evacuation of an acute subdural haematoma. A *subarachnoid haemorrhage* refers to bleeding between the arachnoid and pia mater. This may cause arterial spasm, leading to ischaemic brain damage. It can also lead to obstruction of the flow of cerebrospinal fluid, resulting in communicating high pressure hydrocephalus. An *intracerebral haematoma* is a haemorrhage within the brain caused by a deep contusion or tear in the blood vessels. As with other pathological consequences of TBI, intracerebral haematomata occur most commonly in the frontal and temporal lobes (Gennarelli and Graham, 2005; Le and Gean, 2009).

Primary brain injury: Diffuse neuronal change and axonal injury

The mechanical force of injury may cause more diffuse neuronal membrane disruption (Farkas, 2007). Some cells appear to be able to reorganise, restore their function and thereby survive this disruption, whereas others show persistent membrane dysfunction, with activation of cysteine proteases (calpain and caspase), causing rapid necrotic cell death.

Similarly, mechanical forces can result in scattered and multi-focal axonal change throughout the subcortical white matter, corpus callosum and brain stem, termed *diffuse axonal injury* (DAI). In the most severe injuries, axons may be torn and retract, expelling axoplasm and forming "retraction balls". More commonly, mechanical strains cause focal alteration of the axolemma, or disruption of sodium channels, resulting in an influx of ions such as calcium, that disrupt the cytoskeleton. This results in progressive changes disrupting axonal transport and causing local swelling of the axon, followed by detachment from its downstream segment. Both myelinated and unmyelinated fibres appear to be vulnerable. These processes may take place over several hours or days after injury, creating a potential opportunity for intervention. Various therapies aimed at protecting the mitochondria, including the use of immunophilin ligands, cyclosporin A and FK 506 and hypothermia, are under investigation (Povlishock and Katz, 2005).

Shearing strains are thought to decrease in magnitude from the cortical surface to the centre of the brain (Ommaya and Gennarelli, 1974). They are enhanced along interfaces between substances of different densities and therefore DAI occurs most commonly in the grey–white matter junctions around the basal ganglia, the periventricular zone of the hypothalamus, the superior cerebellar peduncles, the fornices, fibre tracts of the corpus callosum, and in the frontal and temporal poles (Gaetz, 2004).

A consequence of DAI is that of downstream deafferentation or denervation. The downstream axon, disconnected from its sustaining cell body, undergoes wallerian degeneration which may take place over several months after injury. Downstream nerve terminals undergo neurodegenerative change.

Although neoplastic responses are not well understood, there is some evidence to suggest that, in the case of mild–moderate injury, diffuse deafferentation may result in sprouting of adjacent intact nerve fibres, leading to some recovery of synaptic input to the deafferented areas. However, in the case of severe injury, there appear to be maladaptive changes, with fibre ingrowth and changes in cytoarchitecture (Povlishock and Katz, 2005). These processes, and potential means of influencing them, are the focus of continuing experimentation.

Widespread metabolic changes also occur following TBI. Across the spectrum of injury severity, TBI is followed by a short-lived increase in glucose metabolism (a sign of metabolic stress), followed by a decreased rate of glucose metabolism which may last for days or weeks and shows some correspondence with the period of recovery and with outcome. Elevated lactate and glutamate are also evident and higher levels are associated with poorer outcome (Bergsneider, Hovda, and McArthur, 2001).

Petechial white matter haemorrhage

DAI is most commonly associated with injuries involving acceleration–deceleration, such as motor vehicle accidents. Findings on computed tomography or magnetic resonance imaging may include the presence of petechial white matter haemorrhage as well as non-haemorrhagic white matter lesions, diffuse oedema, and small subarachnoid and intraventricular haemorrhages (Povlishock and Katz, 2005). Deeper lesions are indicative of more severe injury (Blackman, Rice, and Matsumoto, 2003; Grados et al., 2001). Adams et al. (1989) refer to three grades of DAI: Grade 1 where focal haemorrhagic lesions are confined to the white matter of the cerebral hemispheres; Grade 2 where there is involvement of the corpus callosum; and Grade 3 where the dorsolateral upper brain stem is involved. However, lesser degrees of DAI may also be seen in some cases of mild head injuries (Bigler, 2008). Over time there is increasing atrophy, the extent of which is correlated with injury severity and outcome (Bigler, 2001a).

Secondary brain injury mechanisms

Both intracranial and extracranial complications may result in secondary brain injury, either as a consequence of cerebral ischaemia or distortion and/or compression of the brain/mass effect. *Cerebral ischaemia*, as a result of inadequate blood flow and consequent tissue hypoxia, is usually the ultimate cause of secondary brain damage associated with TBI. Hypoxic damage is frequently found in the border zones of areas supplied by the major cerebral arteries, particularly in the parasagittal cortex, the hippocampus, the thalamus and basal ganglia (Gennarelli and Graham, 2005). Intracranial complications may include the following:

Brain swelling

There are two mechanisms which lead to an increase in the volume of the brain following TBI. The first is an increase in the cerebral blood volume, termed *hyperaemia*, caused by hypoxia, hypercapnia, or obstruction of major cerebral veins as a result of cerebral oedema. The second is *cerebral oedema*, resulting from an increased volume of intra- or extracellular fluid in the brain tissue. Cerebral oedema may be caused by damage to the walls of cerebral blood vessels, accumulation of fluid within the cell as a result of ischaemia, increased intravascular pressure, or an obstruction to the flow of cerebrospinal fluid. These mechanisms may result in brain swelling of either a localised or a diffuse nature. Damage to the brain tends to be caused by a mass effect, with brain shift and/or raised intracranial pressure, leading to hypoxia/ischaemia.

Infection

Infection, which may develop in the subacute phase after TBI, is a complication associated with skull fracture. It can manifest itself in two forms: *meningitis* and *cerebral abscess*, causing raised intracranial pressure and/or brain shift.

Raised intracranial pressure

Increases in *intracranial pressure* (ICP) are a common consequence of the abovementioned intracranial complications, causing impairment of brain function due to reduction in *cerebral perfusion pressure* and consequently in cerebral blood flow, resulting in ischaemia, and brain shift. Uncontrolled intracranial pressure frequently causes diffuse ischaemic brain damage (Gennarelli and Graham, 2005). Cerebral autoregulation, or the ability of the brain to maintain a constant blood flow to the brain, may be impaired or lost under conditions such as increased intracranial pressure, ischaemia, inflammation or low or high mean arterial pressure, rendering the brain more vulnerable to ischaemia. Reductions in blood flow result in metabolic changes, which ultimately result in neuronal disintegration. Intracranial pressure and associated cerebral perfusion pressure are therefore routinely monitored in severe TBI cases.

Another potential consequence of raised intracranial pressure, haematoma and/or brain swelling is herniation. *Subfalcine herniation* occurs when one cingulate gyrus herniates across the midline. A more serious type is *transtentorial herniation*, where there is downward displacement of the parahippocampal gyrus and uncus of one or both temporal lobes through the tentorial hiatus into the posterior fossa. Compression of the oculomotor nerve, as well as midbrain dysfunction, commonly result from tentorial herniation. Unchecked tentorial herniation leads to a deterioration in brain stem functioning, with consequent respiratory abnormality, hyperventilation, decerebration and, eventually, death. *Tonsillar herniation* occurs when the cerebellum is forced through the foramen magnum, leading to symptoms of vagus nerve compression, hypoxia, oedema of the medulla and, eventually, respiratory arrest and death (Gennarelli and Graham, 2005; Le and Gean, 2009).

Decompressive craniectomy surgery involves temporarily removing a portion of frontal skull bone to increase the volume of the cranial cavity and to decrease intracranial pressure. The procedure carries risks, and the efficacy, optimal timing and surgical methods, and neurological function in the survivors remain uncertain. Whilst some case series and case control studies have shown decreased intracranial pressure and improved neurological outcomes, the only randomised controlled trial in adults to date has suggested that decompressive craniectomy results in poorer functional outcomes (Cooper et al., 2011, 2008).

Apart from damage due to pressure effects, secondary brain injury following TBI is caused by hypoxia, cellular influx of calcium and other ions, release of free radicals and excitotoxic neurotransmitters, and apoptotic cell death, all of which are potentially preventable (Verma, 2000). Results of clinical trials examining the efficacy of drugs that block various ion channels, scavenge free radicals, inhibit excitatory neurotransmitters, or block the internal signals for programmed cell death have, however, been disappointing (Faden, 2001).

A number of reasons for this failure have been put forward, including the differences in therapeutic time windows between animal and human trials and the heterogeneity of neuropathology, which means that treatments focused on one pathological process do not attenuate other processes and thus have little overall impact in humans (Maas, 2001; Narayan, Michel, Ansell, Baethmann, Biegon, Bracken et al., 2002). There is also debate over determination and matching of injury severity levels across sites and studies and of sensitive outcome measures. Efforts towards development of such treatments continues.

Extracranial complications

Extracranial complications may occur where there is multiple trauma. Injuries to other parts of the body may cause blood loss and hypotension, pulmonary injury, aspiration of vomit, or cardiac or respiratory arrest, with consequent hypoxia, causing further brain damage. Thus prevention of these complications in the acute management stages is of paramount importance.

Delayed complications of TBI

Post-traumatic epilepsy

TBI creates an increased risk of epilepsy. Jennett (1979) estimated the overall incidence of post-traumatic epilepsy following non-missile head injury at 5 per cent. He distinguished between *early post-traumatic epilepsy*, which occurs within the first week after injury (most commonly in the first 24 hours), and *late post-traumatic epilepsy*, which typically occurs more than three months post-injury. Protracted seizures carry a risk of further brain injury, as a result of increased metabolic requirements, disruption of spontaneous respiration, and aspiration. Focal motor seizures and partial complex "temporal lobe" seizures are seen most commonly. Children are more susceptible to early epilepsy. Late epilepsy occurs in about 20 per cent of those who experience early epilepsy.

Predisposing factors for epilepsy include the presence of brain contusion with subdural haematoma, skull fracture, greater injury severity and age over 65 years. In a study by Annegers and Coan (2000), the relative risk of seizures was 1.5 following mild TBI (loss of consciousness (LOC) less than 30 minutes), 2.9 following moderate TBI (LOC 30 minutes–1 day) and 17.2 following severe injury (LOC greater than one day). The risk is greatest in the first two years after injury. Another study found that patients with a Glasgow Coma Score (GCS) 3–8 had a cumulative probability of late post-traumatic seizures by 24 months post-injury of 16.8 per cent. The probability was 24.3 per cent for those with GCS score of 9–12 and 8.0 per cent for those with GCS score of 13–15 (Englander et al., 2003), showing that GCS alone does not predict epilepsy risk. In this study one-third of late posttraumatic seizures occurred within a month of injury and 86 per cent within one year. There is also a high risk of recurrence of late onset seizures (Haltiner, Temkin, and Dikmen, 1997).

Although anticonvulsant therapy during the first week after injury may reduce early-onset epilepsy (Temkin et al., 1999), there is no evidence to support prophylactic treatment with anticonvulsants for prevention of late-onset post-traumatic seizures (The Brain Trauma Foundation, The American Association of Neurological Surgeons, and The Joint Section on Neurotrauma and Critical Care, 2000). Whilst no anticonvulsants are without adverse effects, carbamazepine and valproic acid have been found to be relatively free of adverse cognitive effects relative to phenytoin (Dikmen, Temkin, Miller, Machamer, and Winn, 1991; Hessen, Reinvang, and Gjerstad, 2007; Meador, Loring, Huh, Gallagher, and King, 1990). In view of the expense and potential toxicity of anticonvulsants, most clinicians withdraw medications after one to two seizure-free years.

Hydrocephalus

Communicating hydrocephalus, which occurs in 1–2 per cent of cases, results from obstruction to the flow of cerebrospinal fluid by blood in the subarachnoid space. This leads to ventricular enlargement and a consequent decline in cognitive function, gait disturbance and incontinence, although in the case of serious brain injury it may be difficult to discern whether the hydrocephalus is clinically significant. Shunting to treat hydrocephalus is most likely to be effective if there has been evidence of clinical deterioration (Mazzini, 2003). It is important to note that ventricular enlargement can also occur without signs of communicating hydrocephalus, as a result of a general reduction in the bulk of the cerebral white matter (Bigler, 2001b).

Summary of pathophysiological evidence

In summary, the factors causing TBI are complex and numerous, resulting in wide variations in the quantity and distribution of damaged brain tissue. In spite of the apparent heterogeneity of brain injury resulting from blunt trauma to the head, and the difficulties in its delineation, it seems clear from the neuropathological evidence available that diffuse injury is common, and that damage occurs most frequently in the frontal and temporal lobes, the hippocampus, corpus callosum and the basal ganglia. The neurobehavioural significance of this will be discussed in a later section of this chapter.

Neuroimaging and TBI

A number of neuroimaging methods are used in the management of TBI. However, it is not possible to gain an accurate picture of the precise extent of damage to the brain using any of the techniques in current clinical use for studying regional brain morphology and function. *Computed tomography* (CT) is useful in the detection of skull fractures, intracranial haematomas, large contusions, cerebral abscess, hygromas, brain swelling, infarction, ventricular enlargement and atrophy (see Figures 1.1a and 1.1b). It also has the advantages of a relatively rapid scanning time and relative ease of patient monitoring, which are important factors in the acute management phase (Siegel and Alavi, 1990). It can be used to identify possible causes of deterioration or lack of progress in neurological status. However, it is not sensitive in detection of smaller areas of contusion or the diffuse white matter lesions which so frequently occur (Bigler, 2005). Moreover, day-of-injury scans may reveal less injury than becomes evident on subsequent scans.

In comparison, *magnetic resonance imaging* (MRI) is more sensitive, particularly to non-haemorrhagic grey and white matter lesions and isodense collections of blood, and has greater resolution in the brainstem (Le and Gean, 2009; Togal et al., 2008) (see Figure 1.2). However, MRI takes longer to perform and requires that the patient not have any MRI-incompatible implants or equipment. CT is generally used in the acute post-injury stages, and MRI may be more useful over the longer term. Whilst the sensitivity of MRI has increased significantly over the past two decades, it still lacks sensitivity to the microscopic lesions commonly associated with TBI (Bigler, 2005). Flair imaging improves the detection of contusions, white matter

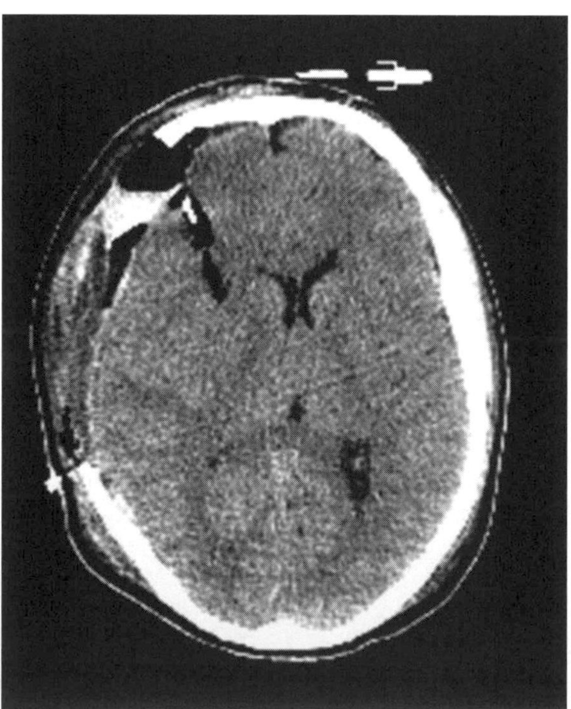

Figure 1.1a CT performed on day of injury at level of basal ganglia, showing extra-axial right acute haematoma with minimal sulcal effacement.

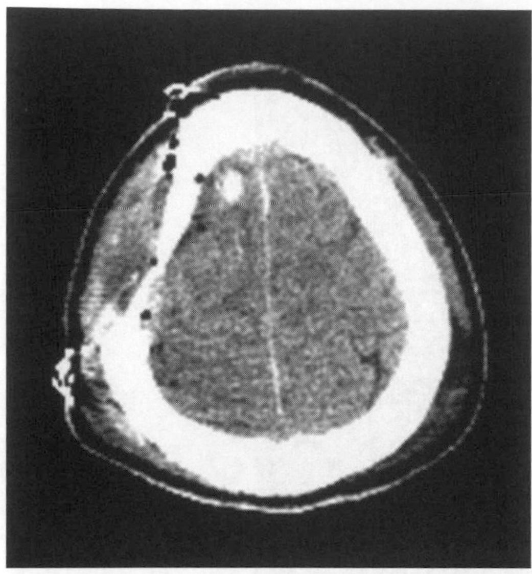

Figure 1.1b Day of injury CT at level of frontal lobes, showing larger right extra-axial haematoma and punctate haemorrhage in right frontal lobe.

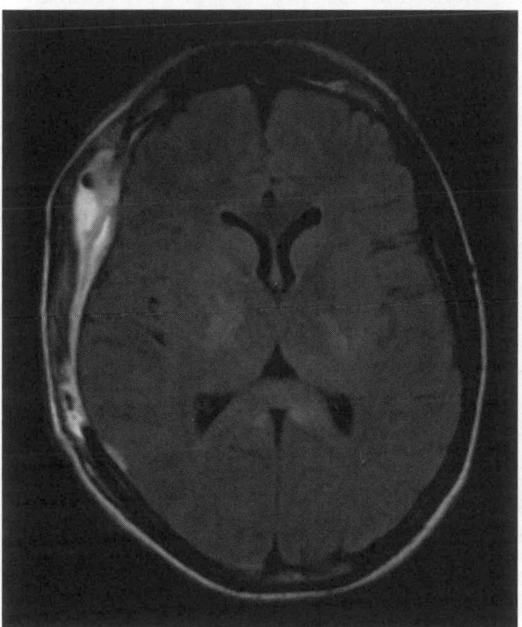

Figure 1.2 MRI performed after right craniectomy with axial flair image at level of basal ganglia, showing bilateral increased signal intensity in basal ganglia and internal capsule.

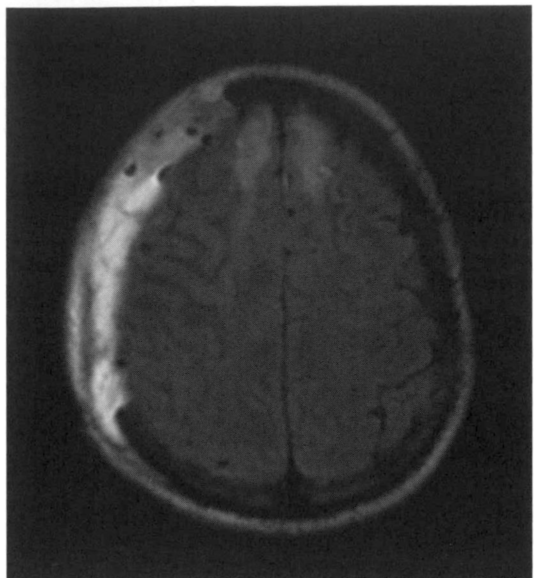

Figure 1.3 Post-operative MRI axial flair image near vertex, showing bilateral increased signal intensity involving white matter and overlying cortex of anterial frontal lobes and small post-operative extracranial haematoma.

shearing injuries and subarachnoid haemorrhage (see Figures 1.3 and 1.4). Gradient-recalled-echo T2*-weighted and susceptibility-weighted MRI are sensitive to the presence of ferritin and haemosiderin, two breakdown products of blood, which may indicate DAI (Le and Gean, 2009) (see Figures 1.5a and 1.5b). These sequences are generally integrated in the one MRI procedure. The absence of positive findings on either CT or MRI does not rule out the presence of lesions, however. Serial scans in individuals with moderate to very severe injuries frequently reveal a gradual reduction in brain tissue volume or atrophy, mostly associated with loss of white matter, which may continue over many months after injury (Bigler, 2005).

Diffusion weighted MRI (DWI), which measures the random motion of water molecules in brain tissue, has been used to calculate lesion size and shown to increase the sensitivity of MRI in detecting DAI (Huisman, Sorensen, Hergan, Gonzalez, and Schaefer, 2003; Le and Gean, 2009). The extent of this has been correlated with outcome (Schaefer, Huisman, Sorensen, Gonzalez, and Schwamm, 2004). Another technique derived from DWI is *diffusion tensor imaging* or DTI. This is now being used to evaluate the integrity of white matter tracts following TBI in the chronic stages, using measures of fractional anisotropy, which measures the preferential motion of water molecules along the white matter axons, as well as axial diffusivity and radial diffusivity (Huisman et al., 2004; Le and Gean, 2009; Skoglund Nilsson,

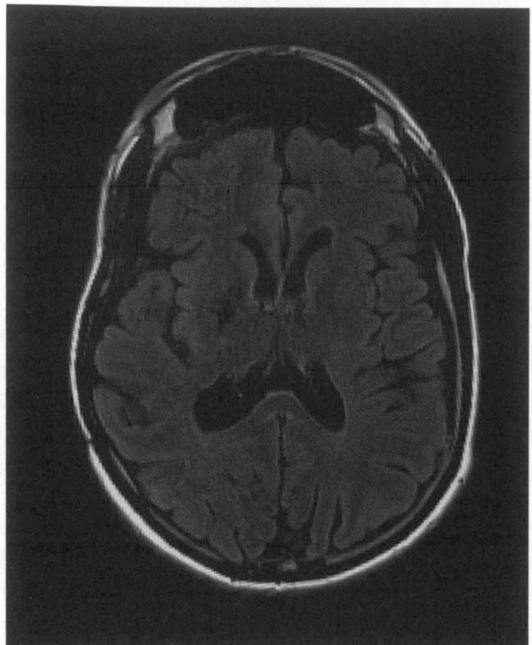

Figure 1.4 Axial flair MRI image two years post-injury at level of basal ganglia, showing focal areas of breakdown products in posterior limb of right internal capsule.

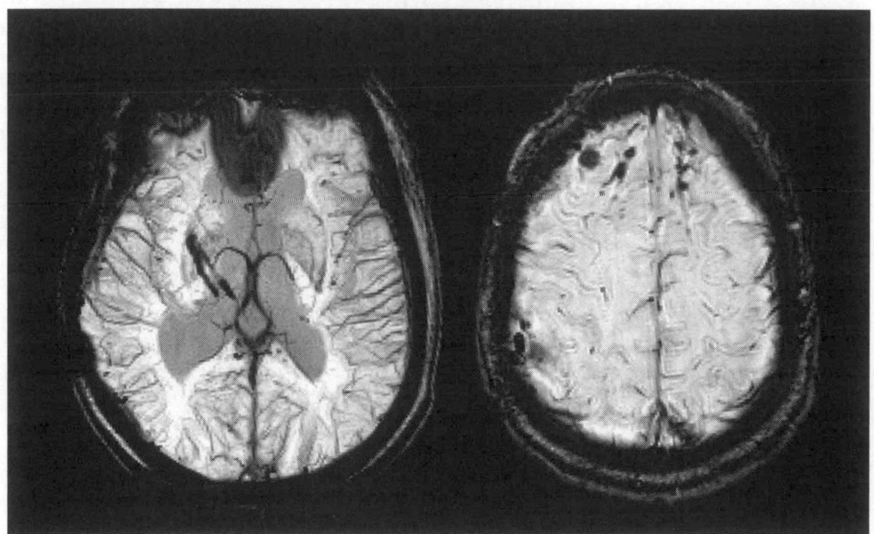

Figure 1.5 Axial susceptibility-weighted MRI images two years post-injury, showing linear haemosiderin staining consistent with haemorrhagic diffuse axonal/ shear injury.

Ljungberg, Jonsson, and Rydenhag, 2008) (see Figure 1.6). Kraus and colleagues (2007) have shown an association between degree of white matter change measured on DTI and extent of cognitive impairment, both being proportional to injury severity. The integrity of thalamic projection fibres measured on DTI has been associated with severity of impairments of executive, attention and memory function (Little et al., 2010b). However it needs to be acknowledged that DTI is not yet standardised, with findings depending on the scanner and software used (Little et al., 2010a).

Some functional imaging techniques provide information regarding metabolic activity in various brain regions, although none of these are routinely available clinically. Measures of cerebral perfusion used to identify compromised brain tissue include *positron emission tomography* (PET), which measures regional metabolic rates for oxygen and glucose, *single photon emission computer tomography* (SPECT) and *perfusion MRI*. Functional MRI studies have shown more widespread cortical activation in TBI individuals performing a mentally effortful task relative to uninjured controls (Christodoulou et al., 2001; Lovell et al., 2007).

Magnetic resonance spectroscopy (MRS) is used to measure metabolites, such as choline (as a measure of membrane injury from DAI), N-acetylaspartate (NAA; as a marker of neuronal health), creatinine (as a marker of energy metabolism), or lactate (as a marker of failed oxidative metabolism), as indicators of pathology which may predict outcome (Shutter, Tong, Lee, and Holshouser, 2006).

Quantitative EEG, *computer-averaged evoked potentials* (EPs), *event-related evoked potentials* (ERPs) and *magnetoencephalography* (MEG) have supplanted the electroencephalogram (EEG) for studying the functional integrity of neural networks non-invasively. However due to their complexity and controversies regarding their relationships with TBI individuals' functional abilities, these methods are not in wide clinical use (Arciniegas, Anderson, and Rojas, 2005). Whilst recent developments in neuroimaging and neurophysiological techniques show promise, neurological, neuropsychological and functional assessment continue to play a vital role in delineating the nature and extent of impairment and disability resulting from TBI.

Recovery from TBI

The mechanisms set in motion when TBI occurs are extremely complex, taking place over hours, days or weeks following injury. They affect not only the neurons directly injured, but also areas of the brain far removed from the lesion site, through processes such as transneuronal degeneration, neurochemical alterations, oedema, raised ICP, and vascular disruption due to haemorrhage or ischaemia (Almli and Finger, 1992; Schoenfeld and Hamilton, 1977).

Once these processes have abated, the nervous system will begin the process of repairing itself. Recovery following TBI generally tends to follow a

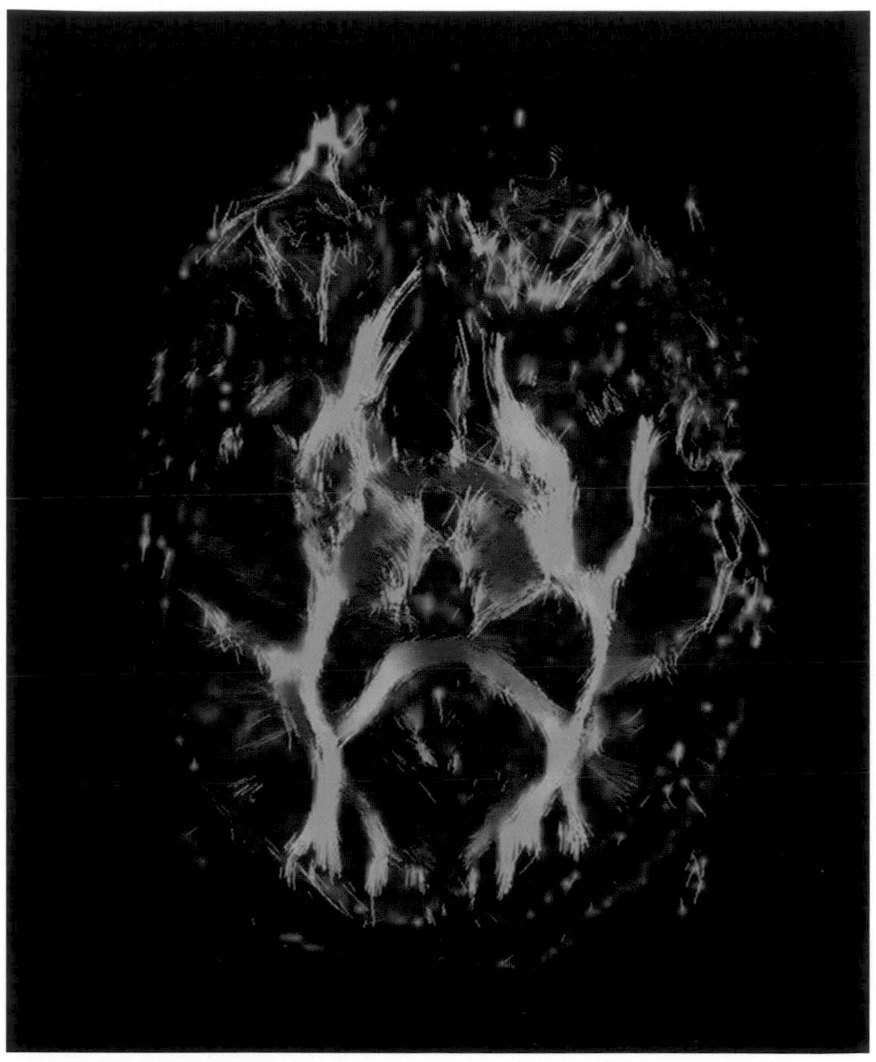

Figure 1.6 Axial diffusion-weighted tensor image (DTI)-based coloured fractional anisotropy (FA) map taken two years post-injury

negatively accelerating curve, which is most rapid in the first three to six months, but may continue for several years after injury (Groswasser Mendelson, Stern, Schecter, and Najenson, 1977; Thomsen, 1984). There is, however, considerable individual variability in recovery curves, so that it is difficult to predict the pattern, time course or ultimate extent of recovery in a given individual (Brooks and Aughton, 1979).

The process of recovery is exceedingly complex. Various functions may follow different time courses of recovery because of differing physiological and structural substrates; specific mechanisms may be pertinent to some functions, but irrelevant to others; individual differences in cerebral organisation may influence recovery, as may genetic and hormonal factors, as well as the age, sex, handedness, intelligence, and motivation of the person sustaining the injury. Other potential sources of variability include the specific aetiology of the lesion(s), their severity and location (Kolb and Cioe, 2004; Kolb, Teskey, and Gibb, 2010).

The mechanisms underlying recovery of function are, as yet, relatively poorly understood. There are a number of proposed mechanisms of recovery from TBI (Finger and Stein, 1982; Kolb and Cioe, 2004). Some of these support the concept of restitution of function to damaged areas, that is, the notion that spontaneous physiological recovery occurs in the damaged area, enabling neural pathways to resume activity and the functions subserved by them to be restored. Others suggest that recovery occurs through the substitution or reorganisation of neural structures and/or functions.

Theories supporting restitution of function

A great deal of the early spontaneous recovery after TBI is probably explained by the resolution of temporary physiological changes, such as oedema, vascular disruption, ICP changes and biochemical alterations, which have caused functional, rather than structural, axonal disruption. This results in the return of temporarily suppressed functions or areas of the brain to normal within the first few hours, days or weeks after injury (Schoenfeld and Hamilton, 1977).

In addition to this resolution, a number of reparative processes are initiated. Whilst these processes rarely, if ever, result in complete restoration of the damaged tissue within the central nervous system, there are regenerative changes that have been associated with behavioural improvement. The presence of regenerative and collateral sprouting into denervated areas has been investigated quite extensively. Evidence from animal studies suggests that the new connections that form are operational (Steward, 1989). However, it remains unclear whether such growth contributes to recovery of function (Almli and Finger, 1992; Kolb et al., 2010). The presence of scar tissue presents a significant barrier to the formation of functional connections. Much research is being undertaken in an attempt to find ways to enhance such regrowth. Experimental attempts have been made to build glial bridges to enable regenerating fibres to grow across areas of scar tissue (Aguayo, 1985). Another potential means of promoting fibre growth is the introduction of neurotrophic factors, such as nerve growth factor, which are produced by the glia in order to promote regenerative growth. Growth factors are also being used to encourage stem cells to differentiate and migrate to the lesioned area (Kolb et al., 2010). Alternatively the action of molecules that inhibit new axonal growth might be inhibited. Studies are also being conducted to investigate what factors influence the formation of new synapses (Kolb and Cioe, 2004). Whilst these research endeavours hold promise, they are still far from clinical implementation in humans.

Theories supporting reorganisation or substitution of function

There are two main classes of substitution theory – those that postulate anatomical reorganisation, and those that postulate behavioural compensation or functional adaptation as mechanisms of recovery.

Anatomical reorganisation

There is a growing body of evidence to suggest that environmental stimulation and specifically behavioural therapies can alter brain function and organisation after injury, termed plasticity. This may occur by the reorganisation of neural circuits within or associated with the damaged area or via the reorganisation of remaining circuits. Studies have shown that increased motor use (e.g., of fingers to play an instrument) or sensory stimulation results in enlargement of the relevant cortical areas devoted to those functions (Elbert, Heim, and Rockstroh, 2001; Nudo, Plautz, and Frost, 2001; Pantev et al., 1998) and changes in synaptic density and organisation (Jacobs and Scheibel, 1993). Genetic changes have also been shown to occur in response to experience (Rampon et al., 2000). When sensorimotor function is impaired by stroke, larger areas of sensorimotor cortical recruitment are evident in both the injured and the contralateral hemisphere, and these show an association with recovery of function. The capacity for reorganisation decreases as the size of the damaged area increases, as the presence of intact tissue appears to be important to allow this reorganisation of function to occur. The extent to which this reorganisation takes place also varies according to genetic differences and pre-injury experience, as well as age (Kolb et al., 2010). Of particular significance in this context, therapy in the form of forced movement has been shown to be necessary to maintain the functions of the undamaged motor cortex and the movements they represent (Kleim et al., 2002). This has led to the development of "constraint-induced movement therapy", where the patient is forced to move an affected limb for several hours each day (Taub and Morris, 2001). It appears that general, non-specific stimulation results in better outcomes, although there is as yet limited evidence indicating what type of therapy is most effective (Kolb et al., 2010).

Age also affects capacity for cerebral plasticity. In infants, if the cerebral cortex is damaged during neural migration, from the third trimester until birth, the outcome will be poorer, whereas if it occurs during the period of neurogenesis in the first two years of life the outcome will be better due to the potential for synaptogenesis. Those aged over 40 are also said to have poorer outcomes (Kolb, 2004). Other factors which may influence potential for cerebral reorganisation include the intelligence of the injured person, their handedness, their sex and their hormonal status. Recent evidence suggests the presence of progesterone immediately post-injury may be advantageous, but the presence of oestrogen may interfere with reorganisation during the recovery process (Kolb, 2004). This raises the potential for pharmacological intervention to facilitate recovery. Trials evaluating the impact of progesterone administered in the acute stages are producing promising findings (Stein, 2001). There is also evidence that certain compounds that facilitate plastic change within the brain, such as amphetamines, may enhance recovery and some preliminary studies support this (Feeney and Sutton, 1987; Goldstein, 2000; Kolb et al., 2010).

Behavioural compensation and functional adaptation

An improved ability to perform a task cannot be accepted as evidence that another part of the brain has taken over the function required to perform that task. It may, alternatively, reflect a change in strategy on the part of the injured individual. Behavioural compensation or functional adaptation is the final explanation of recovery of function. Instead of re-routing connections, brain-injured individuals may develop new solutions to problems using intact structures, that is, they adapt. In order to view this as a possible means of recovery, it is necessary to conceive a function in terms of goals, rather than the means used to attain these goals (Laurence and Stein, 1978). Qualitative analysis of the person's performance will frequently reveal that alternative strategies are being brought into play to make up for the loss of function associated with the brain lesion. It is the nature of these alternative "means" of performing a task that is of particular interest in understanding behavioural compensation as a process of recovery.

There are examples of spontaneous functional adaptation to be found in the literature, both from animal studies (Gentile, Green, Nieburgs, Schmelzer, and Stein, 1978), and human studies (Evans, Wilson, Needham, and Brennall, 2003; Gazzaniga, 1978; Holland, 1982). Luria (1963) has described a number of cases where brain-injured individuals were trained to use alternative modalities in order to perform tasks. As with other theoretical explanations for recovery, there is a need for more carefully controlled and detailed investigation in this area. Whilst improved imaging technology may provide evidence to the contrary, it appears that functional adaptations of various kinds contribute significantly to longer term recovery following TBI. Methods of facilitating restitution of function, anatomical reorganisation and functional adaptation will be explored in further detail in Chapter 4.

Impairment of consciousness

Blunt trauma to the head usually results in immediate loss or impairment of consciousness. The duration and degree of that impairment of consciousness is of major significance in indicating the severity of injury. In the case of mild head injury there may be a clouding of consciousness, where the person is confused and disoriented for a period of time, which they subsequently do not clearly remember. In the case of more severe injuries, coma may persist for days, weeks or months. The essential feature of coma is decreased behavioural responsiveness to external stimuli and inner need.

Coma is graded by measuring the degree of decrease in observable responsiveness to external stimuli. The measure which is most frequently used to grade the depth of coma is the Glasgow Coma Scale (GCS) (Teasdale and Jennett, 1974, 1976). In a small per centage of cases the person with TBI passes from coma into what is termed a *persistent vegetative state*. In this state the person typically shows eye opening, with sleep and wake cycles, and sometimes the ability to "track" (albeit briefly) with the eyes. There may be an ability to make reflex postural adjustments with the limbs, and a range of primitive reflexes may be evident (e.g., bite, grasp), but there is no evidence of responsiveness to their environment (Jennett and Teasdale, 1981). Following emergence from coma, the person who has sustained TBI usually remains confused and disoriented for a period of time, having no capacity to remember ongoing events. This may last for hours, days, weeks or months. The period from the time of injury to the return of the capacity to form new memories is termed *post-traumatic amnesia* (PTA). The duration of PTA is also now widely used as a measure of severity of TBI (Cattelani, Tanzi, Lombardi, and Mazzucchi, 2002; Doig, Fleming, and Tooth, 2001; Fleming, Tooth, Hassell, and Chan, 1999; Sherer et al., 2002a; Sherer, Struchen, and Yablon, 2008; van der Naalt, van Zomeren, Sluiter, and Minderhond, 1999). The assessment and management of patients in coma, low states of awareness and PTA will be discussed in detail in Chapter 2.

Ongoing sensorimotor disabilities

Depending on the location and extent of injury to the brain, a broad range of sensorimotor disabilities may result from TBI. Motor deficits can take the form of weakness or paralysis on one or both sides of the body, incoordination of muscle movements (ataxia), loss of fine and gross motor dexterity, poor balance, and reduced physical endurance. Injury to the nerves which supply the motor apparatus responsible for the production of speech is not uncommon, resulting in a reduced capacity to articulate speech sounds and/or difficulties with phonation, resonance and prosody (dysarthria), and impaired motor programming of articulation (dyspraxia). Swallowing disorders (dysphagia) may also occur.

A broad range of sensory disturbances may be caused by cranial nerve lesions, or injury to subcortical or cortical sensory pathways. Diminished sense of smell can result from olfactory nerve lesions. Visual impairment is particularly common due to a range of causes. Damage to the optic nerve may result in blindness or loss of visual acuity, lesions in the optic pathways in the temporal, parietal or occipital lobes may result in visual field defects, and cranial nerve lesions may lead to a range of eye movement disorders, with blurring of vision or diplopia occurring commonly. Eye movement disorders may also result from damage to the frontal lobes and/or the basal ganglia. Hearing loss occurs in a smaller per centage of cases. It tends to be sensorineural, often bilateral, and associated with transverse petrous fractures. The lesion is most often in the Organ of Corti, which is believed to be damaged by concussion. Conductive deafness may be caused by blood in the middle ear system or disruption of the ossicular chain. Tinnitus occurs frequently, especially following mild head injuries. Vertigo may follow diffuse injury of, or bleeding into, the labyrinth. Injury to the glossopharyngeal nerve, associated with fracture of the base of skull, may produce difficulty in swallowing and loss of taste on the posterior one-third of the tongue, as well as paralysis of some of the pharyngeal muscles. Tactile sensation (pain, temperature and texture) and proprioception (the ability to feel the position of joints and limbs in space) may be impaired as a result of sensory pathway lesions. Comprehensive assessment of sensorimotor problems and provision of appropriate treatment by an interdisciplinary team is an important part of the rehabilitation process. A detailed discussion of these processes is beyond the scope of this book, however.

Cognitive and behavioural sequelae

Following the return of consciousness and orientation, most of those who sustain TBI exhibit a range of ongoing cognitive and behavioural sequelae. These occur in various permutations and combinations, and vary widely in their nature and severity, depending on the location and extent of injury, as well as premorbid characteristics of the injured individual.

Sequelae of mild TBI

Mild TBI is defined as

> those injuries where there is confusion or disorientation, loss of consciousness for 30 minutes or less, PTA for less than 24 hours and/or other transient neurological abnormalities such as focal signs, seizure, and intracranial lesion not requiring surgery; and a GCS score of 13–15 after 30 minutes post-injury or later upon presentation for healthcare. These manifestations must not be due to drugs, alcohol, or medications, or be caused by other injuries, treatment for other injuries (e.g. systemic injuries,

facial injuries or intubation), other problems (e.g. psychological trauma, language barrier or coexisting medical conditions) or penetrating craniocerebral injury (Carroll, Cassidy, Holm, Kraus, and Coronado, 2004a, p. 115).

Neurological deficits are rarely apparent following the acute stages of mild TBI. However, the person may experience a range of symptoms, including headache, dizziness, fatigue, blurred or double vision, sensitivity to noise and/or bright lights, tinnitus, restlessness, insomnia, reduced speed of thinking, concentration and memory problems, irritability, anxiety and depression and poor balance. The most common causes of these injuries are falls and motor vehicle accidents, but a significant proportion of mild TBIs also result from sports-related concussion, cycling accidents, assault and combat in the theatre of war. Typically, individuals who have sustained mild TBI and have no other injuries return home within a few days, with the expectation of resuming their normal activities. In many cases these so-called post-concussional symptoms subside over a period of days or weeks. Neuropsychological studies have confirmed the presence of impaired speed of information processing, attention and/or memory in the early days after injury. Recovery from symptoms and cognitive impairments appears to take place within two weeks following sports-related concussion. In other aetiological groups the time-frame of recovery is more variable, but in the majority of cases symptoms have resolved within three months (Carroll et al., 2004b). However, in 15–25 per cent of cases these difficulties persist and sometimes result in significant ongoing disability and adjustment problems (Carroll et al., 2004b). The cause of such ongoing problems, termed the persistent post-concussive syndrome, remains a subject of much debate. Injury severity measures (i.e. GCS and PTA) do not show a significant association with outcome following mild TBI (Carroll et al., 2004b; Ponsford et al., 2000). Ponsford and colleagues (2000) found that the factors most strongly associated with continuing symptoms following mild TBI were the presence of pre-existing neurological or psychiatric problems, being a student and the presence of other concurrent life stressors. A number of other authors have drawn attention to the overlap of post-concussional symptoms with symptoms associated with pain resulting from other injuries, medication effects, post-traumatic stress, anxiety, depression, pre-accident psychological adjustment issues, individual coping styles, the presence of other stressors and/or litigation/compensation (Arciniegas, Anderson, Topkoff, and McAllister, 2005; Bogod, Mateer, and MacDonald, 2003; Carroll et al., 2004a; Carroll et al., 2004b; Hoge et al., 2008; Mateer, Sira, and O'Connell, 2005; Meares et al., 2006; Meares et al., 2008; Ponsford, 2005; Rose, 2005; Ruff, 2005; Wood, 2004). It would appear that these other issues interact with the effects of mild TBI to exacerbate symptoms and distress and may, in some cases, be the primary factors underpinning persistent post-concussive symptoms.

However, with the use of increasingly sophisticated imaging techniques, such as DTI, MR spectroscopy, MRI-volumetry, gradient echo, diffusion weighted and susceptibility weighted MR scanning sequences, it has become possible to identify cerebral changes which are not evident on CT scans in at least a proportion of mild TBI cases (Bigler, 2008; Cohen et al., 2007; Togal et al., 2008; Wilde et al., 2008; Zhang, Heier, Zimmerman, Jordan, and Ulug, 2006). Moreover, recent studies have provided evidence of greater likelihood of abnormal imaging findings and more significant ongoing neuropsychological problems in individuals with "complicated" mild TBI, suggesting that these injuries occur on a continuum of severity (Lange, Iverson, and Franzen, 2009; Levine et al., 2006; McAllister, Sparling, Flashman, and Saykin, 2001). In a modelling study of concussion, Viano and colleagues (2005) showed 4–5 mm displacements of the hippocampus, caudate, amygdala, anterior commissure and midbrain, which were associated with cognitive and physical symptoms in football players. Bigler (2008) suggests that these same regions are likely to be involved in most concussive injuries to variable degrees, with long-coursing axons such as those in the corpus callosum and anterior commissure particularly vulnerable, and concomitant irritation to the vasculature and the meninges, the extent of which depends on the direction and magnitude of force associated with the injury. These forces disrupt the cytoskeletal architecture, affecting cell function transiently or permanently. According to Giza and Hovda (2004), within 25–50 msec of such an impact there is evidence of transient biomechanically induced ionic disturbance and upregulation of cellular glycolysis, followed by a downregulation in glucose metabolism. The degree to which there are lasting changes depends on the nature and extent of the force applied, and also on factors associated with the person, which may include genetic factors. McAllister and colleagues (2006) have identified genetic polymorphisms modulating central dopaminergic tone, that appear to affect cognitive performance on tests of processing speed, attention and memory following mild or moderate TBI.

Findings regarding the effects of multiple concussive head injuries, most of which have come from sports concussion studies, have been mixed. Results of a recent meta-analysis have suggested that multiple self-reported concussions were associated with poorer performances on tests of delayed memory and executive function (Belanger, Spiegel, and Vanderploeg, 2010). However, the clinical significance of these differences is unclear. Outcomes are likely to depend on the severity of each injury.

Overall, it appears that a number of factors interact to determine the likelihood of continuing post-concussive symptoms. These relate to the person who is injured (age, sex, physical, psychological, cultural, genetic), injury factors (injury force, direction and site, its cause or circumstances, other injuries), and post-injury factors such as pain, post-traumatic stress, environmental demands and expectations, other stressors, and litigation/compensation issues. Further discussion of the causes of ongoing problems following mild TBI and approaches to their management is contained in Chapter 8.

Neurobehavioural consequences of moderate and severe TBI

In the case of moderate and severe TBI, where coma has persisted for more than an hour, and PTA for more than 24 hours, cognitive and behavioural changes are more extensive and persistent than in the case of mild head injury. The nature and degree of these changes vary widely, according to the site and extent of injury. Disorders of language, perception or praxis may result from lesions disrupting the systems responsible for these neuropsychological functions. However, because of the high incidence of DAI, and damage to the frontal and temporal lobes, problems with fatigue, attention, memory, executive function and behavioural regulation are particularly common. Whilst some "executive" problems would be termed "cognitive" and some "behavioural" problems, they will be considered together.

Fatigue

Numerous follow-up studies have reported fatigue to be one of the most common symptoms experienced following mild, moderate and severe TBI, with a reported frequency ranging from 32.4 per cent to 73 per cent (Dikmen, Machamer, and Temkin, 1993; Evans, 1992; Middleboe, Anderson, Birket-Smith, and Friis, 1992; Olver, Ponsford, and Curran, 1996; Ponsford, Olver, and Curran, 1995a; Seel et al., 2003; van der Naalt et al., 1999; van Zomeren and van den Burg, 1985; Vitaz, Jenks, Raque, and Shields, 2003; Ziino and Ponsford, 2005). Despite this, the nature and causes of fatigue remain relatively poorly understood. Results of recent studies suggest that fatigue may result from a number of factors, including impairments of information processing speed, attention and vigilance, sleep disturbance, pain and emotional factors (Ouellet and Morin, 2006; Steele, Ponsford, Rajaratnam, and Redman, 2006; Ziino and Ponsford, 2005, 2006a, 2006b).

Attentional deficits

Attentional problems also occur very frequently at all levels of severity of injury following TBI (Olver et al., 1996; Ponsford et al., 2000; van Zomeren and van den Burg, 1985). This is not surprising, given the neuropathology of TBI, which frequently disrupts attentional neural networks via injury to the fronto-striatal areas, the reticular formation, DAI and disruption of catecholaminergic and serotonergic pathways (Willmott, Ponsford, Hocking, and Schönberger, 2009). An attentional difficulty most commonly reported is reduced speed of information processing, leading to a reduced information processing capacity, with consequent difficulties in focusing on more than one thing at once, or coping with complexity. Poor selective attention (the capacity to focus on some things and screen out others), which can manifest itself as distractibility or poor attention to detail is also reported, along with problems in sustaining attention over time, and difficulty in the allocation of attentional resources in a goal-directed fashion (Ponsford and Kinsella, 1991).

Learning and memory problems

It has already been noted that people with TBI usually have a period of confusion, disorientation and inability to remember ongoing events immediately following their emergence from coma, lasting for days, weeks, or, in the most severe cases, months, known as PTA. There is also frequently impairment of memory for events which immediately preceded the injury, termed retrograde amnesia. The period of retrograde amnesia is variable, being broadly related to the period of unconsciousness. There may be "islands of memory" within the period over which retrograde amnesia extends, and the period of retrograde amnesia tends to "shrink" over time (Russell and Nathan, 1946). The period of persistent retrograde amnesia is usually too brief for it to give a reliable indication of the severity of injury or probable outcome.

After emergence from PTA, many people who have sustained TBI report ongoing difficulties with learning and memory. Indeed, follow-up studies conducted from six months up to seven years after injury have found this to be one of the most frequent subjective complaints of TBI individuals and/or their relatives (Brooks, Campsie, Symington, Beattie, and McKinlay, 1987b; Brown and Nell, 1992; Dikmen, Machamer, Fann, and Temkin, 2010; Olver et al., 1996; van Zomeren and van den Burg, 1985).

As with attentional difficulties, there is potential heterogeneity in the nature and severity of memory difficulties experienced by TBI individuals, depending on the site and extent of injury. Memory problems may manifest as a severe amnesic syndrome, affecting the ongoing storage and retrieval of all types of material, difficulty with either verbal or non-verbal material, or most commonly an inefficient or unreliable memory due to lack of use of organisational strategies and/or attentional problems characteristic of frontal lobe injury (Hoofien, Gilboa, Vakil, and Barak, 2004; Vakil, 2005; Walsh, 1994a). Whatever the nature of the problem, there is usually a marked contrast between the capacity to remember events and skills learned prior to the injury, and the ability to learn and retain new material since the time of injury, the former being relatively preserved. Implicit memory, such as procedural learning, is also relatively spared in many individuals (McCullagh and Feinstein, 2005).

Impaired planning and problem-solving

The high frequency of damage to the frontal lobes associated with TBI means that many of those who have sustained TBI have difficulties in analysing, planning and executing the solutions to problems or complex tasks. They may perform well in structured activities, which require little initiative or direction. However, although there may be a willingness and ability to perform each component of a task, people with planning and problem-solving deficits are frequently unable to generate strategies for efficient task performance, to follow through with the organisation and implementation of complex tasks, or to check for and correct errors. TBI individuals often have difficulty in sustaining performance on tasks. Complex behaviours may dissolve into inert stereotypes. There can be a tendency to lose track of the task at hand, and to respond to distractions or inappropriate cues in the environment. There also tends to be a failure to look ahead, and to use past experience to prepare for anticipated events. People with executive dysfunction have particular difficulty in adapting to new situations (Busch, McBride, Curtiss, and Vanderploeg, 2005; Lezak, Howieson, Loring, Hannay, and Fischer, 2004; Olver et al., 1996; Ponsford et al., 1995a; Walsh and Darby, 1999).

Concrete thinking

Difficulties in forming or dealing with abstract concepts are common. This can result in an inability to generalise from a single instance, or distil the essence of a situation or a conversation, with a tendency to focus on specific, concrete aspects, or be "stimulus-bound". There may also be difficulties in understanding humour or other forms of indirect language. An inability to understand the implications of situations or events is common (Busch et al., 2005; Lezak et al., 2004; Walsh and Darby, 1999). There may be problems in benefiting from experience – in applying old solutions to new situations. Alternatively, there may be an inability to think creatively and generate different solutions to a given problem, with a tendency to repeatedly apply an old, unworkable solution, resulting in failure and frustration.

Lack of initiative

Some of those who have sustained TBI show a lack of initiative or drive in some or all aspects of their behaviour and thought processes. In severe cases there may be a complete inability to initiate speech or any activity without prompting. At a more subtle level, there may be a tendency to lack spontaneity, to be somewhat passive in conversation, to fail to move on to the next task once one is completed, or to move from one step to another within tasks. Relatives may report that the TBI person who was previously active achieves very little in a day and may sit for hours in a chair watching television (Busch et al., 2005; Lezak et al., 2004; Olver et al., 1996; Ponsford et al., 1995a; Walsh and Darby, 1999).

Inflexibility

Inflexibility in thought processes and behaviour may be manifested as difficulty in switching from one task to another, in changing train of thought or shifting "mental set". This may lead to frequent repetition or "perseveration" of the same responses, comments, demands or complaints. There may be an inability to see other people's points of view and a tendency to rely on rigid adherence to routines. Sudden changes in routine may cause the TBI individual to become upset (Busch et al., 2005; Lezak et al., 2004; Olver et al., 1996; Ponsford et al., 1995a; Walsh and Darby, 1999).

Dissociation between thought and action

It is frequently reported that there is a dissociation between what people who have sustained TBI know or say, and how they actually behave. This results in an inability to follow through with instructions, to correct errors or modify behaviour in the light of feedback. This, together with the next few problems, appears to result from a reduced capacity to control, regulate and monitor thought processes and behaviour (Busch et al., 2005; Lezak et al., 2004; Olver et al., 1996; Ponsford et al., 1995a; Walsh and Darby, 1999).

Impulsivity

A reduced capacity to control and monitor behaviour commonly results in impulsivity. There is a difficulty in inhibiting the tendency to respond to problems or situations before taking account of all relevant information, and before thinking of all the possible consequences of one's actions (Busch et al., 2005; Lezak et al., 2004; Olver et al., 1996; Ponsford et al., 1995a; Walsh and Darby, 1999).

Irritability/temper outbursts

One of the most commonly reported problems following TBI is a low tolerance for frustration. Those who have sustained TBI are prone to become irritable and to lose their temper easily (Olver et al., 1996; Ponsford et al., 1995a). The anger may be completely out of proportion to the situation, and there may be physical aggression.

Communication problems

Whilst aphasia is uncommon following TBI, discourse problems are frequently encountered. These can include excessive talking, with poor turn-taking skills, a tendency to repeat oneself or have difficulty keeping to the point (Snow, Douglas, and Ponsford, 1997). Word-finding difficulties and impaired auditory processing are also common. Communication problems following TBI will be discussed in detail in Chapter 5.

Socially inappropriate behaviour

Lack of behavioural control can also lead to an inability to inhibit inappropriate responses, such as swearing, sexual disinhibition, tactlessness or other socially inappropriate behaviours (Kelly et al., 2008; Kelly, Brown, Todd and Kramer, 2008; Olver et al., 1996; Ponsford et al., 1995a). There may be a failure to respond to non-verbal cues given by others, which normally let a person know when it is time to finish a conversation or move on to another topic, or when someone else is feeling uncomfortable with a certain behaviour.

Self-centredness

Those who have sustained severe TBI can be egocentric. This results in a tendency towards demanding, attention-seeking and sometimes manipulative behaviour (Olver et al., 1996; Ponsford et al., 1995a). It can also lead to jealousy, and insensitivity to the feelings or emotional needs of others, as well as a failure to see other people's points of view. This is the source of many relationship problems following TBI.

Changes in affect

TBI can result in a flatness of affect, where there is reduced emotional responsiveness, or an elevation of affect, with euphoria. Reduced emotional control can also lead to a tendency to laugh or cry for no apparent reason, or to show emotions which are quite out of proportion, or inappropriate, to the situation (Lezak et al., 2004).

Lack of insight/self-awareness

Severe TBI frequently results in difficulty perceiving, or a lack of awareness of, changes in cognitive function and behaviour (Fleming and Ownsworth, 2006; Hart, Sherer, Whyte, Polansky, and Novack, 2004b; Prigatano and Fordyce, 1986; Sherer et al., 2003). This leads to a tendency to attempt work or other tasks which are beyond their capabilities. There may also be a failure to recognise how impulsive, irritable, childish or demanding they are in certain situations, with disastrous consequences for interpersonal relationships (Prigatano, 1991). This results in a degree of perplexity in the TBI person, who fails to understand the reasons for failure at work or in social relationships. Occasionally, one sees the emergence of frank delusions (Prigatano, O'Brien, and Klonoff, 1988). Another unfortunate consequence of lack of insight is the inability to understand the need for rehabilitation or other forms of assistance in overcoming limitations.

The cognitive and behavioural changes described above frequently co-exist in a complex fashion, being difficult to disentangle in an individual, particularly as they are imposed upon varying premorbid personality characteristics.

Planning and problem-solving, abstract thinking, initiative, mental flexibility, and control and regulation of thought processes and behaviour have been termed "executive functions" by Lezak et al. (2004), Baddeley (1986) and Stuss and Benson (1986), and this term is now commonly used. Lezak (1978), who has so ably described the problems of those who have sustained TBI, referred to the "characterologically-altered" brain-injured patient.

Consequences of neurobehavioural sequelae for rehabilitation and outcome

The changes in cognition and behaviour outlined in the previous section have been documented in numerous follow-up studies involving moderate and/or severe TBI (Brooks et al., 1987b; Christensen et al., 2008; Dikmen et al., 1993; Dikmen et al., 2003; Draper and Ponsford, 2008; Levin et al., 1990; Millis, 2001; Olver et al., 1996; Tate, Fenelon, Manning, and Hunter, 1991). It is clear that they have a significant impact on the TBI individual's capacity to participate in and benefit from rehabilitation, and to resume previous activities and relationships.

Attentional problems place constraints on the person's capacity to participate in therapy, and memory problems may result in little being retained from one therapy session to the next. A dissociation between thought and action can mean that in spite of good participation in therapy sessions, and apparent willingness to follow instructions or suggestions, there is limited carry-over into other settings. Lack of initiative may necessitate frequent prompting. Behavioural changes can be so difficult to manage that the staff become stressed and the patient receives insufficient rehabilitative therapy. Above all, the individual with TBI may be so lacking in awareness of changes in cognition or behaviour as to lack motivation for therapy, and in some instances to precipitate discharge. These problems, in combination, may result in TBI people receiving inadequate rehabilitation, either because the treating staff feel they are unable to benefit from therapy or are too difficult to manage, or because the injured person refuses to participate.

Many outcome studies have documented the difficulties of those who have sustained moderate or severe TBI in attempting to return to their previous lifestyle (Brooks, McKinlay, Symington, Beattie, and Campsie, 1987a; Dikmen et al., 2003; Draper, Ponsford, and Schönberger, 2007; Jacobs, 1988; Machamer, Temkin, Fraser, Doctor, and Dikmen, 2005; Malec, Smigielski, DePompolo, and Thompson, 1993; Ponsford et al., 1995a; Sherer et al., 2002a; Tate, Broe, Cameron, Hodgkinson, and Soo, 2005; Tate, Lulham, Broe, Strettles, and Pfaff, 1989). Whilst figures for return to employment vary widely, according to the severity of injuries studied, definition of employment, and consideration of pre-injury employment status (Machamer et al., 2005), it appears that the majority of individuals with severe TBI are unable to return to employment (Crepeau and Scherzer, 1993; Kreutzer et al., 2003; Machamer et al., 2005; Ponsford, Olver, Curran, and Ng, 1995b; Sherer et al., 2002b).

Difficulties in making and maintaining relationships, with consequent social isolation and loss of leisure activities, are also common (Oddy, Coughlan, Tyerman, and Jenkins, 1985; Olver et al., 1996; Tate et al., 2005; Winkler, Unsworth, and Sloan, 2006). Psychological problems including reduced self-esteem, depression and anxiety are evident in a significant proportion of cases (Cooper-Evans, Alderman, Knight, and Oddy, 2008; Goodinson, Ponsford, Johnston, and Grant, 2009; Gouick and Gentleman, 2004; Tyerman and Humphrey, 1984). For most injured individuals it is the cognitive and behavioural, rather than the sensorimotor or physical impairments, which are most disabling (Ponsford et al., 1995a). Indeed most people with TBI people make a relatively good physical recovery (Colantonio et al., 2004; Ponsford et al., 1995a).

Because of relationship and social networking difficulties, it is the relatives who often provide the only ongoing support for individuals who have sustained moderate or severe TBI (Kozloff, 1987). Studies focusing on the impact of TBI on family life have shown that it creates significant stress, which does not decrease over time (Ponsford and Schönberger, 2010). These issues will be discussed further in subsequent chapters.

Summary and conclusions

TBI presents unique problems to its survivors, their relatives, and clinicians faced with the task of assisting their rehabilitation. It occurs predominantly in young adults, most commonly males, many of whom may have had limited educational attainment and an unstable work history. Some are still at school or undergoing tertiary training or apprenticeships. Those who are working have not had very long to establish their skills. They may have only recently attained independence from their parents, and are establishing new long-standing relationships. These young people will be confronting their disabilities for decades in a society which most commonly associates disability with the elderly or those with congenital intellectual disabilities.

Above all, however, it is the nature and complexity of the disabilities resulting from TBI which are most challenging. Neuropathological evidence suggests that there are a number of mechanisms of brain injury, some operating at the moment of impact and others as a consequence of intracranial or extracranial complications. This results in marked heterogeneity of injury across individuals. Limitations in the sensitivity of various imaging techniques make delineation of the precise nature and extent of injury in an individual very difficult. However, it is apparent from the neuropathological evidence available that diffuse injury is common, and that damage occurs most frequently in the frontal and temporal lobes, the basal ganglia and hippocampus also being frequently affected in severe cases.

TBI usually results in immediate loss or impairment of consciousness, followed by a period of confusion, known as PTA. The depth or length of coma, and the duration of PTA may be used as measures of severity of TBI.

Following the return of orientation, most of those who sustain TBI exhibit a range of ongoing sensorimotor, cognitive and behavioural sequelae, which vary widely in their severity. Mechanisms of recovery are poorly understood, and there is considerable variability in patterns of recovery. However, recovery from moderate or severe TBI tends to follow a negatively accelerating curve, which is most rapid in the first three to six months, but may continue for several years. In the case of mild TBI, recovery takes place within a couple of months, although some individuals have symptoms which persist beyond this period.

In the majority of cases it is the cognitive, behavioural and emotional changes which are most disruptive and disabling in the long term. These may include deficits of attention, speed of information processing, memory, planning and problem-solving, abstract thinking, initiative, flexibility, and control and regulation of behaviour and thought process, egocentricity, changes in affect and lack of insight. These problems, which occur in differing combinations and in varying degrees of severity, have been shown to have a significant impact on the TBI individual's capacity to participate in and benefit from rehabilitation, and to resume previous activities and relationships. As a consequence, a majority of those who sustain severe TBI are unable to return to employment. Social isolation, loss of leisure activities and difficulty in forming or sustaining relationships are also common. Such disabilities, occurring in young people in the prime of their life, can have a catastrophic impact, not only on the life of the person who has sustained severe TBI, but also on that of their relatives, on whom there may be dependency for the rest of their lives.

It is for these reasons that TBI represents such a unique and complex challenge for rehabilitation professionals, a challenge which in many cases they have not been trained to meet. This text aims to provide some practical guidelines to assist rehabilitation professionals in dealing with some of these challenges.

Principles underlying successful rehabilitation following TBI – the REAL approach

The approach recommended has been termed the REAL approach, signifying REHABILITATION FOR EVERYDAY ADAPTIVE LIVING. The fundamental principles of this approach are outlined below. Practical guidelines for the implementation of the REAL approach are outlined in detail in subsequent chapters.

REHABILITATION

REHABILITATION stands for the team structure and processes mediating interventions which are most likely to result in successful outcomes for TBI individuals. The essential ingredients are interdisciplinary teamwork, involvement of the injured individual and family, and a recognition of the need to evaluate the effectiveness of interventions.

Interdisciplinary teamwork

Good teamwork is essential in the rehabilitation of TBI individuals. The sequelae of TBI impact significantly on one another. In particular, the cognitive, behavioural and emotional changes can affect all aspects of the injured person's rehabilitation. Those participating in the rehabilitation of people who have sustained TBI need to approach their task from a broad and long-term perspective, sharing information, expertise and goals, which, in turn, must be shared with the injured person and the family. The focus of the team's endeavours should be on individuals in the context of their role in the community, rather than on the performance of specific tasks or skills. In this respect, the rehabilitation process needs to be "person-focused", rather than "discipline-focused". This is the essence of what is termed interdisciplinary teamwork, the cornerstone of successful TBI rehabilitation. Clinicians working with TBI individuals need to have a sound understanding of all aspects and implications of TBI. It is important that they have a flexible attitude and are not concerned with role-boundaries, as there will inevitably be considerable overlap in the therapy process. Indeed, this is considered essential to the success of rehabilitation following TBI, especially as TBI individuals have such difficulty in generalising what is learned in one setting to another.

Working with TBI individuals and their families can be a very stressful and thankless task. Interdisciplinary teamwork may alleviate this stress, by providing a supportive network for discussing the uncertainties and frustrations which are encountered. There will, inevitably, be conflicts within the team. Ideally, staff should be given regular opportunities and encouragement to discuss concerns, both with regard to those they are treating and with regard to the team. Burnout is a common problem in such complex and demanding work. Whilst a sound understanding of all the problems associated with TBI, combined with good team communication and support should alleviate this feeling, it may, from time to time, be necessary to encourage clinicians to take a break from working with TBI individuals.

In dealing with these issues, good team co-ordination is essential. The professional background of the team co-ordinator is less important than personal qualities of maturity, good interpersonal skills and an ability to put the goals and development of the team ahead of one's own goals, together with breadth of experience in working with TBI. Team co-ordination is concerned not with directing, but with facilitating and maximising co-operation between team participants, and ensuring that contributions are made by all members of the team. Decisions should be made on a consensus basis, involving input from all team members, and implemented accordingly. An alternative to having a single team co-ordinator is that of assigning individual team members as "case managers" or "key persons". Their roles may include the facilitation, documentation and review of goals, co-ordination of meetings and liaison with the TBI individual and the family. Each rehabilitation team must find what works best for them in this respect. However, it is vital that those who perform these roles have the necessary expertise and personal qualities. The essence is in maintaining good communication between therapists, the TBI individual and the family.

Involvement of the injured individual and family

The injured individual and the family must be seen as equal members of the rehabilitation team, being involved actively, wherever possible, in the processes of assessment, goal-setting, therapy, evaluation and long-term planning. All too frequently these processes are conducted by hospital or rehabilitation staff, with minimal consultation with the injured person and family, who are simply informed of decisions. The negotiation of realistic therapy goals and plans for the future is not always easy, but it needs to be recognised that it is these individuals who will be confronting and dealing with the long-term consequences of the injury directly, not the rehabilitation team. There is no doubt that the motivation and involvement of the injured individual and family in the rehabilitation process will be enhanced by their active participation, and that they will be better prepared to deal with the challenges they will face in the future.

Evaluating the effectiveness of interventions

Whilst evaluation of the effectiveness of interventions is an essential element of the rehabilitation process, it is, for a variety of reasons, also one of the most difficult. A myriad of methodological difficulties face clinicians and researchers in the rehabilitation setting. There is a lack of agreement over definitions and established criteria for measurement. Heterogeneity of injury makes it difficult to study groups. The multifocal nature of the rehabilitation process poses problems for assessment of the impact of specific forms of therapy. It is also difficult to separate effects due to the therapist from those due to the therapy itself, spontaneous recovery or practice effects on repeated measures. Another difficulty is the general lack of research training received by most rehabilitation staff. For all of these reasons there is a significant lack of data regarding the effectiveness of specific forms of intervention following TBI. Many of the studies which have been conducted to date have neglected to assess the impact of the intervention on the daily life and psychosocial adjustment of the injured individual, which is most important.

Maintaining the focus of therapy on the individual in the context of everyday life is likely to facilitate evaluation of its effectiveness. The use of single-case designs will also overcome some of the problems involved. As Wilson (1987b) has pointed out, single-case designs enable the therapist to tailor therapy to the individual's particular needs, and to alter it if it is not working. It is possible to evaluate continuously the person's responses to the intervention, whilst controlling for the effects of practice or spontaneous recovery. It is also possible to ascertain reasons for failure to respond to treatment, and thus establish sources of variability, such as in procedures, patient background, nature and severity of injury, nature of other strengths and weaknesses, and so on. There will be further discussion of methods of evaluating the impact of different forms of therapy throughout this text.

EVERYDAY

EVERYDAY emphasises the need to focus assessment and treatment goals on the individual in the context of everyday life and roles in the community. Many of those who sustain TBI have impaired executive or adaptive functions. As a consequence of this there is difficulty in generalising or adapting what is learned in one situation to another. It is therefore particularly important to focus goals and therapeutic intervention in a very practical way directly on activities performed in their everyday life. Since impaired self-awareness is also common, a focus on everyday living should also maximise the likelihood of the injured individual participating in goal-setting and seeing the relevance of rehabilitation activities.

This focus on everyday life necessitates an understanding of individuals in the context of their previous lifestyle, relationships, abilities, values, personality and behavioural patterns, life goals and roles in the community. This is particularly important in the case of TBI, where the manifestations are heterogeneous and complex, and cannot be divorced from the qualities of the individual who has sustained the injury. Assessment, goal-setting and intervention need to be conducted within this framework.

ADAPTIVE

ADAPTIVE signifies the need to recognise that, whilst there is usually a substantial degree of spontaneous recovery following TBI, there are, following moderate or severe injuries, frequently residual impairments which have a significant impact on the lifestyle of the injured individual. It is unrealistic to imagine that these impairments can be cured or restored to normal through any rehabilitation process. Rehabilitation should aim to facilitate and maximise the extent of recovery, but it should also assist those who are injured to set realistic goals and adapt to whatever limitations affect their ability to function in the community. Such adaptation may involve learning new ways of performing tasks or interacting with others, obtaining prompting, supervision or assistance from other people or devices, or modification of tasks, roles or the environment.

Emotional adaptation to the changes imposed by the injury is just as important as practical adaptation. There is substantial evidence that many individuals with TBI have significant ongoing psychological adjustment difficulties. There is a need for a greater emphasis on ameliorating these problems and providing psychological support to the injured person. Such interventions will usually need to continue or be available over many years. In particular, it is important that the injured individual is given assistance in coming to terms with changes and rebuilding a positive sense of self. Similarly, families and other caregivers deserve active support and assistancc in adapting to the impact of the injury and developing a new identity.

LIVING

LIVING signifies the ongoing and long-term nature of the experience of living with the consequences of TBI in the community. This experience will be unique to the individual, depending not only on the nature and severity of ongoing disability, but also on their previous personality, relationships, values, resources, skills and goals, as well as emotional factors. The extent to which a person with TBI is able to play a meaningful role in the community is also likely to be determined by the availability of practical and emotional supports.

In planning rehabilitation following TBI it is important from the outset, to consider all of these background factors, and to take a long-term view. In setting goals, the rehabilitation team should give careful consideration to the probable needs of the individual in the longer term. As numerous follow-up studies have shown, the recovery process extends over many years and some problems, particularly those of a psychological nature, do not manifest themselves, or become accessible to intervention until several years after injury. Simply training a person to be independent in activities of daily living and setting them up in work, study or avocational activities does not guarantee successful adaptation. The needs and difficulties of these predominantly young individuals will alter as they face a myriad of changes in their lives. The time frame of rehabilitation therefore needs to be a very lengthy one, with follow-up support available indefinitely. It is for this reason that involvement of the family in the rehabilitation process from the early stages is so essential. It is, in many instances, the family who provide most ongoing assistance, both practical and emotional, and carry the burden associated with that. They need to be supported in this role over an extended period and every attempt should be made to alleviate their burden.

2 Assessing and managing impairment of consciousness following TBI

Pamela Snow and Jennie Ponsford

The period in which the TBI survivor is comatose, or is emerging from coma, poses significant challenges, both for relatives and staff. At no other stage in the recovery process is there so much uncertainty, both regarding current level of awareness and what the future will hold. The purpose of this chapter is to describe the features of impaired consciousness at different stages following TBI, together with approaches to assessment and management. The importance of close involvement of family members will be emphasised throughout.

The overwhelming majority of people who become comatose following a TBI emerge from unconsciousness within two weeks. Most will then enter a period of confusion and anterograde amnesia known as post traumatic amnesia (PTA), and will go on to display varying patterns and levels of severity of ongoing disability in the longer term. A small percentage (ranging from 1 to 7 per cent) will enter either a vegetative or minimally conscious state. The common pathways from coma are depicted schematically in Figure 2.1 and form the basis on which emergence from coma will be discussed in this chapter. Death may occur in the acute stages after injury, or many

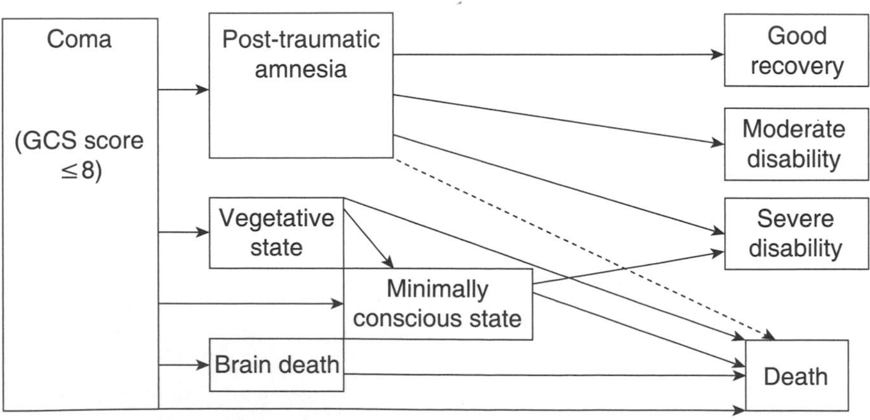

Figure 2.1 Emergence from coma: Common clinical pathways

months later, in which case cause of death is not necessarily recorded as brain injury.

Coma

Coma is widely understood in both lay and medical circles to mean loss of consciousness and is associated with absent, or minimal, responsiveness to external and internal stimuli. It is important to carefully consider the notion "consciousness", both as a basis for understanding coma, and for accurately measuring assessment over time, as even subtle changes may signal improvement or deterioration.

Posner and co-workers (2007) define consciousness as ". . . the full state of awareness of the self and one's relationship to the environment" (p. 5). They note that consciousness has two components: *content* and *arousal*, where content refers to cortically mediated cognitive and affective functions, and arousal refers to the regulation of wakefulness by ascending pathways which arise in the brainstem and course through the diencephalon (thalamus and hypothalamus) to the cortex. Coma is therefore described as ". . . a state of unresponsiveness in which the patient lies with eyes closed and cannot be aroused to respond appropriately to stimuli even with vigorous stimulation" (p. 7). The words "respond appropriately" are important as they make allowance for the fact that aspects of behavioural responsiveness can sometimes be elicited in the comatose patient (e.g., limb withdrawal in response to a painful stimulus), but as depth of coma increases, even limited responses such as these disappear (Posner et al., 2007). Coma reflects loss of function in both the cortex and the brainstem reticular system, and rarely lasts more than two to four weeks (Giacino and Whyte, 2005).

The Glasgow Coma Scale

As noted in Chapter 1, coma is graded by measuring the reduction in observable responsiveness to external stimuli. The measure most commonly used for this purpose is the Glasgow Coma Scale (GCS). The GCS was devised by Teasdale and Jennett in 1974 and revised in 1976 (Teasdale and Jennett, 1974, 1976). It utilises best eye-opening, and best verbal and motor responses, in order to regularly monitor improvement and/or deterioration over time. Responses in each category are ranked and assigned a numerical value, yielding a total score between 3 (a person showing no response on any dimension) and 15 (a person who is alert and well oriented). Teasdale and Jennett (1974) defined coma as the absence of eye-opening, a failure to obey commands, and a failure to give any comprehensible verbal response. This corresponds to a total score of 8 or less on the amended GCS, and constitutes a widely used definition of coma. Box 2.1 displays the dimensions of and scoring key for the GCS.

Box 2.1 Glasgow Coma Scale

Eye Opening	
Spontaneous	E4
To speech	3
To pain	2
Nil	1
Best Motor Response	
Obeys commands	M6
Localises to pain	5
Withdraws to pain	4
Abnormal flexion	3
Extensor response	2
No response	1
Verbal Response	
Oriented	V5
Confused conversation	4
Inappropriate words	3
Incomprehensible sounds	2
None	1

Coma Score: (E + M + V) = 3 to 15.

GCS scores in the first 24 hours after injury are frequently used to grade severity of injury and predict outcome. Scores of 3 to 8 are said to indicate severe injury, 9 to 12 moderate injury, and 13 to 15 mild injury (Jennett and Teasdale, 1981). Because of the potential for deterioration in conscious state within the acute period, however, there has been debate about the optimal time after injury at which the GCS should be derived, i.e. whether this should be at the time when the person is first seen by ambulance officers (the "field" score) or on admission to hospital (Levin and Eisenberg, 1979a; 1979b), prior to resuscitation (Udekwu, Kromhout-Schiro, Vaslef, Baker, and Oller, 2004), following noncranial resuscitation (Marshall et al., 1983), six hours after injury (Jennett, 1976) or as the lowest score in the first 24 hours after injury (Vogenthaler, Smith, and Goldfader, 1989). Davis et al. (2006) showed that GCS scores collected prior to admission to hospital are highly predictive of those on arrival, and scores from both time points are strongly predictive of mortality and need for neurosurgical intervention. They emphasised the need to perform serial GCS assessments in the acute phase, and noted that in spite of its generally good predictive value, "... the use of GCS scores alone in making prehospital triage decisions involves a substantial trade-off between sensitivity and specificity" (p. 988). Rosenfeld (2010) notes that GCS is in fact only one of several early predictive tools, sitting alongside patient age, the occurrence of hypoxia or hypotension, pupil size and reactivity, core body temperature, intracranial pressure, and CT findings. Rosenfeld and others (e.g. Nijboer, van der Naalt, and ten Duis, 2010) acknowledge the particular need for improved early identification of those patients likely to die or survive at best in a vegetative or minimally responsive state. Patients with GCS scores of 3 with fixed, dilated pupils have recently been shown to have "... no appreciable chance of survival" (Chaudhuri, Malhamab, and Rosenfeld, 2009, p. 28), and Chaudhuri et al. (2009) argue that palliative care/organ donation should be the focus of management in these circumstances. Similar findings have been reported by Nijboer and colleagues (2010).

The GCS has been reported to have adequate intra- and inter-rater reliability, provided that trained raters are employed, and the painful stimulus administered is of sufficient intensity (Moppett, 2007). Some important factors will, however, lessen the validity and reliability of the GCS. Ocular trauma or swelling may prevent eye-opening, intoxication with alcohol and/or illicit drugs may interfere with pupil reactivity, the insertion of an endotracheal tube prevents the injured person from responding verbally, and the use of barbiturates and paralysing drugs to lower intracranial pressure immobilises the person. The increasing practice of pre-hospital intubation and administration of sedating drugs has increased the importance of accurate recording of initial GCS scores at the site of injury. While the relationship between field (vs hospital arrival) GCS has been reported as "approximately linear" its relationship with survival is non-linear, with the steepest decline in mortality occurring between scores of 3 and 7 (Moppett, 2007).

It has been postulated (Balestreri et al., 2004; Moppett, 2007) that more aggressive pre-hospital management of brain-injured patients may, over time, lessen the predictive strength of the GCS, given that this is based on data derived from ever-evolving improvements in management during the so-called "golden hour". Further, an individual GCS total score can be comprised of over a hundred possible combinations of best motor, eye-opening and verbal responses. This has led workers such as Healey et al. (2003) to propose that as the motor component contains virtually all of the information contained in the total GCS score, this should replace the full GCS in outcome prediction models. This thinking is also reflected in the development of the Madras Head Injury Prognostic Scale (Ramesh, Thirumaran, and Raja, 2008), which includes GCS best motor response, as well as a range of other patient and trauma-related variables, to yield a total score between 6 and 18. Although its initial validation and predictive use appears promising, further research is needed on its use in first-world countries.

Another attempt to redress some of the prognostic shortcomings of the GCS is the Full Outline of UnResponsiveness (FOUR) Scale (Wijdicks,

Bamlet, Maramattom, Manno, and McClelland, 2005; Wolf, Wijdicks, Bamlet, and McClelland, 2007). This tool evaluates four parameters (eye opening, motor response, brainstem reflexes, and respiration), on a 5-point scale, ranging from zero to four. Although showing initial promise in terms of validity and inter-rater reliability with neurological patients, this tool has not yet been used extensively with large samples of trauma patients (vs patients with acquired brain injuries of other aetiologies, such as haemorrhagic stroke, subarachnoid haemorrhage, and postanoxic encephalopathy). It remains to be seen, therefore, how much it will add above the early GCS data and other physiological and demographic markers of injury severity and prognosis.

The GCS may also not be the most appropriate means of assessing patients with mild TBI (Teasdale, 1995). Professor Teasdale has noted that the definition of mild brain injury in a patient with a GCS score of 13–15 is unsatisfactory because patients with a coma score of 15 make up the overwhelming number of patients classified in this group, so that the inclusion of all patients with a coma score of 13–15 in the same category underestimates the true severity of injury of patients with scores of 13 or 14. Conversely, Teasdale (1995) notes that this classification also gives an impression of undue seriousness to those with a coma score of 15. A further concern with the use of the GCS is the existence of a subgroup of patients experiencing short or negligible coma and prolonged PTA (Wilson, Shiel, Watson, Horn, and McLellan, 1994). It has been demonstrated that a significant proportion of those assigned a GCS score of 15 are actually in PTA, indicating that they may have a more significant brain injury than indicated by the GCS score (Ponsford et al., 2004; Shores et al., 2008).

It is essential that coma-emerging patients at all levels of severity and chronicity are carefully investigated and monitored over time, both medically and with respect to indicators of awareness and responsiveness. This ensures that medical conditions which may compromise cognitive status (e.g., urinary tract infections) are identified and treated. Close monitoring also provides a basis for decisions regarding clinical management, as well as a means of conveying information to families which is as accurate as possible, both diagnostically and prognostically. The task of caring for the coma-emerging patient has, to some extent, been made easier in recent years by the development of increasingly rigorous clinical tools for assessing and monitoring progress and response to interventions over time. Using improved diagnostic criteria, clinicians need to engage in a process of hypothesis testing, employing both behavioural and neurodiagnostic measures. Some of these clinical tools are discussed in this chapter.

Helping the family of the patient who is in coma

The time that the patient spends in coma is frightening and confusing for family members. There is likely to be a high degree of distress and anxiety displayed by relatives, largely over whether or not the injured person is going to survive. During this time families may feel compelled to spend many hours each day at the injured person's bedside, and will eagerly await signs of lightening of conscious state. Wherever practicable, families should be made to feel welcome and useful, as familiar, reassuring figures in the patient's unfamiliar environment. Family members should be encouraged to spend as much, or as little, time at the bedside as they wish, and should also be encouraged to touch and speak to their loved one.

Throughout this time of enormous stress and confusion, a great deal can be done to achieve the trust of family members. Whilst not all members of the treating team have a particular role to play in terms of managing the patient at this stage, those who will soon become involved can introduce themselves to the family, and provide opportunities for relatives to talk about their loved one as the spouse, sibling or parent s/he is, not merely as a patient being kept alive in a sophisticated intensive care unit. There may be pressing practical and financial issues which need to be addressed, and social work assistance should be available to deal with these. The need for readily available emotional support for families at this stressful time cannot be over-emphasised. This is discussed further in Chapter 9.

During the period of coma there may be disagreement between staff and families as to the patient's level of awareness, and familiar faces and voices may evoke more responses than staff will observe during routine care. It is important to involve family members in the assessment process. Staff should not discuss, in the presence of the injured person, any negative views regarding prognosis. The need for consistency in the information conveyed by team members is paramount. Because this information is both complex and emotionally charged, inconsistencies merely perpetuate confusion, and do little to engender trust in the expertise of the treating team as a whole.

As confidence about survival increases, questions regarding the quality of that survival may begin to emerge in the minds of staff. For family members, however, this tends to be a period of enormous relief and renewed hope. Signs of a lightening of conscious state are greeted with excitement and optimism. It is wise to prepare relatives for the fact that consciousness is likely to be regained gradually, with fluctuations and the possible emergence of agitated behaviours. Family members need information which is clear, and care needs to be taken with the use of terms such as "recovery". Clinicians may use this as a synonym for survival, whilst family members will interpret this to mean return to pre-injury level of functioning. It is wiser to use the term "improvement" instead of recovery. Family members may bring considerable pressure to bear on staff in their efforts to be reassured about their loved one's prognosis. In such circumstances, it is advisable to resist the temptation to "guesstimate" outcome. Staff should explain why they do not know the answers to the questions they are being asked, and outline a process by which the relevant issues will be monitored and reviewed. This information will need to be rephrased and repeated many times, and will need to be amended according to changes in the patient's condition. Family members are likely to have lasting memories of the way information was conveyed to them in these early stages, and this may have important implications for the way they view future communications from those caring for their loved one.

Post-traumatic amnesia (PTA)

The majority of TBI survivors do emerge from coma, over widely varying periods of time. Following this, the patient typically passes through a phase of generalised cognitive disturbance, known as PTA. People in this state may be partially or fully conscious, but are confused and disoriented, absorbing little from the environment. There is an inability to store and retrieve new information, and a period of retrograde amnesia is also common. Speech content may be quite confused. Awareness of circumstances is limited. Perception of the new environment and incoming stimuli may be distorted, which serves to increase confusion, perplexity, and sometimes fear. As a result of lack of awareness of the nature of their condition, there is a failure to understand the reasons for being in hospital. Restlessness, agitation, physical and/or verbal aggression are common. If physically capable, people in PTA may wander. The problems may be worse at night, when there are fewer environmental cues to decrease confusion. The person in PTA may also experience delusions and hallucinations. The person does not recall this period afterwards, although they may have "islands" of memory. Some describe it as like being in a dream.

The term "post-traumatic amnesia" was first used by Symonds (1940, p. 77) to refer to ". . . a general defect of cerebral function after consciousness has been regained". However, subsequent definitions have tended to focus on the injured person's disorientation in time, place and person, and/or inability to remember new experiences in an ongoing fashion (Fortuny, Briggs, Newcombe, Ratcliff, and Thomas, 1980; Russell and Nathan, 1946; Russell and Smith, 1961; Schacter and Crovitz, 1977; Schwartz et al., 1998; Shores, 1995; Shores, Marosszeky, Sandanam, and Batchelor, 1986; Symonds and Russell, 1943; Tate et al., 2006). PTA has been said to terminate with the return of continuous memory. Its duration is generally taken to include the full period of coma. The duration of PTA therefore dates from moment of injury until the return of the capacity to store and retrieve new information (Russell and Nathan, 1946).

Russell and his colleagues used the person's retrospective reports to determine the duration of PTA (Russell and Nathan, 1946). However, as Symonds has noted, the presence of "islands of memory" may distort the injured individual's estimate, resulting in a period shorter than the actual length of PTA. Pseudo-reminiscences or confabulation can occur (Forrester, Encel, and Geffen, 1994). Gronwall and Wrightson (1980) and King et al. (1997) found a 21–25 per cent misclassification rate using retrospective as opposed to prospective PTA monitoring. King et al. (1997) also found that retrospective assessment was least effective where PTA duration was less than

24 hours. As Greenwood (1997) has emphasized, in view of the fact that PTA duration is commonly used as an estimate of injury severity, the use of standardised and objective measures for determining its duration is very important.

Assessment of the person in PTA

A number of standardised scales have been developed for measuring the duration of PTA. The first was published by Levin and co-workers in 1979 (Levin, O'Donnell, and Grossman, 1979), the Galveston Orientation and Amnesia Test (GOAT). The GOAT requires the person to give basic biographical information (name, address and birthdate), and assesses orientation for time and place, recollection of events surrounding the accident and admission to hospital, and asks for a description of the first recollection after the injury. The total number of error points is deducted from 100. Scores below 65 are considered to be defective, those from 66 to 75 borderline, and those above 75 normal. The test was designed to be administered at least once daily. Levin, Benton and Grossman (1982a) reported significant associations between the duration of PTA, as measured by the GOAT, and both acute neurological impairment, as measured by the GCS, and the level of overall social and vocational recovery, as rated on the Glasgow Outcome Scale (Jennett and Bond, 1975).

The GOAT has, however, subsequently been criticised by several authors. Gronwall and Wrightson (1980) asserted that recovery of orientation, as assessed on the GOAT, did not necessarily mean that the person had emerged from PTA. The test's reliance on recall of historical memories renders it less sensitive to the presence of anterograde amnesia. Shores, Marosszeky, Sandanam, and Batchelor (1986) pointed out that a normal score could be recorded even if the injured person could not answer the specific amnesia questions, thus arguing that the scale was sensitive only to disorientation, and not to the amnesia which may also be present in PTA. Saneda and Corrigan (1992), Schwartz et al. (1998), Stuss et al. (1999), and Tate et al. (2006) have since confirmed the potential for a temporal dissociation between the recovery of orientation and new learning ability in PTA. Schwartz, Stuss and colleagues (Schwartz et al., 1998; Stuss et al., 1999) found that the ability to recall three words freely after a 24-hour delay occurred consistently after return to normal performance on the GOAT and recommended the use of this protocol, with recall of three pictures recommended in cases where communication problems were present. Wilson, Baddeley, Shiel, and Patton (1992) have also pointed out that people both in and out of PTA are frequently unable to answer questions about the last memory before the accident, or the first memory after the accident.

Shores et al. (1986) extended the earlier work of Fortuny et al. (1980) to produce the Westmead PTA Scale (WPTAS) as a clinical test of orientation, and the ability to lay down memories from one day to the next (Marosszeky,

Ryan, Shores, Batchelor, and Marosszeky, 1998). The WPTAS can be used with only a small amount of training by health professionals, but it is preferable that the scale is administered by the same individual from one day to the next, because of the requirement to remember the examiner's face and name. As shown in Figure 2.2, the test requires injured people to give their age and date of birth, assesses orientation in time and place, the capacity for recall of the examiner's face and name, and for identification, from an array, which three pictures of common objects they have been shown the day before. If patients do not respond spontaneously to the questions asked, they are presented with a multiple choice. For example, if they do not respond to the question, "What is the name of this place?" they may be asked, "Is it home, is it Westmead Hospital or is it Parramatta Hospital?" In the case of failure to spontaneously recall the pictures, a choice is given from the three target pictures and six distractor pictures. From the first day on which a score of 12 is recorded, the three target pictures are changed daily. The procedure is repeated until a perfect score of 12 is obtained on three successive days, with the same set of nine pictures used throughout the task. The period of PTA is said to have ended on the first of these three days.

The psychometric robustness of this scale for discriminating patients in PTA from those out of PTA has been established (Shores, 1995; Shores et al., 1986). However, Tate et al. (2006) have argued that changing the target pictures to be remembered after the first occasion of correct recollection and including these same pictures as foils makes the task of correct recall of the new target pictures more difficult. They compared the administration of this scale with that of an unpublished Modified Oxford PTA Scale (MOPTAS) based on that originally used by Fortuny et al. (1980), which employed a new set of foils each time a new set of pictures had to be recalled. They found no significant difference in the duration of PTA using either scale, although the period from the first score of 12/12 to the attainment of three consecutive 12/12 scores was more protracted in those assessed with the WPTAS. The study findings suggested that in cases where PTA duration exceeds four weeks, emergence has generally occurred by the time 12/12 is first achieved, and this can be taken as indicative of emergence from PTA on either scale.

Despite the above-mentioned limitation, the WPTAS remains the most widely used test for assessing inpatients with moderate to severe TBI in Australian hospitals. The GOAT continues to be widely used in the USA, despite its documented limitations. Another measure developed and used in the US is the Orientation Log or O-Log (Jackson, Novack, and Dowler, 1998). This was designed for use with severely injured populations and also emphasises assessment of orientation, as opposed to the ability to lay down new memories. Given the finding of Tate et al. (2006) of a dissociation between the emergence of orientation and recovery from amnesia in those with severe TBI, with emergence of orientation generally occurring earlier, use of a measure that encompasses both functions would seem more appropriate. Frey, Rojas, Anderson, and Arciniegas (2007) reported that O-Log scores had

Westmead Post Traumatic Amnesia (P.T.A.) Scale

P.T.A. may be deemed to be over on the first of 3 consecutive days of a recall of 12
When a patient scores 12/12, the picture cards must be changed and the date of change noted.
P.T.A. may be deemed to be over on first day of a recall of 12 for those who have been in PTA for > 4 weeks (Tate, R.L. et al. 2006)

Date of Onset: ____________

Initial Examiner: ____________ Alternate face cards used in examiners absence: ____________

Patient Label

	Date:													
1. How old are you?	A													
	S													
2. What is your date of birth?	A													
	S													
3. What month are we in?	A													
	S													
4. What time of the day is it? (Morning / Afternoon / Night)	A													
	S													
5. What day of the week is it?	A													
	S													
6. What year are we in?	A													
	S													
7. What is the name of this place?	A													
	S													
8. Face	A													
	S													
9. Name	A													
	S													
10. Picture I	A													
	S													
11. Picture II	A													
	S													
12. Picture III	A													
	S													
Orientation:	7													
Recall:	5													
Total:	12													

A = Patient's Answer
S = Patient's Score (1 or 0)
* answers if three options given

Adapted by S.Swan, Queensland Health Occupational Therapy Gold Coast Hospital and Royal Brisbane & Women's Hospital, 2009; from Shores, E.A., Marosszeky, J.E., Sandanam, J. & Batchelor, J. (1986). Preliminary validation of a clinical scale for measuring the duration of post-traumatic amnesia. Medical Journal of Australia, 144, 569-572.

Figure 2.2 Westmead PTA Scale

similar sensitivity to PTA duration when compared with the GOAT, however the former appeared to be a better predictor of rehabilitation outcomes (as measured by discharge cognitive status and total FIM scores). The O-Log takes longer to administer than the WPTAS.

The WPTAS is not suitable for assessing people with mild TBI as it is designed to be administered at 24-hour intervals. Ponsford et al. (2004) therefore developed a revised version of the WPTAS, designed to be administered in the Emergency Department (ED) or wherever the injured person is under observation. This version excludes the items assessing memory for the face and name of the examiner and is administered at hourly intervals. Only one score of 12/12 is required to indicate the end of PTA. The Revised WPTAS has shown a stronger association than GCS Scores with cognitive function measured in the ED (Shores et al., 2008). The possible effects of opiates and other drugs or alcohol on scores on these scales need to be borne in mind, however (McCarter, Walton, Moore, Ward, and Nelson, 2007; Meares et al., 2006).

A limitation in using the end of amnesia as the criterion for emergence from PTA is, as Wilson et al. (1992) have pointed out, that there is a small number of TBI survivors who remain so severely amnesic that they never obtain a perfect score on the Westmead PTA Scale. This raises questions as to when "PTA" should be redefined as a severe and chronic amnesic syndrome. In our experience, people who have remained disorientated and amnesic for more than six months following their emergence from coma are likely to exhibit ongoing amnesic difficulties, and therapy should be planned accordingly.

There are also other cognitive and behavioural disturbances associated with PTA, including impairments of perception, speech and executive function, and particularly attention and information processing speed. Wilson et al. (1992) found that most of the measures which differentiated the performances of people in PTA from those of the other groups of amnesic, memory-impaired and orthopaedic controls, namely simple reaction time, speed and accuracy of comprehension, verbal fluency, backward digit span, and delayed recall of prose, placed demands on attention and particularly information processing capacity, speed and accuracy. Stuss et al. (1999) noted that simple attentional functions consistently recovered ahead of more complex attentional functions. As Tate and colleagues (2006) and others have noted, impairments of all of these functions continue beyond emergence from PTA, so there are no criteria for using such tasks to identify the end of PTA. Similarly there is no clear association between cognition and agitation in PTA (Corrigan, Mysiw, Gribble, and Chock, 1992).

There have been a few studies examining the nature of the memory impairment in PTA. Whilst some have argued that PTA is characterised by a failure of consolidation of new information into long-term memory (Shores et al., 1986; Yarnell and Lynch, 1970), others have suggested that the memory disorder in PTA may represent a retrieval problem, resulting from inefficient encoding of memories (Richardson, 2000). Given the fairly generalised nature of the cognitive impairment associated with PTA, it seems arguable that the memory disorder may be characterised by failure of both consolidation and retrieval mechanisms, as well as poor organisation in the encoding of material. There is evidence of relative preservation of motor (procedural) learning skills in PTA (Ewert, Levin, Watson, and Kalisky, 1989). Such findings are similar to those in individuals with an amnesic syndrome of a more permanent nature, such as that associated with Korsakoff's syndrome.

The key to understanding the nature of cognitive and behavioural disturbances in PTA would be to understand their cause. Sadly, little progress has been made towards this end. Because of their agitated and confused state it is very difficult and ethically questionable to subject people in PTA to the imaging procedures which may help to elucidate this. It seems most likely that PTA reflects global metabolic processes which form part of the brain's response to a significant injury (Posner et al., 2007).

PTA duration as a measure of severity of TBI

Duration of PTA has frequently been used by clinicians and researchers as an index of severity of TBI. Associations exist between longer periods of PTA and other clinical indicators of serious brain injury, including skull fracture, intracranial haemorrhage, raised intracranial pressure and presence of residual neurological deficits (Russell and Smith, 1961), lesion volume (Schönberger, Ponsford, Reutens, Beare, and O'Sullivan, 2009) and extent of generalised atrophy, as measured by increased ventricle-to-brain ratio (Bigler, Ryser, Gandhi, Kimball, and Wilde, 2006; Wilde, Bigler, Pedroza, and Ryser, 2006b). A number of studies have also demonstrated significant relationships between the duration of PTA and eventual outcome, as measured by the Glasgow Outcome Scale (GOS) (Bishara, Partridge, Godfrey, and Knight, 1992; Ponsford, Draper, and Schönberger, 2008; Tate et al., 2005), community integration (Doig et al., 2001; Fleming et al., 1999), persistent cognitive dysfunction (Draper and Ponsford, 2008; Wood and Rutterford, 2006a, 2006b), psychosocial dysfunction (Draper and Ponsford, 2007; Tate et al., 2005), or occupational status (Cattelani et al., 2002; Draper et al., 2007; Fleming et al., 1999; Russell and Smith, 1961; Sherer et al., 2002b; van der Naalt et al., 1999). The classification originally proposed by Russell and Smith (1961) and expanded by Jennett and Teasdale (1981) was as follows: less than 5 minutes = very mild; 5–60 minutes = mild; 1–24 hours = moderate; 1–7 days = severe; 1–4 weeks = very severe, and more than 4 weeks = extremely severe.

Many studies have used this classification, which was established on the basis of clinical experience rather than established outcome data. Using residual complaints and return to work two years after injury as outcome criteria, van Zomeren and van den Burg (1985) suggested that 13 days may be more appropriate than seven days as a cut-off point between the severe and very severe categories. A more recent study suggested PTA less than 18 days was associated with a high likelihood of good recovery at one year, less than four weeks meant a good recovery was more likely, and a PTA greater than 56 days resulted in less than 10 per cent likelihood of good recovery on the Extended Glasgow Outcome Scale (Walker et al., 2010b). Another study identified a cut-off PTA of 48 days as indicative of poor employment outcomes and 54 days of the need for supervision one year post-injury (Brown et al., 2005). A further study by the same group showed that one-year employment and global outcomes were predicted by PTA extending into week 4 after injury and independent living by PTA extending into the eighth week post-injury (Brown et al., 2010). No studies to date have clearly established clinically useful criteria at the mild end of the spectrum, although PTA of less than 24 hours results in a strong probability of return to employment or study (Ponsford, Cameron, Fitzgerald, Grant, and Mickocka-Walus, 2011; Ponsford et al., 2000). In light of these findings it would appear that a method of categorisation that discriminates between people with longer PTA duration provides a more accurate indication of clinical outcome. According to this classification, severity of injury, as indicated by PTA duration, is defined as follows: less than 24 hours = mild; 1–7 days = moderate; 1–4 weeks = severe; > 4 weeks = very severe (Arlinghaus, Shoaib, and Trevor, 2005).

Studies have shown that PTA has enhanced predictive ability over GCS when estimating psychosocial, cognitive and functional outcome in TBI survivors (Brown et al., 2005; Cattelani et al., 2002; Doig et al., 2001; Fleming et al., 1999; Sherer et al., 2002a, 2008; van der Naalt et al., 1999). In terms of very long-term outcome, recent studies have shown that PTA is a strong indicator of cognitive function, self-care ability, relationship capacity, living skills, and employability up to 23 years post-injury (Tate et al., 2005; Wood and Rutterford, 2006b).

Unfortunately, variable criteria have been used for measuring PTA duration in outcome studies conducted to date, some relying on questioning of the injured person, others on hospital records, and others having used standardised scales. This places some limitations on the validity and comparability of findings. Whilst the relationship of PTA duration with outcome may have been shown to be statistically significant, and stronger than that of most other individual variables, in most of these studies it explains little more than one-third of the variance in outcome (Bishara et al., 1992; Ponsford et al., 1995b; van Zomeren and van den Burg, 1985). Outcome following TBI is influenced by many variables, relating not only to injury severity, but also to social and demographic factors and the post-injury environment. It is therefore difficult to predict outcome with accuracy in any individual case (Ponsford et al., 1995a; Schönberger, Ponsford, Olver, Ponsford, and Wirtz, 2011). It is certainly unwise for clinicians to convey a definite prognosis based on PTA duration alone to the patient and/or family in the early stages of recovery. Outcome assessment remains to some extent, a subjective assessment; as the late Sir Bryan Jennett rightly observed more than 40 years ago "A different view of recovery may be taken by the doctor, who knows only how bad the patient was after the injury, by the patient, who knows only how good he was before the injury, and by the family, who know something of both" (1972, p. 18).

Management of the person in PTA

Patients in PTA can present a significant management problem for nurses, therapists and families, causing considerable disruption in hospital or rehabilitation wards. As a consequence, it is not uncommon for sedation to be used. However, this tends to not only further reduce the person's level of arousal, but potentially increases confusion and can prolong agitation, as well as exacerbate problems with attention, initiation and fatigue (Cope, 1987). Major tranquillisers may increase the likelihood of post-traumatic epilepsy, and the results of some studies have suggested that they may have a deleterious impact on outcome (Cope, 1987; Feeney, Gonzalez, and Law, 1982; Hoffman, Cheng, Zafonte, and Kline, 2008; Kline, Hoffman, Cheng, Zafonte, and Massucci, 2008). Behavioural principles should be adhered to in interactions with people in PTA, as in other stages of recovery (see Chapter 6). However, due to its usually transient nature and the lack of learning ability on the part of the injured person in this state, the organisation of structured behaviour modification programmes may not be necessary or fruitful and may create unnecessary distress.

The recommended approach to the management of PTA involves creating an environment which minimises agitation. Physical restraint, or lying between the bars of cot sides, tends to compound feelings of agitation and fear. Restless or physically active individuals who are in PTA should be nursed on the floor, with padding around the bed, so they can move about freely without harming themselves. The "Craig Bed", designed by the staff of Craig Hospital in Denver, USA, is ideal for this purpose (see Figure 2.3).

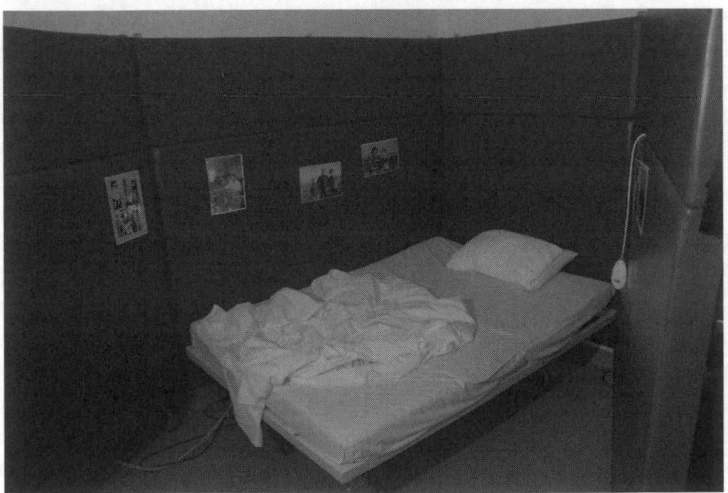

Figure 2.3 Bed for PTA management modified from original Craig Bed

Noise and over-stimulation also tend to exacerbate agitation in people in PTA. It is therefore important to maintain an environment that is as quiet as possible, as well as safe and secure. It is best for people in PTA to have a room to themselves and to remain there as much as possible, to enable the development of familiarity with surroundings. Moving around may only serve to increase confusion. However, people who are physically mobile and want to wander around the ward should be allowed to do so, with appropriate supervision. They should not, however, be allowed to leave the ward area. It is helpful to have an enclosed courtyard area to enable them to spend time outdoors. Electronic surveillance systems represent the ideal method of monitoring the movements of people in PTA, although most units do not have such facilities. If the unit cannot be locked, an alternative may be the use of a bracelet system, whereby a designated staff member takes responsibility for monitoring the whereabouts of the injured person for a specified period, during which a bracelet is worn. This is handed from one staff member to another as each takes responsibility for surveillance of the person concerned.

It is a good idea to have the same staff dealing consistently with the person in PTA. The presence of family, and familiar photographs and possessions around the bed may also be reassuring, as may frequent reminders as to what has happened (e.g., you have been in a car accident), where they are, the time of day, and so on. The number of visitors should be limited, again to avoid over-stimulation. It is best to have one or two visitors at a time, for short periods only, and no visitors if there is obvious fatigue or distress. People in PTA generally fatigue easily, and need much more sleep than usual.

Physiotherapy may be necessary at this stage. If at all possible, this should be conducted on the ward. Taking a person in PTA to a busy physiotherapy department is likely to exacerbate confusion and agitation. It may be helpful for other therapists to establish a supportive relationship through regular, but brief, contacts on the ward. However, it is very important to realise that, whilst in PTA, people will benefit little from therapy which requires active participation, although it is conceivable that there may be some carryover from physiotherapy if motor learning skills remain relatively intact (Ewert et al., 1989).

There is limited evidence to show that individuals in PTA might benefit from "Reality Orientation Therapy" (ROT). According to Moffat (1984, p. 82), ROT, which was designed to assist in the care of confused elderly patients, ". . . aims to maintain or retrain a person's awareness of time, place and current events by incorporating this information in staff interactions with the patient. This structured conversation may be assisted by classroom sessions, the use of external aids, repetition and possibly by specific behavioural training. Whilst there have been reports of improvement in the cognitive function of people in PTA when they were participating in ROT groups (Corrigan, Arnett, Houck, and Jackson, 1985), this has not been differentiated from the cognitive improvement which may occur spontaneously during this phase. There is no evidence showing that use of a calendar enhances orientation (Watanabe, Black, Zafonte, Millis, and Mann, 1998). De Guise and colleagues (2005) reported a clinically, though not statistically, significant reduction in duration of PTA with a structured orientation approach called the "North Star Project", involving placement of a board at the end of the bed to provide frequent prompting of orientation information. Further research into the ways in which ROT could assist at the point of emergence from PTA is clearly needed.

Attempts at assessment of language and other cognitive functions during PTA, and, to a lesser extent, physical abilities, are likely to be thwarted by restlessness, poor concentration, fluctuating levels of arousal, and reduced control over thought processes and behaviour. A picture of severe and generalised impairment may emerge, bearing little resemblance to the pattern of ongoing deficits which is apparent on emergence from PTA. This may result in an unnecessarily gloomy prognosis being conveyed to family members. Many TBI individuals show a rapid improvement in mental state on emergence from PTA. It is, therefore, usually misleading to attempt to assess and prognosticate during PTA. Formal assessment and treatment is likely to serve only to distress the injured person.

Maximising communication success during PTA

It is helpful to remember the close relationship between cognitive status and communication ability during the period of PTA. As GCS scores increase, it is usual to see improvements in both the form and content of verbal output, together with improvements in information processing skills. Communication needs will probably change quite rapidly as the person emerges from PTA. It is important that the relationship between cognition and communication is explained to families, in order to allay anxieties about the sometimes bizarre manifestations of this. The term "aphasia" should not be used to describe the verbal difficulties displayed by the person in PTA. Whilst certain features of these difficulties may resemble aphasia, it is common for many of them to dissipate rapidly following emergence from PTA.

There are a number of ways in which communication with the injured person may be enhanced during the period of PTA. These are summarised below:

- Keep instructions and explanations to a minimum, and deliver them slowly. Allow additional time for the person to respond.
- Establish a reliable yes/no response as early as possible. All staff should take care in framing yes/no, as opposed to forced-choice questions. A yes/no question, for example, might be 'Would you like a drink?", whereas an example of a forced choice question is "Would you like juice or water?". A range of modalities may need to be available to the person to communicate at this level. These include speech, head nodding/shaking,

yes/no boards, thumbs up/down, and any or all combinations which appear to be successful for the person concerned.
- Because of their close relationship with the injured person, family members may be the first to establish a means of communication. Team members need to respect this and build on the work of families.
- Consistently reinforce any communication attempts the injured person makes; however, no attempt should be made to modify content or articulation at this time.

It may be distressing and confusing for family members whose relative swears or uses language otherwise uncharacteristic of their premorbid communication style. Staff should explain that these behaviours reflect the person's reduced control over what is being said, and that as far as possible, they are best ignored at this stage. Other verbal behaviours which may be inadvertently reinforced by family members include perseveration, confabulation and echolalia. Again, these need to be explained in terms of the person's brain injury, and strategies (such as distraction) should be suggested for dealing with them as they arise. It should also be explained to family members that emergent communication skills are likely to fluctuate.

Box 2.2 Summary of principles of management in PTA

- keep noise and stimulation to a minimum
- maintain a safe, secure and familiar environment
- avoid restraint
- allow freedom to wander around the ward area under surveillance
- avoid taking the person from the ward
- keep staff changes to a minimum
- limit the number of visitors and their length of stay
- allow frequent rest times
- reinforce any attempts at communication and keep instructions simple
- provide regular reassurance regarding circumstances
- except for specific needs, do not attempt to assess the injured person
- do not prognosticate
- keep therapy contact brief
- do not allow person to go home

Helping the family of the person in PTA

Families are usually very anxious at this stage to obtain information about the nature of deficits and the likely prognosis. Staff should resist pressure to make predictions. Instead they should use this as an opportunity to explain what PTA is, how the family can assist in appropriate management of their loved one during this phase, and that further assessment and therapy will be conducted following emergence from PTA. Not uncommonly, families ask the same questions over and over, and staff need to be patient with this, and be prepared to reiterate information many times. Understandably, families may also be very keen to see their injured relative being treated intensively, and may even attempt to do this themselves. It is important, therefore, to maintain constant communication between staff and family, so that energies can be harnessed as constructively as possible.

Families may also wish to take their relative home. However, it is unwise to send a person in PTA home for visits, let alone to allow discharge. Although it may seem helpful for the injured person to be in the familiar home environment, such visits lead, more often than not, to over-stimulation. On return to hospital, the person may be more confused, agitated, fatigued and unsettled. Often, people in PTA cannot see the reason for being in hospital, and taking them home for brief visits only unsettles them further. It is also usually extremely stressful for families to try to manage a person in PTA in the home environment. This is not to say that home visits should not occur – indeed they are to be actively encouraged, once there is consistent orientation and awareness of circumstances, and the family seem equipped to cope.

Making the transition to oral feeding

A detailed account of the transition to oral hydration and nutrition is beyond the scope of this chapter. However, key principles associated with this are summarised in Box 2.3 and further detail is available in specialised texts, e.g., Murdoch and Theodoras (2001).

Box 2.3 Making the transition to oral hydration and nutrition during PTA: Key principles

- Before commencing this transition, there needs to be an open discussion by the team (including family) about the risks and benefits of oral intake.
- Be aware of the effect of fluctuating conscious state and fatigue on the safety of oral hydration and nutrition. Be prepared for a stop–start process, and ensure that family members understand this also.
- Evaluate dental status, as this may have changed post injury.
- Visual and auditory distractions in the ward environment may be problematic – minimise these as much as possible.
- Ensure that the skills and expertise of all team members (including family) are called upon – the medical practitioner, SLP, physiotherapist, and OT all have key roles to play.
- Consider the taste, temperature and texture of the foods on offer.

- Generally, commence with foods of the consistency of pureed fruit, rather than thin liquids.
- Be aware that some medications can interfere with the absorption of artificial nutrients.
- Remember that in some cases, dysphagia does not resolve with the end of PTA, in which case ongoing management will need to become the focus.
- Manage primitive oral reflexes and explain their basis and implications to family members.
- Weigh the patient regularly.
- If swallowing problems persist beyond about three months, a Modified Barium Jelly Swallow and/or percutaneous endoscopic gastrostomy (PEG) may be needed.

Vegetative and minimally conscious states after severe TBI

When Jennett and Bond developed the Glasgow Outcome Scale (GOS) in 1975, they described five broad outcome categories after TBI: death, persistent vegetative state (PVS), severe disability (conscious but disabled, often but not always requiring institutional care), moderate disability (disabled but independent to varying degrees), and good recovery (resumption of normal life in spite of "minor neurological deficits"). The GOS has since been widely used in a large number of longitudinal studies examining outcome at various time-points post-injury. However due to its acknowledged lack of reliability and sensitivity to some important aspects of clinical change (Anderson, Housely, Jones, Slattery, and Miller, 1993; Hall, Cope, and Rappaport, 1985) the Glasgow Outcome Scale – Extended (GOSE; Wilson, Pettigrew, and Teasdale, 1998) was developed. The GOSE extends the five GOS categories to eight (dead, vegetative state, lower severe disability, upper severe disability, lower moderate disability, upper moderate disability, lower good recovery and upper good recovery). Questions were added to the structured interview to aid in assigning the "upper" and "lower" distinctions and more detailed guidelines were also developed (Wilson et al., 1998). A reliability study of the GOSE with 50 participants found overall agreement of 78 per cent between two raters and a "very good" kappa value of 0.85 (Wilson et al., 1998). A subsequent study also reported high inter-rater reliability of 0.92 (Pettigrew, Wilson, and Teasdale, 2003).

In the period since development of the GOS and GOSE, there has been considerable debate and more vigorous investigation of the outcome category that Jennett and Bond described as PVS. It is perhaps ironic to reflect on Jennett and Bond's comment (1975, p. 482) that the term *persistent vegetative state* ". . . is the least ambiguous term to describe patients who remain unresponsive and speechless for weeks or months until death after acute brain damage". This false dawn of diagnostic certainty in the 1970s probably reflects the level of reliance at that time on bedside measures of conscious state, and the relative paucity of clinically useful data that could be obtained from neuroimaging approaches or electrophysiological examination. Debate has surrounded the use of the qualifiers such as "persistent" and "permanent", particularly in relation to the time post-injury at which the condition is deemed to be ongoing. Rigorous study of these patients has been hampered by lack of diagnostic clarity, marked inconsistencies in terminology, and the difficulties of studying sufficient numbers of patients with a relatively rare condition.

So what, then, is the origin of the term "persistent vegetative state"? It was proposed by Jennett and Plum in 1972, to describe the small percentage of brain injured people (variously described as between 1 and 7 per cent), who remained in what they termed a state of "wakeful unresponsiveness". Jennett and Plum described a number of common features of the condition they were attempting to characterise, in particular (i) the emergence of eye-opening, initially only in response to pain, but later spontaneously. It was noted that although the person may appear to visually track moving objects, careful observation reveals that this is not sustained beyond a few seconds; (ii) the presence of abnormal motor responses, such as decerebrate rigidity. Primitive reflexes, such as grasping, sucking, and rooting may also be present. Chewing movements and teeth grinding (bruxism) may occur. A noxious stimulus may initially elicit an abnormal extensor response; however, delayed flexion generally occurs. Jennett and Plum noted that "untrained or optimistic" observers are wont to interpret this reflex activity as purposeful behaviour; (iii) the absence of communication, either verbal or non-verbal, although grunting and groaning noises may be heard.

Diagnostic uncertainty has continued to plague those patients who, on the face of it, might be classified as being in a vegetative state, but whose pattern of clinical responsiveness does not necessarily conform to a clear-cut distinction between brainstem-arousal and cortical-awareness. Two major challenges have been a focus of research in the past 15 years – firstly, developing more fine-grained diagnostic categories to allow adequate description of discrete subgroups of patients, according to differences in clinical (and possibly non-clinical) evidence of awareness, and secondly, identifying tools to monitor changes in individual patients, whose level of arousal and/or awareness may alter over time. These endeavours are significant for a number of reasons, most notably to enable a clearer understanding of the pathophysiology of severe brain injury, to enable better prediction of outcome, and to ensure that appropriate rehabilitation resources are made available to patients who may be able to derive benefit, albeit modest in some cases, to achieve gains in independence and quality of life.

The first step in achieving these ends requires greater clarity of terminology to describe patients who are awake, but unable to demonstrate unequivocal cognitive abilities in processing information from their environment or to communicate purposefully to others, even if only on an inconsistent basis. While this may sound relatively straightforward, in practice it can be extremely difficult. Patients with this level of injury severity typically display multiple disabilities, including limb weakness and spasticity, joint contractures, and problems with trunk and head control. It is often difficult to determine the level to which sensory modalities central to communication, i.e. hearing and vision, are preserved. Further, volitional motor responses are typically extremely limited, and those responses which might be employed as evidence of attempted communication are frequently behaviours that would have occurred on a reflex basis anyway, e.g., eye blinking. Appropriate validated tools, skilled practitioners and repeated careful observation are the essential ingredients in this process. Recent evidence suggests that neuroimaging technology (in particular functional MRI) and electrophysiological measures also have a role to play. Each will be considered separately in this chapter, but first, it is important to review shifts in terminology over recent years.

After decades of relative neglect of these patients, three major position papers were published within as many years during the mid-1990s. These position statements were prepared by the American Academy of Neurology (1994), the American Congress of Rehabilitation Medicine (1995), and by a multidisciplinary working party (Andrews, 1996). Unfortunately, as Giacino and Whyte (2005) observed, these parallel efforts served to complicate, rather than simplify the diagnostic landscape, and as a result, the Aspen Neurobehavioral Workgroup (ANW) was formed. The principal function of the ANW was to resolve discrepancies in the first three statements, and deliver consensus on terminology, diagnostic criteria and management guidelines (Giacino and Whyte, 2005). Because of the importance of recognising patients who display some receptive and/or expressive communication ability, the ANW differentiated between patients in a vegetative state (i.e. not displaying signs of awareness) and those who are also severely disabled yet able to respond in some objectively defined meaningful ways. Their distinction between coma, vegetative state, minimally responsive state and the locked-in syndrome is summarised in Table 2.1 below.

The vegetative state

The ANW refined Jennett and Bond's (1975) definition of the vegetative state in a number of important ways. First, they dealt with the issue of the qualifier "persistent", noting that the earlier recommendation that this be applied after 12 months post-injury (Multi-Society Task Force on PVS, 1994a, 1994b) was based on a review of a small numbers of cases and is thus more arbitrarily than empirically derived. Because the term PVS carries with it both a poor prognosis for improvement and a pessimistic outlook on the part of staff and bodies that fund rehabilitation, the ANW recommended that it is more useful to specify the time post-onset and the aetiology of injury. The latter point is important given evidence that non-traumatic causes such as hypoxia carry poorer prognoses for improvement of function. Jennett (2002) suggests that after one month, the qualifier "persistent" can be used, and in the case of

Table 2.1 The Aspen Working Group's differentiation between coma, vegetative state, minimally responsive state, and locked-in syndrome

Condition	*Consciousness*	*Sleep/wake*	*Motor function*	*Auditory function*	*Visual function*	*Communication*	*Emotion*
Coma	None	Absent	Reflex and postural responses only.	None	None	None	None
Vegetative state	None	Present	Postures or withdraws to noxious stimuli. Occasional purposeful movement.	Startle	Startle	None	None
Minimally responsive state	Partial	Present	Localises noxious stimuli. Reaches for objects. Holds or touches objects in a manner that accommodates size and shape. Automatic movements, e.g. scratching.	Localises sound location. Inconsistent command following.	Sustained visual fixation. Sustained visual pursuit.	Contingent vocalisation. Inconsistent but intelligible verbalisation or gesture.	Contingent smiling or crying.
Locked-in syndrome	Full	Present	Quadriplegic	Preserved	Preserved	Aphonic/anarthric Vertical eye movements and blinking usually intact.	Preserved

Source: Giacino et al., 2002, p. 350.

traumatic aetiologies, "permanent" can be used after 12 months. The use of these qualifiers has not, however, been universally adopted, and for purposes of ongoing monitoring and assessment, it may be more beneficial for clinicians to concern themselves with the distinction between vegetative state and minimally conscious state. While retaining features of Jennett and Bond's 1975 description of what they termed the *persistent* vegetative state (most notably spontaneous eye opening, evidence of a sleep–wake cycle, the possible release of some primitive reflexes and lack of reliance on artificial respiration) the ANW's description of the vegetative state further specified that there must be no behavioural evidence of self or environmental awareness. The following diagnostic criteria are therefore central to the ANW definition of vegetative state:

- No evidence of sustained, reproducible, purposeful, or voluntary behavioural responses to visual, auditory, tactile or noxious stimuli.
- No evidence of language comprehension or expression.

Such patients require full and intensive nursing care, being reliant on artificial nutrition and hydration (e.g., via percutaneous endoscopic gastrostomy or "PEG"). Bowel and bladder incontinence are also present.

The minimally conscious state (MCS)

This term was included by the ANW to accommodate the need to differentiate between patients who meet criteria for the diagnosis of vegetative state and those who display some, albeit limited and inconsistent, meaningful responses. As such, the MCS shares with the vegetative state a severe alteration of consciousness, but is differentiated by evidence of ". . . minimal but definite behavioural evidence of self or environmental awareness" (Giacino et al., 2002, pp. 350–351). In this respect it is clinically differentiated from the vegetative state by virtue of a small but demonstrable and reproducible repertoire of behaviours, such as following simple commands, gestural or verbal yes/no responses (even if inaccurate), intelligible verbalisation, and some form of purposeful behaviour, such as contingent vocalisation, smiling or crying in response to input that has some emotional salience, and reaching for objects in a way that signals awareness of the object's size and shape (Giacino et al., 2002). As noted by participants at the ANW in 1994 (see Giacino et al., 1997), however, clear differentiation of the border-zones of the vegetative and minimally conscious state may not be straightforward at all. These workers suggested that clinicians need to consider the relative weighting of *consistency* and *complexity* in the patient's responses, where there is less need to demonstrate consistency of a complex response such as verbalisation, than of a simple response such as a finger movement to command. When patients are able to demonstrate consistent and reliable functional communication, they are deemed to have emerged from the MCS.

In spite of the concerted efforts of multidisciplinary working parties in recent years, there are some persisting tensions around the use of terminology. In Australia, for example, the National Health and Medical Research Council has produced guidelines for assessment and ethical management of patients in a state of *post coma unawareness* (Australian Government National Health and Medical Research Council, 2008). It is pleasing that older terms such as *apallic syndrome*, *coma vigile*, and *akinetic mutism* are no longer in use. However, the *locked-in syndrome* must be clearly distinguished from vegetative/minimally responsive states. This rare syndrome has been discussed in some detail in the literature (e.g., Maguire, Hodges, Medhat, and Redford, 1986; Oboler, 1986; Pearce, 1987; Posner et al., 2007) and usually results from a lesion (infarction, haemorrhage or demyelination) in the ventral pons or medulla. The person is typically quadriparetic and mute, but can demonstrate significantly preserved cognitive abilities via vertical eye movements and/or blinking. Unlike the person in a vegetative or minimally responsive state, the person in a locked-in state is able to give clear signs of awareness of self and the environment. Further, measures of cerebral glucose metabolism in these patients are near normal (Beuthien-Baumann, Holthoff, and Rudolf, 2005). It is also important (but less difficult) to differentiate vegetative/minimally responsive states from *brain death*, which results in the absence of both brainstem and supratentorial function. Brain death is confirmed by the presence of various combinations of coma, apnoea, dilated pupils, absent cephalic reflexes and electrocerebral silence on EEG recording, and is not compatible with survival once artificial respiration is removed (Posner et al., 2007).

Neuropathological changes in vegetative and minimally conscious states after severe TBI

By the mid-1980s, there was some degree of confidence and consensus in rehabilitation circles that patients in a vegetative state (persistent or otherwise) had a poor prognosis for improvement to a level of independence that would involve non-institutional care. There was also a common understanding that the pathophysiology of this condition could be understood in terms of relatively preserved brainstem and hypothalamic (i.e. homeostatic or *vegetative*) functions, against a background of widespread cortical damage. Berrol (1986, p. 9) drew a clear distinction between *arousal* and *awareness* and argued that the former may occur in the presence of adequate brainstem function, where the latter "... implies functioning within the cerebral hemispheres with some cognitive content and ability". This thinking was consistent with Jennett and Plum's description (1972) of these patients as being in a state of "wakeful unresponsiveness". Papanicolaou and colleagues (Papanicolaou, Loring, Eisenberg, Raz, and Contreras, 1986, p. 173) summarised this thinking when they observed that "An intact brainstem ... only increases the likelihood of the patient's survival and has little relevance to the quality of this survival, which depends on hemispheric function". This distinction between widespread cortical damage against a background of relatively intact brainstem function has, however, recently been challenged as an explanatory model of vegetative and minimally conscious states (Posner et al., 2007), as discussed further below.

Postmortem studies of the brains of individuals who have died as a result of TBI have identified diffuse axonal injury (DAI) as an important mechanism underlying impairment of consciousness (Adams, Graham, and Jennett, 2000; Graham, Adams, Murray, and Jennett, 2005; Posner et al., 2007). In a study comparing the brains of 30 patients classified as "Severely Disabled" (SD) with 35 patients who were clinically classified as being in a "Vegetative State" (according to the GOS), Graham et al. found a higher incidence of DAI, especially at the higher grades, and a higher likelihood of abnormalities in the thalamus in patients classified as vegetative, as compared with SD patients, whereas focal damage associated with contusions and intracranial haematomas was more common in the SD group. Ischaemic damage occurred with roughly equal frequency in the two groups.

Data from autopsy studies are important in understanding the pathophysiology of these conditions. However, the day-to-day challenge for clinicians is to gauge remaining brain function using both neurodiagnostic and clinical tools. In the absence of a single, definitive test to determine that a patient is in a vegetative or minimally conscious state, rehabilitation teams need to draw on data from multiple sources. These will be considered below.

Neuroimaging: CT, MRI, fMRI, SPECT

Despite the limitations of CT and MRI scans outlined in Chapter 1, they play an important role in early medical/surgical management, and in detecting causes of deterioration in conscious state (e.g., hydrocephalus, intracranial bleeding). CT scans can provide a useful basis for explaining structural changes to family members. As noted in Chapter 1, however, conscious state may be impaired in the absence of significant changes evident on CT. Therefore, the limitations of CT scans need to be explained to relatives. Whilst their use is not routine in clinical practice, information derived from PET and SPECT scans about cerebral oxygen and glucose metabolism and regional cerebral blood flow can be invaluable. Beuthien-Baumann et al. (2005) found that cerebral glucose metabolism decreases over time in patients diagnosed as vegetative, with reported values between 25 and 71 per cent of those of healthy controls. A group in Oxford (Owen et al., 2006) has used functional MRI (fMRI) to assess the conscious awareness of a 25-year-old woman who met clinical criteria for a vegetative state (VS), following a brain injury sustained as a result of road trauma five months earlier. When she was asked to imagine playing a game of tennis, significant activity was observed in the supplementary motor area. When she was asked to imagine walking through her house, activity was observed in the parahippocampal gyrus, the posterior parietal cortex and the lateral premotor cortex. Most notably, Owen et al. observed that "Her neural responses were indistinguishable from those observed in healthy volunteers performing the same imaginary tasks in the scanner" (p. 1402). However, as others have cautioned (e.g., Panksepp, Fuchs, Garcia, and Lesiak, 2007) it is possible that this patient had been misdiagnosed and was in an MCS rather than a VS.

In a subsequent study of 14 patients, seven of whom were diagnosed as being in a VS, 5 as MCS and 2 as SD, Coleman et al. (2007), examined residual language processing using fMRI techniques. They reported some "islands of preserved function" with respect to speech processing (p. 2502) in some VS patients that could not be elucidated via behavioural responses. However, a number of caveats apply. Firstly, the aetiologies of the brain damage sustained in this group were mixed, including stroke (n=2 VS, 2 MCS patients), cardiac arrest (n=3 VS patients) and diffuse axonal injury following either a fall or a road traffic accident (n=2 VS patients, 3 MCS patients). The three VS patients who showed evidence of speech processing went on to make the most marked behavioural recovery, however two had brain damage resulting from stroke rather than trauma. Secondly, the functional significance of such responses is open to debate given that, as Coleman et al. observe, ". . . our fMRI findings acquired relatively early after their injuries may have simply preceded the natural recovery pattern for these less well-studied aetiologies" (p. 2505). Notwithstanding these caveats, however, such findings call into question the notion that the VS can be accounted for on the basis of an absence of cortical activity in the presence of relatively preserved brainstem function. In fact, the state of current research suggests that the VS represents a type of disconnection syndrome, in which primary somatosensory cortex may be activated, in the absence of activation of cortical association areas (see Giacino, Hirsch, Schiff, and Laureys, 2006 for review). Coleman et al. also caution that the only responses under fMRI conditions that can be interpreted as "significant" are those which are positive, given that negative responses may reflect fluctuating arousal or attention. Hence if this approach is to be used to make important management and or medico-legal decisions, it should be carried out on a repeated basis, in order to reduce the likelihood of false negative responses. Further, in interpreting evidence of cortical activation, a distinction needs to be drawn between perceptual *registration* of information and cognitive *integration*, which requires the activation of complex neural pathways in association regions of the cortex.

Electrophysiological studies

The electroencephalogram (EEG) has a very limited role in the management of people who are emerging from coma and/or those who are in a VS or MCS, due to its many sources of artefact, and inconsistencies between EEG data and behavioural indices (see Ganes and Lundar, 1988; Panksepp et al., 2007). Posner et al. (2007) have observed that the EEG has a role in identifying some treatable conditions after TBI (most notably seizure disorders), but is not a predictive tool with respect to outcome.

Derivatives of the EEG, evoked responses (ERs, also known as evoked potentials) and event-related potentials (ERPs) have, however, been studied extensively as possible predictors of outcome from coma, VS and MCS of varying aetiologies. Evoked potentials are the electrical signals generated by the nervous system in response to sensory stimulation, typically of auditory, visual and general sensory pathways. Brainstem auditory evoked potentials (BAEPs) may be normal in VS/MCS patients, but may also be attenuated, delayed or absent, depending on the nature and severity of brainstem injury (Kobylarz and Schiff, 2005). Somatosensory evoked potentials (SSEPs) have been shown to have predictive value that may be higher than that of clinical measures, however as Kane (2008) has cautioned, their absence may be a negative prognostic indicator, but their presence does not ensure a favourable outcome. This reflects the fact that patients may have extensive brain injury despite preservation of the afferent somatosensory pathways and primary somatosensory cortex.

ERPs differ from evoked responses in that they are of *cortical* origin (and hence are referred to by some workers as "cognitive ERPs") and provide information about processing of the signal and preparation for action at a cortical level (Kotchoubey, 2005). ERPs may be either positive (P) or negative (N) deflections of early, middle and late components, and are taken as measures of signal processing and/or significance. Some ERPs have been studied with particular interest, given their apparent correlations with either poor, or with more positive, outcomes. Three such ERPs are the P3 (a large positive wave with a latency of 300–500 msec), N400, and so-called Mismatch Negativity (MMN). P3 seems to be largely frontal in origin and is regarded as indicating that a stimulus has been "just noticed". N400, on the other hand, is a brain response to verbal and other meaningful stimuli, and depends on the functional integrity of the anterior medial temporal lobe, inferior frontal regions and temporo-parietal junction (Kotchoubey, 2005). Schoenle and Witzke (2004) studied 120 patients grouped into three categories (1) patients in a VS, (2) patients in near VS, and (3) patients not in vegetative state. They found that approximately 12 per cent of VS patients showed clear semantic N400 potentials, which these workers regarded as an indication of semantic processing capabilities. They went on to argue that N400 ERPs should be factored into ethical debates about the management of VS patients. More recently, Vanhaudenhuyse, Laureys, and Perrin (2008) have suggested that the accuracy of ERPs as prognostic tools could be enhanced by increasing the salience of the signals employed, e.g., the patient's own name.

MMN (or "oddball paradigm") is a response to an odd (i.e. unexpected) stimulus in a sequence of stimuli, most commonly visual or auditory, that can be detected irrespective of whether the subject was actively attending to the stimulus. MMN and P3 have been detected in both comatose and VS patients. Recently, for example, Wijnen, van Boxtel, Eilander, and de Gelder (2007) showed that the emergence of MMN (higher amplitudes and lower latencies) in a sample of 10 comatose patients positively predicted emergence from VS to MCS. Others have cautioned that whilst the presence of P3 and MMN is generally regarded as positive prognostically, neither can be taken as a clear indicator of conscious awareness (Kane, 2008; Panksepp et al., 2007). Vanhaudenhuyse et al. (2008) summarise this thinking by stating that ". . . it is very speculative to say that these behaviours are associated to (sic) some kind of consciousness. We can assert that a patient is conscious *only* when she/he communicates her/his contents of consciousness" (p. 263).

Taken together, recent neuroimaging and electrophysiological evidence seems to support the existence of identifiable subgroups of patients who show low levels of responsiveness/retained cortical activity after very severe brain damage. Indeed, it is possible, as Coleman et al. (2007, p. 2504) observed, that rather than there being discrete diagnostic categories such as VS and MCS, there may be a *spectrum* of impairment between coma and the unequivocal evidence of awareness of self and environment exhibited by the patient who attains the GOS "severe disability" level of functioning. Given that the diagnostic boundaries between VS and MCS are generally agreed to be indistinct, this line of thinking may be more helpful to rehabilitation teams than striving to "fit" a patient into a diagnostic category whose boundaries are dynamic and remain contested against a background of ongoing research. It is most important that levels of responsiveness are identified and measured as accurately as possible so that appropriate rehabilitation resources are made available and pessimism on the part of staff and/or funding bodies is not allowed to preclude thorough assessment and close ongoing monitoring. Clinical measurement tools play an important role in this process, and are discussed below.

Clinical measurement tools for use with patients who are in a vegetative or minimally responsive state

VS and MCS patients display behaviours that do not fit neatly into one diagnostic category or another; their performance fluctuates. Incremental change may occur over a long period of time, but only become apparent through careful assessment and accurate recording of responses. A number of clinical measurement tools have been developed for this purpose over the past 20 years. These scales all attempt to describe and objectively measure behaviours which may signal small increments of improvement in conscious state. This is generally achieved by examining each sensory modality (e.g., sight, hearing, touch, taste) in terms of spontaneous and/or criterion-referenced behaviours (i.e. responses which occur in response to a particular stimulus, such as a command). A selected range of these scales is outlined below, in the order in which they first appeared in the literature. A review of these scales and their relative merits is provided by Majerus, Gill-Thwaites, Andrews, and Laureys (2005). Earlier scales aimed at characterising the responses of coma-emerging patients, such as the Disability Rating Scale (Rappaport, Hall, Hopkins, Belleza, and Cope, 1982), the Rancho Levels of Cognitive Functioning Scale (Hagan, 1998) and the Western Neuro Sensory Stimulation Profile (Ansell and Keenan, 1989) preceded the ANW working party on terminology and diagnostic guidelines for VS or MCS patients (Giacino and Whyte, 2005), and hence will not be considered here.

The Coma Recovery Scale – Revised (CRS-R) (revised version published by Giacino, Kalmar, and Whyte, 2004; first published by Giacino, Kezmarsky, DeLuca, and Cicerone, 1991).

The CRS-R comprises 23 items in six subscales concerned with auditory, visual, motor, oromotor, communication, and arousal functions. The three basic scales it shares with the GCS (Teasdale and Jennett, 1974) are further elaborated to allow for the identification of more subtle changes in behavioural responsiveness. Subscales are arranged hierarchically, with reflex activity receiving lower scores, while the higher-scoring responses reflect cognitively mediated volitional responses. Scoring is based on the identification of operationally defined target behaviours, and the scale is administered via a two-step procedure of baseline and subsequent data gathering, in an effort to reduce the likelihood that reflex behaviour is confused with that which is contingent upon a specific stimulus. The CRS-R was designed to be particularly sensitive to the distinction between VS and MCS, and also to identify responses to sensory stimulation approaches. It has strong inter-rater and test re-test reliability, and good concurrent validity with the Disability Rating Scale (DRS; Rappaport et al., 1982).

Sensory Modality Assessment and Rehabilitation Technique (SMART) (Gill-Thwaites and Munday, 1999; 2004)

This tool was designed to identify evidence of awareness via graded assessment of levels of responsiveness in the context of a structured and regulated sensory stimulation programme, and also as a tool to guide rehabilitation efforts. The SMART comprises two major components: (a) the informal gathering of information from family and carers about the patient's premorbid likes and dislikes and current behavioural patterns, and (b) a formal component consisting of a Behavioural Observation Assessment (observation of reflexive, spontaneous and purposeful behaviour during a 10-minute observation period) followed by the SMART Sensory Assessment. The latter is based on the three dimensions of the GCS. The Sensory Assessment is conducted in 10-minute sessions, with equal numbers of sessions in morning and afternoon over a two-week period. In addition to the five sensory modalities, this scale considers motor function, functional communication and wakefulness/arousal and comprises 29 standardised techniques. It is scored on a 5-point hierarchical scale, and has been shown to be both valid and reliable in discriminating evidence of awareness in patients clinically identified as both VS and MCS.

The Wessex Head Injury Matrix (Shiel et al., 2000)

The WHIM has developed out of earlier work by Horn et al. (1993), Shiel, Wilson, Horn, Watson, and McLellan (1994), and Wilson, Shiel, Watson, Horn, and McLellan (1994), concerned with systematic observations of the behaviours that occur spontaneously and/or in response to stimulation in a cohort of 88 initially comatose patients who were followed longitudinally. From these observations, a pool of 145 behaviours was identified. These were ultimately collapsed into six subscales: communication, attention, social behaviour, concentration, visual awareness, and cognition. The 62 items across these six scales were then arranged hierarchically to reflect the sequence of emergence when a patient is recovering from coma. For example, earlier non-verbal, predominantly visual items on the scale proposed by Shiel et al. (2000) record responses to naturally occurring stimuli, or stimuli presented by a therapist (e.g., "Eyes following the person moving into the line of vision"; "Moving a cloth placed over the face"). As recovery progresses, behaviour becomes more interactive, (e.g., "Frowning to show dislike" or "Alerting to a voice outside"). More spontaneous behaviour items are included at the higher levels, (e.g., "Seeking eye contact"). This is followed by the beginning of verbal communication. Items relevant to day-to-day orientation and memory are then included on the scale. The patient's WHIM score reflects the rank order of the most advanced item observed. Hence the WHIM can monitor all stages of recovery from coma, including PTA, as well as being able to detect subtle changes in patients in an MCS. It has been shown to have good inter-rater and test re-test reliability.

Of these three scales, the WHIM is the only one to have clearly been validated on a sample of TBI-only patients. The injury aetiology of the sample studied by Giacino et al. (2004) is not clear, and the sample studied by Gill-Thwaites and Munday (2004) included patients with brain damage of traumatic, anoxic and other medical aetiologies, in unspecified proportions. This is significant inasmuch as patterns of responding are likely to reflect underlying injury pathophysiology. It is hoped that the next decade will see vigorous empirical evaluation of these tools to determine their relative strengths and limitations in the assessment of coma-emerging patients.

The Post-Acute Level of Consciousness scale (PALOC-s) (Eilander et al., 2009)

This scale represents an attempt to address the fact that people who do progress from VS to MCS typically do so slowly and somewhat erratically, hence it is important to be able to capture the range of their responses using psychometrically robust tools. What this scale specifically adds is a further breakdown of the VS and MCS categories. So, for example, VS comprises three levels of responsiveness: (i) hyporesponsive, (ii) reflexive state, and (iii) high active level, and the MCS comprises (i) transitional state, (ii) inconsistent reactions, and (iii) consistent reactions. Eilander et al. (2009) provide behavioural descriptors for each of these levels. This scale also derives three scores for each patient: the "general state", the "best state" and the "worst state". This refinement means that fluctuations in conscious state/responsivity are actively captured. It therefore stands to add considerably to clinical decision making and discussions with family members and funding bodies.

Helping the family of the patient in a minimally conscious state or vegetative state

Whilst the period that the injured person spends in coma is frightening and distressing, it does carry at least an implicit expectation of improvement to a more independent and responsive level of functioning. This hope is usually realised through family members' observations of their loved one and other injured people in the acute care setting, as they begin to show definite signs of awareness. For some families, however, the initial relief in seeing a lightening of conscious state is short-lived, as the injured person has entered a vegetative or minimally conscious state. These families face the prospect of long-term despair, confusion and anger, as they struggle to understand a condition which seems to parody awareness.

Lay people cannot be expected to easily understand or accept explanations from staff that their injured relative's movements, groans, or apparent eye contact are not necessarily purposeful events, particularly as these are the very behaviours that they and the staff had recently greeted as signs of emergence from coma. The term "vegetative" may be a convenient form of medical shorthand to refer to biologically based homeostatic functions, but it does little to comfort or inform family members about their loved one's condition. Indeed, this term has very negative connotations and is arguably unsuitable for use in communicating with families. Regardless of the terminology employed, it is important to explain what the vegetative or minimally conscious states mean, and to outline the possible outcomes, both within 12 months and beyond. Family members will need many months, or even years, to come to terms with such diagnoses and the prognosis associated with them. Whilst this may, to some extent, be assisted by the provision of neuroimaging and electrophysiological data, it may be difficult for relatives to reconcile what they are hearing from staff with what they observe in their loved one from day to day.

Family members often feel that the injured person is aware of their presence and/or is communicating via behaviours such as eye closure or groaning. Indeed, it makes good sense to assume that inconsistent emergence of such behaviours on a purposeful basis is most likely to occur in response to interactions with loved ones – so family observations and feedback should be taken seriously by staff. On the other hand, the patient's failure to communicate may be interpreted by family members as stubbornness, withdrawal or depression. In the case of someone in a minimally conscious state, such explanations cannot be unequivocally ruled out. Differences between the assessment of the injured person by staff and family need not be a source of conflict or hostility, particularly if continued efforts are being made to monitor the injured person using appropriate clinical tools, and provide an optimal management environment. It is helpful if staff are not only consistent in their input to family members, but show a genuine interest in, and make use of, the observations of relatives about the injured person's level of responsiveness. Where good staff–family relationships are cultivated, relatives can be gently educated about the distinction between arousal and awareness and can be asked to monitor signs they see as evidence for either or both of these.

Staff need to be receptive to concerns expressed by family members and, where possible, accommodate their suggestions regarding approaches to the care of the injured person. This demands personal and professional maturity of staff who may, because of their own sense of frustration, sadness and despair about the injured person's condition, find communicating with family members particularly difficult and stressful. Team members need opportunities to discuss their feelings of inadequacy with each other, so that they can continue to provide optimal care to the patient and empathic support to relatives. Family members commonly feel confused and angry about their loved one's condition; angry that the accident occurred, angry that progress is not occurring, angry with staff for not doing a better job and, consciously or unconsciously, angry with the injured person. The latter applies particularly in circumstances where the accident involved excessive alcohol consumption and/or other types of risk-taking behaviour.

It is normal for family members to want to investigate all options which hold some promise of improvement in their loved one's condition. It is most important in these circumstances that staff do not become resentful of relatives for what they may feel is "shopping around". Few of us, in such catastrophic circumstances, would turn our backs on the possibility, no matter how remote, of improving a severely injured relative's condition. Staff can assist relatives by inviting open discussion of alternative, sometimes controversial treatments, and by not rejecting family members (overtly or covertly) for their decision to explore such options.

3 Assessment of participation, activity and cognition following TBI

Sue Sloan and Jennie Ponsford

Introduction

Due to the high frequency of diffuse axonal injury, combined with localised frontal and temporal lobe damage, TBI tends to result in a characteristic range and pattern of cognitive impairments. These include deficits of attention and speed of information processing, learning and memory, and executive functions, which include the ability to think in abstract terms, generate ideas, think flexibly, and plan and solve problems. Executive cognitive deficits are frequently associated with impairments in the ability to self-monitor and regulate behavioural responses. The precise nature and extent of these cognitive problems varies widely, as a function of the location and severity of injury, as well as premorbid and contextual factors. As many follow-up studies have demonstrated, they may affect the individual's capacity to perform activities necessary for independence in daily life and have a more significant impact on long-term psychosocial outcome than do physical disabilities.

Many of these cognitive impairments are not always apparent on standardised neuropsychological assessment, however. Moreover, it is frequently difficult to predict how impairments evident on assessment will specifically affect the individual's daily life and their role performance in community settings. As a consequence of this, the assessment of cognitive difficulties following TBI presents a significant challenge to psychologists and therapists involved in the rehabilitation process, requiring a more direct focus on the everyday life of the individual. Following the principles of the REAL approach, outlined in Chapter 1, the aim of this chapter is to provide guidance in attaining an understanding of the nature of the cognitive difficulties associated with TBI, as well as residual strengths, and their impact on the ability of the individual to function in their chosen life roles and daily activities. The information collected in the course of assessment provides a basis for goal setting, treatment planning and intervention, which will be discussed and expanded in Chapter 4.

The International Classification of Functioning, Disability and Health (ICF) as outlined by the World Health Organization (WHO) (e.g. 2002), provides a useful framework for understanding the manifestations of cognitive difficulties associated with TBI. The ICF is divided into two parts, the first being Functioning and Activity Limitation, which are comprised of Body Systems (i.e. Function and Structure) and Activities/Participation, and the second, Contextual Factors, which includes both Environmental (e.g. social attitudes, architectural features, legal systems, etc.) and Personal Factors (e.g. gender, age, coping styles, education, etc.) Figure 3.1 displays the relationships and interactions between the various components of the ICF.

According to this conceptual structure, injury to a Bodily Structure, such as the brain, affects the function of specific brain areas and results in impairments (e.g., executive function deficits, verbal memory impairment). Activity Limitations stem from combinations of impairments and are the resulting difficulties in performing practical daily tasks (e.g. difficulty with meal preparation, or using the telephone). Participation Restrictions are defined as the social disadvantages for the individual in the context of their valued life roles and responsibilities (e.g. failure to participate in employment, reduced capacity to perform the home maintainer role). Due to their nature and complexity, it is important to assess the manifestations of cognitive sequelae associated with TBI on each of these dimensions. Assessment methods relevant to cognitive function, activity, and participation are outlined in the sections below. Traditionally, assessment starts at the impairment level and the focus on return to life role participation in a community setting typically occurs well into the rehabilitation process. However, such a "bottom-up" or impairment oriented approach often results in a therapy programme with a focus biased towards the person's deficits and lacking functional direction. In order to ensure a focus on meaningful outcomes, rehabilitation needs to begin with a vision of the end in mind. That is, an understanding of the individual's previous or desired life roles within the context of their social and community environments is the key to devising cognitive rehabilitation programmes that result in meaningful outcomes. For this reason, the following sections utilise

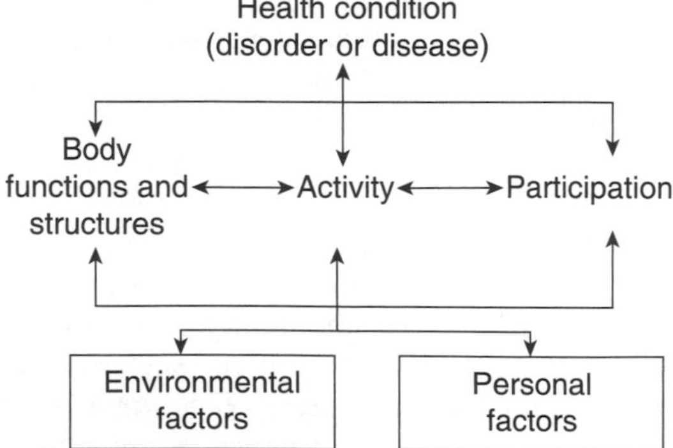

Figure 3.1 The International Classification of Functioning, Disability and Health (ICF)

the WHO framework in a "top-down" approach to address assessment in the following order: participation, activities and cognitive function.

Participation following TBI

Participation Restrictions are defined as "problems an individual may experience in involvement in life situations" (WHO, 2002, p. 10). The consequences of Participation Restriction are that "the individual will be unable to sustain the roles to which he is accustomed or to attain those to which he might otherwise aspire" (WHO, 1980, p. 41). Participation Restrictions reflect a reduction in the ability to participate in a life role to which the person attaches value. Individuals experience Participation Restrictions when they attempt to perform activities within their own cultural/social context. Therefore, Participation Restrictions may not be fully apparent until the person has returned to their community setting. Participation Restriction, formerly referred to as handicap, is thus "a social phenomenon" (WHO, 1980, p. 28).

There is frequent confusion between the concepts of Impairment, Activity Limitation and Participation Restriction. There is a tendency to presume or predict Participation Restriction based on an assessment of the nature and degree of Impairment or Activity Limitation. However, as suggested by the WHO, there is not a simple linear relationship between disease, Impairment, Activity Limitation and Participation Restriction. The same level of Activity Limitation in two different individuals can result in markedly different Participation Restrictions, depending on the expectations, demands upon, and supports available to that individual. Contextual Factors are therefore a crucial determinant of Participation Restriction, and need to be assessed as phenomena in their own right. As a consequence of a failure to consider Participation Restriction, many rehabilitation professionals do not fully understand how individuals with TBI are actually disadvantaged in their social and community context. This results in many well-intentioned rehabilitation efforts having a minimal long-term impact.

Judgements relating to all three concepts of Impairment, Activity Limitation and Participation Restriction depend on deviations from norms. Normative views regarding Participation Restriction are determined either by reference to some "ideal", or to the individual's or society's perceptions as to the degree of disadvantage resulting from the injured person's disabilities and/or impairments. Assessment of Participation Restriction may vary according to the viewpoint from which the disadvantage is perceived, namely, that of the individual, those close to the individual or the community (Noonan, Kopec, Noreau, Singer, and Dvorak, 2009). As the WHO point out, such assessments are difficult to categorise in a reproducible way. Clearly, the establishment of appropriate criteria against which to judge performance in order to assess Participation Restriction presents a complex and difficult challenge. As a consequence, Participation Restriction has historically been very poorly measured. As Whiteneck and Dijkers (2009) point out, it is important to consider both objective and subjective perspectives, and to examine the interaction between the environment and the injured individual's functional impairments and limitations. They argue that there are no existing tools which can properly meet these requirements.

Understanding and assessing Participation Restriction

Studies have shown significant variability in long-term participation outcomes following severe brain injury (Doig et al., 2001; Tate, 2004; Winkler et al., 2006). Although some people are able to re-engage in productive life roles and maintain a network of family and friends, others appear to have limited opportunities for meaningful activity and are socially isolated (Winkler et al., 2006). For people experiencing low community integration, participation in work or education (Avesani, Salvi, Rigoli, and Gambini, 2005; Felmingham, Baguley, and Crooks, 2001; Fleming et al., 1999; Olver et al., 1996; Ponsford et al., 1995b), leisure activities (Brown, Gordon, and Spielman, 2003), and other valued life roles (Hallett, Zasler, Maurer, and Cash, 1994; Sloan, Winkler, and Anson, 2007) is significantly reduced. Loss of life role participation often results in individuals spending large amounts of time alone, engaged in passive activities within the home (Winkler, Unsworth, and Sloan, 2005), failing to integrate into their community (Doig et al., 2001), experiencing social isolation (Elsass and Kinsella, 1987; Olver et al., 1996) and tending to rely more on family for social contact (Eames, Cotterill, Kneale, Storrar, and Yeomans, 1996; Winkler et al., 2005; Winkler et al., 2006). These problems may be further exacerbated for those living in inappropriate accommodation settings, such as residential aged care facilities (Winkler, Sloan, and Callaway, 2007).

The dimension of Participation Restriction following TBI which has been most comprehensively studied is that of employment outcome, which is affected in 50–90 per cent of moderate–severe TBI cases (e.g. Ponsford et al., 1995b; Turner, Ownsworth, Cornwell, and Fleming, 2009). As discussed in Chapter 7, employment outcome is influenced by many factors, including the age of the injured person, injury severity, degree of cognitive impairment, particularly in the areas of attention and executive function, self-awareness, limitation in the performance of activities of daily living, the demands of the job, support from the employer and other behavioural, environmental and social factors (Ownsworth and McKenna, 2004).

Measures of participation

There are a growing number of participation measures available, but few have been comprehensively validated in TBI individuals. The Glasgow Outcome Scale (GOS) (Jennett and Bond, 1975) has been the most widely used scale for assessing global outcome after TBI focusing on injury-related changes in functioning in major life areas, rather than particular symptoms (Wilson, Pettigrew, and Teasdale, 1998). It was designed to be rated by a clinician. Criticisms regarding its unstructured nature and broad categories led to the development of the Glasgow Outcome Scale – Extended (GOSE) (Wilson et al., 1998). The GOSE extends the original five GOS categories to eight (dead, vegetative state, lower severe disability, upper severe disability, lower moderate disability, upper moderate disability, lower good recovery, and upper good recovery). Additional questions were added to the structured interview to aid in assigning the "upper" and "lower" distinctions and more detailed guidelines were also developed, with demonstrated reliability (Wilson et al., 1998).

Other tools for which comprehensive data are available on TBI are the Community Integration Questionnaire (CIQ) and the Craig Handicap Assessment and Reporting Technique (CHART). These measures make comparison with normative data derived from healthy comparison groups and may be criticised because they do not take account of the relative importance of each role to the individual. Nevertheless they do address the most fundamental aspects of participation and have demonstrated validity and reliability in individuals with TBI.

Community Integration Questionnaire (CIQ)

The CIQ (Willer, Rosenthal, Kreutzer, Gordon, and Rempel, 1993) contains 15 items across three subscales: home integration, social integration and productivity. Level of involvement in activities including financial management, grocery shopping, childcare, meal preparation, housework, community access, social activities, employment, study and volunteer work is rated. The total CIQ score ranges from 0 to 29, with higher scores indicating greater integration. The scale was designed for the purposes of programme evaluation in individuals with TBI and it has been shown to be an appropriate instrument in quantifying rehabilitation outcome in TBI individuals at the participatory level (Zhang et al., 2002). However, the scale does not allow for assessment of premorbid role performance, as well as the importance of each activity to the injured person, and it does not elicit the detailed information required for planning individualised community integration programmes.

Craig Handicap Assessment and Reporting Technique (CHART)

Whiteneck, Charlifue, Gerhart, Overholser and Richardson (1992) developed the Craig Handicap Assessment and Reporting Technique (CHART) as a means of quantifying the extent of handicap in individuals with spinal cord injury in a community setting. Using the dimensions of Handicap identified and described by the earlier version of the ICF (WHO, 1980) but excluding Orientation, 27 interview questions identified the degree to which roles were fulfilled in the following domains, using observable criteria: 1) Physical Independence: ability to sustain a customarily effective independent existence;

2) Mobility: ability to move about effectively in his/her surroundings; 3) Occupation: ability to occupy time in the manner customary to that person's sex, age, and culture; 4) Social Integration: ability to participate in and maintain customary social relationships; and 5) Economic Self-Sufficiency: ability to sustain customary socio-economic activity and independence. Each dimension has a maximum possible score of 100 points, representing performance typical of the average non-disabled person, so that higher scores reflect greater participation.

Whiteneck et al. (1992) established the validity and reliability of the CHART for use with spinal cord injured individuals. The inter-rater reliability between injured raters and a family member or other proxy was good on all dimensions except social integration, which varied as a function of how well the proxy knew the person being rated. In 1995, additional questions addressing the domain of cognitive independence were added to CHART and found to be both reliable and valid (Mellick, Walker, Brooks, and Whiteneck, 1999). The CHART has been shown to be a valid measure of outcome in individuals with TBI (Hall, Bushnik, Lakisic-Kazazic, Wright, and Cantagallo, 2001) and to discriminate among various impairment categories in a direction that parallels increasing disability (Walker, Mellick, Brooks, and Whiteneck, 2003).

One potential difficulty with the administration of these scales is in establishing the most relevant or reliable informant. Information regarding Participation is in some cases most accurately obtained by way of a joint interview with the TBI individual and a family member. There is a need for further work on the development of complementary scales, which might also be completed by relatives.

Sydney Psychosocial Reintegration Scale (SPRS)

A scale which allows for comparison of the perspectives of the injured person and a close other is the Sydney Psychosocial Reintegration Scale (SPRS) (Tate, Hodgkinson, Veerbangsa, and Maggiotto, 1999). This is a more recently developed scale designed to assess injury-related changes in functioning in the domains of occupational activity, interpersonal relationships, and independent living skills. Each domain is comprised of four questions rated on a 7-point scale, with higher ratings reflecting better outcome. Scores can be calculated for each domain (ranging from 0 to 24) and an overall score can be calculated. The SPRS has three alternative forms: Form A, which measures change from pre-injury functioning; Form B, which measures current level of functioning; and Form C, which categorises functioning into one of three levels (Tate, Lulham, Broe, Strettles, and Pfaff, 1989; Tate et al., 1999; Tate, Pfaff, Veerabangsa, and Hodgkinson, 2004). Form A of the SPRS has been shown to have high levels of internal consistency; Form B has been shown to have similar psychometric properties (Tate et al., 1999, 2004). The SPRS has both patient and relative versions, allowing for direct comparison of responses and providing a means of assessing the accuracy of the TBI patient's self-reports.

Role Checklist (RC)

Whiteneck and Dijkers (2009) emphasise that according to the ICF framework it is important to assess participation from both objective and subjective perspectives. Thus it is vital to ascertain not only the extent of participation in various roles but how important this is to the injured person, and, arguably, their family. The Role Checklist (RC) (Oakley, Kielhofner, Barris, and Reichler, 1986) assesses this. It measures Participation Restriction from the perspective of the injured individual and elicits information regarding the person's past, present and future participation in life roles (Part 1), and the level of importance the person attributes to each of the roles (Part 2). It details a list of 10 common life roles (student, worker, volunteer, caregiver, home maintainer, friend, family member, religious participant, hobbyist and participant in organisations) and a category of "other". Responses on the RC can be expanded on in a semi-structured interview to provide a detailed understanding of the person's key areas of life role and social participation, their premorbid experiences and their goals for the future. Not only can responses be used to guide the development of meaningful intervention, but the number of roles in which they are participating can be used as a baseline measure from which the success of the intervention can be gauged.

Participation Objective, Participation Subjective (POPS)

A measure designed to be consistent with the ICF Activities/Participation framework is the Participation Objective, Participation Subjective or POPS (Brown et al., 2004). This comprises 26 "items", which are elements of participation (e.g., going to the movies, housework, opportunities to meet new people). Two types of questions are asked for each item. The first question is objective, e.g., how often in a typical month do you go to the movies? The second two questions for each item are subjective: How important is this to your well being? Are you satisfied with your current level of participation, or would you like to be doing more or be doing less? The 26 items are classified into five categories: Domestic Life; Major Life Activities; Transportation; Interpersonal Interactions and Relationships; and Community, Recreational and Civic Life. There are, however, many challenges in assessing the validity and reliability of an instrument such as this (Brown et al., 2004).

Other measures developed more recently which have been based on the ICF Activities/Participation component include the LIFE-H (Fougeyrollas, Noreau, Bergeron, Cloutier, Dion, and St Michel, 1998), IMPACT-S (Post, de Witte, Reichrath, Verdonschot, Wijhuizen, and Perenboom, 2008) and WHODAS II (WHO, 2000). These measures are promising, but they have not been used extensively or validated in groups with TBI.

Use of the ICF framework also requires consideration of the influence of Environmental or Contextual Factors on Participation. Several scales have been developed to measure environmental factors. The Craig Hospital Inventory of Environmental Factors (CHIEF) (Whiteneck, Harrison-Felix, Mellick, Brooks, Charlifue, and Gerhart, 2004) assesses perceived negative environmental influences in five categories: (i) Physical and structural (6 items), (ii) Attitudes and support (5 items), (iii) Services and assistance (7 items), (iv) Policy (4 items), and (v) Work and school (3 items), with a 12-item short form also available. The scale shows good psychometric properties and normative data are available (Whiteneck, Harrison-Felix et al., 2004). The Measure of Quality of the Environment (MQE) (see Fougeyrollas, Noreau and St-Michel, 1997) also assesses the influence of environmental and social factors, including both facilitators and barriers. Measurement of social supports is also pertinent, with one suitable measure being the Social Support Survey (SSS) (Sherbourne and Stewart, 1991), a 19 item self-report scale assessing five dimensions of functional social support: (i) Emotional support (e.g. empathic understanding from other people), (ii) Informational support (e.g. offering of advice), (iii) Tangible supports (e.g. provision of material aid), (iv) Affectionate support (e.g. expression of love), and (v) Positive social interactions (e.g. availability of other people for recreation). Marital status and number of people in whom the person can confide provide contextual background, but are not scored.

A systematic review of participation measures with a range of health conditions (including TBI) as these relate to the ICF is available in Noonan, Kopec, Noreau, Singer, and Dvorak (2009). In assessing Participation Restriction, rehabilitation team members need to be sensitive to the cultural, societal and peer norms that prevail for the injured individual. Such factors may for instance influence cultural expectations for males and females regarding participation in home maintainer and parenting roles. The common demographic features of the TBI population, that is the predominance of young males, may mean the norms of the individual may be very different from those of the rehabilitation staff. Participation and Participation Restriction is likely to change over time as a function of recovery, personal development and life cycle factors, availability of supports and other environmental factors. A comprehensive understanding of the nature and extent of long-term Participation Restriction may not be apparent for many years after injury. However, assessment of Participation/Participation Restriction needs to be undertaken early in the rehabilitation process and continue over an indefinite timeframe. For a comprehensive review of measures for long-term follow-up of community-based individuals the reader is referred to Hall et al. (2001).

Assessment of activity limitation

Activity Limitation is defined as "any difficulties a person may have in executing activities" (WHO, 2002, p. 11). Assessment of Activity/Activity

Limitations, should be undertaken after an understanding of the individual's Participation/Participation Restrictions is obtained, as it involves the identification of limitations in those activities of everyday life that underpin the occupational needs and life roles of the individual, both as they present initially, and as they change over time. A Participation framework enables the therapist to select appropriate activities and tasks for assessment and enriches the understanding of the links between these two domains, which creates a platform for developing relevant interventions. Importantly, equal weight should be given to the identification of the individual's strengths and residual capabilities as well as their limitations.

Use of questionnaires, observational rating scales and checklists

One method of assessing the nature of cognitive difficulties as they are manifested in daily activities is the use of observational rating scales or checklists. These may be completed by therapists or relatives observing the injured person's behaviour or by the injured person themselves. In the domain of attentional behaviour there are two validated scales, the Rating Scale of Attentional Behaviour (Ponsford and Kinsella, 1991) and the Moss Attention Rating Scale (Hart, Whyte, Ellis and Chervoneva, 2009; Whyte, Hart, Bode and Malec, 2003; Whyte, Hart, Ellis, and Chervoneva, 2008). Memory questionnaires include the Subjective Memory Questionnaire (Bennett-Levy and Powell, 1980), the Prospective and Retrospective Memory Questionnaire (Crawford, Smith, Maylor, Della Salla, and Logie, 2003) and the 28-item Everyday Memory Questionnaire developed by Sunderland, Harris, and Baddeley (1983). Royle and Lincoln (2008) have published a 13-item version of this questionnaire which shows satisfactory validity and reliability. There are also several questionnaires designed to assess executive functions in adults, namely the Dysexecutive Questionnaire (DEX) (Wilson, Alderman, Burgess, Emslie and Evans, 1996) from the Behavioural Assessment of the Dysexecutive System (BADS), and the Frontal Systems Behavior Scale (FrSBe) (Grace and Malloy, 2001).

Additionally, there are some more general scales designed to rate the severity of the most common problems associated with TBI, including everyday cognitive difficulties. One of the most widely used scales is the Mayo-Portland Adaptability Inventory (Malec and Lezak, 2003). This scale, now in its fourth revision (MPAI-4) has three subscales: the Ability index, the Adjustment index and the Participation Index. The Ability index rates problems with mobility, use of hands, vision, hearing, dizziness, motor speech, verbal and non-verbal communication and, in the cognitive domain, changes in attention/concentration, memory, fund of information, novel problem-solving and visuospatial abilities in terms of the extent to which they interfere with daily activities. It also has an Adjustment index, assessing impact of anxiety, depression, irritability, pain, fatigue, inappropriate social interactions, sensitivity to mild symptoms, and self-awareness on daily activities. The

Participation index rates ability to initiate and engage in social, leisure, and employment-related activities, and manage transportation and finances. The MPAI-4 shows good psychometric properties.

Another such scale is the Neurobehavioral Functioning Inventory (NFI) (Kreutzer, Seel, and Marwitz, 1999) which has both patient and family versions, designed to document the frequency of common difficulties encountered by people with TBI, including misplacing things, losing track of time, missing appointments, forgetting phone numbers, and having difficulty with word finding. Other items address emotional and behavioural issues like breaking or throwing things, feeling hopeless, restlessness, arguing, and threatening others. Items are organised into six factor analytically derived scales: Depression, Somatic, Memory/Attention, Communication, Aggression and Motor. There is limited documentation of executive difficulties. Normative scales are provided based upon patient age and injury severity.

These scales can be rated either by the injured person, a close other or a clinician. It is important to point out that the reliability of reporting by the injured person may be influenced by their level of self-awareness, which may lead to underestimation of certain problems, or by their emotional state, which may lead to overestimation of problems. Whilst relatives or clinicians may be more reliable, their ratings will be influenced by their opportunities to observe relevant behaviours in various contexts and, for relatives, their emotional state (Draper and Ponsford, 2007). There is no doubt that self-report is important in evaluating problems from the injured person's point of view. However, there is also a significant need for direct behavioural observation of performance of everyday activities.

Assessment of activities of daily living

A distinction is commonly drawn between performance of routine self-care activities such as bathing, dressing, eating and toileting (PADL), and those tasks that are more complex. The latter are referred to as instrumental activities of daily living (IADL) and include domestic tasks such as cooking, laundry and cleaning, as well as shopping and financial management (Law, 1993). These activities are also often classed according to whether they are domestic tasks undertaken in the home (DADL) or activities undertaken in the community setting (CADL).

Assessment begins with identification of the tasks and activities the individual wants, needs and is expected to perform within the domains of personal care, domestic activities, child care, use of transportation, shopping, organisation of daily activities, financial management, sporting, other recreational and social activities, including various modes of communication, employment and study. Assessment of skills related to driving, work and study is discussed in detail in Chapter 7 (return to work, tertiary study is driving) and Chapter 10 (return to school). It is against the background of what was "normal" and "achievable" and "desired" for the person premorbidly that current performance should be evaluated. For instance, before assessing financial management skills it would be important to understand the nature and extent of involvement in these tasks prior to the injury. This approach acknowledges that individuals choose the occupations and activities in which they engage and provides a starting point not only for the assessment (Trombly and Radomski, 2002), but also for the development of an effective therapeutic relationship (Taylor, 2008).

Canadian Occupational Performance Measure (COPM)

The COPM (Law et al., 1998) utilises a semi-structured interview method to assess occupational performance in the areas of activities of daily living, work and leisure. The perception of the person and/or their caregiver should be sought. For each occupational performance area, e.g. cooking, the therapist determines whether the person needs, wants or is expected to perform this activity. If a client needs to do an activity, their perceptions of their current performance are explored through further questioning. If the person is unable to perform the activity at a level satisfactory to them, it is listed as a problem for intervention. Areas listed as problems are then scored by the individual in terms of their importance, their perception of current performance and level of satisfaction with their performance. It is acknowledged that following TBI the individual may not be fully insightful, or ready to address all their limitations. In this approach, the person can commence working on the problems of which they are aware and, at reassessment, changes in their performance can be measured and additional issues that have emerged over the treatment period can be identified (Law et al., 1998; Trombly and Radomski, 2002). Interviews with the injured person and relevant family members are preferably conducted in the home. Areas where assistance is given may be identified through subjective reports and compared with patterns of premorbid behaviour. It is also important to identify the nature and degree of ongoing support and assistance (both paid and unpaid) that is likely to be available and maintained once the person is discharged to the community.

The specific tasks of daily living directly assessed by the therapist will depend on what was identified as relevant at interview. For example, an adolescent living within a family unit may not have been required premorbidly to engage in laundry or cooking activities, or house and garden maintenance, and may not in the foreseeable future. These activities are better assessed at the time they are needed. The person may, however, have been a student and may aim to resume studies. So, the activities involved in this role will need to be comprehensively assessed.

In addition to interview and direct observation, the therapist may use one of the many scales developed to assess activities of daily living, some of which are standardised. Some of the more commonly used measures of PADL, for instance, for which information on reliability and validity is available, include the Barthel Index (Mahoney and Barthel, 1965), The Independent Living

Scale (ILS) (Ashley, Persel, and Clark, 2001; Centre for Neuro Skills, 1986) and the Functional Independence Measure (Granger, Hamilton, Keith, Zielezny, and Sherwin, 1986; Keith, Granger, Hamilton, and Sherwin, 1987). These scales have limitations, both in terms of range of activities and reliability, but nonetheless are widely used to document outcomes.

Personal activities of daily living

Follow-up studies suggest that most TBI individuals do not demonstrate long-term difficulties with personal care tasks (Colantonio et al., 2004; Lippert-Grüner, Lefering, and Svestkova, 2007; Panikoff, 1983; Whiteneck et al., 2004). The more severe the injury, the more likely the person's need for assistance, in both physical and cognitive domains. These findings are not surprising, as basic activities of daily living are typically well learned and performed within familiar environments studded with contextual cues. These factors may mitigate against the effects of residual cognitive impairments, particularly those in the executive domain.

For those individuals who experience long-term difficulties with self-care activities due to cognitive-behavioural impairments, common problems include lack of initiative or poor attention to detail in personal care, resulting in failure to shower regularly, clean teeth or maintain a personal standard of grooming. Such individuals may require verbal cues or encouragement from a carer in order to satisfactorily initiate or complete self-care tasks. Otherwise they may present as unkempt. Conversely, changes in personality, such as rigidity or obsessive attention to detail, may lead to the individual spending an excessive amount of time in personal care activities. Although such a person will present as well groomed, the time spent in the activity may disrupt the normal family routine. Poor self-regulation of behaviour, manifested as impulsivity, may compromise safety in tasks, such as regulating water temperature or using appropriate transfer techniques to compensate for physical disabilities. Difficulty making decisions may be apparent in clothing selections that fail to take account of the weather or activities to be undertaken during the day. These functional difficulties will necessitate a higher level of assistance from a carer than would be predicted on the basis of physical limitations alone.

The unfamiliarity of the hospital setting may add to the person's difficulties in performing personal tasks. Toiletries and towels will be located in unusual places, and the bathroom layout may be unfamiliar. This may result in the level of independence in the familiar home environment being underestimated by the assessor. On the other hand, the strict daily routine and degree of supervision and prompting available in a structured and uncluttered hospital environment may facilitate performance. On return home, when these cues are no longer available and the person is required to self-initiate and schedule these activities, performance may decline. It is important, therefore, to document not only performance of the PADL task itself, but also cues that facilitate performance, and the extent to which novel demands compromise independence. Observations must be made in the home, as well as the hospital setting.

Instrumental activities of daily living

Clinical experience and evidence from follow-up studies indicate that people who have suffered TBI experience a much greater level of ongoing Activity Limitation in more complex domestic and community activities, such as shopping, financial management, transportation or planning leisure activities than is evident in self-care tasks (Colantonio et al., 2004; Jacobs, 1988).

Literature and clinical experience indicate that in understanding the nature of the IADL Limitations experienced by people with TBI, it is particularly important to understand the impact of executive function impairment on performance of everyday activities. Difficulty with planning, organising and problem solving can lead to the person being able to complete basic and well practised activities such as showering, dressing and simple meal preparation, whilst being unable to manage more complex tasks, such as budgeting, meal planning and child-care. Difficulties with idea generation and concrete or inflexible thinking will lead to difficulties with social relationships and managing interactions in the community during activities such as shopping and banking. Difficulties with the initiation of activities and their scheduling within a timeframe can lead to people performing tasks in an erratic or inefficient manner and they may fail to complete the full range of tasks necessary, for instance in a home-maintainer role. Confusingly, people who have been shown to be capable of performing the individual tasks involved in maintaining a clean home (e.g. washing dishes, vacuuming, etc.) may be incapable of reliably initiating and scheduling these activities in order to maintain their home to their previous or current standards. Difficulty with regulating and self-monitoring responses can lead to problems such as impulsive spending and excessive intake of items such as food, drinks and cigarettes. Participation in these activities may be routinely prioritised over other necessary tasks. When people also display trouble learning from their experience, they may continue to repeat the same mistakes and ineffective behavioural routines, despite repeated feedback. The functional manifestations of executive deficits are many and varied, and often the individual's well-learnt skills are relatively preserved, but the person may show significant problems with tasks that are relatively novel. For these individuals the key determinant of their competence is largely their level of familiarity with the task pre-injury. This may result, for instance, in the person being able to manage a complex financial matter, through the application of well-learned routines, but being unable to reliably follow a recipe.

Formal measures of IADL may be insensitive to the cognitive-behavioural problems individuals with TBI experience and they typically sample a small range of preselected tasks which may or may not be relevant to the specific life roles of a given individual. As a consequence of these limitations, therapists tend to obtain assessment information through direct, semi-structured observations of selected tasks. As Law et al. (1998) have argued, the assessment process should be tailored to the daily living skills identified by the client as relevant. This methodology also allows for the identification of any fluctuations in initiative, mood, motivation, fatigue and concentration, which may lead to variations in the day to day performance of, and hence level of assistance required in, daily activities. Such variables need to be isolated through systematic and structured observations, particularly in home settings.

Assessment of Motor and Process Skills (AMPS)

For therapists trained in its use, the AMPS formalises this assessment approach. The AMPS is a systematic, observational assessment that is used to measure performance in goal-directed activities of daily living (Fisher, 1999, 2001). The quality of the person's ADL performance is assessed by rating the effort, efficiency, safety and independence on 16 ADL motor and 20 ADL process skill items, while the person is doing chosen, familiar and life-relevant personal, domestic or community based ADL tasks.

Recording qualitative observations

It is important to conduct this evaluation of performance of relevant activities within the home or other environment in which the task is normally performed. Identification of the components of the specific tasks selected for assessment can be undertaken using the process of activity analysis (e.g. Trombly and Radomski, 2002). The ability of the individual with TBI to perform each of these component tasks should be assessed. The therapist should observe the individual's performance on the task from the point of view of skill competency, rather than identification of impairments. It is usually extremely difficult to make accurate interpretations of underlying impairments, particularly on the basis of observations of the person performing multi-faceted functional tasks. Responses should be recorded in terms of behavioural observations, rather than interpretations of underlying problems. For example, "John commenced dressing after a verbal prompt", rather than "John lacks initiative". This method of assessment is very similar to that recommended for behaviour problems outlined in Chapter 8. For therapists trained in the AMPS a formalised structure for undertaking this form of assessment is provided.

Importantly, the assessment should be extended to ascertain whether the individual is reliably able to demonstrate the same level of task competence in the context of a normal daily routine, as when tasks are performed individually. Frequently the difficulty experienced by the injured person does not relate to performance of the individual task, but to the scheduling of multiple tasks within functional constraints, such as time factors.

Observations of behaviour may be structured and recorded under the following headings, allowing for premorbid abilities and requirements:

Timing

- able to get started on the task
- allows enough time to complete task
- performs task at an appropriate speed
- schedules different elements of the task sequentially or simultaneously as required
- stays focused on the task
- gets going on the task at the appropriate time within the context of an ongoing behavioural routine
- consistently demonstrates an adequate level of competence day-in, day-out despite fluctuations in mood, stress and fatigue.

Preparation

- makes appropriate choices when selecting/prioritising the activity or the content of it
- considers all relevant information in making choices
- obtains all relevant equipment and materials
- organises the work area
- takes and/or gives instructions
- reflects on past performance and considers modifying task if necessary
- anticipates injury-related issues and employs strategies proactively.

Execution

- uses equipment, tools and materials appropriately
- is aware of safety issues as they arise and takes necessary precautions
- detects and corrects mistakes as the activity proceeds
- solves problems as they arise
- deals with frustration adaptively
- seeks help appropriately
- completes all relevant aspects of the task
- uses strategies, methods and systems that allow the task to be performed with greater efficiency.

Completion

- realistically appraises performance and considers strategies to improve
- cleans the work space
- monitors (e.g., waiting for something to cook, set, dry), and comes back to the task and finishes off

- follows up (e.g., putting an ingredient on a shopping list)
- reports back or goes on with the next activity.

The therapist should also seek to identify those contextual factors within the injured person, the environment or the therapist/carer that cause variations in performance from one task or setting to another. The following are examples of the variables which should be carefully considered when assessing Activity Limitation.

Environment

- quiet or distracting
- contextual cues to prompt performance (e.g. familiar setting)
- presence of others (e.g. children, the assessor)
- time of day or day of week the task is performed
- temperature.

Person

- motivation and interest in activity (e.g. whether person perceives the task as relevant to their specific goals or life roles)
- premorbid skill level, influencing familiarity with task
- level of anxiety, depression, etc.
- level of insight, which will interact with motivation and interest
- ability to understand the instructions and purpose of the task
- level of fatigue and stress.

Therapist/carer

- assistance provided by therapist/carer (e.g. physical, verbal)
- relationship with injured person (including level of trust)
- approach to injured person (e.g. encouraging, condescending).

Obtaining quantitative information

Qualitative observations should be supplemented with quantitative information that forms a component of the baseline record of performance. This may include the following:

- time taken to complete task, or components of it
- number of errors made
- number of times specific prompts were given (verbal, written, physical)
- number of steps initiated by the injured person (identified by task analysis).

In summary, the recommended assessment approach relies on the systematic collection of structured behavioural observations of the person engaging in activities of daily living relevant to their current role participation status and future goals. It is vital that this information is supplemented by a knowledge of the "means" by which these "ends" are achieved, that is, the strengths, skills and strategies used by the person to facilitate performance. Furthermore, knowledge of the component skills the person lacks, and the level and nature of the input required from others to complete the task must be obtained. Contextual factors that impact on performance should also be identified. Observations of family members and carers, as well as the individual's own reflections, provide a subjective perspective that enriches the therapist's understanding of Activity Limitations. When combined with the results of neuropsychological assessment of impairment (discussed below) and an understanding of Participation Restrictions (discussed above), the analysis of Activity/Activity Limitations forms a basis for treatment planning, and serves as a baseline for the purposes of evaluating the effectiveness of intervention. There are, however, a number of limitations inherent in this form of behavioural assessment. Due to its subjectivity, it is intrinsically less reliable, potentially affecting the accuracy of assessments from one therapist to another, and reassessments. In this respect, supplementing observations with both quantitative and formal measures becomes extremely important.

Assessment of impairment of cognitive function

The WHO (2002, p. 10) defines impairment as "problems in body function or structure such as significant deviation or loss". Cognitive impairments are deficiencies of neuropsychological function that can be related to damage in specific areas of the brain. Neuropsychological assessment is the method most commonly used to delineate the nature and severity of cognitive impairment following TBI. Whilst neuropsychological assessments should not be used to define Activity Limitation or Participation Restriction, they do provide a relatively standardised and objective means of delineating the specific nature of the cognitive impairments which may underlie disabilities, and thereby provide clues as to the basis of everyday difficulties and possible methods of managing these. Neuropsychological assessments are also able to identify areas of residual cognitive abilities and strengths.

Principles of neuropsychological assessment of TBI individuals have been comprehensively covered in a number of sources, including Walsh (1991; Walsh and Darby, 1999) and Lezak et al. (2004) and they provide detailed guidelines regarding test selection and administration and estimation of premorbid ability levels. This will not, therefore, be covered in great detail in this chapter. Assessment of language and communication skills is covered in Chapter 5. Whilst the discussion in this chapter will focus on assessment of the most common areas of cognitive impairment associated with TBI, it must be understood that impairment of any aspect of cognitive function may occur following TBI.

Initial interview and history

In taking the history, all available information regarding the brain injury and other injuries sustained, surgical intervention, complications, GCS scores, scan results and PTA duration should be gathered. Estimation of PTA duration may be extremely difficult in cases where the injured person underwent surgery, had severe internal injuries and/or was heavily sedated. The injured person's recall of events is likely to be poor under these circumstances, potentially inflating PTA estimates. Further details regarding the estimation of PTA duration are outlined in Chapter 2.

At the initial interview it is important, first, to establish that the person being assessed has emerged from PTA, along the lines suggested in Chapter 2. Neuropsychological assessment is likely to be inconclusive and distressing for the person who is still in PTA, and is therefore not recommended during this phase. It will be necessary to carefully monitor the performance of individuals who have ongoing problems with attention and fatigue, perhaps conducting the assessment over a series of short sessions.

Following a detailed history documenting educational and occupational background and previous learning, neurological, psychiatric and/or substance use problems, detailed and specific examples of functional cognitive and behavioural difficulties experienced at different times since the injury should be obtained to provide clues as to the likely nature of the underlying impairment. These examples later serve as a meaningful basis for feedback from the assessment. In the early stages after injury it is common to find awareness of physical disabilities, but failure to report significant changes in cognition and behaviour. Therefore, the individual's reports need to be treated with caution and verification sought. As an adjunct, questionnaires or rating scales such as the Patient Competency Rating Scale (PCRS) (Prigatano et al., 1986) or the Awareness Questionnaire (Sherer, Bergloff, Boake, High, and Levin, 1998a) may be used with individuals or their caregivers.

It is also important to explore the injured person's psychological reaction to the injury and coping strategies using methods outlined in Chapter 8. The presence of significant emotional disturbance may have an impact on the assessment results. It may also be necessary to consider the possibility of symptom exaggeration or malingering in certain contexts, particularly medico-legal contexts, through the use of tests such as the Test of Memory and Malingering (Tombaugh, 1997) or Green's Word Memory Test (Green and Astner, 1995). Further discussion of assessment of malingering may be found in Lezak (2004) or Strauss and colleagues (Strauss et al., 2006). Finally, it is useful at the initial interview to discuss the injured person's goals and expectations of rehabilitation. Such information is useful, not only in designing the rehabilitation plan, but also in tailoring feedback on completion of the assessment to the individual's level of insight, areas of concern and overall goals.

Wherever possible, the neuropsychologist should speak with a family member to check the accuracy of the information given by the TBI individual, and to obtain their account of the injured person's emergence from coma and PTA, their premorbid personality, behaviour patterns, abilities and interests, and to obtain the family member's perceptions of cognitive and behavioural changes since the injury, and the impact this has had on daily activities and relationships. Previous school reports and academic records should also be obtained wherever possible.

Assessment of attention

The assessment of attention following TBI is not a straightforward task for a number of reasons. Firstly, attention is not a unitary concept. There is little agreement as to definitions or components of attention and there are few established criteria for measurement of these. There is debate as to how to describe the component processes of attention. Whyte, Ponsford, Watanabe and Hart (2010) have suggested that key aspects of attention include arousal, selection, processing speed and strategic control, the latter including the ability to maintain attention to a task; inhibit disruption by distracting influences; shift attention in line with changing goals and priorities; manipulate information currently held in mind (referred to as working memory); and divide attention between two or more task demands. Difficulties sustaining attention, paying attention to more than one thing at a time, ignoring distractions, missing details and slowness in processing incoming information are among the most common sequelae reported by individuals with TBI, close others and rehabilitation therapists (Olver et al., 1996; Ponsford and Kinsella, 1991; van Zomeren and van den Burg, 1985).

A number of experimental studies have found that individuals with TBI are slower to process information (Madigan, DeLuca, Diamond, Tramontano, and Averill, 2000; Ponsford and Kinsella, 1992; Spikman et al., 1996). However, evidence supporting the presence of impairment of other aspects of attention is mixed (Ponsford and Willmott, 2004). Individuals with TBI are not necessarily more susceptible to distraction, even where there are strong conflicting response tendencies, as on the third subtest of the Stroop (Ponsford and Kinsella, 1992; Spikman et al., 1996), although increased sensitivity does emerge when a significant distracting load is added to the Stroop task (Bohnen, Jolles, and Twijnstra, 1992), or where target-distractor similarity is high (Schmitter-Edgecombe and Kibby, 1998). Whyte and colleagues (Whyte, Fleming, Polansky, Cavallucci, and Coslett, 1998; Whyte et al., 1996) developed a naturalistic inattentiveness assessment and were able to demonstrate marked differences in both on-task behaviour and fidgeting behaviour in both distracting and non-distracting environments, between TBI participants and controls. This suggests that the quiet, one-on-one context of neuropsychological assessments minimises the likelihood of inattentive behaviour.

Whilst it has not been possible to demonstrate a consistently greater decline in accuracy or speed of performance over time in individuals with TBI, there is a demonstrated reduction in the level of vigilance, in the form of decreased overall perceptual sensitivity or accuracy. There is also evidence that individuals with TBI expend greater psychophysiological costs to maintain a stable performance. These costs are, in turn associated with increased subjective fatigue (Ziino and Ponsford, 2006b). Regarding strategic control of attention, researchers have suggested that difficulties on complex selective or divided attention tasks are proportionate to the degree of slowing, and that strategic control per se is not impaired (Spikman et al., 1996; Veltman, Brouwer, van Zomeren, and van Wolffelaar, 1996). Others have indicated that additional strategic control deficits are present under conditions of increased task complexity, time pressure, or high working memory load (Dell'Acqua, Stablum, Galbiati, Spannocchi, and Cerri, 2001; Leclercq and Azouvi, 2002; Park, Moscovitch, and Robertson, 1999a; Willmott et al., 2009; Ziino and Ponsford, 2006a).

Given the heterogeneity of TBI, individuals may exhibit any, or all, of the spectrum of attentional difficulties. Therefore, in conducting the neuropsychological assessment of TBI individuals, it is important to observe and record, both quantitatively and qualitatively, a broad range of attentional behaviours, including information processing speed, the ability to focus attention and avoid distraction, the ability to divide attention across more than one task or aspect of a task, to hold and manipulate information in working memory, attention to visual and auditory detail, and the ability to sustain attention. Unfortunately, there is no commonly available neuropsychological test or tests which uniquely tap these behaviours. Rather, the assessment of attentional behaviour will need to be derived from performance across various tests and supplemented by qualitative observations.

A number of tests of speed of information processing have been shown to differentiate TBI individuals from uninjured controls. These include the Wechsler Adult Intelligence Scale (WAIS) Digit Symbol subtest, the oral and written versions of the Symbol Digit Modalities Test (Smith, 1973), the Telephone Search and Map Search subtests from the Test of Everyday Attention (Robertson, Ward, Ridgeway, and Nimmo-Smith, 1994), the Trail Making Test (Reitan and Wolfson, 1985), choice reaction time tasks and the Paced Auditory Serial Addition Test (Gronwall and Sampson, 1974; Ponsford and Kinsella, 1992; Ziino and Ponsford, 2006a). The WAIS Digit Span Backwards subtest is sensitive to impairment of working memory (Draper and Ponsford, 2008). The Test of Everyday Attention (Robertson et al., 1994), has subtests assessing a range of attentional abilities, including selective and divided attention. It is important to remember that absence of evidence of difficulty on these tasks does not preclude the presence of attentional difficulties in the more complex, demanding or distracting situations of everyday life. This underscores the importance of integrating objective findings with subjective and family observations of attentional deficits evident within the person's own functional environmental context

Memory assessment

Ongoing learning and memory difficulties, evident once the individual has emerged from PTA, are commonly observed following TBI. These have been described in detail by a number of authors, and the reader is referred to those sources for a detailed discussion of research in this area (e.g. Baddeley, Wilson, and Watts, 1995; Glisky, 2004; Vakil, 2005; Wilson, 2009). As outlined in Chapter 1, the specific nature of the problems will vary between individuals, and over time within the same individual. Information on the person's ability to learn and remember is vital for planning rehabilitation programmes, so it is important that this area be thoroughly assessed and monitored.

Where the person with TBI has suffered temporal lobe damage, the memory disturbance may be characterised by difficulty storing or consolidating new information. Depending on the site of injury, this may take the form of a general amnesic syndrome or, if there is greater injury in one hemisphere, memory for one class of material (i.e. verbal or non-verbal) may be relatively more impaired than another.

More typically, the brain injured person does not display an amnesic disorder, but their learning of new material (both verbal and non-verbal) is slower and imperfect (Vakil, 2005; Walsh, 1991). Walsh (1991) has suggested that this learning deficit may be due to frontal lobe impairment leading to a difficulty in adequately monitoring performance and detecting errors, then using this error information to modify (i.e. improve) subsequent responses (e.g. learning from their mistakes). People with frontal lobe injuries are also less likely to take an active approach to organising and structuring the material to be learnt. Questioning of the person on completion of a task often reveals an absence of strategies and an unsystematic approach to the learning task. Their difficulties in learning and recalling new information may be seen as secondary to the dysexecutive syndrome described below.

Prospective memory refers to the ability to remember to perform actions at a particular point in the future (Fleming et al., 2008). According to Einstein and McDaniel (1990) prospective memory comprises two subtypes: event-based prospective memory which involves performing a specific action in response to the occurrence of an external event (e.g. passing on a telephone message to your spouse when they return from work) and time-based prospective memory which involves performing an action at a predetermined specified time in the future (e.g. taking medication at 6pm or hanging out the laundry when the washing cycle finishes). Executive functioning plays an important role in prospective memory, and Fleming et al. (2008, p. 824), suggest that "by definition, prospective memory involves executive processes such as planning, disruption of ongoing activity and initiation of an activity".

Kinsella (2010) argues that prospective memory is a complex cognitive skill that requires the interaction between the pre-frontal cortex (executive attention skills) and the hippocampal system (associative retrospective memory). As such, interruption to either of these systems will disrupt prospective memory.

The TBI individual with memory problems will commonly perform better when recall is tested via recognition as compared to free recall (Shimamura, Janowsky, and Squire, 1991), suggesting that more is stored in memory than can be spontaneously retrieved on demand. Memory for the temporal order of events may also be disturbed. In this case the person may be able to remember the individual event, but be unable to accurately state when it occurred, suggesting that the contextual information surrounding that item is lost or unavailable (Shimamura et al., 1991).

The clinician must also examine aspects of attention when making an assessment of memory function. Slowed information processing, reduced selective attention, cognitive fatigue and other attentional difficulties may contribute significantly to poor performances on memory tasks, in that information will be poorly recalled if it was not adequately attended to and processed.

Neuropsychological assessment of memory function should encompass the ability to recall past events, knowledge and skills, to acquire and recall new information of varying complexity and nature and after varying delays, with and without prompting, using any of the commonly used memory tests (e.g., Wechsler Memory Scale, Rey Auditory-Verbal Learning Test, California Verbal Learning Test, Hopkins Verbal Learning Test) as discussed in Lezak (2004) or Strauss et al. (2006). Assessment of prospective memory should be undertaken. Tools include self-report questionnaires, such as the Comprehensive Assessment of Prospective Memory (Fleming et al., 2009); psychometric assessment tools, such as The Memory for Intentions Screening Test (Raskin, 2009); or virtual reality tasks, such as Virtual Week (Rendell and Henry, 2009). Strategies used to actively learn and retrieve information should also be documented.

Executive functions

Executive functions are defined as those higher-order cognitive abilities that encompass the generation, selection, planning and regulation of responses that are goal-directed and adaptive, given the contextual demands placed on the individual. According to Lezak (1983, p. 38), who coined the term, executive functions "enable a person to engage in independent, purposive, self-serving behaviour successfully". As outlined in Chapter 1, executive functions are dependent on the integrity of the pre-frontal regions of the brain and are therefore commonly impaired following TBI.

Executive deficits include "decreased or absent motivation (anergia) and deficits in planning and carrying out the activity sequences that make up goal directed behaviours" (Lezak et al., 2004, p. 36), problem-solving difficulties

(McCarthy and Warrington, 1990), reduced regulation of responses (Luria, 1973), lack of initiative (Stuss and Benson, 1986) and difficulty making decisions (Shallice and Burgess, 1991). Baddeley (1986) termed this collection of cognitive disorders the "dysexecutive syndrome". A number of models of dissociable executive functions have been proposed. For example, Stuss (2007) proposed four separate functional and anatomical domains of executive function: *Executive cognitive functions*, being the cognitive skills required to control and direct lower automatic functions, including planning, monitoring, activating, switching and inhibiting, and mediated by the dorsolateral prefrontal cortex; *Behavioural self-regulatory functions*, linked to the ventral prefrontal cortex and the limbic system, responsible for emotional processing, including the acquisition and reversal of stimulus–reward associations; *Energisation regulating functions* involved in initiating and sustaining behavioural responses required for goal attainment, mediated by medial structures such as the anterior cingulate and superior frontal regions; and *Metacognitive processes*, mediated by the frontal poles, particularly the right frontal pole, responsible for integrating executive cognitive functions and emotional or drive-related inputs and implicated in personality, social cognition, consciousness and self-awareness. Thus, executive difficulties are dissociable and can present as different combinations of the above, or in isolation. The reader is referred to McCloskey, Perkins and Divner (2009, Chapter 2) for a review of key definitions and models.

For the individual with TBI, executive difficulties are frequently pervasive, but variable, as their manifestation is influenced by factors related not only to the extent and location of the injury to the frontal lobes and their connections, but also to the individual's residual strengths, the task being performed and the environmental context. The structure inherent in the task, the level of familiarity with the task and the presence or absence of contextual cues, as well as the intelligence and level of focus of the injured individual, will interact to influence the level of competence displayed at any point in time. These factors need to be borne in mind when conducting the neuropsychological assessment of executive functions. Subtle variations in cognitive demands may lead to variations in performance that are difficult to account for if the examiner relies solely on test scores. The reader is referred to Burgess, Aldernam, Volle, Benoit, and Gilbert (2009) for a recent review of issues in undertaking formalised office-based assessments of executive functions.

Neuropsychological assessment of executive functions requires administration of tests where the material and problems posed are novel to the individual. Additionally, varying levels of task complexity should be administered, and the person's performance interpreted in the light of the degree of complexity they were capable of managing premorbidly. Tests should incorporate components demanding planning, problem solving, abstract thinking, idea generation, flexibility of thinking, and response control, including the ability to inhibit well-learned stereotyped responses. Qualitative observations of the individual's level of initiative, self-monitoring, impulse control, error detection and utilisation, and perseverance should be integrated with quantitative information.

Tests which may be sensitive to executive dysfunction include the WAIS-IV Similarities, Matrix Reasoning and Block Design subtests (Wechsler, 2008); the Porteus Maze Test (Porteus, 1965); the Austin Maze (Walsh, 1991), tests of discursive problem-solving, such as Luria's arithmetical problems (Chistensen, 1984); the Tower of London Task (Shallice and Burgess, 1991); the Wisconsin Card Sorting Test (Milner, 1963); the Stroop Color Word Naming Test (Stroop, 1935); Reitan's Trail Making Test Part B (Reitan and Wolfson, 1985); Delis–Kaplan Executive Function System (Delis, Kaplan, and Kramer, 2001); the Hayling and Brixton Tests (Burgess and Shallice, 1997); and the Controlled Oral Word Association Test (Benton and Hamsher, 1989). It is worth noting that there are several versions of the Stroop test; Lezak et al. (2004) recommend use of the Dodrill (1978) version due to its length (176 items, two trials), as this can reveal difficulties maintaining goal-directed attention.

It must be stressed that all of these tests of executive function are multi-factorial in nature, performance also being affected by other cognitive deficits. For example, performance on the Block Design subtest will be affected by visuo-constructional difficulties, and on the Austin Maze, by visuospatial and non-verbal learning problems. Furthermore, these tests may fail to elicit executive problems, which are nevertheless apparent in the performance of daily activities (Bennett, Ong, and Ponsford, 2005). Indeed, as mentioned earlier in the discussion of attentional assessment, some group studies have failed to differentiate the performance of individuals with severe TBI from that of controls on executive tests including the Tower of London Task, the Stroop, the Wisconsin Card Sorting Test, the Trail Making Test and the Cognitive Estimation Test (Norris and Tate, 2000; Ord, Greve, Bianchini, and Aguerrevere, 2009; Ponsford and Kinsella, 1992).

A number of researchers have attempted to address the limitations of current impairment assessments by devising simulated functional tests. Like neuropsychological measures, the construction and administration of the simulated functional test is psychometrically sound, but the test items and materials are modelled on everyday demands. Some examples of simulated functional assessment batteries include the Rivermead Behavioural Memory Test (Wilson et al., 2008), the Behavioural Inattention Test (Wilson, Cockburn, and Halligan, 1987), the Test of Everyday Attention (Robertson et al., 1994) and the Behavioural Assessment of the Dysexecutive Syndrome (Wilson, Alderman, Burgess, Emslie, and Evans, 1996), which includes the Modified Six Elements Test developed by Burgess and colleagues (2006). These test batteries have greater face validity than conventional neuropsychological tests, and they offer standardised procedures not available when directly observing individuals performing everyday activities. However, these measures retain properties of standard neuropsychological assessment which are not present in natural settings. The tests are, by and large, still administered in quiet, one-to-one, structured settings over a limited time frame, and performance is initiated by the examiner. There is increasing recognition that neuropsychological assessment tools need to incorporate more complex and life-like scenarios, capable of taxing multiple executive processes simultaneously, in order to be more predictive of real world performances (Burgess et al., 2006; Chan, Shum, Toulopoulou, and Chen, 2008; Manchester, Priestley, and Jackson, 2004). The Multiple Errands Test (MET; Alderman, Burgess, Knight, and Henman, 2003; Burgess et al., 2006; Shallice and Burgess, 1991) attempts to address this need by requiring participants to perform errands in a real shopping centre according to certain rules. There have also been a number of virtual reality tasks developed such as the Virtual Street (Titov and Knight, 2005).

By virtue of their standardised nature, however, even these tests cannot be adapted to account for the requirements of the individual's daily life, past experiences, motivation, etc. So although simulated functional tests represent an important move towards improving the ecological validity of neuropsychological impairment assessments, they cannot replace the need for direct assessment of the injured person's performance of everyday activities.

In order to address these limitations and ensure a valid and reliable assessment of executive functions, it is necessary to adopt a broader view of neuropsychological assessment. This involves the use of multiple neuropsychological tests, qualitative analysis of performance and the reports provided by the individual, therapists and family regarding behavioural and emotional changes and the impact of these on daily functioning. In addition to the neuropsychological findings, the consideration of the details of the injury, neurological and neuropsychiatric findings are necessary to ensure an accurate diagnosis.

The role of neuropsychological assessment in the rehabilitation process

Neuropsychological assessment provides a means of measuring, relatively objectively, the injured person's cognitive impairments. Reassessment at intervals allows for objective measurement of change in cognitive function. Results of impairment assessment can help inform an understanding of the underlying nature of the injured person's difficulties in everyday activities. Through the identification of specific strengths, as well as weaknesses, assessment results may be used to assist in the formulation of appropriate management strategies. They may also provide valuable clues as to the aetiology of difficulties, which, in turn, influences treatment. For example, the management of a memory problem related to depression is likely to differ from that of an injury-related memory difficulty.

However, as already mentioned, neuropsychological tests may fail to capture more complex disturbances, particularly those underlying problems with attention, executive function and social behaviours. Moreover, some tasks which are initially sensitive to impairments of, for example, executive function, lose their novelty, and hence their sensitivity, if the person is tested repeatedly over time. This frequently happens through the lengthy course of rehabilitation, and possibly also with repeated assessments for legal proceedings. Another very important issue is that of the power of neuropsychological assessment to predict Activity Limitations and Participation Restriction. Although many of the cognitive functions tapped by the tests are also required to perform everyday tasks, neuropsychological tests clearly do not sample the full range of skills related to everyday living, nor do they assess the individual's performance in the context of their own environment.

Case report – Robert

Robert was a 51-year-old man who sustained a TBI in a motor vehicle accident. GCS was 14 at the accident scene and PTA was 24 hours. Initial CT brain revealed a left frontal haematoma. He also suffered fractures to the face and cervical vertebrae.

Assessment of activity and participation

Prior to the injury, Robert had completed 11 years of schooling and a cabinet-making apprenticeship. He had over 30 years' experience as a cabinet maker and at the time of his injury was working full time in a supervisory role in a workshop making customised kitchens. He was single and lived with his mother, for whom he cared following her stroke several years earlier. He had weekly contact with a wide circle of friends and interests in music, car restoration and golf.

He was assessed four years post-injury and at that time he had resumed driving but had not returned to work. He had lost contact with most of his friends and was not participating in any of his hobbies. He was providing care to his mother but was finding this extremely stressful as he was struggling with the manual handling aspects of this role and was forgetful, for instance in administering her medications.

Direct observation by his occupational therapist, supplemented with subjective reports from Robert, revealed the following profile of Activity Limitations and Participation Restrictions. Robert displayed significant difficulties initiating and following through with the majority of everyday tasks. The only activities that Robert reliably completed were daily personal care activities and walking his dog. These tasks were structured and routine in nature, and the latter was facilitated by the external prompt of his dog's behavioural expectation of a walk. Robert generally failed to reliably initiate most other tasks, particularly the less structured, open-ended tasks that he had to independently schedule and set goals to complete. Tasks such as home and garden maintenance, shopping for new clothes and purchasing a replacement car required a planned and organised approach, with probable changes in strategy and method midway during the execution, as well as complex decision making and prioritising of actions. Robert was overwhelmed by such tasks and some of them had been on his "to do" list for a number of years, with no progress. He had difficulty initiating attendance at a gym, but once started in this routine, he was able to consistently participate. However, if the routine was interrupted (e.g. he missed a day due to ill-health), he was unable to restart it without one-to-one support, despite being motivated and enjoying the benefits of the gym programme. Robert often expressed frustration and incomprehension at his difficulty in initiating and completing tasks that he wanted to do and described feeling "lazy".

Robert also had difficulties with managing the grocery shopping and simple food preparation. For instance, he gave an example where, with the intention of buying ingredients to prepare a meal of steak and vegetables, he went to the supermarket and purchased several kilograms of steak. This was far in excess of his needs and it was only on returning home that he realised he had not purchased the vegetables. That evening, he forgot to cook the steak and instead reverted to purchasing the same take-away chicken meal he had eaten nearly every night for the previous four years. A week later he threw out the steak. Numerous errors were evident in other daily activities; for instance he would return the milk to the refrigerator before he had added it to his coffee, he would often open only one side of the gate before going to drive out, and on one occasion, he "forgot" his mother had been admitted to hospital, only a few hours after he had driven her there.

Robert also reported that he had difficulty making decisions, particularly when he was "on the spot". He realised that he had become extremely indecisive and also had difficulty working out how to get started once he had made a decision. He noted that he now needed more time to think through decisions than he did prior to the accident but, paradoxically, the more he thought about it the less likely he was to undertake the required actions. In contrast, he would often react impulsively to certain triggers (e.g. if a family member asked for help with an urgent home maintenance task) and inevitably make serious errors (e.g. cut a piece of timber the wrong length) as he failed to adequately plan and monitor his actions. In addition to his cognitive difficulties, Robert continued to experience physical problems, including reduced mobility, pain and difficulty lifting.

Robert had a close circle of friends pre-injury, but he now saw them infrequently. He indicated that he was not as tactful when dealing with people as he had been prior to his injury, for example, he would respond angrily and swear at people. He had a low frustration tolerance and at times his responses escalated to outbursts of physical aggression. He also reported communication difficulties, in particular, difficulty "getting his point across", following group conversations, and expressing his thoughts and feelings. Further, Robert reported that he suffered from depression and anxiety and had experienced suicidal thoughts since his injury. He was sleeping approximately 15 hours per day.

Neuropsychological assessment of cognitive function

Robert received a score of 114 on the National Adult Reading Test (Nelson, 1982), within the *High Average* range. The table below provides the age-scaled scores (ASS) obtained on the WAIS-IV, which were found to vary from a high of 15 on Matrix Reasoning to a low of 6 on Symbol Search. This case demonstrates the potential for summary scores (e.g. Full Scale IQ) to be misleading where they mask significant variability in performance across individual subtests.

Subtest	*ASS*	*Subtest*	*ASS*
Picture Completion	14	Similarities	12
Block Design	13	Comprehension	10
Matrix Reasoning	15	Information	11
Perceptual Reasoning Index	**125**	**Verbal Comprehension Index**	**105**
Digit-Symbol Coding	7	Arithmetic	8
Symbol Search	6	Digit Span	13
Processing Speed Index	**81**	**Working Memory Index**	**102**
Full Scale IQ	**106**		

Robert's psychomotor speed was significantly reduced, and rated in the *Low Average* range. Reductions in working memory ability were evident on mental arithmetic tasks, digit backwards, and qualitatively in that he often required repetition of information and task instructions.

Visual abstract reasoning and problem solving was a strength for Robert, scoring in the *Superior* range. His ability to solve complex visuospatial problems on Block Design was consistent with premorbid expectations, although on the last item he demonstrated significant rigidity in his approach. Robert's verbal abilities were mildly reduced on testing, particularly with respect to responding to questions of social conventions and verbal fluency, for which he scored lower than the 40th percentile. Additionally, he made one rule break on each of the letter fluency and category fluency tasks:

	F	*A*	*S*	*FAS Total*	*Animals*
No. of Words	15	12	10	37	25
Norms Mean (SD)				40.5 (10.7)	19.8 (4.2)

His abstract verbal reasoning skills appeared relatively preserved on testing. At a qualitative level, gross receptive and expressive skills were adequate.

Robert demonstrated difficulties with learning and memory, which were clearly affected by attentional demands as he was easily overwhelmed by lengthy verbal information. There was also a failure to organise material and apply strategies to enhance learning. His learning curve plateaued early and he was affected by anterograde interference on the Rey Auditory Verbal Learning test:

Trial	1	2	3	4	5	B	7	Delay	Recognition
Words	4	6	8	9	10	6	6	4	9

Following a delay, Robert's recall of material he had previously acquired was reduced but he was marginally assisted by recognition cues. He was able to learn a simple procedural motor sequence on the Fist Edge Palm task (Christensen, 1974), although again this was effortful; when visual cues were removed, he had difficulty maintaining the sequence without committing errors.

Robert's performance on a range of measures of executive functioning was varied. As noted, Robert demonstrated strengths on complex visuospatial problem solving and visuo-constructional tasks. He was able to self-monitor his performance and change strategies when needed, particularly on structured and untimed tasks, for example, he performed adequately on the Wisconsin Card Sorting Test (WCST) (Heaton, 1981). However, on other cognitively demanding tasks, Robert had difficulty with inhibition, self-monitoring, strategy utilisation, planning, following rules, thinking flexibly, and shifting attention. Inhibition difficulties were particularly evident on the Hayling Sentence Completion Test (Burgess and Shallice, 1997) and the Stroop test (Regard, 1981). Difficulty with switching was noted on Trail Making Test Part B (Partington and Leiter, 1949), where Robert made one sequence error and scored below the 30th percentile, in contrast to his Trails A performance which scored at the 80th percentile.

Test	Score (seconds)	*Norms*	
Stroop			
• Dots	15	13.74 (2.58)	
• Words	19	16.58 (3.34)	
• Colours	47	28.90 (7.62)	6 errors [0.42 (0.77)]
Trails A	27	35.1 (10.6)	80 %ile
Trails B	87	77.7 (23.8)	< 30 %ile 1 error

Conclusion

Relative to the estimate of *High-Average* pre-injury intelligence and several *Superior* scores on the Performance Index of the WAIS-IV, Robert displayed reduced immediate and working memory and slowed speed of information processing. He reported experiencing high levels of cognitive fatigue. Word-finding difficulties were evident conversationally and there were moderate deficits in aspects of executive cognitive function on structured assessment. In particular, he displayed disorganisation and impulsivity in his approach to some, but not all, planning and problem-solving tasks. Of note, the profound problems associated with lack of initiation of daily activities were not apparent on formal assessment. Given the significant Activity Limitations and Participation Restrictions in daily life, these cognitive deficits appeared to be relatively mild in the formal assessment situation. However, it is likely that the focus of the injury he sustained was in a region of the frontal lobes, causing relatively subtle intellectual deficits but severe changes in the regulation of attentional states and the initiation and control of responses. As noted earlier, assessment in a structured and supportive environment is often unable to reveal the extent of these difficulties. Injury to this region is also consistent with the behaviour changes Robert reported, including mood instability, reduced frustration tolerance and impulsive aggressive responses. This executive cognitive dysfunction caused significant disruption of Robert's everyday function and impacted on his ability to engage successfully in the roles of friend, worker, home maintainer and community participant.

The interventions employed to assist Robert to develop his level of participation in the home maintainer role are presented in Chapter 4.

Case report – Sandra

Sandra was a 45-year-old woman who was a pedestrian hit by a train 12 months prior to the current assessment. As a result of this accident she sustained a severe TBI with right frontal lobe contusions and a right parieto-temporal subarachnoid haemorrhage. She also sustained internal injuries. Retrograde amnesia was approximately 10 years and she had a period of PTA lasting more than three months. Prior to the injury, Sandra had completed Year 9 and had worked in factories and as a supermarket cashier. She was not employed at the time of her injury, and was divorced.

At the time of the assessment, Sandra had recently been admitted to a community house where she lived with one other resident, who also had a severe TBI. The residence was a secure setting and she required 24-hour supervision and support, due to her significant cognitive-behavioural problems. She also had no functional vision in her right eye and a visual perceptual impairment.

It was reported that, in the eight weeks since her admission, she had been continually disoriented and the intensity and frequency of her challenging behaviours had escalated. Challenging behaviours included repetitive demands for food and cigarettes and high levels of irritability and agitation. She routinely attempted to abscond from the house and displayed high levels of emotional distress. These issues prompted the referral for neuropsychological and occupational therapy assessments.

Assessment of activity and participation

The community house manager, John, reported that Sandra required prompting to get out of bed and 1:1 support to complete her morning routine.

Although she was able to dress herself, John reported that she selected inappropriate clothes for the weather and each morning insisted she dress to go to work. She became highly agitated when she was told that she would not be going to work. John reported that there was only one staff member on duty during the morning and that Sandra was often left alone for periods of time, while staff attended to the other resident. Once out of bed Sandra would go into the kitchen, where she displayed a number of unsafe behaviours including putting an empty saucepan on a hot stovetop and eating whatever was in the refrigerator, including raw ingredients and dog food. However, in the company of staff, she was generally accepting of their support in the kitchen and she enjoyed helping with domestic chores.

Concern was raised regarding her constantly asking for food and cigarettes throughout the day, although she did not currently smoke. She would pace continuously when not given one-to-one attention and was unable to occupy her own time. Sandra was fixated on ideas such as having to go to work and she continually tried to leave the house. She had no hobbies within the home and staff had been reluctant to take her into the community due to the risk of her absconding. Sandra's mother visited her weekly, but she had no other social contact. John reported that she had had frequent behavioural outbursts, where she had lost her temper, particularly when she was prevented from eating or from leaving the house and when she was re-oriented to her living situation, the current year or the fact that she was unemployed.

Neuropsychological assessment of cognitive function

On the basis of her educational and occupational history it was estimated that Sandra would have been functioning within the *Low Average* range prior to her accident. The following age-scaled scores (ASS) were obtained on the WAIS-IV:

Subtest	*ASS*	*Subtest*	*ASS*
Digit Span	5	Vocabulary	5
Block Design	2	Similarities	6

Auditory attention span was within the *Borderline* range. She was able to repeat five digits forward reliably and three digits backwards unreliably. Qualitatively, Sandra's information processing and psychomotor speed were slowed overall. Sandra was disoriented and densely amnesic and tended to confabulate when unsure of details. On verbal memory tasks she demonstrated rapid forgetting and was only able to recall limited information from two short stories, both immediately after presentation and after a short time delay. Based on her performance on the Hopkins Verbal Learning Test, she appeared to benefit from repetition, but had considerable difficulty spontaneously recalling unstructured information after a delay:

Trial	*1*	*2*	*3*	*Learning*	*Total*	*Delay*	*Recognition*
Score	2	4	5	3	11	0	7/12
Mean*	7.8	9.9	10.9	3.2	28.8	10.3	11.8
SD*	1.7	1.5	1.2	1.5	3.8	1.7	0.4

*Mean and SD based on normative scores

Sandra was disoriented in time and tended to state her age as 35 years, thinking it was approximately 10 years earlier. She would guess the month or day of the week and could not read the time on her watch. She did not know where she was living and, if asked this question, she would look around the room for a cue that would prompt an incorrect answer. Mostly she thought she was visiting at a friend's house and would then state that she was ready to "go home". She was convinced that she was working at a supermarket, a job she held in her early thirties. She would often become highly distressed if she thought she was late for work.

Receptive and expressive language appeared to be intact in conversation. However, Sandra was noted to have difficulty comprehending more complex task instructions. Her expressive vocabulary was within the *Borderline* range and spelling ability was at a Year 6 level. On the Controlled Word Association Test and animal fluency she demonstrated a reduced ability to generate and organise verbal information:

	F	*A*	*S*	*FAS Total*	*Animals*
No. of Words	5	8	5	18	12
Norms Mean (SD)				40.5 (10.7)	19.8 (4.2)

Sandra's ability to recognise actual, familiar objects was intact in context of their use. However, when the object was less familiar or was displayed from an unusual angle she displayed considerable difficulty with recognition and she was unable to recognise pictures of objects. On the Hooper Visual Organisation Test (Hooper, 1958) she obtained a score of 7.5, suggesting a very high probability of impairment. She also tended to focus on one aspect of a visual stimulus, rather than perceiving and integrating all components of the pictorial stimuli, resulting in misperception of common objects. Sandra displayed poor visual tracking and tended to lose her place when scanning an array. Poor perceptual judgement and visuo-motor integration was observed. For example, on written tasks, Sandra had considerable difficulty aligning her responses appropriately on the page and she tended to write over information. Poor depth perception was also observed when she picked up objects.

In terms of executive functioning, Sandra's responses on an abstract verbal reasoning task were impoverished and her performance was within the *Borderline* range. She displayed difficulty flexibly shifting her thinking and was very concrete in her interpretation of information. Her problem solving and planning were extremely impaired.

Conclusion

In summary, neuropsychological assessment revealed significant cognitive deficits in a range of areas including: attention, memory, and executive functions such as verbal reasoning, idea generation, self-monitoring and planning. Sandra was found to be amnesic and disoriented to her current circumstances. She also had visuo-perceptual difficulties. Functionally, she was independent in some basic daily tasks and routines but required 24-hour supervision and support. She was not currently accessing the community due to the risk of her absconding. Sandra was unable to structure or occupy her own time and she displayed a range of significant challenging behaviours. Overall, her life role participation was limited to that of home maintainer and family member.

A number of goals were developed from the neuropsychological and occupational therapy assessments to address the cognitive-behavioural difficulties described above including:

- To reduce Sandra's agitation when presented with orientation information about her current situation via the development of a consistent script detailing her current circumstances to be reinforced by all staff.
- To develop a morning routine to enhance her independence and participation in the home maintainer role, and establish and reinforce limits to her daily intake of food.

The interventions employed to assist Sandra to achieve these goals are presented in Chapter 4.

4 Managing cognitive problems following TBI

Sue Sloan and Jennie Ponsford

Introduction

The cognitive impairments which result from TBI commonly cause ongoing Activity Limitations and Participation Restrictions for the person who is injured, and may create a significant burden for carers and relatives. They also affect the individual's capacity to benefit from other aspects of the rehabilitation process. As outlined in Chapters 1 and 3, the nature and extent of these problems varies according to the site and severity of injury, as well as factors relating to the individual prior to injury, and the environment. Cognitive deficits most frequently include impairments of attention, memory, and executive functions, the latter incorporating the ability to plan and organise, think in abstract terms, initiate, think flexibly, and self-monitor and control thought processes and responses. The nature and complexity of the cognitive impairments associated with TBI renders them particularly difficult to assess, as discussed in the previous chapter. Such difficulties are outweighed only by the challenges presented in rehabilitating these problems and reducing their long-term impact in the context of everyday life.

Approaches to cognitive rehabilitation

According to the 1998 NIH Consensus Statement on Rehabilitation of Persons with Traumatic Brain Injury, *"The goals of cognitive and behavioural rehabilitation are to enhance the person's capacity to process and interpret information and to improve the person's ability to function in all aspects of family and community life"* (1999, p. 978). Stated within the framework of the International Classification of Functioning (ICF) (WHO, 2002), Disability and Health interventions may be aimed at restoring impaired Mental Functions or at reducing Activity Limitations and/or Participation Restrictions. In practice, rehabilitation is often an eclectic combination of each of these approaches. Whilst recognising that the boundaries between approaches to therapy often overlap, in this chapter we will initially outline the evidence for both broad categories of intervention "*cognitive function retraining*", focused on remediating underlying cognitive impairments, and "*functional compensation*", focused on enhancing performance of everyday tasks through the application of compensatory strategies. Utilising the principles of the REAL approach, this chapter aims to establish some guidelines for the design, implementation and evaluation of interventions for individuals with cognitive deficits as a means of promoting independence and enhancing participation in valued life roles.

It has been well established that cognitive deficits show at least some degree of spontaneous recovery in the months and years following TBI. An understanding of this improvement and factors which influence it should inform our interventions. Theories of recovery of function and available research evidence have been discussed in Chapter 1. It is clear that the processes underlying improvements made after injury are complex and are underpinned by a number of different mechanisms. There is a growing body of evidence which suggests that rehabilitative interventions after injury may result in improvements; however, there are also factors not amenable to intervention that will influence outcome, such as the injured person's age, the extent of the injury, hormonal or genetic factors, and the nature of the cognitive functions affected (High, Roebuck-Spencer, Sander, Struchen, and Sherer, 2006; Johansson and Belichenko, 2002; Kleim, 2008; Nudo et al., 2001; Rohling, Beverly, Faust, and Demakis, 2009; Sander, Roebuck, Struchen, Sherer, and High, 2001; Taub and Morris, 2001; Wade, 2003). Capacity for recovery has also been shown to relate to the size of the lesion (Kolb and Cioe, 2004). In view of this, it is possible that individuals with less extensive or more circumscribed lesions might show a greater response to interventions. The extent to which a function might be re-established will also depend upon the extent to which other aspects of the functional system remain intact (Webster and Ungerleider, 2000).

Cognitive function retraining approach

Cognitive retraining is a restorative approach focused on improving or ameliorating specific cognitive functions impaired through injury. Intervention typically involves hierarchically organised training exercises targeting specific cognitive impairments. The procedure is to isolate impairments using detailed psychometric or neuropsychological assessments. The individual is then provided with repeated and highly structured practice on psychometric, computerised or pen-and-paper tasks believed to exercise the area of deficit. Parameters, such as complexity, quantity, speed of presentation, or the amount of cueing, may be gradually altered, depending on the goal of therapy. Such tasks often bear little resemblance to tasks encountered in real-life settings, but it is argued that they exercise the same cognitive processes required to perform functional activities. Proponents of this approach argue that it is more efficient to target underlying impairments, and it is expected that, if therapy results in the restoration of the function, the gains will generalise to a range of unpractised, more functional activities (Mateer, Sohlberg, and Youngman, 1990). This is supported by evidence that such therapy, when carried out intensively in the motor and sensory domains, may facilitate plastic changes in the brain, including synaptic regrowth or compensation by adjacent, intact structures (Kleim, 2008; Kolb, 2004).

Attention retraining

There have been many research studies conducted with TBI individuals which fall under this rubric, with most focusing on the remediation of deficits of attention, generally using computer-mediated tasks (Ben-Yishay, Piasetsky, and Rattok, 1987; Gansler and McCaffrey, 1991; Gray, Robertson, Pentland, and Anderson, 1992; Malec, Jones, Rao, and Stubbs, 1984; Niemann, Ruff, and Baser, 1990; Novack, Caldwell, Duke, Bergquist, and Gage, 1996; Palmese and Rankin, 2000; Park and Ingles, 2001; Park, Proulx, and Towers, 1999b; Ponsford and Kinsella, 1988; Robertson, Gray, and McKenzie, 1988; Ruff et al., 1994; Ruff et al., 1989; Sohlberg and Mateer, 1987; Stablum, Umilta, Mogentale, Carlan, and Guerrini, 2000; Sturm, Willmes, Orgass, and Hartje, 1997; Wood and Fussey, 1987) (For a detailed review see Ponsford and Willmott, 2004). Many of these studies have demonstrated improvement on the trained tasks, where this was measured, and a number also demonstrated gains on neuropsychological measures, most commonly the Paced Auditory Serial Addition Task (PASAT), where the task demands are similar to those of the training tasks (Palmese and Rankin, 2000; Sohlberg and Mateer, 1987; Sohlberg, McLaughlin, Pavese, Heidrich, and Posner, 2000; Stablum et al., 2000). Sturm and colleagues (1997) found specific treatment improvements from training focused either on alertness and vigilance, or on selective and divided attention. In contrast, Novack and colleagues (1996) found no differences in response to focused, hierarchical intervention as compared with general cognitive training. Moreover, Park and colleagues (1999b) found that both individuals with TBI and untrained controls showed similar gains following "Attention Process Training", an attention training package developed by Sohlberg and Mateer (1987), in terms of performance on the PASAT. They argued that the mechanism underpinning improvement is one of specific skill training, which generalises to tasks of a similar nature, rather than improved integrity of underlying damaged attention functions. More recently, however, fMRI studies have demonstrated changes in cerebral activation in response to attentional training. Kim and colleagues (2009) found that improved performances on a visuo-spatial attention task in response to training were accompanied by a decrease in frontal activation and an increase in anterior cingulate and precuneus activation – a pattern that more closely resembled the activation pattern seen in healthy controls performing the same task.

In a meta-analysis of studies of the efficacy of attention training, Park and Ingles (2001) found that significant performance improvements were evident only in the pre- to post-studies of individuals with TBI, but not in the studies which included controls. They concluded that specific-skills training resulted in gains or practice effects on tests of attention similar to the training tasks, but did not have a significant impact on functional outcomes in those treated. Rohling and colleagues (2009) have quantified the significant gains made by untreated controls from pre- to post-testing in a meta-analysis of cognitive rehabilitation studies conducted up to 2002, gains which in the absence of treatment must be attributable to practice effects on assessment measures or spontaneous recovery. After correcting for this they found only a small, though significant, overall effect of cognitive rehabilitation and a specific effect of attentional training. In a large study involving uninjured people, Owen et al. (2010) found that improved performance on trained computerised cognitive tasks did not generalise to untrained tasks.

Relatively few studies have controlled adequately for spontaneous recovery, effects of practice and concurrent therapy or, above all, assessed the degree to which training generalises to aspects of everyday life, and whether gains are maintained over time. Studies which have met all these criteria, particularly in terms of measuring generalisation of effects to everyday life (Ponsford and Kinsella, 1988; Wood and Fussey, 1987), were not able to demonstrate significant functional gains. The importance of controlling for the effects of concurrent therapies is underscored by the findings of Ruff and colleagues (1989), who found no significant difference between neuropsychological gains made by a TBI group receiving intensive neuropsychological training combined with psychotherapy and one receiving psychotherapy and unstructured therapy.

The limited evidence of the remedial effects of attentional training tasks and generalisation of gains to everyday activities most probably reflects the fact that everyday activities are more complex, involving numerous cognitive functions and wide variability in environmental and task demands. In a study of the acquisition of skilled visual search skills, Schmitter-Edgecombe and Beglinger (2001) found that specific training resulted in improved performance on tasks involving the same processes, as long as training was provided in a manner whereby responses to the same classes of stimuli were always the same. Repeated, massed practice on tasks may result in their automatisation, such that they no longer place demands on the controlled processing system, the limited capacity of which interferes with performance of complex tasks requiring divided attention in those with TBI. If the goal of rehabilitation is to improve performance of everyday activities, arguably training should focus on elements of those activities directly, rather than on more abstract tasks.

There is also little evidence that repeated memory drills, such as list-learning tasks, have any impact on performance on untrained memory tasks or everyday memory performance (Glisky, 2004; Rohling et al., 2009; Wilson, 2009). As Glisky (2004) points out, repeated practice of arbitrary materials is unlikely to be effective. Rather, practice needs to be directed towards functionally meaningful activities. Descriptive studies by Sohlberg, White, Evans, and Mateer (1992a; 1992b) in which "prospective memory" was trained by repeatedly asking the patient to perform tasks at specified future times, have revealed mixed results. Whilst there was an increase in the span of prospective memory within the experimental paradigm, evidence of generalisation to naturalistic settings was unclear. The participants were also receiving other forms of therapy concurrently. Most rehabilitation studies in the domains of memory and executive function have utilised compensatory strategies and will be discussed in the next section.

It must be acknowledged that it is not easy to conclusively demonstrate the efficacy of any form of therapy. It is always possible to argue that more intensive or lengthy training may have brought greater gains. However, the cognitive function retraining approach is certainly appealing for a number of reasons. Exercises such as these may serve as a medium for engaging and establishing therapeutic rapport with the injured person. Some will be more motivated to work on a computer than to engage in other aspects of therapy. The retraining tasks also allow therapists to monitor the person's responses relatively objectively and systematically, and provide concrete feedback. Furthermore, this type of therapy is less demanding on the therapist both in terms of time and creative energy, and is therefore less costly. This is a significant factor in many rehabilitation settings, and may be the reason why this approach remains common despite a lack of evidence for its efficacy. Finally, the level of control the therapist can exert over the task and the environment is generally greater than in functional activity, allowing for controlled experimentation with strategies. Practice in implementing strategies may be the reason why some studies have demonstrated gains on training tasks. However, any such improvements in task performance would reflect learning of compensatory strategies, rather than restoration of the underlying cognitive impairment.

By virtue of their executive function difficulties, many people who have sustained TBI will have a very limited capacity to generalise strategies learned during such abstract or de-contextualised training programmes to the real world. As argued by Ylvisaker, Hanks, and Johnson-Greene (2002), it would seem to be more productive and cost-effective in the long term to apply, or extend, such strategy training directly to a wide range of everyday activities which need to be performed by the injured person. In some cases impairment-oriented restorative therapy may be appropriate in the early stages of the rehabilitation process, to focus the injured person's attention on a particular problem, such as visual scanning. However, the cognitive skills learnt in the course of such therapy ultimately need to be applied to real-world activities if they are to result in a significant reduction in the injured person's Activity Limitations and enhance their level of Participation.

Functional compensation approach

The cognitive retraining approach described in the previous section has been developed on the assumption that "recovery" is defined in terms of restoration of the impaired function. As an alternative, the functional compensation approach emphasises "improvement", rather than "recovery", and is focused on teaching the skills required to enhance performance on selected tasks that increase capacity for Activity and Participation across the various domains of life. The WHO (2002) lists these domains as mobility, self-care, domestic life, interpersonal interactions and relationships, major life areas (education, work and employment, and economic life) and community, social and civic life. The functional compensation approach is focused on building the person's strengths to compensate for cognitive impairments and allows the therapist to select training tasks that are meaningful to the individual and relevant to their participation in valued life roles. These may vary in terms of their level of functional relevance and also in the complexity of the compensatory strategies taught. Improvement in task performance may be achieved via a number of means, such as: the development of internal compensatory strategies to aid performance (e.g. mnemonic strategies); the use of external compensatory mechanisms (e.g. use of a diary or whiteboard); environmental restructuring or modification (e.g. reorganisation of cupboards, strategic placement of a calendar-clock); or the provision of structured support of another person.

Ideally, individuals are encouraged to identify and practise functional tasks important in supporting their participation in valued life roles, with practice embedded within day-to-day routines. Tasks are typically modified to improve success in the early stages by downgrading those variables that otherwise make the task too difficult. Through the scaffolding of external support, development of compensatory strategies and repeated practice, the skill is learnt to a level of competency that may then allow the graded withdrawal of external supports.

Compensatory strategies may be broadly categorised into internal or external cognitive skills. Internal compensatory strategies require effortful, conscious control by the individual to modify their approach to the task in a pre-determined fashion and may be helpful for individuals with sufficient awareness, memory and self-monitoring capacity. They draw on the person's cognitive strengths to compensate for their areas of impairment. At the most cognitively demanding level, internal strategies can be used to train the injured person to use self-instructional or self-monitoring strategies in a variety of situations, for example, training a sequence of steps to be followed in different problem-solving situations. At a more basic level, the internal strategies are applied directly to specific daily living tasks, such as the use of a mental checklist to ensure a short sequence of steps is followed for completion of a particular task (e.g. when leaving the house take keys and wallet and lock the door). For the latter, the skills and techniques taught are largely task- and environment-specific, so spontaneous generalisation of gains to untrained tasks and different environments is unlikely to occur. With respect to TBI, numerous studies have demonstrated that compensatory strategies may be used to effectively overcome a range of cognitive difficulties, particularly in the domains of memory and executive function.

Managing memory difficulties

A variety of compensatory strategies have been used in the treatment of memory problems. These have been discussed in detail by Wilson (2009). The most commonly studied internal strategies have involved the use of visual imagery mnemonics to compensate for verbal memory deficits (Kaschel, Della Sala, Cantagallo, and Fahlbock, 2002; Ryan and Ruff, 1988; Stern and Stern, 1989; Thoene and Glisky, 1995; Wilson, 1987a) or verbal mediation or semantic elaboration strategies, such as the PQRST technique, recommended for use by students to improve comprehension and recall of written or lecture material (Glasgow, Zeiss, Barrera, and Lewinsohn, 1977; Wilson, 1987a; Wilson, 2009). Such strategies help organise material to facilitate ease of retrieval. These studies have demonstrated some success in use of the strategies when applied to specific tasks in experimental settings. The study by Kaschel et al. (2002) found that 30 sessions of visual imagery training resulted in improved recall of verbal material in patients with mild brain injury of mixed aetiology, with positive changes in relatives' ratings of the injured person's memory function and gains maintained at three-month follow-up. A well-controlled study by Berg and colleagues (Berg, Koning-Haanstra, and Deelman, 1991) evaluated the use of a range of memory strategies applied to specific difficulties experienced by brain-injured individuals living in the community. They were able to demonstrate more positive effects on memory test performance than those resulting from repeated practice on memory tasks or no treatment. On the other hand, Benedict, Brandt and Bergey (1993) found no significant effects of guided practice in the use of semantic elaboration for recall of word lists, conducted over 13 weeks in a severely amnesic woman.

Findings regarding the day-to-day usefulness of all of these strategies are, at best, mixed (Wilson, 2009). As Glisky (2004) points out, where there is severe medial temporal or hippocampal damage, no matter how good the internal strategies are, new material will not be consolidated. Some strategies may be more likely to assist individuals with memory problems arising from executive function impairment to increase the efficiency of their learning. However, this will only occur when the individual has awareness of their problems and some ability to follow through with what are quite mentally effortful procedures. Many TBI individuals do not have the cognitive capacity to apply such strategies without the structure and prompting provided by the therapist.

An alternative means of compensating for memory problems is the use of external memory aids or cueing devices, such as diaries, timers, alarms and electronic memory aids. Training in the use of these types of strategies is recommended as the most appropriate form of intervention for individuals with severe memory problems (Cicerone et al., 2005; Wilson, 2009). Wilson (1991) found that a significant proportion of memory-impaired individuals followed up 5–10 years after rehabilitation were using memory aids successfully and Evans, Wilson, Needham, and Brennall (2003) found that the use of memory aids was associated with greater independence. A useful development in this category was the NeuroPage (Hersh and Treadgold, 1994). This is an externally programmed paging system, which allows for reminders and cues to appear on a standard pager carried by the injured person. Wilson and colleagues (Wilson, Evans, Emslie, and Malinek, 1997; Wilson, Scott, Evans, and Emslie, 2003), reported that more than 80 per cent of clients provided with a NeuroPage system programmed to prompt the individuals to remember to perform personally relevant, routine daily tasks showed a significant reduction in everyday memory failures whilst using the NeuroPage over a seven-week period, relative to a seven-week baseline. The everyday memory failures increased for some of the participants on return to baseline. A majority of regular users subsequently surveyed found the device useful (Wilson et al., 2003). Unfortunately the use of a centrally programmed paging service is not widely available, however.

Many other electronic devices which can provide prompting are in wide use in the general community. Case series studies employing mobile phones as pagers (Wade and Troy, 2001), a generic paging system (Kirsh, Shenton, and Rowan, 2004) and portable Voice Organizer used to reinforce therapy goals in the hospital setting (Hart, Hawkey, and Whyte, 2002) and in the community (Van Den Broek, Downes, Johnson, Dayus, and Hilton, 2000) have all been shown to enhance the consistency of prospective task performance in individuals with brain injury. A more complex alternative is the use of personal digital assistants (PDAs). Gentry, Wallace, Kvarfordt, and Lynch (2008) found that a sample of 23 community based individuals with severe TBI was able to master the use of the PDA, within three to six 90-minute training sessions, which included a focus on use of the device as a reminder. At eight-week follow-up there were significant gains in self-rated performance of, and participation in, everyday activities across various domains. This sample was somewhat self-selected, however. The use of a PDA or any electronic memory device would be beyond the capability of people with very severe injuries and may also depend on the injured person's prior use of such devices, their simplicity of use and availability of instruction and support in their use (Hart, Buchhofer, and Vaccaro, 2004a; Hart et al., 2002; Hart, O'Neil-Pirozzi, and Morita, 2003).

For many others, a notebook or diary may be more helpful. A survey by Evans and colleagues (2003) showed that the vast majority of people with a brain injury use alarms or watches, followed by wall calendars or charts, lists, notebooks and diaries. The layout of a diary or log-book may significantly influence its usefulness. In a single case study, McKerracher, Powell and Oyebode (2005) demonstrated significantly better prospective memory performance when the diary layout was tailored to the needs of the client, with a daily timetable and daily "to do" list on the same page, as opposed to the standard diary with a weekly timetable and a separate "to do" list. Schmitter-Edgecombe, Fahy, Whelan, and Long (1995) reported that individuals trained in the use of notebooks coupled with the use of wristwatch alarm cues had fewer everyday memory failures than those without these compensatory devices. However, this treatment effect was not sustained at six-month follow-up. Ownsworth and McFarland (1999) also found that use of a diary was more effective when accompanied by additional training in self-management strategies.

A crucial issue in rehabilitation, particularly for those with memory and executive impairments, is how best to teach these individuals new information, strategies or skills. This question has been the focus of an evidence-based review (Ehlhardt et al., 2008). It was concluded on the basis of 20 years of studies that structuring the delivery of information or procedures can facilitate learning. Errorless learning, spaced retrieval and vanishing cues techniques were all shown to be effective in enhancing learning and retention in certain circumstances and these were superior to traditional trial-and-error learning approaches. No single approach was always more effective. The authors concluded that the most effective approach is likely to be a combination of a number of training strategies tailored to the learning circumstances. However, a number of factors were associated with greater success in learning. These included clear delineation of the focus of the intervention, with the use of task analysis prior to multi-step training, the need to conduct training within an ecologically valid context to maximise its relevance to the client and hence client motivation, the importance of constraining errors during the learning process, promoting effortful processing during learning by applying strategies such as visual imagery or elaboration, using multiple exemplars, and providing numerous practice trials distributed over time.

Managing executive dysfunction

As outlined in the previous chapter, the term executive function is a collective term referring to a number of distinguishable processes. These include the cognitive functions of planning, problem-solving and working memory, behavioural self-regulatory functions, activation regulating functions, and metacognitive processes (Cicerone, Levin, Malec, Stuss, and Whyte, 2006). Studies pertaining to rehabilitation of individuals with executive dysfunction may be grouped into those which have attempted to train self-instructional strategies to be applied in a range of situations, termed by some authors metacognitive skills training, and those which have trained strategies specific to a given task or situation. There is a body of work, including randomised controlled trials, group and single case studies that has provided evidence in support of the efficacy of metacognitive skills training, or problem-solving training, in which individuals with executive difficulties are trained to follow a sequence of steps in order to attain a goal (Kennedy et al., 2008b). These steps have included self-monitoring or recording of performance, defining a goal or a problem, selecting a strategy to attain the goal or solve the problem, monitoring its implementation and/or adjusting or modifying the plan based on self-assessment or on external feedback. A number of interventions have demonstrated efficacy, not only in reducing the impact of executive impairment, but also in enhancing participation (Kennedy et al., 2008b). These interventions have focused on various executive functions, including planning, organisation, problem-solving and multi-tasking, as applied to managing social problems (Rath, Simon, Langenbahn, Sherr, and Diller, 2003), attaining functional goals in daily activities (Dawson et al., 2009; Grant, 2008; Levine et al., 2000; Miotto, Evans, Souza de Lucia, and Scaff, 2009; Spikman, Boelen, Lamberts, Brouwer, and Fasotti, 2010; Turkstra and Flora, 2002), generating solutions to problems or making decisions (Cicerone and Giacino, 1992; Cicerone and Wood, 1987; Miotto et al., 2009; von Cramon and Matthes-von Cramon, 1994; von Cramon, Matthes-von Cramon, and Mai, 1991) and verbal reasoning (Delazer, Bodner, and Benke, 1998; Fox, Martella, and Marchand-Martella, 1989; Marshall et al., 2004).

These interventions have been delivered between one and three times per week, with an average of 12 hours of therapy, although some of the more intensive interventions focusing on activities in the community involved 20 hours of intervention or more. Evidence of the generalisation and maintenance of gains has been provided in some of these studies, in the form of improved performance on everyday executive function tasks, namely the Multiple Errands Test (Miotto et al., 2009) or an Executive Secretarial Task (Spikman et al., 2010), enhanced role resumption (Spikman et al., 2010) or by reports from the individual, a family member or therapists. However, in many studies this aspect of outcome measurement has not been experimentally controlled (Kennedy et al., 2008b), so that objective evidence of generalisation is confined to the last two mentioned studies (Miotto et al., 2009; Spikman et al., 2010). Generalisation appears to have been most effective when the intervention has been applied directly to activities or problems in the individual's daily life, as illustrated in the case reports of Dawson and colleagues (2009), Cicerone and Wood (1987) and von Cramon and Matthes-von Cramon (1994). Dawson and colleagues (2009) adapted the CO-OP approach, to achieve success in functional activities which generalised to some untrained activities. This approach has five elements: the client selects the treatment goals; intervention is based on observation of task performance and associated difficulties; use of a global problem-solving strategy (Goal–Plan–Do–Check) and other domain-specific strategies; guidance by the therapist in finding strategies to improve task performance; and involvement of significant others to reinforce use of strategies.

Using a number of dual-task activities, Cicerone (2002) trained four individuals with mild TBI to employ metacognitive strategies to allocate their attention more efficiently and manage the rate of information on tasks requiring them to divide their attention. Training was conducted weekly over 11–27 weeks and was extended to discussion of methods of employing the strategies in everyday activities. There was greater improvement in the treated group on the PASAT and a self-reported reduction in attentional difficulties in their daily lives.

In another study designed to enhance participants' ability to cope with time pressure in the face of slowed information processing, Fasotti, Kovacs, Eling, and Brouwer (2000) provided training in compensatory strategies to slow down the delivery of information, termed Time Pressure Management (TPM). This involved increasing participants' awareness of ways in which mental slowness affected performance of tasks, using self-instruction to take "managing steps" before or during a task to deal with time pressure problems (e.g. asking for repetition or asking another person to slow down their delivery of information), monitoring the implementation of the steps, initially with overt demonstration, then overt self-instruction with written prompts, gradually withdrawn, and finally the application and generalisation of strategies under more distracting conditions (e.g. with a radio playing in the background). Relative to a control group, those who received TPM took more managing steps, resulting in greater and more lasting gains, which generalised to other measures of attention and memory. Those who benefited more showed greater awareness of the need for the strategies and were more assertive in applying the steps in social situations. This technique has recently been applied with some success to reduce mental slowness in an RCT involving stroke patients (Winkens, Van Heugten, Wade, and Fasotti, 2009a; Winkens, Van Heugten, Wade, Habets, and Fasotti, 2009b). These authors emphasise the importance of self-awareness for success of its use, of providing training to recognise situations in which time pressure is a problem, setting realistic goals, applying the strategies to tasks of direct relevance to the injured person, and providing support in learning strategies and monitoring their implementation, first with simple tasks and then with more complex ones across a broad range of settings.

Sohlberg, Sprunk, and Metzelaar (1988) described the use of an external cueing system to improve the verbal initiation and response acknowledgement behaviour of a severely injured male with marked initiation problems. In a group therapy setting, he was given regular cues, written on a card, to monitor firstly, his initiation of conversation, and secondly, his acknowledgement of others talking. There was a significant increase in the target behaviours during intervention. However, performance declined when intervention was withdrawn. No attempt was made to ensure maintenance or generalisation of gains.

Another strategy that has been used to enhance goal attainment was implemented by Manly and colleagues (2002). This involved the provision of external cueing or alerting to interrupt performance of an activity and prompt the injured individual to consider their overall goal. This improved their ability to switch between different aspects of a multi-faceted task, thereby normalising performance. Other studies have suggested that regular paging or SMS alerting can improve recall and attainment of goals (Culley and Evans, 2010; Fish, Manly, and Wilson, 2008).

Factors other than the training itself which may be associated with the successful application of strategies to enhance adaptive function include higher levels of intelligence and education, personal qualities such as determination and persistence, as well as social support and favourable mental health. Schutz and Trainor (2007) attributed the success of a four-step programme training compensation strategies targeting adaptive functions to these factors. Despite persisting executive function impairments the participants described in their own words the ways they deployed and adjusted organisational and self-monitoring strategies to achieve challenging goals in their work, study and social activities.

Influence of self-awareness and insight

Important factors in the success of all interventions are level of self-awareness, and insight and capacity to self-monitor and regulate behavioural responses. The presence of significant impairments in these domains represents major impediments to the success of any interventions focusing directly on cognitive function, as the individual will be less able to acknowledge the existence of the impairment and utilise feedback to modify their performance (Giacino and Cicerone, 2000). Some interventions have been designed to build self-awareness. For instance, Ownsworth, McFarland, and Young (2000) conducted a 16-week group programme designed to improve self-awareness and self-regulation in a group of 21 individuals with chronic acquired brain injury of mixed aetiology. Activities included training in problem-solving and compensatory strategies, as well as role-plays. Participants showed improved knowledge and use of self-regulatory strategies to control emotional and behavioural problems and their self-reported psychosocial function improved immediately post-group, although these gains were not maintained at six-month follow-up.

Ownsworth, Fleming, Desbois, Strong, and Kuipers (2006) targeted error awareness and self-correction in a young man with an extremely severe brain injury on two real-life tasks – cooking at home and voluntary work. There was a reduction in error frequency and increase in spontaneous error correction on the trained tasks, but no generalisation to other tasks. They argued that it was possible to increase on-line awareness, that is awareness of difficulties within a given task, without broader changes in global self-knowledge of deficits. In a subsequent case series these authors demonstrated somewhat greater reductions in errors in a cooking task in response to metacognitive skills training which encouraged the participant to anticipate and self-monitor errors as compared with behavioural practice on the same tasks, with errors corrected by the therapist as they occurred (Ownsworth, Quinn, Fleming, Kendall, and Shum, 2010).

In attempting to understand the factors that underpin improvements in self-awareness, Dirette (2002) conducted detailed interviews with three individuals who were at least six months post-injury and had developed a good level of awareness of their deficits; all described the experience of "critical incidents" linked to "comparing their current level of functioning with their previous level" (p. 865). The experience of these events assisted in building an understanding of the cognitive changes associated with their brain injury. Although having been told by therapists that they had cognitive impairments, "they did not believe it until they tried to do a functional activity outside the rehabilitation setting" (Dirette, 2002, p. 865). This was in contrast to the reports of therapists, who believed that the development of awareness was aided by the clinical testing and discussions that formed part of their intervention. Individuals placed greater emphasis on the feedback gleaned in real-world settings. For instance one client believed her difficulties with cooking were due to the unfamiliarity of the occupational therapy kitchen and it was not until she cooked in her own home that she gained an awareness of her changes in function. Dirette concluded that "the inclusion of familiar tasks in an environment that is familiar to the client may be necessary for developing awareness of cognitive deficits" (2002, p. 868). She cautioned that the timing and structure of intervention is important given the potentially adverse psychological reactions people experience as they develop awareness of their losses. Thus the most appropriate timing and context for therapeutic intervention for cognitive impairments will be influenced by a person's self-awareness and associated emotional state.

Applying functional skills training directly in everyday activities and settings

It is clear from the research discussed to date that real-life experiences are crucial to building insight and also that individuals with executive function impairment who lack self-awareness will be less able to adapt and apply strategies learnt in the therapy setting to their everyday lives. For many individuals it will therefore be more effective to train the use of practical strategies by directly embedding them within a specific functional activity, or a closely simulated task. Kewman and colleagues (1985) trained the driving skills of a brain-injured group, using a shaping procedure. Auditory and visual monitoring tasks, designed to exercise important driving skills, such as keeping track of more than one thing at a time or shifting the focus of attention from one activity to another, were practised whilst the participant was driving a small electric-powered vehicle. The group receiving this training showed significantly greater improvement in performance in on-road driving tests conducted before and after training than a brain-injured control group which drove the car for a similar period of time without performing the monitoring tasks. This finding provides support for the view that greater and more functionally relevant gains can be made by focusing training on the specific skills required to perform a desired activity, rather than on non-functional tasks.

After providing intensive training over a 12-month period, von Cramon and Matthes-von Cramon (1994) were able to demonstrate a significant impact on the work performance of a medical doctor who was exhibiting executive problems nine years post-injury. Problem-solving strategies were applied directly to his work-related difficulties in making histopathological diagnoses using guided verbal self-instruction to analyse each problem, systematically arrive at a solution and check its accuracy. Beginning with spoken self-instruction he was guided to 1) Search systematically for all information available, 2) Separate relevant from irrelevant information and 3) Rate the subjective certainty of each diagnosis and this was gradually faded to internal speech. External guidance from the therapist was gradually withdrawn. Applying this method he progressed from a baseline of less than 4/10 correct to 10/10 correct diagnoses.

Burke, Zencius, Wesolowski and Doubleday (1991) described four case studies in which checklists were used successfully to train injured individuals to follow through with a sequence of tasks in work settings. In all cases, the activity routine was performed without the assistance of the checklist within 12 days. Evans, Emslie, and Wilson (1998) described a case study of a woman with executive impairment where a combination of NeuroPage and a written checklist provided the external cues required to complete a selected range of daily activities. Bergman (1991) designed a customised text writer in order to accommodate the cognitive deficits and use the residual skills of a highly intelligent woman who had sustained severe TBI and was unable to write or use a standard word-processor. The text writer had simplified commands and format, and provided on-screen cues and instructions, thereby minimising cognitive demands. She was able to master the text writer within three training sessions. Follow-up indicated that she used it at least several times daily for a variety of activities in the ensuing months. The text-writer thus greatly enhanced her self-sufficiency and emotional adjustment (Bergman and Kemmerer, 1991).

Where the therapy is focused on skill acquisition in functional activity it is extremely important that clients set their own goals (Dawson et al., 2009; Grant, 2008) and that the activities and targets relate to enhancing the individual's participation in valued life roles. In a series of case studies focused on enhancing functional independence in selected daily activities, Grant (2008) found that when goals were set by the individual (rather than the therapist) they were more likely to be attained. At follow-up, the four participants achieved the expected outcome on the four subgoals that reflected their own goals for the intervention, whereas only two of the eight therapist-derived subgoals were attained.

Sohlberg, Mateer, Penkman, Glang and Todis (1998) outlined a *"Procedural Training and Environmental Support"* programme which maximises functioning in those individuals who are unable to acknowledge or understand their impairments. The focus of this programme is on teaching functional routines to level where they are carried out automatically. Compensatory behaviours are taught at a procedural, implicit level, carers are educated and supported to prompt the individual and environments are structured to cue adaptive behaviours. Ylvisaker and colleagues (2002) have also argued that individuals with chronic impairment who continue to encounter obstacles to successful life role participation require long-term "contextualized" intervention aimed at modifying routines of everyday activity in a wide range of domains including social, vocational and educational participation, carried out in the context of these activities. Individuals who are part of these routines (e.g. family, workmates, carers) become integral in delivering the ongoing support required to enable participation. Feeney, Ylvisaker, Rosen and Greene (2001) demonstrated cost-effectiveness of such a contextualised approach for people with chronic cognitive-behavioural impairment in community settings. Further support for the contextualised paradigm was provided by Braga and Campos da Paz (2000), whose randomised clinical trial indicated the superiority of contextualised cognitive rehabilitation in comparison with traditional rehabilitation in children.

This approach is supported by the findings of Sloan et al. (2009b) in a case series of 85 participants, 59 of whom in the chronic group were an average of 10.2 years post injury. Intervention was based on the Community Approach to Participation model (Sloan, Winkler, and Callaway, 2004) and focused on Participation goals of the individual, with targeted development of the associated skills that underpinned valued role performance. Following a 12-month period of community-based intervention, significant increases were evident in functional independence, community integration, and role participation, with the adoption of an average of one additional life role, relative to their starting point. For some participants, these new roles of volunteer or home maintainer replaced, or expanded to fill the gaps created by the loss of other roles, such as worker or student, and offered the individual routine opportunities for social interaction and community engagement. The authors noted the likelihood that individuals may have a greater readiness for therapy input after a period of time spent living in the community, during which awareness of persistent participation restrictions grows. Increased insight creates opportunities for addressing cognitive-behavioural impairments, social communication skills, and psychological adjustment within the context of functionally meaningful goals for role participation. In a three-year study of 43 people receiving intervention based on the Community Approach to Participation model, these gains were found to occur in the context of an overall reduction in hours of funded support, suggesting that there may be additional cost benefits of long-term community-based intervention (Sloan et al., 2009a).

For individuals with severe, ongoing impairments, the building of specific routines needs to occur in the context of a range of task and environmental modifications and the provision of structured supports (Sloan et al., 2009a). For example, in the case of an injured person in the workplace, duties may be altered so as to minimise demands on memory or initiative, the worker may be placed in a quieter environment to avoid distraction, and other workers may modify their patterns of interaction with the injured person, so as to minimise interpersonal conflict. The work space can be organised in a particular way and the order in which tasks are to be undertaken in the day fixed in a routine. In the home, relatives, or a PDA, may provide the structured prompting of an organised sequence of tasks in order to maximise the injured person's ability to perform personal or domestic activities of daily living. Such adaptations are likely to be necessary in cases where the injured person has severe cognitive deficits, lacks self-awareness, motivation and/or the capacity to adapt, as is frequently the case following severe TBI. Despite this, little emphasis has been given to this approach in the cognitive rehabilitation literature.

Conclusions from the research to date

In general, the research evaluating the impact of interventions for individuals with cognitive impairments, whether focused on retraining the functions themselves or on developing functional compensatory techniques, has had many limitations. Training has frequently been given on artificial tasks in settings which bear limited resemblance to those encountered by the injured person in everyday life. There have been relatively few studies which have comprehensively assessed the ability of the individual to use strategies to overcome everyday difficulties and to sustain gains made from training, and hence evaluated the impact of the intervention in enhancing performance of valued real-world activities and life roles. Studies have shown that most interventions or combinations of interventions may have a positive effect on cognitive function, as measured either neuropsychologically or from the point of view of the treated individual. People with less severe deficits are more likely to benefit from most forms of intervention (Berg et al., 1991; Fryer and Haffey, 1987; Zencius, Wesolowski, and Burke, 1990).

The question of optimal timing of therapeutic intervention is a complex issue, particularly in the case of TBI. As Kolb (2004) has pointed out, because the brain shows enhanced plasticity in the early period after injury, it would seem most advantageous that therapy be provided early, to capitalise on and shape changes that are beneficial. Indeed, there is some evidence to indicate that early intervention may be more effective than late intervention (High et al., 2006; Kleim, 2008; Rohling et al., 2009). However, an important determinant of the ability to benefit from cognitive interventions is self-awareness or insight (Ezrachi, Ben-Yishay, Kay, Diller, and Rattok, 1991; Kovacs, Fasotti, Eling, and Brouwer, 1993; Petrella, McColl, Krupa, and Johnston, 2005; Sherer et al., 1998b). Recovery following TBI is associated with a continuous process of self-discovery, and an increasing level of self-awareness over time after injury may mean that there is a better response to intervention at a later stage. Certainly there is evidence that TBI individuals are able to benefit from rehabilitation many years after injury (High et al., 2006; Sloan et al., 2009b). Whilst increasing self-awareness may enhance the injured person's capacity to benefit from rehabilitation, one of the problems associated with increasing insight over time is that individuals with a more accurate understanding of their limitations and life role changes are more likely to show escalating emotional distress, which may in turn have a negative impact on ability to benefit from therapy (Fleming and Strong, 1999; Heilbronner, Roueche, Everson, and Epler, 1989). As Petrella and colleagues (2005) point out, individuals who are faced with sudden changes in competency as well as uncertainty about the future are very vulnerable. They must reconstruct their self-identity whilst experiencing impairment of the very cognitive abilities required to adapt and adjust to change.

It is clear that no single approach to intervention is suitable for all TBI individuals. The most effective and timely approach will depend on the nature and extent of cognitive and behavioural impairment, particularly skills in the domains of memory, executive cognitive function self-monitoring and awareness of deficits. For those functioning at very low levels in these and other respects, functional compensation, tailored supports and environmental restructuring appear to be most effective in reducing Activity Limitations and Participation Restrictions. People with TBI who have some degree of motivation and self-awareness, as well as a capacity to regulate and monitor their behaviour, may benefit from training in self-instructional or self-regulatory strategies to reduce areas of impairment. The evidence for generalisation of gains to real-world settings is weak, and strategies taught are most likely to be of lasting benefit if they are embedded in functional activities and applied directly in real-world settings. The criterion by which all interventions should ultimately be measured is the impact on everyday activities and role participation.

Some researchers and clinicians working in TBI rehabilitation take the view that compensatory strategies should only be used after all recovery is known to have taken place. However, we would argue that facilitating adaptation to the Activity Limitations and Participation Restrictions caused by an injury should commence early in the rehabilitation process, alongside retraining approaches that are focused on activities of relevance to the injured person. Intervention should be offered over the longer term and be flexible to account for the injured person's recovery, the changes in their life circumstances and goals, as well as the development of insight. Such an approach is likely to maximise the outcome for the injured individual.

Evaluating the impact of interventions

Every effort should be made to objectively assess the impact of the intervention, both in alleviating the specific functional difficulty experienced by the injured person, and in increasing the individual's level of role participation. It is also important to examine whether the effects are maintained over time. In most cases this may be accomplished using single case designs, in the manner suggested by Wilson (1987b) and Tate et al. (2008). It is necessary to have an objective measure of the functional behaviour, obtained in the manner suggested in the previous chapter (e.g. frequency counts of instances of forgetting/prompting made by a caregiver), ideally over a period of time prior to intervention. The measure should continue to be taken throughout the period of intervention and during a follow-up period. It is also useful to ask the injured person and caregivers for their views regarding the problem and the impact of the intervention. This may be done using the Canadian Occupational Performance Measure (COPM) or a standardised questionnaire (see Chapter 3), or questions developed specifically for the purpose. Again, such questions or ratings need to be made after a follow-up period. Neuropsychological measures are not the best measures of the effectiveness of this form of intervention.

Clinical application of Rehabilitation for Everyday Adaptive Living (REAL)

This section will outline how the REAL approach can be used by therapists planning intervention programmes for cognitive deficits following TBI. The core principles of this approach include the need for interdisciplinary teamwork, involvement of family or significant others, evaluation of intervention effectiveness, focusing on the everyday context, making adaptations to overcome residual weaknesses using the individual's strengths, as well as internal or external supports, and the need for a long-term perspective. There are three main components to be considered when planning therapeutic input. These are goal-setting, selecting therapy tasks, and implementing therapy. The latter incorporates provision of therapeutic input that will maximise learning, and selection and implementation of strategies or modifications which are appropriate to the injured person's strengths and weaknesses.

Goal-setting

As goal-setting underpins the treatment process, considerable time needs to be spent formulating goals. This may prove to be a challenging process. It is often difficult to engage the family and TBI individual in realistic goal-setting and all team members may not share the same aims. The following section will address pertinent issues and provide guidelines for setting goals. For the purposes of the following discussion, a goal is defined as a targeted, desired outcome assigned within a time frame. Long-term goals are statements of broad outcomes that encompass expectations of the individual's future roles and responsibilities. Motivation for rehabilitation is likely to be maximised where long-term goals are framed as objectives for increased Participation. This may include goals for return to work or study which are formulated by taking into consideration the TBI individual's identified past, present and future roles and their hopes for enhanced participation, and the family's goals. Other premorbid factors, injury-related variables, such as time since injury, and findings of clinical assessments also need to be taken into account. It is vital that the therapist accepts the broad direction set by the individual and family and avoids the temptation to pass judgement on whether or not they believe the goal is realistic. As the time frame for achieving long-term goals is usually extended, it is possible to define them in relatively broad terms as hopes for the future, for example, "to return to work in six to twelve months".

Ideally, long-term goals are set first, as they provide the direction and context for the development of shorter-term goals, or the steps towards achievement of those broader goals. Typically, to achieve long-term goals, a diverse range of component issues and problems will need to be addressed. Medium-term goals tend to focus on the steps required to address the component problems subsumed by the long-term goal. For instance, to return to work, the individual may need to develop specific job-related skills, acquire a means of transport and adapt to the effects of a memory difficulty. Time frames of weeks to months may be assigned to attain these medium goals. Short-term goals represent a further breakdown of the steps required to achieve the medium- and, in turn, the long-term goals. They focus on very specific outcomes that can be observed and measured behaviourally (e.g. learning to perform a sequence of tasks involved in cutting and planing timber, or learning to use a diary).

In order to arrive at goals that are meaningful to the individual and family, and shared by all members of the treating team, all parties need to be actively involved in the goal-setting process. Ideally, the individual, family and team will share a commitment to the long-term goals. Shorter-term goals may be specific to particular team members, whilst others will be shared across disciplines. For instance, in attaining independence in a mode of transport, it may be necessary to tackle a range of problems, such as reduced mobility, socially inappropriate behaviour and poor planning. Social communication skills developed with the speech pathologist, and cues developed by the physiotherapist to assist the person to ambulate safely in the community, can, for instance, be integrated into travel training activities and practised with the occupational therapist in community settings. This approach helps to ensure that there are opportunities to generalise skills to real-life settings and also provides a meaningful focus for the therapy intervention. It is important to prioritise goals, based on consultation with the injured person, their family and the treating team. Goals also need to reviewed on a regular basis and revised as targets are achieved. A case management structure is helpful to ensure that someone takes responsibility for co-ordinating team planning, securing the input of the TBI individual, mediating between potentially conflicting points of view and making sure all those involved are kept informed on an ongoing basis.

Involving the TBI individual in goal-setting can be a difficult task, as illustrated by the case study of Bradley (below). Goal-setting demands such cognitive processes as abstract thinking, judgement, idea generation and awareness of strengths and weaknesses, any of which may be impaired following TBI. When asked to state their goals, people with TBI may proffer idealised statements or general wishes that fail to reflect an understanding of underlying impairments resulting from the injury. Typically such statements reflect the person's desire to resume a valued life role, or centre on aspects of their current situation which they find particularly challenging. An inpatient immobilised in bed might say he wants to go home, or a severely cognitively impaired individual may say he wants to go back to his previous job or to drive a car. Such goals may not coincide with those of members of the treating team or the family, and may easily be dismissed as being unrealistic. In the resulting void, therapists may be inclined to impose their own goals and assume that the individual would concur if they had insight.

However, therapists' goals, especially those that are focused on a cognitive impairment of which the individual has no awareness, may be perceived as meaningless by the individual, and as a result there may be little active participation in therapy. The therapist needs to be flexible in developing goals and be prepared to view the situation from the perspective of the individual. To successfully set goals it is important that therapists use the language of the TBI individual and accept their desires for re-engagement in past life roles as a starting point to set the long-term goals. The Role Checklist discussed in Chapter 3 is a useful tool for identifying the individual's past and future desired roles. The component steps and pre-requisite skills required to achieve goals for role participation must then be teased out. These become sub-goals to be achieved in the medium to short term. In this way an unrealistic and vague wish becomes a series of smaller, concrete and achievable goals, shared by the individual and therapist. The manner in which the sub-goals contribute to the overall goal needs to be documented explicitly and the individual may need to be referred to this document frequently. The therapist will need to provide an appropriate level of support to help the injured individual to maintain a goal-oriented focus.

Implementing therapy

Selection of therapy tasks

Provided the assessment and goal-setting processes have been followed in the manner suggested, selection of treatment activities should be fairly straightforward. Therapy tasks are chosen from those everyday activities in which the injured person needs to rebuild their skills. Priorities will be set according to the person's overall level of function as well as current and projected demands in the individual's daily life. The specific activities identified should be clearly linked to the longer-term goals for life role participation. Wherever possible, activities should be performed within the context of the normal daily environment and routine, therefore also incorporating activities the individual is able to perform. In order to maximise motivation, activities should be related to the injured person's goals for independence in a clear and concrete manner.

Therapeutic input

Therapeutic input may be provided by therapists, family members, carers or others involved in relevant aspects of the injured person's lifestyle (e.g. fellow workers, friends). It should be given in such a manner as to maximise learning and the attainment of goals. As discussed earlier, the approach taken to therapy will depend on the level of functioning of the injured person. Ways of facilitating the learning process include the following:

- Harness motivation by selecting tasks which are seen as relevant by the injured person. It may be prudent to allow supported risk-taking in order to enhance this aspect, and support the development of self-awareness.
- Break tasks down into steps or components, focusing on one at a time, and gradually linking them together into a routine. Begin with maximal assistance using cues or aids and gradually withdraw these.
- Provide frequent feedback. Feedback should be provided immediately, and in a concrete and uncritical manner. Negative feedback should be preceded by a comment on a positive aspect of performance, and presented in conjunction with constructive suggestions as to how performance may be improved. Wherever possible, it is important to create opportunities for the injured person to receive feedback from peers, fellow workers or family members, as this is likely to be more meaningful.
- Give repeated practice until the skill or strategy is mastered within one context, then provide further practice in a range of other relevant settings.
- Educate the TBI individual and relevant others regarding the nature of changes and specific strengths and weaknesses. Educational input needs to be tailored to the individual's general intelligence, knowledge of TBI, level of cognitive function, degree of insight and emotional status. Written material or tapes may be used. Groups involving other TBI individuals also represent a useful means of enhancing understanding of problems and ways to circumvent them.

Involvement of close others

Families provide a vital role in managing functional cognitive problems, and will continue to do so long after therapy input has ceased. It is important, therefore, that management strategies are devised in consultation with the family or other caregivers, ideally in the home or other relevant context. Family members may be involved in therapy sessions where strategies are modelled and discussed, either in vivo or using videotapes.

An assessment of the overall demands on the family is important, so that a realistic level of involvement can be encouraged. For example, the TBI individual may be lacking in initiative in ADL. Within the hospital it may be possible to introduce a structure to maximise independence to the level where the person requires four specific verbal prompts to get up, shower and dress.

At home, however, the therapist may find that the TBI individual is being fully supervised and physically assisted to perform the same activity. Whilst this may be acceptable for the family in the short term, it is potentially burdensome in the longer term when the family find it difficult to withdraw this level of support.

It is important to try and help the family establish routines that are able to be sustained, and which maximise the independence of the injured person. However, in suggesting alternative approaches it is essential not to denigrate the family's efforts or forcefully present one's own opinion. Mutual exchange of information, and gentle prompting as to the likely consequences of the family's actions, may assist in bringing about consistency between hospital and home. This approach demands humility and flexibility from therapists, who must be willing to subsume their own goals to those of the individual and the family. Ultimately the therapist needs to accept the views of the TBI individual and the family, and search for some common ground on which they can be engaged. Some individuals and families will reject help altogether and this should not be held against them. Therapists should attempt to part on terms that leave the door open to the family should their situation change and they later wish to receive assistance.

Structuring tasks and introducing strategies

Task modifications and strategies designed to compensate for everyday difficulties arising from cognitive impairment cannot be prescribed in the manner of a recipe. The choice, and effectiveness, of strategies will depend not only on the difficulties observed in everyday life, but also on the individual's strengths and residual skills, the nature of their cognitive impairments, the specific demands of the task in question, and environmental variables. An individualised approach that accounts for these factors is recommended.

The process of structuring tasks and introducing strategies commences with an analysis of both the task and the injured person's performance of it. Modifications and strategies need to be introduced in a systematic manner and their effectiveness for the individual evaluated. Modifications can be made at a number of different levels, depending largely on the severity of the injured person's cognitive problems. Firstly, easier versions of the same activity can be selected. Some tasks may be avoided altogether. Secondly, the tasks themselves can be adapted to alter (up- or downgrade) specific cognitive demands. Thirdly, environmental variables can be changed. Fourthly, the input from external sources can be varied in terms of the amount or type of assistance provided. Finally, the methods and cognitive strategies used by the injured person can be altered, drawing on relatively intact abilities. For those individuals with more severe cognitive problems, choices may be restricted to task and environmental modifications, and externally generated prompts. A wider choice of strategy is available for those individuals functioning at a higher level. Overall, the aim of the therapist will be to establish the minimum level of input/adaptation required, to support maximal, sustained independence. Behavioural techniques may be used to assist in training strategies or shaping task modifications. Group discussion may also facilitate the development and acquisition of strategies.

The following section contains some suggested modifications or strategies for dealing with some of the more common cognitive problems associated with TBI. Further examples of the application of the REAL approach to overcoming the impact of cognitive difficulties on the performance of a range of roles are contained in Chapter 7. For ease of organisation, the information in the following section is set out under the headings of attention, memory, executive dysfunction, initiative and insight. However, in this context they are used to categorise functional cognitive behaviours arising from impairments of specific functions, rather than diagnostic labels.

Attentional problems and fatigue

- Build rest-breaks into the activity (e.g. five minutes rest for each 15 minutes).
- Schedule more complex tasks at the time of day when fatigue levels are lowest and there are fewest competing demands.
- Change activities frequently to maintain interest.
- Modify the environment to reduce distractions (e.g. work in a quiet room, facing a wall, reduce interruptions and background noise, clear workspace).
- Modify the task to reduce the amount of information to be processed, or the speed at which it is presented.
- Provide verbal prompts to encourage the person to re-focus on the task and train others to do so.
- Provide verbal or written prompts that assist the person to move from one component of the task to the next in a logical fashion. By removing unstructured periods there is less opportunity for the person to become distracted.
- Allow for repetition of material to be remembered, such as instructions. In work or study environments a dictaphone may be useful to record and replay important material.
- Allow a realistic time-frame for completion of tasks to reduce time pressure and associated stress.
- Train the injured person to ask questions to slow down the delivery of spoken material and clarify points, or introduce other self-talk strategies to maintain the focus of attention (e.g. repeating what has to be done to avoid distraction).
- Train the injured person and others to identify the signs of fatigue and take appropriate action. Stress management, relaxation, mindfulness or meditation techniques may be helpful.
- Structure a graduated return to activities and demands.

Memory and learning difficulties

- If the TBI person is unable to participate actively in applying strategies, use close others to provide necessary prompting or reminding, externally programmed aids, or modify the environment to reduce demands on memory.
- Downgrade the memory demands of the task to a manageable level (e.g. reduce the amount of material to be remembered, reduce the periods of delay between presentation of information and recall, simplify material to be remembered and present information in a logical and structured manner).
- Provide opportunities for repetition of information/frequent practice of tasks.
- Reduce environmental distractions during learning and recall.
- Provide verbal reminders or written prompts and train others to do so.
- Encourage the person to develop a set routine, within which adaptive habits can be trained.
- Identify strategies and techniques used to assist memory before the injury and those employed spontaneously since. These may be broadly divided into internal and external memory aids. Internal aids include mnemonics, such as visual imagery and the PQRST technique. External memory aids include use of a diary, calendar, lists, notes, putting things in special places, as well as a range of programmable electronic or computerised aids.
- Select strategies based on an analysis of the task and the injured person's performance including their overall level of cognitive function (e.g. many internal mnemonic strategies are too demanding cognitively), premorbid strategies, environmental supports and motivation and interest.
- Review methods of applying the strategy and identify anticipated problems (e.g. how will you remember to use the strategy?; what will you write in the diary?). Develop and implement solutions to these problems.
- Provide opportunities to practise relevant tasks during which the person is trained when and how to use memory strategies.
- Involve family members in the implementation of strategies, and have them monitor their use in the home and community. The therapist will also need to observe the use of the strategy in real-world settings.

Executive problems (incorporating impaired planning and organisation, problem-solving and self-monitoring)

- Choose less complex versions of the relevant activity (e.g. select easy recipes).
- Break task into components and present them one at a time.
- Simplify tasks by condensing or eliminating non-vital steps. Once a basic level of skill is obtained, these steps can be reintroduced.

- Provide clear, simple instructions that impart a structure for performance of the task.
- Ensure consistency of approach between therapists and family members.
- Utilise all relevant resources in the individual's environment (e.g. public transport times and routes may be more easily accessed through the Internet than from books of maps and timetables).
- Include familiar activities, triggers, strategies, etc. and draw on pre-morbid skills.
- Provide opportunities for practice in familiar environments.
- Provide external cues that enable the TBI individual to recognise and complete each step of the activity. A regular signal may be used to alert them to check or review what they are doing, to stay on track. External cues may take the form of written checklists (the individual or the therapist may tick off completed steps), verbal prompts (these range from general prompts such as "what comes next?" to specific prompts such as "turn on the oven"), or environmental signals (e.g. setting the oven timer to prompt steps in cooking, SMS or pager messages).
- Behavioural methods outlined in Chapter 6 (such as shaping, chaining) can be used to train the person to perform a routine series of steps in response to a designated trigger.
- "Internal" compensatory strategies can be used for specific situations (e.g. using self-talk to prompt oneself to "slow down" when searching for items in the supermarket).
- "Internal" strategies can also be used more flexibly in a range of situations where the person is able to anticipate problems or adequately self-monitor performance. Such strategies primarily utilise self-talk to cue adaptive behaviours – for example, the "analyse, plan, do, review" approach discussed earlier.

Lack of initiative

- Educate the individual and family as to the nature of the problem, so they understand lack of initiative is not the same as laziness.
- Break down the task into components. Use prompting and reinforcement to shape desired behaviour, chaining steps together, then fading prompts (see Chapter 6).
- Use verbal, written or external prompts. Checklists may be used to check off components of tasks as they are completed. An alarm clock, wrist watch, computer or electronic diary may be programmed to alert the individual to perform specific activities.
- Increase the salience of the task for the individual (e.g. give the person responsibility for preparing breakfast).
- Allow the individual to experience the normal consequences of failure to perform the task. Follow up with feedback and discussion.

- To maximise motivation, make sure tasks are relevant and involve the TBI person in goal-setting and decision-making.

Poor self-awareness

- Delay confronting the person directly with their cognitive problems, and work on disabilities the injured person can recognise (e.g. physical disabilities).
- Convey information about problems in a way that is meaningful, focusing on everyday life activities.
- Allow supported risk-taking within meaningful environments.
- Educate family, friends and peers, and seek their assistance in giving feedback, providing supervision, etc.
- Ask the individual with TBI to monitor and record the incidence of specific behaviours when performing activities.
- Audio- or videotape task performance. In playing back the tape the individual may be asked in a general way to report on "what you notice about the way you performed the activity". Alternatively, self-evaluation may be enhanced by providing some structure to guide observations such as a checklist of behaviour(s) to be self-rated.
- Keep a log book of therapy, domestic and/or community activities in which TBI individuals can record daily experiences in their own words. The injured person may be prompted to include both success and failure in their performance of daily activity. Discussion and questioning aimed at highlighting strengths and weaknesses can be undertaken by the therapist.
- Give feedback immediately, and precede negative comments with positive ones.

Case report – Sandra

The background describing Sandra's injury, the results of neuropsychological and occupational therapy assessments are outlined in a case report in Chapter 3. She had significant deficits of attention, memory, and executive functions such as verbal reasoning, idea generation, self-monitoring and planning, was amnesic and disoriented to her current circumstances and had visuo-perceptual difficulties. Functionally, she was independent in some basic daily tasks and routines but required 24-hour supervision and support and was not accessing the community due to her risk of absconding. Sandra could not structure or occupy her own time and displayed challenging behaviours. Overall, her life role participation was limited to that of home maintainer and family member. Given her profound amnesic disorder, the following strategies were provided to the house staff to assist Sandra's orientation. Staff were asked to provide regular support to ensure Sandra learnt how to utilise these tools to aid her orientation:

Weekly whiteboard: Sandra has a large whiteboard on which her weekly timetable of activities is outlined. The goal of this whiteboard, kept in her bedroom, was to orient Sandra at the start and end of each day as to the activities she would be undertaking. When using the whiteboard, Sandra was prompted to refer to the day/date clock next to the whiteboard to ensure she identified the correct day of the week. At times during the day when she requested to go out or to work, staff would prompt Sandra to refer to her whiteboard to determine the next scheduled activity for the day. Staff were advised not to tell Sandra directly that she does not work. Rather, they were asked to say, "Sandra, let's check the whiteboard. See here, you aren't going to work today, instead this afternoon we are doing the shopping for the household." It was anticipated that initially Sandra would require staff to physically orient her to the whiteboard; however, with repeated prompting over time, she was expected to learn to refer to the whiteboard independently.

Daily whiteboard: A whiteboard was also set up in the lounge room, which detailed the current day, date, and name of the staff member on duty. This whiteboard was to be updated by staff every night so that the information was correct when Sandra got up in the morning. Due to Sandra's visual difficulties, it was important that information on the whiteboard was written clearly, in large font. Again Sandra was referred to this board regularly throughout the day.

Orientation book: An orientation book, which outlined Sandra's life story and contained photographs of her family and current roles (e.g. volunteer work) was developed. This book was kept in her bedroom. Staff read through this book each day with Sandra to assist her to develop a greater level of familiarity and knowledge regarding her circumstances. When Sandra was confused or asked questions about her past or current situation staff encouraged her to get this book and read through it with her.

Sandra had an interest in current events. Watching, reading and talking about the news provided opportunities to expand her interests and also incidentally reinforce current information.

Sandra was not always able to remember day-to-day information reliably. The following strategies were suggested to staff to assist them in prompting Sandra, without triggering distress or a verbal outburst:

When Sandra was asking the same question repeatedly, it was appropriate to ask her to stop and think what that answer may be, rather than jumping in to answer her question straight away. For instance, staff might respond by saying, "What do you think?" Sandra was often able to recall the answer to her own repeated questions. However, when she clearly did not know the answer this was provided to her. A short, simple response was given and staff did not expand on this answer unless Sandra asked a further question.

When Sandra requested food, and she had recently eaten, she was reminded of this. Providing Sandra with the current time of day and informing her of when the next meal will be eaten by way of a question was also useful. e.g. "Sandra, it is 1:00 and we had lunch 30 minutes ago, what time do you think we should have afternoon tea?"

The frequency of her requests for food increased when Sandra was bored, therefore having structured, purposeful activity to occupy her time assisted in decreasing these requests. If Sandra was repeatedly requesting food she was engaged in another activity, such as playing cards or assisting with household tasks, to distract her. Sandra required assistance in independently occupying her own time for short periods.

Case report – Robert

The background describing Robert's injury, the results of neuropsychological and occupational therapy assessments and the goals for intervention are outlined in a case report in Chapter 3. Robert displayed reduced immediate and working memory, slowed speed of information processing, word-finding difficulties, disorganisation, impulsivity, reduced frustration tolerance and experienced high levels of cognitive fatigue. He also had significant problems with initiation in his daily life. These impairments caused significant disruption of Robert's everyday function and impacted on his ability to engage successfully in the roles of friend, worker, home maintainer and community participant.

The intervention described below was developed to support Robert to participate in his role of home maintainer. It was noted that due to his executive cognitive impairments even quite straightforward and familiar activities, such as cleaning the windows, were overwhelmingly difficult for Robert to undertake as he was unable to prioritise and schedule them into his day, despite being capable of physically performing the task. At the commencement of intervention, Robert was supported to identify a list of home-based tasks he wished to complete, which included pruning a lemon tree, clearing out his garage to enable him to park his car, removing a creeper from his garage rear wall, regularly mowing his lawn and developing a vegetable garden. Most of these tasks had been on Robert's "to do list" for a number of years and despite a high level of motivation he had been unable to initiate and complete any of them.

Neuropsychological counselling sessions were held over a two-month period, during which a range of strategies were discussed with Robert, with the goal of him generalising these to the home and so completing his "to do list". These strategies included: selecting one activity for the week and scheduling it in his diary, creating a job-list to be placed on his refrigerator, with the first step of each job written out, writing post-it notes to be stuck on his kitchen bench reminding him of his "job for the week" and setting an alarm in his mobile phone. None of these strategies was successful singly or in combination, despite a high level of motivation and intent. It was clear that Robert was unable to generalise strategies to the home setting as this step in itself required executive function skills including initiation and planning. Given Robert's evident cognitive impairments it was felt he would benefit from the provision of external structuring and prompting such as could be provided by a paid support worker. Although very resistant to this idea initially, he agreed to his occupational therapist establishing a trial of an attendant care worker.

The following guidelines were put in place for the support worker and Robert: The attendant care worker's role was to facilitate Robert's involvement in the task, not to complete tasks for Robert. The support worker should work "side by side" with Robert in both the planning and physical aspects of the tasks. The role was explained as "enabling Robert to do the things he can do, and supporting him to do the things he can't do".

On arrival at Robert's home, the support worker would ask what tasks he would like to complete from the list developed during occupational therapy sessions. Robert was supported to plan the task via prompts in the form of questions. For instance, "What job will you do first?"; "Do you have all the tools for this job?", "Is there somewhere we can put the rubbish?". When Robert was unable to provide an appropriate response the support worker generated an idea and then sought Robert's input. In this way, Robert was empowered to make his own decisions.

The details of the plan for the day were noted and the support worker referred Robert to the written plan, as required. This minimised the number of instructions provided by the worker and allowed Robert to retain a sense of control over the activity.

Jobs were crossed off the list as they were completed. At this time, the support worker could raise any issues that may have arisen during completion of the task (e.g. safety issues with use of the equipment) and invite Robert to reflect on his own performance. Any actions arising from this discussion could be referred to in planning activities in subsequent shifts.

At the end of the shift Robert could be left to complete a task, having been helped to commence it. In this way he could experience a greater sense of independence and accomplishment.

Robert began to look forward to the weekly shift of three hours and felt a greater level of satisfaction in his home maintainer role. His mood improved considerably. He also started to initiate routine tasks, such as mowing the lawn, in the hour before the worker arrived, as Robert felt "it was a waste of the worker's time" to do these tasks in the worker's presence. At the start of each shift he had also identified the outdoor tasks to be completed and he also began to request assistance with spring cleaning activities indoors and with cooking. In this way the role of the support worker gradually expanded and at the end of a six-month period Robert was receiving two three-hour blocks of support each week. It was anticipated that, due to the persistent nature of his executive cognitive deficits, this support would need to be ongoing if his role participation was to be sustained.

Case report – George

George worked as the manager of a video wholesaling business. His job involved researching latest video releases, selecting purchases based on anticipated client demand, ordering, checking off deliveries and arranging distribution to retail outlets. He received and made between 30 and 40 telephone calls per day, and had three people working for him in the business, which he co-owned. Following a TBI six months earlier, George returned to work and reported a number of problems. He said he had difficulty recalling all relevant details of information or instructions, provided over the telephone or in face-to-face interactions. He attempted to compensate by writing everything down, but because of attentional problems he was limited in his ability to take notes at the same time as he held a conversation. He said he tried to make notes at the end of an interaction, but found he was often distracted by subsequent demands. If he held two telephone conversations in quick succession he would confuse the details of the calls. These problems resulted in frequent failure to follow through with instructions and complete the things he was expected or had agreed to do. He made frequent errors. He became anxious about his memory failures and their implications for his vocational future.

Observation of George's work environment and performance in response to specific everyday demands was undertaken by the occupational therapist. A baseline measure was taken. The behaviour selected was "doing the things I said I would do". Over a three-day period George recorded the number of successes and failures that occurred in this category of behaviour. On each of these days he was also asked to select and record in detail one example of difficulty. This information formed the basis of discussions with George, in which the nature of his difficulties, and the conditions under which they occurred, was analysed. Possible strategies to minimise the effects of memory problems were discussed with George, beginning with the identification of premorbidly used aids and techniques. Together, external memory aids were chosen and a routine of recording and checking information was devised.

A desk diary was to be used for planner entries such as appointments, placement of orders and dates of delivery. Additionally, journal entries were made in a notebook with a separate page for each day, and cross referenced with the diary. Journal entries included notes on the content of meetings, conversations and telephone calls. An "action plan sheet" detailed a list of tasks to be carried out that day. The action planner was yellow and was displayed prominently on his desk. It was prepared at the start of each day and included actions relating to things he said he would do, as well as items transferred from his diary and notebook. The action plan was updated throughout the day. George was encouraged to establish priorities, act immediately where appropriate, record the results of his actions, and tick off each item as it was attended to. An answering machine was purchased. This could be switched on if he required time to follow up and finish off details pertaining to one telephone call, before he took a subsequent call. Notes of telephone calls were made in his journal and any follow-up was recorded on the action planner. A dictaphone was also purchased to allow George, with consent, to tape important meetings and conversations. The tapes were used as a back-up to the pen and paper techniques.

George received concurrent intervention for the anxiety he was experiencing in the work situation, specifically that associated with taking phone calls. This was caused by his cognitive difficulties, but ultimately exacerbated them. He was trained in some self-talk strategies to prevent him from panicking whilst on the phone, and given relaxation training to assist his general anxiety levels. Such methods are discussed in detail in Chapter 8.

Reassessment on the baseline measures, regarding George's ability to "do as he said he would" indicated substantial improvement in response to the intervention. However, the additional effort required of George in order to cope with his job resulted in significant compromise of his social and recreational activities. Thus, although he is successfully managing his memory problems, George has required ongoing support to deal with the impact of the head injury on his lifestyle.

Case report – Bradley

Bradley was a motor mechanic of low average premorbid intelligence, who had sustained a severe TBI two months earlier. He did not have much contact with his family. Cognitive problems with attention, memory and executive functions were evident on neuropsychological assessment, and it was anticipated they may have a significant impact on his lifestyle. He had no awareness of them. He was living alone and his only goal was to return to work. He was unwilling to practise domestic, community or vocational tasks in the hospital setting. The occupational therapist's short-term goals were to fully assess the impact of his cognitive deficits on daily tasks, to increase his awareness and understanding of his problems, and to introduce compensatory strategies. Many of the tasks he was asked to perform in the hospital were simulations of real life demands, but Bradley was unable to abstract the reasons for this approach. He reported that he was independent in domestic and community tasks he had undertaken, and would not agree to a home visit. He refused psychological counselling. Bradley was becoming increasingly disillusioned with therapy and had a very poor attendance record. Due to severe orthopaedic injuries involving his left leg it was not anticipated that he would return to work for at least six months, and he required intensive medical treatment and physiotherapy in the interim.

In order to maintain his commitment to the rehabilitation process, and ensure he received treatment for his leg injuries, a team meeting between Bradley and the therapists involved was arranged by the case manager. The team agreed to adopt Bradley's goals and modify or suspend their own. The following example of dialogue with the therapist illustrates how Bradley's goals were identified.

Therapist: "What is the main thing (goal) you want to achieve in the next few months?"
Bradley: "I want to go back to work."
Therapist: "What is stopping you from going to work at the moment?"
Bradley: "They (hospital staff) told me that I cannot lift anything heavy and I forget things. Because of that they say I wouldn't be able to do my job, so they're not letting me go back."
Therapist: "How do you think you would go at work right now?"
Bradley: "No problems."
Therapist: "What parts of your work would be no problem?"
Bradley: "I've been going over my service manuals and can still remember all the car parts and how they are pulled apart, repaired and put back together."
Therapist: "So the information seems familiar when you re-read your manuals, but have you tried to do any mechanical work to test yourself out?"
Bradley: "No, apart from a little job when I helped my brother fix his radiator."
Therapist: "Do you think that practising the things you need to do at work would be an important step before going back to your old job?"
Bradley: "Maybe."
Therapist: "Your physiotherapist tells me that your left leg is still giving you lots of trouble, but that you've missed some of your sessions with her."
Bradley: "Yeah, there's too much waiting around and they make me go and do all these stupid memory games before they let me go to physio."
Therapist: "Would it be better for you if we cut out the memory games and started some work experience, so you can keep up your motor mechanic skills?"
Bradley: "Yes."
Therapist: "Let's start by listing all the different tasks you have to do at work, then we can pick out a few that you can start with . . ."

Goals that were physically oriented and focused on work requirements, such as standing tolerance and endurance, were documented in simple and concrete terms – for example, "to increase the length of time Bradley can stand before needing to rest from 30 to 45 minutes". A time frame of four weeks was set before a review meeting would be held. In the meantime Bradley agreed to attend four times per week for physiotherapy and medical appointments. Occupational and speech therapy sessions were discontinued.

Prior to the next review meeting Bradley initiated an appointment with the case manager. He had realised that his physical limitations would limit the range of tasks he would be able to undertake at work and expressed an interest in doing a computer course to increase his skills in preparation for return to the workforce. He wanted to discuss this in the forthcoming meeting, and requested the assistance of the team in identifying appropriate courses and arranging funding. At the review meeting the physiotherapist reported that Bradley had attended regularly and had made significant progress. His standing tolerance was now 60 minutes. The physiotherapist suggested that two sessions per day working on standing tolerance would be beneficial. He agreed that he would resume occupational therapy, with the focus of the programme being on researching available courses, and practising his computer skills. He also agreed that the occupational therapist would meet with him and his employer to identify tasks he could undertake at work for two hours a week. One hour would be spent on physically oriented tasks and one hour on office-based activities. He also agreed to a home visit to set up a programme of standing practice that would be conducted at home in the context of his daily routine. These interventions offered both Bradley and the occupational therapist an opportunity to gauge the impact of his TBI on a range of functional tasks. Bradley began to report some difficulties he was experiencing. It became clear that Bradley was not shopping or cooking for himself on a regular basis. He reported that he ate cornflakes whenever he got hungry. He had lost a substantial amount of weight. Bradley acknowledged that he would like to eat better, but said he often ran out of money, forgot or couldn't find the time to go shopping. In the course of this discussion, Bradley said that he was tending to spend his fortnightly worker's compensation cheque within the first week, leaving himself very little for the second week. He had accumulated a number of debts, and had to borrow money from friends. His friends were becoming annoyed about this and asking for the money back. This prompted Bradley to seek assistance from the occupational therapist.

Bradley and the occupational therapist worked together to develop some solutions. Bradley kept a record of how he was spending his money over a two-week period. It was apparent that he spent most of it on various social activities, before he had paid bills or bought food. The occupational therapist assisted Bradley to work out a budget for his fortnightly income, setting aside amounts for food and bills, which were to be paid before any money was spent on social activities. Money was also set aside to be banked to pay off old debts. Arrangements were made for Bradley to join a credit union, which would pay his bills, provided Bradley banked a regular weekly amount. Bradley was also encouraged to purchase a diary, which was used to plan the week's activities in detail, setting down times for banking, paying bills, shopping, and performing other necessary tasks. A great deal of time was spent working on ways to ensure Bradley would refer to this diary, and eventually they arrived at a system whereby the alarm on his mobile telephone was programmed to remind him at specified times to refer to his diary. They also put notes in various places in his apartment and developed a standard shopping list for his weekly shopping. The occupational therapist also worked with Bradley on some basic cooking skills, providing him with simple, step-by-step recipes for a small range of meals which he had chosen. She monitored his use of the recipes on a regular basis. She also had him keep continuing records as to how his money was spent over several months, until she felt sure that the routines established were working. In the course of this intervention, Bradley's diary was used to help him plan the necessary phone calls and arrangements to enrol in a computer course, which he carried out successfully.

Conclusions

There are a number of different approaches which may be taken when addressing cognitive dysfunction following TBI. These fall broadly into the categories of restorative therapies, or functional compensation, including environmental manipulation, and the provision of structured supports. A review of the literature indicates that whilst all forms of therapy may be effective in certain contexts, they are likely to have the greatest impact on the individual's participation in life roles if applied directly to the activities underpinning the performance of those roles. The optimal approach will depend on the severity and nature of the injured person's cognitive deficits. Whatever approach is selected, it is important that therapy is focused on real-life difficulties of relevance to the injured person, and that family members, or others close to the injured person, are involved wherever possible. It is also vital that attempts are made to evaluate objectively the impact of the intervention on the everyday life of the injured person and the family.

5 Communication competence following TBI

Assessment and management

Pamela Snow

Communication and TBI: An overview

Communication is a rich and subtle form of higher order human behaviour. It not only commands a central place in a person's ability to negotiate the business of everyday life, but also requires the successful integration of many cultural, cognitive, linguistic and behavioural competencies. Such skills may be impaired as a consequence of TBI, resulting in a complex range of communication difficulties. These include word-finding problems, excessive talkativeness, difficulty staying on topic, poor turn-taking skills, repetitiveness, difficulties thinking of questions or comments to promote and sustain a conversation, problems following conversation in groups or noisy settings, reduced narrative competence, tactlessness, difficulties understanding abstract language, such as metaphor, sarcasm and analogy, and difficulties "reading" facial expressions (see Douglas, 2010; Struchen, 2005; Watts and Douglas, 2006). Other difficulties include problems recalling details of past and present conversations, difficulty perceiving and responding appropriately to non-verbal or situational cues, problems managing appropriate proximity to the other speaker, difficulty modifying tone of voice in relation to the context, and difficulty structuring discourse so that information is conveyed logically and sequentially. Evidence in recent years particularly points to the important role played by impaired *social cognition* in the TBI speaker (e.g. McDonald and Flanagan, 2004; Turkstra, McDonald, and DePompei, 2001; Watts and Douglas, 2006), a topic which will be considered closely here. The assessment and management of such difficulties forms the focus of this chapter.

Impaired ability to retain old, and form new, relationships is central to the long-term psychosocial hardship so frequently reported in follow-up studies of TBI survivors and their close others, and communication difficulties often play key roles in such outcomes (see Togher, McDonald, Tate, Power, and Rietdijk, 2009 for review). Unfortunately, the study of communication following TBI has long been plagued by mixed and sometimes unclear terminology, the literature referring to pragmatics, conversational skills, social skills, cognitive-communicative changes, and/or discourse impairments. In this chapter, "communicative competence" will be considered with respect to prior world knowledge, information processing/executive function skills, social cognition, and linguistic/discourse skills (verbal and non-verbal), as a conceptual framework for understanding the impact of TBI on a speaker. Communicative competence comprises a number of related cognitive, linguistic, behavioural, and cultural awareness skills that need to work synchronously with each other in real time, in order for us to succeed as speakers and listeners in a variety of everyday interactions. Human beings are fundamentally social creatures, who need interpersonal relationships to maintain optimal mental health. Recent evidence in the cognitive neurosciences (e.g. Eisenberger and Lieberman, 2004) indicates that social rejection and physical pain may share similar neural circuitry in healthy controls. What this means for TBI survivors remains to be investigated, but there is no doubt that communication competence plays a key role in outcome, and needs to be considered in relation to many "downstream" sequelae such as loneliness, depression, social anxiety, and substance misuse.

A further challenge for the TBI speaker lies in the fact that everyday communication would be dull indeed if we only ever said exactly what we mean. In fact, we make everyday conversation and other forms of communication e.g. lectures, newspaper articles, television reports, advertisements, e-mails, websites more colourful (but challenging) by using idioms (sayings such as "still waters run deep"), metaphors ("he's a dark horse"), and humour. Jokes, such as puns, may need to be processed at the phonological or semantic level and may also require knowledge of current events – hence the ability to process and retain information heard via television or radio, or read in newspapers and magazines, is critical in enabling us to be connected to others via the medium of humour. All of these creative and enjoyable linguistic devices can, however, compound the task of social inferencing. TBI interferes with the ability to "get" jokes, by virtue of its impact on speed of auditory processing, difficulties shifting mental set, and a tendency to more concrete, rather than abstract, thinking. This in turn decreases the extent to which a person can meaningfully engage with others and experience a sense of connectedness. Connectedness – the feeling of having meaningful attachments to others (family, friends, school/work peers, sporting and other community club peers) – is closely related to mental health across the life-span, and can be extremely difficult to re-create post-TBI (see Engberg and Teasdale, 2004), particularly when maladaptive coping strategies such as substance abuse develop, and/or emotional self-regulation is poor.

In Chapter 3, it was stressed that no formal evaluation should commence until the person has emerged from post traumatic amnesia (PTA), and management of the communication changes associated with PTA is discussed in Chapter 2. Upon emergence from PTA, and prior to the commencement of formal assessment, all relevant biographical, cultural, educational and medical information needs to be collected and carefully considered. The speech-language pathologist (SLP), psychologist, social worker, and other team members should liaise closely in this process, so that assessment information can be interpreted in the light of the unique circumstances of the individual concerned. Positioning the patient and family as experts with respect to what has changed post-injury is critical to establishing a meaningful therapeutic alliance and arriving at treatment goals that have good face validity. Because factors such as premorbid functioning, time since injury, the nature of recovery to date, the development of insight, and the process of spontaneous recovery will all influence communication status, it is vital that assessment and intervention be seen as inextricably related, ongoing processes. A simple "battery approach" to assessment should be avoided, in favour of exploring all available sources of information, quantitative and qualitative.

The International Classification of Functioning, Disability, and Health (ICF) and communication competence after TBI

In Chapter 3, the ICF (WHO, 1980) was considered with respect to TBI and its consequences. This model should be considered alongside the *social model of disability* (Oliver, 1990, p. 2), which holds that disability is ". . . a social state and not a medical condition". This means that difficulties re-entering the community need to be conceptualised as social, political, and attitudinal challenges for the whole community – not just for the affected individual. Many such difficulties stem from problems with communication, and community re-entry should be a focus from the outset when assessment of communicative competence is being planned. Not all impairments apparent on structured testing result in activity or participation limitations for the individual concerned. Conversely, activity or participation limitations may not become apparent in assessment conditions which are sensitive only to impairment – most likely because the test situation is unnaturally quiet, free of distractions, and lacking in everyday realities such as stress and ambiguity, both of which tax already vulnerable information processing skills. Assessment of language skills via selected subtests of aphasia batteries allows specific linguistic impairments (such as reduced auditory processing, or word-finding difficulties) to be isolated and measured (see Table 5.1 for an outline of commonly used assessment approaches).

The extent to which such impairments translate into activity and participation limitations will vary greatly from person to person, however. Assessment therefore needs to be carefully tailored around a range of premorbid and post-injury factors, and clinicians need to focus on the individual and the extent to which the social environment creates or overcomes communication obstacles (see Ma, Threats, and Worrall, 2008 for further elaboration). The use of pragmatic profiles and other measures of functional communication skills may shed some light on everyday communication competence in a range of personally salient contexts. In order for assessment of activity and participation limitations to have authentic meaning (face validity) for the person and communication partners, however, more

Table 5.1 Formal language assessment measures and their role with TBI speakers

Test	*Role in assessing the post-TBI speaker*
Boston Diagnostic Aphasia Examination – 3rd edition: BDAE-3 (Goodglass, Kaplan, and Barresi, 2000)	Enables discrete identification of receptive and expressive language difficulties that may interfere with achievement of communicative competence in challenging real-world contexts.
Boston Naming Test (2nd edition) (Kaplan, Goodglass, and Weintraub, 2001)	Enables identification of word-finding difficulties and exploration of strategies the speaker uses to try to overcome these (e.g. circumlocution, description of use, phonetic or semantic paraphasias etc).
Wiig-Semel Test of Linguistic Concepts (Wiig and Semel, 1976)	Comprehension of logico-grammatical items such as passives, spatial, and temporal relationships. Requires only a yes/no response.
Speed and Capacity of Language Processing (SCOLP) Test (Baddeley, Emslie, and Nimmo-Smith, 1992)	Enables examination of speed of processing of written information, without the contamination of education level, as the stimulus items are all at an early elementary school level, e.g. "Do dogs bark?"
Wechsler Individual Achievement Test –Third Edition (WIAT–III) (Wechsler, 2009a)	*Sub-tests* Listening Comprehension Oral Expression Early Reading Skills Word Reading Pseudoword Decoding Reading Comprehension Oral Reading Fluency Alphabet Writing Fluency Spelling Sentence Composition Essay Composition Math Problem Solving Numerical Operations Math Fluency – Addition Math Fluency – Subtraction Math Fluency – Multiplication *Composites* Oral Language Total Reading Basic Reading Reading Comprehension and Fluency Written Expression Mathematics Math Fluency Total Achievement Useful in examining language-based competencies that are required for return to school and other forms of study (e.g. university, vocational training).

Test	*Role in assessing the post-TBI speaker*
Test of Language Competence – Expanded Edition; TLC-E (Wiig and Secord, 1989)	Subtests include Ambiguous Sentences, Listening Comprehension: Making Inferences, Oral Expression: Recreating Speech Acts, Figurative Language, and a supplemental memory sub-test. Useful in exploring understanding and use of everyday nonliteral linguistic devices such as metaphor and idiom.
Clinical Evaluation of Language Fundamentals – 4th edition (CELF-4); (Semel, Wiig, and Secord, 2006)	Subtests include Concepts and Following Directions, Recalling Sentences, Formulated Sentences, Word Classes (Receptive and Expressive), Expressive Vocabulary, Word Definitions, Understanding Spoken Paragraphs, Sentence Assembly, Semantic Relationships, Number Repetition, Familiar Sequences Phonological Awareness. Note: Includes a *Pragmatics Profile* and the *Observational Rating Scale.* Useful in measuring expressive and receptive language skills, particularly in childhood and adolescence. A Core Language Score can be derived from four sub-tests.

collaborative assessment approaches are required. As time elapses after injury, and opportunities exist for changes to be experienced in the real world, the person and family members are likely to offer first-hand accounts of communication barriers and facilitators in everyday life. These accounts afford rich insights into the lived effects of TBI and provide valuable opportunities to establish ecologically valid intervention goals. The strengths and limitations of a variety of these assessment approaches will be discussed in this chapter.

Communicative competence after TBI: An "iceberg" model

Figure 5. 1 is a schematic representation of a range of factors that contribute to an individual's success as a communication partner. Some of these are observable behaviours (e.g. non-verbal behaviour, turn-taking and repair) while others occur "below the surface", e.g. social inferencing, and the application of stored world knowledge to a particular communicative context. Starting at the base of the iceberg, this model will guide the way in which communicative competence is conceptualised and discussed in this chapter.

"World knowledge" refers to our representation in memory of "facts of the world", e.g. about the distinction between the characteristics of animate and

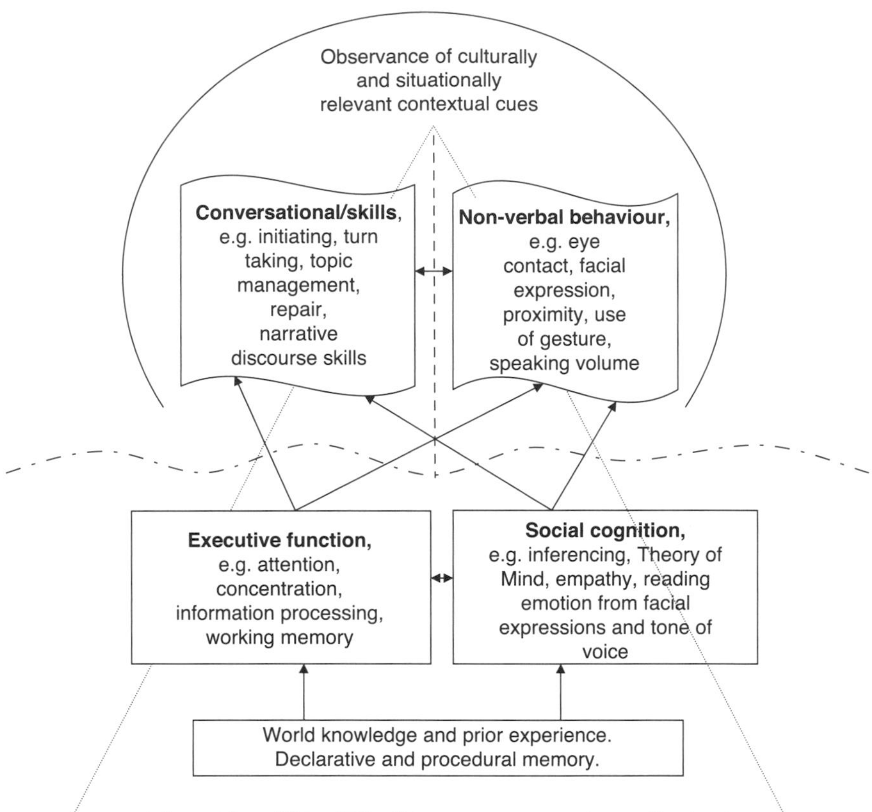

Figure 5.1 The "Communication Iceberg" in TBI. Note the area below the surface is not observable, but accounts for much of what is observed and experienced "above the surface" by communication partners.

inanimate entities, and various assumptions about physical and natural laws that are "understood" and assumed to be true, such as parents being older than their children, daytime being more light than night-time, animals being unable to speak, and so on. Declarative and Procedural memory represent two broad systems of long-term memory (Squire and Zola, 1996). Declarative memory is concerned with items of general knowledge that can be stated, and is typically further sub-divided into Semantic (general factual knowledge) and Episodic (storage of memory of specific events) systems. Procedural memory, on the other hand, concerns unconscious memories of skills that have been acquired (e.g. how to play a musical instrument). World knowledge typically remains intact after TBI, though deficits in declarative memory can hinder communicative competence by virtue of interference with acquisition and retrieval of information in the course of conversation.

The impact of executive function deficits on communicative competence

In Chapter 3, the common executive function sequelae of TBI were outlined, and the importance of detailed neuropsychological assessment was discussed. Although by no means telling the whole story, information derived from neuropsychological assessment forms an important backdrop against which communicative competence can be considered. Communication is not a unitary concept – the role of supporting executive function processes such as attention, working memory, planning and organisation, self-monitoring, and ability to think in the abstract, all need to be considered. The person who displays significant difficulties with attention and concentration, for example, is likely to have difficulties following conversation, particularly in noisy environments, and when several people are taking part in the same conversation. Similarly, the individual with planning and organisational difficulties may not be able to consistently structure ideas so they are presented in a logical, sequential manner for the listener. Self-monitoring difficulties may manifest as repetitiveness, difficulty staying on topic, or poor sensitivity to situational constraints (e.g. use of inappropriate language such as swearing in contexts where this will cause offence or loss of face). Reduced ability to think in the abstract can have debilitating effects on the individual's ability to understand humour, metaphor, sarcasm, and other forms of figurative language – all commonly used in everyday conversation. Egocentricity may manifest as a tendency to want to talk about only certain topics, and difficulty seeing a situation from another person's perspective. All of these difficulties may sit alongside reduced *working memory* – deficits in the system responsible for the temporary storage and manipulation of information so that it can be used in cognitive and communicative tasks (Baddeley, 2003). Everyday reasoning and communication requires that information is rapidly processed and manipulated, thus even subtle decrements in working memory (in particular the so-called "phonological loop" component of the central executive) manifest as communication behaviour which is compromised in some way.

Social cognition: Theory of Mind, social inferencing and reading facial expressions

Social cognition refers to the knowledge, processing, and application of culturally relevant (and often quite subtle) behaviour that assists in establishing and maintaining interpersonal relationships of varying degrees of intimacy and complexity – ranging from superficial "one-off" service encounters, through to grappling with the reactions of a partner during an emotionally charged argument. Social cognition impacts on communication ease and success in many ways in everyday life – from thinking about how an e-mail will "read" at the other end (could unintended offence or confusion be caused?), to being able to fully decode a face-to-face interpersonal situation by considering the verbal content, the speaker's tone of voice and facial expression, and other contextual factors. Social cognition draws on attentional skills and working memory, and encompasses two related constructs that have been shown, over more than a decade, to be of particular relevance to the study of communication competence following TBI: Theory of Mind (ToM) and social inferencing.

Theory of Mind (ToM)

ToM allows us to attribute mental states to others, and to ourselves, and to understand that our own mental state may not always be congruent with that of others (Milligan, Astington, and Dack, 2007). ToM is the basis for human interaction, as it underpins our ability to understand, predict and interpret the beliefs and feelings of others in our world. On the basis of these mental state inferences, we make decisions about our own responses. ToM is relevant to communicative success after TBI because it underpins the ability to draw inferences about what another person is thinking (their mental state), but not explicitly stating, and also addresses the important notion of awareness of *false belief* – knowledge that another person may have a particular belief that is based on an erroneous assumption. ToM also supports the ability to think about how others are thinking about us – and to make modifications in our interpersonal behaviour if we deem that this will be advantageous to our relationships. Under typical circumstances, ToM is evident in the cognitive processes of 4-year-olds. This is testimony to its importance as a foundation for understanding how interactions with others "work", how much information needs to be shared (e.g. on the basis of assumptions made about listener prior knowledge), and why other people react as they do. ToM is important for conversational repair and the saving of face that is so important for communicative success. Sometimes this awareness must occur pre-emptively, while in other situations it takes place in real-time. The following example illustrates ToM as it applies in everyday life.

> *Kim and Toni are work colleagues. Late one afternoon, Kim tells Toni that their boss has called an important meeting for 9:00 the next day. Toni says she will be there, but has a medical appointment first thing in the morning, so will come straight to the meeting when she arrives at work. The following morning, Kim is informed by colleagues that the meeting will now start at 8:30 instead of 9:00. Kim knows that Toni (a) isn't contactable, and (b) can't make an 8:30 meeting, but decides to send her a text message to inform her that the meeting time has changed.*

In this scenario Kim displays sophisticated mentalising skills; she thinks about another person's thinking (Toni's "knowledge" about the meeting start-time is now a false belief), and she displays sensitivity around the fact that it is preferable to not call someone when they have a doctor's appointment. However, her knowledge of the relationship between beliefs and emotional reactions also activates her social problem-solving skills *in advance of a problem actually occurring* – she averts a problem by sending a text message and ensuring that Toni's false belief is rectified before she arrives at work, and the likelihood of interpersonal discord is reduced. Kim is also able to anticipate ("mentalise") a scenario in which Toni's false belief is not rectified, resulting in her being confused at best, and annoyed at worst. This ability to "think about thinking" also overlaps with the domain of empathy, as Kim has mapped Toni's likely *affective* state over her *belief* state. Skills such as these need to be called upon every day in a myriad of home and work interactions, but are highly vulnerable to the effects of brain injury. Their absence in some survivors of TBI makes for many confusing and sometimes quite emotionally painful experiences of communication failure.

In a review of ToM research in the field of TBI, Bibby and McDonald (2005) observed that ToM tasks place implicit language demands on the speaker, as well as taxing working memory. Although its neural substrate is not fully understood, current evidence points to the role of the right ventromedial prefrontal cortex in ToM integrity in the adult (Bibby and McDonald, 2005).

Social inferencing

This refers to the ability to derive intended meaning from incomplete or contradictory verbal/non-verbal information that is shared in a particular social context. Turkstra (2008) has described the need to "fill in the gaps" when critical information is not explicitly provided by the conversation partner. There are many everyday situations in which we need to consider unstated elements of the situation, and weigh these up alongside information that is explicitly stated in order to accurately infer the speaker's intended, versus his/her stated meaning. For example, if you are visiting the home of a friend and you drop and break a wine glass, your host might immediately say "Don't worry about it". Depending on (i) how this is said (warm, reassuring tone, vs icy, business-like tone), (ii) the kinds of accompanying facial expressions (a gentle smile with slightly furrowed brow, accompanied by a slight head shaking motion vs pursed lips, flat intonation, and no movement of the head), and (iii) other contextual factors, such as whether you were there to borrow something or do a favour for your friend, and whether you have broken things there before, your host might be wanting you to infer one of several possible emotional states. These could range from concern for you and your reaction (wanting to minimise your embarrassment), through to annoyance/anger (wanting you to feel remorseful). Failure to integrate the contextual, verbal, and non-verbal (facial expression and tone of voice) cues in the milliseconds available, and arrive at the "right" inference, will damage the relationship in a number of ways.

Similarly, when your boss comes into your office and states "Nice job on the monthly report", this could be a compliment (surface meaning = intended meaning), but it could also be negative feedback being delivered via the linguistic device known as sarcasm, where the surface meaning is the exact *opposite* of the stated meaning. In this scenario, you need to recognise that there is more than one possible meaning, and rapidly draw on prior knowledge, as well as contextual and non-verbal cues conveyed by the speaker (e.g. tone of voice, facial expression, body language), to determine whether your hypothesis is correct. In some situations, it will be necessary to ask for clarification – a communicative task that in itself requires (a) knowledge that there may be more than one possible meaning and (b) higher-order skills such as tact and assertiveness.

The complaints of partners and family members of TBI speakers often reflect the person's difficulty engaging *in vivo* in this high-level processing of both contextual, and verbal and non-verbal information in order to *infer* the speaker's *intended* (though not necessarily overtly *stated*) meaning. Failure to synthesise information correctly creates frustration, embarrassment, and confusion in the real world for TBI survivors and their partners (Bracy and Douglas, 1997). All of us have had moments in which we have misread a social cue and committed a *faux pas* as a result. This can result in considerable anguish, particularly if offence has been caused to another party, or if we have lost face ourselves – it can be very difficult to repair such tears in the social fabric, and indeed doing so often requires a high level of interpersonal skill. For people who have survived TBI, however, such tears can be regular occurrences, and friendships and other social contacts fall away as a consequence. The person him/herself may, however, not make the link between changes in communication behaviour and the loss of social networks.

Reading emotions from facial expressions and tone of voice

An important component skill in perceiving and processing intended speaker meaning is the ability to "read" the emotions behind the sometimes subtle changes in facial expression and tone of voice that occur during conversational interactions. Children who have difficulties making these inferences about another's emotional state receive lower "likeability" scores from their peers than children who do this with ease, and by as early as three years, will be rated as "least liked" by their peers (see Ford and Milosky, 2008 for review). Further compounding their communication difficulties, when children with language impairments make inferencing errors, these tend to be across broad emotional categories, e.g. confusing happy for angry. Ford and Milosky's finding that emotional inferencing skills in pre-school children were strongly predicted by their language skills raises interesting questions about the relationship between these constructs in the adult survivor of TBI. Watts and Douglas (2006), for example, found that facial recognition scores correlated significantly with close-other ratings on the La Trobe Communication Questionnaire (LCQ) (Douglas, O'Flaherty, and Snow, 2000 – see later in this chapter), and Spell and Frank (2000) showed significant associations between difficulties discerning emotion via the auditory channel and performance on a functional measure of communication skill (the American Speech Language Hearing Association Functional Assessment of Communication; ASHA-FACS) (Frattali, Thompson, Holland, Wohl, and Ferketic, 1995). Such findings indicate that recognition of emotional states via both facial expression and prosodic cues are foundational everyday communication skills that need to be closely considered in rehabilitation settings.

TBI can interfere with the ability to process information about affect that is conveyed through changes in facial expression (e.g. Jackson and Moffat, 1987; McDonald, 2005; Prigatano and Pribram, 1982; Spell and Frank, 2000; Watts and Douglas, 2006). However, in assessment situations, the injured person may be shown static stimuli which lack the dynamic movements that contain important additional information. Such images also enable an artificially prolonged exposure to the stimulus. Further, a number of workers have noted that in real life, shifts in a speaker's affective state that are signalled by changes in facial expression are generally accompanied by information that is transmitted simultaneously via the *auditory* channel, for example, changes in speaker volume, rate and intonational contour. It might be expected that this auditory input would provide important contextual information to augment visual information and assist in the processing required to infer the speaker's emotional state. However, there is evidence suggesting that some TBI speakers have *more* difficulty with the dual processing task of managing visual and auditory information simultaneously, as per real life interactions, and a subgroup of people with TBI seems to be particularly poor at decoding affective state from prosodic information alone (McDonald and Saunders, 2005). Not surprisingly, the intensity with which the emotion is depicted also seems to be important, such that low intensity stimuli are more sensitive to the effects of TBI than are high intensity stimuli (Spell and Frank, 2000). This means that in rehabilitation settings, consideration needs to be given not only to addressing recognition of clear depictions of emotion, but also to making decisions about images that may be ambiguous, for example, requiring differentiation between confusion versus annoyance.

In this section, the importance of mentalising and social inferencing for everyday communicative success has been discussed, because so much of what transpires between speakers in everyday conversations is non-literal and/or incomplete. This means therefore that we need to "join the dots" (i.e. draw inferences) based on world knowledge, prior experience, and our reading of situational cues derived from facial expression, tone of voice, and *implied*, rather than stated, meaning. To do so, we must draw on prior knowledge and interpret both verbal and non-verbal cues to process both explicit and implicit meaning. These tasks need to be performed in a matter of milliseconds, while both processing input and formulating output.

Traditional language measures cannot capture these important skills, but new measures have been developed in recent years in an attempt to specifically assess various aspects of social cognition in the TBI speaker. Examples of these measures are discussed later in this chapter.

Conversational and narrative discourse skills

Moving now to the part of our communication iceberg that is above the surface (i.e. able to be observed and directly experienced by others), we need to consider the specific linguistic capabilities that contribute to communicative success.

Conversational skills

Box 5.1 summarises the key conversational discourse difficulties faced by people who have sustained TBI.

Box 5.1 Summary of common difficulties encountered with conversational discourse after TBI

- Problems thinking of things to talk about/ways to start and end a conversation.
- Difficulties organising and structuring one's own ideas into messages that meet listener needs with respect to level of conciseness, and amount of background information required.
- Difficulties maintaining topic focus and executing (and/or responding to) smooth changes in topics.
- A tendency to have difficulties with the rapid information processing demands of normal conversation, resulting in contributions that are delayed or slightly "off target".
- Difficulties conducting conversations in groups or against background noise.
- Difficulties using and understanding linguistic devices such as idiom, metaphor, sarcasm, and humour.
- A tendency to favour certain conversational topics/themes over others and to have difficulty "seeing" another perspective on a topic or making a mental shift from an existing perspective.
- Difficulties with word-finding, resulting in communicative attempts that may be circumlocutory, or marked by longer than normal pauses and hesitations.
- Difficulties inferring speaker intent when this is only indirectly stated.
- Difficulties recognising subtle affective shifts in the conversational partner.

In addition to conversation, we also need to tell (narrate) stories about our experiences, and explain how certain tasks are carried out, via the use of procedural discourse. There is considerably less research evidence on procedural discourse than on narrative discourse, though that which does exist (e.g. Snow et al., 1997) suggests the presence of difficulties in selecting and organising content for the orderly transfer of information to the listener. We will concern ourselves here with narrative discourse, because it has been relatively well studied and occupies a central role in forming and maintaining relationships.

Narrative discourse skills

Narrative discourse refers to the ability to share stories of one's own experiences, by organising and presenting information in a way that is both logical and coherent on the one hand, and interesting for the listener, on the other. Narrative competence begins to emerge in the early pre-school years, and develops in tandem with cognitive skills such as perspective taking, so that appropriate judgements are made about the listener's existing background knowledge. Providing too much, or too little, detail is damaging to the communication exchange, and can result in boredom, annoyance, and/or confusion for the communication partner. Although narrative skill has traditionally been examined in TBI speakers as a monologic skill, in everyday life, narrative production is more complex, because stories are often embedded in conversation. This means that turn-taking, repair, and other reciprocity rules need to be observed, and the speaker must deal with interruptions, and the need to "edit" content according to situational factors. Further, narratives are often co-constructed (e.g. two speakers who have shared a common experience may be relating this to a third party). Competent speakers can produce narratives both as a monologue (e.g. while giving a speech) and as part of a cooperative endeavour during conversation with one or more communication partners.

According to Stein and Glenn (1979), a well-developed narrative episode comprises up to seven logically sequenced story grammar elements: a setting, an initiating event, an internal response, a plan of action, an attempt at action, direct consequences of this action, and protagonists' reactions. It is important to note, though, that narrative form is culturally sensitive; these templates apply for speakers from many Western backgrounds but do not apply universally (Paul, 2007; Stadler and Ward, 2005). Dimensions on which cultures differ can include the degree of audience participation, and the extent to which the story has a single-topic focus, or ranges across a number of interwoven story threads.

Studies of narrative discourse ability following TBI (Coelho, Youse, Le, and Feinn, 2003; Hartley and Jensen, 1991; Jorgensen and Togher, 2009; Snow, Douglas, and Ponsford, 1999) have used a variety of elicitation techniques and stimulus tools (ranging from sharing an account of a holiday, to describing a structured series of sequentially arranged pictures). Narratives once elicited have also been analysed at a variety of levels, ranging from the T-unit (an independent clause and the elements dependent on it), through to productivity measures (e.g. total syllables), propositional analysis, cohesion analyses (global and linguistic), and story structure (e.g. Cannizzaro and Coelho, 2002). There has also been some examination of skill in story generation versus story re-telling, in order to explore the relative cognitive load in different types of narrative tasks (e.g. Coelho, 2002). Although these studies have suggested reduced communicative efficiency and cohesion in the narratives of TBI speakers, it must be remembered that these have largely been elicited as monologues, under experimental conditions. Such conditions do not enable examination of the role of the communication partner in co-constructing a story, nor do they take into account demands on information processing and working memory in situations where there are overlapping utterances between speakers. Further research which looks at narrative discourse under conditions of cognitive load is therefore needed.

In this section, a wide range of factors, existing both below and above "the surface", that contribute to communicative competence have been considered. In addition to the well-documented patterns of executive function and discourse impairment that occur after TBI, it is important to consider also the sociolinguistic profile of the speaker. This reflects demographic factors such as age, gender, education level, cultural background, and occupational standing and will be discussed further in the following section, in which assessment of communication competence following TBI is considered.

Assessing communicative competence: A "top down" approach

Traditionally, assessment of communication following TBI was based on a "bottom up" deficit model, i.e. the patient performed a variety of discrete, mainly microlinguistic tasks, and test or profile responses falling short of a pre-determined norm were indicative of neurogenic "cognitive-communicative" impairment. Important oversights in this approach, however, were firstly the patient's premorbid communicative style and skills, and secondly the acontextual way in which communicative competence was assessed. Both issues will be considered in this section.

By comparing the communication skills of TBI speakers with those of patients from similar sociolinguistic backgrounds who had sustained orthopaedic, rather than brain, injuries, Snow, Douglas and Ponsford (1995; 1997) showed that many apparent "deficits" in communication after TBI may simply reflect the range of normal communication behaviours present in the wider community. Normal communication contains many false starts and minor "errors" and revisions that do not significantly interfere with transmission of ideas between speakers, and do not cause significant breakdown in the interaction, or loss of face for the communication partners. What SLP assessment needs to be sensitive to, then, is *changes* in communication competence post-, as compared to pre-injury, not variants that are within normal limits from a sociolinguistic perspective. Snow et al. found that behaviours of concern in conversation may occur with relatively low frequency, but have a disproportionately negative impact on a communicative exchange, for example, poorly signalled topic changes, inadvertently providing information that is factually incorrect, and providing information in a manner that is confusing and difficult for the listener to follow. Such behaviours are less likely to show up on structured assessment of linguistic micro-skills, but conspire to reduce the satisfaction of communicating with the TBI speaker and are likely to be linked to a dilution of social networks over time (Snow, Douglas, and Ponsford, 1998).

Further, if assessment of communication skills occurs only in a quiet office setting, placing minimal cognitive demands on the person, factors such as concentration, information processing, working memory, idea generation, planning and organisation of verbal output, and self-monitoring ability do not come into play in the way they do during everyday conversation. Assessment in a quiet setting may enhance the reliability of discourse sampling over time, but does little to tax the cognitive and linguistic processes which will be called into play in the real world. SLPs need to directly observe the speaker in real world contexts, rather than eliminate contextual features, or attempt to replicate these in the clinic setting. If this is not done, errors in clinical decision-making will occur.

Administering selected tests designed to evaluate language processing and production skills is important to ensure that underlying, linguistically based deficits (such as word finding problems) are not overlooked in rehabilitation. There is a risk, however, that the inherent structure in this type of testing serves to *obscure*, rather than highlight, communicative difficulties, because language is assessed not as a tool of interaction, but as a collection of discrete skills, such as naming, repetition, or answering largely decontextualised yes/no questions. Indeed, many of the items in these tests require the individual to perform tasks rarely (if ever) performed in the real world, whilst failing to assess the verbal skills the individual is almost certain to require outside the hospital setting.

In order to capture and understand the range and complexity of communication changes that can occur following TBI, clinicians need to employ a flexible, individualised approach to assessment, formulating and testing clinical hypotheses in a systematic fashion. Performing a communication "needs analysis" is a good starting point, that is, finding out what communication demands (spoken and written) this particular person needs to be able to manage, and identifying skill gaps as a basis for determining treatment goals. For example, a trainee chef may be able to successfully deal with a range of graduated clinic-based reading comprehension tasks but be unable to cope with reading instructions in a noisy commercial kitchen. The SLP, in conjunction with other team members, needs to present tasks of immediate relevance (i.e. high face validity) to the individual. Enhancing the ecological validity of rehabilitation promotes engagement and helps staff to determine which cognitive and/or linguistic factors need to be addressed in therapy. Psychometrically based language testing must be aimed at identifying and understanding discourse-level difficulties, and help identify ways of addressing these in therapy.

An important principle in assessing communication skills post-TBI is *triangulation* – the use of multiple data sources and collection tools, to promote the validity and reliability of sampling. In the case of the TBI speaker, this could include structured testing, use of behavioural rating scales, and self and close-other report. Areas of congruence in the data suggest higher validity for the targeting of intervention goals. Above all, an understanding of the cultural, linguistic, cognitive, and social cognition factors that underlie everyday communication difficulties and residual strengths will facilitate the design of individually tailored intervention goals and strategies.

Conversational assessment

Conversation forms the "glue" of everyday interpersonal relationships. It is frequent and pervasive, yet ever-changing, according to a variety of contextual factors. This makes it highly elusive to rigorous assessment and modification. The challenge in assessing conversation lies in doing so in contextually meaningful ways, without interfering with/distorting the very phenomenon under study. Approaches that rely on longhand transcription are not practical in the clinical setting, but clinicians still require tools that allow them to validly and reliably capture discourse behaviours that both uniquely reflect the effects of the person's TBI rather than their premorbid sociolinguistic style, and interfere with communicative success. The focus of assessment should be community re-entry, notably maintaining existing relationships and forming new ones, across a variety of personal, social, educational, vocational, and community domains.

When conversation assessment is carried out in a clinical setting, it has essentially been stripped of any relevance to social roles the person aspires to resume, such as employee, student, or spouse. Further, only limited forms of reinforcement can be provided in a clinical setting, where the interaction is more a semi-structured interview than a conversation. In the real world, reinforcement comes in many guises, overt and covert. These include attention, agreement, shared speaking time, and mutual enjoyment of the topic under discussion. In this sense, pragmatic assessment is guilty of many of the same "relevance crimes" as structured language assessment. A further problem with pragmatic tools is that overall scores may be similar, but qualitatively, the underlying problems identified may vary quite markedly.

Recent developments in discourse assessment following TBI have rightly emphasised the role of the communication partner, contextual features of the interaction, and the need to individualise both assessment and treatment around the particular types of communication exchanges a person needs to master to effect community re-entry. A small selection of more recently developed approaches and tools will be reviewed here.

The work of twentieth-century philosopher of language Paul Grice (1975, 1998) has been highly influential in the assessment of pragmatics/social skill after TBI. Grice postulated that effective conversation is guided by interactants' observance of rules ("maxims") pertaining to the quantity, quality, relation and manner of their discourse. A number of instruments reviewed below stem from Grice's (1975) *Cooperative Principle of Conversation.*

The Profile of Functional Impairment in Communication (PFIC) (Linscott, Knight, and Godfrey, 1997)

Linscott et al. expanded Grice's maxims in an elaborated model of conversation, deriving 10 feature summary scales encompassing specific aspects of communication that are typically impacted by TBI (e.g. logical content, clarity of expression, social style and aesthetics), with 84 specific behaviour items. Each summary scale yields a 5-point summary score ranging from zero ("normal") to 5 ("very severely impaired"). Dahlberg et al. (2006) used the PFIC to explore associations between social-communication skills and psychosocial adjustment. They found that while agreement between the injured person and a significant other about changes in social-communication skill was generally poor, the areas of difficulty identified by clinicians using the PFIC reflected difficulties identified by the TBI speakers (e.g. problems keeping a conversation going, knowing how to end a conversation and/or change topics, and keeping thoughts organised). These findings lend support to the use of the PFIC as a valid clinical tool for identifying treatment priorities. Further research about its sensitivity to clinically meaningful change over time is needed.

The Social Performance Survey Schedule (SPSS) (Lowe and Cautela, 1978)

Recently, Long, McDonald, Tate, Togher and Bornhofen (2008) examined the validity of the SPSS in the assessment of speakers who have sustained TBI. The SPSS is a 100-item questionnaire, on which social competence variables are rated on a 5-point Likert scale. Fifty of the items concern positive (prosocial) behaviours, and 50 negative (antisocial) behaviours. Long et al. found that the positive behaviours scale showed discriminant validity between TBI speakers and non-injured counterparts, but the negative scale did not. They noted that this may reflect the relative lack of positive communication behaviours, rather than the excessive presence of overtly negative behaviours following TBI.

The La Trobe Communication Questionnaire (LCQ)

This tool was developed by Douglas and co-workers (Douglas, Bracy, and Snow, 2007b, 2007a; Douglas et al., 2000) and is a 30-item instrument that has two forms – Form S (self), to be completed by the injured person, and Form O, to be completed by a nominated close other – someone who knew the patient well before the injury and continues to have close contact with him/her following the injury. Most LCQ items are drawn from Grice's (1975, 1998) *Co-operative Principle* of conversation, but additional items pertain to communication behaviours likely to stem from cognitive impairment following TBI, e.g. "Lose track of conversation in noisy places" pertains to distractibility, and "Get side-tracked by irrelevant parts of the conversation" pertains to tangentiality. The factor structure of the LCQ has been described by Douglas et al. (2007a) and by Struchen and co-workers (2008).

The LCQ differs from other SLP measures in a number of ways. Most importantly, it positions the person with TBI and his/her close other as the experts and provides them with a tool to inform the SLP about which communication behaviours have/have not changed following the injury. This is a marked deviation from the tradition of the clinician being the expert, who, following a series of tests, informs the patient and family about the deficits caused by the injury. In this way, the LCQ provides a vehicle for transparently identifying behaviours of concern and fostering three-way discussion (patient, close other and SLP) about setting treatment priorities and identifying meaningful measures of change over time.

In recent years, the growing awareness of the need to specifically measure social cognition skills after TBI has led to the development of specific tools for this purpose. Some examples are briefly reviewed below.

The Awareness of Social Inference Test (TASIT) (McDonald et al., 2006)

This is an audiovisual tool for assessing aspects of social cognition in adults. It comprises three subtests: emotion recognition and two levels of social inferencing ("minimal" and "enriched"), using standardised video vignettes. *Social Inference – Minimal* requires differentiation between sincerity and sarcasm, as well as the ability to deal with paradox. *Social Inferences – Enriched* requires the differentiation between diplomatic lies and sarcasm. McDonald et al. found the TASIT to be valid and reliable for assessing social cognition in a sample of 116 adults with severe TBI (PTA > one day) who were known, on clinical grounds, to have difficulties with social-emotional functioning. Test performances showed minimal practice effects over one week, and scores correlated with neuropsychological measures of speed of information processing, working memory, new learning, and executive functioning. The TASIT takes a little over an hour to administer and could assist in delineating social-emotional inferencing difficulties, and arriving at intervention goals and strategies.

The Video Social Inference Test (VSIT) (Turkstra, 2008)

This measure of social inferencing moves beyond the domains included in the TASIT, to look at inferencing about another's mental state during a social interaction and decisions/predictions regarding future behaviour. In this way, the VSIT seeks to closely replicate the information processing and working memory demands of everyday social interactions, in which reactions are based on responses drawn from rapidly formulated hypotheses about another person's state of mind. All 16 vignettes depict interactions between peers in social interactions in a quiet room. Participants in Turkstra's study were required to make a mental state inference based on the interaction observed and then, keeping this inference in mind, provide an explanation or make a prediction about interactants' behaviour.

Using the principles of the REAL approach to improve communicative competence

The following section summarises suggested strategies for dealing with some of the more common communication problems associated with TBI. For ease of organisation, the information in this section is presented under the headings guiding principles, behavioural/social learning principles and examples of specific approaches. These strategies, and the literature that discusses them, are elaborated further in the remainder of this chapter.

Guiding principles

- Position the patient and family as the experts.
- Engage communication partners as members of the therapy team as early as possible in the rehabilitation process.
- Respect individual differences with regard to premorbid communicative competence, the relative importance of communication skills to this person, at this point in time, and cultural factors that impact on communication.
- Provide relevant education to the injured person and close others about ways in which communication can be affected by TBI, and links between executive dysfunction and communication competence.
- Encourage and assist the person with TBI to develop self-coaching metaphors/analogies that are personally meaningful in order to strengthen communication skills.
- Ensure that intervention goals are derived from triangulated assessment data, taking into account self and close-other report, a needs analysis, performance on structured tests, and observation of the injured person in a range of communicative contexts.
- Use a range of measures that can monitor and gauge change over time.
- Identify and work from strengths.

- Be mindful of the relative importance of impairments, and activity and participation limitations, and target intervention efforts strategically according to the individual's needs at a given time.
- Use treatment materials and approaches that are respectful of the person's age, gender, socio-cultural background, and level of education.

Behavioural/social learning principles

- Provide opportunities for social exchange that are enjoyable, meaningful and motivating to the person concerned.
- Employ specific behavioural approaches, such as modelling, shaping/successive approximation, graded practice/exposure, fading of cues, breaking complex activities down into step-by-step tasks, social reinforcement.
- Provide feedback that is prompt, economical, respectful, and facilitates success on the next attempt.
- Provide opportunities for self-evaluation and self-monitoring.
- Monitor change over time in ways that are meaningful to the injured person.
- Help the injured person to develop self-cuing strategies for specific situations/contexts.

Specific approaches

- Incorporate specific input on perceiving and interpreting social cues/affective states that are conveyed both non-verbally and verbally by other speakers e.g. by using static pictures or video-clips.
- Discuss real and hypothetical communication scenarios with respect to both verbal and non-verbal content – e.g. Why did Person A respond that way to Person B? What did Person B say that was a hint as to how they felt/what they wanted? What could Person A have done to change the outcome?
- Provide opportunities to de-brief on both successful and unsuccessful real-world encounters.
- Incorporate role-plays (scripted and spontaneous).
- Consider the complementary roles of both individual and group work (being mindful of group dynamics and the goals set for each individual).
- Provide training for communication partners in ways of promoting greater independence/success in communication.
- Use audio and video feedback to assist with self-review and self-appraisal.
- Teach tailored strategies for coping with conversation in large groups/noisy settings.
- Practise specific communicative tasks that the person would like to become more skilled/confident with, e.g.

- Starting/ending conversations
- Repairing mis-communication
- Changing/introducing topics
- Making requests
- Seeking information
- Giving and receiving feedback
- Being assertive
- Narrating stories
- Giving instructions
- Following instructions
- Effective listening
- Dealing with challenging communication environments (e.g. talking in crowds or other noisy settings).

Addressing communication problems in context

Communication, by its very nature, is context bound. The medium (spoken vs written or gestured), the purpose (social, commercial, educational, etc.), the nature of the relationship between the partners (equal–unequal, familiar–unfamiliar, friendly–hostile), all interact to shape the way in which topics will be introduced, negotiated, repaired, changed, and terminated. Behaviours which are appropriate in one context (e.g. being at home with family members), will not be appropriate in others (e.g. being in a meeting at work), and great social cost is incurred when we fail to read shifts in contextual cues and adjust communication behaviour accordingly. An inherent challenge, therefore, in rehabilitating communication competence is the fact that a defined set of consistent rules cannot simply be over-learnt and safely applied in a range of settings. Coupled with the notorious lack of generalisation that occurs from one learning context to another after TBI, this means target skills need to be carefully identified by the clinician in consultation with patient and family, and then tackled *in vivo*.

Recent thinking on communication rehabilitation after TBI (e.g. Bellon and Rees, 2006; Dahlberg et al., 2007; McDonald, 2000; Togher, 2000; Ylvisaker, 2003; Ylvisaker, Jacobs, and Feeney, 2003) highlights the importance of facilitating the learning of meaningful skills in meaningful social contexts. In the 1980s and 1990s, it was hoped that isolating and targeting component microlinguistic skills (e.g. word-finding, selective attention, listening comprehension) would result in improved macrolinguisitic performance, across a range of communication contexts. What is much clearer now, is that generalisation of skills acquired in a therapy context to a "real world" context (with all the unpredictability and variability that this entails) is both weak and sporadic. In reviewing over 100 years of learning research, Ylvisaker (2003) has reminded us that even under optimal circumstances (in particular in the absence of a brain injury) transfer of knowledge or skills acquired in one setting to another is disappointingly low.

Promoting communicative competence after TBI means creating opportunities for interaction with a range of communication partners, and re-learning a range of communicative skills (requesting, informing, narrating, questioning, debating, joking, etc.), with the benefit of appropriate partner scaffolding and opportunities for success.

Struchen (2005) observed that many of the TBI intervention approaches traditionally employed by SLPs (e.g. shaping, successive approximation, fading of cues) were borrowed and adapted from related behavioural intervention fields, such as social skill development for people with learning/intellectual disabilities or schizophrenia. These approaches have typically been employed in decontextualised settings, using conversational topics selected and (largely) controlled by the other speaker, and with interactants who are not everyday communication partners (e.g. clinicians). Although there is evidence that the use of specific behavioural approaches can effect change, at least in the short term, issues such as transfer to personally meaningful contexts and long-term maintenance of gains remain ongoing challenges requiring vigorous research. Struchen has provided a useful summary and critique of intervention studies on communication impairment post TBI since the late 1970s. Behavioural approaches probably lend themselves better to the amelioration of specific, discrete deficits and, in that sense, may have direct applicability with more severely injured survivors in whom there are clearly identified behaviours that need to *increase* in frequency (e.g. use of social greetings) or *decrease*, e.g. socially inappropriate language such as swearing.

In reviewing and critiquing social skills training approaches, Ylvisaker (2006, p. 248) observed that "Despite their apparently compelling logic, these programs have been disappointing in their effects for most of the studied populations." The absence of a corpus of robust, well-controlled intervention studies on communication skills post-TBI, together with an increased emphasis on social models of disability, means that these behavioural approaches are no longer the mainstay of rehabilitation. Instead, they are being gradually replaced with more person-centred and ecologically valid approaches that empower the speaker and communication partners to foster everyday communicative success in ways that are personally relevant and rewarding.

Addressing communication in relation to the roles the person wishes to resume means that generalisation is not a postscript to intervention, rather it is the focus from the outset – what Ylvisaker (2006) referred to as a reversal of the traditional emphasis on "impairment-first, participation-later" approaches to rehabilitation. This approach also overcomes TBI survivors' often justified lament that therapy tasks bear little resemblance to situations they face in the real world. Ylvisaker stressed the importance of promoting a robust "sense of self" in the TBI survivor and, to that end, argued for the use of individualised "self-coaching" as a metaphor for self-regulation. In considering the absence of a strong body of literature identifying specific theoretical paradigms/clinical approaches for addressing communication impairment post TBI, Ylvisaker looked closely at the one study identified in Struchen's (2005) systematic review which did provide Level 1 evidence of treatment efficacy. This study, by Helffenstein and Wechsler (1982), emphasised structured review of videotaped interactions, development of alternative scripts, modelling, and guided rehearsal, with control of the "coaching" process being gradually shifted from the clinician to the TBI survivor. Importantly, they showed that not only did communication skills improve (as judged by various observers), but these individuals experienced fewer anxiety symptoms in social situations than controls who did not receive this intervention.

Having employed a range of formal assessment approaches (see Table 5.1) to identify specific linguistic difficulties, and informal measures which inform the development of valid treatment goals, a therapeutic alliance needs to be established between the clinician and TBI speaker. As with all forms of therapeutic relationships, a high degree of warmth, rapport and trust is needed, particularly as a basis for discussion of delicate matters such as interpersonal skills.

It is important that clinicians discuss assessment findings in a spirit of two-way information sharing, problem solving and goal setting. All therapy tasks should have relevance and face validity to the patient, and therapy needs to take place outside the clinic room via a range of real-world exchanges. All activities should be linked to short and long term goals that have been decided on in consultation with the patient and are regularly revisited in the same way.

People who have survived TBI need repeated opportunities to practise and master new skills – in many cases this need goes well beyond the one or two hours a week typically offered in the context of postacute rehabilitation programmes. Just as interpersonal competence is refined over many years of repeated practice, social learning, scaffolding from communication partners, and increasing task complexity during typical development, its rehabilitation requires intensive and sustained opportunities to rehearse and practise skills, ideally with gradually reducing amounts of scaffolding from the communication partner. Working with communication partners in settings that are both relevant and rewarding for the person is central, therefore, to maximising skills that foster, rather than fracture, relationships in the longer term. This important focus is discussed further below.

Working with communication partners in rehabilitation

As noted throughout this chapter, communication skills must, by their very nature, be used in the context of engagement with others. Given the difficulties that TBI survivors often have in being motivated by/benefitting from isolated practice in decontextualised and largely "manufactured" interactions, it makes sense to locate intervention efforts in dyadic interactions that are personally relevant. The argument for this type of approach is further strengthened by the growing evidence (e.g. Dahlberg et al., 2006; Douglas et al., 2007b; Struchen et al., 2008) that both TBI speakers and their close others can readily identify communication behaviours that are problematic in the real world. Ylvisaker and other workers (e.g. Body and Parker, 2005; Goldblum and Alant, 2008; Togher, McDonald, Code, and Grant, 2004) have emphasised the importance of providing specific training to communication partners who have various relationships with the injured speaker – ranging from, but not restricted to, close others (partners, siblings, parents, friends) through to service personnel.

Togher and co-workers (2004) point out that service encounters constitute a significant proportion of everyday communication exchanges, hence their success should foster greater self-efficacy for the TBI survivor in the community, and help to remove barriers to community engagement. They have shown that police can be trained to utilise strategies that promote more efficient telephone interactions with TBI speakers, thus hopefully producing greater communication satisfaction for both parties. Togher et al. also proposed that a variety of communication partners should be included directly in rehabilitation, with consideration of factors such as the power (im)balance between speakers, situational variables, and the degree of familiarity between the parties. Body and Parker (2005) showed that a problem such as topic repetitiveness could be successfully ameliorated by "re-allocating" some of the responsibility for the behaviour to communication partners, and empowering them with specific frameworks and strategies to reduce its negative impact on the exchange. Similar success in engaging communication partners was described by Jorgensen and Togher (2009). These workers found that TBI speakers performed significantly more poorly on monologic narrative tasks than on narratives which were co-constructed with a friend. This finding highlights the importance of identifying strategies and contexts that promote success in the real world. While TBI speakers stand to benefit from the "scaffolding" effect of a friend co-narrating an account of a joint experience, it must nevertheless be noted that in some circumstances speakers must be able to "speak for themselves" and co-narration is actively discouraged (e.g. in police interviews) or not available (e.g. in job interviews).

Understandably, TBI survivors are sometimes very focused on physical goals, such as walking, in the earlier stages of their rehabilitation, and can see little relevance in improving communication skills (particularly where these seem adequate for current day-to-day purposes). With the passage of time, however, these individuals frequently realise that subtle changes in communication affect them in the important social roles or relationships which they are attempting to resume. At this time, they may become receptive to (or actively seek) assistance with communication. For this reason, it is unwise to urge or cajole people to accept therapy for which they are not ready. A negative experience in the early stages may cause reluctance to participate in intervention later on. It is vital that funding bodies also recognise that timing is critical and are flexible in providing support to people whose readiness for therapy may evolve over time.

In addition to assisting the speaker to develop an individualised self-coaching metaphor (as discussed by Ylvisaker, 2006) to increase self-efficacy for communication, clinicians can draw on published communication resources such as *Communicate with Confidence* (Sloan, Mackie, and Chamberlain, 2006). This workbook outlines approaches underpinned by the philosophical stance that *everyone* (regardless of the presence of a TBI) can benefit from some reflection on and refinement of their everyday communication skills, as a basis for improved relationships. *Communicate with Confidence* provides structured listening and talking activities that break complex everyday communication exchanges down into skills that can be rehearsed and evaluated. This workbook goes beyond the basics of social greetings and starting and ending conversations, to take in identifying and responding to emotion words in a communication partner's tone. It promotes experiential learning and also specifically addresses a number of interpersonal behaviours that can be socially damaging, and provides opportunities to identify and practise repair strategies.

People who have difficulties processing information about speaker affective state may need specific assistance identifying and labelling emotions associated with particular facial expressions and tone of voice. Working with good quality, contemporary still images may be appropriate in the first instance, but there should be a progression to dynamic images, with and without audio, depending on which modalities an individual patient seems to struggle with. Some people will also require particular assistance decoding affective information conveyed via tone of voice, e.g. if their work requires significant telephone use.

Whilst it is always important that feedback (verbal, graphic, videotape) be provided to the TBI speaker and family by the therapist, it is also essential to create opportunities for them to give feedback to therapy staff. This can be done informally, via regular discussions and semi-structured interviews. TBI speakers may need assistance evaluating their own performance, for example using rating scales and checklists devised with the therapist's assistance. Clinicians need to promote shared commitment to solution-focused approaches to achieving communication competence. Family members may spend vast amounts of time with the person, and so are well placed to comment about communication skills in a range of settings. They are also frequently resourceful and innovative in suggesting approaches to overcoming difficulties. Discussions with the person and family members often indicate how realistic particular approaches are, in relation to the other constraints they face. Finally, consulting with all parties in this way promotes shared ownership for the outcomes of intervention, and provides a milieu in which decisions regarding current and future intervention efforts can be made with flexibility, ease, and trust.

In assessing the extent to which a person is handicapped by communication difficulties, it is also important to consider the role of motor speech disturbance. Dysarthria frequently results not only in compromised speech intelligibility, but also in reduced speech rate, and inadequate volume. These features will compromise independence in social interaction, particularly with unfamiliar listeners, or in situations where there is even only moderate background noise. Impaired speech intelligibility may lead to assumptions that the person is intoxicated or intellectually impaired, thus restricting the range of social, recreational, educational, and vocational options available. Even where this does not occur, the presence of dysarthria requires greater patience and perseverance on the part of the listener, and in many situations these are not forthcoming. Clinicians need to spend time with communication partners, to develop strategies that optimise success and reduce the frustration and isolation that results from thwarted communication attempts. Use of assistive and augmentative communication approaches should be explored where appropriate. Dysarthria is also commonly associated with eating and swallowing difficulties, which can further impede the person's attempts at social re-integration after TBI. Detailed information on the assessment and management of motor speech disorders after TBI is provided by Yorkston, Beukelman, Strand and Hakel (2010).

The academic and social aspects of return to study (at all levels) are particularly reliant on a range of language-related skills. Academically, these include reading comprehension, note-taking, ability to develop arguments clearly and logically, ability to summarise written and verbal arguments, and ability to understand shades of meaning. Social skills that foster successful return to study include the ability to form and maintain friendships through conversational competence – showing interest in and awareness of others, good topic management skills, and the ability to operate at a range of abstract levels, such as humour, metaphor, and analogy. Increasingly, undergraduate university programmes make use of group-based assignments, so the ability to work and negotiate in a team, and to organise oneself to meet deadlines will be critical to academic success. Whilst some of these skills can be assessed via clinic-based measures, many need to be monitored in the actual context of return to study. As outlined in Chapters 7 and 10, team members will need to liaise closely with teaching staff, in order to determine individual strengths and weaknesses in using language in this way. Clinicians can then provide specific strategies and practice on tasks which are challenging. For further information about return to study after TBI, see Kennedy, Krause and Turkstra (2008a) and Chapters 7 and 10 of this volume.

All intervention needs to be subject to ongoing evaluation in terms of its relevance to specific skills the individual requires, and the extent to which these are being developed. Whilst re-assessment on structured testing at regular intervals is an important aspect of monitoring change, these tests frequently have ceiling and practice effects. Evaluation of the efficacy of therapy, therefore, must have communicative competence and social participation/role resumption as its focus. Just as intervention should be carried out in personally relevant settings, the extent to which the person has achieved and sustained specific communicative competencies needs to be assessed in everyday contexts. This can be done via observation of and interviews with the person and family members, and use of behavioural checklists and questionnaires. Continuous triangulation of assessment information enables ongoing modification to the treatment programme, in response to gains, and/or changes in the environment. They also provide a useful basis for discussion with family members and funding bodies about future therapy.

Case report – Tom*

Tom was 22 when he sustained a very severe TBI. Four years later, he was referred to Speech Pathology and Neuropsychology by his Case Manager after being asked to leave a woodworking group he had been attending for one year. Concerns identified by the woodwork instructor were verbal aggression towards group leaders and inappropriate social communication behaviours towards group participants.

Model for assessing and teaching social communication skills

Integrated social communication assessment and intervention was conducted by the Speech Language Pathologist and Neuropsychologist using the following model of practice (Sloan et al., 2006) (see Figure 5.2).

Assessment

Mapping of Tom's social network (see Sloan et al., 2006) indicated that he had a depleted social network and many of his weekly social contacts occurred in the context of the woodwork group. Maintaining successful participation in this group was identified as a goal of intervention. Tom had limited insight into his pragmatic communication difficulties but did identify that he was dissatisfied with his ability to engage in conversation and was troubled by his conflictual relationships with the woodwork instructors. He said his main goal was to have a girlfriend.

Tom's current greetings and behaviour within the woodwork group were assessed via secondary consultation with the woodwork instructors, discussion with Tom and also direct observation. It was noted that on arrival at the group, Tom spoke exclusively to the female group members. However, he did not typically greet them by saying "Hello", but instead would start by talking

* This case was kindly made available for use in this chapter by Sue Sloan and Jan Mackie. Sue and Jan's generosity in allowing it to be adapted for use here is gratefully acknowledged.

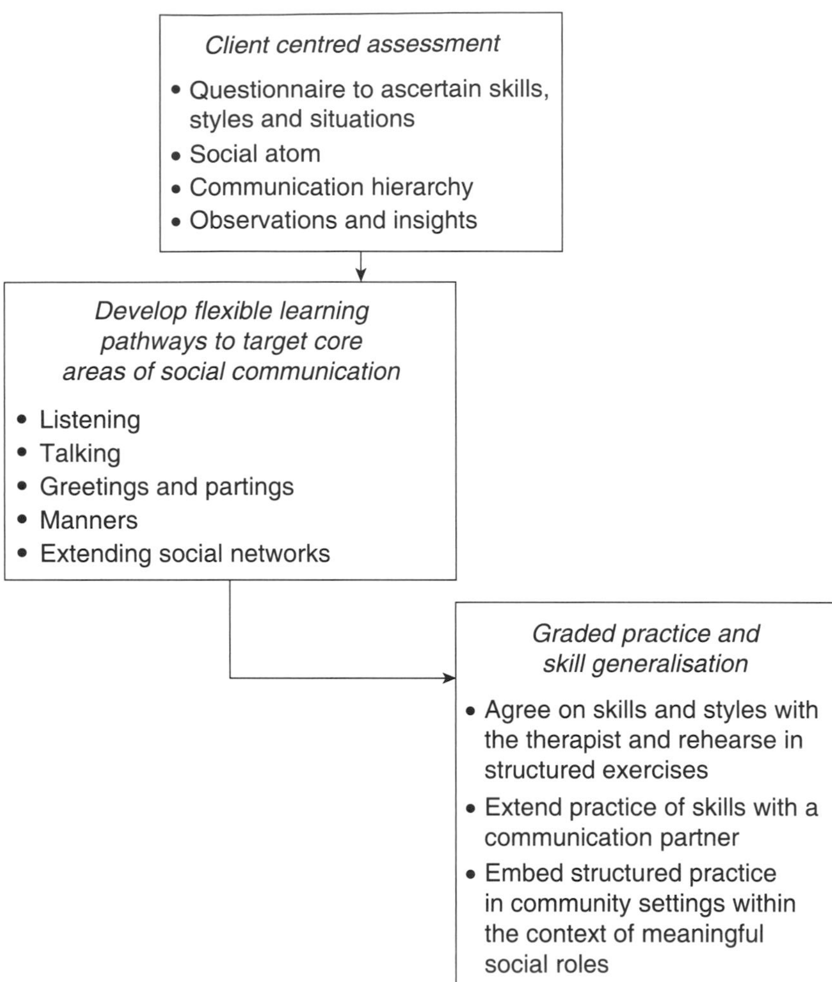

Figure 5.2 Model for assessing and teaching social communication skills (Sloan et al., 2006)

about himself without pausing. His monologue was peppered with personal comments directed at the women and occasionally he would ask an over-familiar question.

At this point staff would attempt to intervene in the interaction and provide Tom with feedback and re-direction. Their feedback centred on telling Tom *what not to do*, rather than *what to do* (e.g. "Don't talk about. . . .") and providing negative commentary on what he said (e.g. "No one is interested in . . ."). Their voice was raised and tone annoyed as they told him to move away and start working on his project. Tom's response to this feedback was to become argumentative and verbally abusive towards the instructors. He would also pick up objects close at hand and slam them down on the work bench. At these times he would storm outside, yelling negative comments about the group. In contrast to these episodes of challenging behaviour, there were days when his participation in the group was more appropriate. This coincided with attendance by a group member with whom he shared an interest in cars. On these days Tom would ignore the women and head straight towards his fellow woodworker and an animated conversation ensued.

The following issues were identified by the therapists:

- lack of suitable social greetings
- not showing general interest in others
- limited and overly personal topics of conversation
- escalating verbal aggression
- unhelpful feedback from instructors.

Intervention

Activities for learning social communication skills utilised the structured worksheets from the resource *Communicate with Confidence* (Sloan et al., 2006). Tom's SLP provided weekly assistance over a period of two months. The neuropsychologist liaised with the SLP and worked in a secondary consultation role with woodwork staff over the same time period.

Issue 1 Tom lacked suitable social greetings

Tom was assisted to reflect on his current greetings and the therapist helped him to explore, and agree on, a new greeting style. In therapy they practised friendly greetings and conversation starters and specifically planned suitable greetings for the woodwork group situation.

Issue 2 Tom did not show interest in others

Therapy focused on the role of listening in communication and Tom was supported to understand the impact of failing to show interest in others on his relationships with instructors and group members. He practised routines to prepare to listen which assisted in shifting his focus to showing interest in others, rather than being interested only in himself. Tom was assisted to establish a system of cue cards on which each group member's name was written and one or two key interests were recorded, as a basis for conversation. Also, Tom was taught non-verbal conversational skills that he could employ to show others that he was interested in them. These included the use of pauses to enable the communication partner to have an opportunity to respond.

Issue 3 Tom used limited and overly personal topics of conversation

A broader range of appropriate topics to talk about were indentified. In order to provide a concrete structure for Tom the topics areas were grouped in the following areas:

- himself, home and family
- his local community
- local and international current events.

Tom was encouraged to ensure his conversation had a balance between each of these topic areas and he was assisted to develop scripts to enable him to start these conversations with confidence. Further, it was identified that, pre-injury, Tom had a core repertoire of polite behaviours, upon which the therapist drew and highlighted as a residual strength. Structured intervention assisted Tom to refresh his use of social skills ("manners") to enable him to foster goodwill in the group situation. The fact that manners can be repeatedly used in a routine way assisted Tom's learning and his practice was further consolidated with a communication partner at home.

Issue 4 Escalating verbal aggression

Staff were assisted to monitor the effect of their own verbal and non-verbal behaviour on Tom's responses, and to keep their speaking volume and tone as friendly as possible, while finding appropriate activities to re-focus Tom's attention and assist him to engage in appropriate activities, e.g. by offering to assist him to locate the necessary materials to pick up from where he left off on the previous day.

Issue 5 Unhelpful feedback from instructors

In order to assist Tom to embed these skills in his role as a woodwork group participant, the instructors were trained to develop a feedback style that he would find both helpful and encouraging. They were assisted to identify key target skills to foster in Tom (e.g. "Let's start the day by saying "Hello" to each other"), concrete examples of *what to say*, rather than what not to say ("Maybe instead of asking if she has a boyfriend, you could ask if she enjoyed the movie the other night"), and to focus on positively reinforcing appropriate communication (e.g. "You've got really great manners Tom").

Outcome

Tom's challenging behaviours diminished and his attendance at the woodwork group was no longer under threat. He greets everyone in the group in a friendly way. He routinely starts a conversation by asking, "How are you?" and follows with a prepared question that focuses on the interests of each group member.

Tom accepts feedback that focuses on his communication strengths and shows no aggression towards group leaders. The group leaders also feel better equipped to deal with this behaviour in a solution-focused way, rather than seeing it as an automatic trigger for exclusion.

This case illustrates the central role played by communication competence in psychosocial outcome after TBI. Tom's difficulty in appropriately initiating conversations, reading cues, and responding to feedback threatened to remove his one social network, thereby creating severe social isolation and increasing his risk of depression, anxiety and/or substance abuse. A collaborative and solution-focused alliance with Tom and his communication partners averted this outcome.

Conclusion

Communication competence underpins a great deal of our everyday endeavours as human beings – our relationships, our work and study, and our ability to navigate our way through various service interactions all hinge on spoken and/or written communication skills. Given that the duration of formal, funded rehabilitation is continuing to decline, it will be increasingly important to maximise the person's engagement with the rehabilitation team. One way of doing this is to recruit friends and family early on in the rehabilitation process and equip them with skills and strategies that promote optimal communication. The evidence is clear that many people who have sustained severe TBI suffer from loneliness and social isolation in the long term, so a sense of interpersonal connectedness should be fostered from the earliest days of rehabilitation. Communication is the principal means by which we form and maintain relationships with others. Rewarding relationships, in turn, foster optimal adjustment and quality of life, and help to buffer against depression and maladaptive coping when other goals cannot be attained.

6 Assessment and management of behaviour problems

Jennie Ponsford

Introduction

One of the greatest sources of stress for those living and working with people who have sustained TBI is dealing with changes in behaviour. Whilst it must be acknowledged that those with TBI are all individuals, and may have displayed antisocial behaviour prior to injury, many outcome studies have shown that significant changes in behaviour and personality are common following TBI. The behavioural changes most frequently documented have been outlined in Chapter 1. They include the development of impulsivity, a low frustration tolerance, verbally threatening or physically aggressive behaviour, non-compliance, disinhibition, inappropriate or irresponsible social behaviour, self-centredness, leading to attention-seeking and/or manipulative behaviour, changes in emotional expression and, at the other end of the spectrum, reduced drive, initiative, and motivation, otherwise termed apathy (Dyer, Bell, McCann, and Rauch, 2006; Kelly, Brown, Todd, and Kremer, 2008; Ponsford et al., 1995a; Ylvisaker et al., 2007).

Such changes occur alone or in combination, and in widely varying degrees. In many instances they are also accompanied by a lack of insight on the part of the injured person, who may therefore fail to acknowledge or understand the differences others perceive. This can result in an unwillingness or inability to modify the difficult behaviour. Poor self-monitoring can mean that even when TBI individuals acknowledge the nature of behavioural difficulties and show a desire to do something to change the situation, they continue nevertheless to behave in the same manner.

There are also complex secondary reactions that emerge in response to the specific problems caused by the injury. For example, a hospitalised TBI individual may behave so inappropriately as to be avoided by staff, family and friends, thereby receiving much less attention. This may lead to the development of maladaptive attention-seeking behaviours, such as constantly screaming out, in order to gain attention. Alternatively, exhibiting aggression in response to pain caused by physiotherapy may result in withdrawal by the physiotherapist and removal of the aversive therapy. Exhibiting the same behaviour in subsequent sessions may enable the injured person to avoid painful therapy sessions. If left to continue without intervention, these behaviours may, in themselves, become part of the person's established behavioural repertoire. In many cases behavioural disturbances are transient, being frequently associated with the emergence from coma and post-traumatic amnesia (PTA) during the early stages of recovery (Brooke, Questad, Patterson, and Bashak, 1992; Sandel and Mysiw, 1996). Appropriate management of agitated behaviour during PTA, as suggested in Chapter 2, and careful management of the transition to a more comprehensive therapy programme following emergence from PTA will, in many cases, circumvent the development of more lasting problems.

Patients in or emerging from PTA are not generally able to cope with the demands of a therapy programme and may become agitated and combative if these are imposed on them (Lequerica et al., 2007). As discussed by Slifer and colleagues (1997), following emergence from PTA, it is very important to increase therapy demands gradually and to monitor the injured person's fatigue and agitation levels as therapeutic activities are introduced. This may be done objectively using the Agitated Behaviour Scale, developed by Corrigan and colleagues (Bogner, Corrigan, Bode, and Heinemann, 2000; Corrigan, 1989).

Ongoing behavioural problems are more likely to occur in those with more severe cognitive disturbances (Bogner, Corrigan, Fugate, Mysiw, and Clinochot, 2001) or as a result of the interaction between pre-injury and contextual issues. Behaviour problems, when severe, can potentially result in danger to the person who has sustained TBI and others, causing stress to hospital or rehabilitation staff and families. As a result, the TBI individual may receive less rehabilitation than required. They also represent major barriers to return to participation in community life, including employment (Winkler et al., 2006). Interventions to change behaviour should only be applied for these reasons. It is not acceptable to attempt to modify a person's behaviour just because it causes inconvenience or is slightly unusual.

If used for the right reasons, the application of appropriate behaviour management strategies can be an important part of the rehabilitation process following TBI. The emphasis of the first section of this chapter will be on dealing with behaviour problems which arise during the course of inpatient rehabilitation, followed by discussion of methods of managing severe behaviour disturbance in the community. There is further discussion of use of anger management strategies following return to the community in Chapter 8.

Education and involvement of staff and family

It is most important that staff, family, friends and others understand the basis of the changes in behaviour being observed following TBI. In particular, it needs to be conveyed that behavioural changes are frequently a direct result of the brain injury itself, occurring as a consequence of reduced tolerance of frustration and reduced control over impulsive, socially inappropriate or aggressive responses. The injured individual is more frequently confronted with frustration due to the presence of cognitive impairments affecting memory, attention and other functions. He or she may not have the capacity to recognise these changes, or to spontaneously modify behaviour. It is also important that staff understand the distinction between the person they are working with and that person's behaviour. Whilst a particular behaviour may be undesirable or offensive, it is not acceptable to generalise from this to make negative judgements about the whole person. Staff need to understand the individual's strengths, as well as weaknesses, and believe that there is some capacity to replace problem behaviours with more adaptive ones.

In the hospital or rehabilitation setting, agreed-upon strategies to address behavioural issues should be applied consistently by the entire treating team if they are to be effective. This means working together in attempting to understand the reasons for the injured person's behaviour, devising a plan for addressing the problem, consistently and cooperatively implementing the plan, checking its progress, making necessary adjustments, and assessing its effectiveness. Such involvement, which should also extend to the family and any others having frequent contact with the injured individual, will maximise the commitment of all team members and the family to the implementation of any procedures agreed upon.

It is also important that all members of the rehabilitation team adhere to an agreed-upon philosophy of managing behavioural issues. Where this is not the case the team co-ordinator should see that the assistance of an appropriately qualified psychologist is sought to provide staff with training and guidance. The application of principles such as those outlined below in daily interactions with TBI patients can in many instances circumvent the development of serious behaviour problems.

Assessment of behaviour problems

Objective recording

Careful assessment should precede attempts to deal with problematic behaviour. An accurate and objective picture of the behaviour in question is best obtained by observation and recording. In order to achieve a clear definition of the behaviour which is causing a problem, staff should be encouraged to record behaviour in observable terms, such as "David hit another patient with his fist", rather than "David had an aggressive outburst"; or "Peter touched the breasts of a female therapy aide", rather than "Peter exhibited inappropriate sexual behaviour". This clearly defines the behaviour of concern, helps to avoid the use of ambiguous terms, such as "aggressive" or "disinhibited", and ensures agreement as to the behaviour being documented.

Once such agreement has been reached, all instances of that behaviour should be recorded over a specified period, such as a day or a week, depending on the frequency with which the behaviour occurs, or by "time-sampling" (Wood, 1987). Time-sampling involves observation and recording of behaviour for specified periods of each day, the times being varied, so that over the period of recording behaviour is sampled across a 12-hour period. Recordings should be accompanied by information as to the time, the setting, the circumstances leading to the behaviour, and what followed. The circumstances should be viewed in the broad, as well as the immediate context. For example, the injured person may have been upset by having a full day of therapy activities or by some other event prior to the incident, such as the failure of a relative to visit. Understanding the antecedents to behaviour will provide many clues as to how to prevent it in future. In recording the consequences of the behaviour, it is important to consider the following:

- whether the person received a pleasant experience or obtained relief from an unpleasant experience as a result of the behaviour
- how people responded to the behaviour
- whether the person avoided doing something as a result of the behaviour
- whether the person obtained access to an activity or object after the behaviour
- what seemed to improve the behaviour, or make it stop? What made it worse?

Recording of the frequency with which the behaviour being modified is exhibited should continue throughout the management phase and for a period after the intervention has ceased.

Two measures have been developed for the purpose of documenting the nature and frequency of injury-related behavioural changes and evaluating interventions. Alderman and colleagues developed a modification of the Overt Aggression Scale (Yudofsky, Silver, Jackson, Endicott, and Williams, 1986), named the Overt Aggression Scale Modified for Neurorehabilitation Rehabilitation (OAS-MNR) (Alderman, Knight, and Morgan, 1997). This enables objective recording of categories of verbal and physical aggression against objects, self and people. It allows for documentation of its frequency and severity, on a four-point scale with verbal descriptors, also recording which of 18 antecedent events preceded the behaviour and which of 14 interventions were used in response to the behaviour. This scale, developed in the context of an inpatient psychiatric setting from brain injured individuals, has established validity and inter-rater reliability and has been shown to be sensitive to the impact of interventions (Alderman, Davies, Jones, and McDonnel, 1999). They have developed and validated a separate scale for recording challenging sexual behaviour – the St Andrew's Sexual Behaviour Assessment (SABA) (Knight et al., 2008).

In Australia, Kelly and colleagues (Kelly, Todd, Simpson, Kremer, and Martin, 2006) have developed a scale which measures a broader range of problem behaviours and is designed for measuring behaviour problems in community settings, termed the Overt Behaviour Scale (OBS). This scale comprises 34 items in nine categories that measure aggression, inappropriate sexual behaviour, perseveration, wandering, inappropriate social behaviour and lack of initiation. It documents the frequency, severity and impact of these behaviours. The OBS has been shown to be sensitive to change following intervention (Kelly et al., 2006).

Consideration of causative factors

There should be careful consideration of factors which may be contributing to the behaviour problem. As Eames (1988) has pointed out, a brain-injured individual's behaviour is the result of a complex interplay of causative factors. First, there are factors relating to the nature of the BRAIN INJURY. Whilst it is impossible to obtain an exact picture of the extent of damage to the brain following TBI, the results of CT and MRI studies, neurological examination and neuropsychological assessment can give some indication as to the nature and severity of injury, and the extent to which different functional systems having some bearing on behaviour may have been affected. For example, brainstem dysfunction may result in reduced alertness and consequent confusion. Injury to limbic structures, especially the amygdala, and the anterior temporal cortex may affect emotional expression and lead to unprovoked outbursts of anger. Damage to the frontal lobes is known to cause a general reduction in the regulation and control of behaviour, leading to a reduced frustration tolerance and impulse control, increased irritability and aggression, disinhibition and other inappropriate behaviour. Responses tend to be disproportionate to the precipitating circumstances. The frontal lobes also play a role in the processing of social information and in regulating social behaviour (Ylvisaker et al., 2007).

Second, there are factors relating to the PERSON who has sustained the brain injury. According to Eames (1988, p. 3), "the family, developmental, medical, psychiatric, and personal histories of the patient all contribute vulnerabilities and predispositions that are likely to be relevant to both the form and the content of any behaviour disorder". It is important to obtain a detailed picture of these aspects of the TBI person's background, including his/her premorbid personality, previous modes of emotional expression, personal and family psychiatric history, cultural background, and pre-injury life circumstances which may be influencing behavioural responses. Consideration of his/her developmental life stage is also relevant, particularly in children and adolescents.

Finally, it is important to consider the CONTEXT within which the disturbed behaviour is occurring. It may be that the level of noise or activity in the environment or the demands of therapy provoke fatigue and associated irritability or agitation. A recent study showed that the majority of aggressive outbursts were associated with demands coming from the environment (Rahman, Oliver, and Alderman, 2010). The experience of being cared for in a setting such as a hospital ward or a rehabilitation unit will almost certainly be unfamiliar and may be extremely threatening. When one has previously had control over one's life, it can be very difficult to accept help or take direction from others. The fact that the majority of those injured are male and the majority of those assisting in their recovery are female may add to this problem, as may the fact that TBI occurs so frequently in adolescence and early adulthood. People from a different cultural background, who may have differing beliefs about illness, injury and recovery may find the experience particularly difficult. In the longer term, it may be necessary to adapt to physical or cognitive limitations, greater dependency on others, a different living situation, a new daily routine or lack thereof, role changes, as well as the loss of the social network which existed prior to the injury. Such experiences undoubtedly contribute to the development of frustration, anger, depression and lack of motivation with associated emotional and behavioural changes.

Pharmacological treatment of behaviour problems

The vast majority of behaviour problems can and should be managed behaviourally or environmentally, particularly when these occur in the acute stages of recovery. In most instances, pharmacological treatment of behaviour problems should be used with TBI patients only after behavioural and environmental approaches have been tried and failed, because of the possibility of its diminishing impact on cognitive function and deleterious effects on recovery.

In many instances, the primary action of a pharmacological agent on one system has associated secondary effects on other systems, so that it is difficult to target a particular problem without influencing other aspects of the patient's functioning. Many TBI individuals experience problems with fatigue, arousal, attention, memory and initiation. Sedation and/or impairment of memory are common side-effects of medications used to control aggressive behaviour, such as major tranquillisers and benzodiazepines. Administration of these medications can exacerbate such problems, sometimes increasing confusion and prolonging agitation, and clouding cognitive recovery (Mysiw and Sandel, 1997). Other common side-effects of drugs used to treat behaviour problems can include a range of motor disturbances and changes in blood pressure. There is evidence that some major tranquillisers are epileptogenic (Cope, 1987). Animal studies have also suggested that they may slow recovery of brain function (Feeney et al., 1982; Hoffman et al., 2008; Kline et al., 2008). Findings from a retrospective study by Mysiw and colleagues (2006) indicate that neuroleptics and benzodiazepines continue to be administered to a significant proportion of patients in the acute stages of recovery and that individuals receiving these medications show longer PTA duration and poorer cognitive recovery than those who do not receive these medications.

Pharmacological intervention is inappropriate for TBI patients who are still in PTA, since their agitation is largely caused by confusion, which may be prolonged by the administration of medications. Pharmacological treatment may need to be considered, as an adjunct to other approaches, at a later stage, where recovery appears to be plateauing, where behavioural or environmental approaches have not been sufficiently successful, and where the behaviour problem, in most instances aggression, is compromising return to the community or long-term placement. The responsibility for prescribing medication should lie with a specialist in rehabilitation medicine or psychiatrist experienced in the management of TBI. As there have been few controlled trials examining the efficacy of pharmacological interventions in the treatment of patients with TBI, there are no diagnostic and treatment guidelines available. Thus great care needs to be exercised by the medical practitioner administering pharmacological treatment, both in commencing treatment and in weaning the TBI person off the medication. It is also very important to assess objectively the impact of the medication on the behaviour in question, using similar methods to those used for evaluating behavioural interventions, and to monitor side-effects.

Careful selection of medication is very important. According to a survey by Fugate and colleagues (1997), specialist physicians working in TBI rehabilitation most commonly prescribed carbamazepine, tricyclic anti-depressants, trazodone, amantadine, and beta blockers in that order for treatment of agitation, and avoided use of neuroleptics, such as haloperidol and benzodiazepines. Non-experts also used some of these medications but also reported using neuroleptics and benzodiazepines. According to an evidence-based review conducted by Warden and others (2006) the majority of studies examining the use of pharmacotherapy for aggression following TBI have significant methodological limitations, such that there was insufficient evident to support standards for treatment of aggression following TBI.

Evidence from their review and another by Fleminger and colleagues (2006) did support guidelines for the use of beta-adrenergic blocking medications, such as propranolol and pindolol for treatment of aggression in patients with TBI. Propranolol reportedly does not significantly alter cognitive function (Yudofsky, Williams, and Groman, 1981), and has been shown to reduce the intensity, but not the frequency of agitated behaviour in TBI subjects, when used in doses of 60 to 420 mg (Brooke, Patterson, Quested, Cardenas, and Farrel-Roberts, 1992). Yudofsky and colleagues (1990) recommend maintenance on the highest dose for eight weeks, prior to determining that the injured person is not responding to the medication. There are, however, some significant contra-indications to its use, including the presence of asthma, severe cardiopulmonary disease, severe diabetes and significant vascular disease (Yudofsky et al., 1990).

According to the review of Warden et al. (2006) other treatments recommended at the option level for aggression included methylphenidate, cranial electrical stimulation, homeopathy, serotonin reuptake inhibitors, valproate, lithium, tricyclic anti-depressants and busiprone. However, further controlled trials are required to further investigate these and other approaches.

Where aggression is thought to be epileptogenic, resulting from temporal lobe damage, an anticonvulsant may be appropriate. According to Warden et al. (2006) valproate and carbamazepine are the anticonvulsants which appear to have no detrimental effects on cognitive function and would therefore be recommended in such cases. Several studies involving single cases or case series have indicated a reduction in aggressive behaviour in patients taking valproate (Geracioti, 1994; Horne and Lindley, 1995; Wroblewski, Joseph, Kupfer, and Kalliel, 1997) and carbamazepine (Azouvi et al., 1999). However, as Fleminger and colleagues (2006) concluded, there have been no randomized controlled trials of the impact of these medications on aggression in individuals with TBI and thus there is no firm evidence that carbamazepine or valproate are effective in management of aggression or agitation following TBI.

Whilst aggression and other so-called behavioural excesses undoubtedly cause significant distress to treating staff and relatives, at the other end of the spectrum reduced drive and initiative or apathy can present a greater barrier to return to independent living and may not respond well to behavioural approaches. Pharmacological interventions used to reduce apathy, and enhance drive and initiative, include the dopaminergic agonists bromocriptine, L-dopa and pergolide, noradrenergic agonists such as desprimine and amitriptyline, and stimulants including amphetamine and methylphenidate (Kant and Smith-Seemiller, 2002; Marin, Fogel, Hawkins, Duffy, and Krupp, 1995; Reinhard, Whyte, and Sandel, 1996). All have had demonstrated effectiveness in single cases, but there have been no large controlled trials to justify any guidelines for management of these behavioural problems.

In cases where the behavioural disturbance is related to a pre-existing psychiatric condition the need for medication may be more pressing and appropriate, although care needs to be taken to establish that side-effects are not increased post-injury and the impact of the medication on cognitive function needs to be monitored. Although individuals with TBI may be more susceptible to medication side-effects there is not consistent evidence to indicate that this is the case (Warden et al., 2006). Whether TBI results in an increased risk of psychosis beyond the immediate post-acute phase of PTA, relative to that seen in the general population, remains to be clearly established, but such disturbances would require prompt pharmacological intervention. On the basis of several uncontrolled case studies, olanzapine has been recommended as a treatment option for psychosis following TBI (Warden et al., 2006).

Contextual approaches to behaviour problems

In many instances, a careful analysis of the context in which the problem behaviour is occurring can provide information which allows the behaviour to be prevented from occurring by changing the injured person's environment in some way. For example, it may be that agitation is precipitated by noise, the presence of too many people, therapy which is placing too many demands, frustration over an inability to communicate or simply fatigue. Confusion may be aggravated by moving the injured individual around the hospital. A mismatch between the demands of the environment and the skills and/or cognitive capacity of the injured person may lead to behavioural problems, including attention-seeking behaviour, aggression or withdrawal. It is frequently possible to reduce a problem significantly by removing precipitating environmental factors, which should become evident during the assessment period, or by providing appropriate environmental supports to reduce stress on the injured person. Such an approach is preferable to trying to alter the behaviour by changing its consequences. When assessing possible reasons for the development of behaviour problems it is also important to consider how comfortable and pleasant the environment is, how stimulating it is, and whether there is adequate privacy. Cultural issues may need to be considered. Additionally, there are issues particularly important in adolescence, such as body image, peer group influence and independence, which may be contributing to the difficulties. Where psychiatric disorder is identified appropriate treatment should be instituted.

Contingency management approaches

If contextual changes alone are insufficient to reduce the problem, it may be necessary to consider other approaches, such as contingency management, based on applied behavioural analysis. Social behaviour is shaped by environmental factors or responses. That is, an individual may be more or less likely to behave in a certain way in the future, depending on the response to that behaviour received in the past. TBI can result in a reduced ability to use feedback to judge the social appropriateness of behaviour. It may be necessary to introduce appropriate contingencies so that more adaptive behaviour can be relearned. Behaviour modification procedures are designed either to increase the probability of desirable behaviours, or to decrease the probability of undesirable behaviours, by altering responses or consequences of that behaviour. Given that many individuals with TBI have significant memory problems it is particularly important that such consequences are *meaningful* (that is, truly desirable/undesirable to the person), that they *immediately* follow the behaviour, and that they are given in an *obvious* way, so there is a clear association between the behaviour and its consequences. They should also be given *frequently* and *consistently* over an extended period, in order to consolidate the response. If the behaviour is not consistently followed by the chosen reinforcer, the problematic behaviour may reappear.

Ideally the reinforcement of behaviour should occur by the least intrusive possible means. The most desirable form of reinforcement in this context is *positive reinforcement*, which may take the form of social praise, encouragement or attention or, if that is insufficient, some material reward. Such rewards may be delivered via a token economy (Wood, 1984). *Negative reinforcement* involves the removal of something undesirable with the same goal. Methods used to decrease the probability of a given behaviour being exhibited again include *negative punishment* or *response cost*, where something desirable is removed, or *positive punishment*, where some undesirable consequence follows a behaviour.

Time-out is a technique used in the management of attention-seeking, aggressive or otherwise disruptive behaviour. This involves the removal of social reinforcement or attention. According to Wood (1984), Time-out-on-the-spot or "TOOTS" involves simply ignoring the undesirable behaviour, if necessary by averting one's gaze or walking away for a few seconds, without saying anything, then continuing the interaction as if nothing had happened. This is the most readily applicable. If this approach is unsuccessful, either because it is too difficult for staff to apply, or the behaviour is too disruptive, situational time-out may need to be applied. This involves physically removing the injured person from the situation, either putting them outside the door or in another room for a few minutes. Again, this should be done without interaction. If situational time-out fails or if there is violent physical aggression, removal of the TBI person to a time-out room for a brief period may be instituted. However, with appropriate environmental control, physical intervention should rarely be required and should be avoided where possible.

Alderman and Ward (1991) advocate the use of *response cost* as an effective technique in those TBI people who have very severe memory deficits and executive problems as a consequence of severe frontal lobe injury. Such individuals sometimes have difficulty in responding to behaviour programmes based on positive reinforcement or time-out. Response cost is believed to be more effective because the consequences are immediate, thereby minimising the limitations imposed by memory problems. Attention is focused on the aberrant behaviour in an exaggerated way, with the introduction of verbal mediation, thereby facilitating the normally limited capacity to use feedback from the environment to modify behaviour. The TBI person plays an active role in the process, which may allow for utilisation of relatively intact procedural learning skills. Alderman and Ward (1991) used a response cost approach in treating a 36-year-old female, AB, who constantly repeated stereotyped verbal phrases. The treatment was conducted in one-hour sessions, five days per week. Following a baseline period spent engaging in a range of therapy tasks, AB was given 50 pence, which could be exchanged for a chocolate bar at the end of each 15-minute trial. However, she lost money if she repeated herself. Each time AB repeated herself, the therapist asked her to state what she had just done and hand over one penny. Written instructions were also kept on the table to remind her of the requirements of the programme. The "cost" of the chocolate was calculated so as to maximise the likelihood of success. It was gradually increased as AB gained control over her verbal behaviour.

At least initially, one behaviour problem should be tackled at a time, and goals should be easy to achieve. Team members and family should be prepared for the possibility that the incidence of the undesirable behaviour may initially increase after the programme has been introduced. At no time should consequences be applied in a punitive fashion. Responses to behaviour should be made quietly and without debate. It is particularly important for everyone involved to remember to give those whose behaviour is being modified lots of attention and praise whenever they are behaving in a desirable fashion. This is one of the most difficult things for staff and others to remember. Not uncommonly, after a positive initial response to the programme, the problem behaviour may re-emerge. Examination of staff and family interactions with the person whose behaviour is being modified may show that they have become less careful about responding positively to desirable behaviour.

In order to be maximally effective, behavioural interventions need to be implemented over an extended period of time. Once success has been achieved there should be a gradual weaning process, the frequency of reinforcement can be reduced, the "cost" of back-up reinforcers increased and any material reinforcement replaced by social reinforcement. Over time, it is important to extend the programme to as many settings as possible in which the TBI person spends time or is likely to in the future. This will maximise the probability of successful generalisation of gains. Involvement of family and friends in this is important. Once the intervention has ceased, it is necessary to continue monitoring the frequency of the target behaviour on an intermittent basis, in order to determine whether gains made are being maintained.

At times it can be difficult to harness the support and cooperation of particular staff or family members involved with the TBI individual. This may lead to inconsistency in the implementation of guidelines, or even active sabotage of the programme. Whilst a staff member may cease treating a person, family members are there to stay. Much time needs to be devoted to working with family so that they understand the reasons for a behavioural programme. A careful judgement needs to be made as to whether it is worth proceeding with a programme under circumstances where it is not supported by the family. Unless the behaviour being modified is restricted to therapy sessions when family are not present, it is usually not worth proceeding.

The development of strategies for contingency management of behaviour following TBI was led by the work of Professors Peter Eames and Rodger Wood (Eames and Wood, 1985b; Wood, 1984, 1987) who developed a structured behavioural token economy programme for individuals with severe behaviour disorders at the Kemsley Unit at St Andrew's Hospital in Northampton, U.K. Such programmes have since been developed in centres in the USA, with reported success in reducing severe behavioural disturbances (Eames and Wood, 1985a). However, it has been argued that these treatments are not successful in a proportion of cases and, particularly in those with frontal lobe injury, may fail to generalise to other environments so that it becomes difficult for these individuals to return to the community (Feeney et al., 2001; Giles and Manchester, 2006; McGlynn, 1990). Moreover, the use of some of the more punitive techniques within these programmes presents some ethical and operational difficulties and may lead to conditioned avoidance, resistance, reduced self-esteem and potential for litigation (Ducharme, 1999; Giles and Manchester, 2006; Rothwell, LaVigna, and Willis, 1999; Ylvisaker, Feeney, and Szekeres, 1998).

Positive behaviour interventions and supports

In recent years there has been increasing use of more positive and collaborative approaches to behaviour management, designed to teach and/or shape adaptive and co-operative social behaviours as well as to promote physical and functional independence. These approaches, as suggested by Ducharme (1999, 2000), Rothwell and colleagues (1999) and Ylvisaker and Feeney (Feeney and Ylvisaker, 1995; Ylvisaker et al., 1998; Ylvisaker et al., 2003), build on the contextual approach outlined earlier. They suggest that behavioural strategies should be based on an analysis of what function the behaviour serves for the person, as a basis for teaching adaptive skills or provision of environmental supports to enable the injured person to achieve the desired end without exhibiting the undesirable behaviour. This ensures a better match between the environment and the injured person's cognitive capabilities. These might include teaching a more effective way of communicating a desire to do something, use of a daily planner or paging system, or strategies for anger control to be used in situations where aberrant responses would usually have occurred. Differential reinforcement, prompting, shaping, chaining, fading, modelling, role play and performance feedback can be used to shape these adaptive responses in naturalistic environments so they come to replace the aberrant behaviours (Ylvisaker et al., 1998; Ylvisaker et al., 2003). These methods will be discussed in more detail below.

At the same time it is also usually necessary to manipulate the environment to remove the conditions precipitating or maintaining the maladaptive behaviour and alter the expectations of others so that the problem behaviour becomes irrelevant. Daily routines may be organised to promote choice, access to meaningful activities and roles, and positive communication from others (Ylvisaker et al., 2003). As suggested by Rothwell et al. (1999), in order to gain short-term control over undesirable behaviour whilst implementing these interventions, it may be necessary to use positive behavioural contingencies, such as differential reinforcement of other/low frequency behaviours which are NOT maladaptive (DRO/DRL), as used with success by Manchester (Manchester, Hodgkinson, and Casey, 1997) and Hegel and Ferguson (2000), or reactive strategies, such as re-direction (use of humour, distraction, physical exercise). These approaches are more collaborative, build positive self-esteem, lead to less conflict and can be readily carried over into community settings. Giles and Manchester (2006) suggest that motivational interviewing may be useful to harness the client's motivation to change and build therapeutic alliance in order to achieve meaningful outcomes in behavioural rehabilitation.

No trials have been conducted which have compared the outcomes from the purely "Operant Neurobehavioral Approach" (ONA) with those from what

Giles and Manchester refer to as the "Relational Neurobehavioral Approach" (RNA) or what Ylvisaker and colleagues (2007) term Positive Behaviour Interventions and Supports (PBIS). According to a review of the evidence for the effectiveness of each of these approaches (Ylvisaker et al., 2007), most studies conducted before 1990 evaluated contingency management or operant approaches, with PBIS interventions beginning to emerge in the 1990s and predominating since 2000. A significant proportion of intervention studies have used a combination of these approaches. Only PBIS approaches have been evaluated in community settings. Studies of both kinds have reported positive behavioural outcomes, but Ylvisaker and colleagues (2007) concluded that methodological problems in the studies limited the conclusions which may be drawn from the evidence to date.

Applications of environmental and behavioural approaches to problems commonly encountered in a general rehabilitation unit

Whilst there are brain injury rehabilitation units which are set up primarily to implement behaviour management approaches, in the majority of rehabilitation centres this is not the case. Staff have to deal with injuries of widely varying severity and presenting a broad range of problems. A number of approaches may be taken in order to achieve goals. This can make it difficult to ensure consistent implementation of formal behaviour modification programmes when these are necessary. However, many problems can be successfully tackled in general rehabilitation units using the principles which have been outlined. Some general guidelines for dealing with specific problems are described below. If these are followed consistently, the need for formal behaviour modification programmes may be circumvented.

Suggested guidelines for dealing with some behaviour problems encountered following TBI

Verbal aggression/irritability

- The most important thing to remember when dealing with aggression of any kind is that it usually occurs as a result of the brain injury. TBI individuals cannot always help it and therefore do not deserve to be blamed.
- Educate all those having contact with the injured person to react to aggressive behaviour in a consistent fashion.
- It is important to ignore angry outbursts, making no direct response. Do not react to aggression by shouting, arguing, hitting back or becoming upset in front of the injured individual. This will only serve to increase the level of agitation and/or reinforce the behaviour. If it is possible, remove the TBI person from the situation that provoked the anger or leave the

situation yourself, as long as this does not place the injured individual or others at any risk. In doing so, make no comment. Return after a couple of minutes, and if the TBI person has calmed down, continue the activity. Respond positively to appropriate behaviour. If abuse continues, postpone the procedures or the interaction, although care must be taken that this does not lead to avoidance behaviour.

- Try to identify the kinds of things that cause the TBI person to become agitated and avoid these. Some precipitating factors may include fatigue, noise, overstimulation, pain, therapy which is too demanding or frustrating, incompatibility with other patients or staff, feeling put down, feeling neglected or having insufficient structured activity. It may also be possible to learn the signals of impending agitation and take steps to calm or reassure the agitated individual, to divert attention, to alter the activity or to remove the individual from the situation. If a particular activity is consistently making a person upset, ask whether this activity is really necessary.
- After calming down, the TBI person is sometimes very apologetic. Use this as an opportunity to suggest better ways of dealing with the situation next time, and make it clear that you are willing to help. Don't be critical and don't hold grudges.
- It is very easy for staff or family to become irritable or angry with a TBI individual for being irritable with them, creating physical and emotional distance. An unfortunate pattern can develop, whereby the TBI person's acting out is met with seclusion, restraints or medication. All of this tends to exaggerate feelings of panic, disorientation, frustration and loneliness, eventually leading to further isolation, restriction and rejection of the person. Good staff and family support and communication are essential to avoid such situations. It is very important that staff and family be able to talk about such feelings.

Physical aggression

- Wherever possible, staff or others should try to identify the presence of agitation before it escalates to physical violence. An attempt should be made to defuse the situation – to gently "talk the person down" in a calm and reassuring fashion. Acknowledge the person's feelings and never confront in any way, or try to reason with the agitated individual. Use isolation or distraction where appropriate. Try to remove any disruptive stimulus or individual. Avoid "cornering" the agitated person.
- The team needs to have an agreed-upon and rehearsed protocol for managing physical violence if it occurs. This may involve implementing time-out procedures, but these should be instituted in a manner that invites compliance rather than conflict.
- Any instance of physical aggression should be documented and its precipitants carefully analysed. The team co-ordinator and treating psychologist should be notified as soon as possible.

- The TBI person will sometimes feel distressed and/or guilty following such an outburst. It is important to provide an opportunity for the TBI person to talk about the incident afterwards if they want to, and explore alternative ways of dealing with the problem.
- All staff involved in the incident should meet with the rest of the team to discuss the incident as soon as possible. They need to discuss why it might have happened, how it might be prevented next time, and how those involved are feeling about the incident. A plan for ongoing management of the problem should be agreed upon. Staff who are upset or fearful should be given individual debriefing.
- It is important that no member of staff is left alone with a TBI person who has become aggressive.
- All staff need to be aware of the procedures for management of aggression, which should be clearly documented and practised regularly.

Socially inappropriate behaviour

- Lack of behavioural control as a consequence of injury to the frontal lobes following TBI can, in addition to irritability and aggression, lead to swearing, sexual disinhibition or other socially inappropriate behaviours. It must be understood that many TBI people are, by virtue of their disability and/or confinement, sexually frustrated. However, because of reduced behavioural control this may be expressed inappropriately. When this occurs the first time, it is best to tell the person quietly that this is not appropriate and proceed with whatever you were doing. Subsequently, ignore the behaviour completely. Any form of reaction, either laughing or becoming embarrassed or angry, may only serve to encourage such behaviour. Try not to take swearing or sexual advances personally.
- Respond to socially appropriate behaviour with attention and praise.
- A designated therapist needs to work collaboratively with the injured individual to understand the reasons for the aberrant behaviour and facilitate the development of more adaptive social behaviours. This may involve altering the demands of social interactions so they become more manageable, or the development of scripts rehearsed in role-play situations, and reinforced in naturalistic settings through prompting, shaping and chaining techniques. The entire therapy team may assist in this process.
- It is important to acknowledge the sexual needs of people with TBI and, wherever possible, to provide outlets for these. This issue is discussed in detail in Chapter 8.

Self-centredness

Those who have sustained frontal lobe injury as a consequence of TBI are prone to be self-centred. This can lead to demanding, attention-seeking and manipulative behaviour. Jealousy, failure to see others' points of view, or insensitivity to the needs and feelings of others may also occur in such cases. Self-centredness is the source of many relationship problems following TBI. There may be a tendency to develop ways of attracting attention from others by joking or clowning around, constant demands for toileting, food or other forms of assistance, swearing, making inappropriate sexual advances, shouting, becoming physically aggressive, engaging in self-abusive behaviour or absconding.

- Whilst it is obviously important to first assess whether the TBI individual is in genuine need of help, staff, families and others need to be sensitive to the development of such behaviour and, whenever it occurs, to ignore it. By reacting, either positively or negatively, one is reinforcing the behaviour by giving the TBI person what they want most, namely attention.
- At the same time it is important to reinforce or reward appropriate and considerate behaviour with praise and attention. If this happens consistently, the injured person will learn that behaving appropriately and considerately brings the reward they want.
- Try to avoid being manipulated in other ways. Staff and family should set consistent rules, for example regarding regular toileting or smoke breaks, and stick to them. Threatening or bargaining with a TBI person on an ad hoc basis is not a good idea.
- It is also important that staff and families do not allow the TBI individual to come to expect all demands to be met. On the other hand, it is not realistic to expect the injured person to respect the rights of staff and family, who have to do some demanding of their own. Those who have sustained TBI can become very dependent on those caring for them. Such relationships may be difficult to sustain, so total dependency on one person is not to be encouraged.

Emotional lability

Emotional lability may continue for some time, causing the TBI individual to laugh or cry too much at inappropriate times. Although the response may be overtly dramatic, the underlying emotion may not be all that strong. It is best to ignore the behaviour when it occurs, and model calm behaviour yourself. On the other hand, be sensitive to the development of depression, which may manifest itself as withdrawal, irritability, loss of appetite, sleep disturbance and a sense of hopelessness.

Lack of drive or initiative

This can present a significant challenge to therapists trying to enhance activity levels and independence. It may be difficult to identify ways of encouraging activity. A combination of pharmacological intervention, regular alerting, and a structured approach to activities with prompting, chaining and fading of prompts as activity sequences are achieved is most likely to bring success. A review of existing evidence for treatments of apathy by Lane-Brown and Tate (2009a) showed that the only treatment evaluated in an RCT was cranial electrotherapy, but there was no clear evidence in support of its efficacy. Lane-Brown and Tate (2009b) reported the success of a single-case intervention in a 32-year-old individual with TBI and low drive, by combining motivational interviewing with compensatory techniques to encourage completion of daily tasks.

Applications of behavioural techniques to achieve therapeutic goals

Shaping and chaining may be a particularly useful means of attaining goals in the areas of physical mobility, activities of daily living, work skills, communication and social skills. Shaping involves the provision of positive reinforcement of either a social or a material nature for successive approximations of a desired behaviour. Chaining involves breaking down the behaviour into a sequence of steps or units which build upon one another. Each step is reinforced until it has been successfully learned, before incorporating the next step. As Wilson (1987b) has illustrated, these methods may be applied in training physical skills needing to be relearned, such as the ability to initiate and carry out a transfer. Chaining procedures may also be used to train specific work skills or a sequence of activities of daily living, such as getting up in the morning, showering and dressing.

Management of behaviour problems in community settings

The management of behaviour problems in community settings presents a new set of challenges. Common presenting problems include poor anger control manifested as verbal or physical aggression, socially inappropriate or demanding behaviour, and lack of initiative in performing a range of tasks, from basic self-care to more complex social or work activities. Of a group of 190 brain-injured individuals referred to a community-based Acquired Brain Injury Behaviour Consultancy service for assistance with behavioural problems, these represented the three most common categories of presenting problems (Kelly et al., 2008). Many of the principles described above can be applied to such problems manifested in nursing homes, community residential facilities in the home (which might include living with family, alone, in a caravan park or rooming house) or work setting. However, a notable difference between these and rehabilitation settings is the lack of availability of structure and trained care staff to implement strategies.

There are few established service models available, but one excellent example comes from the work of Todd, Loewy, Kelly and Simpson (2004). In delivering their community-based behaviour consultancy service, Todd et al. follow a six-stage process: *site visit, crisis management, engagement, intervention, education* and *ongoing review*. Most referrals for assistance will be made at a time of crisis, when the problem behaviour has been manifested over an extended period and people in that person's environment are feeling very stressed and frustrated by it. Interventions previously recommended may have failed, either because they did not take account of the cognitive limitations of the injured person or because they placed unrealistic demands on family or others expected to implement them. There may be no-one to undertake baseline measurements or provide consistent feedback or reinforcement, or those who are available may lack the time or the inclination to do so. A site visit will not only provide a vital opportunity to observe the injured person's behaviour in its natural context, but also help determine the nature of the environment and resources available in which to address the problem. Measures for dealing with the immediate crisis need to be swiftly implemented, including de-briefing, provision of a workable and well-documented strategy for dealing with any behaviours which may present a danger to the injured person or others (physical aggression, absconding), review of medication and alarm systems and/or respite.

In the ensuing assessment period, it is important to engage with the person with TBI to establish his/her strengths, weaknesses, activity patterns, interests and motivations. Those in his or her environment also need to be engaged empathically. They need to be told they are doing a good job. Try to ascertain ways in which the scenario in which the problem behaviour is occurring can be altered, if at all possible by structured observation. This may include changing the daily routine or providing additional activities or supports. Where possible, intervention strategies should target the antecedents of the behaviour, with use of re-framing; for example viewing a weekly bath as a success rather than a failure. Strategies need to be simple and workable for all concerned, with the burden of their implementation kept to a minimum, or they will not be reliably followed through. They need to be clearly communicated to everyone having contact with the individual with an injury. Education of all parties involved as to the effects of brain injury on behaviour and the likely factors contributing to the behaviour problem in this context is vital. Core principles of managing behaviour should be emphasised, including the importance of structure and consistency and the provision of a supportive and positive environment. It needs to be emphasised that the intervention is to "manage" the problem, rather than to "fix it". Ongoing review is paramount, as further problems may emerge with changes in the environment and circumstances of the person with TBI.

Such an approach may also be taken to supporting behavioural change in other settings such as the workplace, involving the employer and fellow employees in providing support to the injured person. This model of intervention is illustrated in a case study by Willis and LaVigna (2003), in which a young man's aggression and socially inappropriate behaviour were managed and significantly reduced in his home and community environment without the use of aversive consequences or physical restraint.

Another very fine example of community-based interventions for behaviour problems comes from the work of Feeney and Ylvisaker (2001). This intervention was conducted as part of a New York State-funded initiative to support individuals with challenging behaviour in the community. The programme philosophy was based on the aforementioned "Positive Behaviour Supports" approach, which takes a contextual approach focused on the person with a disability and the organisation of antecedents of behaviour to create successful positive habits. This includes:

1. efforts to create positive internal setting events before introducing difficult or stressful tasks,
2. allowing the individual with disability as much choice and control as possible,
3. teaching positive communication alternatives to negative behaviour,
4. providing communication partners with scripts that facilitate positive behaviour, rather than triggering negative behaviour,
5. ensuring that the person has positive roles to play in life and is engaged in personally meaningful activities,
6. creating advance scripts for difficult situations
7. helping the person to self-manage difficult situations (Feeney et al., 2001, p. 65).

Specialists collaborate with important people in the life of the person with brain injury to provide them with the understanding, competence and problem-solving skills they need to implement supportive routines. The specialist also provides direct support to the injured person to facilitate optimal achievement of goals, gradually withdrawing support whilst maintaining optimal task performance. This programme was staffed by two psychologists, who implemented the programme via direct involvement with clients and through the running of training workshops. It enabled a high proportion of severely behaviourally disturbed individuals to be managed in the community with substantial cost savings to the government.

There are still a significant number of individuals with a brain injury who continue to live in inappropriate aged care or psychiatric facilities largely because of their behaviour problems which preclude their living in the community. As Kelly and Winkler (2007) have indicated, a significant proportion of those still in confined settings could return to the community, living either with the support of a team such as those described, or in group homes with 24-hour specialised staff. There is a significant need for the development of such services, which would, like the programme of Feeney et al. (2001), provide not only a better quality of life for these predominantly young people but also substantial cost savings.

To date, only one controlled trial of community-based behavioural intervention has been conducted. Carnevale and colleagues (2006) compared the impact of natural setting behaviour management involving education and an individualised behaviour modification programme delivered over eight weeks, with the provision of education about behavioural management alone and with a no-treatment control group in 37 individuals with traumatic and other acquired brain injuries and their caregivers. Although no significant treatment effects were evident at the end of the education-only phase or the individualised behaviour management phase, significant treatment effects in terms of reduction in frequency of disruptive or aggressive behaviours were evident in the individualised treatment group relative to the other groups three months after termination of services. There were no significant changes in caregiver burden or stress, however. Although larger studies are needed, this finding suggests that such interventions may be effective in reducing problematic behaviour.

For those TBI individuals with sufficient cognitive abilities, including some insight and motivation, a range of "cognitive-behavioural" techniques, such as anger management training, may be useful in dealing with behaviour problems. These are discussed further in Chapter 8.

Case report – Tim

Tim was a 29-year-old treefeller, married with two young children, when he sustained an extremely severe head injury in a logging accident. He remained comatose for several weeks, and was subsequently transferred to a rehabilitation unit. Gradual progress was made and, after two months, Tim was eating and drinking well, transferring and walking a few steps with assistance. He was communicating verbally without prompting. However, a few weeks later, Tim became increasingly agitated and uncooperative, with frequent outbursts of both physical and verbal aggression, which included shouting, hitting staff and throwing his food tray across the room. Such behaviour was occurring many times a day, to the point where staff found it difficult to attend to his basic needs. Rehabilitation therapy was gradually ceased. The use of tranquillisers and sedatives resulted in Tim becoming drowsy, and his general level of physical dependency increased. He could no longer walk. There was, however, no decrease in the behaviour problems. Attempts to take him home for visits resulted in aggressive outbursts, directed at both his wife and children. He began to suffer frequent epileptic seizures, thought to be related to the medication.

Fifteen months after his injury the rehabilitation unit began to make arrangements for Tim's transfer to a large psychiatric institution. His family became very distressed at this prospect, as the institution was a long distance from his home, and regular visiting would be impossible. They sought interstate transfer for further assessment and management.

Assessment indicated that Tim had extremely severe and widespread impairment of cognitive function. His level of alertness was reduced and he was very slow in his responses. He was disoriented in time and place, giving his age as 16. He stated that he was married with one child. Whilst he showed recollection of distant past memories, he showed retrograde amnesia for a period of some years. He exhibited no capacity to learn or retain anything new. He appeared to comprehend questions only inconsistently, answering with a yes/no or another one- or two-word response, often a stereotyped phrase. He tended to confabulate. He could not read the names written on his birthday cards. He spent most of his time watching television, never initiating any verbal interaction, apart from shouting. Physically, Tim had a left hemiparesis, affecting the arm more than the leg, trunkal ataxia and general weakness. He was incontinent, needed maximal assistance to transfer, bath and dress, and required supervision when eating.

From observation and questioning of the staff caring for him it became apparent that Tim's shouting and hitting behaviour occurred particularly when he was being handled physically, especially when having his clothes removed for bathing and toileting. He also tended to throw his food across the room when he was being given assistance to eat. He had had no therapy for 12 months because of his aggressive behaviour. Staff were apparently fearful of him and avoided contact, except to carry out duties of care. They had been told that, prior to his injury, Tim had a short fuse and occasionally struck his wife. They considered that his current behaviour was consistent with his premorbid personality, and appeared to believe he had some control over it. His wife had also become quite fearful of him.

Following his admission to the head injury unit, Tim was taken off the medications he was taking and carbamazepine was prescribed. This successfully controlled his epilepsy. He was placed in a single room. His behaviour was observed over a two-week period, during which the usual nursing routines were performed and therapists attempted to assess him. Shouting occurred, on average, eight times daily. Hitting out occurred, on average, twice daily. Consistent with observations at his previous rehabilitation facility, it became clear that Tim tended to become agitated and shout or hit out mainly in the presence of noise and a lot of activity around him, but also when he was being handled physically, when he was being put under pressure to do things quickly, when he was engaged in verbal interaction, or when he was tired. It was also apparent that he liked to gain the attention of staff, and that shouting was used as a means to achieve this. He tended to become agitated when his wife and mother were visiting, which they tended to do at the same time.

At a meeting of all those staff involved in Tim's care, the following management guidelines were agreed upon:

- It is important to remember that Tim is very confused, and cannot remember ongoing events, so he does not fully understand where he is and what is happening. His agitation and aggression are a direct result of his brain injury. He cannot help responding in the way he does. Therefore he does not deserve to be blamed for it.

- Tim's surroundings are to be kept as quiet as possible, with the door to his room closed.
- Preferably only one person is to be with him at a time, and certainly only one person talking to him at once. Overstimulation will make him agitated.
- Approach Tim gently and to explain to him what you are going to do before you do it (e.g. take off his clothes before a bath). Demonstrate or use gesture to help him understand.
- Speak to Tim slowly and wait for him to answer. His thinking is extremely slow and he becomes agitated when he is rushed. Demonstrate or use gesture to help him understand. Similarly, he needs to be given time to perform physical tasks at his own pace.
- Try to spend some "quality" time with Tim, which does not involve care or therapy tasks, and which does not place physical or cognitive demands on him.
- If Tim shouts, ignore it. If he hits out, say nothing, leave the room immediately, closing the door. After two minutes, return as if nothing has happened and continue whatever you were doing. Leave the room again in the same way if the behaviour is repeated.
- It is very important to give Tim attention and praise if he is quiet, co-operative or interacting and not shouting or hitting.
- It is vital that these guidelines be followed consistently.

These guidelines were given to all ward and therapy staff, and they were carefully explained to Tim's wife and mother.

In response to this management, Tim's behaviour problems settled down over a matter of weeks, although he continued to become agitated when his wife and mother visited. It was suggested that they should visit separately, as it was felt that he was having too many conversational demands placed on him. During the third month of his admission there was only one instance of shouting and hitting out. He was also more alert. He was much easier to handle on the ward. He could feed himself using normal cutlery and a non-slip mat, provided only one course was presented at a time and he was left alone. He continued to require assistance in all other activities of daily living. He had brief daily sessions of physiotherapy, occupational therapy and speech therapy, conducted in his room on a one-to-one basis. Physiotherapy focused on hand activities, and practising walking in a frame with assistance. He tolerated daily practice of this without outbursts. However, therapy gains were very slow, due to his poor memory and limited capacity to regulate his behaviour. He appeared to enjoy social contact and played simple games for 15–30 minutes, responding to a calm, friendly approach. He began to spend time in the day room, when it was quiet.

Four months after his admission, Tim was transferred back to the rehabilitation unit from whence he came, in order to be close to his family. He was accompanied by the charge nurse from the head injury unit, who spent time with the staff and others, educating them as to appropriate management of Tim's behaviour. Eight months later, he was reportedly still there, attending the hospital's day centre on a daily basis for ongoing therapy. He had been out on leave with his family, without problems arising. Whilst it was clear that Tim was likely to require institutional care for the foreseeable future, the potential for his placement in a pleasant environment was enhanced by this intervention, which consisted largely of environmental manipulation, combined with some behavioural principles and alteration of his medications.

Case report – Chris

Chris was a 19-year-old apprentice mechanic, living at home in a country town with his family, when he sustained a very severe TBI in a motor vehicle accident, resulting in a coma duration of four weeks. Two months after the injury he was transferred to a rehabilitation centre, but was very aggressive, and urinated and masturbated in public. He was transferred to the local psychiatric centre, because nursing staff could not handle his behaviour. He remained there for six months, receiving some therapy. His behaviour was brought under control to some degree, but he developed some bad habits, such as flicking a cigarette lighter in people's faces. He remained sexually and socially disinhibited. Chris's family felt the environment of the psychiatric centre was not good for Chris and insisted on taking him home. However, they were completely unable to cope with his behaviour. Fourteen months after his injury he was referred for assistance in managing his behaviour.

He was initially assessed at home, but brought into the inpatient setting for initial management of his behaviour. Chris was quite independent physically. However, he exhibited severe receptive and expressive communication difficulties, his speech being quite perseverative. Chris also had a very short attention span, very poor learning and memory capacity, and showed severe planning and self-monitoring problems. His behaviour resembled that of a child. He lacked normal social inhibitions and said "G'day mate!" to everyone he saw. He sought attention from people constantly, and when he did not get a response he would engage in inappropriate behaviour, such as putting his arm around a person he did not know or threatening a punch. He had a low frustration tolerance, and became agitated and aggressive, shouting and threatening to punch them, particularly when he was bored, or when others were aggressive towards him. He became bored easily, requiring frequent changes in activity. He had an obsession with money, spending it freely on food for himself or buying things for others. Chris adored children, and often approached them and gave them sweets or drinks, to the consternation of their parents. If money was left lying around he would take it. He also had an obsession with keys.

It was decided that Chris's aggressive or threatening behaviours, namely shouting, flicking a cigarette lighter, threatening punches and, at times, actually hitting people or damaging property, were the greatest barriers to his capacity to function within his family and the community. A programme was therefore designed to encourage non-aggressive behaviour. Baseline monitoring, carried out daily for a week, indicated that episodes of physical aggression, where Chris hit people or damaged property, occurred four times a week, and in all cases when Chris had been denied something he wanted, such as the right to go and buy something, or when other people reacted aggressively to his threatening behaviour. Shouting or threatening behaviour occurred, on average, six times daily, particularly late in the day, when Chris was bored and restless and not getting one-on-one attention.

A programme of time-out, combined with positive reinforcement for periods of non-aggressive behaviour, delivered via a token economy, was instituted. For all acts of physical aggression, Chris was removed to the time-out room for a period of five minutes. Staff, family and friends were instructed to completely ignore shouting or threatening of punches, or flicking of a cigarette lighter, and to continue with what they were doing, paying no attention to Chris. They were also requested to reinforce non-aggressive, pleasant and helpful behaviour from Chris with attention, smiles and praise. Chris was also to be given one token every 15 minutes, with praise, if there had been no actual or threatened physical or verbal aggression in that period of time. If he did exhibit any of these behaviours during the previous 15 minutes, no token was given. Each token could be cashed in for five cents from the charge nurse on his ward at four designated times in the day. This was his pocket money. Staff, family and friends were asked not to lend or give Chris any other money. A programme of activities was also set up to keep him occupied for much of the day.

These measures resulted in a marked improvement in Chris's behaviour. After three weeks there were no further instances of physical aggression, requiring removal to the time-out room. The shouting and threatening behaviour occurred more frequently in the first few days, on the second day 12 times. In subsequent weeks it gradually dissipated, until by the sixth week it occurred only four times, and by the eighth week only twice. After two weeks, Chris was given tokens every half hour only, and after six weeks at two-hour intervals. After four weeks another target behaviour was added to the programme, namely putting his arm around people. Staff, family and friends were instructed to ignore such behaviour and Chris received no token for the period during which it was exhibited. The frequency of this behaviour also dissipated gradually.

Chris spent a lot of time in the occupational therapy department "helping out". He developed a strong attachment to a male occupational therapist, on whom he began to model his behaviour, and from whom he would accept some direction regarding what was and was not socially acceptable behaviour. After three months in the rehabilitation centre, Chris's behaviour within that setting was quite acceptable. He was slowly weaned off the token economy. This was replaced with social reinforcement. There was, however, no change in his level of cognitive function. He enjoyed physical activities within his capabilities, such as bouncing and throwing a ball and badminton, games such as Uno and bingo, and simple writing activities. He also enjoyed helping put things away, washing up or other simple cleaning tasks. However, due to his short attention span, poor memory and limited capacity to regulate his behaviour, he benefited little from formal therapy.

A decision was made to continue Chris's rehabilitation in his home town. It was considered important to maintain a similar daily routine. A young man who lived in Chris's home town was appointed as an attendant carer, to work with Chris for 30 hours per week. Both he and Chris's parents and sister spent time at the hospital being trained as to how to manage Chris's behaviour and most productively occupy him. He returned home four months after his admission, with regular input maintained between the psychologist and attendant carer. The following letter, written by his attendant 19 months later, attests to the success of his reintegration into the local community:

> I have been working with Chris for the past 19 months and in that time there has been a slow but noticeable improvement in most areas. Chris's speech has improved considerably and I find that the people who we see on a day-to-day basis can on most occasions understand Chris's speech, whereas earlier on people would look to me to help out. He is difficult to understand mainly when he is tired. Chris's attention span has improved and he is now able to stick at tasks much longer, for example he will play Monopoly until other players are worn out. Recently he mowed a pensioner's lawn, which took two hours, and he did not stop until the lawn was completed. He also maintains his attention well in group activities and will join in until exhausted.
>
> Chris's social behaviour has improved markedly and he seems to understand social requirements much more than earlier on. His awareness in this area has been assisted greatly by our regular attendance at the local Community Youth Support Scheme (CYSS). Although it has not been without problems, the attendants and project officers have shown patience and have been a great help in the modifying of Chris's behaviour. Chris also enjoys the interaction with the group of young people and looks forward to "going and seeing his mates". Occasions of aggressiveness, tantrums and swearing are now extremely rare and the CYSS peer group have been largely responsible for this.
>
> In regard to money, Chris receives a weekly amount and we try to regulate his spending so that his money will last the full week. I found early on that it was extremely difficult to stick to a programme, therefore I formulated activities that seemed to be most appropriate on a daily basis. Our activities include basic schoolwork, reading, writing and arithmetic, also working out change, educational games, cooking a balanced meal, doing odd jobs, shopping, maintaining a vegetable garden and fishing. We also attend the local CYSS approximately four half days per week which gives

> us a far greater scope for mental and physical stimulation. Activities at the CYSS include woodwork, leatherwork, oil painting, gardening, group sporting activities, such as cricket, basketball, football, table tennis, group discussion. Chris also participates in a handyman service which the CYSS runs for pensioners – this includes lawn-mowing, wood chopping and gardening. I became a member of the management committee of the CYSS to help continue what I see as a very beneficial support to Chris and young unemployed people.
>
> Overall Chris is a much more aware and happier person than he was 19 months ago and I feel that with continued support his improvement will continue.

Case report – Andrea

Andrea was 18 years old and doing a Business Studies course when she was involved in a motor bike accident. She sustained an extremely severe TBI, with extensive fronto-temporal contusion. She was very slow to recover. She had attended a rehabilitation centre but responded poorly to therapy. At the time of her assessment four years post-injury, Andrea was still dependent in all aspects of personal care, and spent most of her time in a wheelchair, although she could walk with a very poor gait using a frame. She had to share her mother's bed as she so frequently required assistance to go to the toilet during the night. Her mother was exhausted and had had to give up her job to care for Andrea. Her father had moved to another bedroom.

Andrea had severe cognitive impairment. She had an extremely short attention span, was highly distractible and had very slow information processing. She exhibited a severe amnesic syndrome. She was also extremely impulsive. Her speech was dysarthric, rushed and difficult to understand. Behaviourally she was attention-seeking and disinhibited, giggling, making frequent inappropriate comments and often leaving her clothing undone. She ate compulsively, and her weight had gone from 50 to 88 kg, which presented further problems as far as her mobility was concerned.

Following discussion with Andrea's parents, who were clearly highly stressed by the physical demands of her care, achieving independence in transfers, improving her walking gait and independence in toileting, showering and dressing were seen as important initial goals. In order to maximise her ability to participate in further therapeutic or social activities her behaviour in a group or social setting also needed to improve. It was decided to use a token economy to tackle many of these areas. This would provide a structure for therapists to systematically reinforce and shape target behaviours in a concrete and obvious fashion. Verbal prompts were combined with contingent reinforcement. In discussion with Andrea's mother we decided to use her pocket money as back-up reinforcement, as Andrea loved having money to buy magazines. The initial focus of the programme was on transfers.

The transfer process was broken down into steps as follows:

1. Hands off chair
2. Feet together
3. Stand
4. Knees bent (bottom in).

A baseline of the number of verbal prompts needs to perform these steps was taken in physiotherapy daily for the first week. After this the steps were written on a card and rehearsed each time she transferred. Andrea was given a token for each step correctly completed without prompting. The tokens could be exchanged for her pocket money. After the first week the same token system was used for her transfers in occupational therapy, speech therapy, on the ward, and when her mother took her home on weekends. Progress was slow but Andrea gradually mastered the steps. Andrea's mother was heavily involved in the implementation of all these procedures, and was the key to the success of the programme.

After three weeks Andrea was receiving all her tokens consistently, at least within physiotherapy. It was decided she would receive one token for each transfer in which all steps were carried out correctly. Five steps to improve her gait when walking were then introduced as follows, following the same procedures:

1. Frame forward
2. Left leg (forward)
3. Tummy forward
4. Right leg forward
5. Tummy forward.

Again this walking routine was reinforced in other therapy sessions, on the ward and by her mother on weekends. Over time, the tokens were replaced with verbal praise.

Similarly Andrea's showering routine was broken down into steps and she was given a token for each of the steps completed without prompting. Then the dressing routine was added. After 3 months, Andrea was independent in all these areas. Tokens were again replaced with verbal praise for successful completion of each routine.

Andrea's introduction to group interactions was not very successful. She was so disruptive, making inappropriate comments, joking, laughing and touching other group members that she had to be removed from the first group she attended. Given the extent of her lack of self-control we decided to use a response cost approach, whereby something desirable must be given up each time the target behaviour occurs. Alderman and Ward (1992) have suggested that the act of handing over something and stating why assists in shaping the verbal regulation of behaviour.

Two target behaviours were identified: 1. touching other group members and 2. making distracting comments. We began by tackling the touching behaviour. Andrea was given 20 × 5c pieces at the beginning of the session. The instructions were written on a card placed in front of her. Each time she touched another person she was required to hand over 5 cents to one of the therapists running the group and say why she was doing so. The therapist's task was to monitor the incidence of the behaviours. The touching behaviour was eliminated within two sessions. Then making distracting comments was added as a second target behaviour. This proved more difficult for Andrea to eliminate.

A baseline indicated that she was doing this, up to 70 times per session. Each time she interrupted, Andrea was required to hand over 5 cents to the therapist running the group, and say why she was doing so. The instructions were, once again, written on a card in front of her. There was a gradual but substantial decline in the frequency of her interrupting behaviour. The card was no longer needed after the first two week of intervention. Andrea could state her goal independently. After seven weeks the tokens were phased out and replaced with verbal reinforcement and feedback given to Andrea's mother. The same intervention was also instituted in her individual therapy and other group sessions, where interrupting was also a problem. This was also successful. As a consequence, Andrea was able to participate and gain benefit from a broader range of therapeutic activities than she had previously.

Andrea was discharged to the care of her mother and father, who with therapist support supervised practice in the routines learned in the rehabilitation setting. By the time of her discharge Andrea was walking with one elbow crutch, was independent in her morning self-care routine and could make simple snacks for herself. She was able to attend a local drop-in centre and participate in some activities, thereby having enhanced quality of life and far less reliance on parental assistance.

Conclusions

Appropriate intervention for behaviour problems represents an important means of maximising the TBI individual's capacity to benefit from rehabilitation and reintegrate into the community. A careful and objective assessment will provide clues as to the most appropriate form of intervention, whether this involves altering environmental factors, structuring the interactions of others with the TBI person, implementing a contingency programme or taking a more collaborative approach to facilitating positive interactions. It is vital that all those spending time with the individual be actively involved in behavioural interventions. In order to maximise generalisation of gains, the strategies need to be applied in a broad range of settings of relevance to the injured person, with a very gradual weaning process. Except in the presence of frank psychiatric disorders, pharmacological management should only be considered as a last resort, and careful attention needs to be paid to the potential impact of medications on cognitive function.

7 Returning to the community

Jennie Ponsford

Introduction

Of all points in the rehabilitation process following TBI, none is more critical than that at which the individual who has sustained TBI returns to the community, attempting to pick up the threads of a previous lifestyle, or to construct a new life which brings some satisfaction. As a myriad of problems and issues become pertinent at this stage, this is a time when the need for rehabilitation support is paramount. For it is frequently not until this point that the individual with TBI, family, and therapy staff can truly assess and face up to the limitations and lifestyle changes which will confront the injured person.

There is also a danger that services may become fragmented due to funding limitations. It is important, therefore, to make every effort to maintain an integrated system of service delivery after return to the community. The extent and manner to which this is possible will be dictated by what services and funding are available and in many countries this is exceedingly limited. In this respect the "Whatever It Takes" model for community-based services (Willer and Corrigan, 1994) is appropriate. This model, which incorporates many of the same principles as the REAL approach, does not rely on any specific funding sources. Rather, it proposes that a broad range of community resources and natural supports be used to assist those who have sustained TBI to attain self-determined goals, maximising their control over and the quality of their lives. There is a need for recognition of the fact that such resources will, for many, be required for a lifetime.

For individuals who do have access to funding, a number of community integration programme options are now available (Malec and Basford, 1998). These focus on overcoming barriers to return to all aspects of community living. Some highly structured residential programmes, such as those described by Geurtsen, Martina, Van Heugten and Geurts (2008) or Jackson and Manchester (2001), cater to individuals with severe cognitive and/or behavioural disturbance. At the other end of the spectrum are Comprehensive Holistic Day Treatment Programs, such as those developed by Ben-Yishay and Prigatano (Ben-Yishay and Prigatano, 1990; Prigatano et al., 1986) for individuals without severe behavioural problems and with adequate communication skills. These generally involve integrated multi-modal therapy offered to groups of participants over a period of six months, placing significant emphasis on the development of self-awareness though participation in daily group psychotherapy sessions, a so-called "therapeutic milieu" approach. These are described in more detail in Chapter 8. Alternatively, individually tailored interventions may be provided in the community, as described by Ponsford, Harrington, Olver and Roper (2006) and by Sloan and colleagues (Sloan et al., 2009b).

Some outcome studies examining the efficacy of these community re-entry programmes have demonstrated significant gains in independence levels and/or productivity, over and above those which would be expected on the basis of spontaneous recovery (Burke, Wesolowski, and Guth, 1988; Callaway, Sloan, and Winkler, 2005; Cicerone et al., 2008; Cope, Cole, Hall, and Barkan, 1991; Geurtsen et al., 2008; Harrick, Krefting, Johnston, Carlson, and Minnes, 1994; High et al., 2006; Johnston and Lewis, 1991; Klonoff, Lamb, and Henderson, 2000; Mills, Nesbeda, Katz, and Alexander, 1992; Ponsford, 2006; Powell, Heslin, and Greenwood, 2002; Sarajuuri et al., 2005; Sloan et al., 2009b; Vanderploeg et al., 2008). The studies of High et al. (2006), Geurtsen et al. (2008) and Sloan et al. (2009b) showed that significant improvement could be made more than one or three years post-injury, although programme entry within six months of injury resulted in more continuing gains following discharge than in people admitted later (High et al., 2006).

Most studies, however, have not included any control group, with studies by Salazar et al. (2000), Powell et al. (2002), Cicerone et al. (2008) and Vanderploeg et al. (2008) being the only randomised controlled trials (RCTs) evaluating such interventions to date. The first RCT by Salazar et al. (2000), conducted in US Defense Veterans with moderate to severe TBI, showed no differences in one-year employment outcome, fitness for military duty or quality of life following an eight-week intensive multi-disciplinary structured cognitive rehabilitation programme, modelled on the milieu-oriented approach with individual and group sessions addressing physical, cognitive, speech occupational and coping skills, and a home-based programme with weekly telephone advice. More than 90 per cent of both groups were employed at 12-month follow-up, indicating the somewhat unusual nature of this population. Nevertheless this finding was concerning, given that the rehabilitation arm cost more than US$51,000 per veteran.

On the other hand, Powell and colleagues (2002) demonstrated a positive impact of individual community-based interventions (average two weekly sessions) focused on improving independence in daily activities in individuals with very severe injuries, relative to provision of information about resources, measured at two-year follow-up. However, there was no improvement in socialising, productive employment, anxiety or depression, perhaps reflecting the severity of the injuries in those involved. In a less disabled group of individuals with moderate to severe TBI, Cicerone et al. (2008) demonstrated significant gains from a more intensive programme (15 hours per week over 16 weeks) of holistic neuropsychological rehabilitation, as compared with standard rehabilitation, the latter comprising individual discipline specific therapies. Greater improvement was evident on the Community Integration Questionnaire, Perceived Quality of Life Scale and in self-efficacy for managing symptoms and this was maintained at six-month follow-up. On the basis of these studies it is difficult to establish which specific aspects of or approaches to intervention were most effective, and with whom.

In another RCT attempting to shed light on this, conducted in male Defense Veterans with severe TBI, Vanderploeg and colleagues (2008) compared outcomes from daily 1.5–2.5 hours of therapy taking either a cognitive didactic approach focused on practice and use of strategies to overcome cognitive difficulties, or a functional experiential approach utilising errorless learning. They found no significant difference in one-year employment or functional independence outcomes. However, exploratory analyses showed that younger people in the cognitive arm had higher rates of return to work or school whereas patients older than 30 or with higher education in the functional experiential group had higher levels of independent living. Over half of both groups were in independent living and 37.8 per cent were in employment.

Given the mixed findings to date, much further research is required. However, due to ethical constraints and the complexity of dealing with groups of TBI individuals who have heterogeneous abilities and goals, it is difficult to conduct large studies evaluating complex rehabilitative interventions. Single case studies may assist in comparing the efficacy of different approaches. In the absence of such research evidence, the guidelines presented in this chapter have been based on the author's clinical experience. It is acknowledged that these recommendations represent the ideal and that, in many instances, "Whatever It Takes" will be needed to attain maximal independence and fulfilment in terms of living situation, employment, recreation and driving, in the most cost-effective manner possible.

Living skills and accommodation

Whilst a great deal of energy is likely to have been devoted to the development of independence in activities of daily living during the inpatient and outpatient hospital-based rehabilitation phase, it is frequently not until the TBI person has returned to the community that some problems become apparent. Lack of adaptive ability and/or initiative, impulsivity, and attentional and memory difficulties can affect the reliability with which a TBI person can carry out skills learned in rehabilitation. Therefore it is essential that performance of living skills be monitored in community settings, so that necessary supports and/or strategies can be implemented.

There are several ways in which this can be accomplished. For individuals already living in the community, such services may be provided by therapists working with the injured person, family members, and others at the community level, using methods outlined in Chapter 4. Indeed, this is the most desirable approach, because this is the real setting in which the injured person will be living in the future, and there is no need for carry-over from another setting.

Community-based rehabilitation

Ponsford and colleagues (2006) have implemented a community-based model of rehabilitation to replace a more traditional outpatient programme at Epworth Hospital in Melbourne. This aims to assess and conduct therapy within the home, workplace or relevant community setting, with active involvement of the injured individual, relatives and others. During the assessment process, one member of the treating team of therapists interviews the injured person and a close-other, completing the Role Checklist (Oakley et al., 1986) to assess what roles are important to the individual, how these roles were performed prior to injury, and how they are performed now.

Goal-setting

Goals focused on enhancing participation are established on the basis of this analysis, via discussion with the injured person and family, who are thereby actively involved in the goal-setting and rehabilitation process. As discussed in the previous chapter, the use of methods such as Goal Attainment Scaling (GAS) (Kiresuk and Sherman, 1968; Malec, 1999) will facilitate a focus on goals that are relevant and meaningful to the injured person and family as well as measurable. The GAS process involves identifying the overall goal of the intervention, breaking this goal down into a number of individual goals, and then defining specific, measurable outcome criteria for each goal, including the expected outcome, worse than expected and better than expected outcomes, using a 5 point scale, with current status assigned a -1. The individual goals are assessed by comparing the individual's performance with the established GAS 5 point outcome criteria, and the overall goal is evaluated by computing a standardised T-score. Similarly, to assess the efficacy of an intervention across individuals, comparisons can be made between the derived T-scores for each person. GAS thereby has the advantage of enabling comparisons to be made across individuals whose goals and interventions may vary considerably. Unlike other measures, GAS also provides a method for differentiating between goals based upon their relative importance to the overall goal of the intervention. This is achieved through the assignment of weights which are used, in part, to derive the final T-score.

Assessment and intervention

Assessment focuses on identifying the injured person's strengths and weaknesses and the impairments, activity limitations, personal factors and environmental barriers which need to be overcome to attain these goals. Therapeutic interventions take many different forms, but are based within the relevant situation and carried out by the most appropriate team member. As described in Chapter 4, therapy may focus on practising tasks with supervision, prompting and feedback to re-build routines, development of strategies or external aids to reduce the impact of difficulties, or modifying activities and/or the environment. Facilitating appropriate behaviour and social skills in various contexts and dealing with emotional responses, which may become more pronounced with increasing awareness of limitations, are equally important in the process of returning to the community. Generally there is intervention from several disciplines, and referral is also made to local services, with a view to reducing long-term dependency on the rehabilitation centre. Because of the amount of planning and travel time required, the intensity of treatment is much lower than most outpatient programmes, however, with most patients being seen by a given therapist once a week or less. The therapist might conduct a two-hour session in the home and supervise interventions carried out by attendant care workers employed to support their independence and/or family members, who are much more actively involved in their rehabilitation. Although an attempt has been made to conduct physical therapy in the community, a significant number of patients do attend regular physiotherapy sessions at the rehabilitation centre, due to the need for use of equipment.

A study has been conducted comparing outcome following this community-based intervention in participants followed up at two years post-injury with that of a retrospective matched cohort of recipients of a centre-based outpatient rehabilitation programme. Preliminary results, based on the first 77 participants (Ponsford et al., 2006), showed that both groups made similar gains. This resulted in the introduction of changes to the community-based therapy programme to maximise hours of client contact, to allow for continuing contact with other injured individuals, and to provide support in making the transition to the community through participation in a transitions group. In a subsequent evaluation (Ponsford, 2006) including 98 patients and 98 matched controls, injured clients treated in the community showed significantly higher levels of independence in personal ADL and somewhat higher levels of independence in domestic and community ADL. There were no significant differences between groups in terms of employment outcomes or in terms of emotional state. Individuals treated in the community had received fewer therapy sessions and thus treatment costs were lower. Attendant care costs were also lower in the community treatment group. Participants in the community-based programme showed high levels of satisfaction with the programme, indicating that they felt involved in goal-setting and that the programme was generally relevant to their needs. This study has shown that implementation of community-based programmes can be successful, but it is important to maximise contact with trained therapists and allow opportunities for contact with other injured individuals.

Delivering therapy and follow-up support to people in rural areas poses significant challenges. There has been emerging interest in the development of telerehabilitation programmes (Grimes et al., 2000; Kinsella, 1999). Two RCTs have demonstrated that scheduled telephone intervention providing education, reassurance and reactivation following discharge from the hospital for patients with mild TBI (Bell et al., 2008) and Veterans with moderate to severe TBI (Salazar et al., 2000) had a positive impact on one-year outcomes. An increasing number of online services and interventions are becoming available although data as to their efficacy remain limited (Wade, Carey, and Wolfe, 2006a). Fann et al. (2009b) investigated patient treatment-seeking for psychological problems following TBI, and found that patients were less likely to communicate with a clinician over the internet.

Transitional living programmes

Whilst it is arguably preferable to provide all assistance in real settings, this is not always feasible. For individuals who are aiming to live independently in the community, but are not yet able to do so, another means of assessing and retraining living skills may be through a residential transitional living programme. The aim of a transitional living programme is to provide TBI individuals with the experience of living in a shared house or a flat in a residential community. Participants are encouraged to take responsibility for personal and domestic activities, but an appropriately trained staff member is available to observe and assess performance in all areas, including personal care, household planning and budgeting, shopping, cooking, home care, laundry, gardening and maintenance, banking, paying bills, use of public transport, and the ability to manage these within a daily and weekly routine, providing therapy as needed. Other areas which may be addressed include the capacity to get on with others in a household situation, and the pursuit of social and recreational interests, work-related activities or study. Goals are set collaboratively and their attainment evaluated in the manner described for the community-based treatment programme. As in the community-based programme, therapeutic interventions may involve rebuilding routines, with prompting and feedback, developing compensatory strategies, or providing environmental supports. Ultimately, it may become apparent that the TBI individual requires ongoing supervision in certain areas, and this will need to be incorporated into plans for the future living situation.

It is inevitable that some conflicts arise in group living situations. This provides an opportunity to develop and practise interpersonal skills including methods of controlling anger. These skills may be facilitated through regular "house meetings", where household members discuss housekeeping issues, plan social activities, or attempt to resolve conflicts, with facilitation by a staff member. Other pertinent issues are likely to relate to acceptance of, and adjustment to, the changes imposed by the injury. However, in most instances there is a need for individual psychological assistance for brain-injured household members in developing methods of dealing with interpersonal and adjustment difficulties. Such methods will be discussed in detail in Chapter 8.

One of the most difficult tasks for many people who have sustained TBI is using spare time. It is commonly reported that they spend much of the day sitting in front of the television. Finding meaningful ways to occupy time, including the means to regularly access these activities, should represent a major focus of all forms of community-based rehabilitation, as should the development and maintenance of friendships. Ideally this is based on a comprehensive survey of all pre-injury recreational interests and friendships, as discussed later in this chapter. Individuals with TBI need to be assisted in developing skills that will enable social and recreational activities to be planned and carried out as independently as possible. This can be done with a friend or attendant, rather than by organising structured activities for them.

Moving from a transitional living centre into permanent accommodation

People with TBI who aim to live alone may progress from a shared house to a trial in a flat or apartment, where they have total responsibility for all tasks. Supervision can be systematically withdrawn as independence increases, although some ongoing supervision may need to be planned for. Considerable support will be required for the move to the community, in searching for affordable accommodation, negotiating with agents or fellow tenants, purchasing furniture or equipment, and planning and implementing the move. Moving back into previous accommodation, either alone, or with friends or family, involves less planning, but can present other challenges. In particular, fellow tenants or family may have expectations based on the performance or personality of the person with TBI before the injury, which can no longer be met. There is likely to be a need for mutual adjustment to roles and patterns of interactions in the household. For example, a son who was previously independent emotionally, socially and financially, may find himself dependent on ageing parents for supervision in getting around in the community and managing his money. Or a husband who was previously the breadwinner and played an active role in parenting may rely on his wife to fulfil all these responsibilities. The TBI individual may need to accept supervision in certain areas. Family or fellow tenants can be trained to provide necessary prompting, structure and feedback to maximise the TBI person's ability to function, and to respond to certain behaviours in a consistent and constructive fashion. However, ongoing supportive contact by a therapist or support worker is important in the maintenance of such arrangements.

As already noted, the efficacy of transitional living or community re-entry programmes has yet to be fully established. However, a number of cohort studies have shown that the majority of participants in these programmes are able to move on to independent living in the community or achieve a reduction in supervision required (Harrick et al., 1994; Olver, 1991).

For some TBI individuals, return to independent living is not a realistic goal. Ideally, however, they should have the opportunity to live in the community, rather than in an institution. Some individuals who are dependent on assistance and/or supervision for most activities of daily living are able to live with their families. This may be desirable, provided both parties are happy with the arrangement. However, caution should be exerted in allowing care to be provided solely by the family on an ongoing basis. Over time, this may become very burdensome. In many instances the caregivers are elderly parents who have difficulty in meeting the physical and emotional demands of caring for a dependent son or daughter. They become anxious about what will happen when they are no longer able to continue. In others, the burden falls on a spouse, who may already carry the responsibility of caring for children and/or earning the family income. Above all, the TBI person, who was previously an independent member of the household, or may have lived away from the family home, is unlikely to feel happy about being so dependent on care and supervision from parents or spouse.

Attendant care support

The use of attendant care presents the most desirable solution to this problem, if funding is available. Attendant carers can assist a TBI person who wishes to live alone in a house or apartment in the community, or those living with family or friends. Attendant carers may assist in, or supervise the performance of activities of daily living in the home or the community, implement therapeutic exercises, assist the person with TBI in pursuing home-based or community-based activities of interest, including activities of a social, recreational or work-related nature. Above all, an attendant carer may become an important friend to the TBI individual, actively assisting them to re-establish previous activities or social contacts, maintain friendships, or establish new ones.

Desirable qualities in an attendant carer include patience, tolerance, flexibility, initiative and creativity. Above all, an attendant must be compatible with the TBI individual and the family, who should be involved in the selection process.

Following recruitment, attendant carers need therapist input regarding the strengths and weaknesses of the injured person, methods of assisting with physical mobility, activities of daily living, and/or communication, managing problem behaviours and suitable activities of a therapeutic, recreational or social nature. Regular contact should be made with the attendant, the injured individual and the family, to address any problems and develop new activities as appropriate, and to provide assistance and training if there are changes in attendant carers, which are invariably stressful for the injured person and family.

Long-term supervised accommodation

For very severely injured and dependent people with TBI or those without family support, the only available option is care in a supervised setting. Unfortunately, for some this means a geriatric nursing home, where there are rarely suitable social or recreational activities provided. Placement in such settings is completely undesirable and should be avoided. Ideally, long-term accommodation should cater specifically to the needs of TBI individuals. Adequate privacy needs to be provided, with individuals having their own room. An accommodation option being developed increasingly by community groups, case managers, TBI individuals and their families, is a shared home in the community, with necessary assistance from attendant carers. Facilitation of involvement in suitable activities of a social or recreational nature and continuing contact with family and friends is essential. Encouragement should be given to pursue interests or work activities in the local community. As many severe TBI individuals continue to show recovery over many years, it is important that their capabilities and needs are reviewed on a regular basis, and opportunities provided to move to a less supervised living situation if this seems feasible (Winkler et al., 2006).

Case report – Craig*

Craig was injured at the age of 20. Craig had a history of drug and alcohol abuse and had been kicked out of home by his very religious parents. He was hit by a car whilst intoxicated, sustaining a very severe closed head injury and multiple fractures. He remained in PTA for two and a half months. Following a five-week period of acute hospitalisation, Craig had six months of inpatient rehabilitation. He had a significant dysarthria, a right hemiplegia, moderate to severe impairment of learning and memory skills, reduced speed of information processing, poor executive functions including planning and self-monitoring, and a reduced capacity for behavioural self-regulation, which resulted in frequent swearing, sexual disinhibition and other socially inappropriate behaviour. Craig had very little awareness of the cognitive and behavioural changes in himself and was therefore not motivated to work on or use strategies to overcome these problems. He was discharged to live with his family, still requiring daily assistance from an attendant carer. However Craig did not want to live with his family in the long term. He wanted to learn to live independently. To most, this would have seemed a very unrealistic goal, given the severity of his impairments. However, it was put to Craig that he could work towards this goal by attending the Transitional Living Centre (TLC). Although he had no concept of what he needed to achieve in order to live independently he agreed to this plan. He spent a total of nine months there, commencing a year after his injury.

* This case was kindly made available by the staff of the Epworth Hospital Transitional Living Centre.

The goals identified by Craig as being most important were to live independently in a shared house in the community, to have a job, and to have friends and leisure activities. His goal of living in a shared house was given the highest priority initially. This would require him to master many tasks, including personal care, meal preparation, laundry, use of transport to access the community, shopping, budgeting, organisation of the day and paying bills.

Initially Craig was difficult to engage. He did not like the level of supervision at the TLC, and would go out drinking and using marijuana. An agreement was reached that he would spend 5–6 nights per week there if he wanted to stay at the centre and work towards his goals.

The first tasks tackled focused on developing his independent living skills: including getting himself up in the morning, organising his own breakfast and daily plan, and preparing lunch and dinner. Later he learned to use public transport independently, and worked on household cleaning, laundry, shopping, banking and money management. He tended to be impulsive and easily distracted and thus had great difficulty in planning his approach to all these activities – planning shopping, following a list, adhering to budget restrictions, etc. – and required extensive practice in these areas. Each of the tasks was broken down into steps and he initially required maximal prompting to perform the tasks. Checklists were also used to assist him to follow a specific routine, for example in lunch preparation. Every effort was made to use strategies which were familiar to him. For example his family had always used the fridge door for reminders. This was also used in the TLC. Weekly goals were set for accomplishment of specific activities, such as being able to do his washing unaided, cooking a meal for the household, or travelling by train to visit his family.

After four months Craig moved into an apartment at the back of the house, thereby being required to accomplish all domestic tasks without assistance. Staff still assisted him with planning his daily and weekly routine, budgeting and dealing with one-off events. Prior to moving into the apartment, he had developed a repertoire of simple meals. He learned to use a shopping checklist to purchase the required ingredients. With feedback, he learned to be less impulsive, by recording expenditure in a book and keeping receipts. He developed a regular banking routine whereby he withdrew the same amount twice per week and his bills were paid directly. After two months in the apartment he moved into a rented house, sharing with his younger brother and cousin. He required further input in order to establish routines in the new environment. After discharge from the TLC he received regular visits from TLC staff, initially monthly and then six-monthly.

As he mastered this major goal of living independently, the attention of Craig and the TLC staff turned to how he would spend the rest of his time. Over the next three months he commenced voluntary work with disabled children. He also attended a gym several times a week. He later succeeded in getting a job as a cleaner for 10 hours per week. Over time he increased this to 15 hours per week, whilst continuing the voluntary work.

Craig's third goal at the TLC pertained to making friends and in particular finding a girlfriend. Over time he had less contact with his pre-injury group of drug-taking friends and had not established a new network. Socially, he was quite isolated. Craig was able to identify that he had difficulty socialising with friends, but did not understand why. He tended to be very verbose and lacked eye contact. He received frequent feedback from the TLC staff and from other residents of the TLC house in their regular discussion group. He began to develop some awareness of his speech problems. With the aid of some community-based sessions with the speech pathologist and video-taped role-play he began to improve his eye contact and became more aware of others' non-verbal cues to stop talking. His awareness of changes in himself grew as he tackled each of his goals. He became more realistic in his plans and participated more appropriately in group discussions. He expressed a lot of frustration over changes to his lifestyle. Regular sessions were also held involving his family, who became more actively involved in his rehabilitation. As he became closer to his family, and was no longer a drug-user, Craig joined a church youth group and began to make some friends there.

As he began to spend more time in the community, Craig admitted that he had very little confidence in talking to new people, especially women. He would tend to talk about his accident and cover his mouth and he generally avoided talking to women. He admitted that at times he felt very low about this. With input from the psychologist, strategies were discussed whereby Craig was taught to become aware of the signs that he was becoming anxious, such as breathing rapidly or covering his mouth. He practised relaxing by slowing down his breathing and imagining himself in a less threatening situation. He practised talking to women he knew and trusted, such as a female work colleague. His confidence increased gradually. Craig became engaged to a girl he met in his church group. He lived with his brother until they married. He completed a course to become a home care worker, aiming for part-time work, and he continued his voluntary work with disabled children. Over the years, he has maintained contact with staff from the TLC, who have provided support in times of need. Craig is now married with two children, and continues to combine part-time paid employment as a home care worker with voluntary work. The total cost of this rehabilitation programme from the time he went to the TLC was approximately Aust$35,000 (US$22,000).

Return to employment

Although outcome statistics vary significantly according to methodology and the severity of injuries studied, most studies indicate that fewer than half of those who sustain severe TBI are successful in returning to employment in the longer term (Crepeau and Scherzer, 1993; Kreutzer et al., 2003; Machamer et al., 2005; Ownsworth and McKenna, 2008; Ponsford et al., 1995b; Possl, Jurgensmeyer, Karlbauer, Wenz, and Goldenberg, 2001; Shames, Treger, Ring, and Giaquinto, 2007; Sherer et al., 2002a; Sherer et al., 2002b). Moreover, a significant number are not able to maintain employment over time (Kreutzer et al., 2003; Machamer et al., 2005; Olver et al., 1996; Possl et al., 2001; Shames et al., 2007). However, given the established relationship between work involvement and the gratification of basic needs for physical and emotional well-being, as well as family, social, economic and vocational needs, this is a goal which is of central importance to most people who have sustained TBI (Johansson and Tham, 2006; Oppermann, 2004; Shames et al., 2007). Moreover, given the youth of so many TBI individuals who remain unemployed and dependent upon public assistance, "the potential loss in earnings, expense to society, and negative impacts on quality of life to the individual and his or her family members are tremendous" (Abrams, Barker, Haffey, and Nelson, 1993, p. 59).

Factors influencing return to employment

A number of factors have been shown to be significantly correlated with short- and long-term employment outcome. These include the injured person's age, with those over the age of 40 years being less likely to return to work, education, previous employment status and income, severity of injury, degree of resultant cognitive impairment, particularly executive impairment, disability in performing activities of daily living, self-awareness, emotional adjustment and the presence of multiple trauma, particularly spinal and limb injuries (Crepeau and Scherzer, 1993; Gollaher et al., 1998; Machamer et al., 2005; Ownsworth and McKenna, 2008; Ponsford et al., 1995b; Schönberger, Ponsford, Olver, Ponsford and Wirtz, 2011a; Shames et al., 2007; Sherer et al., 2002b). However, each of these factors predicts only a small proportion of the variance, so that it is difficult to make accurate predictions in individual cases (Gollaher et al., 1998; Ponsford et al., 1995b).

Ponsford et al. (1995b) and Possl and colleagues (2001) noted a range of other factors which influenced individual employment outcomes in people with severe TBI. Positive factors included employer support and benefits, and the presence of determination and adaptability on the part of the injured individual. Negative influences were the lack of employer support, presence of continuing problems with fatigue, difficulty learning new information, keeping up with the job due to attentional and memory difficulties, presence of psychiatric illness, substance abuse or other adjustment problems, behavioural and interpersonal difficulties resulting from the injury, and availability of other means of financial support, such as support from a spouse or disability support income. Kendall (2003) found a significant association of vocational adjustment (though not actual employment status) with family and social support and self-esteem.

Models of vocational rehabilitation

Various models of optimising return to employment following TBI have been developed over the past three decades. However, although most report rates of return to productivity ranging from 60 to 80 per cent, as shown in the studies reviewed below, there have been no controlled trials evaluating the efficacy or most effective elements of these programmes.

The milieu-oriented rehabilitation model developed by Ben-Yishay and Prigatano (Ben-Yishay, Silver, Piasetsky, and Rattok, 1987; Klonoff et al., 2000; Prigatano et al., 1986), described earlier and in the next chapter, focuses on cognitive remediation and development of self-awareness and acceptance, followed by voluntary work trials and support in finding employment. Klonoff and colleagues (2000) reported that 76.8 per cent of programme participants were engaged in competitive activity (work or study) up to 11 years after discharge from such a programme.

In 1986, Wehman and his colleagues (1993, 1990) developed the Supported Employment Model for TBI individuals on the premise that they have difficulty in generalising skills learned in rehabilitation settings into the workplace environment. This model allows for assistance in job-searching and intensive on-site job skills training and support by a job coach. It has been shown to be successful (with a 71 per cent job retention rate), and cost-effective, for a significant proportion of individuals, who have not responded to more traditional methods of rehabilitation and would not be considered able to work without on-site support (Wehman et al., 2003). Curl, Fraser, Cook and Clemmons (1996) have used fellow employees as job coaches with some reported success.

Intensive on-site support, such as a job coach, and ongoing follow-up is not necessary in many cases, however. Haffey and Abrams (Abrams et al., 1993; Haffey and Abrams, 1991) developed a "Work Re-entry Program" model for individuals with less catastrophic injuries. This emphasised careful assessment, job development and job analysis processes to match client capabilities with job requirements, but provided less follow-up support on-the-job. Nevertheless, it showed a 68 per cent placement rate and a 75 per cent employment stability rate in clients with a median coma of seven days. These injuries are less severe than those of Wehman et al.'s (1990) Supported Employment sample, which had a mean coma of 53 days. Malec and colleagues developed a medical/vocational case co-ordination system at the Mayo Clinic, in which co-ordinators work with the rehabilitation team early in the rehabilitation process to identify client vocational needs and impediments to return to work (Malec, Buffington, Moessner, and Degiorgio, 2000). Vocational goals are integrated with other rehabilitation goals, referral is made to appropriate rehabilitative and community-based vocational support services, and work-site assessment, workplace education and work trials are provided, with regular follow-up. One-year follow-up of 101 programme participants showed 53 per cent were in independent work and 34 per cent in transitional placement, supported or sheltered work. Outcomes did not differ according to the nature of the rehabilitation programme in which clients were involved. A similar model, the "Program without Walls", has been shown to result in better outcomes relative to the standard US state-run vocational service (O'Neill, Zuger, Fields, Fraser, and Pruce, 2004).

A vocational programme developed in the UK, known as Rehab UK (Murphy et al., 2006), combines elements of all of these programmes, offering a centre-based pre-vocational phase conducted in groups over 12 weeks, focusing on developing compensatory cognitive rehabilitation strategies, social skills, basic numeracy, literacy and IT training, development of self-awareness of the impact of the brain injury, and identification of realistic vocational goals. In the second phase clients are placed in real work settings on a voluntary basis, usually for several months, with the support of a job coach. They continue to receive statutory benefits and attend the centre to work on job-seeking skills. The final phase of the programme involves supported job search with continuing support from the job coach after commencing employment, over an extended period. Average time in the programme is 9–12 months. Murphy and colleagues (Murphy et al., 2006) have reported that 72 per cent of program participants who were a mean of 5.5 years post-injury, were discharged into meaningful independent activity (41 per cent paid work, 16 per cent voluntary work, 15 per cent training or education). Whilst 40 per cent of those returning to work did so at a lower level than prior to injury, 20 per cent had moved to a higher level. It was noted that the cost of the programme would be recouped from savings in Incapacity Benefit in 26 months, but follow-up data were not available.

Whilst there is still a lack of controlled studies demonstrating how well these programmes do relative to no specialised vocational intervention, it would appear that a number of intervention models are successfully placing a significant proportion of their brain-injured clients in meaningful vocational activities, some placing emphasis on preparation before job placement and others on providing on-the-job coaching and support (Hart et al., 2006). The optimal approach for a given individual will depend on a broad range of variables. These include factors relating to the injury, such as the nature and severity of physical, cognitive and behavioural sequelae, particularly the degree of self-awareness; the injured person's premorbid ability levels, personality, adjustment and attitudes; and the nature of the work options available, whether these be through the previous place of employment or from other sources, as well as co-operation from the employer and others supporting the injured person.

Above all, however, the methods used to return the TBI individual to employment will depend on the resources available in terms of private funding and/or publicly-funded vocational rehabilitation services. It is important that those advocating for the injured person try to ensure that large amounts of money are not wasted on expensive vocational assessments which are not of direct benefit to the TBI individual. The procedures suggested below are intended as a guide to maximise successful employment outcomes, but will need to be adapted according to the resources available.

Suggested guidelines for return to employment

The question as to when vocational rehabilitation should begin in order to be maximally effective is not one which is easily answered. The timing of return to employment is likely to be determined by a myriad of variables, including the nature and severity of disabilities, medical and therapy commitments, the kind of work available, and the level of insight, cooperation and motivation of the injured person, family and employer. It is important, however, to begin planning for the TBI individual's vocational future early in the rehabilitation process.

(1) Assessing the worker

A detailed profile of the injured worker's *educational and employment history*, *injuries* and *current capabilities* needs to be obtained. *Physical symptoms* including weakness, sensory changes, pain, fatigue, balance, dizziness, noise intolerance, headaches, visual disturbance and their impact on the worker's ability to stand, walk long distances, bend, squat, lift, climb ladders, work at heights or cope with a noisy environment should be documented, along with any medications required and any required future medical interventions. *Cognitive and behavioural changes* in the domains of attention, processing speed, mental fatigue, memory, visuo-perceptual functions, planning and self-monitoring, initiative and irritability or any other behavioural problems may be determined from neuropsychological assessments, other rehabilitation team members and from the perspective of the injured worker and family. Discussion regarding these changes along with aims and expectations for employment will provide a picture as to the injured client's level of *self-awareness*. If the worker has not worked before or does not have a job to return to, the assessment also needs to encompass an evaluation of client *vocational skills and interests* and documentation of any *previous work experience*. *Ability to drive or use public transport* must also be determined.

(2) Worksite assessment

Return to work in some capacity with a previous employer is more likely to be successful than attempting to find work with a new employer (Johnson, 1987). Therefore, establishing a good relationship with the injured person's previous employer early in the rehabilitation process is important to explain the nature of injuries and the likely time-frame of rehabilitation and to engage them in this process. It is important to establish the employer's willingness to accommodate limitations of the TBI individual, either by modifying the job requirements or by finding alternative duties, as well as acceptance of the need for a graduated return to work. Where this is not the case, it may be necessary to consider alternative employment options, which present more challenges.

Whether the TBI individual is aiming to return to a job held prior to injury or another position selected as potentially suitable, *a detailed analysis of the requirements of the job* will need to be carried out, together with an assessment of *the capacity of the injured worker to perform each of these requirements*. The *physical layout of the workplace* (e.g. access, steps, location of toilets, tea-room) must be considered if mobility is an issue. The assessment of the job needs to include its *physical demands* (requirements for sitting, standing, walking, lifting, bending, climbing, balance, vision, speed of work, etc.) and *cognitive demands* (e.g. concentration, speed of thinking, attention to detail, learning and memory, planning and problem-solving, self-monitoring, multi-tasking, initiating, communicating with or supervising others) and any *safety risks*.

The ability of the injured worker to meet these demands must then be assessed.

(3) Work preparation

Following the philosophy of the REAL approach, outlined in Chapters 1 and 4, it is desirable to introduce real work tasks as early as possible in the rehabilitation process in order to assess and retrain skills and facilitate the development of the TBI individual's awareness of limitations to enable realistic planning. In some cases it may not be in the interests of the person with TBI, or the employer, for this to occur initially in the actual work setting. It may be more appropriate to simulate work requirements in the rehabilitation setting, or to provide unpaid "work experience" in a different setting, as long as the injured person understands the relevance of this. Under these conditions a therapist can assess not only specific work skills, but also the ability of the TBI individual to follow, remember and carry through with instructions, sustain attention to work tasks over time, check for and correct errors, and work at an optimal pace. The injured worker's punctuality may also be assessed, as well as reliability, initiative, and ability to get on with others in the workplace. Difficulties in any of these areas can be addressed gradually, without pressure from the employer. It may be possible to train the TBI individual to perform components of a job in sequence and at an optimal pace under controlled conditions. Speed and accuracy can also be developed over an extended period. The therapist should try to identify whether problem areas are most likely to be overcome by retraining, compensatory techniques, manipulation of the work environment, or altering the job requirements. It is important to focus only on those skills which are involved in the job which the worker will be performing.

(4) Returning to the workplace

The move to the actual work setting requires careful planning. Issues which may need to be addressed beforehand include the organisation of transport, physical access to the worksite, and financial arrangements regarding work subsidies or ongoing disability benefits. If at all possible, a person should be designated to assist in the return-to-work process. Such assistance should, if necessary include the provision of supervision or assistance at the worksite. This return to work specialist should maintain regular contact with the employer, acting as an advocate, and facilitating communication between the injured worker and the employer.

In severe TBI cases, it is important that the employer and fellow employees be given an understanding of the strengths and weaknesses of the injured worker, and how these are likely to affect performance in the workplace. In cases of milder injuries it is more difficult to predict what difficulties, if any, may be manifested and it is preferable to discuss possible injury effects, such as fatigue, in more general terms. Most injured workers initially need to return to work on a part-time basis, gradually increasing hours. Provided the job allows for this, duties may need to be altered or simplified, according to the worker's capabilities. It may be necessary to reduce physical demands of the job, or avoid multi-tasking, the need to work quickly, or to interact with others. Wherever possible, time should be spent with the TBI individual at the worksite, assessing how they are managing, providing feedback, and devising ways of overcoming difficulties. A fellow worker, or site supervisor, might also assist in monitoring the worker's performance in terms of productivity, accuracy, behaviour and any other relevant areas.

(5) Modifying the work environment, skill retraining and the development of compensatory strategies

As discussed in the previous chapter, it is useful to assess the ways in which the worker is best able to learn. For example, it has been shown that some amnesic people have relatively preserved procedural learning skills and may benefit more from "hands-on" experience than verbal instruction. Errorless learning or spaced retrieval may be used to teach discrete information essential for job performance or people's names. Alternatively, compensatory strategies may be developed to enable the worker to perform work tasks independently. These might include the provision of a checklist, or a sequence of cues of a written or pictorial nature to be followed in performing a task. As outlined in Chapter 4, Burke, Zencius, Wesolowski and Doubleday (1991) demonstrated the use of a checklist to be an effective means of training TBI individuals with executive problems to follow a sequence of steps involved in performing a work task. People with memory difficulties may be assisted by the use of a notebook, diary, watch alarm, or electronic appointment minder. A dictaphone can be used to record conversations in meetings, on the telephone, or in lectures, to enable these to be reviewed later. Computer programs designed to check spelling and grammar are useful for detecting errors in word processing.

The work environment may also be modified to minimise the impact of difficulties. Items or geographic locations can be clearly labelled or colour coded. Earplugs may be provided to minimise background noise, or the worker be provided with a quieter or less congested area in which to work. Fellow workers can be given guidelines as to how to minimise and respond to inappropriate behaviour on the part of the TBI individual. Work duties themselves may also be altered to place fewer demands on memory, work speed, planning or initiative.

(6) Review meetings and follow-up support

Regular meetings need to be held between the TBI individual, the employer, and the therapist or job coach to review progress, discuss any problems which are arising and, if appropriate, to upgrade work hours or duties. This also provides employers with an opportunity to give feedback to the injured employee regarding job performance which may not otherwise be communicated. All too frequently an injured worker is dismissed without clear reasons being given, and therefore does not benefit from the experience. The return to work specialist can subsequently clarify the feedback with the injured worker, who may not have fully understood it.

This monitoring needs to continue over an extended period. Many individuals with TBI have difficulty maintaining employment due to ongoing fatigue or cognitive difficulties in performing tasks, interpersonal conflicts, mental health issues, changes in work duties, poor match between worker job preference or ability and the job characteristics or perceived lack of upward mobility (Machamer et al., 2005; Possl et al., 2001; Sale, West, Sherron, and Wehman, 1991). It is extremely important to maintain regular contact in order to address such problems before they result in termination of employment.

Contact should be made with family to ascertain the impact of being in employment on other aspects of the injured person's lifestyle, to ensure that an appropriate work/home balance can be attained. In some cases keeping up with work causes significant stress and fatigue such that there is no energy left for domestic, let alone social or recreational activities. Irritability and substance abuse may result. It may, in the long term, be necessary to cut back on work hours in order to maintain some quality of life and reduce these problems. Return to employment almost invariably precipitates increased awareness of limitations, which is frequently associated with heightened anxiety and depression. Referral should be made for psychological support in dealing with all of these problems as they occur.

In general it is best to avoid the necessity for change in the work routine, and this should be made clear to the injured person and the employer or site supervisor from the outset. It is unwise to allow TBI individuals who have executive or adaptive problems to return to positions which are likely to have variable routines and changing demands, or where the injured worker has an expectation of promotion. If changes are to occur, careful monitoring is particularly important. A scenario which is not uncommon is that of an injured employee who is coping well with a given work routine seeking or being offered a job upgrade or a change in duties. Neither the injured individual nor the employer can anticipate the difficulties likely to be experienced in adapting to such changes. Similarly, problems may occur if there is a change in supervisor. The employer needs to be encouraged to seek advice or support prior to making any such change.

When working with individuals who have sustained TBI, it is also important to accept that for some there are likely to be frequent job changes. This is particularly so when injured workers experience interpersonal difficulties and/or have an unrealistic view of their abilities. Whilst such changes are not desirable, it may still be possible to maintain the injured worker in employment for much of the time, provided the right supports are available to assist in times of difficulty. One of the most important lessons to be learned by those providing support services to TBI individuals is that at least some of these services will be required indefinitely. In short, there is no "cure" for the problems arising from severe TBI. Indeed, it is the expectation of such a cure, and the anticipation that assistance will be time-limited, that is undoubtedly the source of a great deal of frustration for many of those who have sustained TBI, and the people supporting them.

(7) Exploring alternative or new employment options

Over time it will become clear whether the injured worker is likely to be capable of meeting the demands of the position, albeit with some assistance or modifications, or whether an alternative job has to be found. If this is not possible with the current employer, such a position will need to be sought elsewhere. This may necessitate training and assistance in job application, resumé preparation and interview skills. There might be a need for some skill retraining, and arrangements made for such retraining to be funded and undertaken. The extent to which this is feasible will depend on the ability levels of the TBI individual. For some, employment is not going to be a realistic option.

All of these forms of assistance should also be available to TBI individuals who were not working prior to injury, but who now wish to seek employment. These people face a greater challenge than those who were employed prior to injury, because they have no previous experience or behaviour patterns to form a basis for a vocational future, and often have a limited capacity to acquire new skills. There may be a need for a detailed vocational assessment, prevocational skills, training, including preparation of a resumé and job search and interview skills, as well as exposure to a number of different work environments through work experience, prior to selecting a vocational direction, as is the practice at Rehab UK. If an acceptable position can be found, a process similar to that already described could be followed. However, the likelihood of success will be determined by the injured person's level of cognitive, behavioural and emotional functioning.

(8) Sheltered employment

In most instances, sheltered employment is unlikely to present a viable option. Sheltered workshops tend to be geared to the needs of those with congenital intellectual disabilities. TBI people do not generally view themselves as disabled and frequently do not wish to be associated with other disabled groups. Furthermore, such settings usually require the worker to sustain attention to a repetitive task over an extended period, and most people with very severe TBI are not capable of this. Behaviour problems can also present a significant barrier to successful integration into a sheltered employment setting.

Case report – Mark

Mark was 29 years old when he fell off the back of a utility, sustaining a moderate TBI. Initial cognitive assessment identified problems with attention, short-term memory, word-finding and fatigue. He also had diplopia when looking to the right. As a consequence of this he was advised not to drive.

Mark worked as a team leader in the IT industry. He was very ambitious, having been offered a promotion just prior to the accident, and working long hours under great pressure. His job involved multi-tasking, meeting deadlines and supervising two other staff. He was very keen to get back to work and was attempting to check and respond to emails from his hospital bed. The return to work specialist saw him at this time and discussed the return to work process to alleviate his anxiety. He was advised not to return to work until three months post-injury and not to undertake work-related duties in the interim. She contacted his employer to explain that Mark needed time to recover and would not be able to return to work until three months post-injury, without giving any specific details regarding his problems. She visited Mark at home within two weeks of discharge from inpatient rehabilitation. He was reporting fatigue and occasional disorientation and had become less confident about return to work. He was highly anxious.

Three months after the accident the return to work specialist accompanied Mark to the workplace and undertook a detailed analysis of the demands of his job and the environment in which he worked. As he was a valued employee, Mark's employer was willing to modify his job to accommodate Mark's limitations. Mark commenced a graded return to work four months post-accident, working three 4-hour days per week. As he was not driving due to his visual disturbance taxi transport was arranged. Given his problems with attention and processing speed, Mark was assigned an alternative role working on one self-paced project only. Restrictions imposed by the return to work specialist were that he was not to take phone calls, had no responsibility for supervision of others and no deadlines to meet in order to reduce pressure and avoid the need for multi-tasking. He worked from 10 am until 2.30 pm to avoid peak-hour traffic and allow for a half-hour lunch-break to manage fatigue and concentration difficulties. He arranged the more demanding tasks in the mornings and did more routine tasks in the afternoons, since fatigue was an ongoing problem. His insurer provided a 100 per cent wage subsidy for the first four weeks, given that his productivity would be significantly reduced.

When reviewed at week four Mark reported fatigue, slowed thinking, memory difficulties, anxiety and depression. He was falling asleep in the taxi after work. He had lost motivation to work and was feeling he should give it up. He was referred to a psychologist for counselling and continued with the return to work programme. Various strategies for coping with his fatigue, word-finding problems, memory difficulties (e.g. writing things down) and anxiety (e.g. deep breathing) were discussed with him. By week eight his endurance and mood had improved, he was utilising some of the coping strategies, and he was working six-hour days. His duties were gradually upgraded. He commenced taking telephone calls with clients. He was encouraged to plan each phone call and write a list of prompts before the call. He used a strategy of saying he would follow something up and get back to them if he was unsure of anything or needed additional thinking time. He also kept notes of the outcomes of all phone calls. He also kept a list of things to do and planned tasks for the following day at the end of each day at work. His confidence and motivation improved. His vocational allowance was gradually reduced as his hours and duties were upgraded. Over a 12-week period he built up to full-time hours, having returned to his pre-injury role, rather than the one he had been promoted to just before his accident. He was monitored for 21 weeks. He continued to receive psychological support over a three-month period. At a review two years post-injury he was working full-time and had been promoted to team leader. He continued to report memory problems, fatigue and slower thinking. He was still using some of the strategies but managing well.

Case report – Steve

Steve was a 16-year-old school student when he was hit by a car, sustaining a severe TBI. He was intending to pursue a career in school teaching and his school reports suggested he was capable of this. He made a good physical recovery, but developed post-traumatic epilepsy and had severe short term memory difficulties, slowed information processing and difficulty controlling his temper. He experienced social difficulties relating to his peers at school and teachers noted a marked change in personality.

At the time of his injury, Steve had a part time job as a cashier in a local supermarket. His employer described his work as having been of a high standard and felt he had the potential to become a supermarket manager. Due to the strong employer support he was encouraged to return to this job after his injury. A meeting was held with the employer to explain Steve's cognitive and behavioural difficulties and he was assigned to routine, repetitive duties which minimised his interpersonal contact. After leaving school, Steve went to work at the supermarket full-time, because it was clear that he could not cope with further study and because the supermarket work was familiar to him. Duties involved cashier work, stocking shelves and cleaning.

Over the next 15 years Steve contacted or was referred back to the vocational counsellor for assistance with workplace issues at least annually. Ongoing issues included fatigue, poor memory, and inflexible thinking, which resulted in stress when faced with changes in routine or unexpected situations, difficulty multi-tasking, inappropriate social interactions with customers, and occasional anger issues. As a result, although he remained with the same employer, he was often transferred between jobs. Each time this occurred there was a need for vocational input. For example, he was assigned a role as cashier in a petrol outlet. He was forgetful and was observed making sexually inappropriate comments to customers and talking to customers for too long whilst others were waiting, with resultant customer complaints and verbal warnings from the employer. Steve was reporting anxiety and difficulty coping. The speech therapist provided structure, teaching him to speak more quietly, assisting him to develop scripts for addressing customers and routines for checking his cash register measurements, which were often inaccurate. The strategies required constant repetition and were written on cards placed strategically in the workplace, as he would forget them.

Steve had married and had two children and passed his driver's licence. His wife reported concerns regarding his safety due to his impulsivity and limited concentration. Steve was reluctant to reduce his work hours due to financial pressure. He remained determined to stay in employment and has been disappointed by his inability to cope with higher duties. With support from his employer and regular input whenever crises occur, he has so far managed to maintain his job. However, he will always be at risk of losing it.

Returning to tertiary study

A model similar to that outlined for return to employment is applicable to students returning to school or to a tertiary educational environment. Common cognitive difficulties manifested in the educational setting include problems with attention, speed of thinking, learning and memory, fatigue, poor planning and organisational abilities, communication problems and impaired self-awareness. Personality changes, such as impulsivity, irritability and difficulty in getting along with others may affect the injured student's social network.

Tertiary or college students surveyed regarding their experience of return to study have reported a need for increased effort and use of compensatory strategies in their studies, a decline in grades, changes in their educational or vocational goals, a decline in their social and peer group interactions, and a tendency to feel anxious and overwhelmed, with a sense that others do not understand their difficulties (Kennedy et al., 2008a; Maddren, 1996; Stewart-Scott and Douglas, 1998; Todis and Glang, 2008). In our own follow-up study of 62 students 1–5 years post-injury (Ponsford, 2007), 48 per cent indicated they were studying only part-time and 61 per cent had had to apply for special consideration, whereas only 6 per cent had done so prior to the injury. Fifty-six per cent had required individual tuition, as opposed to 9 per cent prior to injury, 87 per cent said they had greater difficulty keeping up with the workload, 85 per cent had greater difficulty learning new information, 83 per cent said they became fatigued more easily and 87 per cent said they needed to expend more effort to pass. Forty per cent said they had greater difficulty getting on with people. With the support provided by our therapists, most were passing their courses despite these difficulties. Students who do *not* receive ongoing support and assistance may experience repeated failure, placing them at risk of developing low self-esteem, becoming socially isolated and losing direction (Hall and DePompei, 1986; Ylvisaker, Hartwick, and Stevens, 1991; Ylvisaker, Todis, Glang et al., 2001). Todis and Glang (2008) found that students who did not receive support were less likely to complete post-secondary education.

A detailed discussion of pertinent issues, with guidelines for returning children and adolescents to school, is set out in Chapter 10. For TBI students returning to, or embarking upon tertiary study, the process is even more difficult for a number of reasons. The demands being made on the student are likely to be greater than at school. The student will be required to concentrate on lectures for periods of at least an hour at a time. Far less structure is provided, the student being required to show considerable initiative and organisational ability to fulfil the requirements of the course. Assessments may only be conducted at lengthy intervals, so that it may be difficult to gauge how the student is coping. There also tends to be less room for flexibility in the curriculum. The student peer group is likely to be far less cohesive and may offer little or no support, reinforcing the sense of isolation experienced by the student. It is therefore not surprising that students who succeed in return to tertiary study are those who possess "a high degree of motivation, positive reframing, flexibility and determination" (Todis and Glang, 2008, p. 262).

There has been little evaluative research conducted regarding the most effective ways of maximising the success of return to tertiary study, although a number of authors have presented case reports to support recommended principles (e.g. Cook, 1991). The guidelines suggested here are consistent with the recommendations of Cook (1991), Hall and DePompei (1986) and Ylvisaker (2001), but are based largely on the author's experience.

It is important early on to recruit the assistance of a disability liaison officer, if such a position exists in the educational institution, and/or at least one teacher or lecturer from the course, making them aware of the likely problems to be faced and discussing the feasibility of a graduated return to study. Aspects of coursework studied previously may be reviewed within the rehabilitation setting, under the supervision of therapists, who can assist the student in developing strategies to cope with potential difficulties. For example, strategies might be devised for recording the content of lectures, such as methods of identifying key themes or words, or the use of audio-taping. It may also be useful to work on written expression, proof reading and summarising skills. Short courses may be undertaken in preparation for return to the former course of study, allowing the student to gain some awareness of problems likely to be encountered and practise compensatory strategies.

On return to study, the student may, in the first instance, attempt only one or two subjects. Supervision will need to be requested of the lecturer, and possibly arrangements made for special tutoring. Ongoing follow-up support is essential. Peer group support may be provided through a study skills group, in which a group of TBI students discuss their difficulties and share ideas as to how to overcome these. Such a group can be a good forum in which to present students with coping strategies, including the use of a diary and action-planner, and methods of organising study time, note-taking, reviewing the content of lectures, essay-writing, coping with fatigue and so on, as well as providing moral support. A "study buddy" may also be recruited to assist in providing accurate lecture material and help with revision for exams.

No matter how much assistance is given to the student, most will feel quite alone within the educational environment, as other students and lecturers are likely to have difficulty in comprehending their problems. It is advisable, therefore, to establish some form of ongoing support on-campus, ideally through a student counselling service, who will need to be educated regarding the consequences of TBI.

It is not uncommon for TBI students who lack awareness of their difficulties to insist on returning to study when it seems clear to others that they will not cope. The experience of failure may be necessary in order to engender a more realistic self-appraisal by the student. However, this can also be a time of enormous stress, and it is vital that students be supported throughout this period, and assisted in the pursuit of alternatives to study if they do fail. Moreover, as the findings of Olver and colleagues (1996) have demonstrated, some students may, with assistance, manage to complete their studies, but have difficulty in obtaining employment afterwards. Ongoing contact needs to be maintained in order to provide necessary support in finding employment, or establishing a meaningful lifestyle.

Case report – Raymond

Raymond was a 24-year-old Vietnamese student who was hit by a car. He sustained a severe TBI, with one day of coma and a PTA duration lasting seven days. Prior to his injury, Raymond was completing the final year of a degree in Electrical Engineering. He had been in Australia, sponsored by a scholarship, for three and a half years. Raymond was sharing an apartment with another Vietnamese student. His family was living in Vietnam. His mother visited for a couple of weeks after his injury. Raymond was described as being intelligent and conscientious in his studies prior to the injury.

Neuropsychological assessment indicated that Raymond was of above average intelligence. His English was good. He had reduced speed of information processing, difficulty sustaining attention due to fatigue, moderately severe difficulties in learning and retaining both verbal and non-verbal material, and reduced planning and problem-solving abilities, poor self-monitoring, as well as word-finding difficulties in English. Raymond showed some awareness of these problems at the time of the assessment, but did not realise their implications for his return to study. He showed no problems physically, or with personal, domestic or community ADL, although he tended to attempt too much and become very fatigued. He was intolerant of noise, and found it difficult to cope on return to his apartment because his flatmate often entertained friends until late at night. He spent a period at the Transitional Living Centre, before moving into an apartment by himself.

Early contact was made with the university, initially with the liaison officer for overseas students, and then with Raymond's lecturers. Because of his scholarship, he would need to return to the course in some capacity within three months, or suspend his enrolment and return to Vietnam. Some familiar coursework was obtained for him to work on in therapy. Raymond was unable to concentrate for more than 30 minutes at a time, becoming overwhelmed and fatigued, and developing headaches and dizziness after this. He was given systematic feedback and reinforcement in order to increase his attention span. Raymond was very keen to complete his course. He could not see the implications of the problems he was experiencing in therapy for his return to study. Against the advice of the therapists, he re-enrolled in two subjects and started attending some lectures. However, he rapidly became overwhelmed by the material presented in lectures and began to realise that he could not cope. Raymond became highly anxious at this stage.

A meeting was arranged between therapists from the hospital, the liaison officer and the course co-ordinator. It was decided that Raymond would attempt one subject, which had the least lecture content. Additional tutoring in that subject was arranged for four hours per week. He also attended the rehabilitation centre twice a week. In addition to carrying out a fitness programme to increase his endurance, Raymond attended a study skills group, where he worked on strategies for note-taking and summarising notes, and structuring study time. With the help of his speech pathologist he worked out a system of tape-recording lectures and reviewing the tape later. He also had sessions with the psychologist to develop self-talk and relaxation strategies to reduce his anxiety when he became overwhelmed. Raymond was also feeling very socially isolated, since he had tended to avoid social situations due to his information processing difficulties. He was encouraged to begin contacting some friends and to go out on weekends, when he felt less tired. He was very self-conscious regarding his slowness in keeping up with conversations. He attended a conversational skills group to boost his abilities and confidence.

Raymond successfully completed the subject and returned to Vietnam for a holiday. He still had three subjects to complete, and it was decided to spread these across the year, rather than attempt them in one semester. Some tutoring was maintained in order to provide back-up support, and Raymond was contacted by his speech pathologist on a regular basis. He required some further input to help him structure his time to meet the demands of the additional subjects. He also attended an evening discussion group to assist him in dealing with some ongoing social difficulties. He had fallen in love with a girl at the rehabilitation centre, but she was not returning his affection, causing him additional stress. As the year progressed, his confidence and coping abilities gradually increased, however. He successfully completed his studies and returned to Vietnam, where he is now working for the government.

Avocational interests

Whether or not return to work or study is possible, recreational interests assume a very important role in the life of a person who has sustained TBI. In spite of this, rehabilitation efforts focusing on this aspect of the TBI individual's lifestyle tend to assume secondary importance. Perhaps reflecting this, in the rehabilitation literature there has been little emphasis on return to leisure pursuits. Results from our own longitudinal follow-up study show that more than one-third of a group of 228 individuals with moderate to severe injuries had not returned to previous leisure interests one, two and five years after injury (Ponsford, 2007). Two other recent studies found that more than 80 per cent of their TBI participants experienced disruption of leisure participation (Bier, Dutil, and Couture, 2009; Wise et al., 2010). These results indicate that TBI has a very significant impact on avocational interests. They underscore the importance of the assessment and development of the TBI individual's ability to pursue previous or alternative recreational activities. Many factors may contribute to difficulties engaging in recreational interests following TBI. These include the presence of physical disabilities, problems with transport, limited finance, impairment of cognition, behaviour and social skills, lack of initiative or self-confidence, poor family or social support, or simply a lack of networking (Bier et al., 2009; Wise et al., 2010). As with all other aspects of return to community living, the extent to which these hurdles can be overcome will be largely determined by the presence of funding support and/or community-based resources for the development of leisure pursuits in young people with disabilities. However, an awareness of the importance of recreation and maintenance of contact with friends in the earlier stages of the rehabilitation will lay a valuable foundation for some success in this domain.

Assessment and rehabilitation of recreational abilities

Individual and group recreational and social activities are frequently organised within rehabilitation programmes in order to provide participants with an opportunity to develop certain skills, or relax and socialise. However, these activities do not necessarily bear a close resemblance to those pursued by the

TBI individual prior to injury, and may not be available after discharge from rehabilitation. It is important that regular individual therapy time be devoted to the assessment and development of the injured person's capacity to pursue activities of relevance and interest to themselves (Blacker, Broadhurst, and Teixeira, 2008; Malley, Cooper, and Cope, 2008). As with other aspects of the TBI individual's lifestyle, a comprehensive assessment of previous recreational and social interests should be made at the time of admission to the rehabilitation programme, and an analysis made of the skills required to participate in such interests. Wherever possible the individual who has sustained TBI should be encouraged and given therapeutic assistance to continue pursuing these interests during the rehabilitation phase.

As it becomes clearer what level of mobility, communication and cognitive function is likely to be reached, an assessment can be made as to which activities may be continued, albeit with some modifications, special equipment or assistance, and rehabilitation goals set accordingly. For the many who are not able to return to previous avocational activities, a comprehensive assessment of their interests and ability to pursue alternatives will be required. Whilst this role may be performed primarily by a recreational therapist or occupational therapist, all team members need to share in the process of formulating and working towards the achievement of such goals. For example, specific assessment and therapeutic input is likely to be required from the physiotherapist when return to sporting activities is being contemplated, and from the speech pathologist when reading or communication skills are involved.

Where a number of TBI individuals have a similar interest, a group may be formed to pursue that interest during the rehabilitation phase, in order to provide an opportunity for skills to be practised. However, wherever possible, the TBI individual needs to be encouraged to pursue avocational activities in the local community, rather than being dependent on the rehabilitation centre. In order to achieve this, the rehabilitation team should apply a similar model of intervention to that applied to return to work or school.

Developing activities at the community level

A great deal of energy will need to be devoted to searching for relevant resources. These should be contacted and educated as to specific needs or limitations of the TBI person. Time needs to be spent with the injured individual engaging in the activity in the community and assisting in overcoming any problems encountered, wherever possible making use of or developing natural supports. An attendant carer may be appointed to provide necessary assistance or preferably friends engaged to help. Above all, ongoing follow-up is essential. Whilst many TBI individuals may be discharged from a rehabilitation programme with a comprehensive set of activities, over time these tend to dissipate for a variety of reasons. The TBI person may not have the initiative or organisational ability to develop alternatives without assistance. Many turn to their families or caregivers for such support in the longer term, but this is not ideal because it adds to their burden and reduces opportunities for both parties to have recreational time on their own.

For individuals who are unable to participate in regular community activities, an appropriate day activities programme may be sought. Ideally, such a programme should cater specifically to the needs of young people with acquired brain injury. TBI individuals are not likely to be successfully accommodated in programmes designed for the elderly disabled or those with congenital disabilities. Young people who have sustained TBI tend not to identify themselves as disabled, frequently do not look disabled and may resent being with other disabled people. They retain the motivations and interests which they held prior to injury. A day programme should enable them to pursue these interests. It needs to provide an appropriate degree of structure, but be sufficiently flexible to allow those who have behaviour problems and limited concentration to participate.

A variety of activities should be available, ranging from productive work tasks to creative activities. One of the greatest needs met by such a programme is for social interaction, and some participants may wish only to sit and smoke, drink coffee, and listen to music. An opportunity should be provided to do this. If a suitable programme can be found, issues of transport and meeting the cost of the programme still need to be dealt with. Since programmes such as these are few and far between, it is more probable that a range of suitable generic activities will need to be sought.

Friendships

A similar emphasis needs to be placed on the facilitation of friendships after injury. Friendships can be affected by many aspects of brain injury. As Fitness (2008) points out, in order to keep friendships going you need to keep in touch and to communicate in person, by email or telephone. You need to self-disclose and to make people feel needed and cared about. You need to provide support and to share activities. You need to plan and do things together and have fun together. Cognitive and behavioural changes may affect the injured person's ability to do these things. Being less able to participate in previously shared social, recreational, work or study-related activities makes it even more difficult. The reality for many individuals with severe TBI is that their friendship network shrinks, or is replaced by more contact with family members.

Friends are rarely informed about the effects of a brain injury or included in rehabilitative activities. When visiting they may become distressed over the changes they perceive, especially when the reasons for these are not explained. They may feel scared or guilty. As Callaway and colleagues (2005) point out, this aspect of rehabilitation is rarely explicitly addressed in rehabilitation. Therapists need to involve friends in the early stages of recovery. This necessitates identifying who they are, with the help of the injured person and family, arranging contact and providing them with information and explanation so they understand the changes they see and know how best to interact with and assist their injured friend. One or two key contacts may be used to communicate with a broader network. Therapy time should be devoted to facilitating maintenance of contact with friends by the injured person. This may be done via email, Facebook, cards, telephone or texting, or even creating a newsletter. Over time, opportunities for regular contact in person need to be created. Joint activities such as creating a scrapbook or website of shared experiences may provide a useful focus. Involving friends in recreational activities helps maintain common ground. Without such common ground it is difficult to sustain friendships. The relationship may need to be renegotiated around a different set of shared interests. Whilst some friends may not remain involved, others may show significant ongoing commitment, if provided with information and support. As with other aspects of returning to the community it is important to provide follow-up to maximise the likelihood of maintaining friendships.

Creating opportunities to make new friends is an equally important focus of therapy. Involvement in leisure pursuits and other avocational activities provides opportunities to make new friends. New friend don't know the "old person", which can be very positive. However, as discussed in Chapter 5, there may be a need to first address communication and social skills issues in order to optimise opportunities to make friends. It is important to overcome barriers and build support structures which facilitate the maintenance of participation in these activities – these might include paid support but more ideally utilise natural supports. Therapy time should be devoted to the identification, education and ongoing assistance of these support persons. As Sloan (2008) has stated, "we need to work with other people in the community, not just the person themselves, and . . . promote social inclusion and a sense of belonging in the community, not just physical access to the community. If we can do all that, we will have some much needed impacts on long-term social outcomes following brain injury."

Driver assessment and rehabilitation

For many young people who have sustained TBI, return to driving represents a major goal. The inability to drive may compound low self-esteem and the injured person's sense of dependency and isolation. However, because of the inherent risks involved in driving, considered assessment is essential. This is frequently difficult to enforce, as in many countries the drivers' licence remains technically valid unless steps are taken to cancel it. There is evidence to suggest that severely brain injured individuals are at greater risk of accidents (Formisano et al., 2005). However the evidence regarding fitness to drive in individuals with mild or moderate injuries is less clear.

The assessment of driving capability is extremely difficult, due to the number, complexity, and frequently abstract nature of the skills involved.

Many of these skills may be impaired following TBI, including motor control and co-ordination, visual perception, speed of information processing, attention, particularly divided attention, memory, behavioural control, planning, judgement, decision-making and self-awareness. Increased fatigue may also present a problem. However, as Brouwer, Withaar, Tant and van Zomeren (2002) have pointed out, the precise manner in which these deficits interfere with the injured individual's actual driving performance is difficult to predict. The presence of a given cognitive deficit may not necessarily result in unsafe driving. For example, a person with a slow reaction time may be able to make allowances for this in their driving. However, if they also have impaired planning, judgement and self-awareness they will be less able to do so (Brouwer et al., 2002). This highlights the significance of executive skills in regulating divided attention, the integrity of which has been shown to be associated with a greater crash rate in simulator driving studies involving individuals with TBI (Cyr et al., 2007) and, in turn, with real-world driving performance (Lew et al., 2005). Moreover, factors unrelated to the injury, such as the injured person's previous driving experience and habits and previous driving infringements have also been shown to play a significant role in post-injury driving performance (Pietrapiana et al., 2005).

Historically, and in some countries to the present time, the decision as to whether an injured person could return to driving has been made by medical practitioners, based on the probability of epilepsy, the patient's neurological status, and speculation as to the nature and manner in which the injured person's cognitive deficits would affect driving capability. However, it is becoming understood that medical assessment alone is not a reliable means of judging driver competence (Brouwer and Withaar, 1997; Fox, Bashford, and Caust, 1992). Neuropsychological assessment has also been used as a predictive tool. Findings in this respect have been mixed. Whilst a number of studies have shown that neuropsychological tests are of limited predictive validity (Brooke, 1992; Brouwer et al., 2002; Fox et al., 1992; Lundqvist and Alinder, 2007), performance on certain tests, including complex reaction time and divided attention tasks, the Trail Making or Color Trails test, WAIS-III Digit Symbol Coding and Matrix Reasoning tasks and the Useful Field of View test, a measure of visual information processing, have shown some association with current (Brouwer and Withaar, 1997; Coleman et al., 2002; Novack et al., 2006) or subsequent (Lundqvist, Alinder, and Ronnberg, 2008) driving behaviour. Self-awareness also appears to play a role (Lundqvist and Alinder, 2007). However, studies to date have been limited by small samples and use of variable tests.

A number of authors have also expressed doubts as to the usefulness of brake reaction time tests and driving simulators in assessing or training the ability to cope on the road (Hopewell and Price, 1985; van Zomeren, Brouwer, and Minderhoud, 1987). However, a study by Lew and colleagues (2005) found some simulator indices (speed and steering control, accidents and vigilance to a divided attention task) predicted ratings of handling of automobile controls, regulation of vehicle speed and direction, higher order judgement and self-control when driving ten months later. In individuals with severe TBI and evidence of significant impairments there is now a growing awareness of the need for multi-disciplinary evaluation, incorporating on-road assessment and training by appropriately qualified instructors. However, as Brouwer and colleagues (2002) have cautioned, not all patients with mild or moderate injuries should be referred for on-road driving assessments, unless there is clear evidence of significant visuo-perceptual, motor, cognitive or behavioural impairments. The presence of mild slowing of information processing speed in the absence of other deficits does not, in their opinion, warrant an on-road assessment.

Recommended driver assessment procedures

In the case of severe TBI it is now generally recommended that assessment not be conducted until several months after injury, during which time the injured individual should be advised not to drive. The first stage in a comprehensive driver evaluation is usually a motor-sensory assessment, encompassing vision, hearing, strength, sensation, range of movement, co-ordination and endurance in arms and legs, neck and trunk, and mobility, with specific identification of whether and how any impairments impact on the injured person's ability to operate and drive a vehicle. Numerous mechanical adaptations are now available to assist in compensating for motor-sensory problems.

Aspects of cognitive function for consideration include the ability to sustain and divide attention, track more than one thing at a time, distractibility, speed of information processing, visual scanning and orientation, memory, impulsivity, planning, anticipation, judgement and decision making, and self-monitoring, as well as behavioural responses under stress, emotional control and self-awareness. Whilst the results of a neuropsychological assessment may assist the driving assessor by pointing to the potential presence of certain difficulties, the actual impact of such impairments on driving performance needs to be assessed on the road. Reaction times may also be assessed using an off-road brake reaction tester, with the introduction of distractions. However, as noted above, the extent to which this may result in unsafe driving may depend on the person's awareness and other executive abilities (Brouwer et al., 2002). Off-road tests of road law and road craft should also be carried out.

Provided a baseline standard has been reached on the off-road assessment, the injured individual may proceed to an on-road assessment. Such assessments must be conducted in a dual-control car by an instructor who is trained in driving assessment, has a good understanding of the impact of brain injury on cognition and behaviour, as well as an understanding of the normal variation in driving habits and behaviour. The test drives are generally graded in terms of their demands, commencing in quiet residential streets and progressing to more complex traffic situations which include busy shopping areas, main roads and inner city streets. An automatic car may be used for the first drive to reduce the demands on the injured person, and a manual car used in subsequent drives. Distractions and other demands may be introduced systematically to assess the injured driver's response to these.

According to the model of car driving put forward by Michon (1979), the task of driving involves three hierarchical levels: the "Strategic level", which involves planning and decision-making regarding the route to be taken, the time of the journey, etc., before driving starts; the "Tactical level", which involves behaviour and decisions in traffic, such as adapting speed to the area, considering when to overtake and switching on headlights to improve visibility; and the "Operational level", which incorporates the actions and decisions involved in driving, such as perception of traffic situations, use of controls and mirrors and generally handling the car. Deficits in speed of processing generally result in problems at the Operational level, whereas executive difficulties impact on the Tactical and Strategic levels, which in turn allow the person to compensate for operational difficulties. Previous driving experience will also assist in compensation for Operational driving difficulties (Brouwer et al., 2002). On-road assessment needs to cover all of these aspects of driving. Given the frequency of executive dysfunction following TBI, it is particularly important to examine planning, anticipation, the ability to adapt to different situations on the road and avoid time pressure. Unfortunately there are no standardised techniques available to make such assessments. Indeed, a significant limitation of most current on-road assessment procedures is the lack of standardised procedures, normative data which clearly differentiate safe from unsafe drivers, and follow-up data regarding actual driving performance. Whilst the conduct of on-road assessment of driving capability has been a very important step forward, much further work is needed in this area before the process can be considered a valid one.

Despite these limitations, studies following up drivers who have returned to driving following off- and on-road driving assessments have generally demonstrated no greater rate of speeding tickets, accidents or near misses than healthy controls (Josman and Katz, 1991; Katz et al., 1990; Schultheis, Matheis, Nead, and DeLuca, 2002). A study by Coleman and colleagues (2002) found that the strongest predictor of driving status and driving frequency in a group of individuals with TBI was their significant other's perception of their fitness to drive, suggesting that some education of significant others as part of the return to driving process may be warranted.

Driver rehabilitation

The question as to whether it is possible to retrain aspects of driving behaviour also remains open, although there is some positive evidence to this effect. Certainly there is considerable scope for overcoming motor-sensory limitations through adaptive modifications to the car. The injured person will need to be trained to use these modifications, and may also learn other compensatory strategies. In some cases the decision is made to grant a restricted licence, allowing driving only during daylight hours, in local or quiet neighbourhoods. Training in the use of satellite navigation may overcome navigational difficulties.

In a controlled study Kewman and colleagues (1985) trained 13 brain-injured subjects in visuo-motor tracking and divided attention skills using a small electric-powered vehicle. They were able to demonstrate a positive impact of this training on on-road driving performance relative to controls.

Driver training programmes are now conducted in many rehabilitation centres. These may incorporate sessions in the classroom and practice in handling and manoeuvring a car, but generally involve on-road instruction. Provision of a series of driving lessons allows further opportunity to observe driver behaviour. Hopewell and Price (1985) reported a return-to-driving rate of 53 per cent following such a driver training programme, although no comparison was made with a matched, untrained sample. The importance of factors such as the nature of cognitive deficits and previous driving experience in determining the ability to benefit from such programmes remains unclear.

The probability of success of driver training or retraining is likely to be maximised if training is focused on the specific limitations of the injured individual. The emphasis of most training programmes described is generally placed on operational aspects of driving, such as handling and manoeuvring the car. As Brouwer and colleagues (Brouwer and Withaar, 1997; Brouwer et al., 2002) point out, given the frequency of executive dysfunction following TBI, there is undoubtedly in many cases a need for development of training strategies focusing on strategic and tactical aspects of driving, such as the Time Pressure Management approach piloted with bicycle riders by Kovacs, Fasotti and colleagues (Fasotti et al., 2000; Winkens et al., 2009a). This approach trains the injured person to anticipate problems associated with time pressure and take necessary steps to avoid them. The success of this training depended on the level of self-awareness of the injured individual, which in itself has been shown to be a significant predictor of driving performance (Lundqvist and Alinder, 2007). It may well also be a highly significant determinant of the degree to which the injured person can adapt to limitations and learn to drive safely.

Conclusions

Considerable time and effort need to be devoted to assisting individuals with TBI to return to a living situation which maximises their independence, work, study, recreational and social interests, and driving. This is best achieved via a thorough assessment of premorbid status in these areas, identification of relevant strengths and weaknesses since the injury, and available supports. Therapeutic input may focus specifically on developing the skills needed to resume activities or develop a new lifestyle, task modification, or the provision of necessary environmental supports. Above all, it is vital to provide ongoing support and assistance over an extended time frame, in order to deal with the inevitable problems and changes which will occur in the lifestyles of TBI individuals and those around them. Given the traditional focus of rehabilitation in the acute phase of recovery, there are likely to be many difficulties in finding the means of meeting all these challenges. In most cases a broad range of community-based resources will need to be tapped, together with the assistance of the injured person's own network of supports.

8 Dealing with the impact of TBI on psychological adjustment and relationships

Jennie Ponsford

Introduction

Psychological reactions to TBI are complex and variable, being determined by a broad range of factors. These include the nature and severity of the injury, the manner in which it was sustained and whether the injured person can recall the accident, as well as the age, developmental stage, previous psychological and social adjustment of the injured person and family, and events since the injury. Psychological consequences of mild TBI differ some-what from those associated with moderate or severe TBI and this will therefore be discussed first. However, the major emphasis of this chapter will be on dealing with emotional and adjustment issues following moderate and severe TBI.

Psychological consequences of mild TBI

As outlined in Chapter 1, mild TBI can result in persisting symptoms, known collectively as the post-concussional syndrome (PCS). These include headache, dizziness, fatigue, visual disturbance, tinnitus, mental slowness, concentration and memory problems, irritability, sensitivity to noise, bustle or light, tinnitus, sleep disturbance, anxiety and depression. Neuropsychological tests may show impaired speed of information processing and attention. It has been proposed that some ongoing symptoms may result from the stress of coping with a reduced information processing capacity, whilst attempting to perform previous roles as before (Gouvier, Cubic, Jones, Brantley, and Cutlip, 1992; van Zomeren and van den Burg, 1985). Certainly there is a strong association between reported ongoing PCS and levels of daily stress and anxiety (Gouvier et al., 1992; Ponsford et al., 2000). However, there is not a strong association between degree of cognitive impairment and reported severity of PCS (Landre, Poppe, Davis, Schmaus, and Hobbs, 2006; Meares et al., 2008; Ponsford et al., 2000). The degree of subjective awareness of limitations is more closely related to subjective distress. Moreover, the association of other factors such as post-traumatic stress, pain from other injuries, other life stressors and previous psychological disturbance with PCS has also been shown to be significant (Meares et al., 2008; Ponsford, 2005; Ponsford et al., 2000).The injury-related symptoms may interact with or be exacerbated by these other factors.

The few studies formally evaluating the impact of interventions for psychological problems following mild TBI have produced mixed findings. Relander, Troupp and Bjorkesten (1972) showed that encouragement to get up as early as possible, education about injury, physiotherapy, and follow-up appointments resulted in more rapid return to work. Bell et al. (2008) showed that follow-up telephone counselling reduced mild TBI-related symptoms at 6 months post-injury. However, trials by Ghaffar and colleagues (2006), and Elgmark Andersson and colleagues (2007), evaluating the efficacy of initial medical evaluation, multidisciplinary treatment comprising patient and family education about mild TBI, individualised psychotherapy, occupational therapy, physiotherapy as needed and follow-up appointments, resulted in no differences on psychological and cognitive measures relative to controls receiving routine care at follow-up six months and one year post-injury respectively. Indeed, in the study by Elgmark Andersson et al. those who had few PCS 2–8 weeks post-injury and declined rehabilitation recovered well, whereas those with several PCS who accepted rehabilitation had still not recovered a year post-injury. Given the emerging link between presence of pre-injury psychiatric issues and ongoing PCS, it may be more rational and cost-effective, as Ghaffar et al. concluded, to target individuals with pre-injury psychiatric problems for more intensive intervention.

Given the lack of strong evidence of efficacy of more intensive interventions and the high volume of individuals with mild TBI, directing such interventions at all patients with mild TBI is arguably neither feasible nor cost-effective in most health care contexts. Recognition of this has led to the development and evaluation of lower cost interventions. Whilst findings have not been universally positive (Alves, Macciocchi, and Barth, 1993), several studies have shown that provision of information about expected symptoms and suggested coping strategies has resulted in fewer reported symptoms, less disruption to social activities and/or lower levels of stress at three or six months post-injury (Mittenberg, Tremont, Zeilinski, Fichera, and Rayles, 1996; Paniak, Toller-Lobe, Durand, and Nagy, 1998; Paniak, Toller-Lobe, Reynolds, Melnyk, and Nagy, 2000; Ponsford et al., 2002; Wade, King, Wenden, Crawford, and Caldwell, 1998). Arguably this information will maximise coping and minimise overreaction and misattribution of symptoms.

For those individuals who continue to report symptoms several weeks after injury, in addition to providing education, it is important to investigate and treat possible comorbid musculoskeletal injuries, pain, sleep disturbances, hearing loss or tinnitus, balance problems, dizziness or vertigo and headache. With respect to cognition, it is neither practical nor necessary to conduct a full neuropsychological assessment in all mild TBI cases (Peloso et al., 2004). However, individuals who are at greater risk of experiencing difficulties following mild TBI, including students or people in very demanding occupations, those with previous injuries or where there are specific questions regarding fitness to return to work or study, may need to be assessed within the first few weeks of injury. Individuals who continue to experience problems

1–3 months post injury should also have a complete neuropsychological assessment. Where litigation is an issue, the possibility of malingering also needs to be considered using appropriate assessment tools (Rose, 2005).

In discussing approaches to dealing with ongoing adjustment difficulties following mild TBI, Cicerone and Tupper (1991) emphasised the importance of modifying the injured individual's belief system regarding the severity of deficits, or the impact of these deficits on daily functioning. There is a need to normalise symptoms, by providing realistic explanation as to their basis. The injured individual may be assisted in learning to regulate their lifestyle to avoid problems (for example, by reducing activity to avoid fatigue or by limiting exposure to environments where there is a lot of noise or interpersonal demands), recognising the early signs of stress and taking steps to avoid it developing. Assistance may be given in developing methods of compensating for cognitive impairments (e.g. by reducing overall workload, introducing a diary, making notes). Somatic and emotional sensitivities may be alleviated by cognitive-behavioural techniques, which assist the injured person to develop a more realistic appraisal of their abilities, tolerate or shift the focus of attention away from their symptoms, and re-establish a sense of mastery over the environment (Mittenberg, Canyock, Condit, and Patton, 2001). The possible presence of Posttraumatic Stress Disorder (PTSD) needs to be considered and treated appropriately. A more detailed discussion of PTSD is contained in the later section on anxiety disorders. In some cases, pre-existing adjustment issues may need to be addressed through more intensive psychotherapy (Ruff, 2005; Wood, 2004).

Emotional reactions to moderate and severe TBI

Numerous studies have documented the significant psychosocial impact of moderate and severe TBI. For many, this results in a decline in vocational status, family or marital relationships, and social or leisure activities (Dikmen et al., 2003; Draper et al., 2007; Machamer et al., 2005; Ponsford et al., 2008; Ponsford et al., 1995a; Tate et al., 2005). A number of authors have also documented psychological consequences, including reduced self-esteem, loneliness and depression (Cooper-Evans et al., 2008; Goodinson et al., 2009; Gouick and Gentleman, 2004; Tyerman and Humphrey, 1984).

Whilst TBI can occur in people of any gender, age or socio-economic class, it is most frequently sustained by adolescent and young adult males (Kraus and McArthur, 1999; O'Rance and Fortune, 2007). They may still be in the process of attaining emotional separation and independence from parental support, establishing an identity, completing study or establishing vocational skills, and forming important social and intimate relationships. The attainment of these milestones is interrupted by the occurrence of TBI. By virtue of their circumstances, as well as physical, emotional and social disabilities, many individuals with TBI have a reduced capacity to resolve age-relevant issues.

Fryer (1989, p. 257) noted that an inability to resolve adolescent issues can result in "lack of purpose, inability to find intimacy with others, and self-defeating behaviour (i.e. substance abuse)". All of these behaviours may also result directly from the brain injury. Rejection by peers and the inability to pursue vocational goals and recreational interests may result in frustration, low self-esteem and social isolation. A new peer group may be formed, but new friendships tend to be more superficial and less enduring (Callaway et al., 2005; Gomez-Hernandez, Max, Kosier, Paradiso, and Robinson, 1997; Oddy, 1984; Oddy et al., 1985). For individuals who were in a long-term relationship or married prior to injury, changes in personality and behaviour may place significant stress on the relationship, which may already be strained by financial hardship and other role changes (Bracy and Douglas, 2002; Burridge, Williams, Yates, Harris, and Ward, 2007; Willer, Allen, Liss, and Zicht, 1991; Winstanley et al., 2006; Wood and Yurdakul, 1997). There may be changes in sexual drive and performance (Ponsford, 2003). Relationships with children may also deteriorate to the point where the person with TBI is competing with them for the attention of their spouse/mother (Thomsen, 1984).

Some findings suggest that a significant proportion of individuals with TBI also come from a lower socioeconomic group, have limited education, unstable employment, previous head injury, drug or alcohol abuse or other psychiatric disorders prior to injury (Kraus and Sorenson, 1994; Robinson and Jorge, 2002), factors that have been shown to be related to poorer post-injury outcome (MacMillan, Hart, Martelli, and Zasler, 2002). The psychosocial and emotional consequences for the individual who has sustained moderate or severe TBI thus represent a complex interplay of changes in cognition, behaviour and personality resulting directly from the brain injury, pre-injury factors and reactive adjustment problems (Cooper-Evans et al., 2008; Gomez-Hernandez et al., 1997).

Studies of psychiatric disorders following TBI suggest that depressive and anxiety disorders and substance use occur with significantly higher frequency than in the general population. These problems, together with poor self-awareness and self-esteem, impaired social or interpersonal skills, anger management problems, marital or relationship difficulties and sexual problems represent the most common psychological issues associated with TBI (Lezak et al., 2004). Approaches to therapy for social or interpersonal skills are described in Chapter 5. Methods of dealing with the other problem areas are discussed below. It must be stressed that all techniques recommended require further experimental validation.

Self-awareness and self-esteem following TBI

Several authors have indicated that unrealistic self-appraisal leads to problems in psychosocial adjustment following moderate or severe TBI (Ezrachi et al., 1991; Fleming and Ownsworth, 2006; Hart et al., 2004b; Prigatano and

Fordyce, 1986; Sherer et al., 2003). Reduced awareness of changes in cognition, behaviour and personality following TBI is thought in most cases to result directly from neurological impairment, particularly impairment of frontal lobe function, rather than from a psychological need to deny the impact of the trauma. However, it is important to be aware of the possibility that denial of deficits could have a psychogenic basis. Lack of insight commonly reduces motivation for rehabilitative therapy, results in unrealistic decisions regarding work or study, and conflict with family members or carers, who may be seen by the injured individual as overly protective or negative.

Numerous studies have shown that when ratings by individuals with TBI are compared with those of their relatives or rehabilitation therapists, the TBI individuals rate themselves as more competent (Hart, Seignourel, and Sherer, 2009; Prigatano, 1986; Sherer et al., 2003). Awareness of cognitive and behavioural changes tends to be poorer than that of physical changes (Fleming and Strong, 1999; Hart et al., 2009). The degree of the discrepancy between the TBI individual and relative ratings is generally associated with severity of cognitive impairment, particularly executive impairment, and negatively correlated with emotional distress (Ben-Yishay and Prigatano, 1990; Cooper-Evans et al., 2008; Prigatano and Altman, 1990; Sherer et al., 2003). The discrepancy tends to decrease over time, suggesting that recovery of cognitive function and exposure to the impact of the injury increase self-awareness (Dirette and Plaisier, 2007; Hart et al., 2009). According to Ezrachi et al. (1991) and Prigatano and Fordyce (1986) the development of realistic self-appraisal is essential if the TBI individual is to return successfully to a productive lifestyle. Studies evaluating the effectiveness of specific cognitive interventions have also identified self-awareness as an essential ingredient to their success (Anson and Ponsford, 2006b; Crosson et al., 1989; Fasotti et al., 2000; Winkens et al., 2009a). Developing awareness is therefore an important component of the rehabilitation process.

Developing self-awareness

Information regarding the causes and nature of the changes resulting from the injury needs to be conveyed to the TBI individual from the time of admission to rehabilitation. Such information and feedback regarding performance should be given in clear and simple terms, repeated as often as necessary and written down. Attempts should be made to demonstrate changes on tasks and in settings that the TBI person was familiar with prior to the injury, and sees as meaningful. Whilst all members of the rehabilitation team will be involved in this process, it may be appropriate to designate a specific member, who has good rapport with the TBI person, to see them on a regular basis to discuss their progress in the programme, problems which are emerging, and to make changes to therapy goals as necessary. However, for a variety of reasons, the severely injured person in the early stages of recovery will rarely be capable of fully comprehending the impact of the injury, let alone accepting it and understanding the implications for the future. Individuals with severe TBI frequently become resentful and even hostile if constantly confronted with their failures. Therefore, therapists should also highlight strengths and positive attributes. There is little to be gained, and a great deal to be lost, by reiterating information and continuing to emphasise problems which the TBI person aggressively refuses to acknowledge. Thus, the manner and frequency with which feedback is given requires careful consideration by the team. Over time, but at a widely varying pace, there are likely to be changes in the injured person's capacity to receive feedback and begin to understand its implications for the future.

It is usually not until TBI individuals have returned to the community and had more direct experience of changes in capabilities, as far as living skills, work, leisure activities and social relationships are concerned, that a more realistic awareness of change is gained (Dirette and Plaisier, 2007). It is for this reason that we would argue that rehabilitation should be conducted in a real and meaningful context as early as possible after injury. As awareness develops, psychological assistance should be made available to support the process of developing a realistic self-appraisal of injury-related changes, whilst minimising loss of self-esteem, since the process of becoming aware of changes can be devastating, provoking what Goldstein (1942) termed a "catastrophic reaction". The writings of Goldstein inspired the work of Ben-Yishay and Prigatano, who view the restoration of the impaired identity or self as a central goal in rehabilitation following brain injury (Ben-Yishay, 2008; Prigatano, 1999). There is a need to bridge the gap between the person's ideal self and their actual self in order to establish a new identity. Gracey and colleagues (Dewar and Gracey, 2007; Gracey et al., 2008; Yeates, Henwood, Gracey, and Evans, 2007) found that individuals with brain injury developed their identity though reflection on their pre-injury selves and participation in activities in a social context that they see as meaningful. However, they require support in this process. Ylvisaker and Feeney (2000), who have also argued that identity can be re-constructed in the context of meaningful activities, have provided some wonderful case examples in which young brain-injured clients have been engaged and motivated by being encouraged to identify themselves with a person they admire and to work on adopting the positive attributes of that person.

The ultimate goal of such therapy is the attainment of some degree of acceptance, and an ability to like the "new" person who has survived the injury. For adolescents and young adults in particular, the therapist needs to be attuned to the impact of the injury on pertinent developmental issues and address these. For some, an important focus may be on body image and forming intimate relationships, for others it will be on having friends and feeling accepted by peers, whilst for others it may be on moving out of home and achieving independence, or on having a job. For many people all of these things will be important. In the process of building self-awareness and a new identity, it is necessary to make a careful assessment of the TBI individual's previous and current psychological state and personality, and methods of coping with stress.

The quality of "therapeutic alliance" has been identified as a key factor in the development of self-awareness, which in turn influences compliance in a rehabilitation context (Schönberger, Humle, and Teasdale, 2006). Clients' predictions about their abilities can be tested collaboratively with the therapist and at a suitable pace for the client. A good working alliance with therapists is associated with more positive self-efficacy and, in turn, with better rehabilitation outcomes (Klonoff et al., 2000).

As will be discussed in detail in Chapter 9, it is also vital that families be involved in the therapeutic process, as the TBI person's emotional state can also be influenced by the manner in which the family has coped with the injury. Many families initially fail to recognise or acknowledge the presence of changes in their relative. When they do recognise such changes, family members and others may also find it very difficult to give the TBI individual realistic feedback. They may require assistance in understanding the importance of feedback and how to give it in a supportive way. The family itself frequently needs to go through a process of re-working its roles, values and identity.

Group therapy to enhance self-awareness and self-esteem

In those individuals who have sufficient language, memory skills and behavioural control, individual therapy may be supplemented with group therapy, which provides an opportunity for peer group feedback and support. Prigatano and Fordyce (1986) recommended that groups focusing on adjustment issues should consist of around six brain-injured individuals and two therapists with background in neuropsychology and clinical psychology. These groups should be closed, to allow for continuity and the development of a sense of trust and belonging. In most holistic programmes, operating in a "Therapeutic Milieu", such groups meet daily or at least several times per week. In addition to achieving some awareness of the impact of the injury on each person's thinking, behaviour, emotional state, and lifestyle, group therapy can provide opportunities to reflect on how these changes might impact on key aspects of life such as work, relationships and leisure, how they are perceived by and affect others, and how they compare with those experienced by other TBI individuals. This experience potentially enhances insight within a supportive environment, reduces the TBI person's sense of isolation, provides an opportunity to work on interpersonal skills, and helps give meaning to their new existence.

Self-esteem may be boosted by exercises in which individuals identify positive attributes in themselves and in one another or talk of their accomplishments. Such exercises represent an important component of the head trauma programmes at the Rusk Institute of Rehabilitation Medicine in New York, developed by Yehuda Ben-Yishay and colleagues (Ben-Yishay,

2000, 2008; Ben-Yishay, Piasetsky, Rattok, Cohen, and Diller, 1980; Daniels-Zide and Ben-Yishay, 2000). Group leaders generally need to be directive, assisting TBI individuals who have difficulty initiating or conveying their thoughts clearly, clarifying what group members say and intervening when group members' comments are perceived as being overly hurtful, aggressive or otherwise inappropriate, as well as keeping the group "on track". It is important to follow up group sessions with individual psychotherapy, focusing on issues arising in the group and/or individual strategies, for example dealing with conflict, becoming more assertive, keeping track of conversations, and assisting the individual to develop realistic plans for their future. According to Ben-Yishay (2008), participants in a therapeutic milieu progress through a hierarchy of six stages: engagement, awareness, mastery, control, acceptance and identity. Following participation in the group programme the focus moves to determining vocational activities that are likely to be manageable and to providing assistance in integration into paid or voluntary work or study. Successful negotiation of these processes is ideally associated with progress though the six stages, although as Ben-Yishay (2008) has observed, not all individuals will attain a re-constituted ego-identity; this depends on the possession of certain premorbid personality characteristics.

The holistic day programmes developed by Ben-Yishay, Prigatano, Klonoff and their colleagues (Ben-Yishay, 2000; Prigatano, 1999) have reported successful outcomes in individual case studies (Ben-Yishay, 2008) and group cohorts (Klonoff et al., 2000). They have since been emulated in many countries by such eminent clinicians as Anne-Lise Christensen, James Malec, Keith Cicerone and Barbara Wilson (Wilson et al., 2000), again reporting positive outcomes (Cicerone et al., 2008; Teasdale and Christensen, 1994). There has, however, been no specific experimental study of the impact of these methods on the development of self-awareness and identity after brain injury, in particular which aspects of the therapy are effective and in whom. Such evaluation is extremely difficult, largely because of the lack of objective measurement tools, particularly in the domain of self-awareness. In those who have sustained very severe TBI with amnesia, attentional problems and very limited behavioural control, attempts to develop realistic self-appraisal, either through individual or group therapy, are very unlikely to be successful. Despite this, their emotional responses are worthy of respect and consideration, and opportunities should be given for ventilation of feelings on a regular basis.

The facilitation of friendships represents another means of enhancing self-esteem. Willer, Allen, Anthony and Cowlan (1993) developed the concept of a "Circle of Support". This is a semi-structured approach to the establishment of a network of friends who meet regularly with the injured person after their return to the community, providing opportunities for them to articulate their goals and dreams and discuss ways of working towards these, as well as potential barriers. It provides a more natural source of social support and positive, but also realistic feedback. The extent to which such circles can be sustained has not been established, however.

Approaches to therapy for specific emotional or interpersonal problems

Individuals with TBI may be at a greater risk of side effects with psychotropic medications, and no pharmacological intervention has been shown to consistently alleviate these problems without significant side-effects (Hiott and Labbate, 2002; Warden et al., 2006). Therefore psychological interventions represent the preferred method of treatment. However, by virtue of their cognitive difficulties, many individuals who have sustained TBI have difficulty in benefiting from traditional psychotherapy, which is heavily reliant on self-awareness, verbal interaction, and a capacity to concentrate on and remember the content of that interaction from one session to the next. Difficulties with executive control of thinking and behaviour may make it difficult to generalise and implement strategies in everyday life.

Cognitive behaviour therapy

There is a lack of strong scientific evidence regarding the success or otherwise of any particular psychotherapeutic approach following TBI. However, cognitive-behavioural techniques lend themselves to dealing with these difficulties quite well. Cognitive behaviour therapy (CBT) focuses on changing unhelpful behaviours and beliefs about the world to reduce negative emotions. Its structured nature allows for the delivery of therapeutic intervention for mental health problems while accommodating the effects of TBI. With CBT, written aids, cues and repetition are fundamental components that can be extended for people with TBI. CBT can also be adapted so it has less emphasis on abstract concepts, by focusing on behavioural strategies (e.g. exposure to feared situations, systematic desensitisation) and the achievement of concrete behavioural goals (Khan-Bourne and Brown, 2003).

It is important at the outset to make a careful assessment of the limitations the TBI person is likely to have in such a therapy situation and to adapt the prescribed techniques as needed. Generally, it is necessary to keep sessions short and build in repetition, writing all important points down in the person's diary or in a special "therapy diary", and using handouts and pictorial aids. The therapist will usually need to focus on very concrete examples and behaviours and may need to be quite directive.

With the agreement of the injured individual, it may be helpful to involve a supportive family member or close friend as a "co-therapist". This person may assist in carrying out homework exercises, where thoughts and behaviour are being monitored, and prompt adherence to guidelines agreed upon in therapy sessions. In a sense, the family member may act as the TBI individual's "frontal lobes", providing feedback in familiar situations, and prompting more adaptive responses. It is, however, extremely important to convey a clear understanding of the aims and process of therapy to the relative who is acting as a co-therapist. Family members may be able to provide valuable information regarding the TBI person's behavioural and emotional responses in a variety of situations, and the triggers and consequences of such responses. They are also likely to be able to help maintain the impact of the intervention in the future, and report on its effectiveness.

The therapist must, however, be sensitive to family dynamics, which may prove to be counterproductive. For example, relatives may deny or have difficulty in accepting the presence of changes in behaviour, therefore being unable to make realistic assessments or give appropriate feedback to the TBI individual. Pre-existing tendencies towards over-protectiveness on the part of parents may result in some ambivalence and even active sabotage of interventions which are likely to result in a greater amount of time being spent by the TBI son or daughter away from the home. The use of a spouse as a co-therapist where there is marital disharmony, particularly involving issues of control or role conflict, may contribute to further disharmony. TBI adolescents may reject the involvement of a family member who is seen as taking control, and this needs to be respected.

CBT has been shown to be effective in the psychological treatment of a range of psychiatric and psychological problems following TBI, including depression (Khan-Bourne and Brown, 2003), anxiety (Hodgson, McDonald, Tate, and Gertler, 2005; Scheutzow and Wiercisiewski, 1999), emotional distress (Bradbury et al., 2008), and anger (Medd and Tate, 2000), as well as poor psychosocial functioning (Ownsworth et al., 2000), self-esteem, problem solving (Rath et al., 2003) and adaptive coping (Anson and Ponsford, 2006a). However, most of the CBT research within the TBI population has been based on case studies. In particular, few studies have examined the impact of psychological treatments for individuals with moderate–severe TBI (Soo and Tate, 2007).

A few group intervention studies have been conducted, focusing on adaptive coping skills, psychosocial functioning, and problem-solving (Anson and Ponsford, 2006a; Ownsworth et al., 2000; Rath et al., 2003). Each of these studies demonstrated gains in use of the skills being taught. However, there was limited evidence of a positive impact on objectively measured anxiety or depression in the groups as a whole. Anson and Ponsford (2006a) used a CBT approach in a group intervention aiming to enhance use of adaptive coping skills following TBI. The 10 sessions focused on understanding the association between thoughts, feelings and bodily sensations; developing strategies for managing anxiety, depression, and anger; for solving problems; and for maximising use of adaptive coping strategies. Whilst there was improvement in use of adaptive coping strategies on completion of the group, this was not necessarily maintained over time. Moreover, levels of anxiety and depression did not change in the group as a whole. However, there was considerable individual variability in response to the group intervention. It was concluded that *individual* counselling, tailored to address individual issues and needs, may be more appropriate for TBI clients. Studies evaluating the efficacy of individual CBT (Bradbury et al., 2008; Bryant, Moulds, Guthrie, and Nixon,

2003; Hodgson et al., 2005) have shown encouraging results, but have involved small samples. At present, there is insufficient evidence to make a gold standard recommendation for the treatment of anxiety and depression following TBI, thus highlighting the need for more research.

Motivational interviewing

One potential limitation of CBT is that it requires active involvement of the client for maximum benefit. Low motivation and engagement can prevent this involvement. Motivational Interviewing (MI) has been used increasingly in recent years to enhance engagement in therapy and motivation to change. MI uses specific strategies to explore and resolve ambivalence to change (Miller and Rollnick, 2002), exploring the pros and cons of change, but leaving it to the client to make the decision to engage in therapy. The use of summaries and worksheets is encouraged since it helps make concepts concrete and provides take-home reminders. Its efficacy has been shown both as a stand-alone treatment, and as a preparatory intervention prior to other treatment such as CBT (Burke, Dunn, Atkins, and Phelps, 2004; Westra and Dozois, 2006). Using MI as a prelude to an empirically validated CBT programme for anxiety, Westra and Dozois (2006) found that in comparison with participants receiving only CBT, those who received MI prior to engaging in CBT had a higher level of self-efficacy (belief in ability to control anxiety), were more compliant with treatment, less likely to drop out of treatment and less anxious at treatment completion. MI has also been used with success in the prevention of alcohol use following TBI (Bombardier and Rimmele, 1999). Bell and colleagues (2008) demonstrated the effectiveness of scheduled telephone counselling based on MI principles in improving overall function and quality of life in a group of 171 individuals with TBI. However, more controlled studies involving CBT and MI are necessary to identify more specifically the influence of different aspects of cognitive function on treatment response.

Depression following TBI

Diagnosing depression

It is now widely recognised that depression is a frequent occurrence following TBI (Ashman et al., 2004; Bombardier et al., 2010; Gould, Ponsford, Johnston, and Schönberger, 2011c; Jorge et al., 2004; Whelan-Goodinson, Ponsford, Johnston, and Grant, 2009a). Whilst there are wide variations in reported rates, most recent studies estimate that between 42 and 53 per cent of individuals with complicated mild to severe TBI experience a depressive disorder in the first year after injury, most commonly Major Depressive Disorder (MDD) (Bombardier et al., 2010; Gould et al., 2011c; Whelan-Goodinson et al., 2009a). There is a steady increase in onset up until 2–3 years post-injury, when the rate tends to plateau (Ashman et al., 2004; Whelan-Goodinson et al., 2009a). However, high rates of depression are still reported between 10 and 30 years post-injury (Draper et al., 2007; Hoofien, Gilboa, Vakil, and Donovick, 2001; Koponen et al., 2002). Depression is comorbid with anxiety in 72–74 per cent of cases (Gould et al., 2011c; Jorge et al., 2004; Whelan-Goodinson et al., 2009a).

Depression may manifest itself in many different ways, resulting in changes in mood, thinking patterns, behaviour and physical well-being. Any or all of the following symptoms may be apparent:

Changes in mood: lowered mood, sadness, tearfulness, flat or blunted affect, irritability.

Changes in thinking patterns: hopelessness, helplessness, worthlessness; pessimism; self-criticism; excessive guilt; self-pity; suicidal thoughts; poor concentration and memory; indecisiveness; worry over health; lack of motivation, interest or pleasure in activities.

Behavioural changes: psychomotor agitation or retardation; reduced attention to physical appearance and hygiene; social withdrawal; relationship difficulties; suicidal behaviour; substance abuse.

Physical symptoms: excessive sleeping, or sleep disturbance, with difficulty falling asleep, frequent waking, nightmares, and/or early morning waking; change in appetite; weight loss or weight gain; elevation of blood pressure; fatigue or loss of energy; psychomotor agitation or retardation.

DSM-IV criteria for a Major Depressive Episode are the presence of five or more of these symptoms during the same two-week period, with at least one of the symptoms being either depressed mood or loss of interest or pleasure, and the symptoms representing a change from previous functioning, not being due to substance abuse, a general medical condition or bereavement, and causing distress or impairment in daily functioning.

Gould and colleagues (2011c) found that depressed mood was the most frequent MDD symptom at six and 12 months post-injury. At six months, the second most frequent MDD symptom was fatigue/loss of energy, whereas at 12 months it was anhedonia (lack of experience of pleasure). There was a 20 per cent reduction in reported thoughts of death and suicide at 12 months from the figure at six months. Psychomotor agitation/retardation was the least frequent symptom at both six and 12 months, with 39 per cent endorsement.

Some of the symptoms of depression are also seen as a direct result of the brain injury itself, such as sleep difficulties, appetite changes and impaired concentration. The clinician should be careful to discriminate between changes which are a direct consequence of the injury, and those reflecting emotional disturbance, on the basis of a careful history, also taking into account the results of other clinical investigations. The development or worsening of such symptoms after injury suggests that they are associated with depression, although appropriate investigations may be necessary to rule out the development of medical complications (e.g. hydrocephalus).

Given the high frequency of pre-injury psychiatric disorders, an assessment should also be made of the injured individual's personality and psychological state in their lifetime prior to injury. In certain cases it may emerge that the injury was the result of a suicide attempt. It is important to obtain an objective picture of the manner and degree to which the depression is manifested. Whilst measures such as the Structured Clinical Interview for DSM-IV Diagnoses (SCID-IV) (First, Spitzer, Gibbon, and Williams, 2002) represent the gold standard diagnostic method, they are time-consuming to administer. Therefore, use of a rating scale may be more pragmatic, with careful consideration of the impact of injury-related symptoms on ratings and the TBI person's cognitive capability of completing such a scale. The Hospital Anxiety and Depression Scale (HADS) (Snaith and Zigmond, 1994) and the Depression Anxiety and Stress Scales (DASS) (Lovibond and Lovibond, 1995) have been validated in the TBI population (Dahm, Ponsford, Wong, and Schönberger, 2009, 2011; Whelan-Goodinson, Ponsford, and Schönberger, 2009b). Both the HADS and DASS depression subscales are relatively free of symptoms that may overlap with injury-related symptoms. However, Whelan-Goodinson and colleagues found that the item regarding "feeling slowed down" was equally endorsed by those with and without depression. Relative to the SCID as a gold standard, the depression subscale of the HADS was associated with a sensitivity of 62 per cent and a specificity of 94 per cent. Using the cut-off of 8 stated in the HADS manual, the risk of having depression given a score of at least 8 was 81 per cent. Using a more conservative cut-off of 12, the risk of having a depressive disorder was 92 per cent (Whelan-Goodinson et al., 2009b). Also using the SCID as the diagnostic measure, the depression subscale of the DASS was found to have a sensitivity of 93 per cent and a specificity of 81 per cent.

Predictors of depression

Relatively little is known of factors (demographic, biological, psychological and social) associated with the development of depression. Jorge and colleagues have suggested that acute onset depressive disorders are associated with lesions and decreased grey matter volume in left dorsolateral frontal and left basal ganglia regions (Fedoroff et al., 1992; Jorge et al., 1993; Jorge et al., 2004) and with decreased hippocampal volume (Jorge, Acion, Starkstein, and Magnotta, 2007). It is hypothesised that frontal systems injury disrupts the neural network important in the regulation of emotional states (Phan, Wager, Taylor, and Liberzon, 2003). On the other hand, depressive disorders developing later are thought to have a psychosocial basis, occurring in response to the experience of disability. Jorge and colleagues (Fedoroff et al., 1992; Jorge et al., 1993) were able to differentiate individuals with these differing patterns of disorder onset based on lesion presence and location.

However, other imaging studies have not replicated this finding to date (Koponen et al., 2006; Salmond, Menon, Chatfield, Pickard, and Sahakian, 2006). The limitations of volumetric imaging studies need to be recognised. The use of Diffusion Tensor Imaging (DTI) to study the integrity of white matter tracts holds greater promise but there have been no definitive DTI findings in the TBI population in relation to psychiatric disorders to date.

Recent studies have identified a strong association between pre-injury psychiatric disorders and the development of post-injury disorders (Bombardier et al., 2010; Gould et al., 2011c; Whelan-Goodinson et al., 2009a), with 74 per cent of individuals with pre-injury psychiatric disorder developing a post-injury disorder in the Gould et al. study. Individuals with a pre-injury disorder tended to exhibit a post-injury disorder earlier after injury, whereas novel depression was more likely to develop 6–12 months post-injury. This finding supports the theory that the 46 per cent of individuals who develop novel depression after TBI do so in response to the experience of disability. Other factors associated with post-injury depression have included female gender, lower education and pain (Whelan-Goodinson, Ponsford, Schönberger, and Johnston, 2010), lower IQ (Salmond et al., 2006), pre-injury unemployment, low income, and minority status (Seel et al., 2003), limb injuries and non-productive coping style (Gould, Ponsford, Johnston, and Schönberger, 2011b). There is also a strong association between the presence of depression and poorer functional outcome (Gould, Ponsford, Johnston, and Schönberger, 2011a; Pagulayan, Hoffman, Temkin, Machamer, and Dikmen, 2008; Whelan-Goodinson, Ponsford, and Schönberger, 2008). The findings of Pagulayan and colleagues and of Schönberger, Ponsford, Gould, and Johnston (2011b) suggest that the presence of perceived functional disability precedes the development of depression – that is, that depression develops in response to the experience of disability after injury.

Treatment of depression

Regarding treatment of depression, Fann and colleagues (2009b) prospectively investigated treatment preferences in the first 12 months following TBI. Physical exercise or counselling with a clinician (in the clinic or over the telephone) were preferred over other treatment modalities, with group therapy the least favoured. Patients were also less likely to communicate with a clinician over the internet. Participants with probable major depression, a history of antidepressant use, or outpatient mental health treatment were more likely to prefer antidepressant treatment. However, preferences may differ between individuals, so they should be given a choice of treatment type.

Whilst medications are commonly prescribed, there is limited evidence supporting any pharmacological intervention following TBI. According to the review by Warden and colleagues (2006), whilst there was no gold standard treatment, options recommended for major depression included the tricyclic antidepressants amitriptyline and desipramine, and the Selective Serotonin

Reuptake Inhibitor (SSRI) sertraline, the latter recommendation based on a successful but non-randomised trial in mild TBI individuals by Fann and colleagues (2000). SSRIs are favoured due to their relative lack of side-effects. Two more recent trials of SSRIs (citalopram and sertraline) in depressed patients with mild to moderate injuries (Rapoport et al., 2008) and in depressed patients with mild, moderate and severe injuries (Ashman et al., 2009) have not shown significantly greater response to SSRIs than in controls. However, results of a double-blinded randomised controlled trial in which sertraline was administered prospectively to 50 TBI individuals *without* depression from an average 21 days post-injury are more promising (Novack, Baños, Brunner, Renfroe, and Meythaler, 2009). They revealed that none of the participants receiving sertraline had depression as measured on the Hamilton Depression Rating Scale at three months, as opposed to 10 per cent of participants given a placebo, a statistically significant difference. However, this intervention did not result in any group differences in depressive symptomatology during the rest of the year after treatment cessation.

As Fann et al. (2009a) concluded, there is clearly a need for more large RCTs evaluating pharmacological treatments for depression following TBI. At present, no pharmacological intervention consistently alleviates depression without side-effects and the use of such interventions should be continuously monitored in each case. Pharmacological treatment should always be managed by a physician who understands the likely impact of such medications on the TBI person's cognitive processes. If TBI individuals have had pre-existing psychiatric conditions for which pharmacological agents were prescribed prior to injury these should be reviewed post-injury, but in many cases continuation of the treatment will be appropriate. Pharmacological intervention is likely to be appropriate in cases where there was an identifiable pre-injury psychiatric diagnosis.

As already discussed, CBT may be a useful means of helping those who have sustained TBI to regain a sense of control and perspective. Following introduction of the cognitive model outlining the association between thoughts, mood, behaviour and physiological changes in the body, the depressed TBI individual may be encouraged, perhaps with the assistance of a relative, to monitor their moods, rate their intensity, and identify and document the thoughts which accompany negative emotions. The therapist may assist them to understand the link between these thoughts and their emotions. The dysfunctional assumptions and core beliefs that underpin these automatic thoughts need to be explored, in order to reduce cognitive distortions and replace dysfunctional thoughts with more constructive ones. Cue cards might be used to prompt more adaptive thinking. The injured person may be encouraged to see that focusing on the injustices of the situation or losses will not provide any answers or help them to feel better. Therapeutic assistance may be given to help the depressed individual to see the differences between the "old" person and the "new" person who has survived the injury in a more positive light, and to begin to measure themselves by what they have achieved since the injury, rather than what they achieved prior to the injury. They should be encouraged to take control over their new lives and be equipped with strategies to solve problems, which are so frequently overwhelming to individuals with brain injuries. The use of adaptive coping strategies such as solving problems, working hard, using humour, physical recreation and seeking relaxing diversions, is to be encouraged. It is also useful to monitor activity levels, and explore ways of increasing the number of meaningful and enjoyable activities in which the person engages. Targets may be set for gradually increasing such involvement. In this respect the therapist may need to work with other members of the rehabilitation team in exploring realistic alternatives. Although there have been no group studies evaluating the use of individual CBT for depression following TBI, Montgomery (1995) reported success in a single case intervention, focused on cognitive reframing, activity scheduling, time management and relaxation skills training. Further detail regarding the use of CBT in the management of depression may be obtained from sources including Beck and colleagues (Beck, Rush, Shaw, and Emery, 1979).

If the depressed person is suicidal, cannot be engaged in – or fails to respond to – psychological therapy, referral to a psychiatrist for pharmacological management will be necessary. Medication may be needed to bring the injured individual to the point of being able to benefit from other forms of therapy. Suicide threats should always be taken seriously, particularly in light of the finding that people with TBI have a risk of death by suicide that is 3–4 times greater than in the general population and significantly higher levels of suicide attempts and suicide ideation (Simpson and Tate, 2007). Family members and members of the rehabilitation team are to be encouraged to contact a mental health professional for assistance.

Anxiety disorders following TBI

Whilst there have been many studies of depression following TBI, anxiety disorders have until recently been relatively under-recognised and under-investigated. Retrospective studies in samples with mild-severe TBI have reported frequencies of 38 per cent up to five years post-injury (Whelan-Goodinson et al., 2009a), 57 per cent up to eight years post-injury (Hibbard, Uysal, Kepler, Bogdany, and Silver, 1998) and 17.4 per cent up to 30 years post-injury (Koponen et al., 2002). A recent prospective study found that anxiety disorders occurred in 44.1 per cent of cases over the first 12 months post-injury (Gould et al., 2011c). The most commonly documented disorders are Generalised Anxiety Disorder (GAD), PTSD, Specific Phobia, Panic Disorder (PD) and Social Phobia, with relatively low rates of Obsessive Compulsive Disorder and Agoraphobia (Deb, Lyons, Koutzoukis, Ali, and McCarthy, 1999; Gould et al., 2011c; Hibbard et al., 1998; Koponen et al., 2002; Whelan-Goodinson et al., 2009a).

PTSD may occur when a person has experienced an event that is outside the range of usual human experience, such as a serious threat to one's life or physical integrity, or that of another person. It is characterised by re-experiences of the trauma (nightmares, flashbacks and/or intrusive recollections of the trauma); avoidance techniques (avoidance of situations that trigger recollections of the event, blocking feelings, feeling detached and estranged from others); and excessive arousal (sleep difficulties, poor concentration and memory, hypervigilance, being easily startled). A crucial issue in the development of this disorder is the individual's perception of what happened. In this sense there is usually some recollection of the events preceding the accident and the sense of impending disaster, if not a recollection of the accident itself and events afterwards. For this reason it was assumed that individuals with TBI could not develop PTSD. However, Bryant and colleagues have now demonstrated in a number of studies that PTSD does occur with significant frequency following mild, moderate and severe TBI (Bryant, 2001). More recently they have argued that mild TBI may be associated with a higher rate of PTSD than in individuals without brain injury because impaired prefrontal networks limit regulation of the amygdala (Bryant, 2008; Bryant et al., 2009). In a prospective study they found that longer PTA was associated with less re-experiencing of symptoms in the acute phase of recovery (Bryant et al., 2009). Eighty per cent of individuals who experience Acute Stress Disorder later develop PTSD after mild TBI (Bryant, 2001).

PD is also said to be associated with lesions involving frontal and medial temporal cortical areas and the limbic system (cingulate gyrus) (Hiott and Labbate, 2002). Injury to the frontal lobes is said to disrupt their inhibitory influence on activity in the amygdala (Bryant et al., 2009). In support of this, Jorge and colleagues found that the presence of acute comorbid GAD and MDD was associated with focal right hemisphere lesions (Jorge et al., 1993).

The strongest predictor of post-injury anxiety disorders is the presence of a pre-injury anxiety disorder, as well as older age and unemployment (Gould et al., 2011b; Whelan-Goodinson et al., 2010). Gould and colleagues (2011c) found that as with depression, onset of anxiety occurred earlier after injury in those with a prior history and later for those without a history. Comorbidity with depression is common, with anxiety disorder emerging either prior to or contemporaneously with depression. As with depression, the presence of anxiety disorders is strongly associated with poorer functional outcomes (Gould et al., 2011a; Whelan-Goodinson et al., 2008). Post-TBI anxiety has debilitating effects on the individual, who tends to have greater functional disability and avoidance of activities due to lower confidence about their abilities to accomplish cognitive and challenging tasks (Hiott and Labbate, 2002; Hodgson et al., 2005).

The symptoms of PTSD may not necessarily be overtly manifested until several months or even a year after severe TBI. Other forms of anxiety may be manifested only after the TBI individual has begun to be involved with activities in the community. GAD, social phobia or PD may occur when the individual experiences difficulty in coping with a situation as a result of cognitive deficits, for example, in social settings, where the injured person may feel self-conscious or have difficulty keeping up with conversations, in the workplace, or when engaging in study activities. Although it is legitimate for the individual to experience anxiety in such a scenario, the response may be significantly out of proportion to the situation due to executive impairments which may reduce the injured person's ability to control the fear response. If not brought under control it can become self-perpetuating, exacerbating the injury-related problems, and lead to avoidance of the stressful situation, and further loss of confidence.

Diagnosis of anxiety disorders

As with depression, anxiety can manifest itself in a number of ways. Depending on the type of disorder it may cause the following changes in feelings, thinking patterns, physical symptoms, and behaviour:

Feelings: out of control, fearful, embarrassed, nervous, tentative, on edge, irritability.

Thinking patterns: anticipation of things going wrong, catastrophising, excessive worry, apprehensive expectation, uncertainty, tending to panic, difficulty concentrating, absent-mindedness, flashbacks.

Behavioural changes: withdrawal, inhibition, restlessness, avoidance, obsessions or compulsions.

Physical symptoms: physiological arousal, with increased heart rate, muscle tension, headache, nausea, trembling, sweating, sensations of shortness of breath, choking, chest pain, nausea, dizziness, fear of dying, numbness or tingling sensations, chills or hot flushes, sweating, sleep disturbance (difficulty falling or staying asleep, restless unsatisfying sleep, nightmares), fatigue.

A diagnosis of GAD would be made on the basis of presence of excessive anxiety and worry that is difficult to control most days over a six-month period with three or more of the symptoms of restlessness, fatigue, difficulty concentrating, irritability, muscle tension and/or sleep disturbance and which interferes with daily functioning. Acute Stress Disorder and PTSD (discussed earlier) are characterised by re-experiencing of a traumatic event, with increased arousal and avoidance of stimuli associated with the trauma. Panic Disorder is characterised by recurrent unexpected panic, Specific Phobia occurs when the anxiety is provoked by exposure to a specific feared object or situation, and Social Phobia where anxiety is provoked by social or performance situations, often leading to avoidance.

In order to obtain a clear picture of symptoms it may be useful to have the injured individual keep a diary, monitoring and recording the situations in which the anxiety occurs, any associated thoughts, feelings, bodily sensations and behaviour, and rating its severity. This places a realistic perspective on the problem, which in itself may help to alleviate some anxiety.

As indicated earlier, the gold standard method for diagnosing these disorders is the SCID, although it is recommended that there be consultation with close relatives and medical records in order to verify symptom reporting. However, self-administered rating scales are also available for use in the assessment process, bearing in mind the fact that some symptoms may be directly attributable to the injury. Many of the somatic complaints that are common sequelae of head injury are also symptoms of anxiety, including vertigo, stomach problems, heartbeat irregularities and headache. As mentioned above, the validity of the HADS (Snaith and Zigmond, 1994) and the DASS (Lovibond and Lovibond, 1995) has been examined in the TBI population (Dahm et al., 2011; Whelan-Goodinson et al., 2009b). The Anxiety subscale of the HADS is a less reliable indicator of anxiety in the TBI population showing a sensitivity of 75 per cent and a specificity of 77 per cent. Using the cut-off of 8 stated in the HADS manual, the risk of having anxiety is only 57 per cent. A cut-off score of 15 was required to achieve a 92 per cent likelihood of correct diagnosis (Whelan-Goodinson et al., 2009b). Dahm and colleagues (2011) found that the Stress scale of the DASS demonstrated similar sensitivity and specificity to the HADS Anxiety scale in predicting diagnosis of an anxiety disorder and was more sensitive than the DASS Anxiety Scale, though the validity of the latter scale improved when items relating to certain types of somatic symptoms were excluded.

Management of anxiety disorders

There is even less evidence regarding the efficacy of pharmacological interventions for anxiety than for depression following TBI, predicating a need for further studies. In non-injured people, SSRIs have been used to successfully treat social phobia, PD, OCD, GAD and PTSD (Hiott and Labbate, 2002). SSRIs are the medication most recommended for TBI individuals, given the side effects observed in the use of tricyclics and benzodiazepines (Scheutzow and Wiercisiewski, 1999). However, sertraline, an SSRI, was no more effective than placebo in reducing anxiety following mild to severe TBI (Ashman et al., 2009).

The extent to which psychological interventions are successful is likely to depend on the injured person's level of cognitive functioning, particularly the ability to learn, self-monitor and carry through with intentions. The aim of anxiety management is to give the client control over the anxiety, rather than to abolish it completely. In implementing CBT for anxiety, it is important to educate the injured person about the physiology of the anxiety response, and the role that thoughts can play in perpetuating that response. They need to understand that avoidant behaviour is not helpful. Having them keep a diary, monitoring the situations in which anxiety occurs, associated thoughts, feelings, bodily sensations and behaviours, and rating its severity will serve as a means of enhancing this understanding. Such records can be used as a basis for challenging and disputing irrational thoughts which are fuelling anxiety.

Assistance may be given to interpret situations in alternative ways, and thereby develop more positive self-talk and coping statements. Again, cue cards may be useful in implementing such coping strategies.

One method of alleviating symptoms of anxiety is muscle relaxation. This can provide a distraction from anxious thoughts as well as decrease bodily symptoms, such as muscle tension. Relaxation can usually be facilitated by deep breathing. The relaxation technique needs to be adapted to suit the individual, particularly in the light of specific cognitive or behavioural limitations. For those who fatigue easily and tend to fall asleep during relaxation sessions it may be necessary to make changes to positioning, lighting and timing of sessions. Relaxation instructions should be taped for practice at home. It is useful to develop both a longer and a shorter version, the latter being suitable for use in anxiety-provoking situations. It may be possible to teach the injured person to pick up the early signs of anxiety, so that relaxation techniques can be applied before the anxiety takes over. This requires some self-monitoring capability, however. Practice should be provided in the application of relaxation in stressful situations, using mental imagery, role-play or real-life situations.

Some TBI individuals have difficulty in benefiting from relaxation techniques, particularly using imagery, because they are unable to focus and maintain attention to a sufficient degree. Careful guiding of relaxation procedures is important in such cases, with frequent cueing. A useful alternative may be physical exercise. Distraction and cognitive restructuring may be used to attain control over the thoughts which accompany and perpetuate anxiety. It may be possible to teach the injured individual strategies for re-focusing thoughts, either onto the immediate surroundings, listing things or reciting a poem. It is generally helpful to work with the injured person to take a graded approach to involvement in activities, for example for those with social anxiety and avoidance, organising one-on-one social engagements, rather than going to parties, whilst monitoring their anxiety levels and use of coping strategies. Work on avoidance needs to begin early in the intervention process. As in the case of other cognitive-behavioural strategies, the assistance of a relative or friend may be sought to help in the implementation of these strategies. It may also be helpful to provide training in specific skills, such as conversational or social skills, or assertiveness skills.

Learning strategies for managing cognitive difficulties may also alleviate anxiety; for example memory strategies, such as note-taking or recording of meetings or telephone conversations for subsequent review, use of organisational systems to reduce the necessity to deal with unexpected demands, and time pressure management strategies such as asking questions to slow down the delivery of information (Winkens et al., 2009a). It may also be possible to make certain external modifications, for example, to a work or study regime, to reduce the demands on the injured individual and thereby reduce anxiety. Assistance in planning and time-tabling daily activities could also serve to alleviate anxiety.

As with other forms of psychological therapy there has been little research evaluating the impact of interventions for anxiety in TBI individuals. In the only group study to date, Hodgson and colleagues (2005) conducted a RCT of a CBT intervention for managing social anxiety following predominantly mild brain injury in 12 people. Their CBT programme included components such as relaxation training, cognitive restructuring, assertiveness skills and graded exposure. Participants' cognitive limitations were accommodated using various strategies including the use of external aids, repeated repetitions of treatment materials and shorter sessions. They reported a significant improvement on measures of general anxiety, depression and transient mood for the treatment group compared to wait-list control which was maintained at a one-month follow-up. Further studies are required to examine the impact of CBT in larger samples and in more severely injured individuals.

Treatment of PTSD generally involves graded exposure therapies to assist the individual in gradually confronting the stimuli they would otherwise seek to avoid. They are encouraged to talk about the traumatic events, both within therapy and at home. The aim is to reduce post-traumatic reactions, such as flashbacks, intrusive memories and startle responses through habituation, and thereby bring about extinction of the conditioned aversive arousal response. Desensitisation therapy may be carried out using imagination during relaxation exercises, or through graduated exposure to real-life situations. CBT involving education about trauma reactions, progressive muscle relaxation training, imaginal exposure to trauma memories, cognitive restructuring and graded invivo exposure to avoided situations, has been shown to be effective in treating Acute Stress Disorder and preventing PTSD following general trauma (Bryant, Sackville, Dang, Moulds, and Guthrie, 1999) and mild TBI (Bryant, Moulds, Guthrie, and Nixon, 2003). Whether such therapy could be successful in individuals with more severe TBI, who have more significant cognitive impairments, remains to be demonstrated.

Substance abuse

A significant proportion of individuals with TBI have a history of substance abuse, with reported rates from retrospective studies between 32 and 41 per cent (Ashman et al., 2004; Hibbard et al., 1998; Whelan-Goodinson et al., 2009a). Whilst higher than general community rates, these rates are similar to those of demographically similar non-injured controls (Kreutzer, Witol, and Marwitz, 1996a; Ponsford, Whelan-Goodinson, and Bahar-Fuchs, 2007). High rates of pre-injury alcohol abuse (7–10.8 per cent) and alcohol dependence (24.1–29 per cent) have been reported (Jorge, Starkstein, Arndt, Moser, and Crespo-Facorro, 2005; Whelan-Goodinson et al., 2009a). Almost one-third of individuals report use of drugs, predominantly marijuana, cocaine, and amphetamines, during the three months before injury (Bombardier, Rimmele, and Zintel, 2002; Bombardier, Temkin, Machamer, and Dikmen, 2003).

Between 30 and 50 per cent of individuals with a TBI are intoxicated at the time of injury (Corrigan, Rust, and Lamb-Hart, 1995; Golan et al., 2007; Parry-Jones et al., 2006; Shandro et al., 2009), which is positively associated with greater initial injury severity (Turner, Kivlahan, Rimmele, and Bombardier, 2006). Substance abuse has been shown to have a deleterious effect on medical, neurological, neurobehavioural, and functional outcomes (Parry-Jones et al., 2006). Longitudinal studies have shown that alcohol and drug use decline in the first year post-injury but climb back towards pre-injury levels in the second year, with those most at risk of heavy post-injury alcohol use being young males who engaged in heavy pre-injury substance use (Bombardier et al., 2003; Kreutzer et al., 1996b; Ponsford et al., 2007).

Despite this, screening and treatment for alcohol and drug use do not occur routinely in rehabilitation settings. CBT, brief interventions including MI and the provision of information have had demonstrated efficacy in the general population of substance abusers. However, there have been few studies evaluating the efficacy of interventions to reduce substance use after TBI. In one of the more intensive interventions, Vungkhanching and colleagues (2007) found that a 12-session Skills-based Substance Abuse Prevention Counselling (SBSAPC) programme significantly decreased alcohol and drug use, increased coping skilfulness and maintenance of employment at 9-month follow-up, relative to a non-intervention group. Another community-based intervention, named the TBI Network, provided assessment, planning, outreach, social and emotional support, job development and advocacy to individuals with comorbid TBI and substance abuse problems over 6 months, resulting in increased abstinence rates, decreased frequency and quantity of alcohol consumed, and a 30 per cent increase in employment relative to initial assessment (Corrigan et al., 1995). In other interventions involving TBI individuals with comorbid substance abuse problems, Delmonico and colleagues (1998) reported success using a group psychotherapy model based on the philosophy of "harm reduction". Heinemann and colleagues found comprehensive case management to be beneficial in the areas of community integration, physical well-being, and life satisfaction although there was no benefit in terms of decreased substance use (Heinemann, Corrigan, and Moore, 2004).

Such intensive interventions are neither feasible nor cost-effective for individuals without entrenched substance abuse problems, who may nevertheless return to heavy drinking after injury. Several researchers have examined the use of brief MI within the TBI population. In a small study Bombardier and Rimmele (1999) tested brief MI as a means of preventing a return to alcohol abuse and found 75 per cent of those who received the intervention reported drinking less than one drink during a typical week at one year follow-up, compared to 55 per cent of individuals who did not receive any intervention. However, there is a lack of published data evaluating the effectiveness of written or verbal information regarding alcohol use following TBI. Results of a recent study comparing the efficacy of a one-off brief MI together with an information booklet produced by Corrigan and colleagues from the Ohio Valley Medical Center, as compared with provision of the information booklet alone or with treatment as usual, showed a trend for less frequent alcohol use in both the intervention groups, although this did not reach statistical significance (Ponsford, Tweedly, and Lee, 2010; Tweedly, Ponsford, and Lee, in press). It may be that provision of information is as effective as is the use of a brief MI. It is to be hoped that more systematic practices may be introduced to minimise the risk of post-injury substance use.

Anger management

Problems in controlling anger are commonly experienced by those who have sustained severe TBI. Such difficulties persist over many years after injury. They contribute to problems in establishing and/or sustaining employment, personal relationships, and social or leisure pursuits (Ownsworth and McKenna, 2008; Winkler et al., 2006). They also represent a significant source of stress to family members (Ergh et al., 2002; Ponsford et al., 2003; Testa et al., 2006). Approaches to controlling anger, and dealing with other behaviour problems manifested in the earlier stages of recovery, or within the rehabilitation setting, have been outlined in detail in Chapter 6. As discussed in that chapter, these methods can be adapted for use in community settings. TBI individuals who remain very severely impaired from a cognitive point of view, with little or no insight, memory or capacity for self-control, cannot be actively engaged in overcoming their behavioural problems. The behavioural methods discussed in Chapter 6 may be applied in collaboration with carers and family members. TBI individuals who have returned to the community and who have some awareness of their problem and motivation for change may be able to participate more actively in the therapy process, monitoring their own behavioural responses and applying various coping skills, with the assistance of a family member. In such cases, a cognitive-behavioural approach to anger management, as outlined by Novaco (1975), may be a useful alternative. Both single case and group studies have suggested that such methods can be used successfully to reduce anger problems in people with TBI (Lira, Carne, and Masri, 1983; McKinlay and Hickox, 1988; Medd and Tate, 2000; Uomoto and Brockway, 1992; Walker et al., 2010a). The following guidelines are based on these reports, together with the author's experience.

Suggested guidelines for improvement of anger control

Interventions for anger following TBI should be preceded by the taking of a comprehensive history to ascertain the extent to which anger problems may have existed before injury, whether and how these have changed since the injury, and how they are affecting the injured person and others, also exploring possible mood changes. It is important to clarify how the anger is being manifested behaviourally (e.g. shouting, throwing objects, hitting others) and discuss methods currently being used to resolve the anger. The responses of others may be contributing to the problem, and this may become one focus of therapy. It is also useful at this stage to reach agreement as to what is an acceptable level of aggression in the household or elsewhere. This may represent the goal for treatment.

This may be followed by education as to the ways in which TBI may contribute to anger control problems – including the role of fronto-limbic injury in reducing anger control as well as increased sensitivity to noise and crowds, but also discussing the potential role of mood changes or substance use. A model of anger may be presented, showing how an angry response can be triggered and how thoughts during the decision phase may influence the anger response. Consistent with the cognitive-behavioural model, this would be followed by exploration and monitoring of the cognitive, physical and emotional changes that occur when the person first becomes angry, during the anger outburst and afterwards.

It is helpful to have the injured person (and family member if present) keep a diary of angry outbursts, precipitating external circumstances as well as thoughts, feelings and behaviours that led to them and were experienced during the angry outburst, and what happened afterwards, over a period of a week initially, but ideally throughout the intervention period. This record can be used as a baseline, to identify the circumstances which provoke anger, and ways in which thoughts, feelings, behaviours, and environmental factors including the responses of others can either fuel the anger or have a calming influence.

This record provides a basis for educating the person with TBI (and family member) as to how to avoid provoking anger. For example, it may be that angry outbursts tend to occur when there is a lot of noise and bustle, such as when the television is on and small children are around, or when particular issues are being discussed, when the TBI individual is having trouble keeping up with a conversation or is being criticised for making mistakes or is tired or has been drinking. Steps can be taken to modify the environment or other people's interactions with the injured individual to avoid causing frustration.

Following anger management guidelines suggested by Novaco (1975), in those individuals with sufficient self-monitoring capabilities, it is important to encourage awareness of thoughts, feelings and bodily sensations which signal an impending outburst of anger. These can be used as cues for the implementation of strategies to circumvent the outburst. Such strategies may include deep breathing or removing themselves from the situation, either to a designated space in the house or by going for a walk. When the injured individual is not able to do this alone, the assistance of the family member may be sought, firstly to identify behaviours which signal impending anger. The family member can remove the trigger, for example by changing the subject or turning off the television, or prompting the TBI person to use whatever strategy has been agreed upon. This may be done using an agreed verbal cue which has been rehearsed in therapy sessions. If necessary, family members may need to physically leave the situation themselves. Alternatively the injured person may develop self-talk or cognitive challenging strategies or assertiveness skills to utilise in certain anger-provoking situations. Coping skills should be practised in progressively more anger-provoking situations using role-play techniques.

McKinlay and Hickox (1988) have summarised the steps involved in this anger management process with the acronym ANGER:

A – Anticipate the trigger situations.
N – Notice the signs of rising anger.
G – Go through your "temper routine" (which includes relaxation or breathing exercises, and finding an alternative way of handling the situation).
E – Extract yourself from the situation, if all else fails.
R – Record how you coped: What lessons can you learn for next time?

If therapy is being conducted with both the injured person and a family member together it may be useful to see each individually at times to discuss specific concerns or issues. Where the anger has been contributing significantly to social isolation, it is important, as the anger is brought under control, to increase involvement in enjoyable activities. Follow-up sessions after the strategies have been implemented successfully are also crucial to ensure that their use is maintained. In this respect it is useful to ask the parties involved to keep a record of angry outbursts for a week prior to attending a follow-up session.

CBT for anger management may also be delivered in a group format. In an uncontrolled trial, Walker and colleagues (2010a) have reported the success of 12 weekly sessions based on a modified CBT model similar to that outlined above, as evidenced by decreased anger frequency and increased attempts at anger control. Changes were maintained at follow-up assessment.

Marital and relationship problems

The negative impact of TBI on marital relationships has been extensively documented (Bracy and Douglas, 2002; Burridge et al., 2007; Lezak, 1978; Peters, Stambrook, Moore, and Esses, 1990). Whilst there are relatively few divorces in the early years after injury, there are, in cases of extremely severe TBI, many more in the longer term (Tate et al., 1989; Thomsen, 1984; Wood and Yurdakul, 1997). There is also substantial evidence of a decline in the quality of marital relationships, with spouses reporting reduced quality of communication, loss of emotional support and companionship, and greater dependency and insecurity on the part of the injured spouse (Willer et al., 1991). For the TBI partner there may also be significant role changes. Loss of the capability of earning an income to support the family, managing the family finances, managing the household and engaging in parental activities can be a major source of stress and loss of self-esteem within the relationship

(Willer et al., 1991). This may be particularly so in people from different cultural backgrounds, which place great emphasis on the performance of certain roles (Saltapidas and Ponsford, 2008). Almost inevitably, couples have to come to terms with some temporary or permanent change following TBI.

Couples need support in dealing with these changes, not only individually, but also together. In many cases couples may not have been communicating honestly and clearly with each other. The injured person's spouse may be afraid of hurting the TBI partner or provoking an angry outburst by discussing changes in personality and behaviour. There is evidence to suggest that families become more controlled and less openly communicative over time after injury, developing rigid rules to avoid behavioural outbursts (Ponsford and Schönberger, 2010). The TBI individual may feel insecure in the relationship, having lost control in areas previously considered important.

It is important, therefore, to facilitate communication between couples, helping them develop skills in speaking honestly and directly, listening to and validating each other, as outlined by Montgomery and Evans (1983). Active guidance will be needed to assist in reaching solutions to problems. In particular, couples may benefit from assistance in mutually defining new roles and responsibilities within the relationship, not necessarily excluding the TBI partner from involvement in family decisions. As with other psychological therapy, the therapist needs to have a good understanding of changes in cognition and behaviour, so that unrealistic demands are not placed on the couple and the person with TBI is able to participate fully/appropriately.

With the active cooperation of the non-injured spouse, however, and repetition and structure, supplemented with simple written notes, slow progress may not necessarily be impeded. The therapist may need to have additional sessions with the uninjured partner in order to achieve this. A co-therapist may be recruited to work with the TBI person individually. Where irritability is a significant problem, anger management techniques or other behavioural strategies, as outlined earlier, will need to be introduced.

One of the most important components of marital therapy in these circumstances is to facilitate the couple in giving each other positive feedback, rather than focusing always on negative changes. For a variety of reasons it is likely that they are not able to pursue social or recreational activities together, which may have been an important basis of shared pleasure in the relationship. The therapist can assist the couple in seeing the importance of sharing enjoyable time together and finding new ways of doing this. Where the injured partner is very dependent upon the spouse, it is also important, however, to schedule time for them to spend engaging in social or recreational activities separately. Not uncommonly, TBI individuals become jealous when their spouse wants to pursue outside activities. This results in increasing social isolation and bitterness on the part of the care-giving partner, with consequent stress on the relationship. The need for the caregiver to have free time must be discussed openly in therapy. The uninjured partner may need some individual training in assertiveness skills in order to deal with such issues. Introduction of the couple to a support group involving other couples in which one partner has sustained TBI may also be mutually beneficial, as will referral for practical assistance in dealing with financial or legal problems, another significant source of stress.

Inevitably, some relationships fail after TBI, either because of the extent of cognitive and behavioural change in the TBI partner, or because of an inability of either party to adapt to role changes in the relationship. Both partners will require considerable support in making such a decision. The uninjured spouse will experience much guilt, and may be offered little support by the family of the TBI partner. For the injured individual, there may be a great deal of anger and bitterness, due to an inability to see the point of view of the partner. There will also be many practical issues to be resolved, such as who will provide care or supervision for the TBI individual, and how access to children can be arranged. Financial settlement may be complicated by legal claims for compensation. These issues are explored further in the next chapter.

For individuals not in a long-term relationship at the time of injury, there are likely to be many difficulties in establishing relationships, as a consequence of changes in sexual behaviour and self-confidence, in addition to other personality changes affecting interpersonal relationships. These need to be addressed, both in the context of individual therapy and group therapy, focusing on the development of insight, self-esteem and interpersonal skills in the manner outlined in other sections of this chapter, and Chapter 5.

Sexuality following TBI

In spite of the importance of sexuality for all people, but particularly adolescents and young adults, sexual issues are rarely addressed adequately following TBI. TBI potentially disrupts many important aspects of sexuality, including social and relationship skills, self-esteem, and behavioural control, as well as libido and the physical capacity to perform sexually. TBI frequently causes damage to limbic structures, including the hippocampus, septal complex, amygdala, and hypothalamus, as well as the thalamus, cingulum and frontal lobes – all of which have been shown to be involved, either directly or via hormonal mechanisms, in the regulation of sexual responses (Horn and Zasler, 1990). Changes in motor control or sensation or pain may further interfere with the ability to engage in or take pleasure from sexual activity. In some instances, sexuality may not have been fully developed or expressed prior to injury, thus adding to the complexity of the rehabilitation process.

Research on changes in sexuality associated with TBI

TBI may result in either a loss of sex drive or increased sexual desire. Increased sex drive is associated with frontal lobe impairment and may be evident in individuals with very severe TBI. However, a decrease in sex drive appears to be more common. Ponsford (2003) investigated changes in sexual behaviour, affect, self-esteem and relationship quality, and their interrelationships in individuals with moderate–severe TBI 1–5 years post-injury, relative to demographically similar controls. Significant sexual changes were reported by more than 50 per cent of TBI participants. Between 36 and 54 per cent of the TBI group reported a decrease in the importance of sexuality, opportunities and frequency of engaging in sexual activities, reduced sex drive, a decline in their ability to give their partner sexual satisfaction, to engage in sexual intercourse, enjoyment of sexual activity, ability to stay aroused and to climax. The frequencies of such negative changes were significantly higher than those reported by controls and far outweighed the frequency of increases on these dimensions, which was reported by around 10 per cent of TBI participants. Fatigue was the most frequently documented contributing factor for both TBI participants and controls, but it was reported with twice the frequency in the TBI group. Decreased mobility, pain and loss or decrease in sensitivity were significant contributors for up to one-third of TBI participants. These physical factors may potentially be investigated further with a view to their alleviation. TBI participants aged 46–55 reported the greatest decreases in quality and frequency of their sexual experiences, a decline which was not so evident in the control group.

Just under half of the TBI participants reported decreased self-confidence, sex appeal, higher levels of depression, and decreased communication levels and relationship quality with their sexual partner. About one-third of the group attributed the decline in the quality of their sexual experiences to these factors. There were also significant associations between the presence of anxiety and depression and scores on most items from the sexuality questionnaire. Those taking antidepressants were more likely to report a decline in their sexuality, although it was not clear whether this was due to the presence of depression or the medication itself. Otherwise, medication did not appear to have a significant impact on sexuality. The findings of this study are consistent with those of previous studies (Kreuter, Dahllof, Gudjonsson, Sullivan, and Siosteen, 1998; Kreutzer and Zasler, 1989; Sandel, Williams, Dellapietra, and Derogatis, 1996).

Addressing sexual issues in the rehabilitation setting

In spite of the reported frequency of change in sexual behaviour following TBI, in many instances sexual issues are not even discussed in the course of rehabilitation. Rehabilitation staff tend to feel uncomfortable and ill-prepared in discussing sexual concerns with patients. This problem is exacerbated by the fact that the majority of staff are female and the majority of those injured are male. There is little privacy and opportunity for sexual expression within the hospital environment. The majority of TBI individuals do not have an ongoing sexual relationship and have little prospect of forming one in the foreseeable future. Expressions of sexual frustration are frequently interpreted by rehabilitation staff in a judgemental fashion.

As with other aspects of the rehabilitation programme, it is important that the rehabilitation team reach some understanding and agreement as to their approach to issues of sexuality. This process will necessitate education in aspects of sexuality and how it may be affected by TBI, training in basic counselling, social and behavioural skills, and clarification of values along the lines suggested by Blackerby (1990), Medlar and Medlar (1990) and Simpson (2001). There must be a commitment to the philosophy developed by the team, so that personal attitudes are not imposed upon TBI individuals and their families. Whilst it is important that certain individuals within the team develop specific expertise in dealing with sexual problems, it must be recognised that sexual issues may be raised with any team member. Therefore, information, resources and education need to be made available to the entire rehabilitation team, as well as the injured individuals and their partners or families. The "You and Me" programme, developed by Simpson (1999) represents one very good example of such a resource.

TBI individuals and their families may not see the need or wish to confront sexual problems during the rehabilitation phase. However, it is important that a team member draws their attention to the possibility of changes in sexual behaviour early on, indicating a preparedness to discuss such issues if and when they arise in the future. Many will not raise concerns until permission is given to talk about such matters.

Assessment and therapy for sexual problems

Zasler and Horn (1990) have presented a detailed account of the causes, nature and management of sexual problems associated with TBI. Organic causes include endocrine dysfunction, sensori-motor problems, cognitive and behavioural impairment, bowel and bladder dysfunction, changes in libido and genital dysfunction. It is important to make a comprehensive assessment covering all of these areas as a means of determining appropriate intervention.

Where sensorimotor problems or genital dysfunction are interfering with the capacity to perform sexual acts, advice may be needed regarding alternative positioning, the use of assistive devices, artificial lubricants and/or alternative means of obtaining sexual satisfaction. Hormonal imbalance may be treated successfully with hormone replacement therapy. The possible negative influence of medications must also be considered (Zasler and Horn, 1990). Where sexual problems are related to behavioural disinhibition as a result of fronto-temporal injury, behavioural methods may be applied along the lines outlined in Chapter 6. Zasler and Horn point out the importance of distinguishing hypersexuality, thought to be associated with limbic dysfunction, from disinhibition and in turn, from sexual frustration.

From the findings of Ponsford (2003) it is clear that self-confidence, emotional and relationship problems, and stress commonly cause a decline in the quality of sexual drive and behaviour. It is important to explicitly explore and attempt to address these issues within the rehabilitation process. However, since many of these issues will only be manifested following return to the community, it is also vital to convey to the injured person a willingness to assist with such problems in the future and provide resources for future support in dealing with these issues.

There is some evidence to suggest that the partners of brain-injured individuals also experience a reduction in sex drive for a variety of reasons (Rosenbaum and Najenson, 1976). These include stress due to increased responsibilities, loss of attraction to the disabled partner, a perception of personality change in the TBI partner, with a consequent decline in the quality of the relationship, and depression. Where such non-organic factors are thought to be contributing to the problem, intervention will need to focus in these areas.

As a result of their physical, cognitive and/or behavioural disabilities, the unfortunate reality for many of those who have sustained TBI is that there may be few opportunities to experience a sexual relationship. This leads to considerable frustration, particularly where masturbation is considered unacceptable or cannot be achieved due to physical disability. There may be a need to give permission to explore alternatives or to teach specific sexual skills. Referral to a sex therapist may assist in this process, as staff may not feel comfortable in this role. Depending on local laws and moral and ethical views, the use of a surrogate sexual partner or referral to a massage parlour to assist in the development of appropriate sexual skills may be considered in certain instances. Whilst the rights and privacy of the TBI individual must always be respected, it may in some instances also be necessary to involve the family in such decisions.

Birth control

Assessment and advice regarding appropriate methods of birth control and protection from sexually transmitted diseases are a very important component of sexual rehabilitation for all TBI individuals who are potentially sexually active. This is particularly so where there is an increase in sex drive, or where the TBI individual is prone to impulsive behaviour and lacks the capacity for self-regulation. Whilst the rights of the TBI individual must be respected, physical and cognitive limitations must be taken into account when determining a suitable form of contraception. Where unplanned pregnancy occurs there will be a need for counselling to assist the TBI person in deciding whether to terminate or proceed with the pregnancy, and referral made to appropriate support services.

Case report – Danielle

Danielle was aged 19 when she sustained a severe TBI, with 55 days of PTA and multiple fractures in a motor vehicle accident. She was from the country and had completed her final year at school a year beforehand. She had taken a year off and done voluntary work overseas, returned and moved to the city to work as a receptionist. She was about to commence a course in Disability Studies. After one month in the acute hospital she had six months of inpatient rehabilitation. She had a left-sided weakness. Neuropsychological assessment revealed her to be of average intelligence. She exhibited severe memory impairments – worse in the verbal than non-verbal domain – slow information processing, and planning and problem-solving difficulties. After inpatient rehabilitation she spent five months at a transitional living centre, working on her independent living skills as she planned to move back into a house in the community. She moved into a house with a group of young people but found she did not cope well as she was lacking in self-confidence. She had issues with her body image, being self-conscious about the look of her nose which had been fractured. She was not drinking alcohol and found it difficult to go to pubs and to make conversation in social situations. She felt people thought she was stupid. This was a big change from her previous outgoing personality. She moved from the shared house to live with a 40-year-old woman and spent most of her time with her as this was easier than mixing with young people.

She did a fitness course to see how she would cope with study. As she managed this, the following year she enrolled in a Social Sciences degree. She found herself very nervous and lacking confidence in class, afraid to ask questions or participate in discussions and worried what others would think of her. She began to avoid going to lectures, preferring to download the notes. She was also overwhelmed by the amount of work and had difficulty taking notes.

At this point, 18 months post-injury, her psychologist commenced CBT, conducted over nine sessions, with some adaptations to allow for her cognitive limitations. The focus of this was on teaching her to monitor her thoughts and emotions, evaluating unhelpful thoughts (e.g. "I am stupid") and developing more positive thoughts (e.g. "Although I have some memory loss, I can still go to uni and I am achieving good grades"). She received training in relaxation which was practised daily at home. Social skills training was also provided to address issues such as poor eye-contact and difficulties with generating social conversation. She had graded exposure to various social activities (beginning with telephoning a close friend, progressing to going to a party, and then having friends over for dinner), and educational activities (talking with other students, asking questions of lecturers outside class, progressing to asking questions in class).

Danielle found it hard to remember the content of therapy from one session to the next and sometimes forgot to do homework exercises. There was a need to repeat the content of the previous session at the beginning of each new session. Handouts were given in each session, and compiled into a manual of therapy tips. Her mobile phone was programmed to remind her to complete homework. More positive thoughts were written on cue cards and kept in Danielle's purse for quick access. Progress was slow as a consequence of her poor memory. Nevertheless Danielle did benefit from the therapy, showing a significant reduction in her feelings of stress, depression and anxiety, as measured in the DASS, over the course of therapy. By the end of therapy (week 12), the DASS scores were all within the *normal* range. She maintained the improvement at follow-up and also continued to report an increase in use of productive coping strategies and in participation in social and university-related activities. Danielle also reported during the follow-up interview that she was feeling more confident about expressing her opinion in class. She continued her course to completion, studying part-time until the final year and worked part-time as a therapy aide. She got her drivers' licence back and developed a relationship with a boyfriend from her home town, whom she visited regularly on weekends. This intervention circumvented the development of significant social withdrawal due to anxiety.

Case report – Julie

Julie was a 45-year-old senior primary school teacher, who was married with no children. She had sustained a severe TBI and multiple fractures in a car accident six months earlier. Neuropsychological assessment had indicated that she was of superior intelligence, but she had residual difficulties with attention, speed of information processing, and planning and self-monitoring on complex or novel tasks. Shortly after discharge from outpatient rehabilitation she became highly stressed and depressed and sought counselling.

Whilst able to manage her domestic routine she had found she became easily fatigued and relied on her husband for a lot more assistance, whereas she had previously been energetic, independent and the dominant partner in the relationship. She felt much more emotional and found it difficult to cope with being reliant on her husband. She had also become more irritable. She described being able to physically feel the anger rising in her stomach and felt unable to control it. Her previously active social life had had to be significantly curtailed because she got too tired. She had also given up many of the activities which she and her husband previously enjoyed, such as bushwalking. Her activities were limited by pain and restriction of movement in fracture sites and visual problems, as well as fatigue.

Julie had returned to work at her school for two half-days per week. As she was unable to take a class she worked in the library. She experienced significant coping difficulties due to her cognitive impairments, as well as fatigue. Having been a high-achieving, career-oriented person prior to her injury, Julie found the experience of not coping highly stressful and became very anxious. She was prone to outbursts of anger and tearfulness and had occasional panic attacks. She worried what her fellow teachers and the parents thought of her, sensing that they did not understand the nature of her difficulties.

Julie thus presented with symptoms of anxiety and depression and low self-esteem. When at school, and when faced with anything out of her normal routine at home, she became extremely tense and had difficulty concentrating. She repeatedly made negative comments about herself and her situation, and had a very pessimistic view of the future. The concentration and memory difficulties she reported were out of proportion to those apparent on neuropsychological assessment. She was tending to withdraw from social contact. Her relationship with her husband had deteriorated and she had lost interest in sex. In spite of her fatigue, she was having difficulty sleeping and her appetite had decreased.

In the initial sessions, Julie was given an opportunity to vent her anger over the accident and its effects. Initially, Julie was worried that she may have been responsible, and expressed guilt about the burden she had placed on her husband. However, shortly afterwards she received a letter from a witness indicating that the accident had been due to irresponsibility on the part of another driver. She developed extreme anger towards this person.

Julie was introduced to the concept of self-talk and her attention was drawn to the influence her negative self-talk was having on her emotional state. As a homework exercise she monitored her emotional outbursts, recording the precipitating circumstances, what she was saying to herself at the time, and the nature and degree of her emotional response. These records were reviewed in therapy, with a view to challenging negative self-talk and replacing it with more constructive thoughts. A number of coping statements were developed for Julie to use in stressful situations. These were rehearsed through role-play. The therapist also pointed out how little her anger over the accident was achieving, other than making her feel bad. They developed some coping statements to replace these angry thoughts.

Julie was taught relaxation techniques, which she practised with the aid of a tape whilst resting each afternoon, and again when she was awake at night. She practised inducing a relaxed state by taking deep breaths. She used this, in addition to her coping statements, to assist her to calm down when she became anxious at school, or when she felt angry.

From the records she had kept it became apparent that Julie became most anxious, upset or angry when she was tired. At times she was clearly attempting more than she could reasonably manage. She began to monitor her activity levels. Her time at school was kept to two half days until her stamina and familiarity with the work had increased. She slept each afternoon and spent time exercising. She was encouraged to pursue social activities with friends, as these were important to her, but to do this only on weekends, when she could have additional rest.

Some therapy time was spent reviewing Julie's strengths and weaknesses. She made lists of these and was surprised at the number of strengths she could find in herself. She identified her motivation, determination, initiative, conscientiousness, intelligence and self-awareness as strengths. Discussion focused on how she could use these strengths to rebuild a meaningful life for herself. Over time it was becoming clear that she was unlikely to be able to return to full-time work. However, an opportunity presented itself at the school to develop a programme for gifted children. She was able to use her considerable experience to do this very successfully and on a part-time basis. She received positive feedback from the school administration and the parents for her initiatives, and subsequently admitted that she had found this work in some ways more challenging than her classroom teaching.

Some joint sessions were held with Julie's husband in order to address the relationship difficulties. They had not been communicating very clearly since the injury. He had never been one to talk about things, and she had felt too insecure about the relationship to do so. The couple had been unable to have children due to her infertility. Although her husband had indicated that he was quite happy not to have children, Julie felt she had let him down. Now she felt of no use to him in other respects, being reliant on him for assistance, and unable to participate in activities they had found enjoyable. Therefore she thought it would have been better if she had died in the accident, so that he could start a new life and have a family. Julie was encouraged to express her feelings to her husband in therapy. She was surprised to hear him reiterate his genuine relief at not having children. He told her how reliant he had always been on her to take the lead in the relationship. He felt it had been worthwhile for him to have to take greater responsibility now. He was also able to tell Julie how much he valued her in spite of the changes since her injury.

He was, however, having difficulty coping with Julie's anger and mood swings, often taking her anger personally. Julie agreed that he should assist her in minimising or dealing with such outbursts, by encouraging her to regulate her activity levels, break down seemingly overwhelming tasks and take deep breaths or walk away to circumvent angry outbursts. He indicated that he had not fully understood Julie's limitations until the therapy sessions. He was encouraged to give Julie positive feedback for her achievements as frequently as possible.

Some time was also spent discussing ways in which Julie and her husband could increase time spent in pleasurable activities together. Rather than attempting bushwalking, they took shorter walks locally on weekends. Julie was encouraged to organise one social activity each weekend, also allowing adequate time for rest and recruiting help from others, for example to wash dishes or bring a dessert. The couple reported after these sessions that their sex life had improved, largely as a consequence of the general improvement in the relationship, and of Julie being more relaxed.

This intervention initially spanned nine months, but therapeutic contact continued over a period of three years. As Julie faced new challenges and crises she was still prone to become depressed and angry. However, she generally responded well to the therapy. Three years after her injury Julie wrote the following message on a Christmas card:

> Thank you very much for helping me back on the planet. I feel I have a future now – perhaps not as financially rewarding and very different, but one that provides new challenges and rewards. I may even end up like that butchered flowering gum I was waxing lyrical about, and give and consequently get more from life. Thank you also for including my husband

in assisting my emotional recovery. I believe it has strengthened our partnership.

Case report – Michael

Michael was an 18-year-old apprentice fitter and turner when he was injured in a motor car accident. He was in coma for about one week and had a period of PTA lasting 25 days. His inpatient hospitalisation and rehabilitation lasted seven weeks and he continued outpatient therapy for a further six months. After seven months of rehabilitation, he had made a good recovery physically, but showed persisting cognitive difficulties with attention, processing speed, verbal learning and memory, word-finding, affecting his conversational skills, inflexible thinking and planning difficulties. After a five-month work trial, he was coping with full-time work at his previous level. He had also returned to driving. However, he lacked confidence socially, because of his difficulty in generating conversation.

When reviewed four months after discharge from outpatient therapy, and a year post-injury, Michael reported experiencing a number of adjustment problems and was referred for psychological counselling. Although coping with full-time work, he was not enjoying his apprenticeship. He reported difficulty getting along with workmates and initiating conversations in social situations, such as parties. He found it difficult not drinking, as his social life had previously revolved around the local pub, and he did not feel comfortable sitting in the pub and not drinking alcohol. He noted that his friends had drifted away, and he was more socially isolated. At the time of his injury he had been in a two-year relationship and his girlfriend had ended the relationship shortly after his discharge from hospital, increasing his social isolation. As a consequence of these problems he had become depressed.

Michael's difficulties were tackled on a number of levels. The most pressing problem appeared to be his conversational difficulties and consequent social anxiety. He was referred back to his speech pathologist, who worked with him intensively to practise generating conversation on a range of topics. Role-play and video-taped feedback was used to facilitate this. "In vivo" practice occurred on weekends and was reviewed the following week. Michael's psychologist trained him in relaxation techniques, which he practised daily. She had him monitor his thinking in social situations. It became apparent that he was very self-conscious socially. He tended to avoid approaching people, especially women, and, when engaged in conversation he tended to panic, saying to himself, "I can't think of what to say. They must think I'm so hopeless and boring." These thoughts were interfering with his ability to get on with the conversation. Michael and his psychologist worked together to generate some competing and more positive thoughts, such as, "I'm going to stay calm and take this one step at a time." They rehearsed these along with his conversational strategies.

Michael was invited to attend a support group for young people who had sustained TBI. This provided an opportunity to discuss the difficulties they had experienced since discharge from rehabilitation. Michael was very reassured by the fact that many of the others in the group had been experiencing similar problems, and this boosted his confidence. It also made it easier for him to accept the changes in himself, of which he had become so painfully aware. Some group sessions were spent focusing on each individual's strengths. Michael began to appreciate that he still had many residual abilities and was very fortunate, relative to others in the group, to be able to continue pursuing his vocational goal to become a fitter and turner. Group members shared their individual strategies for dealing with problems of a cognitive or interpersonal nature. He contributed enthusiastically to the discussion and received positive feedback, which further enhanced his self-esteem. It also provided an opportunity to rehearse the conversational skills he had learned in individual therapy.

Michael was encouraged to become involved in some local sporting activities, which he had previously enjoyed, but which he had given up after the injury, due to problems with fatigue. He began playing squash competitively. Although initially reluctant, he joined a local youth group. This provided a forum in which to meet people and practise his conversational skills. Michael required considerable support with this initially. He was very inexperienced sexually, which added to his anxiety with regard to forming new relationships with women. Several sessions were spent assisting Michael to work through and clarify his feelings regarding sexual relationships.

Michael has required counselling on an intermittent basis over a number of years. He completed his apprenticeship and started a new job, but had some problems adapting to this. His social network remains very limited and he still lacks a close friend in whom to confide. He has shown a tendency to lack judgement in his choice of friends, to become overly intense about relationships and very upset when the friendship drifts apart. He has had a couple of relationships with girls much younger than he, each lasting a couple of months, but these have not been very successful. He continues to experience anxiety in unfamiliar situations and when placed under pressure. Michael developed paranoid ideation and continues to receive psychiatric treatment. Thus, in spite of an excellent recovery in terms of performance of activities of daily living, Michael's psychological adjustment is far from good. He is likely to require intermittent psychological support for many years to come.

Conclusions

The importance of addressing the myriad psychological and adjustment problems faced by TBI individuals cannot be overemphasised. At an appropriate time after injury, all those who have sustained TBI should have access to counselling and/or group therapy to enhance the development of self-awareness, whilst maximising self-esteem and providing an opportunity to rebuild a new sense of self. Individual assessment and therapy should also be available on an ongoing basis to deal with the development of depression, anxiety, anger and other interpersonal problems, relationship difficulties and changes in sexuality. Approaches to therapy need to be adapted to the specific strengths and weaknesses of the injured person, cognitive-behavioural interventions being potentially useful. Involvement of a close other in such interventions may be helpful in some cases.

9 Working with families

Jennie Ponsford

Introduction

TBI can create a significant burden for the families of those who are injured, as it is they who most frequently must provide long-term support, socialisation and assistance to the TBI individual. Indeed the impact of TBI for relatives can be as devastating as for the person who is injured. This has been comprehensively documented in numerous outcome studies conducted over the past three decades (Brooks et al., 1987b; Douglas and Spellacy, 1996; Ergh et al., 2002; Kreutzer, Gervasio, and Camplair, 1994b; Kreutzer et al., 2009b; Machamer, Temkin, and Dikmen, 2002; Oddy, Humphrey, and Uttley, 1978; Perlesz, Kinsella, and Crowe, 1999, 2000; Ponsford and Schönberger, 2010; Ponsford et al., 2003; Testa et al., 2006; Thomsen, 1984; Wells, Dywan, and Dumas, 2005; Willer et al., 1991; Winstanley et al., 2006). It is therefore essential to extend rehabilitation efforts to the family, as well as to the person with TBI. This chapter aims to outline common family reactions to the occurrence of TBI, their evolution over time, sources of stress at different stages in the recovery process, and long term changes in family behaviour. This will be followed by discussion of ways in which the burden of families may be minimised.

Common family responses to TBI

The occurrence of TBI creates an immediate crisis for relatives, potentially disrupting established relationships, roles, expectations and goals within the family unit. Emotional reactions are likely to be heightened by the fact that the injury occurred suddenly and may have been avoidable. Family responses to TBI have not been subjected to rigorous research. There have, however, been a number of models or stage theories put forward to describe or conceptualise their reactions over time. In a critique of these models, Rape, Bush and Slavin (1992) identified six stages of family adjustment which were included in most of the models. These include (1) the initial shock response; (2) emotional relief, denial and unrealistic expectations; (3) bargaining, mourning or working through; and (4) acceptance and restructuring. It is important to recognise that these models have not been empirically tested. There are likely to be differences in the sequence and rate at which families pass through such phases, and not all families will experience any or all of these emotional responses. Factors such as the pre-existing family structure, cohesion, coping skills and available resources significantly influence family responses.

Initially, families tend to experience a state of shock. The impact of seeing the injured relative fighting for life creates anguish, confusion, feelings of helplessness and frustration. In many instances a very bleak outlook is given by doctors. All that is wished for is that the injured family member will survive.

Once the immediately life-threatening phase is passed there is frequently a sense of relief. As the TBI family member emerges from coma, and initially recovers relatively rapidly, there are likely to be feelings of expectancy, optimism, and hope for full recovery. As Romano (1974) has described, there is a tendency to deny or ignore obvious changes in cognition and behaviour. Denial of the consequences of TBI may be strengthened by a number of factors. Early predictions that the patient might die, remain comatose, or never walk and talk again may have proven to be incorrect, justifying a loss of faith in further medical predictions. It is, in reality, extremely difficult to prognosticate with any degree of accuracy regarding outcome. Families are frequently told that recovery may continue over a couple of years, and that the final outcome is uncertain. This engenders hope. Many of the problems are relatively intangible. It is much easier to focus on physical disability, which may show relatively rapid improvement, than on cognitive and behavioural changes, which tend to be more persistent but are less readily apparent. There may be strong spiritual beliefs, a sense of faith that determination and hard work will overcome any problems, or an expectation that future advances in medical science will result in a cure for the damage incurred.

Denial can be a source of considerable conflict in the relationship between family members and rehabilitation staff. However, denial may serve a beneficial purpose in the early stages of recovery, as families are trying to cope emotionally with the idea that life may never be the same again. Professionals working with families need to understand and respect this. Attempts to confront denial frequently undermine the relationship between rehabilitation staff and family. Relatives may come to view staff as pessimistic, and lose faith in their commitment to making the best of the injured family member's future. It is preferable to provide family members with opportunities to experience the changes in their injured relative and provide supportive input as and when appropriate. Awareness of the reality of the impact of the injury tends not to come until after the TBI individual has been discharged from hospital, at which point families experience more directly the injured family member's coping difficulties and cognitive-behavioural changes. As a result, depression and/or anger may develop. Anger may be directed at themselves, another family member, rehabilitation staff, the driver of a vehicle involved in the accident, or others, in an attempt to attribute blame for the accident or its consequences. In many instances there are legitimate grounds for such anger, when the party identified as having been responsible for the accident is found to have been behaving irresponsibly and/or under the influence of alcohol or other substances. There may be feelings of guilt or regret over whether something could have been done to prevent the injury. Experiencing negative feelings about the burden imposed by the injured family member, whose survival was so much wanted, may also cause guilt.

There is likely to be significant disruption of relationships and roles which existed in the family prior to injury. Middle-aged or elderly parents, who were making plans for retirement, or enjoying new-found freedom since adult children have left the family home, may be faced with caring for a newly dependent son or daughter at the expense of their own health and needs. They will be concerned as to what will happen to the injured child or adult when they can no longer provide the care that is needed. However, where both parents are still alive they are able to support each other and share the burden to some extent.

Spouses carry a somewhat different burden from that of parents. Where there are children, the spouse of an injured individual must take on the role of both parents, supporting the children as well as the newly injured husband or wife. Additionally, there are responsibilities for running the household, dealing with financial matters and earning an income for the family. The spouse who is injured may be childish, self-centred and irritable, and therefore unable to offer the emotional support which formed an integral part of the relationship prior to injury.

Children of a TBI person may also have to take on new responsibilities. The uninjured parent is frequently absent, visiting at the hospital. When at home, he or she is likely to be tired, irritable and emotionally drained, having limited energy to devote to dealing with issues of importance to the children. The children may experience, therefore, not only a loss of affection and support from the injured parent, but also from the one who is not injured. The mother or father who has sustained an injury may be irritable or aggressive towards the children, unpredictable in his or her responses and no longer willing or able to share activities with them.

Faced with such changes, children may find it difficult or embarrassing to invite their friends into the home. As a consequence, children might drift away from home and withdraw from their parents, particularly if they are adolescents. They may be reluctant to share their feelings with others and tend to deny what is happening and avoid dealing with it. Younger children can develop behaviour problems in such circumstances. Siblings of those injured may also feel neglected and forced to take on additional responsibilities.

Whatever the constellation of the family unit, there is evidence from a number of sources to suggest that it becomes increasingly isolated, as support from hospital and rehabilitation staff becomes no longer available. Friends and relatives, who initially rallied around, become less attentive. There is a growing awareness of the inadequacies of the TBI individual in coping with activities of a social, vocational or recreational nature, so that increasing amounts of time are spent in the home. Caregivers may have to give up their own employment and leisure interests, providing care at the expense of their own health, needs and emotional well-being. As a consequence, the family unit may gradually withdraw from social contact (Kozloff, 1987; Oddy, 1984).

For many, there is eventually a growing awareness of the permanence of the situation and the need to become reconciled to lasting changes in the injured family member, the family's roles and relationships. Relatives may experience grief over the loss of cherished qualities in the injured family member and unfulfilled potential. However, as Perlesz, Furlong and McLachlan (1989) have pointed out, grieving is extremely difficult when it has to be done in the presence of the person who is being grieved for. There is a need not only to mourn the person who was prior to injury, but to adjust to the new person who has survived the injury. The fact that there may be little physical change in the injured individual may prevent or interfere with the grieving process.

With the growing understanding of the new identity of the injured family member, there is, eventually, a need for permanent readjustment of expectations of the injured individual, a redefining of relationships and roles and restructuring of the family environment. The extent to which this can be effectively accomplished will depend on many factors, including the family's resources, coping styles and organisation, whether the family has been able to grieve effectively, the importance placed on qualities which have been lost, attitudes towards newly acquired behaviours, and the flexibility of family beliefs (Perlesz et al., 1989). As Verhaeghe and colleagues (2002) point out, the grieving process is disrupted by the fact that the injured family member is still present and the family is confronted repeatedly with their loss, perhaps even more so over time as the injured person fails to achieve life goals such as a career, marriage and having children. This makes it potentially more difficult for them to come to terms with their losses than they might with a death. It means that long-term support is frequently required.

The impact of TBI on marital, sibling and parent–child relationships

Early studies focusing on very severely injured groups of TBI individuals documented high rates of marital breakdown more than five years following severe TBI, ranging from 78 per cent in those with very severe disabilities (Thomsen, 1984) to 42 per cent in those with "good" outcomes (Tate et al., 1989; Wood and Yurdakul, 1997). However more recent studies, which have recruited consecutive series of patients across a broader spectrum of injury severity, have shown a different picture. Ponsford (2007) found that of a cohort of 228 individuals with moderate–severe TBI followed up at one, two and five years post-injury, only 12 per cent were separated, divorced or widowed at one year post-injury, 11 per cent at two years and 21 per cent at five years, whilst of the 128 individuals in the same group who were single at the time of injury,

9 per cent had married at one year, 11 per cent at two years and 20 per cent at five years post-injury. Of another sub-group from the same rehabilitation cohort followed up at 10 years post-injury only 16 per cent were separated, divorced or widowed. It could be argued that these lower rates reflected the fact that this group had all had access to comprehensive rehabilitation and a system of ongoing supports. However a US study by Kreutzer and colleagues (2007) also found that, of a group of 120 individuals with mild–severe TBI who had been married pre-injury and were followed up 30–96 months post-injury, only 25 per cent had separated or divorced. Marital stability was associated with being married longer before injury, older age, less severe injury and non-violent injury. Another US study (Arango-Lasprilla et al., 2008) also found that only 15 per cent of a group of 977 individuals with primarily moderate to severe TBI had separated or divorced two years post-injury, with being male, younger age, moderate injury and violent injury cause associated with greater marital instability. In minority cultural groups those with greater disability were more likely to remain married. These findings do not suggest that people with TBI are at greater risk of divorce than the general population. Where divorce does occur it tends to be in cases of very severe injury and it may not occur until many years after injury. In the early years there is hope of recovery. The decision to end a marriage to a severely brain-injured person is rarely taken without significant guilt and often as a last resort when all other possible solutions have been tried, possibly as a means of protecting children from emotional distress.

There is, nevertheless, substantial evidence to suggest that spouses of those with moderate to severe TBI experience considerable stress and that the quality of the marital relationship may change. Peters et al. (1990) found that spouses of severely head-injured husbands reported greater disagreement, difficulty reaching joint decisions, fewer overt acts of physical and verbal affection and had significantly lower overall "dyadic adjustment" scores than spouses of moderately or mildly injured husbands. Bracy and Douglas (2002) found that wives of TBI husbands reported greater marital dissatisfaction and poorer communication with their partner than spouses of orthopaedically injured controls and used avoidance coping to deal with recurring marital problems. Burridge and colleagues (2007) noted that greater reduction in relationship satisfaction evident in couples in which one partner had a brain injury was associated with poorer socio-emotional functioning, especially empathetic skill.

Willer et al. (1991) reported that wives of TBI husbands identified the loss of emotional support, sharing, and companionship as significant problems, after changes in personality, cognition, insight, and reduced financial resources. On the other hand, the husbands of TBI wives expressed more concern over dependency, insecurity, overprotectiveness, and reluctance to leave the home on the part of the injured wife, in addition to mood swings. Douglas (1987) noted that families of husbands with severe TBI appeared to experience more stress, conflict, were more socially isolated, and generally less cohesive than families where the injured member was an adult child. It must be noted, however, that by virtue of the fact that they were still living together two years after injury, these families may have represented a somewhat biased sample.

Such findings support the view that spouses carry a greater long-term burden than parents. A number of studies have found significantly higher levels of distress in spouses than in parents of head-injured adults (Gervasio and Kreutzer, 1997; Hall et al., 1994; Panting and Merry, 1972; Rosenbaum and Najenson, 1976; Thomsen, 1984), although not all studies have found this to be the case (Allen, Linn, Gutierrez, and Willer, 1994; Brooks et al., 1987b; Kreutzer et al., 2009b; Oddy et al., 1978; Ponsford and Schönberger, 2010; Ponsford et al., 2003). There is agreement, however, that the nature of the burden experienced by spouses is likely to be different from that of parents. In addition to caring for the injured family member and dealing with changes in personality and behaviour, spouses must frequently take on many additional responsibilities to ensure that the personal, financial and practical needs of the family are met, and may no longer have their social, affectional and sexual needs met by their injured partner (Kreutzer, Kolakowsky-Hayner, Demm, and Meade, 2002; Tyerman, Young, and Booth, 1994). Thomsen (1984, p. 264) reported that, "Spouses considered themselves to be the only grown-ups in the family". Spouses may be less able to tolerate childish, demanding and irritable behaviour than parents, who are possibly relatively better equipped to resume their former caregiving role, and are often assisted and supported in this task by their spouse. In her eloquent description of the stresses faced by family members of those with TBI, Lezak (1978) noted that the spouses of TBI individuals find themselves in a social "limbo", being able neither to mourn their loss nor form new relationships, experiencing guilt and a sense of isolation. There may be little support from the extended family, who, by virtue of their lack of regular involvement, might show limited understanding of the changes in the TBI family member and the stress these have created for the immediate family.

Nevertheless, there is also considerable evidence of ongoing stress in families where parents are caring for a head-injured son or daughter. Many such parents are near or at retirement age and may have failing health. They tend to be greatly concerned about the eventual fate of their adult child. Jacobs (1988) noted the high frequency with which one parent gave up a job in order to care for a head-injured son or daughter.

A number of studies have shown that, whilst stress levels seem to be greatest in people involved in a direct caregiving role (Kreutzer et al., 2009b; Perlesz et al., 2000; Ponsford and Schönberger, 2010; Ponsford et al., 2003), significant stress may be evident in other relatives and in secondary and tertiary caregivers (Gan, Campbell, Gemeinhardt, and McFadden, 2006; Perlesz et al., 2000). Siblings express similar concerns regarding their injured brother's future care and autonomy and their own responsibility in that regard (Willer, Allen, Durnan, and Ferry, 1990). One study has suggested the presence of high levels of stress in the siblings of those injured (Orsillo, McCaffrey, and Fisher, 1993). Siblings report feeling neglected by health professionals (Harrington, 2007b). There is also evidence of conflict between TBI individuals and siblings, who may eventually express jealousy and disapproval of the central role played by the TBI family member and withdraw their support (Kozloff, 1987; Oddy, 1984). Others express admiration of their injured sibling's achievements (Harrington, 2007b).

Unfortunately there has been relatively little formal documentation of the long-term impact of TBI on the children of those who sustain it. In her 10–15 year follow-up study of extremely severely injured TBI people and their families, Thomsen (1984, p. 264) noted that, "The relationship between the patients and their children developed badly in all cases . . .". Pessar, Coad, Linn and Willer (1993) examined 24 families in which one parent was brain-injured. Reports of the uninjured parent indicated that most of the children experienced negative behavioural change after the parent's injury. Problems included a decline in the relationship with the injured parent, acting out behaviour and emotional problems. Poorer outcomes were correlated with the gender of the injured parent, those having significant problems tending to have injured fathers, compromised parenting ability of the injured parent, compromised parenting performance by the uninjured parent, and the presence of depression in the uninjured parent.

As discussed by Urbach et al. (1994), children will show differential responses to the experience of having a head-injured parent according to their age and developmental stage. In the pre-school aged child, the development of trust, self-image and autonomy may be affected by the inconsistent and unpredictable behaviour of a head-injured parent. School-aged children may be subjected to abuse and/or competition with the injured parent and experience consequent shame, resentment and guilt. Adolescents are more likely to have support outside of the family and their self-image is less vulnerable to parental responses, but they may respond by acting out and/or avoiding time spent at home. Children of all ages may have to take on executive responsibilities beyond those normally expected. A small qualitative study investigating the experience of school-aged children of a parent with severe TBI revealed that children expressed a sense of grief and social isolation, often also dealing with violence and fears of family disintegration (Butera-Prinzi and Perlesz, 2004). It needs to be noted, however, that all of the studies conducted to date in siblings or children of brain-injured individuals have been conducted with selected samples likely to be biased towards those experiencing difficulties. There is a need for much further research in this area.

Sources of stress on families following TBI

Many studies have documented elevated levels of anxiety, depression and/or psychiatric "caseness" in relatives of those with TBI, with 25–30 per cent showing problems at clinically significant levels and 60–80 per cent reporting some degree of emotional distress (Anderson et al., 2002; Brooks, Campsie, Symington, Beattie, and McKinlay, 1986; Brooks et al., 1987b; Douglas and Spellacy, 1996; Ergh et al., 2002; Hall et al., 1994; Harris, Godfrey, Partridge, and Knight, 2001; Jacobs, 1988; Kreutzer, Gervasio, and Camplair, 1994a; Kreutzer et al., 2009b; Machamer et al., 2002; Marsh, Kersel, Havill, and Sleigh, 1998; Oddy et al., 1978; Perlesz et al., 2000; Ponsford and Schönberger, 2010; Ponsford et al., 2003; Schönberger, Ponsford, Olver, and Ponsford, 2010; Testa et al., 2006; Thomsen, 1984; Willer et al., 1991; Winstanley et al., 2006). This stress appears to persist over time, up to at least seven years after injury. There is also evidence of unhealthy family functioning, which is associated with the presence of anxiety and depression in relatives (Ergh et al., 2002; Gan et al., 2006; Nabors, Seacat, and Rosenthal, 2002; Ponsford et al., 2003; Sander et al., 2002; Testa et al., 2006; Winstanley et al., 2006).

It would appear from the research to date that the major sources of stress in families of TBI individuals are changes in emotional control, personality or behaviour, particularly irritability and aggression, and cognitive difficulties, such as slowness and memory problems. Other factors associated with increased stress include a lack of availability of social support and practical supports in caring for the injured person, the necessity for role changes in the household (i. e. relatives giving up work to care for them, wives having to take over the responsibility for financial management), financial issues, the injured person being the father of young children, a lack of marital cohesion and increased marital conflict (Anderson et al., 2002; Brooks et al., 1986; Brooks et al., 1987b; Douglas and Spellacy, 1996; Ergh et al., 2002; Hall et al., 1994; Hanks, Rapport, and Vangel, 2007; Jacobs, 1988; Kreutzer et al., 1994a; Kreutzer et al., 2009a; Machamer et al., 2002; Marsh et al., 1998; Moore, Stambrook, and Peters, 1993; Nabors, Seacat, and Rosenthal, 2002; Oddy et al., 1978; Ponsford and Schönberger, 2010; Ponsford et al., 2003; Testa et al., 2006; Thomsen, 1984; Willer et al., 1991).

Another very significant source of variation is the family's inherent capacity to cope with such changes, which is likely to be related to personalities and general stability within the family. Sander and colleagues (2003) have provided evidence to suggest that families of those with TBI may have had higher rates of pre-injury stress and/or unhealthy family functioning, meaning they are less well-equipped to cope with the impact of an injury in a family member. A number of authors have drawn attention to the significant influence of family functioning in determining the family's adaptation to TBI, in both adults and children (Curtiss, Klemz, and Vanderploeg, 2000; Kozloff, 1987; Max, Castillo, Robin, and others, 1998; Perlesz, 1999; Yeates, Taylor, Drotar, and others, 1997; Zarski, DePompei, and Zook, 1988). For many families, particularly those with pre-existing problems, TBI increases their vulnerability, making them weaker and more dysfunctional. Therefore it is important to consider pre-existing problems as a factor contributing to family stress after injury.

The picture is not always negative, however, or may not remain so. As Perlesz et al. (1999, 2000) have cogently pointed out, there has been a focus in the literature to date on emphasising the negative consequences of injury. The fact that many families cope well and the majority do not exhibit clinically significant anxiety or depression needs to be highlighted more strongly. Ponsford et al. (2003) found that the family functioning reported by relatives of individuals with moderate to severe TBI, as measured on the Family Assessment Device (FAD) was, on average, not significantly different from that in other normative samples. A number of authors have observed that some families appear to cope surprisingly well, and may actually become stronger and more resilient in the face of the chronic challenges presented by TBI (Brooks, 1984; Douglas, 1994; Perlesz, 1999; Perlesz et al., 1999). The adjustment process may take place over many years, however. This points to the need to take a very long-term view in terms of availability of support and assistance. Finally, it must be noted that not all changes in personality following TBI are necessarily negative. Occasionally families report that their injured relative has become more even-tempered or compliant, or has a more positive outlook on life after having survived and recovered from such trauma.

Another source of stress commonly reported by families of TBI individuals is poor communication with health professionals involved in treating the injured relative (Oddy et al., 1978). This may reflect a lack of adequate communication by staff, a failure to understand or remember information given, or the presence of denial as a defence mechanism. It is probable that all of these explanations are true for a proportion of cases. This finding highlights the need for the rehabilitation team to give special attention to the manner and timing of information provision.

Many families experience great concern regarding availability of suitable accommodation and/or supervision for the TBI individual, should they be no longer able to provide the care that is needed. Financial and legal problems frequently add further to the burden of the families, who may have little understanding of such matters and few resources with which to obtain assistance.

Methods of coping with TBI in the family

The responses of the family may have as significant an impact on the TBI individual's psychosocial adjustment as the specific disabilities resulting from the injury. Effective use of problem-solving and behavioural coping strategies by the family in response to TBI has been associated with lower levels of depression in the person who sustained the TBI (Leach, Frank, Bouman, and Farmer, 1994). Sander and colleagues (2002) have demonstrated a strong association between unhealthy family functioning and rehabilitation outcome. Hence the importance of focusing on the family system as part of the rehabilitation process.

Zarski and colleagues (1988) have suggested that families which respond by focusing on and organising around the limitations of the TBI member are least likely to be able to deal with injury-related changes and most likely to use denial as a major block to family reintegration. From studies examining the impact of illness or disability on family adjustment, it is apparent that those families who adapt best are those who support one another, openly express feelings and emotions, and are flexible in the face of change. They tend not to view the disability as harmful or challenging to family life, are able to discuss it openly, appreciate the affected family member's residual capabilities and allow them a continuing role in the household. These families also appreciate the need to remain involved in activities outside of the home. The presence of strong religious beliefs is also common (Martin, 1988; Power, 1985). It would appear that such patterns may also characterise well-adjusted families following TBI (Douglas, 1994; Harrington, 2007a; Perlesz, 1999). Kosciulek (1997) and Minnes and colleagues (2000) concluded that the ability of the family to positively appraise or "reframe" their situation, to manage tension, and to seek spiritual support were associated with more positive family outcomes following TBI. Blais and Boivert (2005, 2007) and Rivara and colleagues (2007) found that family coping style, and in particular use of problem-solving skills, positive reinterpretation, and low use of avoidant coping and magical thinking, resulted in better psychological adjustment regardless of the severity of disability. In exploring the complexity of family responses to trauma, Perlesz (1999) noted that many families acknowledge positive aspects of their experience of trauma, whilst still exhibiting clinically significant anxiety and/or depression. Cultural factors, availability of practical assistance and social support have also been identified as very significant factors in determining the style and level of family coping and adjustment (Carnes and Quinn, 2005; Douglas and Spellacy, 1996; Ergh, Hanks, Rapport, and Coleman, 2003; Ergh et al., 2002; Nabors et al., 2002; Wade et al., 2004).

Douglas (1987) found that the family environments of a group of individuals with severe to very severe TBI were characterised by significantly higher levels of control than normal, suggesting that set rules and procedures were used to run family life to a greater extent than in normal families. This finding has been supported by recent data from Ponsford and Schönberger (2010) showing that families of those with TBI are more likely to have set rules for control of behaviour than the norm. The families in the study by Douglas were also less likely to make spontaneous decisions or change daily routines within the family. Such changes were likely necessary in order to meet the needs of the injured relative who, by virtue of problems with memory, executive function and behavioural control, is likely to function best within a stable and well-controlled setting. These families also tended to be less open or expressive of feelings, and to communicate less about concerns and problems, perhaps in an attempt to adapt to increased friction and strained relationships. Finally, there was evidence of less participation of such families in activities outside the family environment.

In a study involving married couples where one partner had a TBI, Willer et al. (1991) found that able-bodied husbands reported suppression of their feelings when reacting to mood swings as the most effective coping strategy.

Other strategies included being careful not to attribute all family problems to the head injury, mutually defining new roles and responsibilities, support groups for their wives, and maintaining a sense of humour. Wives of injured husbands reported their most effective coping strategy to be the development of a realistic but optimistic outlook. The development of assertiveness skills in relation to husband, health care providers, in-laws and insurance representatives was also identified as important. Ranked third was the need to allow the injured husband to become independent, followed by the need to take time for one's self and for family outings. Participation in support groups was identified as another significant coping strategy.

Restructuring of the family environment may, in some cases, involve marital separation or a move of the injured family member to alternative accommodation. Finding a suitable long-term placement for a dependent spouse or adult child is likely to be a difficult and stressful task, often necessitating further rehabilitative assessment and therapy.

How to help families

Given their crucial long-term role as caregivers, decision-makers and providers of support to those who sustain TBI, families deserve to be involved, supported and assisted throughout the phases of acute care, rehabilitation and beyond. Indeed this is an essential component of the REAL approach to rehabilitation following TBI. Involvement with and assistance to families may take a number of forms. These include provision of information regarding TBI and its impact on the injured family member, active involvement in goal-setting and the therapy process itself, supportive counselling and, if deemed necessary, family therapy. The amount of intervention required may depend on the nature and extent of disability in the TBI individual, how the family was functioning prior to the injury, and how the "family system" is affected by the injury.

As with many other aspects of TBI rehabilitation, there has been relatively little research evaluating the impact of specific family interventions on the injured individual and the family. Those studies that have been conducted have generally had methodological limitations. There is a significant need for more systematic data on which to base family assistance. The approach recommended here has been based on the existing evidence from the literature, together with the author's experience.

Early intervention

As noted in Chapter 2, provision of information and support should begin in the intensive care unit. High rates of anxiety, depressive and post-traumatic stress symptoms have been identified in the relatives of patients treated in intensive care (Paparrigopoulos et al., 2006). Families frequently report traumatic memories of how they were treated by medical or other hospital staff in this acute stage, in "being prepared for the worst", which can have a lasting impact on their attitudes to health professionals. Whether such memories are well-founded or reflect their confused state of mind at the time is unclear. However, in view of their fragile state, families are likely to be assisted by the presence of a support worker who understands their situation and has time to explain and interpret the sometimes overwhelming information provided by doctors. Neurosurgical staff face the difficult and stressful task of minimising the likelihood of mortality and morbidity in the injured patient. It is difficult for them to look after families as well. This is acknowledged by Marks and Daggett (2006), who evaluated the implementation of a critical care plan for families of patients with severe TBI. This comprised the provision of health information, emotional support, involvement in patient care tasks, encouragement to families to look after themselves, working as a team to train families to take over long-term care of the patient, and linking them with community-based resources for support and assistance. Nursing staff involved in this evaluation suggested that a designated person not involved in caring for the patient should undertake the role of communicating with families.

When the TBI individual emerges from coma of significant duration, referral will, hopefully, be made for rehabilitation, either in another unit of the same hospital or at another centre. Having just got to know and trust the staff in the neurosurgical unit, families are faced with a new environment, many new faces, and a change in routine. It is important that families are welcomed into the rehabilitation setting by a team member who is identified as someone to whom the family can turn for information, assistance and support throughout the rehabilitation period. Such continuity of involvement is important. This person should provide the family with orientation to the ward and therapy areas, the treatment programme and staff who will work with the injured person. These staff should also take time to introduce themselves and explain their role. A written booklet containing information about TBI and its consequences, and how the rehabilitation programme works is helpful. It is likely that by this stage close family members are feeling exhausted, having spent day and night at the bedside. There may also be pressure for them to return to work. It will be important to families to see their injured relative settled into the new environment, but once this has been achieved, they should be given permission to spend less time at the hospital, provided they feel comfortable with this.

Family assessment

A comprehensive assessment should be made of the family's constellation, the roles played by different members, including the one who has been injured, the nature of relationships and communication within the family. It is also important to consider other stresses on the family. The Head Injury Family Interview (Hi-Fi) was developed by Kay and colleagues (1995) as a structured interview to guide the collection of background information from individuals with TBI and their families and document the impact of the injury on family members.

Where staff with the appropriate family assessment skills are available, the clinical interview may be supplemented by the use of a standardised assessment tool to examine objectively the family system and the responses of individuals to the injury. Such methods include self-report measures and observational techniques. No such tools have been specifically designed for use with the TBI population. The Family Assessment Device (FAD) (Epstein, Baldwin, and Bishop, 1983) is a self-report questionnaire designed to assess the six dimensions of the McMaster Model of Family Functioning and overall level of family functioning. The dimensions assessed include Problem Solving, Communication, Roles Dimension, Affective Responsiveness, Affective Involvement, Behaviour Control and General Functioning. It has been the measure most frequently used to study responses of family members across different disability groups, including those with TBI. It has been shown to have good psychometric properties (Bishop and Miller, 1988; Perlesz et al., 1999). Numerous recent studies have documented high rates of unhealthy functioning on FAD subscales in families of those with TBI, although there has been some variation in the subscales most affected (Anderson et al., 2002; Bragg, Klockars, and Berninger, 1992; Ergh et al., 2002; Kreutzer et al., 1994b; Ponsford et al., 2003; Sander et al., 2002; Testa et al., 2006; Winstanley et al., 2006). Perlesz and colleagues (1999) noted that the length and linguistic complexity of the questionnaire may be problematic and recommended the use of the short form 12-item General Functioning subscale as an alternative to the full FAD.

The Family Environment Scale (FES) (Moos and Moos, 1981) is another measure used in a small number of studies to measure interpersonal relationships, personal growth and basic organisational structure of the family following TBI (Douglas and Spellacy, 1996; Perlesz and O'Loughlan, 1998, 2000). It has been shown to discriminate TBI families from controls, although it has been suggested that its factor structure requires further investigation. FACES III (Olson, 1986), a measure based on the Circumplex model, has been used by Maitz (1991) to study family cohesion and marital conflict in TBI couples.

In the course of the initial assessment period, families may want to discuss the circumstances of the accident and their feelings about this. The emotional reactions and needs of children and siblings should also be explored. It is important to establish what resources are available to the family, financially, in terms of support and assistance from extended family or friends, and whether they are able to have time off from employment. Arrangements may need to be made for home help, financial or legal assistance. The family's cultural background and beliefs and their value system should also be assessed in detail and taken into consideration in planning the rehabilitation process and optimal modes of communicating with the family. Where English is not spoken, it is important to ensure clear communication, using an interpreter, and involving a social worker who understands their cultural background. This person can convey to the rehabilitation team an understanding of family reactions to the injury and attitudes to the rehabilitation process, as well as act as an advocate for the family. Wherever possible, written information should be translated into the family's native language.

Family members usually represent an invaluable source of information regarding the TBI individual's previous lifestyle, abilities, behaviour and personality. Such information is a vital aspect of the REAL approach, to enable the team to set realistic and appropriate goals. It is important to gain an understanding of the family's perception of the impact of the injury on the injured individual, physically, cognitively and behaviourally. Their expectations regarding the rehabilitation process, its goals and outcome, and their role in that process should also be explored. In many instances families may have quite different priorities and expectations from those of rehabilitation staff. Although these may seem inappropriate or unrealistic, they are likely to be maintained and conveyed to the TBI family member, even in the face of logical argument to the contrary by team members. The views of the family deserve respect and consideration from the rehabilitation team. Wherever possible an attempt should be made to negotiate goals which incorporate the aims and priorities of the family, as well as the TBI person. In some cases, the family's wishes and needs may not be congruent with, or in the best interests of the injured person. In others the views of different family members may conflict with one another. Where this is seen to be the case, active family participation in goal-setting and therapy is less helpful.

Provision of feedback and discussion of goals

In the early stages of rehabilitation the TBI individual may be exhibiting ongoing confusion, disorientation and agitation characteristic of post-traumatic amnesia (PTA). As outlined in Chapter 2, attempts to assess and treat the injured person at this stage are likely to result in a picture of global impairment and increasing agitation. Having had the expectation that rehabilitation was to commence in earnest, families may be disappointed at the lack of therapist involvement and the lack of information available. It is therefore important that staff explain the nature of PTA, and try to focus the family's attention on appropriate management of the TBI person during this phase of recovery, rather than attempting to assess or treat the injured individual.

Following emergence from PTA, a more detailed assessment by appropriate team members should be possible. The results of this assessment should be conveyed in a manner whereby it is most likely to be understood by the family, who will have differing capacities to absorb such information. Some will cope with a meeting involving the entire family and rehabilitation team. Others will be overwhelmed by such an occasion and cope better with a smaller meeting with one or two key staff. Whatever the nature of the meeting, this should be backed up with written notes in the family's native language. It may also be helpful to have a tape of the meeting made available to enable the family to review the meeting or others to hear the team's feedback.

Whether the TBI family member should be present at family meetings is a matter for the family and the rehabilitation team to assess and discuss beforehand. It may prove to be too overwhelming or embarrassing for the injured person. Family members may not feel comfortable about asking certain questions or discussing particular changes in the presence of the injured individual. It may be more appropriate to hold a separate meeting tailored to the capabilities of the TBI person. On the other hand, it can be upsetting for TBI individuals to know that others are talking about them without their presence. It is important that team members introduce themselves and explain their role. Information should be conveyed clearly, avoiding the use of jargon. Above all, the messages conveyed need to be consistent. The views of the family (and the injured person, if present) regarding changes they see and progress being made should also be sought. Such a meeting can serve as a means of jointly determining appropriate goals and discussing how these are to be achieved. Family members should be encouraged to raise other issues of concern to them. These discussions need to be backed up with individual contact in order to assess the extent to which the family have understood or felt comfortable about discussing all relevant issues. The meetings frequently raise significant emotional responses which may need to be explored. Family meetings should be held on a regular basis, in order to review progress and set new goals. Discharge tends to create a great deal of anxiety for families, so it is particularly important to communicate frequently as this point approaches.

Family members are likely to ask what the eventual outcome will be. However, as many outcome studies have borne out, such predictions, even after the patient has emerged from coma and commenced active rehabilitation, are fraught with uncertainty (Ponsford et al., 1995b). Moreover, families may not be ready to deal with the answers to their questions. For these reasons it is unwise to prognosticate in these early stages of recovery. Rather, clear information should be conveyed as to the nature of the injured person's injuries, what is being done to help, and the likely time frame over which treatment and improvement are likely to occur. Staff need to be prepared to repeat information many times over an extended period, as families do not always take it in. Even when it is written down there is no guarantee that it has been understood.

Coping with denial

Not uncommonly, families will refuse to acknowledge the significance of the injuries, apparently failing to hear what medical and rehabilitation staff have told them. Their view of the TBI individual's capacity to recover and resume previous activities seems quite unrealistic. Such denial may be viewed negatively by rehabilitation staff. However, continuing to confront relatives with "the facts", as seen by therapy staff, is rarely beneficial and may alienate the family from the rehabilitation team. Preserving an open relationship between therapists and family is crucial to the success of the rehabilitation programme. Whilst having little knowledge of head injury, they know a great deal about the injured individual and are likely to be actively involved in a caretaking, supervisory or supportive role in the long term.

In the majority of instances it is not possible to provide the family with facts about the future. For many families, denial develops as an adaptive mechanism, maintaining family stability whilst they are dealing with such sudden and devastating changes. Moreover, with time, education, active involvement in the rehabilitation process, and experience of living with their injured family member, many families do become more realistic. When this occurs they are most likely to share their worries about the future with team members who have treated them with trust and respect.

When denial continues over a prolonged period it can become more problematic. It may affect the family's willingness to be involved in the rehabilitation programme. It also becomes difficult for the team to make plans for the future. Prolonged denial may indicate the need for structured family intervention.

In view of the fact that it is the family who are most likely to provide long-term care and/or support to the injured individual, it is vital that, under these circumstances, family members be actively involved in the therapy process at all stages. All too frequently relatives are seen as an irritating presence by rehabilitation staff, who want to get on with their job in peace. Clearly, there will be times when therapists need to work with the TBI individual alone, especially when the presence of others causes distraction or behaviour problems. However, participation of family members in relevant aspects of the rehabilitation programme will enhance their awareness of the TBI person's strengths and weaknesses, and their ability to assist in minimising the impact of the disabilities. It also presents an opportunity to model strategies of managing behavioural or emotional difficulties. Indeed, relatives may be invaluable as co-therapists in dealing with such problems. The exception to this is when family dynamics are such that this is not in the best interests of the injured person.

Planning for return to the community is easier when the family has had ongoing involvement in the programme. Family involvement and consultation becomes increasingly important at the time of discharge, as families need to be prepared to take over the supportive role which has been performed by the rehabilitation staff. This is often a stressful time, as families begin to realise the long-term changes they are facing. Staff should make themselves available for consultation and support after discharge from the programme. However, it is also important to link the family with appropriate resources in their local community, so as to minimise dependency on hospital-based services.

The principles of working with families outlined here are embodied in the Interdisciplinary Family Intervention Program or PRIFAM, an education program delivered electronically to health professionals working with TBI individuals and their families by Lefebvre and colleagues (2007). An evaluation of the delivery of this program showed that it fostered the forging of an interdisciplinary partnership between health professionals and families. These principles are also espoused by Kreutzer and colleagues (2010).

Family education and support groups

It is likely to be helpful to enable families to talk with one another during and after the rehabilitation phase, sharing information and emotional support. The general community tends to have little knowledge of TBI and its consequences, so that friends and other family members may not understand what the injured person and family are going through. The issues addressed by family support groups will vary according to the setting, time since injury and nature of the relationship with the TBI family member. In the acute stages of recovery, families may be less ready to discuss their emotional reactions to the trauma, still focusing intensely on the needs of the injured family member. They may, however, benefit from educational input, both in structured form from members of the rehabilitation team or community agencies, and from other families who have already had the experience. Topics of interest may include mechanisms of TBI, management of coma and PTA, medical complications, such as epilepsy, the nature and management of disorders of mobility, communication, swallowing, cognition, behaviour and emotion, vocational issues, accessing community resources, and financial and legal issues. It is wise to tailor the content of educational sessions to the needs of the group. Supplementary notes are also helpful, as many issues may not be fully understood until much later. Such educational sessions may form a basis for broader discussion of issues relevant to individual group members, leading to a sharing of information and support.

Depending on the time since injury and their stage of adjustment, families may benefit from the opportunity of sharing their emotional reactions to the situation and discussing the impact of the injury on the family. Suitably trained rehabilitation professionals should take a facilitative role in this process, to ensure that all families are encouraged to participate actively and that all relevant issues are covered. Some issues raised may need to be taken up individually. Such groups may help families to realise that their experiences and reactions are shared by others. This relieves their sense of isolation and provides family members with a feeling that they are accepted and understood.

The issues of importance to spouses of TBI individuals may be somewhat different from those of parents of injured adolescents or adults. Spouses may feel uncomfortable about discussing relationship issues or their feelings about changes in behaviour and personality. It is therefore useful to enable spouses to talk with one another, providing relief from the guilt which many experience regarding their negative feelings about the injured partner.

Many families form strong bonds through participation in family groups. Such relationships provide a useful resource for the future, when there is no longer active rehabilitation support. In this respect it is useful for support groups to be ongoing, so that families may return in times of need. If this is not possible within the rehabilitation setting, referral should be made to an accessible community-based group. Indeed it is after return to the community that family support groups may be most helpful, as there is likely to be less support from other sources, and family members may be more ready to benefit from them.

A study by Singer et al. (1994) compared the impact of two kinds of support groups for parents of children or young adults with severe brain injury. One group participated in a psychoeducational stress management programme that emphasised instruction in coping skills and group sharing of methods of coping. The second was an informational support group, in which parents identified topics they wished to discuss and were encouraged to share their feelings. Parents in the stress management group showed significant reductions in depressive and anxiety symptoms, whereas the informational and support group did not. As the authors acknowledged, the conclusions from the study were limited by the small size of the groups and the varying aetiologies of brain injury represented. Moreover, the informational support group may have brought other benefits to its participants (e.g. increased knowledge or social support base). However, these preliminary findings suggest that training in adaptation and coping skills may be a worthwhile focus of family support groups.

Other studies have evaluated educational interventions for carers. A controlled pilot study evaluating the impact of an eight-session group intervention comprising didactic presentation with handouts containing exercises and advice on coping strategies, group discussion, and role play for dealing with impaired memory and executive function and emotional problems, delivered separately to brain-injured individuals and their carers, showed a reduction in psychological distress in carers following educational input, although this did not reach statistical significance. A small RCT compared education alone with education combined with education in behaviour management on the premise that the latter might be more effective in reducing carer burden, but obtained no significant differences on the measures used (Carnevale, Anselmi, Buischio, and Millis, 2002). In another study, problem-solving training provided in the home reduced depression and health complaints and dysfunctional problem-solving styles in family caregivers of people with TBI relative to general education (Rivara, Elliott, Berry, and Grant, 2008). Systems of web-based information and on-line support for family carers have also been shown to be useful for providing social support, information and guidance (Rotondi, Sinkule, and Spring, 2005). A manualised intervention, the Brain Injury Family Intervention (BIFI) (Kreutzer et al., 2009c), comprising sessions in the home with the injured person and caregiver discussing injury consequences, ways of coping with change and managing stress, problem-solving and looking after one's self, resulted in fewer reported unmet needs and obstacles to obtaining services, but no changes in family functioning, satisfaction or caregiver distress. A version of this intervention for families of adolescents with TBI has also been developed (Gan, Gargaro, Kreutzer, Boschen, and Wright, 2010).

Educational programmes for parents of children with brain injuries have also shown demonstrated efficacy, including an interactive multimedia intervention known as Brain Injury Partners, which provided parents of children with TBI with training in educational advocacy skills (Glang, McGlaughlin, and Schroeder, 2007). Implementation of a seven-session online problem-solving intervention for parents of children with TBI (Wade et al., 2006a; Wade, Michaud, and Brown, 2006b) resulted in a reduction in child behaviour problems and reported improvements in parental problem-solving skills post-intervention, though not at follow-up.

Multifamily group interventions, which have a strong psychoeducational and problem-solving focus, originally developed for families of individuals with mental health problems, have more recently been applied to the families of those with brain injury. Charles (2007) describes such a group for families with children, where one parent has had a brain injury. This provided an opportunity for these families, not only to gain information about brain injury, but also to share their difficulties, which included a high frequency of violence, so that they no longer felt alone or ashamed. Evaluation of a multiple family group intervention conducted with 27 survivors of brain or spinal cord injury and 28 caregivers over 12–18 months (Rodgers et al., 2007) revealed a decrease in depressive symptoms and anger towards others, an increase in life satisfaction in those injured, and a reduction in burden for caregivers. Themes emerging from a qualitative evaluation of this group included normalisation of the caregiving experience, socialisation, enhancement of coping skills and education about the injuries. Further research is required to evaluate the effectiveness of such groups.

Grieving and the readjustment process – supportive counselling and family therapy

Even those families who show relatively healthy functioning are greatly stressed by the occurrence of TBI. Provision of supportive counselling is a useful means of assisting them to adjust to the impact of the injury, both in terms of the emotional reactions of individual family members and of the family system itself. Where there are pre-existing problems in the family, or where family reactions to the injury are considered to be maladaptive, formal family therapy may be appropriate.

Supportive counselling should provide an opportunity for family members to express and work through their emotional responses at different stages, including feelings of anxiety, helplessness, hope, denial, depression, guilt, anger, loss and grief. The counsellor will need to be flexible in this respect, as individuals within the family are likely to be experiencing differing responses at a given point in time. Many will not be ready to talk about their feelings until long after the injured relative has been discharged. Counselling also provides a forum in which to raise practical problems, particularly those occurring after discharge, and to discuss issues regarding management of the newly acquired disabilities of the TBI individual within the family.

Assistance may be required in restructuring the family system. As the family initially mobilises itself to deal with the crisis, this involves changes which are seen as temporary. Family members tend to put aside their own interests and needs in order to give maximum support to the injured relative. Such sacrifices cannot usually be sustained without a significant physical or emotional toll. At some point, longer term adaptations need to be made. However, it is usually not possible to consider long-term changes until the family has realised the permanency of the situation. A great deal of work may first be required to assist the family in becoming realistic and grieving effectively. As Perlesz et al. (1989) have pointed out, grieving the losses resulting from TBI is complicated by the prolonged period of uncertainty regarding outcome. This tends to encourage unrealistic hope for recovery. It is also very difficult to "mourn in the presence of the one being mourned for". This is particularly so when the changes being mourned are relatively intangible alterations in personality, behaviour and cognition, rather than physical disability or disfigurement. The restructuring process may not begin, therefore, until many years after injury and may never be fully accomplished.

Many dimensions of the family system may be affected by TBI. In particular, there is likely to be a need for significant reorganisation of roles and relationships, as well as modes of communication, decision-making and problem-solving. The extent to which such changes can be made successfully will depend on the quality of functioning in these areas prior to the injury, and the family's level of cohesion and adaptability. Coping with role changes has been identified as a significant source of stress, particularly by spouses of those who have sustained TBI. The extent to which family members can successfully adopt new roles will depend on the flexibility of family beliefs, which may be influenced by cultural background, individuals' experience in adopting different roles and the extent to which resources can be utilised to provide information and support. For example, a wife who has never worked, has been reliant on her husband for management of the family finances, and has difficulty asserting herself is going to find it much more difficult to take responsibility in these areas than one who has well-developed professional skills and previously played an active role in decision-making and financial management. Similarly, fathers who have had previous involvement in child-rearing will adapt better to increased responsibilities in this area than those who for cultural or other reasons consider that to be a female domain.

Some families will achieve these adaptations without assistance. Others will do so with supportive assistance of various kinds, such as the aforementioned BIFI (Kreutzer et al., 2002) which includes 16 intervention topics, self-evaluation tools and treatment strategies for families of those with TBI. The use of this tool has not been formally evaluated, however. Albert and colleagues (2002) describe the development and evaluation of a social work liaison program, which commenced during inpatient treatment, comprising caregiver education and designation of a support worker to support each family caregiver up until and following discharge, with an average of 12 calls made within the first 13 months post-discharge. Caregivers were encouraged to call the social workers but only 15 per cent of calls were initiated by families, highlighting the importance of providing proactive support. The focus of calls shifted from rehabilitation to discharge-planning to personal counselling and finally to family adjustment issues, with 25 per cent of calls devoted to counselling. This social work liaison program resulted in improved outcomes on measures of burden, satisfaction and mastery and higher ratings of quality of life relative to an historical comparison cohort.

Family therapy is one means of assisting families who have not been able to grieve effectively and to resolve maladaptive patterns of communication and interaction which impede the adjustment of the injured individual and/or the family. A forum is provided in which family conflicts can be re-enacted and more adaptive strategies developed for resolving issues. Cultural influences and family belief systems can be explored. Families are encouraged to understand that the problems they are experiencing are often more related to the resources, coping styles and organisation of the family system, than to the limitations of the injured family member. For example an injured relative may be emotionally dependent and demand constant attention. A spouse or parent may reinforce this behaviour to avoid further distress in the family. "The result is a dysfunctional circularity, whereby the overprotectiveness will foster further dependency and resentment and elicit additional overprotectiveness" (Zarski et al., 1988, p. 32).

An attempt may therefore be made to shift the focus from the brain injury and its negative consequences to the family system itself. Following from this, the family is encouraged to accept the new identity of the injured relative, without constantly making comparison with pre-injury qualities. The extent to which the family members "normalise" their altered situation and accept the TBI family member will partly determine whether a positive self-image can be adopted by the injured individual. As Perlesz et al. (1989) point out, the family itself also has to develop a new identity. Family therapy aims to assist families to focus on their strengths and come to recognise ways in which they have grown through the experience of TBI.

No controlled trials have been conducted to evaluate the impact of family therapy on the long-term adjustment of TBI individuals and their families, and there is a need for such research to validate its use. However, the results of case studies seem promising (Perlesz, 1999; Perlesz et al., 1989). A significant problem in some cases is convincing families to accept the need for intervention. Unfortunately those who have had the most long-standing problems may be the most resistant in this respect. It is particularly important, however, that family therapy services be provided by clinicians who are skilled in this area and understand TBI and its consequences. The referring agency should provide background relating to the injury and its effects. Because of the long time-frame over which these adaptations are made, it is also vital that access to both supportive counselling and family therapy services be available over an indefinite period after injury. For some families it may be ten years before they are ready to benefit from such assistance.

Advocacy and support agencies

The heterogeneity and complexity of problems which result from TBI places considerable demands on families, not only in terms of their interactions with the injured individual, but also in terms of the necessity to deal with many different professionals and agencies. Both they and the person who is injured are likely to be faced with choices regarding appropriate forms of treatment, who will deliver it and how long it should continue. In many instances there is a need for ongoing negotiation with insurance agencies in order to obtain funding. Later, decisions may be required regarding long-term care, guardianship and legal issues. By virtue of limitations in their background knowledge and capacity to comprehend information provided, the majority of families and TBI individuals are ill-equipped to make such decisions. Emotional distress adds further to their difficulties. In order to ensure that the TBI individual receives the best possible services it is important that assistance is offered to both the injured person and the family through explanation, interpretation, and advocacy. Where no family support exists, advocacy for the person who has sustained the injury becomes even more important.

This form of support is frequently offered during the rehabilitation phase, but after discharge the TBI individual and the family have few resources on which to draw. In this respect, agencies such as Headway in Britain, the National Head Injuries Foundation (NHIF) in the USA and Brain Injury Australia offer invaluable service, in assisting brain-injured individuals and their families to negotiate their way through rehabilitation services and options for long-term accommodation and support, to become better informed, and to deal with financial, guardianship and legal issues. Some of these organisations also provide a support network in the form of regional support groups. However, the most important function of these organisations is that of drawing the attention of the public and the government to the unique and devastating consequences of TBI, and the policies and services which are required to meet the needs of TBI individuals and their families. Rehabilitation professionals working with TBI have an obligation to contribute to such efforts.

Legal issues

TBI individuals and their families confront a range of legal issues. These vary from one country to another, but generally include proceedings relating to motor vehicle or work-related injuries, issues of competency, financial management, guardianship and the right to make decisions regarding treatment. In the early stages of recovery from TBI sustained in a motor vehicle accident, police may wish to interview the injured person regarding the circumstances of the accident. This can be distressing and bewildering for the TBI individual, who may still be confused and is likely to have no recollection of these events. Police should be encouraged to wait until there has been sufficient cognitive recovery to allow the injured person to cope with such an interview. It will also be important to make them aware of the cognitive limitations of the person who has sustained the injury, particularly the fact that recollection of the events surrounding the accident is never likely to be possible.

TBI individuals may find their inability to recall the accident and period afterwards quite distressing. Both they and their families may go to considerable lengths to find an explanation as to how it happened and who was responsible. There is frequently extreme anger towards the party deemed responsible, particularly where negligence and excessive alcohol or other substances are allegedly involved. This tends to be fuelled by the legal processes. Even where charges are laid and a conviction made, the punishment is rarely considered to be adequate relative to the losses incurred. In some instances there may be a continuing desire to retaliate. Counselling may be necessary in order to work through these feelings. It is important to encourage the TBI individual and the family to see that ongoing anger is likely to be destructive to themselves; that they need to put the accident behind them and focus on the future.

Many countries still have an adversarial system in which compensation is awarded on the basis of proven responsibility for the injury as well as degree of impairment. Legal proceedings usually continue over many years, often commencing at the point when the TBI individual and the family were beginning to adjust to the impact of the injury and look to the future. A multitude of assessments may be conducted, requiring the injured person and/or the family to reiterate the history and consequences of the injury many times. There may be pressure to prove the degree of disability, leading at times to exaggeration of problems and discouragement of return to previous activities, such as work, in order to maximise compensation. This can be extremely counterproductive.

Some of the most disabling impairments resulting from TBI, particularly changes in cognition, personality, and behaviour, will not be evident on physical examination or even standardised psychological assessment, and they may not be accurately reported by the TBI individual. Unless the examinations are carried out by practitioners who are skilled in the area of TBI, the degree of impairment and disability may be significantly underestimated. Clinicians are commonly required to estimate the degree of impairment of various functions in per centage terms, a practice of questionable efficacy. There is a need for development of methods specifically applicable to those who have sustained TBI and for use by suitably experienced practitioners.

Frequently the only parties to benefit from these processes are the lawyers. It is important that the rehabilitation facility encourage the family to use lawyers who have a good understanding of TBI, and who are willing to work with treating staff to maximise the interests of the TBI individual and the family. A no-fault system of compensation is desirable. This provides immediate funding for rehabilitation and other injury-related services, without the need to establish responsibility for the injury. Such a system, administered by the Transport Accident Commission, has been operating cost-effectively in the State of Victoria in Australia, since 1981.

The awarding of financial compensation may bring with it new stresses and responsibilities for the injured individual and the family, sometimes with associated bitterness over its inadequacy to compensate for losses. Advice will be needed regarding methods of preserving capital to provide for long-term needs. There is frequently concern regarding the TBI person's ability to manage even day-to-day finances or to make decisions regarding large sums of money. The assessment of these and other decision-making capabilities relating to the affairs of TBI individuals is extremely difficult, especially in cases where deficits are relatively subtle. There are few established guidelines. However, it is recommended that the process should involve not only neuropsychological assessment, but also assessment of daily functioning in these areas, in the manner suggested in Chapter 3.

The process of assessing competency is often complicated by lack of insight on the part of the injured individual, leading to considerable conflict with family members and relevant authorities. In this respect it may be unwise for family members to take on the task of guardianship. Moreover, some families may be overprotective, and use this as a means of exerting control over the injured relative. Many TBI individuals are capable of managing all or part of their affairs, either alone or with assistance. Any restriction of rights should only be imposed after careful consideration.

It is not uncommon for TBI individuals who lack awareness of problems resulting from the injury to refuse treatment. In many instances their rights in this regard have to be respected. Indeed, there may be little to be gained in attempting to treat an individual who is actively resistant. However, where there is a perceived threat to the well-being of that individual or others, the family, a guardian or doctors may need to intervene on their behalf. Unfortunately, current procedures for the implementation of such intervention tend to be complicated, traumatic and counterproductive to the interests of the TBI individual. There is a need to address this issue, whilst protecting the interests of the person who has sustained the injury.

Finally, some TBI individuals have increased involvement with police and the legal system as a result of behaviour problems or substance abuse. It is important that they be given access to appropriate advocacy services and that the potential influence of the brain injury on behaviour be given consideration.

Case report – Abdul

Abdul was 34 years old when he sustained an extremely severe TBI in a motor car accident. Coma lasted one month and PTA four and a half months. Abdul had emigrated to Australia from Turkey nine years earlier, and met and married his Turkish wife two years later. He was a professional soccer player and also worked in a factory. His wife was a welfare worker. They both spoke fluent English. The couple had two sons, the elder of whom was aged five at the time of his father's injury. He was a passenger in the car when the accident occurred. Although uninjured, he was trapped in the car for 40 minutes and experienced much distress at witnessing his injured, unconscious father, whom he idolised. The second child had been born only a few weeks prior to the accident.

Abdul's wife, Fatima, initially spent day and night at the bedside. As the couple had no family in Australia, she relied on assistance from friends to mind the children. She was first told that Abdul was unlikely to survive. After two days his condition had stabilised, but doctors indicated that he was likely to remain severely disabled, if not comatose. However, relieved that he had survived, and knowing that Abdul was a fit and determined person, Fatima felt very hopeful that he would recover. She was under a great deal of stress, trying to juggle the needs of her new baby and older son with hospital visits, but in the first few weeks friends were very helpful. The hospital social worker arranged for additional support from a Turkish welfare agency. Fatima wanted to spend as much time with Abdul as possible, as she felt it was important that he was stimulated and that he was most likely to respond to her voice. After a month, Abdul began to respond, first by opening and tracking with his eyes, and later following some simple commands. However, he remained mute for some time, which made Fatima very anxious.

Six weeks after the injury, whilst still in this state, Abdul was transferred for rehabilitation. Before he was transferred Fatima visited the hospital and was shown around by a social worker. She was also given a manual containing information about the programme and about TBI. She read this avidly, and also went to the medical library and sought out further information about TBI. As he was still in PTA, Abdul was initially managed only on the ward, receiving short sessions of physiotherapy, and having brief visits from the psychologist and other therapists. A small meeting was held to explain the nature of the injury and PTA, and to introduce the therapists to Fatima. Abdul remained restless and agitated for the next two months. Although able to speak, his speech was very confused. Fatima became frustrated at the lack of progress and worried that he should be receiving more therapy.

Four and a half months after the injury, therapists determined that Abdul was no longer in PTA and conducted full assessments. Abdul was found to have severe and extensive cognitive impairments, affecting his expressive and receptive language abilities, with poor word-finding and paraphasias (as much in Turkish as in English), a short attention span, distractibility, slow information processing, very poor learning and memory skills, visuo-constructional difficulties, a tendency to perseverate, extreme impulsivity, and a lack of ability to plan and self-monitor his behaviour or thought processes. He was also prone to laugh or cry uncontrollably at times. He showed virtually no awareness of his cognitive limitations, was extremely self-centred, and had a low tolerance of frustration.

Physically, Abdul was also significantly disabled, being confined to a wheelchair and requiring assistance in all aspects of his care. This information was conveyed to Fatima. It was emphasised that the problems were severe, but that further recovery would be expected. Unfortunately progress was extremely slow. Reassessment conducted after a further three months, and then six months of therapy indicated only small gains. Lack of initiative and impulsivity were presenting significant barriers to physical progress, and Abdul was still dependent in many aspects of self-care.

Fatima felt it would assist her husband's progress if she took him home. The rehabilitation team were worried as to how she would cope with Abdul as he was, but as this was very important to her they agreed. Abdul was discharged to attend daily outpatient therapy eleven months after his injury. At this stage Fatima was still hopeful of significant further gains, as she had been told that recovery usually continued for at least two years. However, things did not go as she had hoped. Abdul was very demanding at home, expecting his wife to attend to his every need. He constantly competed with the children for her attention, and argued with his elder son, for example over what television programme they would watch. He was completely unable to see how much stress she was under, trying to work full-time, care for two young children and for him. When he was frustrated he became very aggressive towards Fatima and his elder son. Fatima also reported that her husband had become very demanding sexually, which added to her stress.

A behavioural programme was instituted to try and increase Abdul's independence in the home. Fatima found it difficult to follow the guidelines consistently, due to the many competing demands on her attention and time. The couple were also seen together for counselling in an attempt to enhance Abdul's understanding of the impact of his behaviour, to develop anger management techniques, discuss their sexual problems and Fatima's concern over his intolerance of and lack of affection towards his elder son. Over an extended period some gains were made in terms of Abdul's independence in performing self-care activities, but he remained extremely egocentric and demanding. He would agree to attempt certain strategies in therapy, but was not able to carry them out consistently at home.

Fatima was also seen individually to provide her with a supportive outlet, a forum in which she could discuss concerns regarding the children and assist her to develop her assertiveness with Abdul. She was particularly self-conscious in dealing with the sexual problem, as this was an area in which she had always felt inadequate. She also attended a support group with several other spouses of severely injured husbands. She was still determined that the family would stay together and seemed desperate to try any intervention which might improve things. She explained that, as a Turkish wife, it would be unheard of for her to desert her husband. Abdul's elder son suffered ongoing emotional and behavioural problems after the injury. He was exceptionally intelligent, and this may have added to his difficulties. He was referred to a specialised children's counselling service. The younger son was less affected because he was still very young, and had not known his father prior to the injury.

Two years after the injury, Abdul had made only small gains and the same patterns of behaviour remained. The family was referred for family therapy, but Abdul refused to attend after the first two sessions. Fatima was beginning to express intense feelings of anger and resentment towards her husband. She finally began to acknowledge the fact that her husband was unlikely to recover much further. She became extremely depressed, as she began to grieve for the husband she had lost. A Turkish attendant carer had been employed in an effort to relieve her burden, but Abdul still insisted that his wife perform many tasks for him, as he felt this was the duty of a Turkish wife. Having made little progress over the previous six months, he was referred for outpatient therapy at a day centre in his local community. His attendant carer was encouraged to involve him in a number of other activities, such as watching his soccer team.

Five years after the injury, Fatima finally decided she could no longer live with her husband due to his difficult behaviour. She had long since "separated" from him on an emotional level, but had, for a long time, struggled with her feelings of guilt. She eventually made this decision, not only because of the stress the changes in her husband had created for her, but more particularly because of its impact on the children. The children went to live with her.

A Turkish housekeeper was employed to cook and clean for Abdul, and an attendant carer was appointed for 30 hours per week to assist him in getting around in the community. Once alone, he did more for himself and showed a surprising ability to organise his day-to-day activities. He was, however, extremely angry with his wife, as he felt it was her duty to stay with him. He telephoned her constantly, usually with requests for money. He tended to spend his weekly income quickly because most days he took himself by taxi to a Turkish restaurant for lunch. He would have no money left to pay the bills. Out of guilt, Fatima would pay the bills. Abdul also wanted to be a father to his children. Although worried about their welfare, Fatima allowed the two boys to go and stay with their father on weekends. Abdul developed a close bond with his younger son but continued to have conflict with his elder son. Financial settlement of their separation and divorce was complicated by legal proceedings relating to the accident. Abdul eventually received a substantial settlement, some of which was allocated to pay expenses for the children, such as their education.

Abdul's elder son had significant adjustment problems over the next ten years, engaging in frequent antisocial behaviour. He dropped out of school and only had intermittent contact with his father. The younger son continued to visit Abdul every second weekend. Fatima gradually rebuilt a life for herself, but still worried a great deal about Abdul. She had had a couple of relationships, of which Abdul angrily disapproved, but did not remarry. Abdul returned to Turkey for six months in the hope of finding a new wife, but returned alone. He had continuing conflict with the court which held his money in trust, as he wanted more control over his money. Both Abdul and his wife required counselling and assistance of various kinds on a number of occasions over the years after their separation.

Conclusions

There is substantial evidence that TBI has a significant impact on caregivers, and on the family as a whole. The long-term psychosocial adjustment of the person who is injured will to some extent be determined by the levels of adjustment and coping of the family unit. Follow-up studies also indicate that family members provide most ongoing support of a practical, social and emotional nature to the TBI individual. Therefore it is paramount that the family unit be as involved in the rehabilitation process as the injured person. This means frequent provision of clear information regarding TBI and its impact on the injured family member, active involvement in goal-setting and the therapy process itself, access to supportive counselling, and assistance in finding and dealing with service agencies and dealing with financial and legal issues. There is a need to recognise that the adjustment process for families is likely to be a very lengthy one. Access to family therapy services should be available to assist families who have difficulty in grieving, or adjusting roles and expectations of the injured individual within the family following injury. All forms of family support need to be available over the lifespan of the person with TBI.

10 Traumatic brain injury in children

Jennie Ponsford

Introduction

Whilst many of the issues and management strategies outlined in previous chapters also apply to children who sustain TBI, and certainly to adolescents, in a number of ways paediatric head injury differs from that in adults. There is, as a consequence, a need for research regarding sequelae of TBI, course of recovery, intervention strategies and long term needs in the paediatric population. It is also necessary to develop rehabilitation and support services focusing specifically on this group. The aim of this chapter is to explore issues and needs of particular relevance to brain-injured children. Its focus will be on children up to the age of 15 years. Many of the issues pertinent to older adolescents have been explored in detail in Chapter 8.

Causes of injury

Findings from epidemiological studies have indicated that the causes of TBI in children differ from those in adults, and within children differ according to chronological age. Motor vehicle accidents are responsible for a significant, but smaller proportion of cases (Brink, Imbus, and Woo-Sam, 1980; Levin et al., 1992; Rutter, Chadwick, Shaffer, and Brown, 1980). In most instances the child has been injured as a pedestrian, rather than as a passenger. Studies from the United States report a higher incidence of motor vehicle accidents compared with Australian studies (e.g. Crowe, Babl, Anderson, and Catroppa, 2009; Kraus, Rock, and Hemyari, 1990).

Child abuse is the cause of injury in almost 25 per cent of paediatric TBI cases younger than 2 years (Gennarelli and Graham, 2005). In pre-school age children (0–4 years), falls and other accidents in the home account for a large proportion of cases. In school-aged children a higher proportion of injuries result from accidents outside the home, such as falls, moving objects such as a bat or a ball striking the head, and automobile accidents where the child was a cyclist or a pedestrian. In adolescents there is a dramatic increase in head injuries where the adolescent was a driver or passenger, and alcohol or drugs are involved (Levin et al., 1992). As in adults, the number of male children and adolescents who sustain head injuries consistently and significantly outweighs the number of females, although the ratios vary across age-groups, and this relationship is not found in children under 2 years (Crowe et al., 2009). It is estimated that 80–90 per cent of paediatric TBIs admitted to hospital are mild in severity, 7–8 per cent moderate and 5–8 per cent severe (Crowe et al., 2009; Kraus, 1995).

Pathophysiology

There are also pathophysiological differences in the impact of TBI in children relative to adults. Differences in aetiology between adults and children may contribute to such variation (Bruce, 1995). Further, pathophysiological differences within children as a group relate to differences in age-related causes of head injury as noted above as well as age related differences in pathobiology and response to injury (see Adelson, 2010). In particular, injury due to abuse in younger children is more likely to occur in the context of repetitive trauma, and reduced medical attention at the time of injury, which are thought to lead to an increased role of hypoxemia in the pathophysiology of non-accidental TBI (Berger, Beers, Richichi, Weisman, and Adelson, 2007).

Falls or low speed accidents may result in less severe rotational acceleration than that associated with motor vehicle accidents. Although the skull of a child is less rigid than that of an adult and cerebral convolutions are relatively shallow, which may provide a cushioning effect, it has been suggested that the greater flexibility of the skull leads to increased deformation of the skull and more generalised shearing within the cortex (Jennett, 1972). A relatively lower incidence of haematomas and a higher incidence of diffuse cerebral swelling has been found in children relative to adults, with diffuse injury manifested most commonly as diffuse axonal injury or vascular injury (Bruce et al., 1979; Levin et al., 1993). Levin and colleagues (1993) found that lesions were most frequent in the dorsolateral and orbital frontal regions, in frontal lobe white matter, and in isolated posterior regions. There is also evidence of injury involving the cerebellum (Spanos et al., 2007). More recent DTI studies show reduced size and microstructural changes in the anterior commissure (Wilde et al., 2006a), in frontal and supracallosal areas (Wozniak et al., 2007) and in posterior callosal regions after paediatric TBI, suggesting arrested development, decreased organisation, and disrupted myelination (Ewing-Cobbs et al., 2008). As in adults, the depth of brain lesion is related to functional outcome (Levin et al., 1997a). In children with severe injuries, poor outcomes have been associated with impaired cerebral autoregulation including elevated intracranial pressure and hypotension early after injury (Chaiwat, Sharma, Udomphorn, Armstead, and Vavilala, 2009; Philip, Udomphorn, Kirkham, and Vavilala, 2009; Slawik et al., 2009; Zebrack et al., 2009) and a Glasgow Coma Scale (GCS) score of 5 or less (Chung et al., 2006). Children also show increased likelihood of early post-traumatic seizures (Annegers, Hauser, Coan, and Rocca, 1998).

Pre-disposing factors

Some studies have found that children who sustain TBI are more likely to come from socially disadvantaged families and have premorbid emotional, behavioural and/or learning difficulties (Anderson et al., 1997; Brown, Chadwick, Shaffer, Rutter, and Traub, 1981; Klonoff, 1971; Max et al., 1999; Rivara et al., 1993; Yeates et al., 2005), although other studies have not had this finding (Pelco, Sawyer, Duffield, Prior, and Kinsella, 1992). The implications of the presence of pre-existing difficulties are somewhat more complex for children than they are in adults. These will be explored in a later section of this chapter.

Recovery

For many years it was believed that children recover better from TBI than adults. Indeed mortality rates following paediatric head injury are lower than in adults (Bruce, Schut, Bruno, Wood, and Sutton, 1978). Children may also show more impressive resolution of focal motor and sensory deficits (Bruce et al., 1979; Levin, Ewing-Cobbs, and Eisenberg, 1995). Variations in aetiology may also contribute to such differences. However, these differences cannot necessarily be assumed to be true for cognitive functions.

There seems to be a complex relationship between age at injury and developmental milestones. Some research on early versus late brain injury in animals (Kennard, 1936, 1938, 1940) has suggested that the immature brain exhibits greater potential for recovery. On the other hand, it is also known that immature organs and those undergoing development are the most susceptible to damage (Dobbing, 1968; Johnson and Almli, 1978). More recent studies have shown the principle of greater plasticity for the young brain to be an oversimplification of the complex interaction of variables that must be considered. Damage to the young brain may disrupt the future acquisition of abilities. Goldman (1971, 1974) suggested that some of the apparent recovery in young animals immediately following brain injury may be the result of the functional immaturity of that brain area. Behavioural deficits may not appear until a later age, when those areas would normally become functional. Even Kennard's research showed late-developing deficits in infant-lesioned monkeys. This issue may be particularly pertinent to TBI, where injury to the frontal lobes is common. Since some frontal lobe functions may develop later than other functions, deficits may not manifest themselves immediately following injury, but may develop over time.

Goldman (1971, 1974) hypothesised that the young animal brain has areas not yet "committed" to a specific function that can sometimes take over the functions usually performed by an area that has been damaged. The potential for plasticity and reorganisation needs to be considered with respect to the time of injury and the age of establishing developmental milestones within different domains, including motor function, language and cognition (e.g. Forsyth, 2010). For example, in humans the right cerebral hemisphere can subsume language functions following early damage to the left hemisphere (Milner, 1974). However, such development is generally accomplished at the expense of other normally right hemisphere functions (Teuber, 1975; Woods and Teuber, 1973). These children's overall abilities are also compromised (Milner, 1974; Woods and Teuber, 1973).

Many studies have now demonstrated long-term neuropsychological deficits following severe TBI in children (Anderson and Catroppa, 2005, 2007; Anderson, Catroppa, Morse, Haritou, and Rosenfeld, 2005; Babikian and Asarnow, 2009; Catroppa and Anderson, 2004, 2005; Chadwick, Rutter, Brown, Shaffer, and Traub, 1981; Donders and Warschausky, 2007; Horneman and Emanuelson, 2009; Jaffe et al., 1993; Knights et al., 1991; Levin, Eisenberg, Wigg, and Kobayashi, 1982b; Muscara, Catroppa, and Anderson, 2008a; Nadebaum, Anderson and Catroppa, 2007; Prior, Kinsella, Sawyer, Bryan, and Anderson, 1994; Slomine et al., 2002; Van Heugten et al., 2006; Yeates et al., 2002). Whilst early studies were limited by excessive reliance on IQ tests and lack of control groups, there are now several lines of evidence suggesting a causal link between brain injury and cognitive impairment in children. The presence of a recovery curve adds support to this link. A number of studies have shown substantial improvement in cognitive functions over time after injury, particularly during the first one to two years post-injury (Anderson, Catroppa, Morse, Haritou, and Rosenfeld, 2005, 2009b; Chadwick et al., 1981; Ewing-Cobbs et al., 2004; Jaffe et al., 1993; Van Heugten et al., 2006; Yeates et al., 2002), but continuing up to five years after injury (Klonoff, Low, and Clark, 1977).

There is evidence from these studies of a relationship between severity of injury, as measured by initial GCS scores, duration of coma or post-traumatic amnesia (PTA) and degree of neuropsychological impairment (Babikian and Asarnow, 2009). Children with severe injuries show slower recovery and poorer cognitive outcomes up to five years post-injury than children with mild or moderate injuries (Anderson et al., 2009b; Ewing-Cobbs et al., 2004; 2006). In Anderson and colleagues' (2009b) study, recovery trajectories were associated with injury severity over the first 30 months after injury. From 30 months to five years after injury, progress was stable – that is, the children did not fall further behind their peers. Thus it would appear that severely injured children lose ground relative to their peers mainly during the early years after injury, after which they begin to make appropriate developmental gains, but do not catch up. Only injury severity (as determined by GCS score) and acute cognitive performance were strong predictors of five-year outcomes. However, it is important not to make generalisations about the predictability of injury severity on outcomes in younger children given that there is a lack of valid and reliable assessments of injury severity in younger children (Adelson, 2010).

Cognitive sequelae of mild TBI in children

As in adults, mild TBI causes a range of post-concussional symptoms in the early days after injury, particularly headaches, dizziness and fatigue (Ayr, Yeates, Taylor, and Browne, 2009; Farmer, Singer, Mellits, Hall and Charney, 1987; Ponsford et al., 1999). There is some evidence that, like adults, children experience deficits in speed of information processing and attention early after injury. However, evidence from controlled prospective studies of children with uncomplicated mild TBI suggests that these deficits resolve within the first week after injury in the majority of cases and there is no evidence of persisting sequelae three months post-injury or beyond (Anderson et al., 2005; Babikian and Asarnow, 2009; Bijur and Haslum, 1995; Chadwick et al., 1981; Fay et al., 1993; Knights et al., 1991; Ponsford et al., 1999; Prior et al., 1994). In Ponsford et al.'s (1999) study the children who had persisting sequelae showed a higher incidence of previous head injury, learning difficulty and/or premorbid stressors, such as family problems, causing emotional or behavioural problems. Stress or pain from other injuries may also contribute to persisting symptoms (Luis and Mittenberg, 2002). The presence of these problems appears to interact with, exacerbate or cause persisting problems following mild TBI.

In studies including children with complicated mild TBI, where there is evidence of damage on CT or MRI (a group that may also be classified as moderately severe), there is some evidence of more persisting sequelae, particularly in children of lower IQ (Fay et al., 2010; Levin et al., 2008; Yeates et al., 2009). Premorbid functioning also moderates outcome from complicated mild TBI. Fay et al. (2010) found that low cognitive functioning and injury severity interacted, such that children with complicated mild TBI were particularly at risk for developing worse outcome, relative to children of similar cognitive ability and mild uncomplicated injuries and also children of similar cognitive ability and orthopaedic injury (Fay et al., 2010). In light of this finding, there is clearly a possibility of persisting problems in certain mild TBI cases.

Some recent studies have raised the possibility that mild TBI in children may place them at greater risk of long-term problems (Hessen et al., 2007). In a birth cohort study of children aged 14 to 16 years, McKinlay and colleagues (2009) found that children who had been hospitalised for mild TBI during preschool years were more likely to show symptoms of attention deficit/hyperactivity disorder, conduct disorder/oppositional defiant disorder, substance abuse, and mood disorder. However, given the association of mild TBI with a higher frequency of these problems, one cannot necessarily assume a causative connection.

Cognitive deficits displayed by children following moderate or severe TBI

Recovery following moderate to severe TBI occurs more slowly and there is much more evidence of cognitive impairments associated with these injuries

(Babikian and Asarnow, 2009). Whilst many studies have documented cognitive impairments on IQ tests, recent studies have shown that, as in adults, the most commonly documented cognitive impairments in children with moderate to severe TBI are in the domains of memory, attention, executive function and some associated language skills. Although some studies find visuo-spatial impairments are not common (Babikian and Asarnow, 2009), others report consistent findings of reduced performances on tests of non-verbal intellectual abilities (see Taylor, 2010 for summary).

Memory impairments

Disorders of new learning and memory have been identified as amongst the most common cognitive deficits following TBI in children both acutely and over at least five years post-injury (Anderson and Catroppa, 2007; Babikian and Asarnow, 2009; Catroppa and Anderson, 2002, 2007; Di Stefano et al., 2000; Jaffe et al., 1992; Kinsella et al., 1997; Levin and Eisenberg, 1979b; Levin et al., 1996). This is consistent with the recent finding that volume loss is greatest in the hippocampus (Wilde et al., 2007), although an earlier study found a closer association of learning impairment with frontal lesions (Di Stefano et al., 2000).

Not all aspects of memory are equally affected, however. Studies have generally shown that the acquisition of verbal material, such as a word list, over a series of trials and its recall after a delay is most affected in children with severe TBI (Anderson and Catroppa, 2007; Di Stefano et al., 2000; Jaffe et al., 1992; Kinsella et al., 1997; Levin et al., 1982b; Levin et al., 1996). Anderson and Catroppa (2007) found that visual memory, immediate memory, measured on digit span forwards, and working memory, measured on digits backwards, were not impaired five years post-injury. Other studies have demonstrated problems in working memory, measured on the n-back task, in children with severe TBI (Chapman et al., 2006; Levin et al., 2002; Levin et al., 2004a). Mandalis and colleagues (2007) found impaired performance on a measure of Phonological Loop function, related to poor encoding and acquisition on a new verbal learning task in children with moderate to severe TBI.

There is evidence that prospective memory may also be impaired following TBI in children (McCauley and Levin, 2004; McCauley, McDaniel, Pedroza, Chapman, and Levin, 2009). However, as in adults, procedural memory appears to be relatively unaffected, which has implications for rehabilitation (Ward, Shum, Wallace, and Boon, 2002).

Attentional difficulties

Parents and teachers commonly report continuing attentional problems in children with moderate and severe TBI over at least four years post-injury (Catroppa and Anderson, 2005; Yeates et al., 2005). Findings from neuropsychological studies have been somewhat variable, however. This is partly due to problems in the definition of attention, its multi-dimensional nature, and lack of agreement as to how to measure its various aspects. Measures of attention most commonly used with children have included tests of processing speed, such as reaction time or Coding and Symbol Search subtests from the WISC, the Trail Making Test, letter cancellation, digit span tasks, continuous performance/vigilance measures, the Contingency Naming test and subtests from the Test of Everyday Attention for children (TEA-Ch).

Numerous studies employing these measures have shown reduced speed of performance across a broad range of injury severity and over periods of up to five years post-TBI (Anderson and Pentland, 1998; Catroppa and Anderson, 2005; Catroppa, Anderson, Morse, Haritou, and Rosenfeld, 2007; Chadwick et al., 1981; Jaffe et al., 1992; Knights et al., 1991; Nadebaum et al., 2007). As in adults these impairments are most evident on complex tasks and may not be evident on tests of simple reaction time (Catroppa and Anderson, 2005).

Researchers have demonstrated impairment of both selective and sustained attention on the Continuous Performance Test (CPT), showing more missed responses and an increasing number of misses over time (Anderson and Pentland, 1998; Catroppa and Anderson, 2005; Dennis, Wilkinson, Koski, and Humphreys, 1995). Impaired response inhibition has also been evident on this task (Catroppa and Anderson, 2005) and on the Opposite Worlds subtest from the TEA-Ch, another test of inhibitory control. An fMRI study demonstrated several areas of greater activation in frontal and parietal regions in children with TBI performing the CPT relative to controls (Kramer et al., 2008). These findings contrast with those obtained in imaging studies of Attention-Deficit/Hyperactivity Disorder where under-activation of the attention network has been documented.

As in adults it is difficult to separate impairments in shifting or dividing of attention from impairments in processing speed and attentional capacity (Catroppa and Anderson, 2005). However children with severe TBI perform more poorly on the DT subtest from the TEA-Ch, a measure of divided attention (Nadebaum et al., 2007). It has been argued that as sustained attention and the ability to shift and divide attention do not develop fully until later in childhood, deficits may only emerge in older children (Catroppa and Anderson, 2005; Catroppa et al., 2007). All forms of attentional impairment are most evident in children with severe injuries, but also in children with moderate injuries. The possible influence of pre-injury attentional disturbances should also be considered in individual cases (Yeates et al., 2005).

Language impairment

Whilst verbal functions have been reported to be less affected than other abilities, there is evidence of linguistic impairment following severe TBI. As Ewing-Cobbs and Barnes (2002) point out, the nature of these will depend on many factors, including the child's age at injury, presence of focal versus diffuse injury and stage of linguistic development, with skills already acquired and consolidated most resistant to injury, and those developing at the time of injury most vulnerable, followed by skills which have yet to develop. Focal injury occurring perinatally is least likely to result in significant impairments, as there is potential for reorganisation, whereas children with diffuse injuries do not fare as well. Children with TBI seldom exhibit aphasic syndromes. However, deficits at the lexical or word level, including impaired visual confrontation naming, object description, verbal fluency and writing to dictation, may occur, particularly in pre-school children with severe injuries (Anderson et al., 1997; Ewing-Cobbs et al., 1997). These younger children also fare badly in reading, as word decoding skills have not yet been developed.

These impairments are less likely in school-aged children or adolescents (Chadwick et al., 1981; Ewing-Cobbs, Levin, Eisenberg, and Fletcher, 1987), although they may show more subtle receptive or expressive difficulties over time, particularly manifested as reduced expressive naming and word fluency (Dennis, 1992; Jordan and Murdoch, 1990; Jordan, Ozanne, and Murdoch, 1988, 1990; Levin, Song, Ewing-Cobbs, Chapman, and Mendelsohn, 2001a; Winogron, Knights, and Bawden, 1984). Older children may also show reading comprehension difficulties, which may be associated with impaired processing speed (Ewing-Cobbs and Barnes, 2002).

As in adults, older children and adolescents are more likely to exhibit problems with discourse, that is, telling a story or participating in a conversation, and have difficulty using language to communicate effectively (Chapman et al., 1992; Chapman et al., 2006; Chapman et al., 2001; Chapman et al., 2004; Dennis and Barnes, 1990; Ewing-Cobbs and Barnes, 2002). Some of the difficulties evident include difficulty interpreting ambiguous sentences and metaphors, drawing inferences and producing discourse segments, and recalling the semantic content of and preserving the gist of stories (Ewing-Cobbs and Barnes, 2002). A number of cognitive impairments may contribute to discourse problems, including impaired self-regulation and problem-solving (Chapman et al., 2004), monitoring and detection of semantic anomalies (Hanten et al., 2004), working memory (Chapman et al., 2006), and processing speed (Ewing-Cobbs and Barnes, 2002). Impaired interpretation of facial expressions may also contribute to this difficulty (Bornhofen and McDonald, 2008). Impairments of executive function have been shown to contribute to language difficulties in children, as well as in adults.

Executive dysfunction

Given the vulnerability of the frontal lobes to injury, as in adults, children with TBI are likely to experience executive dysfunction. Diamond (1988) has suggested that the pre-frontal cortex mediates the performance of behavioural tasks as early as the first year of life. Executive difficulties have been reported by the parents of children across all levels of TBI severity, but are most common following severe TBI (Anderson and Catroppa, 2005; Sesma,

Slomine, Ding, McCarthy, and Children's Health After Trauma Study, 2008). However, the probability and manifestations of executive dysfunction depend on the age of the child at injury, and interact with cognitive development prior to injury. The fact that executive functions develop gradually throughout childhood and adolescence adds to the risk of executive function deficits for all TBI children, either immediately following injury, or in the future, as they may fail to develop normally. Executive functions are the skills required to attain a future goal, which may include attentional control, strategic planning and problem-solving, cognitive flexibility and concept formation (Anderson and Catroppa, 2005). Executive function is thus a multi-dimensional construct and there is little agreement as to the definitions and methods of measuring these constructs, with most tests tapping into several constructs. Consequently it is difficult to compare findings across studies. Furthermore, although in clinical settings disturbances in behavioural aspects of executive function may be seen in the presence of intact cognitive aspects of executive functions, research studies typically report on combined measures of cognitive and behavioural aspects of executive functioning. Findings from such studies are difficult to interpret.

In children with moderate, and particularly with severe injuries, impairments have been demonstrated on tests measuring strategic planning and problem-solving, including the Austin Maze (Prior et al., 1994), Tower of London task (Levin et al., 1997b), Rey Complex Figure (Anderson and Catroppa, 2005), Porteus Maze test (Levin, Song, Ewing-Cobbs, and Roberson, 2001b), Block Design (Nadebaum et al., 2007), a party planning task (Todd, Anderson, and Lawrence, 1996), cognitive flexibility and mental speed, including the Trail Making test, Contingency Naming test (Anderson and Catroppa, 2005; Jaffe et al., 1992) and TEA-Ch DT test (Nadebaum et al., 2007), and abstract or logical reasoning or concept formation, including the Wisconsin Card Sorting Test (Levin et al., 1997b; Prior et al., 1994; Slomine et al., 2002), Twenty Questions (Levin et al., 1997b), Verbal Fluency (Anderson and Catroppa, 2005; Levin et al., 2001a; Slomine et al., 2002), Progressive Figures, Colour Form and Category Test (Jaffe et al., 1992), Matching Familiar Figures, and Similarities (Chadwick et al., 1981). Levin and colleagues (1997b) showed that the presence of frontal lesions on MRI was associated with impairments on the Wisconsin Card Sorting and Tower of London tasks.

Studies have shown that Verbal Fluency performance was poorest and recovery was slower in younger than in older children with severe TBI (Levin et al., 2001a; Slomine et al., 2002), possibly reflecting their reduced opportunities for language development prior to injury. However, older children who had left frontal lesions performed worse, highlighting the potential impact of functional commitment of the left frontal region at the time of injury. Anderson and colleagues (2005) found that children with severe injuries showed the greatest recovery on executive measures over two years after injury, but continued to exhibit the most significant impairments. In a 7–10 year follow-up of children injured between ages 8 and 12, following transition into adulthood the group differences had diminished somewhat, although the severely injured participants showed executive dysfunction in some tasks (Muscara et al., 2008a). Overall there has not been a lot of evidence to support the idea that executive difficulties worsen with increasing time post-injury, as development occurs. Rather, they seem to be most influenced by injury severity and by initial age at injury. Family functioning may also influence the manifestations of executive dysfunction (Nadebaum et al., 2007).

A number of more recent studies employing experimental tasks have demonstrated reduced error monitoring, leading to problems in adjusting behaviour as the situation demands (Ornstein et al., 2009), impaired response inhibition (Leblanc et al., 2005), and a decreased ability to regulate behaviour from within in order to achieve a goal, with dependency on environmental cues (Cook, Chapman, and Levin, 2008). Children with frontal lesions also show poorer socialisation, more maladaptive behaviours and greater overall disability than injured children without frontal lesions (Levin et al., 2004b). There is increasing awareness of the social difficulties experienced by children with TBI. Prigatano and Gupta (2006) found that children with severe TBI had fewer friends than uninjured children. Social difficulties have been shown to be associated with the above-mentioned executive self-regulatory difficulties and poor social problem-solving, with greater reliance on avoidant or aggressive, rather than assertive approaches to social problem-solving (Ganesalingam, Yeates, Sanson, and Anderson, 2007; Hanten et al., 2008; Muscara, Catroppa, and Anderson, 2008b). Social adjustment problems are in turn exacerbated by family environmental factors, such as lower socioeconomic status, lack of family resources and poor family functioning (Yeates et al., 2004).

Interaction between age and recovery

An issue which is debated in the literature is that of whether the age of the child affects potential for recovery. Do those who are younger show greater potential for recovery? Do younger children suffer more generalised cognitive impairment? Are those abilities which are best-established at the time of injury (e.g. language) least likely to be affected? Whilst earlier studies using IQ tests did not find evidence of poorer cognitive outcome in children injured at a younger age (Chadwick et al., 1981; Klonoff, 1971; Klonoff et al., 1977; Knights et al., 1991), findings from recent studies suggest that children sustaining severe TBI at younger age do experience more significant cognitive impairments in the longer term. It is also important to consider the possibility that indicators of injury severity may not accurately represent the severity of injury in younger children.

Severe TBI sustained in the pre-school years (age 3–7) has been shown to result in poorer outcomes relative to children aged 8–12 years, who in turn showed poorer outcome than children aged 12–15 (Anderson et al., 2005;

Ewing-Cobbs et al., 2004). Age at injury is less predictive of outcomes for children with mild or moderate TBI, although Ewing-Cobbs et al. (2004) found that younger children with mild to moderate TBI showed less achievement over time in Arithmetic and Reading Decoding than older children. Anderson and colleagues found that infants aged 0–2 years with moderate TBI showed poorer outcomes than did older children with injury of similar severity. Another study focused only on children aged 4 months to 7 years (Ewing-Cobbs et al., 1997) did not show any differences in outcome across this age-range, with all severely injured children showing equally poor outcomes across a range of domains relative to children with mild and moderate injuries. Recovery was evident over the first six months after injury but not thereafter, so there was little evidence of catch-up. Another study (Donders and Warschausky, 2007) comparing outcomes from injury sustained at age 6–12 years with that from injury between 16 and 20 years found no group differences in overall cognitive ability, post-injury education or vocational accomplishments. However, the early-onset group demonstrated worse outcomes in higher-level cognitive skills, social integration, driving, and legal guardianship. These findings, together, suggest that early brain injuries may disrupt the acquisition of some skills and have a worse overall impact on cognitive outcome.

Scholastic performance following TBI

One very significant difference between children and adults is that children must go to school. In this setting they are expected to learn and acquire new skills, not just resume a familiar routine in the home or at work. Impairment of memory, attention and speed of thinking, so essential for the acquisition of new skills in the educational setting, may significantly affect progress at school, and thereby have lasting effects on the child's future. In this respect the impact of TBI in a child may be greater than in an adult. There may be cumulative effects over time, leading to delays or even failure to acquire certain cognitive skills. It has been suggested that pre-schoolers, in whom cognitive skills are developing rapidly, may be at risk for developing the most significant academic delays (Anderson, Catroppa, Morse, Haritou, and Rosenfeld, 2000; Ewing-Cobbs et al., 2004). Numerous studies have shown persistent delays in reading, arithmetic performance and other school-related tasks in severely head-injured children (Catroppa and Anderson, 2007; Catroppa et al., 2009; Chadwick et al., 1981; Ewing-Cobbs et al., 2004; Ewing-Cobbs et al., 2006; Hawley, 2004; Jaffe et al., 1993; Kinsella et al., 1995; Kinsella et al., 1997; Knights et al., 1991).

There is also evidence that a significant proportion of children with TBI have been considered by their teachers to be experiencing difficulties with schoolwork, have required placement in special classes, or have shown limited academic achievement (Anderson, Brown, Newitt, and Hoile, 2009a; Chadwick et al., 1981; Ewing-Cobbs et al., 2006; Kinsella et al., 1995; Kinsella et al., 1997; Klonoff et al., 1977; Knights et al., 1991). Some of these studies have included children with moderate or even mild injuries (Anderson et al., 2009a; Klonoff et al., 1977). Although the presence of comorbidities always needs to be borne in mind, the presence of even mild impairments of attention, processing speed, memory, or executive function may have an impact on school performance.

Deficits in scholastic achievement may take some time to become apparent – sometimes a year or more after injury (Jaffe et al., 1993). Moreover, the pattern of skill deficits is frequently somewhat uneven, with arithmetic being most vulnerable to disruption by TBI, due to its demands on mental speed, working memory and problem-solving skills, whereas word recognition skills may be less impaired (Ewing-Cobbs et al., 2004). Measures of scholastic achievement may not capture the difficulties that children experience with learning in the classroom after injury. Ewing Cobbs et al. (2004) found that cognitive variables such as phonological processing and verbal memory accounted for more variability in academic scores than did duration of impaired consciousness and socioeconomic status. Other studies have also found that severity of verbal memory impairment at 6, 12 and 24 months post-injury is associated with poorer performance on academic measures (Catroppa and Anderson, 2007; Kinsella et al., 1997) and with special education placement (Kinsella et al., 1997; Miller and Donders, 2003) in severely injured children. In the study by Catroppa and colleagues, pre-injury academic ability was also influential. This should always be taken into consideration.

Behavioural and psychiatric sequelae of TBI in children

Methodological problems plagued many early studies of behaviour change following TBI in children. The issue is complicated by the finding mentioned earlier that children who sustain TBI have a greater likelihood than others of having behavioural or emotional disturbance prior to injury and coming from families in psychosocial adversity (Anderson et al., 1997; Brown et al., 1981; Klonoff, 1971; Max et al., 1999; Rivara et al., 1993; Yeates et al., 2005). Studies that have controlled for the influence of these factors and for the effects of general trauma show higher rates of behavioural disturbance in children with severe, but not mild TBI (Anderson, Miorse, Catroppa, Haritou, and Rosenfeld, 2004; Brown et al., 1981; Chapman et al., 2010; Fletcher, Ewing-Cobbs, Miner, Levin, and Eisenberg, 1990; Fletcher et al., 1996; Kinsella, Ong, Murtagh, Prior, and Sawyer, 1999; Knights et al., 1991; Schwartz et al., 2003; Yeates et al., 2005). These problems were evident across all age-groups in the first year after injury and persisted for at least four years after injury. These studies have found that the presence of pre-existing behavioural problems and socioeconomic disadvantage were still the most significant risk factors for post-injury behavioural disturbance, along with injury severity. Concurrent factors may also include weakness in working memory and adaptive behaviour skills, poorer behaviour and school competence, and adverse family functioning (Schwartz et al., 2003; Taylor et al., 2001). Kinsella and colleagues (1999) highlighted the influence of parental coping on behaviour disturbance in children with severe TBI.

Examination of the nature of behaviour change in these studies reveals higher rates of externalising behaviours, including delinquent, aggressive and ADHD-type behaviours (Chapman et al., 2010; Max et al., 2005b; Schwartz et al., 2003; Yeates et al., 2005) and socially disinhibited behaviours (Brown et al., 1981). In pre-school age children these problems have been shown to increase somewhat over time (Chapman et al., 2010). It would be reasonable to conclude that this pattern, which bears a close relationship to the so-called frontal lobe syndrome seen in adults, occurs as a direct result of brain injury. In support of this are the findings of recent studies, cited earlier, showing reduced response inhibition and impaired self-monitoring and self-regulation of thinking and behaviour (Cook et al., 2008; Leblanc et al., 2005; Ornstein et al., 2009). Max and colleagues (2005a; 2006) documented personality change in 22 per cent of children with TBI in the first six months and 12–13 per cent between 6 and 24 months post-injury, and found this to be significantly associated with injury severity and the presence of superior frontal gyrus injury, although pre-injury adaptive function became influential in the second year after injury (Max et al., 2005a; 2006).

Levin and colleagues (2007) found that 86.4 per cent of children with pre-injury ADHD had the diagnosis 12 months after injury, as compared with 14.5 per cent of children without pre-injury ADHD, in whom the diagnosis was associated with greater injury severity, greater and more frequent fluctuations in hyperactive symptoms, and poorer socioeconomic status. Similarly, Max et al. (2005c) found that so-called secondary ADHD, diagnosed in children without premorbid ADHD, occurred in 16 per cent of children with TBI in the first six months after injury, 15 per cent of children 6–12 months after injury and in 21 per cent in the second year after injury. Socioeconomic status and orbitofrontal gyrus lesions significantly predicted secondary ADHD occurring in the first six months post-injury. Pre-injury adaptive function was a consistent predictor and pre-injury psychosocial adversity was the most significant predictor of secondary ADHD in the second year after injury. Thus it appears that pre-frontal structural changes as well as psychosocial factors play a role in the evolution of this condition.

As Fletcher and colleagues (1990) have noted, behavioural change in children with TBI is more variable than it is in adults. This may partly reflect the insensitivity of measures used, but may also reflect the fact that children are more vulnerable emotionally and behaviourally, and their behaviour may be influenced by many factors other than the brain injury itself. Such factors include the child's pre-injury personality, social circumstances, and the way in which the family copes with the injury. Numerous studies have now found that, in addition to injury severity, better overall pre-injury family functioning, a high level of family cohesion, positive family relationships and lower levels of "control" (family hierarchy and rules that are rigid) are significantly associated with good adaptive functioning, social competence and global functioning in the injured child (Brown et al., 1981; Gerrard-Morris et al., 2010; Kinsella et al., 1999; Max et al., 1999; Rivara et al., 1993; Yeates et al., 2004; Yeates et al., 1997).

Changes in parental handling of children with TBI are common during the two years after injury (Brown et al., 1981; Chapman et al., 2010). Parents may show a decreased use of discipline and be overprotective. There is evidence that more permissive parenting styles are associated with greater behavioural disturbance following TBI in children (Chapman et al., 2010). There may also be a decline in family relationships following the injury, which may contribute to behavioural disturbance in the injured child (Brown et al., 1981; Chapman et al., 2010; Taylor et al., 2001). Children have particular emotional and psychological needs at different stages of development, and the injury may prevent these needs being met. Young children, forced to be in hospital for long periods, may experience separation anxiety and develop fears of death, medical procedures and pain. Older children and adolescents suffer from being different from their peers. Poor body image and social isolation can result in significant loss of self-esteem, anxiety and depression. The process of becoming independent of parental support and influence, so central during adolescence, is significantly disrupted by TBI. Resultant "acting-out" behaviour may be exacerbated by a reduction in behavioural control resulting from frontal lobe injury.

In a study of psychiatric disorders following paediatric TBI, Bloom and colleagues (2001) found that ADHD and depressive disorders were the most common lifetime and novel diagnoses in the first year after injury. A wide variety and high rate of novel psychiatric disorders were identified, with 74 per cent of these disorders persisting in 48 per cent of the injured children. Internalising disorders were more likely to resolve than externalising disorders. In a longitudinal outcome study, Anderson and colleagues (2009a) have found that survivors of severe TBI followed up into early adulthood have, in addition to limited educational and vocational attainments, a relatively high rate of mental health problems, which also developed in some participants with moderate injuries.

Summary of differences between TBI in children and adults

There are a number of differences between the impact of TBI in children and in adults. The causes of injury are more variable in children, and their pathophysiological responses to injury differ. Whilst there is some evidence to suggest that children have an increased probability of survival and show better motor-sensory recovery, it is clear that, like adults, children suffer ongoing impairment of cognitive function following severe TBI. From group studies there is little evidence of lasting cognitive or behavioural impairment as a result of mild TBI, although this may occur following complicated mild TBI or where there are pre-existing vulnerabilities. The pattern of cognitive deficits following moderate to severe TBI depends to some extent on the age of the child and the level of premorbid cognitive development. It does resemble that seen in adults in certain respects, in that memory, attention, speed of information processing and executive function appear to be particularly affected in proportion to injury severity. Behavioural changes are also common following severe TBI in children, and are influenced not only by injury severity, but also by pre-injury behaviour as well as psychosocial and family circumstances.

Both cognitive and behavioural deficits in children with TBI are more complex and variable than in adults because they must be viewed within the context of a dynamic developmental process. Maturational, psychosocial and cognitive factors interact with injury far more in children than in adults. A child's deficits can only be viewed in relation to pre-traumatic levels of development and behaviour. Infants and young children must not only regain former functions, but also continue to acquire new skills to set a foundation for further development. There is a growing body of evidence to suggest that pre-school children are more vulnerable to cognitive dysfunction and a failure to acquire new skills over time. Finally, children may be more vulnerable emotionally and behaviourally, being disproportionately affected by the impact of their injuries on their families and on their social relationships.

The REAL approach to assessment and rehabilitation of children with TBI

It is clear that the needs of children with TBI differ from those of adults in a number of ways, which means that specialised assessment and rehabilitation services are extremely important. The need to follow the principles of the REAL approach to rehabilitation following TBI is possibly even greater in children than in adults. The complexity of the problems being confronted necessitates teamwork across a range of disciplines. It is essential that family are involved at all levels of assessment and management. They need to provide a comprehensive understanding of the child's personality, behaviour patterns and abilities prior to injury, to be active participants in the therapy process and to assist in planning for the child's future.

Children with TBI can be accurately assessed only within the context of their previous developmental stage and behaviour patterns. For social and emotional reasons it is particularly important to return children to their normal environment as early as possible. There is thus even greater pressure to conduct the rehabilitation process within the context of the child's everyday life. The fact that the child usually returns to the school environment, and potentially develops increasing scholastic difficulties over time, necessitates the provision of ongoing assistance extending into adulthood. Psychological support is also essential, since TBI children and adolescents may be particularly vulnerable emotionally. The following sections contain suggested guidelines for the implementation of the REAL approach as it applies to children with TBI, with particular emphasis on those aspects of assessment and rehabilitation which are unique to children and their families, and which have not been discussed in other chapters.

Assessment following paediatric TBI

The staff assessing and treating an acutely injured child should have special expertise in working with children. In particular, they need to be capable of understanding the child's developmental level physically, linguistically, cognitively, behaviourally and emotionally.

Given the clear relationship between indices of injury severity and outcome, there is, as with adults, a need to use objective measures of coma and PTA. However, these should be appropriate to the child's abilities. Some items from the GCS, such as the ability to obey commands or give an appropriate verbal response, are inappropriate as applied to young children, especially under the age of two years. If the GCS is to be used, the verbal response would need to be scored by giving the child a score of five if there is any vocalisation and zero if no crying occurs. The motor component of the scale may be applied after the first few months of life, leaving out the response to command. The best motor response is said to be a powerful predictor of outcome (Bell and Britton, 1989). Raimondi and Hirschauer (1984) developed the Children's Coma Scale to be used with infants and toddlers. The scale ranges from 3 to 11 points and includes such items as "cries" for the best verbal response and "flexes/extends" for the best motor response. Scores on this scale correlated moderately well with global categories of outcome. A similar scale has been developed by Hahn and colleagues (1988). Although the usefulness of these Children's Coma Scales in understanding recovery patterns remains to be fully established, the development and use of age-appropriate scales is to be encouraged.

Similar problems apply with the use of adult measures of PTA to assess children. The Westmead PTA Scale has been validated for use in children over the age of seven years (Marosszeky et al., 1993). Two versions of this have been developed and piloted for use with children aged 4–6 years. The first is the Starship Post-Traumatic Amnesia Scale (Fernando, Eaton, Faulkner, Moodley, and Setchell, 2002) assessing orientation (How old are you? What did you last eat? Where do you live? Why are you in hospital? What is your mother's/father's name? Is it daytime or nighttime?), memory for the examiner's name and face and three target pictures. The other is the Westmead Post-traumatic Amnesia Scale for Children (WPTAS-C; Rocca, Wallen, and Batchelor, 2008), which comprises two orientation (How old are you? What is the name of this place?) and four memory questions, including two items remembering pictures of familiar objects. A children's version of the Galveston Orientation and Amnesia Test, known as the Children's Orientation and Amnesia Test (COAT) has also been developed (Ewing-Cobbs, Levin, Fletcher,

Miner, and Eisenberg, 1990). The COAT consists of a series of simple questions examining temporal orientation, recall of autobiographical information, and immediate and short-term memory. Norms are available which permit specification of the degree of PTA in children as young as three years. Iverson, Iverson and Barton (1994) have provided reference data for interpreting COAT scores of children with TBI who have learning disabilities. However, this scale lacks sensitivity to the ability to lay down new memories, having only one item assessing this (recall of the examiner's name). Further validation is required to assess the sensitivity of all of these scales to presence of PTA in young children. Moreover, despite the potential usefulness of PTA as a marker of severity, this is limited by developmental constraints on orientation and memory functioning in children. Therefore, whilst injury in children 0–3 years is common and the brain at this age is particularly vulnerable to injury, it is not understood whether PTA is a valid construct in these younger children.

Assessment of a child's feeding capacity and communication skills must also be appropriate to that child's developmental stage, as should any augmentative communication systems that are developed by the speech pathologist. Typical aphasia batteries and tests designed for children with congenital language impairments focus on knowledge of linguistic codes (syntax, morphology, lexicon). These are generally less useful for assessing the language disturbances of children with TBI than an assessment of the child's potential to learn language, as well as the ability to process, mentally manipulate and produce language in an efficient and organised manner (Baxter, Cohen, and Ylvisaker, 1985).

Following the principles of the REAL approach, the assessment of other cognitive deficits should also take place within the context of the child's premorbid level of ability. Statements that a child is functioning "within normal limits" on an IQ test do not reflect the degree of loss to a child who was previously functioning in the superior range. Conversely, the finding that a child who now demonstrates a borderline IQ was also borderline before the injury may suggest that the injury is less likely to interfere with school progress.

In the absence of a reliable measure of premorbid IQ, other information sources should be used to assess premorbid functioning. School records may offer an estimate of the child's previous scholastic performance in a variety of domains. Parental reports and checklists can also be useful sources of information, particularly for children who have not yet started school. Parental questionnaires should provide information about developmental milestones, educational history (e.g. remedial classes) and psychosocial factors, including pre-injury behaviour and family functioning. Interview formats such as the Vineland Adaptive Behaviour Scale (Sparrow, Balla, and Cicchetti, 1984) and the Adaptive Behaviour Assessment System Second Edition (ABAS 2) assess functioning in areas such as communication and daily living skills. The Connors Parent Questionnaire (Connors, 1973) and the Child Behaviour Checklist (Achenbach, 1983) are commonly used to assess emotional/behavioural functioning.

These questionnaires should be completed as close as possible to the time of injury and use the same informant over serial administrations (Rutter et al., 1980). The limitations of these relatively subjective methods of reporting, as discussed earlier in relation to assessment of behaviour change, need to be borne in mind. Parents may overrate the child's premorbid ability, underrate problems after injury, or fail to report on problems not covered on a checklist or questionnaire. Teacher checklists can offer a measure of behaviours, such as attention and peer interaction, both pre- and post-injury, although once again there are limitations in the use of subjective reports.

In recent years, there have been gains in the development of age-appropriate measures of specific cognitive abilities, particularly attention and processing speed (e.g. TEA-Ch), learning and memory (e.g. Children's Memory Scale) and executive function (e.g. Contingency Naming Test). Tests of social skills and social problem-solving are under development (Ganesalingam et al., 2007). However, consistent with the REAL philosophy, the assessment process should extend beyond the structured one-to-one test situation, which may not elicit distractibility and other attentional problems, organisational and adaptive difficulties, subtle problems with memory, information processing and communication, or the effects of fatigue. Furthermore, many cognitive tests assess skills or knowledge acquired prior to the injury, rather than the child's capacity to learn new information or skills. It is essential that therapists and teachers work together systematically to assess skills in these and other areas, particularly the child's ability to cope with increasing demands in terms of speed and complexity of information to be absorbed, distractions, organisational and adaptive functions and initiative. Identification of strengths and weaknesses within the classroom setting provides a structure for classroom-based intervention (Ylvisaker et al., 2005). This may involve task modification, cueing and/or compensatory strategies. It is also vital that reassessment be conducted at regular intervals over a number of years, so that relevant changes can be made as the child develops and recovers. Skills which fail to develop or be acquired at a later stage may be detected and appropriate support given.

In assessing behaviour, it is important to take careful account of the child's developmental level. Behavioural assessment should be based on observation, together with reports from parents, teachers and any others involved with the child. Because of the possibility of pre-existing behaviour problems, a careful history needs to be taken. Consideration should be given to the impact of speech and motor deficits, family stress, coping and the other factors within the child's life that may be impacting on behaviour. An assessment should also be made of the child's emotional state, to detect changes in mood or self-esteem, anxiety and depression.

Developmental considerations also influence the assessment and treatment of motor dysfunction. Infants and young children must not only regain former developmental and motor functions, but also develop additional motor skills to set a foundation for further development. Older children, on the other hand, must relearn previously integrated movements. Children's motivation in treatment will vary with chronological and developmental age. A seven-year-old child, for instance, may be interested only in getting back on a bike, whereas an adolescent may be concerned primarily with physical appearance.

Rehabilitation

A model for paediatric rehabilitation described by King and colleagues (2002) embodies the principles of the REAL approach. This holistic model proposes the use of a broad range of services delivered in both a family-centred and interdisciplinary fashion, in the context of the home and community, to address the child's impairments and activity limitations, but above all aims to maximise the child's participation in all aspects of community life. These are the principles that should guide rehabilitation of children following TBI, beginning in the acute stages of recovery.

Being in hospital can be very frightening for a child, although this will vary depending on their age and stage in development. Every effort should be made to surround the child with familiar objects and have family members present and involved in the child's care. Parents will be extremely anxious, so staff need to take every opportunity to explain what is going on and answer questions. Further discussion of issues pertaining to the families of TBI children is contained in a later section of this chapter. Other issues of relevance to management in the acute stages of recovery have been explored in detail in Chapter 2.

It is in the injured child's interests socially and emotionally to return home as soon as possible. However, children with severe TBI should not be discharged before the family understands how to manage them and appropriate arrangements have been made for ongoing therapy and other necessary support services. Discharge will not be appropriate if the child is still in PTA. Having a child who is in PTA at home places a very heavy burden on families, may lead to overstimulation of the child and the development of behaviour problems, which might have been avoided. Like adults, children in PTA need a quiet, familiar and well-structured environment, which can be manipulated to minimise agitation and the potential development of maladaptive behaviours. Further, once at home, ongoing assessment of PTA is not possible.

In planning for discharge there is a need to seek out facilities for rehabilitation in the home and/or in outpatient settings nearby. Given the general lack of specialised paediatric rehabilitation facilities catering to children with TBI, this is likely to be difficult. However, it is not appropriate to mix children with adults in a rehabilitation setting. Children need far more structure and should be able to mix with their peers, rather than adults with TBI. Paediatric rehabilitation facilities should also provide for play therapy and educational assessment. Additionally, as children with brain injury and their families often have complex needs, which change as the children develop, transition back to and through school, and seek new experiences, specific resources and skills are required to care for and monitor the paediatric population.

Where specialised community-based facilities do not exist, services from a number of sources will need to be co-ordinated. These may include medical, nursing and therapy services, psychological assessment and guidance, normal school services, special education assistance and integration support. Given the lack of specialised paediatric rehabilitation facilities suitable for children with TBI, the "Whatever it Takes" model of Willer and Corrigan (1994), discussed in Chapter 7, is likely to be particularly applicable. Good case management is seen to be an essential component to the provision of a co-ordinated service. It is acknowledged that the guidelines suggested in this chapter represent the ideal, and that in many cases hospitals and families will need to seek out whatever services are available to fulfil the injured child's needs.

Interventions for cognitive difficulties

A detailed discussion of interventions for cognitive impairments following TBI is contained in Chapter 4. As in adults, there is limited evidence from randomised controlled trials of the efficacy of any specific therapies in alleviating cognitive difficulties associated with TBI in children. Approaches parallel those taken in adults, including both restorative and compensatory methods. Restorative methods may take the form of retraining in specific skills or the use of pharmacological interventions. As in adults there is some evidence supporting use of stimulants, methylphenidate or dexamphetamine in alleviating attentional problems (Bakker and Waugh, 2000). Compensatory approaches may include provision of prompting from picture sequences or age-appropriate self-instructional methods (Lawson and Rice, 1989), modifications to the environment, including simplifying or slowing down tasks, removing distractions, or providing prompting or other cues developed in an age-appropriate fashion, such as use of picture sequences instead of written steps (Savage, DePompei, Tyler, and Lash, 2005; Ylvisaker et al., 1998). Wilson, Emslie, Quirk and Evans (2001) have shown that children as young as eight years can benefit from the Neuropage, a computerised reminder paging system.

On the basis of an evidence-based review of paediatric rehabilitation studies conducted between 1980 and 2006, Laatsch et al. (2007) made only three practice recommendations. The first was that attention remediation may assist in recovery. Recent studies have replicated this finding of a potential benefit in children with TBI from cognitive training on cognitive function, and have shown maintenance at six months after completion, although the extent to which this translates to functional change is, as in adults, poorly understood (Van 't Hooft, 2010). The pertinent issues pertaining to this research have been discussed in chapter four. It is particularly important to provide training on tasks that are of direct relevance to the child. The second recommendation is that parents or guardians attending Emergency Departments would most likely benefit from the provision of information regarding the effects of mild TBI, the latter research having been conducted by Ponsford et al. (2001). The third is that families should be involved in the rehabilitation process. This is discussed further in the next section.

Role of families

Parents should be provided with detailed information regarding progress, play an active role in the choices made regarding the rehabilitation of their child, and be involved in the therapy process. They will be the most important therapists for the child in the years to come. Further, depending on the age of the child at injury, and in the case of younger children, the home may be the primary context in which the child interacts. As with adults, some families may place unrealistic or inappropriate demands on the injured child and others may be overprotective. Such situations need to be handled carefully and tactfully, as it is extremely important to maintain open communication and a sense of trust. In view of the established association between parenting, family coping and other environmental factors, and the development of ongoing behavioural and psychiatric sequelae, early family intervention will hopefully minimise the development of such problems. Guidance and support should be given in the appropriate management of behaviour, following the principles outlined in Chapter 6. In reviewing behavioural interventions for children as well as adults, Ylvisaker and colleagues (2007) concluded that there was support for provision of behavioural intervention, applied behaviour analysis and positive behavioural interventions and supports, much of which might take place most constructively within the context of the family. With the growing awareness of the causes and significance of social problem-solving difficulties and social anxiety in children with TBI, some research groups are developing interventions for these problems, although this work is in its infancy. Parents require assistance in dealing with the emotional responses of the injured child. It is important that families gain an understanding of the ways in which the child's behaviour and emotions may be influenced by the injury, as well as changes in circumstances and the nature of interactions of others. The structured routine which was present in the hospital needs, as far as possible, to be maintained in the home. Siblings, teachers and any others having frequent contact with the child should also be involved in this process.

There is preliminary evidence supporting the efficacy of on-line family support programmes and of parenting skills training programmes that encourage positive parenting behaviours (Wade et al., 2006a; Wade, Oberjohn, Burkhardt, and Greenberg, 2009). However, these programmes require a significant time commitment and access to the internet and, therefore, are not suitable for all families. There is a need for such interventions to be available in various modalities.

Suggested guidelines for integration to school

For children who are of school age at the time of injury, return to school is an important part of their rehabilitation. For those who have not yet started school, this transition will be even more challenging. Because of the unique demands of a learning environment, the consequences of inadequate preparation for, or inappropriate timing of, commencement or return to school can be quite disastrous. Teachers are usually extremely busy, having many different demands placed upon them. They may not spontaneously ask questions about what to expect from a TBI child or adolescent, or how to handle forthcoming problems, either because of a lack of understanding of such injuries, particularly where there has been a good physical recovery, or a reluctance to reveal uncertainty about managing the educational domain. Where there has been inadequate preparation for school re-entry, problems that develop may be presented more in the form of complaints about the TBI student's failure to carry out tasks or comply with school rules, rather than as problems the staff might have in understanding the needs of the student.

Early contact should be made with the school to establish good communication and encourage the involvement of teachers and fellow students in the rehabilitation process. They should be encouraged to visit the injured student in hospital to provide a network of support, and to gain an understanding of the injury and the recovery process. Together with family members, they will be crucial in assisting the injured student's adaptation. It is helpful to hold a meeting involving teachers, therapists and the family early in the rehabilitation phase. This provides an opportunity to convey information regarding the nature of injuries and the possible time frame of the rehabilitation process. However, more importantly, it provides a forum in which the rehabilitation team can learn more about the student, and all parties can participate in setting goals and planning how these are to be achieved. Teachers may be asked to provide a profile of the student's previous strengths and weaknesses, together with samples of work completed prior to injury.

When it is felt that the injured child or adolescent is ready, a visiting teacher may, in close liaison with the school, begin to assess the student's ability to cope with schoolwork and at what level. If no visiting teacher is available, therapists will need to do this in liaison with the child's teacher. Appropriate tasks may then be introduced within the home or therapy setting. It is usually best to begin with schoolwork which the student with TBI has performed some time prior to injury, to maximise the possibility of success. It is likely to be very stressful for the student to experience failure with work which had previously presented little difficulty. Therefore this process needs to be taken very gradually.

Returning to the school environment

For children and adolescents, school meets many needs for socialisation and peer-group identification, as well as education. It is therefore particularly important that plans for return to the school environment be made as soon as it is felt that the student will cope in some capacity. Careful preparation is necessary. If it is possible, members of the rehabilitation team should visit the school, assessing the injured student's ability to manage the physical environment, timetable, subject content and transport. This enables potential problem areas to be pinpointed, so that therapists can work with teachers, fellow students, the family and the injured student to devise solutions to these. The student should also have opportunities to visit the school prior to returning. An attempt should be made to identify sources of support for the student, such as a school chaplain or counsellor.

Rehabilitation staff, as well as the visiting teacher, need to meet with teachers involved with the student, providing information regarding the injured student's current strengths and weaknesses, current cognitive fatigue levels, and information regarding what specific problems are anticipated. They may work with the teachers to develop ways in which these can be circumvented or overcome, and plan an appropriate schedule of classes. It may be helpful for therapists to observe the child in the classroom to offer further practical advice. However, it is important not to go into the school environment with an attitude of superiority, issuing instructions to teachers and others at the school. Wherever possible the skills and experience of the teachers need to be harnessed to solve problems. Nevertheless, in some schools teachers will be stressed and under-resourced, having little additional time or energy available to give to an injured student. The approach taken to school reintegration will need to take account of this.

Classmates can also prove invaluable in the rehabilitation process, and they should be involved, along with the TBI student, as much as possible. They will usually be able to make suggestions or provide practical assistance in solving a range of problems. "Buddies" may help carry books, make sure the TBI student doesn't forget things, or get lost around the school, and has someone to sit with during breaks. Such a network of support from classmates is particularly important for the TBI student, who usually feels different from everyone else, due to prolonged absence and newly acquired scars or disabilities. It is important to devote therapeutic time to the active facilitation of the injured child or adolescent's friendship network, particularly given the evidence that social difficulties, including making friends, are an ongoing problem after TBI in children (Muscara et al., 2008b; Prigatano and Gupta, 2006).

Most students will need to return to school gradually, because of limited concentration and a tendency to fatigue. The school, therefore, needs to be prepared to be flexible, and to reduce demands on the student. This may involve reducing the number of subjects studied, or changing them to suit new limitations. Subjects initially studied should be selected based on an analysis of the cognitive demands they make. For example, it would not be wise for a student with memory and executive difficulties to initially attempt a subject where there is a large amount of material to be learned and significant demands are made upon organisational and conceptual abilities.

For TBI students with planning difficulties, there will be an increased need for structure. Returning to school, with its inherent schedule of classes to some extent provides this. However, activities and assignments within classes may need additional structuring. For example, TBI students may have particular difficulty in writing an essay without some assistance as to how to plan and structure it, and they may not be able to utilise free time effectively. During instruction, the teacher's directions need to be specific, and clear expectations about the task are required. Instructions may need to be written down in a step-by-step fashion, or presented pictorially for those with reading difficulties. Problems in integrating material through specific modalities, such as reading, can be overcome through the use of other modalities, such as audiotapes. Oral tests may be given. Where memory is a problem, material will need to be simplified, repeated and written down, so that the student can review it. The student may benefit from the use of a diary, although diary use would need to be trained. Teachers should avoid using rote memory tasks to measure learning. For older students, help may be given to organise material and develop ways of enhancing storage and recall of material using mnemonics or cues.

Above all, students with TBI need accommodation and time – time to make up what has been missed, extended time in testing and completion of assignments, time taken by teachers for repetition of directions and additional assistance, time to get from one place to another, time to recover. The provision of all this support to the TBI student is likely to place a great burden on the classroom teacher. If funding can be procured, this burden will be substantially relieved by the provision of an integration aide to assist the student in the classroom. Such an aide, who might be funded either through the educational system, or by an insurer, can perform a similar role to that of a job coach in the employment setting. The integration aide, whether appointed by the school, the insurer or the rehabilitation team, will require input from the rehabilitation team along the lines of that given to an attendant carer. The aide should have a comprehensive understanding of the student's cognitive strengths and weaknesses and appropriate ways of handling problems with mobility, communication and behaviour.

The integration aide may need to be present in the classroom at all times, actively facilitating the student's participation in lessons. Alternatively, the aide may give the student additional coaching or present what is being taught in a way in which it is more likely to be understood or remembered. A well-trained integration aide can be a very useful source of guidance to fellow students and teachers as to how best to manage behaviour problems. The aide can also act as an advocate for the student. Some brain-injured students, particularly adolescents, feel very self-conscious about having an integration aide with them in the classroom. This needs to be given careful consideration, as it is important not to further lower the student's self-esteem. In such cases the aide may have to work with the student outside the classroom.

As with return to work programmes, frequent contact between all those involved in the process of return to school is important. If possible, regular meetings need to be held between the teachers, the integration aide and rehabilitation staff, as well as the parents, with the TBI student present if appropriate. The aim of such meetings should be to review progress and make necessary adjustments, as well as address any problems. Parental feedback is particularly important. A student may appear to be coping whilst at school, but be exhausted, irritable and moody at home. This is generally an indication that too many demands are being made on the injured student.

Over time many brain-injured students will be able to cope with increased demands and will no longer require therapy. Adjustments to the curriculum should be made accordingly. Later, decisions may need to be made as to whether the student should progress to the next level. Such decisions should always be given very careful consideration, weighing the advantages of peer group support against the impact of increasing demands on the student's self-esteem. These decisions are particularly important at crucial developmental transition points (such as from primary to high school). At these times it is important to reassess the injured child's ability to meet the new and increased demands.

Whilst every effort needs to be made to return and maintain TBI students at their previous school, in a minority of cases, where there is very severe physical disability and a need for ongoing therapy, it may be necessary to move to a "special" school. Just as much care needs to be taken in the integration of TBI students into special schools as into regular schools. Whilst special schools may be geared to cope with the needs of disabled students, the teachers do not necessarily have any greater understanding of the impact of TBI, or how to manage the unique problems associated with TBI, particularly those of a behavioural nature. Ongoing support from the rehabilitation team is very important.

Transition to the workplace

Making the transition from school to the workplace is another point at which intervention is likely to be necessary. A child with TBI may have been managing relatively well with structured supports and the supervision provided in the school environment, and the need for assistance in the next phase may be neglected. The findings of Anderson and colleagues (2009a) highlight the poor vocational outcomes following TBI sustained in childhood. It is essential that the adolescent leaving school receives appropriate vocational assessment and assistance in making the transition to employment, tertiary study or avocational activities in the manner outlined in Chapter 7.

Case report – Laura

Laura was aged four years when she was hit by a car reversing in a supermarket car park, sustaining a severe TBI. She and her older brother were living with their mother. Their father, a heavy drinker, had left a year previously. Laura was upset by this and had started bed-wetting. She was attending kindergarten and according to her mother had settled in and was reportedly coping satisfactorily. She had become interested in books and was learning to read some words. Following the accident, Laura remained drowsy and confused for 10 days. A CT scan had revealed cerebral swelling, which gradually subsided. She was in the acute hospital throughout this period, her bed being placed in a quiet area. Her mother stayed with her, whilst her grandparents minded her brother. Her mother was extremely stressed, feeling guilty that she had not been properly supervising Laura at the time of the accident and worried what the future would hold.

During her hospital stay, Laura was visited by therapists, but no cognitive or language assessment was conducted. Physically, she had some balance problems and clumsiness, but was otherwise recovering satisfactorily. She also made quite rapid gains cognitively after her emergence from PTA. However, it was apparent that she lacked concentration, and was somewhat impulsive and irritable. Laura was discharged home shortly after emerging from PTA. Arrangements had been made for her to attend a rehabilitation centre with paediatric facilities for ongoing assessment and therapy on an outpatient basis.

Interviews were conducted with her mother regarding her developmental history, her behaviour and cognitive abilities prior to and since the injury. Laura's mother noted that she was managing well physically and could feed and dress herself as before. However, she had become extremely irritable, and the bed-wetting already present had worsened. Uncontrollable temper tantrums had become a frequent occurrence in response to the slightest frustration. Her mother also reported that Laura was more active than she had been, and could not sit and concentrate on an activity for any length of time.

Assessment by the physiotherapist revealed that Laura's balance problems were resolving. Neuropsychological assessment showed that Laura was of average ability, and most skills were at or near expected age levels. However, marked attentional difficulties and some impulsivity were noted. She also lacked persistence with difficult tasks. Laura's mother had counselling to assist her in dealing with her guilt and the day-to-day problems of coping with Laura. Laura's older brother also attended some sessions, to enable him to discuss the impact of Laura's injury on the family and to help him attain an understanding of the nature and effects of Laura's injury.

Six weeks after her injury, Laura returned to kindergarten, initially for two hours per day in the mornings, followed by a rest, and some therapy sessions in the afternoon. A meeting was held with the kindergarten teacher to explain the effects of the head injury and she was given guidelines for managing Laura's restless behaviour. She reported over time that Laura had difficulty engaging in cooperative play and had a low tolerance for frustration. She had lost interest in looking at books. However, Laura improved over time and was able to spend full mornings there within six weeks.

The following year Laura was due to start school. On the advice of the therapists, Laura's mother spoke with various schools to ascertain their willingness to provide support for children with difficulties. She identified a school not too far from where they lived. At the start of the school year, a meeting was held, involving Laura's class teacher, mother and father, therapists, and the neuropsychologist. An explanation of TBI and Laura's current strengths and weaknesses was given by the therapists.

Laura initially settled in reasonably well with the support of her teacher, who made sure she sat at the front of the class, and set firm limits on her behaviour. However, her restlessness continued to be a problem and Laura's progress in reading and mastering mathematical concepts was limited. An integration aide was appointed to spend some one-on-one time with her to go over the material covered in class. She created games to facilitate the learning of spelling and arithmetic and used a sticker system to reward Laura for even the smallest accomplishments. Her mother also used some of these systems to encourage her to read picture books at home.

At the end of the school year, Laura was still behind academically. It was apparent that she was still slow to learn, although she had made some progress with the assistance of her integration aide. Because of concerns over her self-esteem and the fact that she had recently made a friend, it was decided to allow her to move up to the next grade. The integration support was maintained for the whole of the following year.

It is now three years since Laura's injury. Her progress at school has been slow and she has repeated one grade. She still receives tutoring twice a week. Her mother reports that she is not the same child as before the injury. She remains irritable in the evenings, being obviously very tired at the end of the day. Her mother has frequent battles with her over the smallest matters. Laura fights with her brother constantly, as he has become intolerant of her unpredictable behaviour. She has also suffered emotionally, having no close friends and little confidence in her ability to learn. Some days she does not want to go to school. Clearly, Laura and her family will require follow-up monitoring, assessment and support for the duration of her education.

Case report – Chris

Chris was 14 and a Year 8 student, living with his parents and two brothers, when he was hit by a car whilst riding his bike. He sustained a severe TBI with initial GCS of 5, PTA lasting 25 days and CT scan showing left frontal contusion. He had seven weeks of inpatient rehabilitation. He had decreased arm strength and co-ordination, poor trunk control and decreased running ability. Neuropsychological assessment revealed impairments of information processing speed, attention, verbal learning and memory, word-finding, written expression, reading, arithmetic, and planning and problem-solving. Behaviourally he was restless, distractible, and impulsive, with a low frustration tolerance. He showed limited awareness of these changes and just wanted to get out of hospital. He had daily therapy sessions focused on improving his mobility, strength and co-ordination and addressing his cognitive difficulties using computer-based and pen and paper activities. He was given training in internal recall strategies and use of a diary. He attended a conversational skills group twice weekly. Daily occupational therapy focused on breakfast and snack preparation and road safety. The neuropsychologist provided advice regarding behaviour management.

Seven weeks post-injury Chris was discharged home. A community integration team took over his management. Chris's major goals were to resume his roles at home in his family, to return to his major sporting interests in skateboarding and cycling, to socialise with his friends and to return to school.

With regard to home and family life, Chris required supervision in most activities due to his impulsiveness and forgetfulness. With his mother's help a written weekly programme of tasks done at home was created. An attendant carer was present 8–10 am daily to support him in making breakfast and snacks, cleaning up and preparing to go to therapy. The initial goal was to make breakfast with no more than two prompts daily. After several weeks he was able to independently make his breakfast. The family was provided with strategies to manage his short temper. He did not like his brothers accompanying him home from school which was necessary for his safety.

With regard to returning to skateboarding and cycling, the main impediments were poor co-ordination and balance. To address these Chris attended centre-based physiotherapy three times weekly, which included both individual therapy and participation in running, circuit and balance groups. He had ten bike education sessions. He had pre-skateboarding training focused on high level balance and postural control, followed by skateboarding training. He got back to these activities.

With regard to socialising, Chris initially felt very socially isolated. A buddy was organised at school and a meeting was held with his friends to explain his injuries, how best to help him and how to avoid arguments in the playground. A graded return to spending recess and lunchtime at school was organised. After his return to school he showed a lot of attention-seeking and disruptive behaviour which interfered with his participation in classes. The neuropsychologist liaised with teachers and friends to develop consistent means of responding to this, ensuring that others did not react to his behaviour and that he was quietly asked to leave the room. With this support his behaviour settled down. Although he lost a lot of friends due to conflicts, he became calmer over time and gradually re-established a small friendship network.

With regard to the goal of returning to study, the impediments were his lack of safety in crossing roads to get to school, his language problems, including poor literacy, his limited memory and concentration, impulsivity, and inappropriate attention-seeking and disruptive behaviour. The speech pathologist focused therapy on his language, attentional and memory skills, initially undertaking computerised and pen and paper tasks, with the goal of working independently for increasing periods of time, and providing training in internal recall strategies and use of a diary. They began reviewing his schoolwork at the rehabilitation centre. He had a lot of difficulties with language-based tasks. However, Chris felt he would cope if he could just get back to school. A school visit was organised to ascertain barriers to return to school, discuss Chris's strengths and weaknesses and identify which aspects of the curriculum he might best manage initially. Education sessions were held with all his teachers, as well as his friends. An integration aide was appointed, initially for 8 but increasing to 13 hours per week as his time at school increased. He started attending school for the three least demanding subjects – Art, Physical Education and Home Economics. The attendant carer accompanied him to school to ensure his safety on the roads. The following semester he increased to five subjects – English, Maths, Health and Human Development, Woodwork and Music. Due to his distractibility there was a constant need for the attendant carer to cue him to return to tasks. His behaviour was frequently disruptive and the aide systematically removed him from class when this happened and praised him when his behaviour was good. In order to cope with his memory problems the aide encouraged him to use his school diary to record verbal instructions and assisted him to organise his notes and handouts into folders. He did not like having the aide, but was able to be convinced to tolerate the situation.

Neuropsychological reassessment revealed improvements but persisting problems with language, reasoning, memory and processing speed, strengths in visuo-spatial skills, and significant continuing problems with verbal processing, distractibility and doing two things at once. He progressed to Year 9, with the integration aide present for 17 hours per week during academic subjects of English, Maths, Science and Social Studies to keep him on task, prompt use of diary and help him complete homework. Due to reduced confidence in his verbal skills he was encouraged to complete oral tasks in written format and read this out. He did not require an integration aide for the practical subjects (Woodwork, Automechanics, Music, Physical Education). He excelled at woodwork and wanted to pursue a trade.

At the end of Year 10 he made the transition to a trade-based pre-apprenticeship course. A disability liaison officer from the technical school was involved, and his teachers were made aware of the possibility of difficulties, especially with coursework material. He completed this course and then made the transition to the workplace successfully, requiring minimal assistance, although again this was offered and he was regularly followed up. He had matured over time and had a couple of girlfriends. He has successfully completed two years of his carpentry apprenticeship. Without this support Chris would possibly have dropped out of school, developed significant anger management problems and had limited prospect of entering the workforce.

Family needs

Although there have been many studies investigating the impact of TBI in adolescents and adults on the family, there has been much less research on family reactions to the occurrence of TBI in a child. Families of young children who are injured are said to experience similar emotional reactions, and pass through similar phases of adjustment to relatives of TBI adults (Martin, 1988; Waaland and Kreutzer, 1988). These reactions have been discussed in detail in Chapter 9. There is increasing evidence that families who function well prior to injury cope best with the trauma, and this, in turn, leads to a better outcome in the injured child (Rivara et al., 1993). There are some ways, however, in which the needs and stresses of parents of young children may differ from those of the relatives of adults who have sustained TBI.

As the natural caregivers, parents of children with TBI must, in the acute stage, relinquish the care of their child to the treatment team, seeing their child subjected to a bewildering set of high technology medical procedures. While being given complex information about the child's injury, treatment and prognosis, parents are likely to be wrestling with feelings of loss, fear, denial and anger. They may have difficulty understanding the information and explanation given by doctors, who can usually spare only limited time while the injured child is in danger. As with adults, empathic listening, repetition, clarification of information and reassurance need to be available to parents at this and all stages of recovery. Every effort should be made to involve parents in the care of their child at all stages of recovery.

Initially, parents are likely to wish only that the child will survive, but may ask key questions that contain elements of their own hopes for the child, such as going to university or becoming an athlete. Parents of children with lasting disabilities will never see their child grow up to fulfil their dreams and have to adjust their ambitions. Instead of hoping for a professional career for their child, there may only be hope that the child will live independently. Many hopes may be replaced by fears. Under these circumstances there can be an enormous sense of grief over unfulfilled potential. Guilt is another common reaction. As a parent's role includes nurturance and protection, injury to a child may indicate to the parents that they have failed in this role, whatever the circumstances of the accident. Such emotional responses may accentuate denial and anger and prolong the adjustment process.

In addition to dealing with the injured child and their own emotional responses, parents have the stresses of responsibilities to the rest of the family. One parent, usually the mother, tends to spend more time with the injured child. There tends to be a significant and lengthy disruption to normal family functioning. Siblings, having experienced the trauma of seeing their injured brother or sister in hospital, may harbour fantasies and fears which create anxiety for them. They receive less attention from their parents and may develop feelings of jealousy. Siblings of children who sustain TBI need to be given opportunities to discuss their perceptions and feelings about the injured brother or sister, and the impact of the injury on the family and themselves. Siblings are frequently remarkably ill-informed regarding the nature of the injury and prognosis. Whilst parents and rehabilitation staff may feel this is protecting them, it can engender anxiety. An effort should also be made to preserve the routine of siblings as much as possible. Parents need to be encouraged and given the necessary support to set aside time with them.

The greatest victim of disrupted family life under these circumstances is usually the parents' time to themselves, both as a couple and individually. Other children and family business are cared for at the expense of the couple's personal needs. Marital stress is common, particularly in troubled marriages, but also in healthy ones. Resentment may develop when parents have differing perceptions of the injured child's disabilities and needs. Counselling should be made available to emphasise the importance of ongoing communication and mutual support. Discussion with other parents of injured children may also prove helpful. Parents need to hear that it is both necessary and important for them to take care of themselves, and to fulfil needs other than simply eating and sleeping. For many parents this is very difficult, as time away from the injured child may be very painful, at least in the early stages of recovery.

As discussed in Chapter 9, counselling or family therapy may be necessary to assist the family as a whole to grieve effectively, and to redefine and restructure family relationships and roles. In view of the vulnerability of injured children behaviourally and emotionally, the importance of maximising family coping after injury cannot be overemphasised. Families of children who sustain TBI are likely to face even greater stresses than those of adults with TBI in obtaining adequate services for the injured child. Appropriate rehabilitation services for children who sustain TBI are few and far between. Due to a relative lack of knowledge regarding TBI in children, the quality of therapy and educational services available tends to be limited. Moreover, the needs of the child will change significantly over time. Each developmental level will bring with it the potential emergence of new cognitive deficiencies, and behavioural and emotional changes. As time passes, vocational, avocational, social and relationship issues will become more important than educational issues. There will be concern over the future care of a severely disabled child, should the parents be no longer able to provide this.

Ideally, assistance in dealing with the myriad issues needs to be available to families throughout the lifespan of the injured child. In the case of severe disability, there will also be a need to provide access to respite care, in addition to attendant care. It is vital to link families of injured children with a network of ongoing social and emotional supports. As mentioned in the previous chapter, educational programmes for parents of children with brain injuries have also shown some demonstrated efficacy (Glang et al., 2007; Wade et al., 2006a; Wade et al., 2006b). Further development and evaluation of such programmes is to be encouraged.

Conclusions

The impact of TBI is somewhat different in children from that in adults. Whilst children appear to have a lower mortality and show a better motor-sensory recovery, there is clear evidence of lasting impairment in the domains of memory, attention, speed of performance, abstract thinking and executive function. These have long term effects on academic attainment. Behaviour problems are also common following severe TBI, but they follow a less predictable pattern, being associated with premorbid behavioural patterns and family functioning, as well as the injury and emotional factors. Overall it would appear that the manifestations of TBI in children, both cognitively and behaviourally, depend, first, on the severity of injury, second on age at injury and third on the child's pre-injury cognitive behavioural and psychosocial functioning, including the socioeconomic and family environment. There is a need for skilled and careful assessment in all these areas, including a comprehensive assessment of the child's physical, linguistic, cognitive, academic and behavioural functioning prior to injury, as well as social and family functioning. Rehabilitation facilities need to cater specifically to children, and have the flexibility to work in the community. Attention should be paid to the child's social and emotional adjustment throughout the rehabilitation process. Return to school must be carefully planned, with follow-up support available over many years, as the demands on the child change. Given the impact of family functioning on outcome following paediatric TBI, ongoing family support is also vital.

References

Abrams, D., Barker, L. T., Haffey, W., and Nelson, H. (1993). The economics of return to work for survivors of traumatic brain injury: Vocational services are worth the investment. *Journal of Head Trauma Rehabilitation, 8*(4), 59–76.

Achenbach, T. M., and Edelbrook, C. (1983). *Manual for the child behaviour checklist and revised behaviour profile*. Burlington: University of Vermont.

Adams, J. H., Doyle, D., Ford, I., Gennarelli, T. A., Graham, D. I., and McLellan, D. R. (1989). Diffuse axonal injury in head injury: definition, diagnosis and grading. *Histopathology, 15*(1), 49–59.

Adams, J. H., Graham, D. I., and Jennett, B. (2000). The neuropathology of the vegetative state after acute brain insult. *Brain, 123*, 1327–1338.

Adelson, P. D. (2010). Clinical trials for pediatric TBI. In V. Anderson and K. O. Yeates (Eds.), *Pediatric traumatic brain injury: New frontiers in clinical and translational research* (pp. 54–67). New York: Cambridge University Press.

Aguayo, A. J. (1985). Axonal regeneration from injured neurons in the adult mammalian central nervous system. In C. W. Cotman (Ed.), *Synaptic plasticity* (pp. 457–484). New York: Guilford Press.

Albert, S. M., Im, A., Brenner, L., Smith, M., and Waxman, R. (2002). Effect of social work liaison program on family caregivers to people with brain injury. *Journal of Head Trauma Rehabilitation, 17*(2), 175–189.

Alderman, N., Burgess, P. W., Knight, C., and Henman, C. (2003). Ecological validity of a simplified version of the multiple errands shopping test. *Journal of the International Neuropsychological Society, 9*(1), 31–44.

Alderman, N., Davies, J. A., Jones, C., and McDonnel, P. (1999). Reduction of severe aggressive behaviour in acquired brain injury: case studies illustrating clinical use of the OAS-MNR in the management of challenging behaviours. *Brain Injury, 13*(9), 669–704.

Alderman, N., Knight, L., and Morgan, C. (1997). Use of a modified version of the Overt Aggression Scale in the measurement and assessment of aggressive behaviours following brain injury. *Brain Injury, 11*, 503–523.

Alderman, N., and Ward, A. (1991). Behavioural treatment of the dysexecutive syndrome: reduction of repetitive speech using response cost and cognitive overlearning. *Neuropsychological Rehabilitation, 1*, 65–80.

Allen, K., Linn, R. T., Gutierrez, H., and Willer, B. S. (1994). Family burden following traumatic brain injury. *Rehabilitation Psychology, 39*(1), 29–48.

Almli, R. C., and Finger, S. (1992). Brain injury and recovery of function: Theories and mechanisms of functional reorganization. *Journal of Head Trauma Rehabilitation, 7*(2), 70–77.

Alves, W., Macciocchi, S. N., and Barth, J. T. (1993). Postconcussive symptoms after uncomplicated MHI. *Journal of Head Trauma Rehabilitation, 8*, 48–59.

American Academy of Neurology (1994). Multi-society Task Force Report on PVS. Medical aspects of the persistent vegetative state. *New England Journal of Medicine, 330*, 1499–1508.

American Congress of Rehabilitation Medicine (1995). Recommendations for use of uniform nomenclature pertinent to patients with severe alterations in consciousness. *Archives of Physical Medicine and Rehabilitation, 76*, 205–209.

Anderson, M. I., Parmenter, T. R., and Mok, M. (2002). The relationship between neurobehavioural problems of severe traumatic brain injury (TBI), family functioning and the psychological well-being of the spouse/caregiver: path model analysis. *Brain Injury, 16*(9), 743–757.

Anderson, S. I., Housely, A. M., Jones, P. A., Slattery, J., and Miller, J. D. (1993). Glasgow Outcome Scale: An inter-rater reliability study. *Brain Injury, 7*, 309–317.

Anderson, V., Brown, S., Newitt, H., and Hoile, H. (2009a). Educational, vocational, psychosocial, and quality-of-life outcomes for adult survivors of childhood traumatic brain injury. *Journal of Head Trauma Rehabilitation, 24*(5), 303–312.

Anderson, V., and Catroppa, C. (2005). Recovery of executive skills following paediatric traumatic brain injury (TBI): a 2 year follow-up. *Brain Injury, 19*(6), 459–470.

Anderson, V., and Catroppa, C. (2007). Memory outcome at 5 years post-childhood traumatic brain injury. *Brain Injury, 21*(13–14), 1399–1409.

Anderson, V., Catroppa, C., Morse, S., Haritou, F., and Rosenfeld, J. V. (2000). Recovery of intellectual ability following traumatic brain injury in childhood: Impact of injury severity and age at injury. *Pediatric Neuropsychology, 32*, 282–290.

Anderson, V., Catroppa, C., Morse, S., Haritou, F., and Rosenfeld, J. V. (2005). Functional plasticity or vulnerability after early brain injury? *Paediatrics, 116*(6), 1374–1382.

Anderson, V., Catroppa, C., Morse, S., Haritou, F., and Rosenfeld, J. V. (2009b). Intellectual outcome from preschool traumatic brain injury: a 5-year prospective, longitudinal study. *Pediatrics, 124*(6), 1064–1071.

Anderson, V., Morse, S. A., Klug, G., Catroppa, C., Haritou, F., Rosenfeld, J. V. et al. (1997). Predicting recovery from head injury in school-aged children: A prospective analysis. *Journal of the International Neuropsychological Society, 3*, 568–580.

Anderson, V., and Pentland, L. (1998). Residual attention deficits following childhood head injury: Implications for ongoing development. *Neuropsychological Rehabilitation, 8*, 283–300.

Anderson, V. A., Miorse, S. A., Catroppa, C., Haritou, F., and Rosenfeld, J. V. (2004). Thirty month outcome from early childhood head injury: A prospective anlaysis of neurobehavioural recovery. *Brain, 127*, 2608–2620.

Andrews, K. (1996). International Working party on the management of the Vegetative State: Summary report. *Brain Injury, 10*(11), 797–806.

Annegers, J. F., and Coan, S. P. (2000). The risks of epilepsy after traumatic brain injury. *Seizure, 9*(7), 453–457.

Annegers, J. F., Hauser, W. A., Coan, S. P., and Rocca, W. A. (1998). A population-based study of seizures after traumatic brain injury. *New England Journal of Medicine, 338*, 20–24.

Ansell, B. J., and Keenan, J. E. (1989). The Western Neuro Sensory Stimulation Profile: A tool for assessing slow-to-recover head-injured patients. *Archives of Physical Medicine and Rehabilitation, 70*, 104–108.

Anson, K., and Ponsford, J. (2006a). Evaluation of a coping skills group following traumatic brain injury. *Brain Injury, 20*(2), 167–178.

Anson, K., and Ponsford, J. (2006b). Who benefits? Outcome following a coping skills group intervention for traumatically brain injured individuals. *Brain Injury, 20*(1), 1–13.

Arango-Lasprilla, J. C., Ketchum, J. M., Dezfulian, T., Kreutzer, J. S., O'Neil-Pirozzi, T. M., Hammond, F. et al. (2008). Predictors of marital stability 2 years following traumatic brain injury. *Brain Injury, 22*(7–8), 564–574.

Arciniegas, D. B., Anderson, C. A., and Rojas, D. C. (2005). Electrophysiological techniques. In J. Silver, T. W. McAllister and S. C. Yudofsky (Eds.), *Textbook of traumatic brain injury* (pp. 135–157). Arlington, VA: American Psychiatric Publishing, Inc.

Arciniegas, D. B., Anderson, C. A., Topkoff, J., and McAllister, T. W. (2005). Mild traumatic brain injury: a neuropsychiatric approach to diagnosis, evaluation and treatment. *Neuropsychiatry, Disability and Treatment, 1*(4), 311–327.

Arlinghaus, K. A., Shoaib, A. M., and Trevor, R. P. (2005). Neuropsychiatric Assessment. In J. M. Silver, T. W. McAllister and S. C. Yudofsky (Eds.), *Textbook of traumatic brain injury* (pp. 59–78). Washington, DC: American Psychiatric Publishing.

Ashley, M. J., Persel, C. S., and Clark, M. C. (2001). Validation of an independent living scale for post-acute rehabilitation applications. *Brain Injury, 15*(5), 435–442.

Ashman, T. A., Cantor, J. B., Gordon, W. A., Spielman, L., Flanagan, S., Ginsberg, A. et al. (2009). A randomized controlled trial of sertraline for the treatment of depression in persons with traumatic brain injury. *Archives of Physical Medicine and Rehabilitation, 90*(5), 733–740.

Ashman, T. A., Spielman, L. A., Hibbard, M. R., Silver, J. M., Chandna, T., and Gordon, W. A. (2004). Psychiatric challenges in the first 6 years after traumatic brain injury: cross-sequential analyses of Axis I disorders. *Archives of Physical Medicine and Rehabilitation, 85*, 36–42.

Australian Government National Health and Medical Research Council (2008). Ethical Guidelines for the Care of People in Post-Coma Unresponsiveness (Vegetative State) or a Minimally Responsive State, from <http://nrv.gov.au/_files_nhmrc/_gsdata_/_saved_/file/publications/synopses/e81.pdf>

Australian Institute of Health and Welfare (2004). *Australia's health 2004*. Canberra: AIHW.

Avesani, R., Salvi, L., Rigoli, G., and Gambini, M. G. (2005). Reintegration after severe brain injury: a retrospective study. *Brain Injury, 19*(11), 933–939.

Ayr, L. K., Yeates, K. O., Taylor, H. G., and Browne, M. (2009). Dimensions of postconcussive symptoms in children with mild traumatic brain injuries. *Journal of the International Neuropsychological Society, 15*(1), 19–30.

Azouvi, P., Jokic, C., Attal, N., Denys, P., Markabi, S., and Bussell, B. (1999). Carbamazepine in agitation and aggressive behaviour following severe closed-head injury: results of an open trial. *Brain Injury, 13*(10), 797–804.

Babikian, T., and Asarnow, R. (2009). Neurocognitive outcomes and recovery after pediatric TBI: meta-analytic review of the literature. *Neuropsychology, 23*(3), 283–296.

Baddeley, A. D. (1986). *Working memory*. Oxford: Clarendon Press.

Baddeley, A. (2003). Working memory: looking back and looking forward. *Nature Reviews Neuroscience, 4*(10), 829–839.

Baddeley, A., Emslie, H., and Nimmo-Smith, I. (1992). *The speed and capacity of language-processing test*. Bury St Edmunds: Thames Valley Test Company.

Baddeley, A., Harris, J., Sunderland, A., Watts, K., and Silson, B. A. (1987). Closed head injury and memory. In H. S. Levin, J. Grafman and H. M. Eisenberg (Eds.), *Neurobehavioural recovery from head injury* (pp. 295–317). New York: Oxford University Press.

Baddeley, A. D., Wilson, B. A., and Watts, F. N. (1995). *Handbook of memory disorders*. Chichester and New York: Wiley and Sons.

Bakker, K., and Waugh, M. C. (2000). Stimulant use in paediatric acquired brain injury: Evaluation of a protocol. *Brain Impairment, 1*, 29–36.

Balestreri, M., Czosnyka, M., Chatfield, D. A., Steiner, L. A., Schmidt, E. A., Smielewski, P. et al. (2004). Predictive value of Glasgow Coma Scale after brain trauma: Change in trend over the past ten years. *Journal of Neurology, Neurosurgery and Psychiatry, 75*, 161–162.

Baxter, R., Cohen, S. B., and Ylvisaker, M. (1985). Comprehensive cognitive assessment. In M. Ylvisaker (Ed.), *Head injury rehabilitation: Children and adolescents* (pp. 247–274). Boston: College Hill Press.

Beck, A. T., Rush, A. J., Shaw, B. F., and Emery, G. (1979). *Cognitive therapy of depression*. New York: Guilford Press.

Belanger, H. G., Spiegel, E., and Vanderploeg, R. D. (2010). Neuropsychological performance following a history of multiple self-reported concussions: A meta-analysis. *Journal of the International Neuropsychological Society, 16*, 262–267.

Bell, B. A., and Britton, J. (1989). Mechanisms of trauma. In D. A. Johnson, D. Uttley and M. Wyke (Eds.), *Children's head injury: Who cares?* (pp. 1–11). London: Taylor and Francis.

Bell, K., Hoffman, J., Temkin, N., Powell, J., Fraser, R., Esselman, P. et al. (2008). The effect of telephone counselling on reducing posttraumatic symptoms after mild traumatic brain injury: A randomised trial. *Journal of Neurology, Neurosurgery and Psychiatry, 79*(11), 1275–1281.

Bellon, M. L., and Rees, R. J. (2006). The effect of context on communication: A study of language and communication skills of adults with acquired brain injury. *Brain Injury, 20*(10), 1069–1078.

Bennett-Levy, J., and Powell, G. E. (1980). The Subjective Memory Questionnaire (SMQ). An investigation into the self-reporting of real-life memory skills. *British Journal of Social and Clinical Psychology, 19*, 177–188.

Ben-Yishay, Y. (2000). Post-acute neuropsychological rehabilitation. In A. Christensen and B. Uzzell (Eds.), *International handbook of neuropsychological rehabilitation* (pp. 131–139). New York: Kluwer Academic/Plenum Publishers.

Ben-Yishay, Y. (2008). Foreword. *Neuropsychological rehabilitation, 18*(5–6), 513–521.

Ben-Yishay, Y., Piasetsky, E. B., and Rattok, J. (1987). A systematic method for ameliorating disorders in basic attention. In M. J. Meier, A. L. Benton and L. Diller (Eds.), *Neuropsychological rehabilitation* (pp. 165–181). New York: Churchill Livingstone.

Ben-Yishay, Y., Piasetsky, E. B., Rattok, J., Cohen, H., and Diller, L. (1980). Developing a core "curriculum" for group-exercises designed for head trauma patients who are undergoing rehabilitation. In Y. Ben-Yishay (Ed.), *Working approaches to remediation of cognitive deficits in brain damaged persons (Rehabilitation Monograph No. 61)* (pp. 175–234). New York: New York University Medical Centre, Institute of Rehabilitation Medicine.

Ben-Yishay, Y., and Prigatano, G. P. (1990). Cognitive remediation. In M. Rosenthal, E. R. Griffith, M. R. Bond and J. D. Miller (Eds.), *Rehabilitation of the adult and child with traumatic brain injury* (pp. 393–400). Philadelphia: Davis.

Ben-Yishay, Y., Silver, S. M., Piasetsky, E., and Rattok, J. (1987). Relationship between employability and vocational outcome after intensive holistic cognitive rehabilitation. *Journal of Head Trauma Rehabilitation, 2*(1), 35–48.

Benedict, H. B., Brandt, J., and Bergey, G. (1993). An attempt at memory retraining in severe amnesia: An experimental single-case study. *Neuropsychological Rehabilitation, 3*, 37–51.

Benedict, R. H. B., Schretlen, D., Groninger, L., and Brandt, J. (1998). Hopkins Verbal Learning Test – Revised: Normative data and analysis of inter-form and test-retest reliability. *The Clinical Neuropsychologist, 12*(1), 43–55.

Bennett, P. C., Ong, B. E. N., and Ponsford, J. (2005). Assessment of executive dysfunction following traumatic brain injury: Comparison of the BADS with other clinical neuropsychological measures. *Journal of the International Neuropsychological Society, 11*(05), 606–613.

Benton, A. L., and Hamsher, K. d. S. (1989). *Multilingual aphasia examination* (2nd ed.). San Antonio, TX: The Psychological Corporation.

Berg, I. J., Koning-Haanstra, M., and Deelman, B. G. (1991). Long-term effects of memory rehabilitation: A controlled study. *Neuropsychological Rehabilitation, 1*, 97–111.

Berger, R. P., Beers, S., Richichi, R., Weisman, D., and Adelson, D. (2007). Serum biomarker concentrations and outcome after pediatric traumatic brain injury. *Journal of Neurotrauma, 24*, 1793–1801.

Bergman, M. M. (1991). Computer enhanced self-sufficiency: Part 1. Creation and implementation of a text writer for an individual with traumatic brain injury. *Neuropsychology, 5*, 17–23.

Bergman, M. M., and Kemmerer, A. G. (1991). Computer enhanced self-sufficiency: Part 2. Uses and subjective benefits of a text writer for an individual with traumatic brain injury. *Neuropsychology, 5*, 25–28.

Bergsneider, M., Hovda, D., and McArthur, D. I. (2001). Metabolic recovery following human traumatic brain injury based on FDG-PET: Time course and relationship to neurological disability. *Journal of Head Trauma Rehabilitation, 16*, 135–148.

Berrol, S. (1986). Evolution and the persistent vegetative state. *Journal of Head Trauma Rehabilitation, 1*(1), 7–13.

Beuthien-Baumann, B., Holthoff, V. A., and Rudolf, J. (2005). Functional imaging of vegetative state applying single photon emission tomography and positron emission tomography. *Neuropsychological Rehabilitation, 15*(3/4), 276–282.

Bibby, H., and McDonald, S. (2005). Theory of mind after traumatic brain injury. *Neuropsychologia, 43*, 99–114.

Bier, N., Dutil, E., and Couture, M. (2009). Factors affecting leisure participation after a traumatic brain injury: an exploratory study. *Journal of Head Trauma Rehabilitation, 24*(3), 187–194.

Bigler, E. (2001a). Quantitative magnetic resonance imaging in traumatic brain injury. *Journal of Head Trauma Rehabilitation, 16*(2), 117–134.

Bigler, E. D. (2001b). The lesion(s) in traumatic brain injury: Implications for clinical neuropsychology. *Archives of Clinical Neuropsychology, 16*, 95–131.

Bigler, E. D. (2005). Structural Imaging. In J. M. Silver, T. W. McAllister and S. C. Yudofsky (Eds.), *Textbook of traumatic brain injury* (pp. 79–106). Arlington, VA: American Psychiatric Publishing, Inc.

Bigler, E. D. (2007). A motion to exclude and the "fixed" versus "flexible" battery in "forensic" neuropsychology: Challenges to the practice of clinical neuropsychology. *Archives of Clinical Neuropsychology, 22*(1), 45–51.

Bigler, E. (2008). Neuropsychology and clinical neuroscience of persistent post-concussive syndrome. *Journal of the International Neuropsychological Society, 14*, 1–22.

Bigler, E. D., Ryser, D., Gandhi, P., Kimball, J., and Wilde, E. A. (2006). Day-of-injury computerized tomography, rehabilitation status, and development of cerebral atrophy in persons with traumatic brain injury. *American Journal of Physical Medicine and Rehabilitation, 85*, 793–806.

Bijur, P. E., and Haslum, M. (1995). Cognitive, behavioral, and motoric sequelae of mild head injury in a national birth cohort. In S. Broman and M. E. Michel (Eds.), *Traumatic head injury in children*. New York: Oxford University Press.

Bishara, S. N., Partridge, F. M., Godfrey, H., and Knight, R. G. (1992). Post-traumatic amnesia and Glasgow Coma Scale related to outcome in survivors in a consecutive series of patients with severe closed-head injury. *Brain Injury, 6*, 373–380.

Bishop, D., and Miller, I. W. (1988). Traumatic brain injury: Empirical family assessment techniques. *Journal of Head Trauma Rehabilitation, 3*(4), 16–30.

Blacker, D., Broadhurst, L., and Teixeira, L. (2008). The role of occupational therapy in leisure adaptation with complex neurological disability: a discussion using two case study examples. *NeuroRehabilitation, 23*(4), 313–319.

Blackerby, W. F. (1990). A treatment model for sexuality disturbance following brain injury. *Journal of Head Trauma Rehabilitation, 5*(2), 73–82.

Blackman, J. A., Rice, S. A., and Matsumoto, J. A. (2003). Brain imaging as a predictor of early functional outcome following traumatic brain injury in children, adolescents, and young adults. *Journal of Head Trauma Rehabilitation, 18*(4), 493–503.

Blais, M. C., and Boivert, J. M. (2005). Psychological and marital adjustment in couples following traumatic brain injury (TBI): a critical review. *Brain Injury, 19*(4), 1223–1235.

Blais, M. C., and Boivert, J. M. (2007). Psychological adjustment and marital satisfaction following head injury. Which critical personal characteristics should both partners develop? *Brain Injury, 21*(4), 357–372.

Bloom, D. R., Levin, H. S., Ewing-Cobbs, L., Saunders, A. E., Song, J., Fletcher, J. M. et al. (2001). Lifetime and novel psychiatric disorders after pediatric traumatic brain injury. *Journal of the American Academy of Child and Adolescent Psychiatry, 40*(5 May), 572–579.

Body, R., and Parker, M. (2005). Topic repetitiveness after traumatic brain injury: An emergent, jointly managed behaviour. *Clinical Linguistics, 19*(50), 379–392.

Bogner, J. A., Corrigan, J. D., Bode, R. K., and Heinemann, A. W. (2000). Rating scale analysis of the agitated behavior scale. *Journal of Head Trauma Rehabilitation, 15*(1), 656–669.

Bogner, J. A., Corrigan, J. D., Fugate, L., Mysiw, W. J., and Clinchot, D. (2001). Role of agitation and prediction of outcomes after traumatic brain injury. *American Journal of Physical Medicine and Rehabilitation, 80*(9), 636–644.

Bogod, N. M., Mateer, C. A., and MacDonald, S. W. S. (2003). Self-awareness after traumatic brain injury: A comparison of measures and their relationship to executive function. *Journal of the International Neuropsychological Society, 9*(3), 450–458.

Bohnen, N., Jolles, J., and Twijnstra, A. (1992). Modification of the Stroop Color Word Test improves differentiation between patients with mild head injury and matched controls. *The Clinical Neuropsychologist, 6*, 178–184.

Bombardier, C. H., Fann, J. R., Temkin, N. R., Esselman, P. C., Barber, J., and Dikmen, S. S. (2010). Rates of major depressive disorder and clinical outcomes following traumatic brain injury. *JAMA, 303*, 1938–1945.

Bombardier, C. H., and Rimmele, C. T. (1999). Motivational interviewing to prevent alcohol abuse after traumatic brain injury: A case series. *Rehabilitation Psychology, 44*(1), 52–67.

Bombardier, C. H., Rimmele, C. T., and Zintel, H. (2002). The magnitude and correlates of alcohol and drug use before traumatic brain injury. *Archives of Physical Medicine and Rehabilitation, 83*(12), 1765–1773.

Bombardier, C. H., Temkin, N. R., Machamer, J., and Dikmen, S. S. (2003). The natural history of drinking and alcohol-related problems after traumatic brain injury. *Archives of Physical Medicine and Rehabilitation, 84*(2), 185–191.

Borgaro, S. R., and Prigatano, G. P. (2002). Early cognitive and affective sequelae of traumatic brain injury: A study using the BNI Screen for Higher Cerebral Functions. *Journal of Head Trauma Rehabilitation, 17*(6), 526–534.

Bornhofen, C., and McDonald, S. (2008). Emotion perception deficits following traumatic brain injury: a review of the evidence and rationale for intervention. *Journal of the International Neuropsychological Society, 14*(4), 511–525.

Bracy, C., and Douglas, J. (1997). Marital dyad perception of injured partners' communication following severe traumatic brain injury. *Brain Impairment, 6*, 1–12.

Bracy, C. A., and Douglas, J. M. (2002). Comparison of a group of long-term TBI marital dyads with a control group of orthopaedic marital dyads, on measures of marital satisfaction, marital coping, and perception of husbands' communication skills. *Brain Impairment, 3*(1), 71.

Bradbury, C. L., Christensen, B. K., Lau, M. A., Ruttan, L. A., Arundine, A. L., and Green, R. E. (2008). The efficacy of cognitive behaviour therapy in the treatment of emotional distress after acquired brain injury. *Archives of Physical Medicine and Rehabilitation, 89*(12 Suppl), S61–S68.

Braga, L. W., and Campos da Paz, A. (2000). Neuropsychological pediatric rehabilitation. In A. L. Christensen and B. Uzzell (Eds.), *International Handbook of Neuropsychological Rehabilitation*. New York: Kluwer Academic/Plenum Publishers.

Bragg, R. M., Klockars, A. J., and Berninger, B. W. (1992). Comparison of families with and without adolescents with traumatic brain injury. *Journal of Head Trauma Rehabilitation, 7*(4), 94–108.

Brain Injury Association of America (2011, 6th February). BIAA Adopts New TBI Definition. Retrieved 24 March 2011, from http://www.biausa.org/AnnouncementRetrieve.aspx?ID=66290

Brandt, J. (1991). The Hopkins Verbal Learning Test: Development of a new memory test with six equivalent forms. *The Clinical Neuropsychologist, 5*(2), 125–142.

Brink, J. D., Imbus, C., and Woo-Sam, J. (1980). Physical recovery after severe head trauma in children and adolescents. *Journal of Paediatrics, 97*, 721–727.

Broe, G. A., Tate, R. L., Ross, G., Tregeagle, S., and Lulham, J. (1981). The nature and effects of brain damage following severe head injury in young subjects. In

T. A. R. Dinning and T. J. Connelly (Eds.), *Head injuries. An integrated approach* (pp. 92–97). Brisbane: John Wiley and Sons.

Brooke, M. M., Patterson, D. R., Quested, K. A., Cardenas, D., and Farrel-Roberts, L. (1992). The treatment of agitation during initial hospitalization after traumatic brain injury. *Archives of Physical Medicine and Rehabilitation, 73*, 917–921.

Brooke, M. M., Questad, K. A., Patterson, D. R., and Bashak, K. J. (1992). Agitation and restlessness after closed head injury: a prospective study of 100 consecutive admissions. *Archives of Physical Medicine and Rehabilitation, 73*(4), 320–323.

Brooke, M. M., Quested, K.A., Patterson, D.R., and Valois, T.A. (1992). Driving evaluation after traumatic brain injury. *American Journal of Physical Medicine and Rehabilitation, 71*, 177–182.

Brooks, D. N., and Aughton, M. E. (1979). Psychological consequences of blunt head injury. *International Rehabilitation Medicine, 1*, 160–165.

Brooks, D. N., Campsie, L., Symington, C., Beattie, A., and McKinlay, W. (1986). The five-year outcome of severe blunt head injury: A relative's view. *Journal of Neurology, Neurosurgery and Psychiatry, 49*, 764–770.

Brooks, D. N., McKinlay, W., Symington, C., Beattie, A., and Campsie, L. (1987a). Return to work within the first seven years of head injury. *Brain Injury, 1*, 5–19.

Brooks, N. (1984). Head injury and the family. In N. Brooks (Ed.), *Closed head injury: Psychological, social, and family consequences* (pp. 123–147). Oxford: Oxford University Press.

Brooks, N., Campsie, L., Symington, C., Beattie, A., and McKinlay, W. (1987b). The effects of severe head injury on patient and relative within seven years of injury. *Journal of Head Trauma Rehabilitation, 2*(3), 1–13.

Brouwer, W., and Withaar, F. K. (1997). Fitness to drive after traumatic brain injury. *Neuropsychologial Rehabilitation, 7*(3), 177–193.

Brouwer, W. H., Withaar, F. K., Tant, M. I. M., and van Zomeren, A. H. (2002). Attention and driving in traumatic brain injury: A question of coping with time-pressure. *Journal of Head Trauma Rehabilitation, 17*(1), 1–15.

Brown, A. W., Malec, J. F., Mandrekar, J., Diehl, N. N., Dikmen, S. S., Sherer, M. et al. (2010). Predictive utility of weekly post-traumatic amnesia assessments after brain injury: A multicentre analysis. *Brain Injury, 24*(3), 472–478.

Brown, A. W., Malec, J. F., McClelland, R. L., Diehl, N. N., Englander, J., and Cifu, D. X. (2005). Clinical elements that predict outcome after traumatic brain injury: A prospective multicentre recursive partitioning (decision-tree) analysis. *Journal of Neurotrauma, 22*, 1040–1051.

Brown, D. A., Chadwick, O., Shaffer, D., Rutter, M., and Traub, M. (1981). A prospective study of children with head injuries. III. Psychiatric sequelae. *Psychological Medicine, 11*, 63–78.

Brown, D. S. O., and Nell, V. (1992). Recovery from diffuse traumatic brain injury in Johannesburg: A concurrent prospective study. *Archives of Physical Medicine and Rehabilitation, 73*, 758–770.

Brown, M., Dijkers, M.P.J.M., Gordon, W.A., Ashman, T., Charatz, H., and Cheng, Z. (2004). Participation Objective, Participation Subjective: A measure of participation combining outsider and insider perspectives. *Journal of Head Trauma Rehabilitation, 19,* 459–481.

Brown, M., Gordon, W. A., and Spielman, L. (2003). Participation in social and recreational activity in the community by individuals with traumatic brain injury. *Rehabilitation Psychology, 48*(4), 266–274.

Bruce, D. A. (1995). Pathophysiological responses of the child's brain following trauma. In S. H. Broman and M. E. Michel (Eds.), *Traumatic head injury in children* (pp. 40–51). New York: Oxford University Press.

Bruce, D. A., Raphaely, R. C., Goldberg, A. I., Zimmerman, R. A., Bilaniuk, L. T., Schut, L. et al. (1979). Pathophysiology, treatment and outcome following severe head injury in children. *Child's Brain, 5*, 174–191.

Bruce, D. A., Schut, L., Bruno, L. A., Wood, J. H., and Sutton, L. N. (1978). Outcome following severe head injuries in children. *Journal of Neurosurgery, 48*, 679–688.

Bruns, J., Jr, and Hauser, W. (2003). The epidemiology of traumatic brain injury: A review. *Epilepsia, 44*(supplement 10), 2–10.

Bryant, R. A. (2001). Posttraumatic stress disorder and traumatic brain injury: can they co-exist? *Clinical Psychology Review, 21*, 931–948.

Bryant, R. A. (2008). Disentangling Mild Traumatic Brain Injury and Stress Reactions. *The New England Journal of Medicine, 358*(5), 525–527.

Bryant, R. A., Creamer, M., O'Donnell, M., Silove, D., Clark, C. R., and McFarlane, A. C. (2009). Post-traumatic amnesia and the nature of post-traumatic stress disorder after mild traumatic brain injury. *Journal of the International Neuropsychological Society, 15*, 862–867.

Bryant, R. A., Moulds, M., Guthrie, R., and Nixon, R. D. V. (2003). Treating acute stress disorder following mild traumatic brain injury. *American Journal of Psychiatry, 160*, 585–587.

Bryant, R. A., Sackville, T., Dang, S. T., Moulds, M., and Guthrie, R. (1999). Treating acute stress disorder: an evaluation of cognitive behaviour therapy and supportive counselling techniques. *American Journal of Psychiatry, 156*, 1780–1786.

Burgess, P. W., Alderman, N., Forbes, C., Costello, A., Coates, L. M.-A., Dawson, D. R. et al. (2006). The case for the development and use of "ecologically valid" measures of executive function in experimental and clinical neuropsychology. *Journal of the International Neuropsychological Society, 12*(2), 194.

Burgess, P. W., Alderman, N., Volle, E., Benoit, R. G., and Gilbert, S. J. (2009). Mesulam's frontal lobe mystery re-examined. *Restorative Neurology and Neuroscience, 27*(5), 439–506.

Burgess, P. W., and Shallice, T. (1997). *The Hayling and Brixton Tests*. Bury St Edmunds: Thames Valley Test Company Limited.

Burke, B. L., Dunn, C. W., Atkins, D. C., and Phelps, J. S. (2004). The emerging evidence base for Motivational Interviewing: A meta-analytic and qualitative Inquiry. *Journal of Cognitive Psychotherapy, 18*(4), 309–322.

Burke, W. H., Wesolowski, M. D., and Guth, M. L. (1988). Comprehensive head injury rehabilitation: an outcome evaluation. *Brain Injury, 2*, 313–322.

Burke, W. H., Zencius, A. H., Wesolowski, M. D., and Doubleday, F. (1991). Improving executive function disorders in brain-injured clients. *Brain Injury, 5*, 241–252.

Burridge, A. C., Williams, W. H., Yates, P. J., Harris, A., and Ward, C. D. (2007). Spousal relationship satisfaction following acquired brain injury: The role of insight and socio-emotional skill. *Neuropsychological Rehabilitation, 17*(1), 95–105.

Busch, R. M., McBride, A., Curtiss, G., and Vanderploeg, R. D. (2005). The components of executive functioning in traumatic brain injury. *Journal of Clinical and Experimental Neuropsychology, 27*, 1022–1032.

Buschke, H., and Fuld, P. A. (1974). Evaluating storage, retention, and retrieval in disordered memory and learning. *Neurology, 24*, 1019–1025.

Butera-Prinzi, F., and Perlesz, A. (2004). Through children's eyes: children's experience of living with a parent with an acquired brain injury. *Brain Injury, 18*(1), 83–101.

Callaway, L., Sloan, S., and Winkler, D. (2005). Maintaining and developing friendships following severe traumatic brain injury: Principles of occupational therapy practice. *Australian Occupational Therapy Journal, 52*(3), 292–295.

Cannizzaro, M., and Coelho, C. (2002). Treatment of story grammar following traumatic brain injury: a pilot study. *Brain Injury, 16*(2), 1065–1073.

Carnes, S. L., and Quinn, W. H. (2005). Family adaptation to brain injury: Coping and psychological distress. *Families, Systems and Health, 23*(2), 186–203.

Carnevale, G. J., Anselmi, V., Buischio, K., and Millis, S. (2002). Changes in ratings of caregiver burden following a community-based behaviour management program from persons with traumatic brain injury. *Journal of Head Trauma Rehabilitation, 17*(2), 83–95.

Carnevale, G. J., Anselmi, V., Johnston, M. V., Busichio, K., and Walsh, V. (2006). A natural setting behavior management program for persons with acquired brain injury. *Archives of Physical Medicine and Rehabilitation, 87*, 1289–1297.

Carroll, L. J., Cassidy, J. D., Holm, L., Kraus, J., and Coronado, V. G. (2004a). Methodological issues and research recommendations for mild traumatic brain injury: the WHO Collaborating Centre Task Force on Mild Traumatic Brain Injury. *Journal of Rehabilitation Medicine, 36*(Suppl 43), 113–125.

Carroll, L. J., Cassidy, J. D., Peloso, P. M. et al (2004b). Prognosis for mild traumatic brain injury: Results of the WHO Collaborating Centre Task Force on Mild Traumatic Brain Injury. *Journal of Rehabilitation Medicine, 43*(Suppl), 84–105.

Catroppa, C., and Anderson, V. (2002). Recovery in memory function in the first year following TBI in children. *Brain Injury, 16*(5), 369–384.

Catroppa, C., and Anderson, V. (2004). Recovery and predictors of language skills two years following pediatric traumatic brain injury. *Brain and Language, 88*(1), 68–78.

Catroppa, C., and Anderson, V. (2005). A prospective study of the recovery of attention from acute to 2 years following pediatric traumatic brain injury. *Journal of the International Neuropsychological Society, 11*(1), 84–98.

Catroppa, C., and Anderson, V. (2007). Recovery in memory function, and its relationship to academic success, at 24 months following pediatric TBI. *Child Neuropsychology, 13*(3), 240–261.

Catroppa, C., Anderson, V. A., Morse, S. A., Haritou, F., and Rosenfeld, J. V. (2007). Children's attentional skills 5 years post-TBI. *Journal of Pediatric Psychology, 32*(3), 354–369.

Catroppa, C., Anderson, V. A., Muscara, F., Morse, S. A., Haritou, F., Rosenfeld, J. V. et al. (2009). Educational skills: long-term outcome and predictors following paediatric traumatic brain injury. *Neuropsychological Rehabilitation, 19*(5), 716–732.

Cattelani, R., Tanzi, F., Lombardi, F., and Mazzucchi, A. (2002). Competitive re-employment after severe traumatic brain injury: Clinical, cognitive and behavioural predictive variables. *Brain Injury, 16*(1), 51–64.

Centre for Neuro Skills (1986). *Independent Living Scale*. California: Centre for Neuro Skills.

Chadwick, O., Rutter, M., Brown, G., Shaffer, D., and Traub, M. (1981). A prospective study of children with head injuries. II. Cognitive sequelae. *Psychological Medicine, 11*, 49–61.

Chaiwat, O., Sharma, D., Udomphorn, Y., Armstead, W. M., and Vavilala, M. S. (2009). Cerebral hemodynamic predictors of poor 6-month Glasgow Outcome Score in severe pediatric traumatic brain injury. *Journal of Neurotrauma, 26*(5), 657–663.

Chan, R., Shum, D., Toulopoulou, T., and Chen, E. (2008). Assessment of executive functions: Review of instruments and identification of critical issues. *Archives of Clinical Neuropsychology, 23*, 201–216.

Chapman, L. A., Wade, S. L., Walz, N. C., Taylor, H. G., Stancin, T., and Yeates, K. O. (2010). Clinically significant behaviour problems during the initial 18 months following early childhood traumatic brain injury. *Rehabilitation Psychology, 55*(1), 48–57.

Chapman, S. B., Culhane, K. A., Levin, H. S., Harwood, H., Mendelsohn, D., Ewing-Cobbs, L. et al. (1992). Narrative discourse after closed head injury in children and adolescents. *Brain and Language, 43*, 42–65.

Chapman, S. B., Gamino, J. F., Cook, L. G., Hanten, G., Li, X., and Levin, H. S. (2006). Impaired discourse gist and working memory in children after brain injury. *Brain and Language, 97*(2 May), 178–188.

Chapman, S. B., McKinnon, L., Levin, H. S., Song, J., Meier, M. C., and Chiu, S. (2001). Longitudinal outcome of verbal discourse in children with traumatic brain injury: three-year follow-up. *Journal of Head Trauma Rehabilitation, 16*(5), 441–455.

Chapman, S. B., Sparks, G., Levin, H. S., Dennis, M., Roncadin, C., Zhang, L. et al. (2004). Discourse macrolevel processing after severe pediatric traumatic brain injury. *Developmental Neuropsychology, 25*(1–2), 37–60.

Charles (2007). Families living with acquired brain injury: A multiple family group experience. *Neurorehabilitation, 22*(1), 61–76.

Chaudhuria, K., Malhamab, G. M., and Rosenfeld, J. (2009). Survival of trauma patients with coma and bilateral fixed dilated pupils. *Injury, 40*(1), 28–32.

Christensen, A. (1984). *Luria's Neuropsychological investigation* (2nd ed.). Bogtrykker, Vojens: P.J. Schmidts.

Christensen, A.-L. (1974). *Luria's Neuropsychological investigation*. Risskov, Denmark: Munksgaard.

Christensen, B. K., Colella, B., Inness, E., Hebert, D., Monette, G., Bayley, M. et al. (2008). Recovery of cognitive function after traumatic brain injury: A multilevel modeling analysis of Canadian outcomes. *Archives of Physical Medicine and Rehabilitation, 89*(Supplement 2), S3–S15.

Christodoulou, C., DeLuca, J., Ricker, J. H., Madigan, N. K., Bly, B. M., Lange, G. et al. (2001). Functional magnetic resonance imaging of working memory impairment after traumatic brain injury. *Journal of Neurology, Neurosurgery & Psychiatry, 71*(2), 161–168.

Chung, C. Y., Chen, C. L., Cheng, P. T., See, L. C., Tang, S. F., and Wong, A. M. (2006). Critical score of Glasgow Coma Scale for pediatric traumatic brain injury. *Pediatric Neurology, 34*(5), 379–387.

Cicerone, K., Levin, H., Malec, J., Stuss, D., and Whyte, J. (2006). Cognitive Rehabilitation Interventions for Executive Function: Moving from Bench to Bedside in Patients with Traumatic Brain Injury. *Journal of Cognitive Neuroscience, 18*(7), 1212–1222.

Cicerone, K. D. (2002). Remediation of "working attention" in mild traumatic brain injury. *Brain Injury, 16*(3).

Cicerone, K. D., Dahlberg, C., Malec, J. F., Langenbaum, D. M., Felicetti, T., Kneipp et al. (2005). Evidence-based cognitive rehabilitation: Updated review of the literature from 1998 through 2002. *Archives of Physical Medicine and Rehabilitation, 86*, 1681–1692.

Cicerone, K. D., and Giacino, J. T. (1992). Remediation of executive deficits after traumatic brain injury. *NeuroRehabilitation, 2*, 12–22.

Cicerone, K. D., Mott, T., Azulay, J., Sharlow-Galella, M. A., Ellmo, W. J., Paradise, S. et al. (2008). A randomized controlled trial of holistic neuropsychologic rehabilitation after traumatic brain injury. *Archives of Physical Medicine and Rehabilitation, 89*(12), 2239–2249.

Cicerone, K. D., and Tupper, D. E. (1991). Neuropsychological rehabilitation: Treatment of errors in everyday functioning. In D. E. Tupper and K. D. Cicerone (Eds.), *The neuropsychology of everyday life: Issues in development and rehabilitation* (pp. 271–291). Boston: Kluwer Academic Publisher.

Cicerone, K. D., and Wood, J. C. (1987). Planning disorder after closed head injury: A case study. *Archives of Physical Medicine and Rehabilitation, 68*, 111–115.

Coelho, C. (2002). Story narratives of adults with closed head injury and non-brain-injured adults influence of socioeconomic status, elicitation task, and executive functioning. *Journal of Speech, Language and Hearing Research, 45*, 1232–1248.

Coelho, C., Youse, K., Le, K., and Feinn, R. (2003). Narrative and conversational discourse of adults with closed head injuries and non-brain-injured adults: A discriminant analysis. *Aphasiology, 17*(5), 499–510.

Cohen, B. A., Inglese, M., Rusinek, H., Babb, J. S., Gossman, R. L., and Gonen, O. (2007). Proton MR spectroscopy and MRI-volumetry in mild traumatic brain injury. *American Journal of Neuroradiology, 28*, 907–917.

Colantonio, A., Ratcliff, G., Chase, S., Kelsey, S., Escobar, M., and Vernich, L. (2004). Long term outcomes after moderate to severe traumatic brain injury. *Disability and Rehabilitation, 26*(5), 253–261.

Coleman, M. R., Rodd, J. M., Davis, M. H., Johnsrude, I. S., Menon, D. K., Pickard, J. D. et al. (2007). Do vegetative patients retain aspects of language comprehension? Evidence from fMRI. *Brain, 130*, 2494–2507.

Coleman, R. D., Rapport, L. J., Ergh, T. C., Hanks, R. A., Ricker, J. H., and Millis, S. R. (2002). Predictors of driving outcome after traumatic brain injury. *Archives of Physical Medicine and Rehabilitation, 83*(October), 1415–1422.

Connors, C. (1973). Rating scales for use in drug studies in children. *Psychopharmacology Bulletin, 9*(Special Supplement), 24–84.

Cook, J. (1991). Higher education: An attainable goal for students who have sustained head injuries. *Journal of Head Trauma Rehabilitation, 6*(1), 64–72.

Cook, L. G., Chapman, S. B., and Levin, H. S. (2008). Self-regulation abilities in children with severe traumatic brain injury: a preliminary investigation of naturalistic action. *Neurorehabilitation, 23*(6), 467–475.

Cooper, D. J., Rosenfeld, J. V., Murray, L., Arabi, Y. M., Davies A, D'Urso, P. et al. (2011). Multicenter, prospective randomized trial of early Decompressive Craniectomy in patients with severe traumatic brain injury (DECRA) and refractory intracranial pressure. *New England Journal of Medicine,* Accepted 17 March.

Cooper, D. J., Rosenfeld, J. V., Murray, L., Wolfe, R., Ponsford, J., Davies, A. et al. (2008). Early decompressive craniectomy for patients with severe traumatic brain injury and refractory intracranial hypertension – a pilot randomised trial. *Journal of Critical Care, 23*, 387–393.

Cooper-Evans, S., Alderman, N., Knight, C., and Oddy, M. (2008). Self-esteem as a predictor of psychological distress after severe acquired brain injury: An exploratory study. *Neuropsychological Rehabilitation, 18*(5–6), 607–626.

Cope, D. N. (1987). Psychopharmacologic considerations in the treatment of traumatic brain injury. *Journal of Head Trauma Rehabilitation, 2*(4), 1–5.

Cope, D. N., Cole, J. R., Hall, K. M., and Barkan, H. (1991). Brain injury: analysis of outcome in a post-acute rehabilitation system. Part 1: General analysis. *Brain Injury, 5*, 111–125.

Corrigan, J. D. (1989). Development of a scale for assessment of agitation following traumatic brain injury. *Journal of Clinical and Experimental Neuropsychology, 11*, 261–277.

Corrigan, J. D., Arnett, J. A., Houck, L. J., and Jackson, R. D. (1985). Reality orientation for brain injured patients: Group treatment and monitoring of recovery. *Archives of Physical Medicine and Rehabilitation, 66*, 626–630.

Corrigan, J. D., Mysiw, W. J., Gribble, M. W., and Chock, S. K. L. (1992). Agitation, cognition and amnesia during post-traumatic amnesia. *Brain Injury, 6*, 155–160.

Corrigan, J. D., Rust, E., and Lamb-Hart, G. L. (1995). The nature and extent of substance abuse problems in persons with traumatic brain injury. *Journal of Head Trauma Rehabilitation, 10*, 29–46.

Crawford, J. R., and Allan, K. M. (1997). Estimating premorbid IQ with demographic variables: Regression equations derived from a UK sample. *The Clinical Neuropsychologist, 11*, 192–197.

Crawford, J., Smith, G., Maylor, F., Della Salla, S., and Logie, R. (2003). The Prospective and retrospective memory Questionnaire (PRMQ): Normative data and latent structure in a large non-clinical sample. *Memory, 11*(3), 261–275.

Crepeau, F., and Scherzer, P. (1993). Predictors and indicators of work status after traumatic brain injury: A meta-analysis. *Neuropsychological Rehabilitation, 3*, 5–35.

Crosson, B., Barco, P. P., Velozo, C., Bolesta, M. M., Cooper, P. V., Werts, D. et al. (1989). Awareness and compensation in post-acute head injury rehabilitation. *Journal of Head Trauma Rehabilitation, 4*(3), 46–54.

Crowe, L., Babl, F., Anderson, V., and Catroppa, C. (2009). The epidemiology of paediatric head injuries: Data from a referral centre in Victoria, Australia. *Journal of Paediatrics and Child Health, 45*, 346–350.

Culley, C., and Evans, J. J. (2010). SMS text messaging as a means of increasing recall of therapy goals in brain injury rehabilitation: a single-blind within-subjects trial. *Neuropsychological Rehabilitation, 20*(1), 103–119.

Curl, R., Fraser, R., Cook, R., and Clemmons, D. (1996). Traumatic brain injury vocational rehabilitation: Preliminary findings from the co-worker as trainer project. *Journal of Head Trauma Rehabilitation, 11*(1), 75–85.

Curtiss, G., Klemz, S., and Vanderploeg, R. D. (2000). Acute impact of severe traumatic brain injury on family structure and coping responses. *Journal of Head Trauma Rehabilitation, 15*, 1113–1122.

Cyr, A. A., Stinchcombe, A., Gagnon, S., Marshall, S., Hing, M. M., and Finestone, H. (2007). Driving difficulties of brain-injured drivers in reaction to high-crash-risk simulated road events: A question of impaired divided attention? *Journal of Clinical and Experimental Neuropsychology, 31*(4), 472–482.

Dahlberg, C. A., Cusick, C. P., Hawley, L. A., Newman, J. K., C.E., M., Harrison-Felix, C. L. et al. (2007). Treatment efficacy of social communication skills training after traumatic brain injury: A randomized treatment and deferred treatment controlled trial. *Archives of Physical Medicine and Rehabilitation, 88*(12), 561–1573.

Dahlberg, C., Hawley, L., Morey, C., Newman, J., Cusick, C. P., and Harrison-Felix, C. (2006). Social communication skills in persons with post-acute traumatic brain injury: Three perspectives. *Brain Injury, 20*(4), 425–435.

Dahm, J., Ponsford, J., Wong, D., and Schönberger, M. (2009, September,). Utility of the Depression Anxiety Stress Scales in assessing depression and anxiety following traumatic brain injury. Paper presented at the 44th Annual Conference of the Australian Psychological Society, Darwin.

Dahm, J., Ponsford, J., Wong, D., and Schönberger, M. (2011, 11–12 July). Utility of the Depression Anxiety Stress Scales in assessing depression and anxiety following traumatic brain injury. Paper presented at the 8th conference of the WFNR Neuropsychological Rehabilitation Special Interest Group, Rotorua, New Zealand.

Daniels-Zide, E., and Ben-Yishay, Y. (2000). Therapeutic Milieu Day Program. In A. Christensen and B. Uzzell (Eds.), *International handbook of neuropsychological rehabilitation* (pp. 183–193). New York: Kluwer Academic/Plenum Publishers.

Davis, D., Serrano, J. A., Vilke, G. M., Sise, M. J., Kennedy, F., Eastman, A. B. et al. (2006). The predictive value of field versus arrival Glasgow Coma Scale score and TRISS calculations in moderate-to-severe traumatic brain injury. *The Journal of Trauma: Injury, Infection, and Critical Care, 60*(5), 985–990.

Dawson, D. R., Gaya, A., Hunt, A., Levine, B., Lemsky, C., and Polatajko, H. J. (2009). Using the cognitive orientation to occupational performance (CO-OP) with adults with executive dysfunction following traumatic brain injury. *Canadian Journal of Occupational Therapy, 76*(2), 115–127.

De Guise, E., Leblanc, J., Feyz, M., Thomas, H., and Gosselin, N. (2005). Effect of an integrated reality orientation programme in acute care on post-traumatic amnesia in patients with traumatic brain injury. *Brain Injury, 19*(4), 263–269.

Deb, S., Lyons, I., Koutzoukis, C., Ali, I., and McCarthy, G. (1999). Rate of psychiatric illness 1 year after traumatic brain injury. *American Journal of Psychiatry, 156*, 374–378.

Delazer, M., Bodner, T., and Benke, T. (1998). Rehabilitation of arithmetical test problem solving. *Neuropsychological Rehabilitation, 8*, 401–412.

Delis, D. C., Kaplan, E., and Kramer, J. H. (2001). *Delis Kaplan Executive Function System (DKEFS)*. San Antonio, TX: The Psychological Corporation.

Delis, D. C., Kramer, J. H., Kaplan, E., and Ober, B. A. (1987). *California Verbal Learning Test*. San Antonio, TX: The Psychological Corporation.

Dell'Acqua, R., Stablum, F., Galbiati, S., Spannocchi, G., and Cerri, C. (2001). Selective effect of closed-head injury on central resource allocation: evidence from dual-task performance. *Experimental Brain Research, 136*(3), 364–378.

Delmonico, R. L., Hanley-Peterson, P., and Englander, J. (1998). Group psychotherapy for persons with traumatic brain injury: Management of frustration and substance abuse. *Journal of Head Trauma Rehabilitation, 13*(6), 10–22.

Dennis, M. (1992). Word finding in children and adolescents with a history of brain injury. *Topics in Language Disorders, 13*, 66–82.

Dennis, M., and Barnes, M. A. (1990). Knowing the meaning, getting the point, bridging the gap and carrying the message: Aspects of discourse following closed head injury in childhood adolescence. *Brain and Language, 39*, 428–446.

Dennis, M., Wilkinson, M., Koski, L., and Humphreys, B. P. (1995). Attention deficits in the long term afte childhood head injury. In S. H. Broman and M. R. Michel (Eds.), *Traumatic head injury in children* (pp. 165–187). New York: Oxford University Press.

Dewar, B.-K., and Gracey, F. (2007). Am not was: Cognitive behaviour therapy for adjustment and identity change following herpes simplex encephalitis. *Neuropsychological Rehabilitation, 17*, 602–620.

Di Stefano, G., Bachevalier, J., Levin, H. S., Song, J. X., Scheibel, R. S., and Fletcher, J. M. (2000). Volume of focal brain lesions and hippocampal formation in relation to memory function after closed head injury in children. *Journal of Neurology, Neurosurgery and Psychiatry, 69*(2), 210–216.

Diamond, A. (1988). Differences between adult and infant cognition: Is the crucial variable presence or absence of language? In L. Weiskrantz (Ed.), *Thought Without Language* (pp. 337–370). New York: Oxford University Press.

Dikmen, S., Machamer, J., Fann, J. R., and Temkin, N. R. (2010). Rates of symptom reporting following traumatic brain injury. *Journal of the International Neuropsychological Society, 16*, 401–411.

Dikmen, S., Machamer, J., and Temkin, N. (1993). Psychological outcome in patients with moderate to severe brain injury. *Brain Injury, 7*(113–124).

Dikmen, S. S., Machamer, J. E., Powell, J. M., and Temkin, N. R. (2003). Outcome three to five years after moderate to severe traumatic brain injury. *Archives of Physical Medicine and Rehabilitation, 84*, 1449–1457.

Dikmen, S. S., Temkin, N. R., Miller, B., Machamer, J., and Winn, H. R. (1991). Neurobehavioral effects of phenytoin prophylaxis of posttraumatic seizures. *JAMA, 265*, 1271–1278.

Dirette, D. (2002). The development of awareness and the use of compensatory strategies for cognitive deficits. *Brain Injury, 16*(10), 861–871.

Dirette, D., and Plaisier, B. R. (2007). The development of self-awareness of deficits from 1 week to 1 year after traumatic brain injury: Preliminary findings. *Brain Injury, 21*, 1131–1136.

Dobbing, J. (1968). Vulnerable periods in developing brain. In A. N. Davison and J. Dobbing (Eds.), *Applied neurochemistry*. Oxford: Blackwell.

Dodrill, C. B. (1978). A neuropsychological battery for epilepsy. *Epilepsia, 19*, 611–623.

Doig, E., Fleming, J., and Tooth, L. (2001). Patterns of community integration 2–5 years post-discharge from brain injury rehabilitation. *Brain Injury, 15*(9), 747–762.

Donders, J., and Warschausky, S. (2007). Neurobehavioral outcomes after early versus late childhood traumatic brain injury. *Journal of Head Trauma Rehabilitation, 22*(5), 296–302.

Douglas, J. M. (2010). Relation of executive functioning to pragmatic outcome following severe traumatic brain injury. *Journal of Speech, Language and Hearing Research, 53*(2), 365–382.

Douglas, J. M., Bracy, C. A., and Snow, P. C. (2007a). Exploring the factor structure of the La Trobe Communication Questionnaire: Insights into the nature of communication deficits following traumatic brain injury. *Aphasiology, 21*(12), 1181–1194.

Douglas, J. M., Bracy, C. A., and Snow, P. C. (2007b). Measuring perceived communicative ability after traumatic brain injury: reliability and validity of the La Trobe Communication Questionnaire. *Brain Injury, 22*(1), 31–38.

Douglas, J. M., O'Flaherty, C. A., and Snow, P. C. (2000). Measuring perception of communicative ability: The development and evaluation of the La Trobe Communication Questionnaire. *Aphasiology, 14*, 251–268.

Douglas, J. M., and Spellacy, F. J. (1996). Indicators of long-term family functioning following severe traumatic brain injury. *Brain Injury, 10*(11), 819–839.

Douglas, M. J. (1987). Perceptions of family environment among severely head-injured patients and their relatives. Unpublished master's thesis. University of Victoria, British Columbia, Canada.

Douglas, M. J. (1994). Indicators of long-term family functioning following severe TBI. Unpublished PhD thesis. University of Victoria, British Columbia, Canada.

Draper, K., and Ponsford, J. (2007). Long-term outcome following traumatic brain injury: How should this be measured? *Neuropsychological Rehabilitation, 19*(5), 645–661.

Draper, K., and Ponsford, J. (2008). Cognitive functioning and outcome 10 years following traumatic brain injury. *Neuropsychology, 22*(5), 618–625.

Draper, K., Ponsford, J., and Schönberger, M. (2007). Psychosocial and emotional outcome following traumatic brain injury. *Journal of Head Trauma Rehabilitation, 22*(5), 278–287.

Ducharme, J. M. (1999). A conceptual model for treatment of externalizing behaviour in acquired brain injury. *Brain Injury, 13*(9), 645–668.

Ducharme, J. M. (2000). Treatment of maladaptive behavior in acquired brain injury: remedial approaches in postacute settings. *Clinical Psychology Review, 20*(3), 405–426.

Dyer, K. F., Bell, R., McCann, J., and Rauch, R. (2006). Aggression after traumatic brain injury: analysing socially desirable responses and the nature of aggressive traits. *Brain Injury, 20*(11), 1163–1173.

Eames, P. (1988). Behavior disorders after severe head injury: Their nature and causes and strategies for management. *Journal of Head Trauma Rehabilitation, 3*(3), 1–6.

Eames, P., Cotterill, G., Kneale, T. A., Storrar, A. L., and Yeomans, P. (1996). Outcome of intensive rehabilitation after severe brain injury: a long-term follow-up study. *Brain Injury, 10*, 631–650.

Eames, P., and Wood, R. (1985a). Rehabilitation after severe brain injury: a follow-up study of a behaviour modification approach. *Journal of Neurology, Neurosurgery and Psychiatry, 48*(7), 613–619.

Eames, P., and Wood, R. L. (1985b). Rehabilitation after severe brain injury: A special-unit approach to behaviour disorders. *International Rehabilitation Medicine, 7*, 130–133.

Ehlhardt, L. A., Sohlberg, M. M., Kennedy, M., Coelho, C., Ylvisaker, M., Turkstra, L. et al. (2008). Evidence-based practice guidelines for instructing individuals with neurogenic memory impairments: What have we learned in the last 20 years? *Neuropsychological Rehabilitation, 18*(3), 300–342.

Eilander, H. J., van de Wile, M., Wijers, M., van Heugten, C. M., Buljevac, D., Lavrijsen, J. C. M. et al. (2009). The reliability and validity of the PALOC-s: A post-acute level of consciousness scale for assessment of young patients with prolonged disturbed consciousness after brain injury. *Neuropsychological Rehabilitation, 19*(1), 1–27.

Einstein, G. O., and McDaniel, M. A. (1990). Normal aging and prospective memory. *Journal of Experimental Psychology: Learning, Memory and Cognition, 16*, 717–726.

Eisenberger, N. I., and Lieberman, M. D. (2004). Why rejection hurts: A common neural alarm system for physical and social pain. *Trends in Cognitive Sciences, 8*(7), 294–300.

Elbert, T., Heim, S., and Rockstroh, B. (2001). Neural plasticity and development. In C. A. Nelson and M. Luciana (Eds.), *Handbook of developmental cognitive neuroscience* (pp. 191–204). Cambridge, MA: MIT Press.

Elgmark Andersson, E., Emanuelson, I., Bjorklund, R., and Stalhammar, D. A. (2007). Mild traumatic brain injuries: the impact of early intervention on late sequelae. A randomized controlled trial. *Acta Neurochirurgica, 149*(2), 151–159; discussion 160.

Elsass, L., and Kinsella, G. (1987). Social interaction following severe closed head injury. *Psychological Medicine, 17*(67–78).

Engberg, A. W., and Teasdale, T. W. (2004). Psychosocial outcome following traumatic brain injury in adults: A long-term population-based follow-up. *Brain Injury, 18*(6), 533–545.

Englander, J., Bushnik, T., Duong, T. T., Cifu, D. X., Zafonte, R., Wright, J. et al. (2003). Analyzing risk factors for late posttraumatic seizures: A prospective, multicenter investigation. *Archives of Physical Medicine and Rehabilitation, 84*(3), 365–373.

Epstein, N. B., Baldwin, L. M., and Bishop, D. S. (1983). The McMaster Family Assessment Device. *Journal of Marital and Family Therapy, 9*(2), 171–180.

Ergh, T. C., Hanks, R. A., Rapport, L. J., and Coleman, R. D. (2003). Social support moderates caregiver life satisfaction following traumatic brain injury. *Journal of Clinical and Experimental Neuropsychology, 25*(8), 1090–1101.

Ergh, T. C., Rapport, L. J., Coleman, R. D., and Hanks, R. A. (2002). Predictors of caregiver and family functioning following traumatic brain injury. *Journal of Head Trauma Rehabilitation, 17*(2), 155–174.

Evans, J. J., Emslie, H., and Wilson, B. A. (1998). External cueing systems in the rehabilitation of executive impairments of action. *Journal of the International Neuropsychological Society, 4*(04), 399–408.

Evans, J. J., Wilson, B. A., Needham, P., and Brentnall, S. (2003). Who makes good use of memory aids? Results of a survey of people with acquired brain injury. *Journal of the International Neuropsychological Society, 9*, 925–935.

Evans, R. W. (1992). The post-concussion syndrome and sequelae of mild head injury. *Neurologica Clinics, 10*, 815–847.

Ewert, J., Levin, H. S., Watson, M. G., and Kalisky, Z. (1989). Procedural memory during post-traumatic amnesia in survivors of severe closed head injury. *Archives of Neurology, 46*, 911–916.

Ewing-Cobbs, L., and Barnes, M. (2002). Linguistic outcomes following traumatic brain injury in children. *Seminars in Pediatric Neurology, 9*(3), 209–217.

Ewing-Cobbs, L., Barnes, M., Fletcher, J. M., Levin, H. S., Swank, P. R., and Song, J. (2004). Modeling of longitudinal academic achievement scores after paediatric traumatic brain injury. *Developmental Neuropsychology, 25*(1 and 2), 107–133.

Ewing-Cobbs, L., Fletcher, J. M., Levin, H. S., Francis, D. J., Davidson, K., and Miner, M. E. (1997). Longitudinal neuropsychological outcome in infants and preschoolers with traumatic brain injury. *Journal of the International Neuropsychological Society, 3*(6), 581–591.

Ewing-Cobbs, L., Levin, H., Fletcher, J., Miner, M., and Eisenberg, H. (1990). The Children's Orientation and Amnesia test: relationship to acute severity and to recovery of memory. *Neurosurgery, 27*, 683–691.

Ewing-Cobbs, L., Levin, H. S., Eisenberg, H. M., and Fletcher, J. M. (1987). Language functuions following closed head injury in children and adolescents. *Journal of Clinical and Experimental Neuropscyhology, 9*, 575–592.

Ewing-Cobbs, L., Prasad, M. R., Kramer, L., Cox, C. S. J., Baumgartner, J., Fletcher, S. et al. (2006). Late intellectual and academic outcomes following traumatic brain injury sustained during early childhood. *Journal of Neurosurgery Pediatrics, 105* (4 Suppl), 287–296.

Ewing-Cobbs, L., Prasad, M. R., Swank, P., Kramer, L., Cox, C. S., Jr., Fletcher, J. M. et al. (2008). Arrested development and disrupted callosal microstructure following pediatric traumatic brain injury: relation to neurobehavioral outcomes. *Neuroimage, 42*(4), 1305–1315.

Ezrachi, O., Ben-Yishay, Y., Kay, T., Diller, L., and Rattok, J. (1991). Predicting employment in traumatic brain injury following neuropsychological rehabilitation. *Journal of Head Trauma Rehabilitation, 6*(3), 71–84.

Faden, A. L. (2001). Neuroprotection and traumatic brain injury. *Archives of Neurology, 58*, 1553–1555.

Fann, J. R., Hart, T., and Schomer, K. G. (2009a). Treatment for depression after traumatic brain injury: a systematic review. *Journal of Neurotrauma, 26*(2), 2383–2402.

Fann, J. R., Jones, A. L., Dikmen, S. S., Temkin, N. R., Esselman, P. C., and Bombardier, C. H. (2009b). Depression treatment preferences after traumatic brain injury. *Journal of Head Trauma Rehabilitation, 24*(4), 272–278.

Fann, J. R., Uomoto, J. M., and Katon, W. J. (2000). Sertraline in the treatment of major depression following mild traumatic brain injury. *Journal of Neuropsychiatry and Clinical Neurosciences, 12*(2), 226–232.

Farkas, O. (2007). Cellular and subcellular change evoked by diffuse traumatic brain injury: a complex web of change extending far beyond focal damage. *Neurotrauma, 161*, 43–59.

Farmer, M. Y., Singer, H. S., Mellits, E. D., Hall, D., and Charney, E. (1987). Neurobehavioural sequelae of minor head injuries in children. *Paediatric Neuroscience, 13*, 304–308.

Fasotti, L., Kovacs, F., Eling, P. A. T. M., and Brouwer, W. H. (2000). Time pressure management as a compensatory strategy training after closed head injury. *Neuropsychological Rehabilitation, 10*, 47–65.

Fay, G. C., Jaffe, K. M., Polissar, N. L., Liao, S., Martin, K. M., Shurtleff, H. A. et al. (1993). Mild paediatric traumatic brain injury: A cohort study. *Archives of Physical Medicine and Rehabilitation, 74*, 895–901.

Fay, T. B., Yeates, K. O., Taylor, H. G., Bangert, B., Dietrich, A., Nuss, K. E. et al. (2010). Cognitive reserve as a moderator of postconcussive symptoms in children with complicated and uncomplicated mild traumatic brain injury. *Journal of the International Neuropsychological Society, 16*(1), 94–105.

Fedoroff, J. P., Starkstein, S. E., Forrester, A. W., Geisler, F. H., Jorge, R. E., Arndt, S. V. et al. (1992). Depression in patients with acute traumatic brain injury. *The American Journal of Psychiatry, 149*, 918.

Feeney, D. M., Gonzalez, A., and Law, W. A. (1982). Amphetamine, haloperidol, and experience interact to affect rate of recovery after motor cortex injury. *Science, 217*, 855–857.

Feeney, D. M., and Sutton, R. L. (1987). Pharmacotherapy for recovery of function after brain injury. *Critical Reviews in Neurobiology, 3*, 135–197.

Feeney, T. J., and Ylvisaker, M. (1995). Choice and routine: antecedent behavioral interventions for adolescents with severe traumatic brain injury. *Journal of Head Trauma Rehabilitation, 10*, 67–86.

Feeney, T. J., Ylvisaker, M., Rosen, B. M., and Greene, P. (2001). Community supports for individuals with challenging behaviors after brain injury: An analysis of the New

York State Behavioral Resource Project. *Journal of Head Trauma Rehabilitation, 16*(1), 61–75.

Felmingham, K. L., Baguley, I. J., and Crooks, J. (2001). A comparison of acute and post discharge predictors of employment 2 years after traumatic brain injury. *Archives of Physical Medical Rehabilitation, 82*, 435–439.

Fernando, K., Eaton, L., Faulkner, M., Moodley, Y., and Setchell, R. (2002). Development and piloting of the Starship Post-Traumatic Amnesia Scale for children aged between four and six years. *Brain Impairment, 3*, 34–41.

Finger, S., and Stein, D. G. (1982). *Brain damage and recovery*. New York: Academic Press.

First, M. B., Spitzer, R. L., Gibbon, M., and Williams, J. B. W. (2002). *Structured Clinical Interview for DSM-IV-TR Axis I Disorders, Research Version, Non-patient Edition. (SCID-I/NP)*. New York: Biometrics Research, New York State Psychiatric Institute.

Fish, J., Manly, T., and Wilson, B. A. (2008). Long-term compensatory treatment of organizational deficits in a patient with bilateral frontal lobe damage. *Journal of the International Neuropsychological Society, 14*, 154–163.

Fisher, A. G. (1999). *Assessment of motor and process skills* (3rd ed.). Fort Collins, CO: Three Star Press.

Fisher, A. G. (2001). *Assessment of Motor and Process Skills. Volume 1: Development, standardisation and administration manual* (5th ed.). Fort Collins, CO: Three Star Press.

Fitness, J. (2008, 15th August). *The art of friendship and intimacy.* Paper presented at the Eighth Annual Workshop of the Victorian Brain Injury Recovery Assoc. Inc., Melbourne.

Fleming, J., Kennedy, S., Fisher, R., Gill, H., Gullo, M., and Shum, D. (2009). Validity of the Comprehensive Assessment of Prospective Memory (CAPM) for use with adults with traumatic brain injury. *Brain Impairment, 10*(1), 34–44.

Fleming, J., and Ownsworth, T. (2006). A review of awareness interventions in brain injury rehabilitation. *Neuropsychological Rehabilitation, 16*, 474–500.

Fleming, J., Riley, L., Gill, H., Gullo, M. J., Strong, J., and Shum, D. (2008). Predictors of prospective memory in adults with traumatic brain injury. *Journal of the International Neuropsychological Society, 14*(5), 823–831.

Fleming, J., and Strong, J. (1999). A longitudinal study of self-awareness: Functional deficits underestimated by persons with brain injury. *Occupational Therapy Journal of Research, 19*(1), 3–17.

Fleming, J., Tooth, L., Hassell, M., and Chan, W. (1999). Prediction of community integration and vocational outcome 2–5 years after traumatic brain injury rehabilitation in Australia. *Brain Injury, 13*(6), 417–431.

Fleminger, S., Greenwood, R., and Oliver, D. L. (2006). Pharmacological management for agitation and aggression in people with acquired brain injury. *Cochrane Database Systematic Review, 18*(4), CD003299.

Fletcher, J. M., Ewing-Cobbs, L., Miner, M. E., Levin, H. S., and Eisenberg, H. M. (1990). Behavioral changes after closed head injury in children. *Journal of Consulting and Clinical Psychology, 58*, 93–98.

Fletcher, J. M., Levin, H. S., Lachar, D., Kusnerik, L., Harward, H., Mendelsohn, D. et al. (1996). Behavioral outcomes after pediatric closed head injury: relationships with age, severity, and lesion size. *Journal of Child Neurology, 11*(4), 283–290.

Ford, J. A., and Milosky, L. M. (2008). Inferring emotional reactions in social situations. Differences in children with language impairment. *Journal of Speech, Language and Hearing Research, 46*, 21–30.

Formisano, R. F., Bivona, U., Brunelli, S., Giustini, M., Longo, E., and Taggi, F. (2005). A preliminary investigation of road traffic accident rate after severe brain injury. *Brain Injury, 19*(3), 159–163.

Forrester, G., Encel, J. C., and Geffen, G. (1994). Measuring post-traumatic amnesia (PTA): an historical review. *Brain Injury, 8*, 175–184.

Forsyth, R. J. (2010). Back to the future: rehabilitation of children after brain injury. *Archives of Disease in Childhood, 95*(7), 554–559.

Fortuny, L. A., Briggs, M., Newcombe, F., Ratcliff, G., and Thomas, C. (1980). Measuring the duration of post-traumatic amnesia. *Journal of Neurology, Neurosurgery, and Psychiatry, 43*, 377–379.

Fougeyrollas, P., Noreau, L., Bergeron, H., Cloutier, R., Dion, S-A., and St-Michel, G. (1998). Social consequences of long term impairments and disabilities: Conceptual approach and assessment of handicap. *International Journal of Rehabilitation Research, 21,* 127–141.

Fougeyrollas, P., Noreau, L., and St-Michel, G. (1997). The Measure of the Quality of Environment. *ICIDH and Environmental Factors International Network, 9,* 32–39.

Fox, G. M., Bashford, G., M., and Caust, S. L. (1992). Identifying safe versus unsafe drivers following brain impairment: the Coorabel Programme. *Disability and Rehabilitation, 14*, 140–145.

Fox, R. M., Martella, R. C., and Marchand-Martella, N. E. (1989). The acquisition, maintenance and generalization of problem-solving skills by closed head injured adults. *Behavioural Therapy, 20*, 61–76.

Frattali, C. M., Thompson, C. M., Holland, A. L., Wohl, C. B., and Ferketic, M. M. (1995). The FACS of life ASHA FACS – a functional outcome measure for adults. *ASHA, 37*(4), 40–46.

Frey, K. L., Rojas, D. C., Anderson, C. A., and Arciniegas, D. B. (2007). Comparison of the O-Log and GOAT as measures of posttraumatic amnesia. *Brain Injury, 21*(5), 513–520.

Fryer, J. (1989). Adolescent community integration. In P. Bach-y-Rita (Ed.), *Traumatic brain injury* (pp. 255–286). New York: Demos Publications.

Fryer, L. J., and Haffey, W. J. (1987). Cognitive rehabilitation and community readaptation: Outcomes from two program models. *Journal of Head Trauma Rehabilitation, 2*(3), 51–63.

Fugate, L., Spacek, L. A., Kresty, L. A., Levy, C. E., Johnson, J. C., and Mysiw, J. W. (1997). Measurement and treatment of agitation following traumatic brain injury: II. A survey of the brain injury special interest group of the American Academy of Physical Medicine and Rehabilitation. *Archives of Physical Medicine and Rehabilitation, 78*, 924–928.

Gaetz, M. (2004). The neurophysiology of brain injury. *Clinical Neurophysiology, 115*, 4–18.

Gan, C., Campbell, K. A., Gemeinhardt, M., and McFadden, G. T. (2006). Predictors of family functioning after brain injury. *Brain Injury, 20*(6), 587–600.

Gan, C., Gargaro, J., Kreutzer, J. S., Boschen, K. A., and Wright, F. V. (2010). Development and preliminary evaluation of a structured family system intervention for adolescents with brain injury and their families. *Brain Injury, 24*(4), 651–663.

Ganes, T., and Lundar, T. (1988). EEG and evoked potentials in comatose patients with severe brain damage. *Electroencephalography and Clinical Neurophysiology, 69*, 6–13.

Ganesalingam, K., Yeates, K. O., Sanson, A., and Anderson, V. (2007). Social problem-solving skills following childhood traumatic brain injury and its association with self-regulation and social and behavioural functioning. *Journal of Neuropsychology, 1*(Pt 2), 149–170.

Gansler, D. A., and McCaffrey, R. J. (1991). Remediation of chronic attention deficits in traumatically brain injured patients. *Archives of Clinical Neuropsychology, 6*, 335–353.

Gazzaniga, M. S. (1978). Is seeing believing: notes on clinical recovery. In S. Finger (Ed.), *Recovery from brain damage* (pp. 410–414). New York: Plenum Press.

Gennarelli, T. A., and Graham, D. I. (2005). Neuropathology. In J. M. Silver, T. W. McAllister and S. C. Yudofsky (Eds.), *Textbook of traumatic brain injury* (pp. 27–50). Arlington, VA: American Psychiatric Publishing.

Gentile, A. M., Green, S., Nieburgs, A., Schmelzer, W., and Stein, D. G. (1978). Disruption and recovery of locomotor and manipulatory behaviour following cortical lesions in rats. *Behavioural Biology, 22*, 417–455.

Gentry, T., Wallace, J., Kvarfordt, C., and Lynch, K. (2008). Personal digital assistants as cognitive aids for individuals with severe traumatic brain injury: A community-based trial. *Brain Injury, 22*(1), 19–24.

Geracioti, T. D. (1994). Valproic acid treatment of episodic explosiveness related to brain injury. *Journal of Clinical Psychiatry, 55*(9), 416–417.

Gerrard-Morris, A., Taylor, H. G., Yeates, K. O., Walz, N. C., Stancin, T., Minich, N. et al. (2010). Cognitive development after traumatic brain injury in young children. *Journal of the International Neuropsychological Society, 16*(1), 157–168.

Gervasio, A. H., and Kreutzer, J. S. (1997). Kinship and family members' psychological distress after traumatic brain injury: A large sample study. *Journal of Head Trauma Rehabilitation, 12*(3), 14–26.

Geurtsen, G. J., Martina, J. D., Van Heugten, C. M., and Geurts, A. C. (2008). A prospective study to evaluate a new residential community reintegration programme for severe chronic brain injury: The Brain Integration Programme. *Brain Injury, 22*(7–8), 543–554.

Ghaffar, O., McCullagh, S., Ouchterlony, D., and Feinstein, A. (2006). Randomized treatment trial in mild traumatic brain injury. *Journal of Psychosomatic Research, 61*(2), 153–160.

Giacino, J. T., Ashwal, S., Childs, N., Cranford, R., Jennett, B., Katz, D. I. et al. (2002). The minimally conscious state: Definition and diagnostic criteria. *Neurology, 58*(3), 349–352.

Giacino, J. T., and Cicerone, K. D. (2000). Varieties of deficit unawareness after brain injury. *Journal of Head Trauma Rehabilitation, 13*(5), 1–15.

Giacino, J. T., Hirsch, J., Schiff, N., and Laureys, S. (2006). Functional neuroimaging applications for assessment and rehabilitation planning in patients with disorders of consciousness. *Archives of Physical Medicine and Rehabilitation, 87*(12, Suppl), 67–76.

Giacino, J. T., Kalmar, K., and Whyte, J. (2004). The JFK Coma Recovery Scale-Revised: Measurement characteristics and diagnostic utility. *Archives of Physical Medicine and Rehabilitation, 85*(12), 2020–2029.

Giacino, J. T., Kezmarsky, M. A., DeLuca, J., and Cicerone, K. D. (1991). Monitoring rate of recovery to predict outcome in minimally responsive patients. *Archives of Physical Medicine and Rehabilitation, 72*, 897–901.

Giacino, J. T., and Whyte, J. (2005). The vegetative and minimally conscious states: Current knowledge and remaining questions. *Journal of Head Trauma Rehabilitation, 20*(1), 30–50.

Giacino, J. T., Zasler, N. D., Katz, D. I., Kelly, J. P., Rosenberg, J. H., and Filley, C. M. (1997). Development of practice guidelines for assessment and management of the vegetative and minimally conscious states. *Journal of Head Trauma Rehabilitation, 12*(4), 79–89.

Giles, G. M., and Manchester, D. (2006). Two approaches to behavior disorder after traumatic brain injury. *Journal of Head Trauma Rehabilitation, 21*(2), 168–178.

Gill-Thwaites, H., and Munday, R. (1999). The Sensory Modality Assessment and Rehabilitation Technique (SMART): A Comprehensive and integrated assessment and treatment protocol for the vegetative state and minimally responsive patient. *Neuropsychological Rehabilitation, 9*(3–4), 305–320.

Gill-Thwaites, H., and Munday, R. (2004). The Sensory Modality Assessment and Rehabilitation Technique (SMART): A valid and reliable assessment for vegetative state and minimally conscious state patients. *Brain Injury, 18*(12), 1255–1269.

Giza, C. C., and Hovda, D. (2004). Pathophysiology of traumatic brain injury. In M. Lovell, R. J. Echemendia, J. T. Barth and M. W. Collins (Eds.), *Traumatic brain injury in sports: An international and neuropsychological perspective* (pp. 45–70). Lisse, The Netherlands: Swets and Zeitlinger.

Glang, A., McGlaughlin, K., and Schroeder, S. (2007). Using interactive multimedia to teach parent advocacy skills: An exploratory study. *Journal of Head Trauma Rehabilitation, 22*(3), 198–205.

Glasgow, R. E., Zeiss, R. A., Barrera, M., and Lewinsohn, P. M. (1977). Case studies on remediating memory deficits in brain damaged individuals. *Journal of Clinical Psychology, 33*, 1049–1054.

Glisky, E. L. (2004). Disorders of Memory. In J. Ponsford (Ed.), *Cognitive and behavioral rehabilitation: From neurobiology to clinical practice* (pp. 100–128). New York: Guilford Press.

Golan, J. D., Marcoux, J., Golan, E., Schapiro, R., Johnston, K. M., and Maleki, M. et al. (2007). Traumatic brain injury in intoxicated patients. *The Journal of Trauma: Injury, Infection, and Critical Care, 63*(2), 365–369.

Goldblum, G., and Alant, E. (2008). Sales assistants serving customers with traumatic brain injury. *Brain Injury, 23*(1), 87–109.

Goldman, P. S. (1971). Functional development of the prefrontal cortex in early life and the problem of neuronal plasticity. *Experimental Neurology, 32*, 366–387.

Goldman, P. S. (1974). An alternative to developmental plasticity: Heterogeneity of C.N.S. structures in infants and adults. In D.G. Stein, J.J. Rosen and N. Butters (Eds.), *Plasticity and recovery of function in the central nervous system* (pp. 149–174). New York: Academic Press.

Goldstein, K. (1942). *After-effects of brain injuries in war: Their evaluation and treatment*. New York: Grune and Stratton.

Goldstein, L. B. (2000). Effects of amphetamines and small related molecules on recovery after stroke in animals and man. *Neuropharmacology, 39*, 852–859.

Gollaher, K., High, W., Sherer, M., Bergloff, P., Boake, C., Young, M. E. et al. (1998). Prediction of employment outcome one to three years following traumatic brain injury. *Brain Injury, 12*(4), 255–263.

Gomez-Hernandez, R., Max, J. E., Kosier, T., Paradiso, S., and Robinson, R. G. (1997). Social impairment and depression after traumatic brain injury. *Archives of Physical Medicine and Rehabilitation, 78*, 1321–1326.

Goodglass, H., Kaplan, E., and Barresi, B. (2000). *Boston diagnostic aphasia examination* (3rd ed.). Philadelphia: Lippincott Williams and Wilkins.

Goodinson, R., Ponsford, J., Johnston, L., and Grant, F. (2009). Psychiatric disorders following traumatic brain injury: Their nature and frequency. *Journal of Head Trauma Rehabilitation, 24*(5), 324–332.

Gouick, J., and Gentleman, D. (2004). The emotional and behavioural consequences of traumatic brain injury. *Trauma, 5*, 285–292.

Gould, K. R., Ponsford, J., Johnston, L., and Schönberger, M. (2011a). The relationship between psychiatric disorders and one-year psychosocial outcome. *Journal of Head Trauma Rehabilitation, 26*(1), 79–89.

Gould, K. R., Ponsford, J. L., Johnston, J., and Schönberger, M. (2011b). Predictive and associated factors of psychiatric disorders after traumatic brain injury: A prospective study. *Journal of Neurotrauma, 28*(7),1149–1154.

Gould, K. R., Ponsford, J. L., Johnston, L., and Schönberger, M. (2011c). The nature, frequency and course of psychiatric disorders in the first year after traumatic brain injury, a prospective study. *Psychological Medicine, 41*(10), 2099–2109.

Gouvier, W. D., Cubic, B., Jones, G., Brantley, P., and Cutlip, Q. (1992). Postconcussion symptoms and daily stress in normal and head-injured college populations. *Archives of Clinical Neuropsychology, 7*, 193–211.

Grace, J., and Malloy, P.F. (2001). *Frontal Systems Behavior Scale (FrSBe): Professional Manual*. Lutz, FL: Psychological Assessment Resources.

Gracey, F., Palmer, S., Rous, B., Psaila, K., Shaw, K., O'Dell, J. et al. (2008). "Feeling part of things": Personal construction of self after brain injury. *Neuropsychological Rehabilitation, 18*(5/6), 627–650.

Grados, M. A., Slomine, B. S., Gerring, J. P., Vasa, R., Bryan, N., and Denckla, M. B. (2001). Depth of lesion model in children and adolescents with moderate to severe traumatic brain injury: use of SPGR MRI to predict severity and outcome. *Journal of Neurology, Neurosurgery and Psychiatry, 70*(3), 350–358.

Graham, D. I. (1999). Pathophysiological aspects of injury and mechanisms of recovery. In M. Rosenthal, E. A. Griffith, J. S. Kreutzer and B. Pentland (Eds.), *Rehabilitation of the adult and child with traumtic brain injury* (pp. 19–41). Philadelphia: F.A. Davis and Company.

Graham, D. I., Adams, J. H., Murray, L. S., and Jennett, B. (2005). Neuropathology of the vegetative state after head injury. *Neuropsychological Rehabilitation, 15*(3–4), 198–213.

Granger, C. V., Hamilton, B. B., Keith, R. A., Zielezny, M., and Sherwin, F. S. (1986). Advances in functional assessment for medical rehabilitation. *Topics in Geriatric Rehabilitation, 1*, 59–74.

Grant, M. K. (2008). *The rehabilitation of executive deficits following traumatic brain injury* (Doctoral Dissertation). Melbourne: Monash University.

Gray, J. M., Robertson, I. H., Pentland, B., and Anderson, S. J. (1992). Microcomputer based cognitive rehabilitation for brain damage. A randomized group controlled trial. *Neuropsychological Rehabilitation, 2*, 97–116.

Green, P., and Astner, K. (1995). *Manual: Word Memory Test (Research Form I) Oral Administration*. Durham, NC: CogniSyst.

Greenwood, R. (1997). Value of recording duration of post-traumatic amnesia. *Lancet, 349*(9058), 1041–1042.

Grice, H. P. (1975). Logic in conversation. In P. Cole and J. Morgan (Eds.), *Studies in syntax and semantics* (Vol. 3, pp. 41–58). New York: Academic Press.

Grice, H. P. (1998). Logic and conversation. In A. Kasher (Ed.), *Pragmatics. Critical concepts* (pp. 145–161). London: Routledge.

Grimes, G., Dubois, H., Grimes, S. J., Greenleaf, W. J., Rothenburg, S., and Cunningham, D. (2000). Telerehabilitation services using web-based telecommunication. *Study of Health Technology Information, 70*, 113–118.

Gronwall, D. M., and Sampson, H. (1974). *The psychological effects of concussion*. Auckland: Auckland University Press/Oxford University Press.

Gronwall, D. M., and Wrightson, P. (1980). Duration of post-traumatic amnesia after mild head injury. *Journal of Clinical Neuropsychology, 2*, 51–60.

Groswasser, Z., Mendelson, L., Stern, M., Schecter, I., and Najenson, T. (1977). Re-evaluation of prognostic factors in rehabilitation after severe head injury. *Scandinavian Journal of Rehabilitation Medicine, 9*, 147–149.

Haffey, W. J., and Abrams, D. L. (1991). Employment outcomes for participants in a brain injury work reentry program: Preliminary findings. *Journal of Head Trauma Rehabilitation, 6*(3), 24–34.

Haffey, W. J., and Johnston, M. V. (1990). A functional assessment system for real-world rehabilitation outcomes. In D. E. Tupper and K. D. Cicerone (Eds.), *The neuropsychology of everyday life: Assessment and basic competencies* (pp. 99–123). Boston, MA: Kluwer Academic Publishers.

Hagan, C. (1998). *The Rancho levels of cognitive functioning*. Downey, CA: Rancho Los Amigos Medical Center.

Hahn, Y. S., Chyng, C., Barthel, M. J., Bailes, J., Flannery, A. M., and McLone, D. G. (1988). Head injuries in children under 36 months of age. Demography and outcome. *Child's Nervous System, 4*, 34–40.

Hall, D. E., and DePompei, R. (1986). Implications for the head injured reentering higher education. *Cognitive Rehabilitation, May/June*, 6–8.

Hall, K. M., Bushnik, T., Lakisic-Kazazic, B., Wright, J., and Cantagallo, A. (2001). Assessing traumatic brain injury outcome measures for long-term follow-up of community-based individuals. *Archives of Physical Medicine and Rehabilitation, 82*(3), 367–374.

Hall, K., Cope, D. N., and Rappaport, M. (1985). Glasgow Outcome Scale and Disability Rating Scale: Comparative usefulness in following recovery in traumatic head injury. *Archives of Physical Medicine and Rehabilitation, 66*, 3, 35–37.

Hall, K. M., Karsmark, P., Stevens, M., Englander, J., O'Hare, P., and Wright, J. (1994). Family stressors in traumatic brain injury: A two-year follow-up. *Archives of Physical Medicine and Rehabilitation, 75*, 876–884.

Hallett, D. J., Zasler, N. D., Maurer, P., and Cash, S. (1994). Role change after traumatic brain injury in adults. *American Journal of Occupational Therapy, 48*(3), 241–246.

Haltiner, A., Temkin, N., and Dikmen, S. (1997). Risk of seizure recurrence after the first late posttraumatic seizure. *Archives of Physical Medicine and Rehabilitation, 78*(835–840).

Hanks, R. A., Rapport, L. J., and Vangel, S. (2007). Caregiving appraisal after traumatic brain injury: The effects of functional status, coping style, social support and family functioning. *NeuroRehabilitation, 22*(1), 43–52.

Hanten, G., Dennis, M., Zhang, L., Barnes, M., Roberson, G., Archibald, J. et al. (2004). Childhood head injury and metacognitive processes in language and memory. *Developmental Neuropsychology, 25*(1–2), 85–106.

Hanten, G., Wilde, E. A., Menefee, D. S., Li, X., Lane, S., Vasquez, C. et al. (2008). Correlates of social problem solving during the first year after traumatic brain injury in children. *Neuropsychology, 22*(3), 357–370.

Harrick, L., Krefting, L., Johnston, J., Carlson, P., and Minnes, P. (1994). Stability of functional outcomes following transitional living programme participation: 3-year follow-up. *Brain Injury, 8*, 439–447.

Harrington, H. (2007a). The family's positive experience: After a member sustains a traumatic brain injury – What makes the difference. Paper presented at the 30th Annual Brain Impairment Conference, Brisbane, Australia.

Harrington, H. (2007b, May). The siblings' experience when their brother or sister sustains a traumatic brain injury. Paper presented at the 30th Annual Brain Impairment Conference, Brisbane, Australia.

Harris, J. K., Godfrey, H. P., Partridge, F. M., and Knight, R. G. (2001). Caregiver depression following traumatic brain injury (TBI): a consequence of adverse effects on family members? *Brain Injury, 15*(3), 223–238.

Hart, T., Buchhofer, R., and Vaccaro, M. (2004a). Portable electronic devices as memory and organizational aids after traumatic brain injury: a consumer survey study. *Journal of Head Trauma Rehabilitation, 19*(5), 351–365.

Hart, T., Dijkers, M., Fraser, R., Cicerone, K., Bogner, J. A., Whyte, J. et al. (2006). Vocational services for traumatic brain injury: treatment definition and diversity within model systems of care. *Journal of Head Trauma Rehabilitation, 21*(6 Nov–Dec), 467–482.

Hart, T., Hawkey, K., and Whyte, J. (2002). Use of a portable voice organizer to remember therapy goals in traumatic brain injury rehabilitation: A within-subjects trial. *Journal of Head Trauma Rehabilitation, 17*(6), 556–570.

Hart, T., O'Neil-Pirozzi, T., and Morita, C. (2003). Clinician expectations for portable electronic devices as cognitive-behavioural orthoses in traumatic brain injury rehabilitation. *Brain Injury, 17*(5), 401–411.

Hart, T., Seignourel, P. J., and Sherer, M. (2009). A longitudinal study of awareness of deficit after moderate to severe traumatic brain injury. *Neuropsychological Rehabilitation, 19*(2), 161–176.

Hart, T., Sherer, M., Whyte, J., Polansky, M., and Novack, T. A. (2004b). Awareness of behavioural, cognitive, and physical deficits in acute traumatic brain injury. *Archives of Physical Medicine and Rehabilitation, 85*, 1450–1456.

Hart, T, Whyte J, Ellis C, Chervoneva I. (2009). Construct validity of an attention rating scale for traumatic brain injury. *Neuropsychology*, 23, 729–735.

Hart, T, Whyte J, Millis S, Bode R, Malec J, Richardson RN, and Hammond F. (2006). Dimensions of disordered attention in traumatic brain injury: Further validations of the Moss Attention Rating Scale. *Archives of Physical Medicine and Rehabilitation*, 87, 647–55.

Hartley, L. L., and Jensen, P. J. (1991). Narrative and procedural discourse after closed head injury. *Brain Injury, 5*, 267–285.

Hawley, C. A. (2004). Behaviour and school performance after brain injury. *Brain Injury, 18*(7), 645–659.

Healey, C., Osler, T. M., Rogers, F. B., Healey, M. A., Glance, L. G., Kilgo, P. D. et al. (2003). Improving the Glasgow Coma Scale score: Motor score alone is a better predictor. *The Journal of Trauma: Injury, Infection, and Critical Care, 54*(4), 671–680.

Heaton, R. (1981). *Wisconsin Card Sorting Test Manual*. Odessa, FL: Psychological Assessment Resources, Inc.

Hegel, M. T., and Ferguson, R. J. (2000). Differential reinforcement of other behavior (DRO) to reduce aggressive behavior following traumatic brain injury. *Behavior Modification, 24*(1), 91–101.

Heilbronner, R. L., Roueche, J. R., Everson, S. A., and Epler, L. (1989). Comparing patient perspectives of disability and treatment effects with quality of participation in a post-acute brain injury rehabilitation programme. *Brain Injury, 3*(4), 387–395.

Heinemann, A. W., Corrigan, J. D., and Moore, D. (2004). Case management for traumatic brain injury survivors with alcohol problems. *Rehabilitation Psychology, 49*(2), 156–166.

Helffenstein, D. A., and Wechsler, F. S. (1982). The use of Interpersonal Process Recall (I.P.R.) in the remediation of interpersonal and communication skill deficits in the newly brain-injured. *Clinical Neuropsychology, 4*, 139–143.

Hersh, N., and Treadgold, L. (1994). NeuroPage: The rehabilitation of memory dysfunction by prosthetic memory and cueing. *NeuroRehabilitation, 4*, 187–197.

Hessen, E. L. M., Reinvang, I., and Gjerstad, L. I. (2007). Influence of major antiepileptic drugs on neuropsychological function: Results from a randomized, double-blind, placebo-controlled withdrawal study of seizure-free epilepsy patients on monotherapy. *Journal of the International Neuropsychological Society, 13*, 393–400.

Hibbard, M. R., Uysal, S., Kepler, K., Bogdany, J., and Silver, J. (1998). Axis I psychopathology in individuals with traumatic brain injury. *The Journal of Head Trauma Rehabilitation, 13*, 24–39.

High, W. M. J., Roebuck-Spencer, T., Sander, A. M., Struchen, M. A., and Sherer, M. (2006). Early versus later admission to postacute rehabilitation: impact on functional outcome after traumatic brain injury. *Archives of Physical Medicine and Rehabilitation, 87*(3), 334–342.

Hiott, D., and Labbate, L. A. (2002). Anxiety disorders associated with traumatic brain injuries. *NeuroRehabilitation, 17*(4), 345–355.

Hodgson, J., McDonald, S., Tate, R., and Gertler, P. (2005). A randomised controlled trial of a cognitive behavioural therapy program for managing social anxiety after acquired brain injury. *Brain Impairment, 6*, 169–180.

Hoffman, A. N., Cheng, J. P., Zafonte, R. D., and Kline, A. E. (2008). Administration of haloperidol and risperidone after neurobehavioral testing hinders the recovery of traumatic brain injury-induced deficits. *Life Sciences, 83*(17–18), 602–607.

Hoge, C. W., McGurk, D., Thomas, J. L., Cox, A. L., Engel, C. C., and Castro, C. A. (2008). Mild traumatic brain injury in US soldiers returning from Iraq. *New England Journal of Medicine, 358*(5), 453–463.

Holland, A. L. (1982). Observing functional communication of aphasic patients. *Journal of Speech and Hearing Disorders, 47*, 50–56.

Hoofien, D., Gilboa, A., Vakil, E., and Barak, O. (2004). Unawareness of cognitive deficits and daily functioning among persons with traumatic brain injuries. *Journal of Clinical and Experimental Neuropsychology, 26*, 278–290.

Hoofien, D., Gilboa, A., Vakil, E., and Donovick, P. J. (2001). Traumatic brain injury 10–20 years later: A comprehensive outcome study of psychiatric symptomatology, cognitive abilities, and psychosocial functioning. *Brain Injury, 15*, 189–209.

Hooper, H. E. (1958). *The Hooper Visual Organisation Test Manual.* Beverly Hills, CA: Western Psychological Services.

Hopewell, C. A., and Price, R. J. (1985). Driving after head injury. *Journal of Clinical and Experimental Neuropsychology, 7*, 148.

Horn, L. J., and Zasler, N. D. (1990). Neuroanatomy and neurophysiology of sexual function. *Journal of Head Trauma Rehabilitation, 5*(2), 1–13.

Horn, S., Shiel, A., McLellan, L., Campbell, M., Watson, M., and Wilson, B. (1993). A review of behavioural assessment scales for monitoring recovery in and after coma with pilot data on a new scale of visual awareness. *Neuropsychological Rehabilitation, 3*, 121–137.

Horne, M., and Lindley, S. E. (1995). Divalproex sodium in the treatment of aggressive behaviour and dysphoria in patients with organic brain syndrome. *Journal of Clinical Psychiatry, 56*(9), 430–431.

Horneman, G., and Emanuelson, I. (2009). Cognitive outcome in children and young adults who sustained severe and moderate traumatic brain injury 10 years earlier. *Brain Injury, 23*(11), 907–914.

Huisman, T. A., Schwamm, L. H., Schaefer, P. W., Koroshetz, W. J., Shetty-Alva, N., Ozsunar, Y. et al. (2004). Diffusion tensor imaging as potential biomarker of white matter injury in diffuse axonal injury. *American Journal of Neuroradiology, 25*(3), 370–376.

Huisman, T. A., Sorensen, A. G., Hergan, K., Gonzalez, R. G., and Schaefer, P. W. (2003). Diffusion-weighted imaging for the evaluation of diffuse axonal injury in closed head injury. *Journal of Computer Assisted Tomography, 27*(1), 5–11.

Iverson, G. L., Iverson, A. M., and Barton, E. A. (1994). The Children's Orientation and Amnesia Test: Educational status is a moderator variable in tracking recovery from TBI. *Brain Injury, 8*, 685–688.

Jackson, H. F., and Manchester, D. (2001). Towards the Development of Brain Injury Specialists. *Neurorehabilitation, 16*, 27–40.

Jackson, H. F., and Moffat, N. J. (1987). Impaired emotional recognition following severe head injury. *Cortex, 23*(2), 293–300.

Jackson, W. T., Novack, T. A., and Dowler, R. N. (1998). Effective serial measurement of cognitive orientation in rehabilitation: The orientation log. *Archives of Physical Medicine and Rehabilitation, 79*(6), 718–721.

Jacobs, B., and Scheibel, A. B. (1993). A quantitative dendritic analysis of Wernicke's area in humans. *Journal of Comparative Neurology, 32*, 83–96.

Jacobs, H. E. (1988). The Los Angeles Head Injury Survey: Procedures and preliminary findings. *Archives of Physical Medicine and Rehabilitation, 69*, 425–431.

Jaffe, K. M., Fay, G. C., Polissar, N. L., Martin, K. M., Shurtleff, H. A., Rivara, J. B. et al. (1992). Severity of paediatric traumatic brain injury and early neurobehavioral outcome: a cohort study. *Archives of Physical Medicine and Rehabilitation, 73*, 540–547.

Jaffe, K. M., Fay, G. C., Polissar, N. L., Martin, K. M., Shurtleff, H. A., Rivara, J. B. et al. (1993). Severity of paediatric traumatic brain injury and neurobehavioral recovery at one year – a cohort study. *Archives of Physical Medicine and Rehabilitation, 74*, 587–595.

Jennett, B. (1972). Head injuries in children. *Developmental Medicine and Child Neurology, 14*, 137–147.

Jennett, B. (1972). Some aspects of prognosis after severe head injury. *Scandinavian Journal of Rehabilitation Medicine, 4*, 16–20.

Jennett, B. (1976). Assessment of severity of head injury. *Journal of Neurology, Neurosurgery, and Psychiatry, 39*, 647–655.

Jennett, B. (1979). Posttraumatic epilepsy. *Advances in Neurology, 22*, 137–147.

Jennett, B. (2002). *The vegetative state: Medical facts, ethical and legal dilemmas*. New York: Cambridge University Press.

Jennett, B., and Bond, M. (1975). Assessment of outcome after severe brain damage. *Lancet, 1*, 480–487.

Jennett, B., and Plum, F. (1972). Persistent vegetative state after brain damage. A syndrome in search of a name. *Lancet, 1*, 734–737.

Jennett, B., and Teasdale, G. (1981). *Management of head injuries*. Philadelphia: Davis.

Johansson, B. B., and Belichenko, P. V. (2002). Neuronal plasticity and dendritic spines: Effect of environmental enrichment on intact and post-ischemic rat brain. *Journal of Cerebral Blood Flow and Metabolism, 22*, 89–96.

Johansson, U., and Tham, K. (2006). The meaning of work after acquired brain injury. *The American Journal of Occupational Therapy, 60*(1), 60–69.

Johnson, D., and Almli, C. R. (1978). Age, brain damage, and performance. In S. Finger (Ed.), *Recovery from brain damage* (pp. 115–134). New York: Plenum Press.

Johnson, R. (1987). Return to work after severe head injury. *Disability Studies, 9*, 49–54.

Johnston, M. V., and Lewis, F. D. (1991). Outcomes of community re-entry programmes for brain injury survivors. Part 1: Independent living and productive activities. *Brain Injury, 5*, 141–154.

Jordan, F., and Murdoch, B. (1990). A comparison of the conversational skills of closed head injured children and normal children. *Australian Journal of Human Communication Disorders, 18*(1), 69–82.

Jordan, F. M., Ozanne, A. E., and Murdoch, B. E. (1988). Long term speech and language disorders subsequent to closed head injury in children. *Brain Injury, 2*, 179–185.

Jordan, F. M., Ozanne, A. E., and Murdoch, B. E. (1990). Performance of closed head injured children on a naming task. *Brain Injury, 4*, 147–154.

Jorge, R. E., Acion, L., Starkstein, S. E., and Magnotta, V. (2007). Hippocampal Volume and Mood Disorders After Traumatic Brain Injury. *Biological Psychiatry, 62*, 332–338.

Jorge, R. E., Robinson, R. G., Arndt, S. V., Forrester, A. W., Geisler, F., and Starkstein, S. E. (1993). Comparison between acute- and delayed-onset depression following traumatic brain injury. *Journal of Neuropsychiatry and Clinical Neurosciences, 5*, 43–49.

Jorge, R. E., Robinson, R. G., Moser, D., Tateno, A., Crespo-Facorro, B., and Arndt, S. V. (2004). Major depression following traumatic brain injury. *Archives of General Psychiatry, 61*, 42–50.

Jorge, R. E., Starkstein, S. E., Arndt, S., Moser, D., and Crespo-Facorro, B. (2005). Alcohol misuse and mood disorders following traumatic brain injury. *Archives of General Psychiatry, 62*(7), 742–749.

Jorgensen, M., and Togher, L. (2009). Narrative after traumatic brain injury: A comparison of monologic and jointly-produced discourse. *Brain Injury, 23*(9), 727–740.

Josman, N., and Katz, N. (1991). A problem-solving version of the Allen Cognitive Level Test. *The American Journal of Occupational Therapy, 45*, 331–338.

Kane, N. (2008). Evoked potentials and the prognosis of comatose patients receiving intensive care. *Advances in Clinical Neurosciences and Rehabilitation, 8*(2), 14–15.

Kant, R., and Smith-Seemiller, L. (2002). Assessment and treatment of apathy syndrome following head injury. *NeuroRehabilitation, 17*(4), 325–331.

Kaplan, E., Goodglass, H., and Weintraub, S. (2001). *Boston Naming Test* (2nd ed.). Philadelphia: Lippincott, Williams and Wilkins.

Kaschel, R., Della Sala, S., Cantagallo, A., and Fahlbock, A. (2002). Imagery mnemonics for the rehabilitation of memory: a randomised group controlled trial. *Neuropsychological Rehabilitation, 12*, 127–153.

Katz, R. T., Golden, R. S., Butter, J., Tepper, D., Rothke, S., Holmes, J. et al. (1990). Driving safety after brain damage: Follow-up of twenty-two patients with matched controls. *Archives of Physical Medicine and Rehabilitation, 71*(February), 133–137.

Kay, T., Cavallo, M. M., Ezrachi, O., and Vavagiakis, P. (1995). The head injury family interview: a clinical and research tool. *Journal of Head Trauma Rehabilitation, 10*(2), 12–31.

Keith, R. A., Granger, C. V., Hamilton, B. B., and Sherwin, F. S. (1987). The functional independence measure: a new tool for rehabilitation. *Advances in Clinical Rehabilitation, 1*, 6–18.

Kelly, G., Brown, S., Todd, J., and Kremer, P. (2008). Challenging behaviour profiles of people with acquired brain injury living in community settings. *Brain Injury, 22*(6), 457–470.

Kelly, G., Todd, J., Simpson, G., Kremer, P., and Martin, C. (2006). The overt behaviour scale (OBS): A tool for measuring challenging behaviours following ABI in community settings. *Brain Injury, 20*(3), 307–319.

Kelly, G., and Winkler, D. (2007). Long-term accommodation and support for people with higher levels of challenging behaviour. *Brain Impairment, 8*(3), 262–275.

Kendall, E. (2003). Predicting vocational adjustment following traumatic brain injury: A test of a psychosocial theory. *Journal of Vocational Rehabilitation, 19*, 31–45.

Kennard, M. A. (1936). Age and other factors in motor recovery from precentral lesions in monkeys. *American Journal of Physiology, 115*, 138–146.

Kennard, M. A. (1938). Reorganization of motor function in the cerebral cortex of monkeys deprived of motor and pre-motor areas in infancy. *Journal of Neurophysiology, 1*, 477–496.

Kennard, M. A. (1940). Relation of age to motor impairment in man and in subhuman primates. *Archives of Neurology and Psychiatry, 44*, 377–397.

Kennedy, M., Krause, M., and Turkstra, L. (2008a). An electronic survey about college experiences after traumatic brain injury. *NeuroRehabilitation, 23*, 219–231.

Kennedy, M. R. T., Coelho, C., Turkstra, L., Ylvisaker, M., Sohlberg, M. M., Yorkston, K. et al. (2008b). Intervention for executive functions after traumatic brain injury: A systematic review, meta-analysis and clinical recommendations. *Neuropsychological Rehabilitation, 18*(3), 257–299.

Kewman, D. G., Seigerman, C., Kintner, H., Chu, S., Henson, D., and Reeder, C. (1985). Simulation training of psychomotor skills: Teaching the brain-damaged to drive. *Rehabilitation Psychology, 30*, 11–27.

Khan-Bourne, N., and Brown, R. G. (2003). Cognitive behavioural therapy for the treatment of depression in individuals with brain injury. *Neuropsychological Rehabilitation, 13*, 89–107.

Kim, H., Yoo, W. K., Ko, M. H., Park, C. H., Kim, S. T., and Na, D. L. (2009). Plasticity of the attentional network after brain injury and cognitive rehabilitation. *Neurorehabilitaiton and Neural Repair, 23*(5), 468–477.

King, G., Tucker, M. A., Baldwin, P., Larry, K., LaPorta, J., and Martens, L. (2002). A life needs model of pediatric service delivery: services to support community participation and quality of life for children and youth with disabilities. *Physical and Occupational Therapy in Pediatrics, 22*(2), 53–77.

King, N. S., Crawford, S., Wenden, F. J., Moss, N. E., Wade, D.T., and Caldwell, F. E. (1997). Measurement of PTA: how reliable is it? *Journal of Neurology, Neurosurgery and Psychiatry, 62*(1), 38–42.

Kinsella, A. (1999). Disabled populations and telerehabilitation – new approaches. *Caring, 18*(8), 20–22, 24, 26–27.

Kinsella, G., Ong, B., Murtagh, D., Prior, M., and Sawyer, M. (1999). The role of the family for behavioral outcome in children and adolescents following traumatic brain injury. *Journal of Consulting and Clinical Psychology, 67*(1), 116–123.

Kinsella, G., Prior, M., Sawyer, M., Murtagh, D., Eisenmajer, R., Anderson, V. et al. (1995). Neuropsychological deficit and academic performance in children and adolescents following traumatic brain injury. *Journal of Pediatric Psychology, 20* (6 Dec), 753–767.

Kinsella, G. J. (2010). Everyday memory for everyday tasks: Prospective memory as an outcome measure following TBI in older adults. *Brain Impairment, 11*(1), 37–41.

Kinsella, G. J., Prior, M., Sawyer, M., Ong, B., Murtagh, D., Eisenmajer, R. et al. (1997). Predictors and indicators of academic outcome in children 2 years following traumatic brain injury. *Journal of the International Neuropsychological Society, 3*(6), 608–616.

Kiresuk, T. J., and Sherman, R. E. (1968). Goal attainment scaling: A general method for evaluating comprehensive community mental health programs. *Community Mental Health Journal, 4*(6), 443–453.

Kirsh, N., Shenton, M., and Rowan, J. (2004). A generic "in-house" alphanumeric paging system for prospective activity impairments after traumatic brain injury. *Brain Injury, 18*, 725–734.

Kleim, J. A. (2008). Principles of experience-dependent neural plasticity: Implications for rehabilitation after brain damage. *Journal of Speech, Language and Hearing Research, 51*(February), 5225–5239.

Kleim, J. A., Barbay, S., Cooper, N. R., Hogg, T. M., Reidel, C. N., Remple, M. S. et al. (2002). Motor-learning dependent synaptogenesis is localized to functionally reorganized motor cortex. *Neurobiology of Learning and Memory, 77*, 63–77.

Kline, A. E., Hoffman, A. N., Cheng, J. P., Zafonte, R. D., and Massucci, J. L. (2008). Chronic administration of antipsychotics impede behavioral recovery after experimental traumatic brain injury. *Neuroscience Letters, 448*(3), 263–267.

Klonoff, H. (1971). Head injuries in children: Predisposing factors. *American Journal of Public Health, 61*, 2404–2417.

Klonoff, H., Low, M. D., and Clark, C. (1977). Head injuries in children: a prospective five-year follow-up. *Journal of Neurology, Neurosurgery, and Psychiatry, 40*, 1211–1219.

Klonoff, P. S., Lamb, D. G., and Henderson, S. W. (2000). Milieu-based neurorehabilitation in patients with traumatic brain injury: Outcome up to 11 years post discharge. *Archives of Physical Medicine and Rehabilitation, 81*(November), 1535–1537.

Knight, C., Alderman, N., Johnston, C., Green, S., Birkett-Swan, L., and Yorsten, G. (2008). The St Andrew's Sexual Behaviour Assessment (SASBA): Development of a standardised recording instrument for the measurement and assessment of challenging sexual behaviour in people with progressive and acquired neurological impairment. *Neuropsychological Rehabilitation, 18*(2), 129–159.

Knights, R. M., Ivan, L. P., Ventureyra, E. C. G., Bentivoglio, C., Stoddart, C., Winogron, W. et al. (1991). The effects of head injury in children on neuropsychological and behavioural functioning. *Brain Injury, 5*, 339–351.

Kobylarz, E. J., and Schiff, N. D. (2005). Neurophysiological correlates of persistent vegetative and minimally conscious states. *Neuropsychological Rehabilitation, 15*(3/4), 323–332.

Kolb, B. (2004). Mechanisms of cortical plasticity. In J. Ponsford (Ed.), *Cognitive and behavioral rehabilitation: From neurobiology to clinical practice* (pp. 30–58). New York: Guilford Press.

Kolb, B., and Cioe, J. (2004). Neuronal organisation and change after neuronal injury. In J. Ponsford (Ed.), *Cognitive and behavioural rehabilitation: From neurobiology to clinical practice* (pp. 7–29). New York: Guilford Press.

Kolb, B., Teskey, G. C., and Gibb, R. (2010). Factors influencing cerebral plasticity in the normal and injured brain. *Frontiers in Human Neuroscience, 4*(November), Article 204.

Koponen, S., Taiminen, T., Kurki, T., Portin, R., Isoniemi, H., Himanen, L. et al. (2006). MRI findings and Axis I and II psychiatric disorders after traumatic brain injury: a 30-year retrospective follow-up study. *Psychiatry Research, 146*(3), 263–270.

Koponen, S., Taiminen, T., Portin, R., Himanen, L., Isoniemi, H., Heinonen, H. et al. (2002). Axis I and II Psychiatric disorders after traumatic brain injury: A 30-year follow-up study. *American Journal of Psychiatry, 159*, 1315–1321.

Kosciulek, J. F. (1997). Relationship of family schema to family adaptation to brain injury. *Brain Injury, 11*(11), 821–830.

Kotchoubey, B. (2005). Event-related potential measures of consciousness: two equations with three unknowns. *Progress in Brain Research, 150*, 427–444.

Kovacs, F., Fasotti, L., Eling, P., and Brouwer, W. (1993). Strategy training to compensate for mental slowness in head injured patients. Paper presented at the International Brain Injury Forum: The quest for better outcomes, Oxford.

Kozloff, R. (1987). Networks of social support and outcome from severe head injury. *Journal of Head Trauma Rehabilitation, 2*(3), 14–23.

Kramer, M. E., Chiu, C. Y., Walz, N. C., Holland, S. K., Yuan, W., Karunanayaka, P. et al. (2008). Long-term neural processing of attention following early childhood traumatic brain injury: fMRI and neurobehavioral outcomes. *Journal of the International Neuropsychological Society, 14*(3), 424–435.

Kraus, J. F. (1995). Epidemiological features of brain injury in children: Occurrence, children at risk, causes and manner of injury, severity and outcomes. In S. H. Broman and M. E. Michel (Eds.), *Traumatic head injury in children* (pp. 21–39). New York: Oxford University Press.

Kraus, J. F., and McArthur, D. L. (1999). Incidence and prevalence of, and costs associated with traumatic brain injury. In M. Rosenthal, E. R. Griffith, J. S. Kreutzer and B. Pentland (Eds.), *Rehabilitation of the adult and child with traumatic brain injury* (pp. 3–17). Philadelphia: FA Davis.

Kraus, J. F., Rock, A., and Hemyari, P. (1990). Brain injuries among infants, children, adolescents, and young adults. *American Journal of Diseases of Children, 144,* 684–691.

Kraus, J. F., and Sorenson, S. B. (1994). Epidemiology. In J. M. Silver, S. C. Yudofsky and R. E. Hales (Eds.), *Neuropsychiatry of traumatic brain injury* (pp. 3–42). Washington, DC: American Psychiatric Press, Inc.

Kraus, M. F., Susmaras, T., Caughlin, B. P., Walker, C. J., Sweeney, J. A., and Little, D. M. (2007). White matter integrity and cognition in chronic traumatic brain injury: a diffusion tensor imaging study. *Brain, 130*(10), 2508–2519.

Kreuter, M., Dahllof, Gudjonsson, G., Sullivan, M., and Siosteen, A. (1998). Sexual adjustment and its predictors after traumatic brain injury. *Brain Injury, 12*, 349–368.

Kreutzer, J. S., Gervasio, A. H., and Camplair, P. S. (1994a). Patient correlates of caregivers' distress and family functioning after traumatic brain injury. *Brain Injury, 8*, 211–230.

Kreutzer, J. S., Gervasio, A. H., and Camplair, P. S. (1994b). Primary caregivers' psychological status and family functioning after traumatic brain injury. *Brain Injury, 8*, 197–210.

Kreutzer, J. S., Kolakowsky-Hayner, S. A., Demm, S. R., and Meade, M. A. (2002). A structured approach to family intervention after brain injury. *Journal of Head Trauma Rehabilitation, 17*(4), 347–369.

Kreutzer, J. S., Livingston, L. A., Everley, R. S., Gary, K. W., Arango-Lasprilla, J. C., Powell, V. D. et al. (2009a). Caregivers' concerns about judgement and safety of patients with brain injury: A preliminary investigation. *Physical Medicine and Rehabilitation, 1*(August), 723–728.

Kreutzer, J. S., Marwitz, J. H., Hsu, N., Williams, K., and Riddick, A. (2007). Marital stability after brain injury: An investigation and analysis. *NeuroRehabilitation, 22*(1), 53–59.

Kreutzer, J. S., Marwitz, J. H., Walker, W., Sander, A., Sherer, M., Bogner, J. A. et al. (2003). Moderating factors in return to work and job stability after traumatic brain injury. *Journal of Head Trauma Rehabilitation, 18*(2), 128–138.

Kreutzer, J. S., Rapport, L. J., Marwitz, J. H., Harrison-Felix, C., Hart, T., Glenn, M. et al. (2009b). Caregivers' well-being after traumatic brain injury: A multi-center prospective investigation. *Archives of Physical Medicine and Rehabilitation, 90*(June), 939–946.

Kreutzer, J., Seel, R., and Marwitz, J. (1999). *The Neurobehavioral Functioning Inventory.* San Antonio, TX: The Psychological Corporation.

Kreutzer, J. S., Stejskal, T. M., Ketchum, J. M., Marwitz, J. H., Taylor, L. A., and Menzel, J. C. (2009c). A preliminary investigation of the brain injury family intervention: Impact on family members. *Brain Injury, 23*(6), 535–547.

Kreutzer, J. S., Witol, A. D., and Marwitz, J. H. (1996a). Alcohol and Drug Use Among Young Persons with Traumatic Brain Injury. *Journal of Learning Disabilities, 29*(6), 643–651.

Kreutzer, J. S., Witol, A. D., Sander, A. M., Cifu, D. X., Harris Marwitz, J., and Delmonico, R. (1996b). A prospective longitudinal multicenter analysis of alcohol use patterns among persons with traumatic brain injury. *Journal of Head Trauma Rehabilitation, 11*, 58–69.

Kreutzer, J. S., and Zasler, N. D. (1989). Psychosexual consequences of traumatic brain injury: methodology and preliminary findings. *Brain Injury, 3*, 177–186.

Kreutzer, J. S., Marwitz, J. H., Godwin, E. F., and Arango-Lasprilla, J. C. (2010). Practical approaches to effective family intervention after brain injury. *Journal of Head Trauma Rehabilitation, 25*(2), 113–120.

Laatsch, L., Harrington, D., Hotz, G., Maracantuomo, J., Mozzoni, M., Walsh, V. et al. (2007). An evidence-based review of cognitive and behavioural rehabilitation treatment studies in children with acquired brain injury. *Journal of Head Trauma Rehabilitation, 22*, 248–256.

Landre, N., Poppe, C. J., Davis, N., Schmaus, B., and Hobbs, S. E. (2006). Cognitive functioning and postconcussive symptoms in trauma patients with and without mild TBI. *Archives of Clinical Neuropsychology, 21*(4), 255–273.

Lane-Brown, A., and Tate, R. (2009a). Interventions for apathy after traumatic brain injury. *Cochrane Database Systematic Review, April 15*(2), CD006341.

Lane-Brown, A., and Tate, R. (2009b). Treatment for apathy syndrome following traumatic brain injury. Paper presented at the 32nd Brain Impairment Conference, Sydney.

Lange, R. T., Iverson, G. L., and Franzen, M. D. (2009). Neuropsychological functioning following complicated vs uncomplicated mild traumatic brain injury. *Brain Injury, 23*(2), 83–91.

Laurence, S., and Stein, D. (1978). Recovery after brain damage and the concept of localization of function. In S. Finger (Ed.), *Recovery from brain damage: Research and theory* (pp. 369–407). New York: Plenum Press.

Law, M. (1993). Evaluating activities of daily living: Directions for the future. *The American Journal of Occupational Therapy, 47*, 233–237.

Law, M., Baptiste, S., Carswell, A., McColl, M. A., Polatajko, H., and Pollock, N. (1998). *Canadian Occupational Performance Measure* (2nd ed. Rev. ed.). Ottawa: CAOT Publications ACE.

Lawson, M. J., and Rice, D. N. (1989). Effects of training in use of executive strategies on a verbal memory problem resulting from closed head injury. *Journal of Experimental and Clinical Neuropsychology, 11*, 942–854.

Le, T. H., and Gean, A. D. (2009). Neuroimaging of traumatic brain injury. *Mount Sinai Journal of Medicine, 76*, 145–162.

Leach, L. R., Frank, R. G., Bouman, D. E., and Farmer, J. (1994). Family functioning, social support and depression after traumatic brain injury. *Brain Injury, 8*, 599–606.

Leblanc, N., Chen, S., Swank, P. R., Ewing-Cobbs, L., Barnes, M., Dennis, M. et al. (2005). Response inhibition after traumatic brain injury (TBI) in children: impairment and recovery. *Developmental Neuropsychology, 28*(3), 829–848.

Leclercq, M., and Azouvi, P. (2002). Attention after traumatic brain injury. In M. Leclercq and P. Zimmermann (Eds.), *Applied Neuropsychology of Attention* (pp. 257–279). Hove: Psychology Press.

Lefebvre, H., Pelchat, D., and Levert, M. J. (2007). Interdisciplinary family intervention program: a partnership among health professionals, traumatic brain injury patients, and caregiving relatives. *Journal of Trauma Nursing, 14*(2), 100–113.

Lequerica, A. H., Rapport, L. J., Loeher, K., Axelrod, B. N., Vangel, S. J. J., and Hanks, R. A. (2007). Agitation in acquired brain injury: impact on acute rehabilitation therapies. *Journal of Head Trauma Rehabilitation, 22*(3), 177–183.

Levin, H., Hanten, G., Max, J., Li, X., Swank, P., Ewing-Cobbs, L. et al. (2007). Symptoms of attention-deficit/hyperactivity disorder following traumatic brain injury in children. *Journal of Developmental and Behavioral Pediatrics, 28*(2 Apr), 108–118.

Levin, H. S., Aldrich, E. F., Saydairi, C., Eisenberg, H. M., Foulkes, M. A., Bellefleur, M. et al. (1992). Severe head injury in children: Experience of the Traumatic Coma Data Bank. *Neurosurgery, 31*, 435–443.

Levin, H. S., Benton, A. L., and Grossman, R. G. (1982a). *Neurobehavioral consequences of closed head injury*. New York: Oxford University Press.

Levin, H. S., Culhane, K. A., Mendelsohn, D., Lilly, M. A., Bruce, D., Fletcher, J. M. et al. (1993). Cognition in relation to magnetic resonance imaging in head-injured children and adolescents. *Archives of Neurology, 50*, 897–905.

Levin, H. S., and Eisenberg, H. M. (1979a). Neuropsychological impairment after closed head injury in children and adolescents. *Journal of Paediatric Psychology, 4*, 389–402.

Levin, H. S., and Eisenberg, H. M. (1979b). Neuropsychological outcome of closed head injury in children and adolescents. *Child's Brain, 5*, 281–292.

Levin, H. S., Eisenberg, H. M., Wigg, N. R., and Kobayashi, K. (1982b). Memory and intellectual ability after head injury in children and adolescents. *Neurosurgery, 11*, 668–673.

Levin, H. S., Ewing-Cobbs, L., and Eisenberg, H. M. (1995). Neurobehavioral outcome fo paediatric closed head injury. In S. H. Broman and M. E. Michel (Eds.), *Traumatic head injury in children* (pp. 70–94). New York: Oxford University Press.

Levin, H. S., Fletcher, J. M., Kusnerik, L., Kufera, J. A., Lilly, M. A., Duffy, F. F. et al. (1996). Semantic memory following pediatric head injury: relationship to age, severity of injury, and MRI. *Cortex, 32*(3), 461–478.

Levin, H. S., Gary, H. E., Eisenberg, H. M., Ruff, R. M., Barth, J. T., Kreutzer, J. et al. (1990). Neurobehavioural outcome one year after severe head injury. *Journal of Neurosurgery, 73*, 699–709.

Levin, H. S., Hanten, G., Chang, C. C., Zhang, L., Schachar, R., Ewing-Cobbs, L. et al. (2002). Working memory after traumatic brain injury in children. *Annals of Neurology*, *52*(1 July), 82–88.

Levin, H. S., Hanten, G., Roberson, G., Li, X., Ewing-Cobbs, L., Dennis, M. et al. (2008). Prediction of cognitive sequelae based on abnormal computed tomography findings in children following mild traumatic brain injury. *Journal of Neurosurgery Pediatrics, 1*(6), 461–470.

Levin, H. S., Hanten, G., Zhang, L., Swank, P. R., Ewing-Cobbs, L., Dennis, M. et al. (2004a). Changes in working memory after traumatic brain injury in children. *Neuropsychology, 18*(2), 240–247.

Levin, H. S., Mendelsohn, D., Lilly, M. A., Yeakley, J., Song, J., Scheibel, R. S. et al. (1997a). Magnetic resonance imaging in relation to functional outcome of pediatric closed head injury: a test of the Ommaya-Gennarelli model. *Neurosurgery, 40*(3), 432–440.

Levin, H. S., O'Donnell, V. M., and Grossman, R. G. (1979). The Galveston Orientation and Amnesia Test. *Journal of Nervous and Mental Disease, 167*, 675–684.

Levin, H. S., Song, J., Ewing-Cobbs, L., Chapman, S. B., and Mendelsohn, D. (2001a). Word fluency in relation to severity of closed head injury, associated frontal brain lesions, and age at injury in children. *Neuropsychologia, 39*(2), 122–131.

Levin, H. S., Song, J., Ewing-Cobbs, L., and Roberson, G. (2001b). Porteus Maze performance following traumatic brain injury in children. *Neuropsychology, 15*(4), 557–567.

Levin, H. S., Song, J., Scheibel, R. S., Fletcher, J. M., Harward, H., Lilly, M. et al. (1997b). Concept formation and problem-solving following closed head injury in children. *Journal of the International Neuropsychological Society, 3*(6), 598–607.

Levin, H. S., Zhang, L., Dennis, M., Ewing-Cobbs, L., Schachar, R., Max, J. et al. (2004b). Psychosocial outcome of TBI in children with unilateral frontal lesions. *Journal of the International Neuropsychological Society, 10*(3), 305–316.

Levine, B., Fujiwar, E., O'Connor, C., Richard, N., Kovacevic, N., Mandic, M. et al. (2006). In vivo characterisation of TBI neuropathology with structural and functional neuroimaging. *Journal of Neurotrauma, 23*, 1396–1411.

Levine, B., Robertson, I. H., Clare, L., Carter, G., Hong, J., Wilson, B. A. et al. (2000). Rehabilitation of executive functioning: An experimental-clinical validation of goal management training. *Journal of the International Neuropsychological Society, 6*, 299–312.

Lew, H. L., Poole, J. H., Lee, E. H., Jaffe, D. L., Huang, H. C., and Brodd, E. (2005). Predictive validity of driving-simulator assessments following traumatic brain injury: A preliminary study. *Brain Injury, 19*(3), 177–188.

Lezak, M. D. (1978). Living with the characterologically altered brain injured patient. *Journal of Clinical Psychiatry, 39*, 592–598.

Lezak, M. D. (1983). *Neuropsychological assessment* (2nd ed.). New York: Oxford University Press.

Lezak, M. D., Howieson, D. B., Loring, D. W., Hannay, H. J., and Fischer, J. S. (2004). *Neuropsychological assessment* (4th ed.). New York: Oxford University Press.

Linscott, R. J., Knight, R. G., and Godfrey, H. P. D. (1997). The Profile of Functional Impairment in Communication (PFIC): A measure of communication impairment for clinical use. *Brain Injury, 10*(6), 397–412.

Lippert-Grüner, M., Kuchta, J., Hellmich, M., and Klug, N. (2006). Neurobehavioural deficits after severe traumatic brain injury (TBI). *Brain Injury, 20*(6), 569–574.

Lippert-Grüner, M., Lefering, R., and Svestkova, O. (2007). Functional outcome at 1 vs. 2 years after severe traumatic brain injury. *Brain Injury, 21*(10), 1001–1005.

Lira, F. T., Carne, W., and Masri, A. M. (1983). Treatment of anger and impulsivity in a brain damaged patient: A case study applying stress inoculation. *Clinical Neuropsychology, 5*, 159–160.

Little, D. M., Kraus, M. F., Jiam, C., Moynihan, M., Siroko, M., Schulze, E. et al. (2010a). Neuroimaging of hypoxic-ischemic brain injury. *Neurorehabilitation, 26*(1 Jan), 15–25.

Little, D. M., Kraus, M. F., Joseph, J., Geary, E. K., Susmaras, T., Zhou, X. J. et al. (2010b). Thalamic integrity underlies executive dysfunction in traumatic brain injury. *Neurology, 74*(7), 558–564.

Long, E., McDonald, S., Tate, R., Togher, L., and Bornhofen, C. (2008). Assessing social skills in people with very severe traumatic brain injury: Validity of the Social Performance Survey Schedule (SPSS). *Brain Impairment, 9*(4), 274–281.

Lovell, M. R., Pardini, J. E., Welling, J., Collins, M. W., Bakal, J., Lazar, N. et al. (2007). Functional brain abnormalities are related to clinical recovery and time to return-to-play in athletes. *Neurosurgery, 61*(2), 352–359; discussion 359–360.

Lovibond, S. H., and Lovibond, P. F. (1995). *Manual for the Depression Anxiety Stress Scales* (2nd ed.). Sydney Psychology Foundation.

Lowe, M. R., and Cautela, J. R. (1978). A self-report measure of social skill. *Behavior Therapy, 9*(4), 535–544.

Luis, C. A., and Mittenberg, W. (2002). Mood and anxiety dsorders following paediatric traumatic brain injury. *Journal of Clinical and Experimental Neuropscyhology, 24*, 240–270.

Lundqvist, A., and Alinder, J. (2007). Driving after brain injury: Self-awareness and coping at the tactical level of control. *Brain Injury, 21*(1109–1117).

Lundqvist, A., Alinder, J., and Ronnberg, J. (2008). Factors influencing driving 10 years after brain injury. *Brain Injury, 22*(4), 295–304.

Luria, A. R. (1963). *Recovery of function after brain injury*. New York: Macmillan.

Luria, A. R. (1973). The frontal lobes and the regulation of behaviour. In K. H. Pribram and A. R. Luria (Eds.), *Psychophysiology of the frontal lobes* (pp. 3–26). New York: Academic Press.

Ma, E. P.-M., Threats, T. T., and Worrall, L. E. (2008). An introduction to the International Classification of Functioning, Disability and Health (ICF) for speech-language pathology: Its past, present and future. *International Journal of Speech-Language Pathology, 10*(1–2), 2–8.

Maas, A. L. (2001). Neuroprotective agents in traumatic brain injury. *Expert Opinion on Investigational Drugs, 10*(4), 753–767.

Machamer, J., Temkin, N., and Dikmen, S. (2002). Significant other burden and factors related to it in traumatic brain injury. *Journal of Clinical and Experimental Neuropsychology, 24*(4), 420–433.

Machamer, J., Temkin, N., Fraser, R., Doctor, J., and Dikmen, S. (2005). Stability of employment after traumatic brain injury. *Journal of the International Neuropsychological Society, 11*, 807–816.

MacMillan, P. J., Hart, R. P., Martelli, M. F., and Zasler, N. D. (2002). Pre-injury status and adaptation following traumatic brain injury. *Brain Injury, 16*(1), 41–49.

Maddren, E. K. (1996). *Return to study following mild-moderate traumatic brain injury: A practical team-based approach*. Paper presented at the 5th Conference of the International Association for the Study of Traumatic Brain Injury and 20th Conference of the Australian Society for the Study of Brain Impairment, Melbourne.

Madigan, N. K., DeLuca, J., Diamond, B. J., Tramontano, G., and Averill, A. (2000). Speed of information processing in traumatic brain injury: Modality-specific factors. *Journal of Head Trauma Rehabilitation, 15*, 943–956.

Maguire, T. J., Hodges, D. L., Medhat, M. A., and Redford, J. B. (1986). Transient locked-in syndrome and phenobarbitol. *Archives of Physical Medicine and Rehabilitation, 68*, 566–567.

Mahoney, F., and Barthel, D. (1965). Functional evaluation: The Barthel Index. *Maryland State Medical Journal, 14*, 56–61.

Maitz, E. A. (1991). Family systems theory applied to head injury. In J. M. Williams and T. Kay (Eds.), *Head injury: A family matter* (pp. 65–80). Baltimore: Paul H. Brookes.

Majerus, S., Gill-Thwaites, H., Andrews, K., and Laureys, S. (2005). Behavioral evaluation of consciousness in severe brain damage. *Progress in Brain Research, 150*, 397–413.

Malec, J., Jones, R., Rao, N., and Stubbs, K. (1984). Video-game practice effects on sustained attention in patients with cranio-cerebral trauma. *Cognitive Rehabilitation, 2*(4), 18–23.

Malec, J. F. (1999). Goal attainment scaling in rehabilitation. *Neuropsychological Rehabilitation, 9*(3/4), 253–275.

Malec, J. F., and Basford, J. S. (1998). Postacute brain injury rehabilitation. *Archives of Physical Medicine and Rehabilitation, 77*, 198–207.

Malec, J. F., Buffington, A. L. H., Moessner, A. M., and Degiorgio, L. (2000). A medical/vocational case coordination system for persons with brain injury: An evaluation of employment outcomes. *Archives of Physical Medicine and Rehabilitation, 81*(August), 1007–1015.

Malec, J. F. and Lezak, M. D. (April, 2003). *Manual for the Mayo-Portland Adaptability Inventory (MPAI-4)*. http://www.tbims.org/combi/mpai

Malec, J. F., Smigielski, J. S., DePompolo, R. W., and Thompson, J. M. (1993). Outcome evaluation and prediction in a comprehensive-integrated post-acute outpatient brain injury rehabilitation programme. *Brain Injury, 7*, 15–29.

Malley, D., Cooper, J., and Cope, J. (2008). Adapting leisure activity for adults with neuropsychological deficits following acquired brain injury. *NeuroRehabilitation, 23*(4), 329–334.

Manchester, D., Hodgkinson, A., and Casey, T. (1997). Prolonged severe behavioural disturbance following traumatic brain injury: What can be done? *Brain Injury, 11*(8), 605–617.

Manchester, D., Priestley, N., and Jackson, H. (2004). The assessment of executive functions: coming out of the office. *Brain Injury, 18*(11), 1067–1081.

Mandalis, A., Kinsella, G., Ong, B., and Anderson, V. (2007). Working memory and new learning following pediatric traumatic brain injury. *Developmental Neuropsychology, 32*(2), 683–701.

Manly, T., Hawkins, K., Evans, J., Woldt, K., and Robertson, I. H. (2002). Rehabilitation of executive function: facilitation of effective goal management on complex tasks using periodic auditory alerts. *Neuropsychologia, 40*, 271–281.

Marin, R. S., Fogel, B. S., Hawkins, J., Duffy, J., and Krupp, B. (1995). Apathy: a treatable syndrome. *Journal of Neuropsychiatry, 7*(1), 23–30.

Marks, J. P., and Daggett, L. M. (2006). A critical pathway for meeting the needs of families of patients with severe traumatic brain injury. *Journal of Neuroscience Nursing, 38*(2), 84–89.

Marosszeky, N. E. V., Batchelor, J., Shores, E. A., Marosszeky, J. E., Klein-Boonschate, M., and Fahey, P. P. (1993). The performance of hospitalised, non head-injured children on the Westmead PTA Scale. *The Clinical Neuropsychologist, 7*(1), 85–95.

Marosszeky, N. E. V., Ryan, L., Shores, E. A., Batchelor, J., and Marosszeky, J. E. (1998). *The PTA Protocol: Guidelines for using the Westmead Post-Traumatic Amnesia (PTA) Scale*. Sydney: Wild and Wooley.

Marsh, N., Kersel, D. A., Havill, J. H., and Sleigh, J. W. (1998). Caregiver burden at 1 year following severe traumatic brain injury. *Brain Injury, 12*(12), 1045–1059.

Marshall, L. F., Becker, D. P., Bowers, S. A., Cayard, C., Eisenberg, H., Gross, C. R. et al. (1983). The National Traumatic Coma Data Bank. Part 1: Design, purpose, goals, and results. *Journal of Neurosurgery, 59*, 276–284.

Marshall, R. C., Karow, C. M., Morelli, C. A., Iden, K. K., Dixon, J., and Cranfill, T. B. (2004). Effects of interactive strategy modeling on problem-solving by persons with traumatic brain injury. *Aphasiology, 18*, 650–673.

Martin, D. A. (1988). Children and adolescents with traumatic brain injury: Impact on the family. *Journal of Learning Disabilities, 21*, 464–470.

Mateer, C. A., Sira, C. S., and O'Connell, M. E. (2005). Putting Humpty Dumpty together again. The importance of integrating cognitive and emotional interventions. *Journal of Head Trauma Rehabilitation, 20*(1), 62–75.

Mateer, C. A., Sohlberg, M. M., and Youngman, P. K. (1990). The management of acquired attention and memory deficits. In R. L. Wood and I. Fussey (Eds.), *Cognitive rehabilitation in perspective* (pp. 68–95). London: Taylor and Francis.

Max, J. E., Levin, H. S., Landis, J., Schachar, R., Saunders, A., Ewing-Cobbs, L. et al. (2005a). Predictors of personality change due to traumatic brain injury in children and adolescents in the first six months after injury. *Journal of the American Academy of Child and Adolescent Psychiatry, 44*(5), 434–442.

Max, J. E., Levin, H. S., Schachar, R. J., Landis, J., Saunders, A. E., Ewing-Cobbs, L. et al. (2006). Predictors of personality change due to traumatic brain injury in children and adolescents six to twenty-four months after injury. *The Journal of Neuropsychiatry and Clinical Neurosciences, 18*(1), 21–32.

Max, J. E., Roberts, M. A., Koele, S. L., Lindgren, S. D., Robin, D. A., Arndt, S. et al. (1999). Cognitive outcome in children and adolescents following severe traumatic brain injury: influence of psychosocial, psychiatric, and injury-related variables. *Journal of the International Neuropsychological Society, 5*(1), 58–68.

Max, J. E., Schachar, R. J., Levin, H. S., Ewing-Cobbs, L., Chapman, S. B., Dennis, M. et al. (2005b). Predictors of attention-deficit/hyperactivity disorder within 6 months after pediatric traumatic brain injury. *Journal of the American Academy of Child and Adolescent Psychiatry, 44*(10), 1032–1040.

Max, J. E., Schachar, R. J., Levin, H. S., Ewing-Cobbs, L., Chapman, S. B., Dennis, M. et al. (2005c). Predictors of secondary attention-deficit/hyperactivity disorder in children and adolescents 6 to 24 months after traumatic brain injury. *Journal of the American Academy of Child and Adolescent Psychiatry, 44*(10), 1041–1049.

Max, J. F., Castillo, C. S., Robin, D. A., and others (1998). Predictors of family functioning after traumatic brain injury in children and adolescents. *Journal of the American Academy of Child and Adolescent Psychiatry, 37*, 83–90.

Mazzini, L. et al., (2003). Posttraumatic hydrocephalus: a clinical, neuroradiologic, and neuropsychologic assessment of long-term outcome. *Arch Phys Med Rehabil, 84*(11), 1637–1641.

McAllister, T. W., Flashman, L. A., McDonald, B. C., and Saykin, A. J. (2006). Mechanisms of working memory dysfunction after mild and moderate TBI: Evidence for functional MRI and neurogenetics. *Journal of Neurotrauma, 23*, 1450–1467.

McAllister, T. W., Sparling, M. B., Flashman, L. A., and Saykin, A. J. (2001). Neuroimaging findings in mild traumatic brain injury. *Journal of Clinical and Experimental Neuropsychology, 23*, 775–791.

McCarter, R., Walton, N., Moore, C., Ward, A., and Nelson, I. (2007). PTA testing, the Westmead Post Traumatic Amnesia Scale and opiate analgesia: A cautionary note. *Brain Injury, 21*(13–14), 1393–1397.

McCarthy, R. A., and Warrington, E. K. (1990). *Cognitive neuropsychology: A clinical introduction*. San Diego, CA: Academic Press.

McCauley, S. R., and Levin, H. S. (2004). Prospective memory in pediatric traumatic brain injury: a preliminary study. *Developmental Neuropsychology, 25*(1–2), 5–20.

McCauley, S. R., McDaniel, M. A., Pedroza, C., Chapman, S. B., and Levin, H. S. (2009). Incentive effects on event-based prospective memory performance in children and adolescents with traumatic brain injury. *Neuropsychology, 23*(2), 201–209.

McCloskey, G., Perkins, L. A., and Divner, B. V. (2009). *Assessment and intervention for executive function difficulties*. New York: Taylor and Francis.

McCullagh, S., and Feinstein, A. (2005). Cognitive Changes. In J. M. Silver, T. W. McAllister and S. C. Yudofsky (Eds.), *Textbook of traumatic brain injury* (pp. 321–335). Arlington, VA: American Psychiatric Publishing, Inc.

McDonald, S. (2000). Putting communication disorders in context after traumatic brain injury. *Aphasiology, 14*, 339–347.

McDonald, S. (2005). Are you crying or laughing? Emotional recognition deficits after severe traumatic brain injury. *Brain Impairment, 6*(1), 56–67.

McDonald, S., Bornhofen, C., Shum, D., Long, E., Saunders, C., and Neulinger, K. (2006). Reliability and validity of the awareness of social inference test (TASIT): a clinical test of social perception. *Disability and Rehabilitation, 28*(24), 1529–1542.

McDonald, S., and Flanagan, S. (2004). Social perception deficits after traumatic brain injury: The interaction between emotion recognition, mentalising ability and social communication. *Neuropsychology Review, 18*, 572–579.

McDonald, S., and Saunders, J. C. (2005). Differential impairment in recognition of emotion from still, dynamic and multi-modal displays in people with severe TBI. *Journal of the International Neuropsychological Society, 11*, 392–399.

McGlynn, S. M. (1990). Behavioural approaches to neuropsychological rehabilitation. *Psychological Bulletin, 108*, 420–441.

McKerracher, G., Powell, T. J., and Oyebode, J. (2005). A single case experimental design comparing two memory notebook formats for a man with memory problems caused by traumatic brain injury. *Neuropsychological Rehabilitation, 15*(2), 115–128.

McKinlay, A., Grace, R., Horwood, J., Fergusson, D., and MacFarlane, M. (2009). Adolescent psychiatric symptoms following preschool childhood mild traumatic brain injury: evidence from a birth cohort. *Journal of Head Trauma Rehabilitation, 24*(3), 221–227.

McKinlay, W. M., and Hickox, A. (1988). How can families help in the rehabilitation of the head injured? *Journal of Head Trauma Rehabilitation, 3*(4), 64–72.

Meador, K. J., Loring, D. W., Huh, K., Gallagher, B. B., and King, D. W. (1990). Comparative cognitive effects of anticonvulsants. *Neurology, 40*(391–394).

Meares, S., Shores, E., Batchelor, J., Baguley, I. J., Chapman, J., Gurka, J. et al. (2006). The relationship of psychological and cognitive factors and opioids in the development of the postconcussion syndrome in general trauma patients with mild traumatic brain injury. *Journal of the International Neuropsychological Society, 12*(6), 792–801.

Meares, S., Shores, E. A., Taylor, A. J., Batchelor, J., Bryant, R. A., Baguley, I. J. et al. (2008). Mild traumatic brain injury does not predict acute postconcussion syndrome. *Journal of Neurology, Neurosurgery and Psychiatry, 79*(3), 300–306.

Medd, J., and Tate, R. (2000). Evaluation of an anger management therapy programme following acquired brain injury: A preliminary study. *Neuropsychological Rehabilitation, 10*, 185–201.

Medlar, T., and Medlar, J. (1990). Nursing management of sexuality issues. *Journal of Head Trauma Rehabilitation, 5*(2), 46–51.

Mellick, D., Walker, N., Brooks, C. A., and Whiteneck, G. (1999). Incorporating the cognitive independence domain into CHART. *Journal of Rehabilitation Outcome Measures, 3*(3), 12–21.

Michon, J. A. (1979). *Dealing with changes: Summary report of a workshop at the Traffic Research Centre.* Groningen: State University, Groningen, The Netherlands.

Middleboe, T., Anderson, H. H., Birket-Smith, M., and Friis, M. L. (1992). Minor head injury: impact on general health after 1 year: A prospective follow-up study. *Acta Neurologica Scandinavica, 85*(1), 5–9.

Miller, L. J., and Donders, J. (2003). Prediction of Educational Outcome After Pediatric Traumatic Brain Injury. *Rehabilitation Psychology, 48*(4), 237–241.

Miller, W. R., and Rollnick, S. (2002). *Motivational interviewing: Preparing people for change* (2nd ed.). New York: Guilford Press.

Milligan, K., Astington, J.W., and Dack, L.A. (2007). Language and Theory of Mind: Meta-analysis of the relation between language ability and false-belief understanding. *Child Development*, *78*(2), 622–646.

Millis, S. R., Rosenthal, M., Novack, T. A., Sherer, M., Nick, T. G., Kreutzer, J. S. et al. (2001). Long-term neuropsychological outcome after traumatic brain injury. *Journal of Head Trauma Rehabilitation, 16*(4), 343–355.

Mills, V. M., Nesbeda, T., Katz, D. I., and Alexander, M. P. (1992). Outcomes for traumatically brain-injured patients following post-acute rehabilitation programmes. *Brain Injury, 6*, 219–228.

Milner, B. (1963). Effects of brain lesions on card sorting. *Archives of Neurology, 9*, 90–100.

Milner, B. (1974). Hemispheric specialisation: Scope and limits. In F. O. Schmitt and G. G. Worden (Eds.), *The neurosciences: Third study program*. Cambridge, MA: MIT Press.

Minnes, P., Graffi, S., Nolte, M. L., Carlson, P. and Harrick, L. (2000). Coping and stress in Canadian family caregivers of persons with traumatic brain injury. *Brain Injury, 14*, 737–748.

Miotto, E., Evans, J. J., Souza de Lucia, M. C., and Scaff, M. (2009). Rehabilitation of executive dysfunction: A controlled trial of an attention and problem-solving treatment group. *Neuropsychological Rehabilitation, 19*(4), 517–540.

Mittenberg, W., Canyock, E., Condit, D., and Patton, C. (2001). Treatment of post-concussion syndrome following mild head injury. *Journal of Clinical and Experimental Neuropsychology, 23*(6), 829–836.

Mittenberg, W., Tremont, G., Zeilinski, R. E., Fichera, S., and Rayles, K. R. (1996). Cognitive-behavioural prevention of postconcussion syndrome. *Archives of Neurology, 11*, 139–145.

Moffat, N. (1984). Strategies of memory therapy. In B. A. Wilson and N. Moffat (Eds.), *Clinical management of memory problems* (pp. 63–88). London: Croom Helm.

Montgomery, B., and Evans, L. (1983). *Living and loving together*. Melbourne: Nelson Publishers.

Montgomery, G. K. (1995). A multi-factor account of disability after brain injury: implications for neuropsychological counselling. *Brain Injury, 9*(5), 453–469.

Moore, A., Stambrook, M., and Peters, L. (1993). Centripetal and centrifugal family life cycle factors in long-term outcome following traumatic brain injury. *Brain Injury, 7*, 247–256.

Moos, R. H., and Moos, B. S. (1981). *Family Environment Scale*. Palo Alto, CA: Consulting Psychologists Press.

Moppett, I. K. (2007). Traumatic brain injury: Assessment, resuscitation and early management. *British Journal of Anaesthesia, 99*(1), 18–31.

Multi-Society Task Force on PVS (1994a). Medical aspects of the persistent vegetative state (First of two parts). *The New England Journal of Medicine, May 26*, 1499–1508.

Multi-Society Task Force on PVS (1994b). Medical aspects of the persistent vegetative state (Second of two parts). *The New England Journal of Medicine, June 2*, 1572–1579.

Murdoch, B. E., and Theodoras, D. (2001). *Traumatic brain injury: Associated speech, language, and swallowing disorders*. Australia: Singular Publishing.

Murphy, L., Chamberlain, E., Weir, J., Berry, A., Nathaniel-James, D., and Agnew, R. (2006). Effectiveness of vocational rehabilitation following acquired brain injury: preliminary evaluation of a UK specialist rehabilitation programme. *Brain Injury, 20*(11), 1119–1129.

Muscara, F., Catroppa, C., and Anderson, V. (2008a). The impact of injury severity on executive function 7–10 years following pediatric traumatic brain injury. *Developmental Neuropsychology, 33*(5), 623–636.

Muscara, F., Catroppa, C., and Anderson, V. (2008b). Social problem-solving skills as a mediator between executive function and long-term social outcome following paediatric traumatic brain injury. *Journal of Neuropsychology, 2*(1), 445–461.

Mysiw, J., and Sandel, E. (1997). The agitated brain injured patient. Part 2: Pathophysiology and treatment. *Archives of Physical Medicine and Rehabilitation, 78*, 213–220.

Mysiw, W. J., Bogner, J., Corrigan, J., Fugate, L., Clinchot, D., and Kadyan, V. (2006). The impact of acute care medications on rehabilitation outcome after traumatic brain injury. *Brain Injury, 20*(9), 905–911.

Nabors, N., Seacat, J., and Rosenthal, M. (2002). Predictors of caregiver burden following traumatic brain injury. *Brain Injury, 16*(12), 1039–1050.

Nadebaum, C., Anderson, V., Catroppa, C. (2007). Executive function outcomes following traumatic brain injury in young children: A five year follow-up. *Developmental Neuropsychology, 32*(2), 703–728.

Narayan, R. K., Michel, M. E., Ansell, B., Baethmann, A., Biegon, A., Bracken, M .B. et al. (2002). Clinical trials in head injury. *Journal of Neurotrauma, 19*(5), 503–557.

Nelson, H. E. (1982). *National Adult Reading Test: Test manual*. Slough: NFER-Nelson.

Niemann, H., Ruff, R. M., and Baser, C. A. (1990). Computer-assisted attention retraining in head-injured individuals: A controlled efficacy study of an outpatient program. *Journal of Consulting and Clinical Psychology, 58*, 811–817.

NIH Consensus Development Panel on Rehabilitation of Persons With Traumatic Brain Injury (1999). Rehabilitation of Persons With Traumatic Brain Injury. *JAMA: The Journal of the American Medical Association, 282*(10), 974–983.

Nijboer, J. M. M., van der Naalt, J., and ten Duis, H.-J. (2010). Patients beyond salvation? Various categories of trauma patients with a minimal Glasgow Coma Score. *Injury; International Journal of the Care of the Injured, 41*, 52–57.

Noonan, V. K., Kopec, J. A., Noreau, L., Singer, J., and Dvorak, M. F. (2009). A review of participation instruments based on the International Classification of Functioning, Disability and Health. *Disability and Rehabilitation, 31*(23), 1883–1901.

Norris, G., and Tate, R. L. (2000). The Behavioural Assessment of the Dysexecutive Syndrome (BADS): Ecological, Concurrent and Construct Validity. *Neuropsychological Rehabilitation, 10*(1), 33–45.

Novack, T. A., Banos, J. H., Alderson, A. L., Schneider, J. L., Weed, W., Blankenship, J. et al. (2006). OFOV performance and driving ability following traumatic brain injury. *Brain Injury, 20*(5), 455–461.

Novack, T. A., Baños, J. H., Brunner, R., Renfroe, S., and Meythaler, J. M. (2009). Impact of early administration of sertraline on depressive symptoms in the first year after traumatic brain injury. *Journal of Neurotrauma, 26*(11), 1921–1928.

Novack, T. A., Caldwell, S. G., Duke, L. W., Bergquist, T. F., and Gage, R. J. (1996). Focused versus unstructured intervention for attention deficits after traumatic brain injury. *Journal of Head Trauma Rehabilitation, 11*(52–60).

Novaco, R. (1975). *Anger control: The development and evaluation of an experimental treatment*. Lexington, MA: Lexington Books.

Nudo, R. J., Plautz, E. J., and Frost, S. B. (2001). Role of adaptive plasticity in recovery of function after damage to motor cortex. *Muscle and Nerve, 24*, 1000–1019.

O'Neill, J., Zuger, R., Fields, A., Fraser, R., and Pruce, T. (2004). The Program Without Walls: Innovative approach to state agency vocational rehabilitation of persons with traumatic brain injury. *Archives of Physical Medicine and Rehabilitation, 85*(Suppl 2), S68–S72.

O'Rance, L., and Fortune, N. (2007). Disability in Australia: acquired brain injury (Vol. Cat. no. AUS 96). Canberra: AIHW.

Oakley, F., Kielhofner, G., Barris, R., and Reichler, R. K. (1986). The Role Checklist: Development and empirical assessment of reliability. *Occupational Therapy Journal of Research, 6*, 157–170.

Oboler, S. K. (1986). Brain death and persistent vegetative states. *Clinics in Geriatric Medicine, 2*, 547–576.

Oddy, M. (1984). Head injury and social adjustment. In N. Brooks (Ed.), *Closed head injury: Psychological, social and family consequences* (pp. 108–122). London: Oxford University Press.

Oddy, M., Coughlan, T., Tyerman, A., and Jenkins, D. (1985). Social adjustment after closed head injury: a further follow-up seven years after injury. *Journal of Neurology, Neurosurgery, and Psychiatry, 48*, 564–568.

Oddy, M., Humphrey, M., and Uttley, D. (1978). Stresses upon the relatives of head-injured patients. *British Journal of Psychiatry, 133*, 507–513.

Oliver, M. (1990). The individual and social model of disability. Retrieved 15 November 2009, from www.leeds.ac.uk/disability-studies/archiveuk/Oliver

Olson, D. H. (1986). Circumplex model VII: Validation studies and FACES III. *Family Process, 25*, 337–351.

Olver, J. (1991). Towards community re-entry. Preliminary evaluation of Bethesda Hospital's Transitional Living Program. *Think Magazine, June,* 28–29.

Olver, J. H., Ponsford, J. L., and Curran, C. (1996). Outcome following traumatic brain injury: A comparison between 2 and 5 years after injury. *Brain Injury, 10*, 841–848.

Ommaya, A. K., and Gennarelli, T. A. (1974). Cerebral concussion and traumatic unconsciousness: Correlation of experimental and clinical observations on blunt head injuries. *Brain, 97*, 633–654.

Oppermann, J. D. (2004). Interpreting the meaning individuals ascribe to returning to work after traumatic brain injury: a qualitative approach. *Brain Injury, 9*(September), 941–955.

Ord, J. S., Greve, K. W., Bianchini, K. J., and Aguerrevere, L. (2009). Executive Dysfunction in Traumatic Brain Injury: The Effects of Injury Severity and Effort on the Wisconsin Card Sorting Test. *Journal of Clinical and Experimental Neuropsychology, 29*, 1–11.

Ornstein, T. J., Levin, H. S., Chen, S., Hanten, G., Ewing-Cobbs, L., Dennis, M. et al. (2009). Performance monitoring in children following traumatic brain injury. *Journal of Child Psychology and Psychiatry and Allied Disciplines, 50*(4), 506–513.

Orsillo, S. M., McCaffrey, R. J., and Fisher, J. M. (1993). Siblings of head-injured individuals: A population at risk. *Journal of Head Trauma Rehabilitation, 8*(1), 102–115.

Osterrieth, P. A. (1944). Le test de copie d'une figure complexe. *Archives of Psychology, 30*(206–353).

Ouellet, M. C., and Morin, C. M. (2006). Subjective and objective measures of insomnia in the context of TBI. *Sleep Medicine, 7*(6), 486–497.

Owen, A. M., Coleman, M. R., Boly, M., Davis, M. H., Laureys, S., and Pickard, J. D. (2006). Detecting awareness in the vegetative state. *Science, 313*, 1402.

Owen, A. M., Hampshire, A., Grahn, J. A., Stenton, R., Dajani, S., Burns, A. S. et al. (2010). Putting brain training to the test. *Nature, 465*(10), 775–779.

Ownsworth, T., Fleming, J., Desbois, J., Strong, J., and Kuipers, P. (2006). A metacognitive contextual intervention to enhance error awareness and functional outcome following traumatic brain injury: A single case experimental design. *Journal of the International Neuropsychological Society, 12*, 54–63.

Ownsworth, T., and McKenna, K. (2004). Investigation of factors related to employment outcome following traumatic brain injury: a critical review and conceptual model. *Disability and Rehabilitation, 26*(13), 765–783.

Ownsworth, T., Quinn, H., Fleming, J., Kendall, M., and Shum, D. (2010). Error self-regulation following traumatic brain injury: a single case study evaluation of metacognitive skills training and behavioural practice interventions. *Neuropsychological Rehabilitation, 20*(1), 59–80.

Ownsworth, T. L., and McFarland, K. (1999). Memory remediation in long-term acquired brain injury: two approaches in diary training. *Brain Injury, 13*, 605–626.

Ownsworth, T. L., McFarland, K., and Young, R. M. (2000). Self awareness and psychosocial functioning following acquired brain injury: An evaluation of a group support programme. *Neuropsychological Rehabilitation, 10*(5), 465–484.

Pagulayan, K. F., Hoffman, J. M., Temkin, N. R., Machamer, J. E., and Dikmen, S. S. (2008). Functional limitations and depression after traumatic brain injury: Examination of the temporal relationship. *Archives of Physical Medicine and Rehabilitation, 89*, 1887–1892.

Palmese, C. A., and Raskin, S. A. (2000). The rehabilitation of attention in individuals with mild traumatic brain injury, using the APT-II programme. *Brain Injury, 14*(6), 535–548.

Paniak, C., Toller-Lobe, G., Durand, A., and Nagy, J. (1998). A randomized trial of two treatments for mild traumatic brain injury. *Brain Injury, 12*, 1011–1023.

Paniak, C., Toller-Lobe, G., Reynolds, S., Melnyk, A., and Nagy, J. A. (2000). A randomized trial of two treatments for mild traumatic brain injury. 1 year follow-up. *Brain Injury, 14*, 219–226.

Panikoff, L. B. (1983). Recovery trends of functional skills in the head-injured adult. *The American Journal of Occupational Therapy, 37*, 735–743.

Panksepp, J., Fuchs, T., Garcia, V. A., and Lesiak, A. (2007). Does any aspect of mind survive brain damage that typically leads to a persistent vegetative state? Ethical considerations. *Philosophy, Ethics, and Humanities in Medicine, 2*(32).

Pantev, C., Oostenveld, R., Engelien, A., Ross, B., Roberts, L. E., and Hoke, M. (1998). Increased auditory cortical representation in musicians. *Nature, 392*, 811–814.

Panting, A., and Merry, P. (1972). The long-term rehabilitation of severe head injuries with particular reference to the need for social and medical support for the patient's family. *Rehabilitation, 38*, 33–37.

Papanicolaou, A. C., Loring, D. W., Eisenberg, H. M., Raz, N., and Contreras, F. L. (1986). Auditory brain stem evoked responses in comatose head injured patients. *Neurosurgery, 18*(2), 173–175.

Paparrigopoulos, T., Melissaki, A., Efthymiou, A., Tsekou, H., Vadala, C., Kribeni, G. et al. (2006). Short-term psychological impact on family members of intensive care unit patients. *Journal of Psychosomatic Research, 61*(5), 719–722.

Park, N. W., and Ingles, J. L. (2001). Effectiveness of attention rehabilitation after an acquired brain injury: A meta-analysis. *Neuropsychology, 15*(2), 199–210.

Park, N. W., Moscovitch, M., and Robertson, I. H. (1999a). Divided attention impairments after traumatic brain injury. *Neuropsychologia, 37*(10), 1119–1133.

Park, N. W., Proulx, G., and Towers, W. (1999b). Evaluation of the Attention Process training programme. *Neuropsychological Rehabilitation, 9*, 135–154.

Parry-Jones, B. L., Vaughan, F. L., and Cox, W. M. (2006). Traumatic brain injury and substance misuse: A systematic review of prevalence and outcomes research (1994–2004). *Neuropsychological Rehabilitation, 16*(5), 537–560.

Partington, J. E., and Leiter, R. G. (1949). Partington's Pathway Test. *The Psychological Service Centre Bulletin, 1*, 9–20.

Paul, R. (2007). *Language disorders from infancy through adolescence: Assessment and intervention* (3rd ed.). St. Louis, MO: Mosby.

Pearce, J. M. S. (1987). The locked-in syndrome. *British Medical Journal, 294*, 198–199.

Pelco, L., Sawyer, M., Duffield, G., Prior, M., and Kinsella, G. (1992). Premorbid emotional and behavioural adjustment in children with mild head injuries. *Brain Injury, 6*(1), 29–37.

Peloso, P. M., Carroll, L. J., Cassidy, J. D., Borg, J., von Holst, H., Holm, L. et al. (2004). Critical evaluation of the existing guidelines on mild traumatic brain injury. *Journal of Rehabilitation Medicine*(43 Suppl), 106–112.

Perlesz, A. (1999). Complex responses to trauma: Challenges in bearing witness. *Australian and New Zealand Journal of Family Therapy, 20*(1), 11–19.

Perlesz, A., Furlong, M., and McLachlan, D. (1989). Family-centred rehabilitation: Family therapy for the head injured and their relatives. In R. Harris, R. Burns and R. Rees (Eds.), *Recovery from brain injury: Expectations, needs and processes* (pp. 180–191). Adelaide: Institute for the Study of Learning Difficulties.

Perlesz, A., Kinsella, G., and Crowe, S. (1999). Impact of traumatic brain injury on the family: A critical review. *Rehabilitation Psychology, 44*(6–35).

Perlesz, A., Kinsella, G., and Crowe, S. (2000). Psychological distress and family satisfaction following traumatic brain injury: injured individuals and their primary, secondary, and tertiary caregivers. *Journal of Head Trauma Rehabilitation, 15*(3), 909–929.

Perlesz, A., and O'Loughlan, M. (1998). Changes in stress and burden in families seeking therapy following traumatic brain injury. *International Journal of Rehabilitation Research, 21*, 339–354.

Pessar, L. F., Coad, M. L., Linn, R. T., and Willer, B. S. (1993). The effects of parental traumatic brain injury on the behaviour of parents and children. *Brain Injury, 7*, 231–240.

Peters, L., Stambrook, M., Moore, A., and Esses, L. (1990). Psychosocial sequelae of head injury: Effects on the marital relationship. *Brain Injury, 4*, 39–47.

Petrella, L., McColl, M. A., Krupa, T., and Johnston, J. (2005). Returning to productive activities: Perspectives of individuals with long-standing acquired brain injuries. *Brain Injury, 19*(9), 643–655.

Pettigrew, L. E. L., Wilson, J. T. L., and Teasdale, G. M. (2003). Reliability of ratings on the Glasgow Outcome Scales from in-person and telephone structured interviews. *Journal of Head Trauma Rehabilitation, 18*, 252–258.

Phan, K. L., Wager, T., Taylor, S. F., and Liberzon, I. (2003). Functional neuroanatomy of emotion: A meta-analysis of emotion activation studies in PET and fMRI. *Neuroimage 16*, 331–348.

Philip, S., Udomphorn, Y., Kirkham, F. J., and Vavilala, M. S. (2009). Cerebrovascular pathophysiology in pediatric traumatic brain injury. *Journal of Trauma-Injury Infection and Critical Care, 67*(2 Suppl), S128–S134.

Pietrapiana, P., Tamietto, M., Torrini, G., Mezzanato, T., Rago, R., and Perino, C. (2005). Role of premorbid factors in predicting safe return to driving after severe TBI. *Brain Injury, 19*(3), 197–211.

Ponsford, J. (2003). Sexual changes associated with traumatic brain injury. *Neuropsychological Rehabilitation, 13*(1–2), 275–289.

Ponsford, J. (2005). Rehabilitation interventions after mild traumatic brain injury. *Current Opinion in Neurology, 18*(6), 692–697.

Ponsford, J. (2006). Community-based rehabilitation following traumatic brain injury. Paper presented at the Fourth World Congress for Neurorehabilitation, Hong Kong, 12–16 February 2006.

Ponsford, J. (2007). *Monash-Epworth Rehabilitation Research Centre Head Injury Outcome Project Report* (Research Report).

Ponsford, J., Cameron, P., Fitzgerald, M., Grant, M., and Mickocka-Walus, A. (2011). Long term outcomes after uncomplicated mild traumatic brain injury: A comparison with trauma controls. *Journal of Neurotrauma,* 28(6), 937–948.

Ponsford, J., Draper, K., and Schönberger, M. (2008). Functional outcome 10 years after traumatic brain injury: Its relationship with demographic, injury severity, and cognitive and emotional status. *Journal of the International Neuropsychological Society, 14*, 233–242.

Ponsford, J., Facem, P. C., Willmott, C., Rothwell, A., Kelly, A.-M., Nelms, R. et al. (2004). Use of the Westmead PTA scale to monitor recovery of memory after mild head injury. *Brain Injury, 18*(6), 603–614.

Ponsford, J., Harrington, H., Olver, J., and Roper, M. (2006). Evaluation of community-based rehabilitation following traumatic brain injury. *Neuropsychological Rehabilitation, 16*(3), 315–328.

Ponsford, J., and Schönberger, M. (2010). Long-term family functioning following traumatic brain injury. *Journal of the International Neuropsychological Society, 16*, 1–12.

Ponsford, J., Tweedly, L., and Lee, N. (2010). Investigation of a brief intervention to minimize alcohol use following traumatic brain injury. Paper presented at the 7th Satellite Symposium on Neuropsychological Rehabilitation, Krakow, Poland, 5–6 July 2010.

Ponsford, J., Whelan-Goodinson, R., and Bahar-Fuchs, A. (2007). Alcohol and drug use following traumatic brain injury: A prospective study. *Brain Injury, 21*(13), 1385–1392.

Ponsford, J., and Willmott, C. (2004). Rehabilitation of non-spatial attention. In J. Ponsford (Ed.), *Cognitive and behavioural rehabilitation: From neurobiology to clinical practice* (pp. 299–342). New York: Guilford Press.

Ponsford, J., Willmott, C., Rothwell, A., Cameron, P., Ayton, G., Nelms, R. et al. (2001). Impact of early intervention on outcome after mild traumatic brain injury in children. *Pediatrics, 108*(6), 1297–1303.

Ponsford, J., Willmott, C., Rothwell, A., Cameron, P., Kelly, A. M., and Nelms, R. (2002). Impact of early intervention on outcome following mild head injury in adults. *Journal of Neurology, Neurosurgery and Psychiatry, 73*(3), 330–332.

Ponsford, J., Willmott, C., Rothwell, A., Cameron, P., Kelly, A. M., Nelms, R. et al. (2000). Factors influencing outcome following mild traumatic brain injury in adults. *Journal of the International Neuropsychological Society, 6*(6), 568–579.

Ponsford, J. L., and Kinsella, G. (1988). Evaluation of a remedial programme for attentional deficits following closed head injury. *Journal of Clinical and Experimental Neuropsychology, 10*, 693–708.

Ponsford, J. L., and Kinsella, G. (1991). The use of a rating scale of attentional behaviour. *Neuropsychological Rehabilitation, 1*, 241–257.

Ponsford, J. L., and Kinsella, G. (1992). Attentional deficits following closed-head injury. *Journal of Clinical and Experimental Neuropsychology, 14*(5), 822–838.

Ponsford, J. L., Olver, J. H., and Curran, C. (1995a). A profile of outcome: 2 years after traumatic brain injury. *Brain Injury, 9*(1), 1–10.

Ponsford, J. L., Olver, J. H., Curran, C., and Ng, K. (1995b). Prediction of employment status two years after traumatic brain injury. *Brain Injury, 9*, 11–20.

Ponsford, J. L., Olver, J. H., Ponsford, M., and Nelms, R. (2003). Long-term adjustment of families following traumatic brain injury where comprehensive rehabilitation has been provided. *Brain Injury, 17*(6), 453–468.

Ponsford, J. L., Willmott, C., Rothwell, A., Cameron, P., Ayton, G., Nelms, R. et al. (1999). Cognitive and behavioral outcome following mild traumatic head injury in children. *Journal of Head Trauma Rehabilitation, 14*(4), 360–372.

Porteus, S. (1965). *Porteus Maze Test: Fifty years' application*. Palo Alto, CA: Pacific.

Posner, J. B., Saper, C. B., Schiff, N., and Plum, J. B. (2007). *Plum and Posner's Diagnosis of Stupor and Coma.* New York: Contemporary Neurology.

Possl, J., Jurgensmeyer, S., Karlbauer, F., Wenz, C., and Goldenberg, G. (2001). Stability of employment after brain injury: A 7-year follow-up study. *Brain Injury, 15*(1), 15–27.

Post, M.W.M., de Witte, L.P., Reichrath, E., Verdonschot, M.M., Wijhuizen, G.J., and Perenboom, R.J.M. (2008). Development and validation of IMPACT-S, an ICF-based questionnaire to measure activities and participation. *Journal of Rehabilitation Medicine, 40,* 620–627.

Povlishock, J., and Katz, D. I. (2005). Update of neuropathology and neurological recovery after traumatic brain injury. *Journal of Head Trauma Rehabilitation, 20*(1), 76–94.

Powell, J., Heslin, J., and Greenwood, R. (2002). Community based rehabilitation after severe brain injury: a randomised controlled trial. *Journal of Neurology, Neurosurgery and Psychiatry, 72*, 193–202.

Power, P. W. (1985). Family coping behaviours in chronic illness: A rehabilitation perspective. *Rehabilitation Literature, 46*, 78–83.

Prigatano, G. (1986). A patient competency rating. In G. P. Prigatano and others (Eds.), *Neuropsychological rehabilitation after brain injury* (pp. 143–151). Baltimore: Johns Hopkins University Press.

Prigatano, G. P. (1991). Disturbances of self-awareness of deficit after traumatic brain injury. In G. P. Prigatano and D. L. Schacter (Eds.), *Awareness of deficit after brain injury* (pp. 111–126). New York: Oxford University Press.

Prigatano, G. P. (1999). *Principles of neuropsychological rehabilitation*. Oxford: Oxford University Press.

Prigatano, G. P., and Altman, I. M. (1990). Impaired awareness of behavioural limitations after traumatic brain injury. *Archives of Physical Medicine and Rehabilitation, 71*, 1058–1064.

Prigatano, G. P., and Fordyce, D. J. (1986). Cognitive dysfunction and psychosocial adjustment after brain injury. In G. P. Prigatano et al. (Eds.), *Neuropsychological rehabilitation after brain injury* (pp. 1–17). Baltimore: Johns Hopkins University Press.

Prigatano, G. P., and Gupta, S. (2006). Friends after traumatic brain injury in children. *Journal of Head Trauma Rehabilitation, 21*(6), 505–513.

Prigatano, G. P., O'Brien, K. P., and Klonoff, P. S. (1988). The clinical management of delusions in post acute traumatic brain injured patients. *Journal of Head Trauma Rehabilitation, 3*(3), 23–32.

Prigatano, G. P., and others (1986). *Neuropsychological rehabilitation after brain injury*. Baltimore: Johns Hopkins University Press.

Prigatano, G. P., and Pribram, K. H. (1982). Perception and memory of facial affect following brain injury. *Perceptual and Motor Skills, 54*(3), 859–869.

Prior, M., Kinsella, G., Sawyer, M., Bryan, D., and Anderson, V. (1994). Cognitive and psychosocial outcome after head injury in children. *Australian Psychologist, 29*(2), 116–123.

Raghupathi, R. (2004). Cell death mechanisms following traumatic brain injury. *Brain Pathology, 14*, 215–222.

Rahman, B., Oliver, C., and Alderman, N. (2010). Descriptive analysis of challenging behaviours shown by adults with acquired brain injury. *Neuropsychological Rehabilitation, 20*(2), 212–238.

Raimondi, A. J., and Hirschauer, J. (1984). Head injury in the infant and toddler. *Child's Brain, 11*, 12–35.

Ramesh, V. G., Thirumaran, K. P., and Raja, M. C. (2008). A new scale for prognostication in head injury. *Journal of Clinical Neuroscience, 15*, 1110–1113.

Rampon, C., Jiang, C. H., Dong, H., Tang, Y. P., Lockhart, D. J., Schultz, P. C. et al. (2000). Effects of environmental enrichment on gene expression in the brain. *Proceedings of the National Academy of Science (USA), 97*, 12880–12884.

Rape, R. N., Bush, J. P., and Slavin, L. A. (1992). Toward a conceptualization of the family's adaptation to a member's head injury: A critique of developmental stage models. *Rehabilitation Psychology, 37*(1), 3–22.

Rapoport, M., Chan, F., Lanctot, K., Herrmann, N., McCullagh, S., and Feinstein, A. (2008). An open-label study of citalopram for major depression following traumatic brain injury. *Journal of Psychopharmacology, 22*(8 Nov), 860–864.

Rappaport, M., Hall, K. M., Hopkins, K., Belleza, T., and Cope, D. N. (1982). Disability rating scale for severe head trauma: Coma to community. *Archives of Physical Medicine and Rehabilitation, 63*, 118–123.

Raskin, S. A. (2009). Memory for Intentions Screening Test: psychometric properties and clinical evidence. *Brain Impairment, 10*(1), 23–33.

Rath, J. F., Simon, D., Langenbahn, D. M., Sherr, R. L., and Diller, L. (2003). Group treatment of problem-solving deficits in outpatients with traumatic brain injury: A randomised outcome study. *Neuropsychological Rehabilitation, 13*, 461–488.

Regard, M. (1981). *Cognitive rigidity and flexibility: A neuropsychological study.* Unpublished PhD Dissertation, University of Victoria.

Reinhard, D. L., Whyte, J., and Sandel, M. E. (1996). Improved arousal and initiation following tricyclic antidepressant use in severe brain injury. *Archives of Physical Medicine and Rehabilitation, 77*(1), 80–83.

Reitan, R., and Wolfson, D. (2004). Theoretical, methodological and validational bases of the Halstead-Reitan neuropsychological test battery. In M. Hersen (Ed.), *Comprehensive Handbook of Psychological Assessment* (Vol. 1, pp. 105–131). New Jersey: John Wiley and Sons, Inc.

Reitan, R. M., and Wolfson, D. (1985). *The Halstead-Reitan Neuropsychological Test Battery*. Tucson, AZ: Neuropsychology Press.

Relander, M., Troupp, H. A., and Bjorkesten, G. (1972). Controlled trial of treatment for cerebral concussion. *British Medical Journal, 4*(5843, Dec. 30), 777–779.

Rendell, P. G., and Henry, J. D. (2009). A review of Virtual Week for prospective memory assessment: clinical implications. *Brain Impairment, 10*(1), 14–22.

Rey, A. (1959). *Le test de copie d'une figure complexe*. Paris: Editions du Centre de Psychologie Appliquée.

Rey, A. (1964). *L'Examen clinique en psychologie*. Paris: Presses Universitaires de France.

Richardson, J. T. E. (2000). *Clinical and neuropsychological aspects of closed head injury* (2nd ed.). Hove: Psychology Press.

Rimel, R. W., and Jane, J. A. (1984). Patient characteristics. In M. Rosenthal, E. R. Griffith, M. R. Bond and J. D. Miller (Eds.), *Rehabilitation of the head injured adult* (pp. 9–20). Philadelphia: Davis.

Rivara, J. B., Jaffe, K., Fay, G. C., Polissar, N. L., Martin, K. M., Shurtleff, H. A. et al. (1993). Family functioning and injury severity as predictors of child functioning one year following traumatic brain injury. *Archives of Physical Medicine and Rehabilitation, 74*, 1047–1055.

Rivara, P., Elliott, T. R., Berry, J. W., Grant, J. S., and Oswald, K. (2007). Predictors of caregiver depression among community-residing families living with traumatic brain injury. *NeuroRehabilitation, 22*, 3–8.

Rivara, P. A., Elliott, T. R., Berry, J. W., and Grant, J. S. (2008). Problem-solving training for family caregivers of persons with traumatic brain injuries: a randomized controlled trial. *Archives of Physical Medicine and Rehabilitation, 89*(5), 931–941.

Robertson, I., Gray, J. M., and McKenzie, S. (1988). Microcomputer-based cognitive rehabilitation of visual neglect: three multiple-baseline single-case studies. *Brain Injury, 2*, 151–163.

Robertson, I. H., Ward, T., Ridgeway, V., and Nimmo-Smith, I. (1994). *The Test of Everyday Attention*. Bury St. Edmunds: Thames Valley Test Company.

Robinson, R. G., and Jorge, R. E. (2002). Longitudinal course of mood disorders following traumatic brain injury. *Archives of General Psychiatry, 59*(1), 23–24.

Rocca, A., Wallen, M., and Batchelor, J. (2008). The Westmead Post-Traumatic Amnesia Scale for Children (WPTAS-C) aged 4 and 5 years old. *Brain Impairment, 9*(1), 14–21.

Rodgers, M. L., Strode, A. D., Norell, D. M., Short, R. A., Dyck, D. G., and Becker, B. (2007). Adapting multiple family group treatment for brain and spinal cord injury: intervention development and preliminary outcomes. *American Journal of Physical Medicine and Rehabilitation, 86*(6), 482–492.

Rohling, M. L., Beverly, B., Faust, M. E., and Demakis, G. (2009). Effectiveness of cognitive rehabilitation following acquired brain injury: A meta-analytic re-examination of Cicerone et al.'s (2000, 2005) systematic reviews. *Neuropsychology, 23*(1), 20–39.

Romano, M. D. (1974). Family response to traumatic head injury. *Scandinavian Journal of Rehabilitation Medicine, 6*, 1–4.

Rose, J. M. (2005). Continuum of care model for managing mild traumatic brain injury in a workers' compensation context: A description of the model and its development. *Brain Injury, 19*(1), 29–39.

Rosenbaum, M., and Najenson, T. (1976). Changes in life patterns and symptoms of low mood as reported by wives of severely brain-injured soldiers. *Journal of Consulting and Clinical Psychology, 44*, 881–888.

Rosenfeld, J. V. (2010). How confident can we be in predicting outcome in patients with a minimal Glasgow Coma Score? *Injury, 41*, 50–51.

Roth, P., and Farls, K. (2000). Pathophysiology of traumatic brain injury. *Critical Care Nursing Quarterly, 23*, 14–25.

Rothwell, N. A., LaVigna, G. W., and Willis, T. J. (1999). A non-aversive rehabilitation approach for people with severe behavioural problems resulting from brain injury. *Brain Injury, 13*(7), 521–533.

Rotondi, A. J., Sinkule, J., and Spring, M. (2005). An interactive Web-based intervention for persons with TBI and their families: use and evaluation by female significant others. *Journal of Head Trauma Rehabilitation, 20*(2), 173–185.

Ruff, R. (2005). Two decades of advances in understanding of mild traumatic brain injury. *Journal of Head Trauma Rehabilitation, 20*(1), 5–18.

Ruff, R., Mahaffey, R., Engel, J., Farrow, C., Cox, D., and Karzmark, P. (1994). Efficacy of THINKable in the attention and memory retraining of traumatically head-injured patients. *Brain Injury, 8*, 6–14.

Ruff, R. M., Baser, C. A., Johnson, J. W., Marshall, L. F., Klauber, S. K., Klauber, M. R. et al. (1989). Neuropsychological rehabilitation: An experimental study with head-injured patients. *Journal of Head Trauma Rehabilitation, 4*(3), 20–36.

Russell, W. R., and Nathan, P. W. (1946). Traumatic amnesia. *Brain, 69*, 280–300.

Russell, W. R., and Smith, A. (1961). Post-traumatic amnesia in closed head injury. *Archives of Neurology, 5*, 16–29.

Rutter, M., Chadwick, O., Shaffer, D., and Brown, G. (1980). A prospective study of children with head injuries: I. Design and methods. *Psychological Medicine, 10*, 633–646.

Ryan, T. V., and Ruff, R. M. (1988). The efficacy of structured memory retraining in a group comparison of head trauma patients. *Archives of Clinical Neuropsychology, 3*, 165–179.

Salazar, A. M., Warden, D. L., Schwab, K., Spector, J., Braverman, S., Walter, J. et al. (2000). Cognitive rehabilitation for traumatic brain injury: A randomized trial. Defense and Veterans Head Injury Program (DVHIP) Study Group. *JAMA: The Journal of the American Medical Association, 283*(23), 3123–3124.

Sale, P., West, M., Sherron, P., and Wehman, P. (1991). Exploratory analysis of job separations from supported employment for persons with traumatic brain injury. *Journal of Head Trauma Rehabilitation, 6*(3), 1–11.

Saling, M. M. (1994). Report writing in neuropsychology. In S. Touyz, D. Byrne and A. Gilandas (Eds.), *Neuropsychology in clinical practice* (pp. 394–400). Sydney: Harcourt Brace.

Salmond, C. H., Menon, D. K., Chatfield, D. A., Pickard, J. D., and Sahakian, B. J. (2006). Cognitive reserve as a resilience factor against depression after moderate/severe traumatic brain injury. *Journal of Neurotrauma, 23*(7), 1049–1058.

Saltapidas, H., and Ponsford, J. (2008). The influence of cultural background on experiences and beliefs following traumatic brain injury and their association with outcome. *Brain Impairment, 9*(1), 1–13.

Sandel, M. E., and Mysiw, W. J. (1996). The agitated brain injured patient. Part 1: definitions, differential, diagnosis, and assessment. *Archives of Physical Medicine and Rehabilitation, 77*, 617–623.

Sandel, M. E., Williams, K. S., Dellapietra, L., and Derogatis, L. R. (1996). Sexual functioning following traumatic brain injury. *Brain Injury, 10*(10), 719–728.

Sander, A. M., Caroselli, J. S., High, W. M., Becker, C., Neese, L., and Scheibel, R. (2002). Relationship of family functioning to progress in a post-acute rehabilitation programme following traumatic brain injury. *Brain Injury, 16*(8), 649–657.

Sander, A. M., Roebuck, T. M., Struchen, M. A., Sherer, M., and High, W. M. (2001). Long-term maintenance of gains obtained in post-acute rehabilitation by persons with traumatic brain injury. *Journal of Head Trauma Rehabilitation, 16*(4), 356–373.

Sander, A. M., Sherer, M., Malec, J. F., High, W. M., Thompson, R. N., Moessner, A. M. et al. (2003). Preinjury emotional and family functioning in caregivers of persons with traumatic brain injury. *Archives of Physical Medicine and Rehabilitation, 84*(2), 197–203.

Saneda, D. L., and Corrigan, J. D. (1992). Predicting clearing of post-traumatic amnesia following closed-head injury. *Brain Injury, 6*, 167–174.

Sarajuuri, J. M., Kaipio, M. L., Koskinen, S. K., Niemela, M. R., Servo, A. R., and Vilkki, J. S. (2005). Outcome of a comprehensive neurorehabilitation program for patients with traumatic brain injury. *Archives of Physical Medicine and Rehabilitation, 86*(December), 2296–2302.

Savage, R. C., DePompei, R., Tyler, J., and Lash, M. (2005). Paediatric traumatic brain injury: A review of pertinent issues. *Paediatric Rehabilitation, 8*(92–103).

Schacter, D. L., and Crovitz, H. F. (1977). Memory function after closed head injury: a review of quantitative research. *Cortex, 13*, 150–176.

Schaefer, P. W., Huisman, T. A., Sorensen, A. G., Gonzalez, R. G., and Schwamm, L. H. (2004). Diffusion-weighted MR imaging in closed head injury: high correlation with initial Glasgow coma scale score and score on modified Rankin scale at discharge. *Radiology, 233*(1), 58–66.

Scheutzow, M. H., and Wiercisiewski, D. R. (1999). Panic disorder in a patient with traumatic brain injury: a case report and discussion. *Brain Injury, 13*(9), 705–714.

Schmitter-Edgecombe, M., and Beglinger, L. (2001). Acquisition of skilled visual search performance following severe closed head injury. *Journal of the International Neuropsychological Society, 7*(5), 615–630.

Schmitter-Edgecombe, M., Fahy, J. F., Whelan, J. P., and Long, C. J. (1995). Memory remediation after severe closed head injury: Notebook training versus supportive therapy. *Journal of Consulting and Clinical Psychology, 63*(3), 484–489.

Schmitter-Edgecombe, M., and Kibby, M. (1998). Visual selective attention after severe closed head injury. *Journal of the International Neuropsychological Society, 4*, 144–159.

Schoenfeld, T. A., and Hamilton, L. W. (1977). Secondary brain changes following lesions: A new paradigm for lesion experimentation. *Physiology and Behaviour, 18*, 951–967.

Schoenle, P. W., and Witzke, W. (2004). How vegetative is the vegetative state? Preserved semantic processing in VS patients – evidence from N 400 event-related potentials. *NeuroRehabilitation, 19*(4), 329–334.

Schönberger, M., Humle, F., and Teasdale, T. W. (2006). The development of the therapeutic working alliance, patients' awareness and their compliance during the process of brain injury rehabilitation. *Brain Injury, 20*, 445–454.

Schönberger, M., Ponsford, J., Olver, J., and Ponsford, M. (2010). A longitudinal study of family functioning after TBI and relatives' emotional status. *Neuropsychological Rehabilitation, 20*(6), 813–829

Schönberger, M., Ponsford, J., Olver, J., Ponsford, M., and Wirtz, M. (2011a). Prediction of functional and employment outcome one year after Traumatic Brain Injury: A Structural Equation Modelling approach. *Journal of Neurology, Neurosurgery and Psychiatry, 82,* 936–941.

Schönberger, M., Ponsford, J., Reutens, D., Beare, R., and O'Sullivan, R. (2009). The relationship between age, injury severity and MRI findings following traumatic brain injury. *Journal of Neurotrauma, 26*, 2157–2167.

Schönberger, M., Ponsford, J. L., Gould, K. R., and Johnston, L. (2011b). The temporal relationship between depression, anxiety and functional status after traumatic brain injury: A cross-lagged analysis. *Journal of the International Neuropsychological Society, 17,* 1–11.

Schultheis, M. T., Matheis, R. J., Nead, R., and DeLuca, J. (2002). Driving behaviors following brain injury: Self-report and motor vehicle records. *Journal of Head Trauma Rehabilitation, 17*(1), 38–47.

Schutz, L. E., and Trainor, K. (2007). Evaluation of cognitive rehabilitation as a treatment paradigm. *Brain Injury, 21*(6), 545–557.

Schwartz, L., Taylor, H. G., Drotar, D., Yeates, K. O., Wade, S. L., and Stancin, T. (2003). Long-term behavior problems following pediatric traumatic brain injury: prevalence, predictors, and correlates. *Journal of Pediatric Psychology, 28*(4), 251–263.

Schwartz, M. L., Carruth, F., Binns, M. A., Brandys, L., Moulton, R., Snow, W. G. et al. (1998). The course of post-traumatic amnesia: Three little words. *Canadian Journal of Neurological Science, 25*(2), 108–116.

Seel, R. T., Kreutzer, J. S., Rosenthal, M., Hammond, F. M., Corrigan, J. D., and Black, K. (2003). Depression after traumatic brain injury: A national institute on disability and rehabilitation research model systems multicenter investigation. *Archives of Physical Medicine and Rehabilitation, 84*(2), 177–184.

Semel, E., Wiig, E. H., and Secord, W. A. (2006). *Clinical evaluation of language fundamentals* (4th ed.). Toronto, Canada: The Psychological Corporation/A Harcourt Assessment Company.

Sesma, H. W., Slomine, B. S., Ding, R., McCarthy, M. L., and the Children's Health After Trauma Study Group (2008). Executive functioning in the first year after pediatric traumatic brain injury. *Pediatrics, 121*(6), e1686–1695.

Shallice, T., and Burgess, P. W. (1991). Deficits in strategy application following frontal lobe damage in man. *Brain, 114*(2), 727–741.

Shames, J., Treger, I., Ring, H., and Giaquinto, S. (2007). Return to work following traumatic brain injury: Trends and challenges. *Disability and Rehabilitation, 29*(7), 1387–1395.

Shandro, J. R., Rivara, F. P., Wang, J., Jurkovich, G. J., Nathens, A. B., and MacKenzie, E. J. (2009). Alcohol and risk of mortality in patients with traumatic brain injury. *Journal of Trauma-Injury Infection and Critical Care, 66*(6), 1584–1590.

Sherbourne, C. D., and Stewart, A. L. (1991). The MOS Social Support Survey. *Social Science in Medicine, 32*(6), 705–714.

Sherer, M., Bergloff, P., Boake, C., High, W., and Levin, E. (1998a). The Awareness Questionnaire: Factor structure and internal consistency. *Brain Injury, 12*, 63–68.

Sherer, M., Boake, C., Levin, E., Silver, B. V., Ringholz, G., and High, W. M. (1998b). Characteristics of impaired awareness after traumatic brain injury. *Journal of the International Neuropsychological Society, 4*, 380–387.

Sherer, M., Hart, T., Nick, T. G., Whyte, J., Thompson, R. N., and Yablon, S. A. (2003). Early impaired self-awareness after traumatic brain injury. *Archives of Physical Medicine and Rehabilitation, 84*, 168–176.

Sherer, M., Novack, T. A., Sander, A. M., Struchen, M. A., Alderson, A., and Nakase Thompson, R. (2002a). Neuropsychological assessment and employment outcome after traumatic brain injury: A review. *The Clinical Neuropsychologist, 16*(2), 157–178.

Sherer, M., Sander, A. M., Nick, T. G., High, W. M., Malec, J. F., and Rosenthal, M. (2002b). Early cognitive status and productivity outcome after traumatic brain injury: Findings from the TBI Model Systems. *Archives of Physical Medicine and Rehabilitation, 83*, 183–192.

Sherer, M., Struchen, M. A., and Yablon, S. A. (2008). Comparison of indices of traumatic brain injury severity: Glasgow Coma Scale, length of coma and post-traumatic amnesia. *Journal of Neurology, Neurosurgery and Psychiatry, 79*(Oct 10), 678–685.

Shiel, A., Horn, S. A., Wilson, B. A., Watson, M. J., Campbell, M. J., and Mclellan, D. L. (2000). The Wessex Head injury matrix (WHIM) main scale: A preliminary report on a scale to assess and monitor patient recovery after severe head injury. *Clinical Rehabilitation, 14*, 408–416.

Shiel, A., Wilson, B. A., Horn, S., Watson, M., and McLellan, D. L. (1994). A scale to identify and evaluate cognitive behaviours after severe head injury. Paper presented at the Sixteenth European Conference of the International Neuropsychological Society, Angers, France.

Shimamura, A. P., Janowsky, J. S., and Squire, L. R. (1991). What is the role of frontal lobe damage in amnesic disorders? In H. S. Levin, H. M. Eisenberg and A. L. Benton (Eds.), *Frontal lobe functioning and dysfunction*. Oxford: Oxford University Press.

Shores, E. A. (1995). Further concurrent validity on the Westmead PTA Scale. *Applied Neuropsychology, 2*, 167–169.

Shores, E. A., Lammel, A., Hullick, C., Sheedy, J., Flynn, M., Levick, W. et al. (2008). The diagnostic accuracy of the Revised Westmead PTA Scale as an adjunct to the Glasgow Coma Scale in the early identification of cognitive impairment in patients with mild traumatic brain injury. *Journal of Neurology, Neurosurgery and Psychiatry, 79*(10), 1100–1106.

Shores, E. A., Marosszeky, J. E., Sandanam, J., and Batchelor, J. (1986). Preliminary validation of a scale for measuring the duration of post-traumatic amnesia. *Medical Journal of Australia, 144*, 569–572.

Shum, D., Fleming, J., and Neulinger, K. (2002). Prospective memory and traumatic brain injury: A review. *Brain Impairment, 3*(1), 1–16.

Shutter, L., Tong, K. A., Lee, A., and Holshouser, B. A. (2006). Prognostic role of proton magnetic resonance spectroscopy in acute traumatic brain injury. *Journal of Head Trauma Rehabilitation, 21*(4), 334–349.

Siegel, A., and Alavi, A. (1990). Brain imaging techniques. *Physical Medicine and Rehabilitation: State of the Art Reviews, 4*, 433–446.

Simpson, G., and Tate, R. (2007). Suicidality in people surviving a traumatic brain injury: prevalence, risk factors and implications for clinical management. *Brain Injury, 21*(13–14), 1335–1351.

Simpson, G. K. (1999). *You and me. An education program about sex and sexuality after traumatic brain injury*. Sydney: Brain Injury Rehabilitation Unit.

Simpson, G. K. (2001). Addressing the sexual concerns of persons with traumatic brain injury in rehabilitation settings: A framework for action. *Brain Impairment, 2*(2), 97–108.

Singer, G. H. S., Glang, A., Nixon, C., Cooley, E., Kerns, K. A., Williams, D. et al. (1994). A comparison of two psychosocial interventions for parents of children with acquired brain injury: An exploratory study. *Journal of Head Trauma Rehabilitation, 9*(4), 38–49.

Skoglund, T. S., Nilsson, D., Ljungberg, M., Jonsson, L., and Rydenhag, B. (2008). Long-term follow-up of a patient with traumatic brain injury using diffusion tensor imaging. *Acta Radiol, 49*(1), 98–100.

Slawik, H., Salmond, C. H., Taylor-Tavares, J. V., Williams, G. B., Sahakian, B. J., and Tasker, R. C. (2009). Frontal cerebral vulnerability and executive deficits from raised intracranial pressure in child traumatic brain injury. *Journal of Neurotrauma, 26*(11), 1891–1903.

Slifer, K. J., Tucker, C. L., Gerson, A. C., Sevier, R. C., Kane, A. C., Amari, A. et al. (1997). Antecedent management and compliance training improve adolescents' participation in early brain injury rehabilitation. *Brain Injury, 11*(12), 877–889.

Sloan, S. (2008, 15 August). Friendships and social networks following brain injury: Issues and Interventions. Paper presented at the Eighth Annual Workshop of the Victorian Brain Injury Recovery Assoc. Inc, Melbourne.

Sloan, S., Callaway, L., Winkler, D., McKinley, K., Ziino, C., and Anson, K. (2009a). Changes in care and support needs following community-based intervention for individuals with acquired brain injury. *Brain Impairment, 10*(3), 295–306.

Sloan, S., Callaway, L., Winkler, D., McKinley, K., Ziino, C., and Anson, K. (2009b). The Community Approach to Participation: Outcomes following acquired brain injury intervention. *Brain Impairment, 10*(3), 282–294.

Sloan, S., Mackie, J., and Chamberlain, S. (2006). *Communicate with confidence*. Kew, Victoria: Skilled Life Press.

Sloan, S., Winkler, D., and Anson, K. (2007). Long-term outcome following traumatic brain injury. *Brain Impairment, 8*(3), 251–261.

Sloan, S., Winkler, D., and Callaway, L. (2004). Community integration following severe traumatic brain injury: outcomes and best practice. *Brain Impairment, 5*(1), 12–29.

Slomine, B. S., Gerring, J. P., Grados, M. A., Vasa, R., Brady, K. D., Christensen, J. R. et al. (2002). Performance on measures of "executive function" following pediatric traumatic brain injury. *Brain Injury, 16*(9), 759–772.

Smith, A. (1973). *Symbol digit modalities test*. Los Angeles: Western Psychological Services.

Snaith, R. P., and Zigmond, A. S. (1994). *The Hospital Anxiety and Depression Scale with the Irritability-Depression-Anxiety Scale and the Leeds Situational Anxiety Scale: Manual*. Slough: NFER-Nelson.

Snow, P., Douglas, J., and Ponsford, J. (1995). Discourse assessment following traumatic brain injury: A pilot study examining some demographic and methodological issues. *Aphasiology, 9*(4), 365–380.

Snow, P., Douglas, J., and Ponsford, J. (1997). Procedural discourse following traumatic brain injury. *Aphasiology, 11*(10), 947–967.

Snow, P., Douglas, J., and Ponsford, J. (1998). Conversational discourse abilities following severe traumatic brain injury: A follow-up study. *Brain Injury, 12*(11), 911–935.

Snow, P. C., Douglas, J. M., and Ponsford, J. L. (1999). Narrative discourse abilities following severe traumatic brain injury: A longitudinal study. *Aphasiology, 13*(7), 529–551.

Sohlberg, M. M., and Mateer, C. A. (1987). Effectiveness of an attention-training program. *Journal of Clinical and Experimental Neuropsychology, 9*, 117–130.

Sohlberg, M. M., Mateer, C. A., Penkman, L., Glang, A., and Todis, B. (1998). Awareness intervention: Who needs it? *The Journal of Head Trauma Rehabilitation, 13*(5), 62–78.

Sohlberg, M. M., McLaughlin, K. A., Pavese, A., Heidrich, I., and Posner, M. I. (2000). Evaluation of attention process training and brain injury education in persons with acquired brain injury. *Journal of Clinical and Experimental Neuropsychology, 22*(5), 626–656.

Sohlberg, M. M., Sprunk, H., and Metzelaar, K. (1988). Efficacy of an external cuing system in an individual with severe frontal lobe damage. *Cognitive Rehabilitation, 6*, 36–40.

Sohlberg, M. M., White, O., Evans, E., and Mateer, C. (1992a). Background and initial case studies into the effects of prospective memory training. *Brain Injury, 6*, 129–138.

Sohlberg, M. M., White, O., Evans, E., and Mateer, C. (1992b). An investigation of the effects of prospective memory training. *Brain Injury, 6*, 139–154.

Soo, C., and Tate, R. (2007). Psychological treatment for anxiety in people with traumatic brain injury [Systematic Review]. *Cochrane Database of Systematic Reviews* 2007, Issue 3. Art. No.: CD005239. DOI: 10.1002/14651858.CD005239.pub2.

Spanos, G. K., Wilde, E. A., Bigler, E. D., Cleavinger, H. B., Fearing, M. A., Levin, H. S. et al. (2007). Cerebellar atrophy after moderate-to-severe pediatric traumatic brain injury. *American Journal of Neuroradiology, 28*(3), 537–542.

Sparrow, S., Balla, D., and Cicchetti, D. (1984). *Vineland Adaptive Behaviour Scales*. Circle Pines, MN: American Guidance Service.

Spell, L. A., and Frank, E. (2000). Recognition of nonverbal communication of affect following traumatic brain injury. *Journal of Nonverbal Behaviour, 24*, 285–300.

Spikman, J. M., Boelen, D. H. E., Lamberts, K. F., Brouwer, W. H., and Fasotti, L. (2010). Effects of a multifaceted treatment program for executive dysfunction after acquired brain injury on indications of executive functioning in daily life. *Journal of the International Neuropsychological Society, 16*(1), 118–129.

Spikman, J. M., van Zomeren, A. H., and Deelman, B. G. (1996). Deficits of attention after closed-head injury: slowness only? *Journal of Clinical and Experimental Neuropsychology, 18*(5), 755–767.

Squire, L. R., and Zola, S. M. (1996). Structure and function of declarative and nondeclarative memory systems. *Proceedings of the National Academy of Sciences of the United States of America, 93*(24), 13515–13522.

Stablum, F., Umilta, C., Mogentale, C., Carlan, M., and Guerrini, C. (2000). Rehabilitation of executive deficits in closed head injury and anterior communicating artery aneurysm patients. *Psychological Research, 63*(3–4), 265–278.

Stadler, M. A., and Ward, G. C. (2005). Supporting the narrative development of children. *Early Childhood Education Journal, 33*, 73–80.

Steele, D., Ponsford, J., Rajaratnam, S., and Redman, J. (2006). Self-reported changes to night-time sleep following traumatic brain injury. *Archives of Physical Medicine and Rehabilitation, 87*(2), 278–285.

Stein, D. G. (2001). Brain damage, sex hormones and recovery: a new role for progesterone and estrogen? *Trends in Neuroscience, 24*(7), 386–391.

Stein, N. L., and Glenn, C. G. (1979). An analysis of story comprehension in elementary school children. In R. O. Freedle (Ed.), *New directions in discourse processing* (pp. 53–120). New Jersey: Ablex Publishing Corporation.

Stern, J. M., and Stern, B. (1989). Visual imagery as a cognitive means of compensation for brain injury. *Brain Injury, 3*, 413–419.

Steward, O. (1989). Reorganization of neuronal connections following CNS trauma: Principles and experimental paradigms. *Journal of Neurotrauma, 6*(2), 99–152.

Stewart-Scott, A. M., and Douglas, J. M. (1998). Educational Outcome for Secondary and Postsecondary Students Following Traumatic Brain Injury. *Brain Injury, 12*(4), 317–331.

Strauss, E., Sherman, E. M. S., and Spreen, O. (2006). *A compendium of neuropsychological tests: Administration, norms, and commentary* (3rd ed.). New York: Oxford University Press.

Stroop, J. R. (1935). Studies of interference in serial verbal reactions. *Journal of Experimental Psychology, 18*, 643–662.

Struchen, M. A. (2005). Social communication interventions. In J. R. High, A. M. Sander, M. A. Struchen and K. A. Hart (Eds.), *Rehabilitation for traumatic brain injury* (pp. 88–117). Oxford: Oxford University Press.

Struchen, M. A., Clark, A. N., Sander, A. M., Mills, M. R., Evans, G., and Kurtz, D. (2008). Relation of executive functioning and social communication measures to functional outcomes following traumatic brain injury. *NeuroRehabilitation, 23*(2), 185–198.

Sturm, W., Willmes, K., Orgass, B., and Hartje, A. (1997). Do specific attention deficits need specific training? *Neuropsychological Rehabilitation, 7*, 81–193.

Stuss, D. T. (2007). New approaches to prefrontal lobe testing. In B. L. Miller and J. Cummings (Eds.), *The human frontal lobes: Functions and disorders* (2nd ed., pp. 292–305). New York: Guilford Press.

Stuss, D. T., and Benson, D. F. (1986). *The frontal lobes*. New York: Raven Press.

Stuss, D. T., Binns, M. A., Carruth, F. G., Levine, B., Brandys, C. E., Moulton, R. T. et al. (1999). The acute period of recovery from traumatic brain injury: Posttraumatic amnesia or posttraumatic confusional state? *Journal of Neurosurgery, 90*(4), 635–643.

Symonds, C. P., and Russell, W. R. (1943). Accidental head injuries: Prognosis in Service Patients. *Lancet, 1*, 7–10.

Tabar, K. H., Warden, D. L., and Hurley, R. A. (2006). Blast-related traumatic brain injury: what is known? *Journal of Neuropsychiatry and Clinical Neurosciences, 18*(2), 141–145.

Tate, R. (2004). Assessing support needs for people with traumatic brain injury: the Care And Needs Scale (CANS). *Brain Injury, 18*(5), 445–460.

Tate, R., McDonald, S., Perdices, M., Togher, L., Schultz, R., and Savage, S. (2008). Rating the methodological quality of single-subject designs and n-of-1 trials: Introducing the Single-Case experimental design (SCED) Scale. *Neuropsychological Rehabilitation, 18*(4), 385–401.

Tate, R. L., Broe, G. A., Cameron, I. D., Hodgkinson, A. E., and Soo, C. A. (2005). Pre-injury, injury and early post-injury predictors of long-term functional and psychosocial recovery after severe traumatic brain injury. *Brain Impairment, 6*, 75–89.

Tate, R. L., Fenelon, B., Manning, M. L., and Hunter, M. (1991). Patterns of neuropsychological impairment after severe blunt head injury. *The Journal of Nervous and Mental Disease, 179*, 117–126.

Tate, R. L., Hodgkinson, A., Veerabangsa, A., and Maggiotto, S. (1999). Measuring psychosocial recovery after traumatic brain injury: Psychometric properties of a new scale. *Journal of Head Trauma Rehabilitation, 14*, 543–557.

Tate, R. L., Lulham, J. M., Broe, G. A., Strettles, B., and Pfaff, A. (1989). Psychosocial outcome for the survivors of severe blunt head injury: The results from a consecutive series of 100 patients. *Journal of Neurology, Neurosurgery, and Psychiatry, 52*, 1128–1134.

Tate, R. L., Pfaff, A., Baguley, I. J., Marosszeky, J. E., Gurka, J. A., Hodgkinson, A. E. et al. (2006). A multicentre, randomised controlled trial examining the effect of test procedures measuring emergence from post-traumatic amnesia. *Journal of Neurology, Neurosurgery, and Psychiatry, 77*, 841–849.

Tate, R. L., Pfaff, A., Veerabangsa, A., and Hodgkinson, A. E. (2004). Measuring psychosocial recovery after brain injury: Change versus competency. *Archives of Physical Medicine and Rehabilitation, 85*, 538–545.

Taub, E., and Morris, D. M. (2001). Constraint-induced movement therapy to enhance recovery after stroke. *Current Atherosclerosis Reports, 3*, 279–286.

Taylor, H. G. (2010). Neurobehavioral outcomes of pediatric traumatic brain injury. In V. Anderson and K. O. Yeates (Eds.), *New frontiers in pediatric traumatic brain injury* (pp. 145–168). New York: Oxford University Press.

Taylor, H. G., Yeates, K. O., Wade, S. L., Drotar, D., Stancin, T., and Burant, C. (2001). Bidirectional child-family influences on outcomes of traumatic brain injury in children. *Journal of the International Neuropsychological Society, 7*, 753–767.

Taylor, R. (2008). *The intentional relationship: Occupational therapy and use of self.* Philadelphia: Davis.

Teasdale, G. (1995). Head injury. *Journal of Neurology Neurosurgery and Psychiatry, 58*(5), 526–539.

Teasdale, G., and Jennett, B. (1974). Assessment of coma and impaired consciousness: A practical scale. *Lancet, 2*, 81–84.

Teasdale, G., and Jennett, B. (1976). Assessment and prognosis of coma after head injury. *Acta Neurochirurgica, 34*, 45–55.

Teasdale, T. W., and Christensen, A. L. (1994). Psychosocial outcome in Denmark. In A. L. Christensen and B. P. Uzzell (Eds.), *Brain injury and neuropsychological rehabilitation: International perspectives* (pp. 235–244). Hillsdale, NJ: Lawrence Erlbaum Associates.

Temkin, N. R., Dikmen, S. S., Anderson, G. D., Wilensky, A. J., Holmes, M. D., Cohen, W. et al. (1999). Valproate therapy for prevention of posttraumatic seizures: a randomized trial. *Journal of Neurosurgery, 91*(4), 593–600.

Testa, J. A., Malec, J. F., Moessner, A. M., and Brown, A. W. (2006). Predicting family functioning after TBI: impact of neurobehavioral factors. *Journal of Head Trauma Rehabilitation, 21*(3), 236–247.

Teuber, H. L. (1975). Recovery of function after brain injury in man, *Ciba Foundation Symposium no. 34: Outcome of severe damage to the central nervous system* (pp. 159–190). Amsterdam: Elsevier.

The Brain Trauma Foundation, The American Association of Neurological Surgeons, and The Joint Section on Neurotrauma and Critical Care (2000). Role of antiseizure prophylaxis following head injury. *Journal of Neurotrauma, 17*(6–7), 549–543.

The Psychological Corporation (2001). *Wechsler Test of Adult Reading*. San Antonio, TX: Author.

Thoene, A. I. T., and Glisky, E. L. (1995). Learning of name-face associations in memory impaired patients: A comparison of different training procedures. *Journal of the International Neuropsychological Society, 1*, 29–38.

Thomsen, I. V. (1984). Late outcome of very severe blunt head injury: a ten to fifteen year second follow-up. *Journal of Neurology, Neurosurgery, and Psychiatry, 47*, 260–268.

Titov, N., and Knight, R. G. (2005). A computer-based procedure for assessing functional cognitive skills in patients with neurological injuries: The virtual street. *Brain Injury, 19*(5), 315–322.

Todd, J., Loewy, J., Kelly, G., and Simpson, G. (2004). Managing challenging behaviour: Getting interventions to work in non-specialised community settings. *Brain Impairment, 5*(1), 42–52.

Todd, J. A., Anderson, V. A., and Lawrence, J. (1996). Planning skills in head injured adolescents and their peers. *Neuropsychological Rehabilitation, 6*, 81–99.

Todis, B., and Glang, A. (2008). Redefining success: results of a qualitative study of postsecondary transition outcomes for youth with traumatic brain injury. *Journal of Head Trauma Rehabilitation, 23*(4), 252–263.

Togal, N. B., Hakyemez, B., Erdogan, C., Bulut, M., Koksal, O., Akkose, S. et al. (2008). MR imaging in the detection of diffuse axonal injury with mild traumatic brain injury. *Neurology Research, 30*(9), 974–978.

Togher, L. (2000). Giving information: The importance of context on communicative opportunity for people with traumatic brain injury. *Aphasiology, 14*(4), 365–390.

Togher, L., McDonald, S., Code, C., and Grant, S. (2004). Training communication partners of people with traumatic brain injury: A randomised controlled trial. *Aphasiology, 18*(4), 313–335.

Togher, L., McDonald, S., Tate, R., Power, E., and Rietdijk, R. (2009). Training communication partners of people with traumatic brain injury: Reporting the protocol for a clinical trial. *Brain Impairment, 10*(2), 188–204.

Tombaugh, T. N. (1997). The Test of Memory Malingering (TOMM): Normative data from cognitively intact and cognitively impaired individuals. *Psychological Assessment, 9*(3), 260–268.

Trombly, C. A., and Radomski, M. V. (2002). *Occupational therapy for physical dysfunction* (5th ed.). Philadelphia: Lippincott, Williams and Wilkins.

Turkstra, L., McDonald, S., and DePompei, R. (2001). Social information processing in adolescents: Data from normally developing adolescents and preliminary data from their peers with traumatic brain injury. *Journal of Head Trauma Rehabilitation, 16*(5), 469–483.

Turkstra, L. S. (2008). Conversational-based assessment of social cognition in adults with traumatic brain injury. *Brain Injury, 22*(5), 397–409.

Turkstra, L. S., and Flora, T. L. (2002). Compensating for executive function impairments after TBI: A single case study of functional intervention. *Journal of Communication Disorders, 35*, 467–482.

Turner, A. P., Kivlahan, D. R., Rimmele, C. T., and Bombardier, C. H. (2006). Does Preinjury Alcohol Use or Blood Alcohol Level Influence Cognitive Functioning After Traumatic Brain Injury? *Rehabilitation Psychology, 51*(1), 78–86.

Turner, B., Ownsworth, T., Cornwell, P., and Fleming, J. (2009). Reengagement in Meaningful Occupations During the Transition From Hospital to Home for People With Acquired Brain Injury and Their Family Caregivers. *The American Journal of Occupational Therapy, 63*(5), 609.

Tweedly, L., Ponsford, J., and Lee, N. Investigation of the effectiveness of brief interventions to reduce alcohol consumption following Traumatic Brain Injury (in press). *Journal of Head Trauma Rehabilitation*, Accepted 30 May 2012.

Tyerman, A., and Humphrey, M. (1984). Changes in self concept following severe head injury. *International Journal of Rehabilitation Research, 7*, 11–23.

Tyerman, A., Young, K., and Booth, J. (1994). *Change in family roles after severe traumatic brain injury*. Paper presented at the Fourth Conference of the International Association for the Study of Traumatic Brain Injury.

Udekwu, P., Kromhout-Schiro, S., Vaslef, S., Baker, C., and Oller, D. (2004). Glasgow Coma Scale Score, mortality, and functional outcome in head-injured patients. *The Journal of Trauma: Injury, Infection, and Critical Care, 56*(5), 1084–1089.

Uomoto, J. M., and Brockway, J. A. (1992). Anger management training for brain injured patients and their family members. *Archives of Physical Medicine and Rehabilitation, 73*, 674–679.

Urbach, J. R., Sonenklar, N. A., and Culbert, J. P. (1994). Risk factors and assessment of children of brain-injured parents. *Journal of Neuropsychiatry, 6*, 289–295.

Vakil, E. (2005). The effect of moderate to severe traumatic brain injury (TBI) on different aspects of memory: A selective review. *Journal of Clinical and Experimental Neuropsychology, 27*(8), 977–1021.

Van Den Broek, M. D., Downes, J., Johnson, Z., Dayus, B., and Hilton, N. (2000). Evaluation of an electronic memory aid in the neuropsychological rehabilitation of prospective memory deficits. *Brain Injury, 14*, 435–462.

van der Naalt, J., van Zomeren, A. H., Sluiter, W. J., and Minderhoud, J. M. (1999). One year outcome in mild to moderate head injury: The predictive value of acute injury characteristics related to complaints and return to work. *Journal of Neurology, Neurosurgery and Psychiatry, 66*(2), 207–213.

Van Heugten, C., Hendriksen, J., Rasquin, S., Dijcks, B., Jaeken, D., and Vles, J. (2006). Long-term neuropsychological performance in a cohort of children and adolescents after severe paediatric traumatic brain injury. *Brain Injury, 20*(9), 895–903.

van Zomeren, A. H., Brouwer, W. H., and Minderhoud, J. M. (1987). Acquired brain damage and car driving: A review. *Archives of Physical Medicine and Rehabilitation, 68*, 697–705.

van Zomeren, A. H., and van den Burg, W. (1985). Residual complaints of patients two years after severe head injury. *Journal of Neurology, Neurosurgery and Psychiatry, 48*, 21–28.

Van't Hooft, I. (2010). Neuropsychological rehabilitation in children with traumatic brain injuries. In V. Anderson and K. O. Yeates (Eds.), *Pediatric traumatic brain injury: New frontiers in clinical and translational research* (pp. 169–191). New York: Cambridge University Press.

Vander Schaaf, S. (1990). An operational model of lifelong living. *Journal of Head Trauma Rehabilitation, 5*(1), 40–46.

Vanderploeg, R. D., Schwab, K., Walker, W. C., Fraser, J. A., Sigford, B. J., Date, E. S. et al. (2008). Rehabilitation of traumatic brain injury in active duty military personnel and veterans; Defense and Veterans Brain Injury Center randomized controlled trial of two rehabilitation approaches. *Archives of Physical Medicine and Rehabilitation, 89*(December), 2227–2238.

Vanhaudenhuyse, A., Laureys, S., and Perrin, F. (2008). Cognitive event-related potentials in comatose and post-comatose states. *Neurocritical Care, 8*, 262–270.

Veltman, J. C., Brouwer, W., van Zomeren, A. H., and van Wolffelaar, P. C. (1996). Central executive aspects of attention in subacute severe and very severe closed head injury patients: Planning, inhibition, flexibility, and divided attention. *Neuropsychology, 10*, 357–367.

Verhaeghe, S., Defloor, T., and Grypdonck, M. (2002). Stress and coping among families of patients with traumatic brain injury: a review of the literature. *Journal of Clinical Nursing, 14*(8), 1004–1012.

Verma, A. (2000). Opportunities for neuroprotection in traumatic brain injury. *Journal of Head Trauma Rehabilitation, 15*(5), 1149–1161.

Viano, D. L., Casson, I. R., Pellman, E. J., Zhang, L., King, A. L., and Yang, K. H. (2005). Concussion in professional football: brain responses by finite element analysis. part 9. *Neurosurgery, 57*, 891–916.

Vitaz, T. W., Jenks, J., Raque, G. H., and Shields, C. B. (2003). Outcome following moderate traumatic brain injury. *Surgical Neurology, 60*, 285–291.

Vogenthaler, D. R., Smith, K. R., Jr., and Goldfader, P. (1989). Head injury, an empirical study: Describing long-term productivity and independent living outcome. *Brain Injury, 3*, 355–368.

von Cramon, D. Y., and Matthes-von Cramon, G. (1994). Back to work with a chronic dysexecutive syndrome? (A case report). *Neuropsychological Rehabilitation, 4*, 399–417.

von Cramon, D. Y., Matthes-von Cramon, G., and Mai, N. (1991). Problem-solving deficits in brain-injured patients: A therapeutic approach. *Neuropsychological Rehabilitation, 1*, 45–64.

Vungkhanching, M., Heinemann, A. W., Langley, M. J., Ridgely, M., and Kramer, K. M. (2007). Feasibility of a skills-based substance abuse prevention program following traumatic brain injury. *Journal of Head Trauma Rehabilitation, 22*(3), 167–176.

Waaland, P. K., and Kreutzer, J. S. (1988). Family response to childhood traumatic brain injury. *Journal of Head Trauma Rehabilitation, 3*(4), 51–63.

Wade, D. T. (2003). Stroke rehabilitation: The evidence. In R. J. Greenwood, M. P. Barnes, T. M. McMillan and C. D. Ward (Eds.), *Handbook of neurological rehabilitation* (2nd ed., pp. 487–504). Hove: Psychology Press.

Wade, D. T., King, N. S., Wenden, F. J., Crawford, S., and Caldwell, F. E. (1998). Routine follow up after head injury: a second randomised controlled trial. *Journal of Neurology, Neurosurgery and Psychiatry, 65*(2 Aug), 177–183.

Wade, S. L., Carey, J., and Wolfe, C. R. (2006a). An online family intervention to reduce parental distress following pediatric brain injury. *Journal of Consulting and Clinical Psychology, 74*(3), 445–454.

Wade, S. L., Michaud, L., and Brown, T. M. (2006b). Putting the pieces together: preliminary efficacy of a family problem-solving intervention for children with traumatic brain injury. *Journal of Head Trauma Rehabilitation, 21*(1), 57–67.

Wade, S. L., Oberjohn, K., Burkhardt, A., and Greenberg, I. (2009). Feasibility and preliminary efficacy of a web-based parenting skills program for young children with traumatic brain injury. *Journal of Head Trauma Rehabilitation, 24*(4), 239–247.

Wade, S. L., Stancin, T., Taylor, H. G., Drotar, D., Yeates, K. O., and Minich, N. M. (2004). Interpersonal stressors and resources as predictors of parental adaptation following paediatric traumatic brain injury. *Journal of Consulting and Clinical Psychology, 72*(5), 776–784.

Wade, T. K., and Troy, J. C. (2001). Mobile phones as a new memory aid. *Brain Injury, 15*, 305–320.

Walker, A. J., Nott, M. T., Doyle, M., Onus, M., McCarthy, K., and Baguley, I. J. (2010a). Effectiveness of a group anger management programme after severe traumatic brain injury. *Brain Injury, 24*(3), 517–524.

Walker, N., Mellick, D., Brooks, C. A., and Whiteneck, G. G. (2003). Measuring participation across impairment groups using the Craig Handicap Assessment Reporting Technique. *American Journal of Physical Medicine and Rehabilitation, 82*(12), 936–941.

Walker, W. C., Ketchum, J. M., Marwitz, J. H., Chen, T., Hammond, F., Sherer, M. et al. (2010b). A multicentre study on the clinical utility of post-traumatic amnesia duration in predicting global outcome after moderate-severe traumatic brain injury. *Journal of Neurology, Neurosurgery and Psychiatry, 81*, 87–89.

Walsh, K. (1994a). Neuropsychological assessment of patients with memory disorders. In S. Touyz, D. Byrne and A. Gilandas (Eds.), *Neuropsychology in clinical practice* (pp. 107–127). Sydney: Academic Press.

Walsh, K. W. (1994b). *Neuropsychology: A clinical approach* (3rd ed.). Edinburgh: Churchill Livingstone.

Walsh, K. W. (Ed.). (1991). *Understanding brain damage: A primer of neuropsychological evaluation* (2nd ed.). Edinburgh: Churchill Livingstone.

Walsh, K. W., and Darby, D. (1999). *Neuropsychology: A clinical approach.* (4th ed.) Edinburgh: Churchill Livingstone.

Ward, H., Shum, D., Wallace, G., and Boon, J. (2002). Pediatric traumatic brain injury and procedural memory. *Journal of Clinical and Experimental Neuropsychology, 24*(4), 458–470.

Warden, D. L., Gordon, B., McAllister, T. W., Silver, J. M., Barth, J. T., Bruns, J. et al. (2006). Guidelines for the pharmacologic treatment of neurobehavioral sequelae of traumatic brain injury. *Journal of Neurotrauma, 23*(10), 1468–1501.

Watanabe, T., Black, K., Zafonte, R., Millis, S. R., and Mann, N. (1998). Do calendars enhance posttraumatic temporal orientation? A pilot study. *Brain Injury, 12*, 81–85.

Watts, A., and Douglas, J. M. (2006). Interpreting facial expression and communication competence following severe traumatic brain injury. *Aphasiology, 20*(8), 707–722.

Webster, M. J., and Ungerleider, L. G. (2000). Neuroanatomy of visual attention. In R. Parasuraman (Ed.), *The attentive brain* (pp. 19–34). Cambridge, MA: The MIT Press.

Wechsler, D. (2008). *Wechsler Adult Intelligence Scale: Fourth edition.* Sydney: NCS Pearson, Inc.

Wechsler, D. (2009a). *Wechsler Individual Achievement Test: Third edition (WIAT-III).* Austin, TX: Pearson Assessment.

Wechsler, D. (2009b). *Wechsler Memory Scale: Fourth edition.* San Antonio, TX: Pearson.

Wehman, P., Kregel, J., Keyser-Marcus, L., Sherron-Targett, P., Campbell, L., West, M. et al. (2003). Supported employment for persons with traumatic brain injury: A preliminary investigation of long-term follow-up costs and program efficiency. *Archives of Physical Medicine and Rehabilitation, 84*(February), 192–196.

Wehman, P., Kregel, J., Sherron, P., Nguyen, S., Kreutzer, J., Fry, R. et al. (1993). Critical factors associated with the successful supported employment placement of patients with severe traumatic brain injury. *Brain Injury, 7*, 31–44.

Wehman, P., Kreutzer, J., West, M., Sherron, P., Zasler, N., Groah, C. et al. (1990). Return to work for persons with traumatic brain injury: a supported employment approach. *Archives of Physical Medicine and Rehabilitation, 71*, 1047–1052.

Wells, R., Dywan, J., and Dumas, J. (2005). Life satisfaction and distress in family caregivers as related to specific behavioural changes after traumatic brain injury. *Brain Injury, 19*(3), 1105–1115.

Westra, H. A., and Dozois, D. J. (2006). Preparing clients for cognitive behavioral therapy: A randomized pilot study of motivational interviewing for anxiety. *Cognitive Therapy and Research, 30*(4), 481–498.

Whelan-Goodinson, R., Ponsford, J., Johnston, L., and Grant, F. (2009a). Psychiatric disorders following traumatic brain injury: Their nature and frequency. *Journal of Head Trauma Rehabilitation, 24*, 324–332.

Whelan-Goodinson, R., Ponsford, J., and Schönberger, M. (2008). The association between psychiatric state and outcome following traumatic brain injury. *Journal of Rehabilitation Medicine, 40*(10), 850–857.

Whelan-Goodinson, R., Ponsford, J., and Schönberger, M. (2009b). Validity of the Hospital Anxiety and Depression Scale to assess depression and anxiety following traumatic brain injury as compared with the Structured Clinical Interview for DSM-IV. *Journal of Affective Disorders, 114*(1), 94–102.

Whelan-Goodinson, R., Ponsford, J., Schönberger, M., and Johnston, L. (2010). Predictors of psychiatric disorders following traumatic brain injury. *Journal of Head Trauma Rehabilitation, 25*(5), 320–329.

Whiteneck, G., Brooks, C. A., Mellick, D., Harrison-Felix, C., Terrill, M. S., and Noble, K. (2004). Population-based estimates of outcomes after hospitalization for traumatic brain injury in Colorado. *Archives of Physical Medicine and Rehabilitation, 85*, 73–81.

Whiteneck, G. G., Charlifue, S. W., Gerhart, K. A., Overholser, J. D., and Richardson, G. N. (1992). *Guide for use of the CHART Craig Handicap Assessment and Reporting Technique*. Englewood, CO: Craig Hospital.

Whiteneck, G., and Dijkers, M. P. (2009). Difficult to measure constructs: Conceptual and methodological issues concerning participation and environmental factors. *Archives of Physical Medicine and Rehabilitation, 90*(11, Supplement 1), S22–S35.

Whiteneck, G. G., Gerhardt, K. A., and Cusick, C. P. (2004). Identifying environmental factors that influence the outcomes of people with traumatic brain injury. *Journal of Head Trauma Rehabilitation, 19*(3), 191–204.

Whiteneck, G. G., Harrison-Felix, C. L., Mellick, D. C., Brooks, C. A., Charlifue, S. W., and Gerhart, K. A. (2004). Quantifying environmental factors: A measure of physical, attitudinal, service, productivity, and policy barriers. *Archives of Physical Medicine and Rehabilitation, 85*, 1324–1335.

WHO (1980). *International Classification of impairments, disabilities, and handicaps: A manual of classification relating to the consequences of disease*. Geneva: World Health Organization.

WHO (2002). *Towards a Common Language for Functioning, Disability and Health ICF*. Geneva: World Health Organization.

Whyte, J., Fleming, M., Polansky, M., Cavallucci, C., and Coslett, H. B. (1998). The effects of visual distraction following traumatic brain injury. *Journal of the International Neuropsychological Society, 4*, 127–136.

Whyte , J., Hart, T., Bode, R.K., and Malec, J. F. (2003). The Moss Attention Rating Scale for traumatic brain injury: initial psychometric assessment. *Archives of Physical Medicine and Rehabilitation, 84*, 268–76.

Whyte , J., Hart, T., Ellis, C.A., and Chervoneva, I. (2008). The Moss Attention Rating Scale for traumatic brain injury: further explorations of reliability and sensitivity to change. *Archives of Physical Medicine and Rehabilitation, 89*, 966–73.

Whyte, J., Polansky, M., Cavallucci, C., Fleming, M., Lhulier, J., and Coslett, H. B. (1996). Inattentive behaviour after traumatic brain injury. *Journal of the International Neuropsychological Society, 2*, 274–281.

Whyte, J., Ponsford, J., Watanabe, T., and Hart, T. (2010). Traumatic Brain Injury. In W. R. Frontera, J. D. Delisa, B. M. Gans, N. A. Walsh and L. Robinson (Eds.), *Delisa's physical medicine and rehabilitation: Principles and practice* (5th ed., pp. 575–623). Philadelphia: Wolters Kluwer, Lippincott Williams and Wilkins.

Wiig, E. H., and Secord, W. A. (1989). *Test of language competence – expanded edition*. San Antonio, TX: The Psychological Corporation.

Wiig, E. H., and Semel, E. M. (1976). *Language disabilities in children and adolescents*. Columbus, OH: Charles E. Merrill Publishing Company.

Wijdicks, E. F. M., Bamlet, W. R., Maramattom, B. V., Manno, E. M., and McClelland, R. L. (2005). Validation of a new coma scale: The FOUR score. *Annals of Neurology, 58*, 585–593.

Wijnen, V. J. M., van Boxtel, G. J. M., Eilander, H. J., and de Gelder, B. (2007). Mismatch negativity predicts recovery from the vegetative state. *Clinical Neurophysiology, 118*, 597–605.

Wilde, E. A., Bigler, E. D., Haider, J. M., Chu, Z., Levin, H. S., Li, X. et al. (2006a). Vulnerability of the anterior commissure in moderate to severe pediatric traumatic brain injury. *Journal of Child Neurology, 21*(9), 769–776.

Wilde, E. A., Bigler, E. D., Hunter, J. V., Fearing, M. A., Scheibel, R. S., Newsome, M. R. et al. (2007). Hippocampus, amygdala, and basal ganglia morphometrics in children after moderate-to-severe traumatic brain injury. *Developmental Medicine and Child Neurology, 49*(4 Apr), 294–299.

Wilde, E. A., Bigler, E. D., Pedroza, C., and Ryser, D. (2006b). Post-traumatic amnesia predicts long-term cerebral atrophy in traumatic brain injury. *Brain Injury, 20*, 695–699.

Wilde, E. A., McCauley, S. R., Hunter, J. V., Bigler, E. D., Chu, Z., Wang, Z. J. et al. (2008). Diffusion tensor imaging of acute mild traumatic brain injury in adolescents. *Neurology, 70*(12), 948–955.

Willer, B., Allen, K., Durnan, M., and Ferry, A. (1990). Problems and coping strategies of mothers, siblings and young adult males with traumtic brain injury. *Canadian Journal of Rehabilitation, 3*(3), 167–173.

Willer, B., and Corrigan, J. D. (1994). Whatever It Takes: a model for community-based services. *Brain Injury, 8*, 647–659.

Willer, B., Rosenthal, M., Kreutzer, J. S., Gordon, W. A., and Rempel, R. (1993). Assessment of community integration following rehabilitation for traumatic brain injury. *Journal of Head Trauma Rehabilitation, 8*(2), 75–87.

Willer, B. S., Allen, K., Anthony, J., and Cowlan, G. (1993). *Circles of support for individuals with acquired brain injury. Manual*. State University of New York at Buffalo, Buffalo, NY: Rehabilitation Research and Training Center on Community Integration of Persons with Traumatic Brain Injury.

Willer, B. S., Allen, K. M., Liss, M., and Zicht, M. S. (1991). Problems and coping strategies of individuals with traumatic brain injury and their spouses. *Archives of Physical Medicine and Rehabilitation, 72*, 460–468.

Willis, T. J., and LaVigna, G. W. (2003). The safe management of physical aggression using multi-element positive practices in community settings. *Journal of Head Trauma Rehabilitation, 18*(1), 75–87.

Willmott, C., Ponsford, J., Hocking, C., and Schönberger, M. (2009). Factors contributing to attentional impairments following traumatic brain injury. *Neuropsychology, 23*(4), 424–432.

Wilson, B., Alderman, N., Burgess, P. W., Emslie, H., and Evans, J. J. (1996). *Behavioural Assessment of the Dysexecutive Syndrome*. Bury St Edmunds: Thames Valley Test Company.

Wilson, B., Greenfield, E., Clare, L., Cockburn, J., Baddeley, A., Watson, P. et al. (2008). *Rivermead Behavioural Memory Test (RBMT-III)*. London: Pearson Assessment.

Wilson, B. A. (1987a). *Rehabilitation of memory*. New York: Guilford Press.

Wilson, B. A. (1987b). Single-case experimental designs in neuropsychological rehabilitation. *Journal of Clinical and Experimental Neuropsychology, 9*, 527–544.

Wilson, B. A. (1991). Long-term prognosis of patients with severe memory disorders. *Neuropsychological Rehabilitation, 1*, 117–134.

Wilson, B. A. (2009). *Memory rehabilitation. Integrating theory and practice*. New York: Guilford Press.

Wilson, B. A., Baddeley, A., Shiel, A., and Patton, G. (1992). How does post-traumatic amnesia differ from the amnesic syndrome and from chronic memory impairment? *Neuropsychological Rehabilitation, 2*, 169–256.

Wilson, B. A., Cockburn, J., and Halligan, P. W. (1987). *The Behavioural Inattention Test*. Bury St. Edmunds: Thames Valley Test Company.

Wilson, B. A., Emslie, H. C., Quirk, K., and Evans, J. J. (2001). Reducing everyday memory and planning problems by means of a paging system. A randomised controlled crossover study. *Journal of Neurology, Neurosurgery and Psychiatry, 70*, 477–482.

Wilson, B. A., Evans, J., Brentnall, S., Bremner, S., Keohane, C., and Williams, H. (2000). The Oliver Zangwill Center for Neuropsychological Rehabilitation. In A. Christensen and B. Uzzell (Eds.), *International handbook of neuropsychological rehabilitation* (Vol. 231–246). New York: Kluwer Press/Plenum Publishing.

Wilson, B. A., Evans, J. J., Emslie, H. C., and Malinek, V. (1997). Evaluation of NeuroPage: A new memory aid. *Journal of Neurology, Neurosurgery and Psychiatry, 63*, 113–115.

Wilson, B. A., Scott, H., Evans, J., and Emslie, H. C. (2003). Preliminary report of a NeuroPage service within a health care system. *NeuroRehabilitation, 18*, 3–8.

Wilson, B. A., Shiel, A., Watson, M., Horn, S., and McLellan, L. (1994). Monitoring behaviour during coma and posttraumatic amnesia. In A.-L. Christensen and B. Uzzell (Eds.), *Brain injury and neuropsychological rehabilitation: International perspectives* (pp. 85–98). Hillsdale, NJ: Lawrence Erlbaum Associates.

Wilson, J. T. L., Pettigrew, L. E. L., and Teasdale, G. M. (1998). Structured interviews for the Glasgow Outcome Scale and the Extended Glasgow Outcome Scale: Guidelines for their use. *Journal of Neurotrauma, 15*, 573–585.

Winkens, I., Van Heugten, C. M., Wade, D. T., and Fasotti, L. (2009a). Training patients in Time Pressure Management, a cognitive strategy for mental slowness. *Clinical Rehabilitation, 23*(1), 79–90.

Winkens, I., Van Heugten, C. M., Wade, D. T., Habets, E., and Fasotti, L. (2009b). Efficacy of time pressure management in stroke patients with slowed information processing: a randomized controlled trial. *Archives of Physical Medicine and Rehabilitation, 90*(10), 1672–1679.

Winkler, D., Sloan, S., and Callaway, L. (2007). Younger people in residential aged care: support needs, preferences and future directions. Melbourne: Summer Foundation Ltd.

Winkler, D., Unsworth, C., and Sloan, S. (2005). Time use following a severe traumatic brain injury. *Journal of Occupational Science, 12*(2), 69–81.

Winkler, D., Unsworth, C., and Sloan, S. (2006). Factors that lead to successful community integration following severe traumatic brain injury. *Journal of Head Trauma Rehabilitation, 21*, 8–21.

Winogron, H. W., Knights, R. M., and Bawden, H. N. (1984). Neuropsychological deficits following head injury in children. *Journal of Clinical Neuropsychology, 6*, 269–286.

Winstanley, J., Simpson, G., Tate, R., and Myles, B. (2006). Early indicators and contributors to psychological distress in relatives during rehabilitation following severe TBI: Findings from Brain Injury Outcomes Study. *Journal of Head Trauma Rehabilitation, 21*(6), 453–456.

Wise, E. K., Mathews-Dalton, C., Dikmen, S., Temkin, N., Machamer, J., Bell, K. et al. (2010). Impact of traumatic brain injury on participation in leisure activities. *Archives of Physical Medicine and Rehabilitation, 91*(9), 1357–1362.

Wolf, C. A., Wijdicks, E. F. M., Bamlet, W. R., and McClelland, R. L. (2007). Further validation of the FOUR Score Coma Scale by intensive care nurses. *Mayo Clinic Proceedings, 82*(4), 435–438.

Wood, R. L. (1984). Behaviour disorders following severe brain injury: their presentation and psychological management. In N. Brooks (Ed.), *Closed head injury: Psychological, social and family consequences* (pp. 195–219). Oxford: Oxford University Press.

Wood, R. L. (1987). *Brain injury rehabilitation: A neurobehavioural approach*. London: Croom Helm.

Wood, R. L. (2004). Understanding the "miserable minority": a diasthesis-stress paradigm for post-concussional syndrome. *Brain Injury, 18*(11), 1135–1153.

Wood, R. L., and Fussey, I. (1987). Computer-based cognitive retraining: a controlled study. *International Disability Studies, 9*(4), 149–153.

Wood, R. L., and Rutterford, N. A. (2006a). Demographic and cognitive predictors of long-term psychosocial outcome following traumatic brain injury. *Journal of the International Neuropsychological Society, 12*, 350–358.

Wood, R. L., and Rutterford, N. A. (2006b). The long term effect of head trauma on intellectual abilities: A 16 year outcome study. *Journal of Neurology, Neurosurgery and Psychiatry, 77*(10), 1180–1184.

Wood, R. L., and Yurdakul, L. K. (1997). Change in relationship status following traumatic brain injury. *Brain Injury, 11*(7), 491–502.

Woods, B. T., and Teuber, H. L. (1973). Early onset of complementary specialisation of cerebral hemispheres in man. *Transactions of the American Neurological Association, 98*, 113–117.

World Health Organization. (2000). *Disability Assessment Schedule. WHODAS II.* http://www.who.int/icidh/whodas/index.html.

Wozniak, J. R., Krach, L., Ward, E., Mueller, B. A., Muetzel, R., Schnoebelen, S. et al. (2007). Neurocognitive and neuroimaging correlates of pediatric traumatic brain injury: a diffusion tensor imaging (DTI) study. *Archives of Clinical Neuropsychology, 22*(5), 555–568.

Wroblewski, B. A., Joseph, A. B., Kupfer, J., and Kalliel, K. (1997). Effectiveness of valproic acid on destructive and aggressive behaviours in patients with acquired brain injury. *Brain Injury, 11*(1), 37–47.

Yarnell, P. R., and Lynch, S. (1970). Retrograde memory immediately after concussion. *Lancet, 1*, 863–864.

Yeates, K. O., Armstrong, K., Janusz, J., Taylor, H., Wade, S., Stancin, T. et al. (2005). Long-term attention problems in children with traumatic brain injury. *Journal of the American Academy of Child and Adolescent Psychiatry, 44*(6), 574–584.

Yeates, K. O., Swift, E., Taylor, H. G., Wade, S. L., Drotar, D., Stancin, T. et al. (2004). Short- and long-term social outcomes following pediatric traumatic brain injury. *Journal of the International Neuropsychological Society, 10*(3), 412–426.

Yeates, K. O., Taylor, H., Wade, S. L., Drotar, D., Stancin, T., and Minich, N. (2002). A prospective study of short- and long-term neuropsychological outcomes after traumatic brain injury in children. *Neuropsychology, 16*(4), 514–523.

Yeates, K. O., Taylor, H. G., Drotar, D., Wade, S. L., Klein, S., Stancin, T. et al. (1997). Preinjury family environment as a determinant of recovery from traumatic brain injuries in school-aged children. *Journal of the International Neuropsychological Society, 3*, 617–630.

Yeates, K. O., Taylor, H. G., Rusin, J., Bangert, B., Dietrich, A., Nuss, K. et al. (2009). Longitudinal trajectories of postconcussive symptoms in children with mild traumatic brain injuries and their relationship to acute clinical status. *Pediatrics, 123*(3), 735–743.

Yeates, P., Henwood, K., Gracey, F., and Evans, J. (2007). Awareness of disability after acquired brain injury (ABI) and the family context. *Neuropsychological Rehabilitation, 17*(2), 151–173.

Ylvisaker, M. (2003). Context-sensitive cognitive rehabilitation after brain injury: Theory and practice. *Brain Impairment, 4*(1), 1–16.

Ylvisaker, M. (2006). Self-Coaching: A context-sensitive, person-centred approach to social communication after traumatic brain injury. *Brain Impairment, 7*(3), 246–258.

Ylvisaker, M., Adelson, P. D., Braga, L. W., Burnett, S. M., Glang, A., Feeney, T. et al. (2005). Rehabilitation and ongoing support after pediatric TBI: twenty years of progress. *Journal of Head Trauma Rehabilitation, 20*(1), 95–109.

Ylvisaker, M., and Feeney, T. J. (2000). Construction of identity after traumatic brain injury. *Brain Impairment, 1*, 12–28.

Ylvisaker, M., Feeney, T. J., and Szekeres, S. (1998). Social-environmental approach to communication and behavior. In M. Ylvisaker (Ed.), *Traumatic brain injury rehabilitation: Children and adolescents* (pp. 271–298). Newton, MA: Butterworth-Heinemann.

Ylvisaker, M., Hanks, R., and Johnson-Greene, D. (2002). Perspectives on rehabilitation of individuals with cognitive impairment after brain injury: rationale for

reconsideration of theoretical paradigms. [Review]. *Journal of Head Trauma Rehabilitation, 17*(3), 191–209.
Ylvisaker, M., Hartwick, P., and Stevens, M. (1991). School reentry following head injury: Managing the transition from hospital to school. *Journal of Head Trauma Rehabilitation, 6*(1), 10–22.
Ylvisaker, M., Jacobs, H., and Feeney, T. J. (2003). Positive supports for people who experience behavioral and cognitive disability after brain injury: A review. *Journal of Head Trauma Rehabilitation, 18*(1), 7–32.
Ylvisaker, M., Todis, B., Glang, A., Urbanczyk, B., Franklin, C., De Pompei, R. et al. (2001). Educating students with TBI: themes and recommendations. *Journal of Head Trauma Rehabilitation, 16*, 76–93.
Ylvisaker, M., Turkstra, L., Coehlo, C., Yorkston, K., Kennedy, M., Sohlberg, M. M. et al. (2007). Behavioural interventions for children and adults with behavioural disorders after TBI: A systematic review of the evidence. *Brain Injury, 21*(8), 769–805.
Yorkston, K. M., Beukelman, D. R., Strand, E. A., and Hakel, M. (2010). *Management of motor speech disorders in children and adults* (3rd ed.). Austin, TX: Pro-Ed Inc.
Yudofsky, S., Silver, J. M., and Hales, R. E. (1990). Pharmacologic management of aggression in the elderly. *Journal of Clinical Psychiatry, 51*, 22–28.
Yudofsky, S., Williams, N., and Groman, J. (1981). Propranolol in the treatment of rage and violent behaviour in patients with chronic brain syndrome. *American Journal of Psychiatry, 138*, 218–220.
Yudofsky, S. M., Silver, J. M., Jackson, W., Endicott, J., and Williams, D. (1986). The Overt Aggression Scale for objective recording of verbal and physical aggression. *American Journal of Psychiatry, 143*, 35–39.
Zarski, J. J., DePompei, R., and Zook, A. (1988). Traumatic head injury: Dimensions of family responsivity. *Journal of Head Trauma Rehabilitation, 3*(4), 31–41.
Zasler, N. D., and Horn, L. J. (1990). Rehabilitative management of sexual dysfunction. *Journal of Head Trauma Rehabilitation, 5*(2), 14–24.
Zebrack, M., Dandoy, C., Hansen, K., Scaife, E., Mann, N. C., and Bratton, S. L. (2009). Early resuscitation of children with moderate-to-severe traumatic brain injury. *Pediatrics, 124*(1), 56–64.
Zencius, A., Wesolowski, M. D., and Burke, W. H. (1990). A comparison of four memory strategies with traumatically brain-injured clients. *Brain Injury, 4*, 33–38.
Zhang, L., Abreu, B. C., Gonzales, V., Seale, G., Masel, B., and Ottenbacher, K. J. (2002). Comparison of the Community Integration Questionnaire, the Craig Handicap Assessment and Reporting Technique, and the Disability Rating Scale in Traumatic Brain Injury. *Journal of Head Trauma Rehabilitation, 17*(6), 497–509.
Zhang, L., Heier, L. A., Zimmerman, R. D., Jordan, B., and Ulug, A. M. (2006). Diffusion anisotropy changes in the brains of professional boxers. *American Journal of Neuroradiology, 27*, 2000–2004.
Ziino, C., and Ponsford, J. (2005). Measurement and prediction of subjective fatigue following traumatic brain injury. *Journal of the International Neuropsychological Society, 11*, 416–425.
Ziino, C., and Ponsford, J. (2006a). Selective Attention Deficits and Subjective Fatigue following Traumatic Brain Injury. *Neuropsychology, 20*(3), 383–390.
Ziino, C., and Ponsford, J. (2006b). Vigilance and fatigue following traumatic brain injury. *Journal of the International Neuropsychological Society, 12*, 100–110.

Author index

Subject index